JEWS AND THE LAW

JEWS AND THE LAW

edited by

Ari Mermelstein
Victoria Saker Woeste
Ethan Zadoff
Marc Galanter

Legal History & Biography Series

QUID PRO BOOKS
New Orleans, Louisiana

Copyright © 2014 by Ari Mermelstein, Victoria Saker Woeste, Ethan Zadoff, and Marc Galanter. All rights reserved. Individual chapters are also copyright © their respective authors. No part of this book may be reproduced or utilized in any form or by any means, electronic or mechanical, including photocopying, copying its digital form, recording, or by any information storage and retrieval system, without permission in writing from the publisher or the chapter author.

Published in 2014 by Quid Pro Books.

ISBN 978-1-61027-227-8 (pbk)
ISBN 978-1-61027-229-2 (hbk)
ISBN 978-1-61027-228-5 (ebk)

QUID PRO BOOKS
Quid Pro, LLC
5860 Citrus Blvd., Suite D-101
New Orleans, Louisiana 70123
www.quidprobooks.com

qp

Publisher's Cataloging-in-Publication

Mermelstein, Ari.

Jews and the law / ed. by Ari Mermelstein, Victoria Saker Woeste, Ethan Zadoff, and Marc Galanter.

p. cm. — (Legal history & biography)

Includes bibliographical references.

ISBN 978-1-61027-227-8 (pbk)

1. Jews—United States—Identity. 2. Ethnic relations—United States. 3. Judaism—United States. I. Woeste, Victoria Saker. II. Zadoff, Ethan. III. Galanter, Marc. IV. Title. V. Series.

E184.J4.M49 2014   305'.04'135—dc22
                                     2014133972

The cover design is based on the painting "Moses Smashing the Tablets of the Law" (1659), by Rembrandt Harmenszoon van Rijn (1606–1669). This image and other images in the volume derive from material not currently falling under copyright protection; no copyright is claimed in the foundational work.

Contents

Introduction • Victoria Saker Woeste 1

Jewish Lawyers in Life and Practice

Jews in the German Legal Professions: Emancipation,
 Assimilation, Exclusion • Kenneth Ledford 13

Louis Marshall, Julius Henry Cohen, Benjamin Cardozo, and the
 New York Emergency Rent Laws of 1920 • Samuel Levine 37

The Jewish Law Firm: Past and Present • Eli Wald 65

Jewish Lawyers for Causes of the Political Right • Ann Southworth 125

Jews, Antisemitism, and Legal Development

Gentleman's Agreement: The Antisemitic Origins of Restrictions
 on Stockholder Litigation • Lawrence Mitchell 141

From Emancipation to Assimilation: Is Secular Liberalism Still
 Good for Jewish Lawyers? • Russell Pearce and Adam Winer 171

Hating the Law for Christian Reasons: The Religious Roots
 of American Antinomianism • Jay Michaelson 207

Lawyer Jokes and the Jewish Question: Jews, Lawyers, and
 Legalism in American Life • Marc Galanter 279

Legalism and the Jews

Jews and Legal Realism • Morton Horwitz 309

Jews and American Legal Pluralism • Dalia Tsuk Mitchell 321

Texts, Values, and Historical Change: Reflections on the
 Dynamics of Jewish Law • David Berger 347

Israeli Lawyers and the Failed Jewish Revolution
 of 1948 • Assaf Likhovski 359

About the Editors 385

PERMISSIONS

The following chapters, in part or in whole, have already been published. We are grateful to the holders of the original copyrights for permitting their republication in this volume:

David Berger, "Texts, Values, and Historical Change: Reflections on the Dynamics of Jewish Law." Pages 201–16 in *Radical Responsibility: Celebrating the Thought of Chief Rabbi Lord Jonathan Sacks.* Edited by Michael J. Harris, Daniel Rynhold, and Tamra Wright. Jerusalem: Maggid, 2012.

Samuel J. Levine, "Louis Marshall, Julius Henry Cohen, Benjamin Cardozo, and the New York Emergency Rent Laws of 1920: A Case Study in the Role of Jewish Lawyers and Jewish Law in Early Twentieth-Century Public Interest Litigation." *Journal of the Legal Profession* 33 (2008): 1–29.

Lawrence E. Mitchell, "Gentleman's Agreement: The Anti-Semitic Origins of Restrictions on Stockholder Litigation." *Queen's Law Journal* 36 (2010): 71–116.

Eli Wald, "The Jewish Law Firm: Past and Present," based on "The Rise of the Jewish Law Firm or Is the Jewish Law Firm Generic?" *UMKC Law Review* 76 (2008): 885–938.

Jews and the Law

INTRODUCTION

Victoria Saker Woeste[*]

Jews are a people of law, and law defines who the Jewish people are and what they believe. The scholarly work in this anthology contributes to the deepening sophistication and complexity of our understanding of what it is to be Jewish and, more problematically, what it means to be at once Jewish and participate in secular legal systems as lawyers, judges, legal thinkers, civil rights advocates, and teachers.

A century or so ago, such a thing as a "Jewish law firm" was not only not rare, it was commonplace. Today, there are far fewer identifiably Jewish firms in the major cities of the United States. As American Jews gained in economic and professional mobility, Jewish lawyers rose to claim a spot at the practicing bar. In the last forty years, that place has been right alongside the elite non-Jewish lawyers who dominated large law firms. A pronounced self-awareness, if not self-consciousness, accompanied the rise of Jews in the American legal profession in the first decades of the twentieth century.[1] The essays in this book trace the history and chart the sociology of the Jewish legal profession over time, revealing new stories and dimensions of this significant aspect of the American Jewish experience and at the same time exploring the impact of Jewish lawyers and law firms on American legal practice.

Of course, our subject defies easy definition. There are myriad ways in which it is possible to talk about the "Jewish legal profession." There also are just as many ways in which that phrase falls apart, as a historical construct and as an observable sociological phenomenon. The reason for that mutability is the problematic nature of Jewish identity as it was understood in the civic community. To be Jewish was not just to observe a particular religious faith. Well into the 1950s and 1960s, it also conferred a racial identity, one that was omnipresent in such important markers of belonging as the U.S. Census, immigration quotas, military service, and private education. Even more difficulty arises from the fact that no one can choose the color of their skin, but people can choose to observe Orthodox Judaism—or not—thus rendering Jewishness an even more fluid category of identity as long as Jews were treated as a separate racial group. As that racial categori-

---

[*] Research Professor, American Bar Foundation.

[1] The best (and so far only) book-length history of Jewish lawyers remains Jerold S. Auerbach, *Unequal Justice: Lawyers and Social Change in Modern America* (New York: Oxford University Press, 1976).

zation changed over time, so too did the cultural recognition and understanding of Jewishness.

As many of our contributors observe, changes in American legal philosophy also helped shape Jewish identity. Jurisprudentially, Russell Pearce and Adam Winer note, the rise of secular liberalism "served as the ideological catalyst for Jewish success" in the legal profession in the twentieth century, but it also "weaken[ed] Jewish identity in a way that denies Jewish lawyers—and American Jews generally—a valuable resource for finding meaning in their lives, for maintaining a Jewish identity, and for continuing their commitments to equal justice under law."[2] An important question raised in many of the essays in this collection is where do Jewish lawyers find meaning and identity, not just today, but historically?

The latest research in the history, sociology, and demography of the Jewish law firm has a great deal to tell us as we pursue an answer to that question. In his pathbreaking study of the Jewish experience within the American legal system, Jerold Auerbach notes that the "entry of Jews into the legal profession was prolonged and painful, strewn with obstacles of exclusion and discrimination set by law schools and law firms."[3] It was easier for acculturated German Jews to get into Dwight Law School (which eventually became Columbia Law School) in the 1870s than it would be for them to get into Harvard just ten years later. Barriers to entry were thrown up rapidly in the last decades of the nineteenth century and the first thirty years of the twentieth. Overt antisemitic discrimination hardened after 1900, taking the forms of admission quotas in education, exclusions in hiring, and outright bars to government service. One generation's worth of these practices produced a startling profile. By the 1930s, more than half the lawyers in New York's Five Boroughs were Jewish, yet most of them attended low-status law schools, practiced in solo offices, and did not earn incomes comparable to white Anglo-Saxon lawyers.[4] Most obstacles to social and professional equality for Jewish Americans finally began to dissipate after World War II; thus, the necessity for Jews to form separate law firms, particularly in major urban markets, gradually receded. Yet law remained the last bastion of respectable antisemitism.[5]

Many of the prominent all-Jewish firms that characterized the bar of New York City before World War II remained fixtures of the professional landscape after mid-century. Before then, during the interwar period, so-called "white-shoe" law firms (where the white elites practiced) grew apace, but Jewish firms grew faster despite discrimination or, equally likely,

---

[2] Russell G. Pearce and Adam Winer, "From Emancipation to Assimilation: Is Secular Liberalism Still Good for Jewish Lawyers?" 171.

[3] Quoted in Pearce and Winer, "From Emancipation to Assimilation," 186.

[4] Lawrence E. Mitchell, "Gentleman's Agreement: The Antisemitic Origins of Restrictions on Stockholder Litigation," 152.

[5] Pearce and Winer, "From Emancipation to Assimilation," 189.

because of it.⁶ Today, the hiring practices and practice portfolios of the distinguished older Jewish law firms look much like those of other corporate law firms. Thanks to a host of studies, we know a great deal about the Jewish law firm and its trajectory in the twentieth century.⁷ As Eli Wald, Auerbach's successor as the biographer of the Jewish legal profession, puts it, Jewish firms gained their foothold by supplying, just as black firms did for African American lawyers, "an oasis of comfort and security in what was correctly perceived to be a hostile and anti-Semitic legal environment."⁸

The new work showcased in this collection provides a healthy contrast to the conventional study of Jewish lawyers, which tends to focus on biographies of famous individual Jews such as Louis Brandeis, Felix Frankfurter, and Benjamin Cardozo. Their rise to public prominence in the first half of the twentieth century was predicated on the notion that being Jewish was compatible with being American, according to Auerbach, because the two traditions had a common emphasis on constitutionalism, legalism, and social justice.⁹ Not only have historians challenged that assumption, but also Jewish lawyers themselves disagreed about the forced binary of this line of thinking and about the degree to which one's Jewishness could be sublimated to one's civic citizenship. Disagreements such as these arose as a consequence of the fact that not all prominent Jews were religiously observant; some of the old guard remained faithful to Orthodox Judaism while many of the lawyers who came of age in the immediate post–Civil War era cleaved to Reform Judaism.¹⁰

According to Pearce and Winer, Jews played an "important role" in promoting secular liberalism and benefitted from its success.¹¹ The rise of secular liberalism and the decline of explicit antisemitism as a barrier to Jews in the legal profession were synchronous developments. By the late 1960s, twenty percent of America's 350,000 lawyers were Jewish.¹² This impressive fact not only marks a generational triumph over discrimination, but it also illustrates dramatically the degree to which Jews became lawyers in numbers disproportionate to their share of the general population. Once, such predominance would have given rise to conspiracy theories and backlash. No longer. Pearce and Winer remark that "today in the US, antisemi-

---

⁶ Ibid.

⁷ Mitchell, "Gentleman's Agreement"; Eli Wald, "The Jewish Law Firm: Past and Present."

⁸ Eli Wald, "The Rise and Fall of the WASP and Jewish Law Firms," *Stanford Law Review* 60 (2008): 1865.

⁹ Auerbach, *Rabbis and Lawyers: The Journey from Torah to Constitution* (Bloomington: Indiana University Press, 1990), 17.

¹⁰ Jonathan Sarna, *American Judaism: A History* (New Haven: Yale University Press, 2005); Victoria Saker Woeste, *Henry Ford's War on Jews and the Legal Battle Against Hate Speech* (Stanford, CA: Stanford University Press, 2012).

¹¹ Pearce and Winer, "From Emancipation to Assimilation," 180.

¹² Ibid., 181 n. 61.

tism has diminished significantly to the point where it is not a significant stumbling block to Jews individually or collectively."[13]

There are many reasons for this development, and one has to do with Jews' own political and religious preferences. According to Ann Southworth's study of conservative cause lawyers, most Jewish lawyers are political liberals and practice in the Reform tradition (if they are observant). There simply aren't that many conservative, Orthodox Jewish lawyers and of those who are, very few are cause lawyers in the conventional sense. As a result, Jack Greenberg is more typical of American Jewish lawyers than, for example, the conservative law professor Richard Epstein; but neither exemplifies a particular archetype of Jewish lawyer. That is precisely because, as Pearce and Winer have observed, "the decline of religion [in public space of legal practice] ... removed barriers"[14] to Jewish participation in the profession. It matters far less for the characteristics of their public identities that Greenberg and Epstein are Jews than that they are liberal and conservative, politically.

The early twentieth-century civil rights leader Louis Marshall would have approved. His legal philosophy, activism, and law practice were all predicated on the assumption that one's Jewish faith and a public life in the legal profession were entirely compatible. In terms of being a lawyer, one's Judaism was irrelevant; to be a Jew, one had only to worship in one's own way. Not all of his contemporaries agreed with this formulation of the delicate balance between religion and citizenship. Indeed, it would appear from the trajectory of work studying the Jewish legal profession that over the twentieth century, Jewishness became sublimated to American legalism and constitutionalism. That sublimation, it could be argued, was the price of Jewish inclusion in a society that, heterogeneous or not, insisted on drawing sharp lines based on color, religion, and national origin.[15]

If Russell Pearce and Adam Winer, Ann Southworth, Dalia Tsuk Mitchell, Eli Wald, and others in this anthology are correct (and they are engaged by Morton Horwitz, who disagrees in substantial particulars), then the next step is to produce an interpretive synthesis of the social scientific analysis of Jewish lawyers' involvement in particular practice areas such as establishment clause litigation.[16] Such a synthesis should integrate historical and theoretical work on the nature of the "dual allegiance" of Jewish civic identity, meaning the tension that arises between secular citizenship and Jewish religious law.[17] In short, the major questions that should next be addressed are: do Jews practice a particular area of law (and is it because they are Jewish that they are drawn to those practice areas); and how has

---

[13] Ibid., 181.

[14] Ibid., 190.

[15] Woeste, *Henry Ford's War on Jews*, 53–88.

[16] Morton Horwitz, "Jews and Legal Realism."

[17] Jonathan Sarna, "Two Jewish Lawyers Named Louis," *American Jewish History* 94 (2008): 1–19.

the assimilation of Jews into the American legal profession changed the self-identification of Jewish lawyers, by which I mean their relation of law as a career to their religious affiliation. The essays that follow prepare the way for serious consideration of these issues.

These papers are the result of a conference on "Jews and the Legal Profession," hosted by Cardozo Law School in October 2006. Suzanne Last Stone of Cardozo and Marc Galanter of the University of Wisconsin Law School organized and convened the meeting, which drew scholars from a myriad of disciplines, including law, history, and sociology. Originally conceived as a follow up to and an extension of an earlier conference taking up much the same themes, the Cardozo meeting aspired not only to draw attention to the burgeoning literature on Jewish lawyers in American law practice but also to the historical and jurisprudential contributions Jews have made to legal development in both the United States and abroad.

The book is organized in three overlapping categories: Jewish Lawyers in Life and Practice; Jews, Antisemitism, and Legal Development; and Legalism and the Jews. These categories are didactic, but not inflexibly drawn; the essays often reference each other and draw on themes across the book. The logic behind the organization scheme is to present the reader with an accessible point of entry: the experience of Jews as ordinary lawyers and judges in Europe and North America over the last two centuries. Next is a section of essays that look at patterns of antisemitic bias and discrimination and their impact on Jewish law practice and legal change. From there we proceed to a concluding section of essays that delve deeply into the jurisprudential sources and origins of law and probe Jewish influence on legal ideas over time and the impact of secular legal systems on notions of Jewishness and Jewish conceptions of self.

Jewish Lawyers in Life and Practice

This section presents essays that document the participation in or exclusion from of Jews in the practice of law. These essays range broadly over time and place, from Germany to early twentieth-century America to modern U.S., and examine Jews' experience with the structural barriers to law practice. Inclusion of Jews at all levels of the legal profession, but particularly the practicing bar and judiciary, was closely linked to the political viability of liberalism. As long as Germany professed a belief in meritocracy, Kenneth Ledford persuasively argues, Jews could and did ascend to positions in law, including private practice and magistrates. Yet Ledford takes care to point out that the story is complicated, not merely a progression from exclusion to inclusion to exclusion. As he argues, "Despite the well-deserved reputation of the Weimar Republic as an era of rampant antisemitism and right-wing political justice, Jewish legal professionals during the republic solidified their position within their fields."[18]

---

[18] Kenneth F. Ledford, "Jews in the German Legal Professions: Emancipation, Assimilation, Exclusion," 30.

In a fascinating study of litigation challenging post–World War I emergency rent laws, Samuel J. Levine considers whether a prominent Jewish lawyer sought to influence the famous Jewish judge sitting on the case by citing to Jewish legal sources. In the process, Levine reveals the underlying struggle of late Progressive-Era lawyers to influence judicial decision-making, to "'get the judges away from the prevailing lawyers' bias against the laws and bring into play the forces of history.'"[19] In a case that pitted the property rights of landlords against the state, the lawyers were playing out one of the most significant jurisprudential arguments of the first half of the twentieth century.

Based on interviews with several dozen lawyers who practiced law between 1945 and 1965, Eli Wald's research explores the relationships between firms, practice areas, and Jewish representation among firm members. Until well into the 1970s, Jews were underrepresented in large white-shoe law firms and overrepresented in individual law practice. Wald finds that once discrimination against Jews began to ebb, this imbalance between large firms and individual practices began to even out. But inclusion in Manhattan's legal elites did not necessarily mean an acceptance of Jews as such; rather, it reflected a higher level of competition for first-rate legal services and qualified lawyers to perform them. Perhaps the best indicators of Jewish inclusion in the modern era are Ann Southworth's revelations about conservative Jewish lawyers and Jewish lawyers who work for right-wing political organizations. By working for causes not traditionally identified with liberal or progressive interests, a small but influential group of Jewish lawyers has broken a long-standing stereotype, increased the diversity of practice areas, and widened the range of political activism in which Jewish lawyers engage.[20]

Jews, Antisemitism, and Legal Development

In this section, four essays consider the concurrent streams of legal change and antisemitism. They elaborate on the findings of the articles in the first section on the demographics of law practice, while pointing the way towards themes taken up in section three: legalism, Jews' particular conceptions of law and legal ideas, and the philosophical genealogy of modern secular liberalism.

Lawrence Mitchell's piece examines New York's 1944 law prohibiting litigation by stockholders, which he argues the state's legal profession and corporate elites purposefully directed at a plaintiff's bar consisting over-

---

[19] Samuel J. Levine, "Louis Marshall, Julius Henry Cohen, Benjamin Cardozo, and the New York Emergency Rent Laws of 1920: A Case Study in the Role of Jewish Lawyers and Jewish Law in Early Twentieth-Century Public Interest Litigation," 63, quoting Julius Henry Cohen, *They Builded Better Than They Knew* (New York: Julian Messner Inc., 1946), 170.

[20] Eli Wald, "The Jewish Law Firm: Past and Present"; Ann Southworth, "Jewish Lawyers for Causes of the Political Right."

whelmingly of Jewish attorneys. Mitchell's analysis of the influence and power of structural racism reveals how ingrained were attitudes that regarded certain practice areas as low-brow and undignified. These attitudes almost always aligned with antisemitic biases against Jewish lawyers, most of whom were sole practitioners. Even an apparently rational legislative act, he argues, "can conceal depths of discrimination and bigotry."[21]

Similarly, the emergence of secular liberalism, which freed modern democracies from the fundamentalist impulses of pre-modern religious morality, redounded to the detriment of lawyers, particularly Jewish lawyers. According to Pearce and Winer, secular liberalism requires an abandonment of the religious or moral conception of the public good. As a result, Jewish lawyers' embrace of secular liberalism required them to abandon their profession of their Jewishness in the public sphere. The more that the American state became disconnected from universal notions of a public good, the harder it became for Jewish lawyers to act on Jewish mores in their capacities as lawyers. This development, Pearce and Winer argue, has contributed to the emergence of the widely held view of lawyers as "hired guns."[22]

Jay Michaelson shares Pearce and Winer's concern about the cultural perceptions of lawyers as utilitarian tradespeople for hire, and he maps that specific perception onto the larger debate between legalism (strict adherence to the letter of the law) and the common sense understanding of law's spirit, or intent. The anti-lawyer ethos has colored public perceptions of such varied events as the Clinton impeachment trial of 1998, the function and role of juries and equity courts, and the adoption of the common law. Michaelson reads these histories against the backdrop of St. Paul's rejection of legalism, which he argues infiltrated American notions of constitutional, statutory, and common law and contributed to the ascendance of secular jurisprudence. Michaelson mourns the "lost souls" of Jewish lawyers who cleaved to secular jurisprudence to gain admission to the legal profession. Anti-legalism, he concludes, need not displace Jewishness, in another attempt to reconcile the twin poles of Jewish identity and national citizenship.[23]

Anti-legalism also figures into the popularity and significance of lawyer jokes, as Marc Galanter recounts. His essay provides an anthropology of the forms of humor and satire that have historically been aimed at Jewish lawyers. Galanter peels through the superficial to reach the deeper meaning of the genre. Jokes about staged accidents and fraud comment seriously on perceptions of litigiousness and ambulance-chasing. They also reveal the deep-seated prejudice against Jewish lawyers, whom the barbs often

---

[21] Lawrence E. Mitchell, "Gentleman's Agreement: The Antisemitic Origins of Restrictions on Stockholder Litigation," 170.

[22] Pearce and Winer, "From Emancipation to Assimilation," 177.

[23] Jay Michaelson, "Hating the Law for Christian Reasons: The Religious Roots of American Antinomianism," 270–78.

associate with both those phenomena. Ultimately, Galanter suggests, the prevalence of jokes as a form of commentary on the legal profession marks the ascendance of legalism in everyday life. Jews, as lawyers and litigants, are now an unremarkable part of that transformation.[24]

Legalism and the Jews

In this section, the final four essays of the collection continue Pearce and Winer's and Michaelson's discussions of the enduring tensions between Jewish identity, Jewish religious sensibilities, and Jewish morality on the one hand and the triumph of secular liberalism, anti-legalism, and relativism. In a short rumination on the most important legal and jurisprudential debate of the past 150 years, Morton Horwitz charts the influence of Jews on legal realism and the sociological jurisprudence movement that preceded it. He then links a number of prominent Realist Jewish lawyers and judges to what Peter Novick termed "cognitive relativism," the idea that "categories of thought and frames of reference are socially and historically contingent." The holding power of cognitive relativism so strongly influenced Realist Jews that they used it to shape essential thinking about modernism itself.[25] Dalia Tsuk Mitchell, also centrally fascinated by the interaction of Jews and legal realism, finds in mid-twentieth-century jurisprudence a search for a lasting, defensible theory of social inclusion. In her telling, Harold Laski, Morris Cohen, and Cohen's son Felix were all searching for an expression of secular sovereignty that would not only embrace Jews but other minority groups as well. But it was Robert Cover, writing in the early 1990s, who explicitly recognized the Jewish contribution to legal pluralism—as well as the Jewishness of the notion of pluralism itself.[26]

David Berger's thought piece on Jewish law teaches us a lesson in rabbinical legal decision-making. Berger's intent is to provoke readers to understand the frictions between Orthodox Judaism and Reform Judaism as an ongoing search for religious unity and harmony, even though it is tempting to characterize them as factions battling it out for religious supremacy and legal rectitude. The internal discords within Judaism, Berger suggests, stretch back to the Middle Ages and beyond, and their very existence points to the exercise of latitude and discretion in unexpected ways. Rabbis took into consideration "concerns that [were] not part of the narrow textual discourse," especially when asked to interpret religious law (as opposed to biblical texts) in cases having to do with economic well-being. Even the textualists (today, we might substitute the disciples of "original intent") could find ways to make concessions outside the realm of canonical teachings, when to do so suited more pressing communal needs.[27]

---

[24] Marc Galanter, "Lawyer Jokes and the Jewish Question: Jews, Lawyers, and Legalism in American Life."

[25] Morton Horwitz, "Jews and Legal Realism," 310.

[26] Dalia Tsuk Mitchell, "Jews and American Legal Pluralism."

[27] David Berger, "Texts, Values, and Historical Change: Reflections on the Dynamics of

Likewise, Assaf Likhovski charts a historical moment when fundamentalists, textualists, and Jewish legalists forewent the opportunity to remake the Israeli legal system in the image of Jewish religious law. The creation of the state of Israel created an internal divide between those attached to the letter of the law and those devoted to its spirit; it was lawyers and secular Zionists who populated the latter group and ensured that Israel would be governed by secular law. Israeli lawyers chose their professional identity over Jewish nationalism and the possibility of creating a legal system based on religious morality. They did so in part to preserve their monopoly over legal knowledge and the delivery of legal services, Likhovski argues, but the result, in the end, owed as much if not more to the sharply shifting cultural and political forces shaping post-1948 Israeli society. The most important of these was the quickly emerging dominance of secular law; its rise meant that the revolutionary moment came and went without a revolution.[28]

All of the essays in the second and third sections of the collection thus seek to map out the continuing, historically recurrent tensions between the letter of the law and its spirit; further, they then seek to show that those tensions have driven the course of the modernization of law and jurisprudence, how that process has unfolded in different places and times, and, most critically of all, how Jewish lawyers and legal thinkers have been primary agents in breaking down those tensions. Read together, the essays collected here push us to recognize the historical contingency of Jewish identity—and its inseparability from transformations in legal knowledge across the world.

Many institutions and individuals came together for the common purpose of staging the 2006 conference that inspired these scholars to produce these essays. In addition to Suzanne Last Stone and Marc Galanter, the organizers, I wish to thank the David Berg Foundation, which underwrote a large proportion of the conference costs, and the Leonard and Bea Diener Institute of Jewish Law at Benjamin N. Cardozo Law School. Co-sponsors included the Yeshiva University Center for Jewish Law and Contemporary Civilization at Cardozo Law School; the the American Association of Jewish Lawyers and Jurists; the Institute on Religion, Law, and Lawyers' Work at Fordham Law School; the Program on the Legal Profession at Harvard Law School; and the Center for Professional Values and Practice at New York Law School. Ethan Zadoff took on the lion's share of copy editing during the volume's early stages. Ari Mermelstein alone deserves credit for bringing this book to publication. His patience and dedication are a model of scholarly collaboration. I am grateful to him for keeping the faith.

V.S.W.
April 2014

Jewish Law," 351, 356–58.

[28] Assaf Likhovski, "'The Time Has Not Yet Come to Repair the World in the Kingdom of God': Israeli Lawyers and the Failed Jewish Revolution of 1948," 360, 369–72, 383.

Jewish Lawyers in Life and Practice

Jews in the German Legal Professions: Emancipation, Assimilation, Exclusion

Kenneth F. Ledford*

By June 1905, District Court Judge Franz Paul Rosenthal in the Neubrandenburg Prussian provincial town of Landsberg an der Warthe had grown frustrated that his career advancement had ground to a halt in such a minor town. At the relatively young age of 57, he petitioned his supervising judge of the local superior court for permission to retire, citing a physician's opinion that his chronic lower-back pain, swollen legs, nervous agitation, deafness, and insomnia rendered him unfit to fulfill his professional duties.[1] The supervising judge forwarded the petition to the court of appeal for the district, the *Kammergericht* in Berlin, along with a cover letter that devoted a whole paragraph describing Rosenthal's service as a one-year volunteer in the Prussian army during the Franco-Prussian War of 1870–1871.[2] The supervising judge tactfully mentioned a disciplinary transfer imposed in 1883 and Rosenthal's history of health problems, and then he endorsed the petition to retire, recommending that upon retirement, Rosenthal be honored with conferral of the Order of the Red Eagle, Fourth Class. The *Kammergericht* President approved the request, Rosenthal received his medal, retired effective October 1, and moved to Berlin.

But the supervising judge's letter had not told the whole story, nor was Rosenthal yet ready for repose. Two years afterward, in November 1907, he wrote to the Prussian Minister of Justice Maximilian von Beseler to seek reappointment as judge at some district or superior court in the vicinity of Berlin, so that he could be near his adult children. According to Rosenthal, an extended cure in Italy had so restored his "strong constitution" that he was ready to return to the bench.[3] The Justice Minister turned to the presid-

---

* Department of History and School of Law, Case Western Reserve University, Cleveland, Ohio.

[1] Letter from Landgerichtspräsident Landsberg to Kammergerichtspräsident Berlin, 30 June1905, I. HA, Rep. 97 Personalia/Kammergericht, Nr. 362: Akten des Königlichen Kammergerichts betreffend Dr. Franz Paul Rosenthal, Amtsgerichtsrat in Landsberg a/W, Bl. 25, Geheimes Staatsarchiv Preußischer Kulturbesitz (hereafter "GStA"), Berlin.

[2] According to Rosenthal's personnel file, he had received the Campaign Medallion received by all troops active in the campaign, and later the Reserve Army Award Second Class; service with more than routine valor would have resulted in award of the Iron Cross, either First or Second Class, indicating that Rosenthal's participation was rather ordinary. Unpaginated, undated Personnel Data Sheet (Personalnachweis), I. HA 97, Nr. 362, first leaf, GStA, Berlin.

[3] Letter from Rosenthal to Justice Minister von Beseler, 3 November 1907, I. HA, Rep.

ing judge (President) of the *Kammergericht* in Berlin for his opinion of Rosenthal's petition, and that judge responded in a most revealing fashion.

In the opening recitation of Rosenthal's vital statistics, the presiding judge included not only his date of birth but his religious confession, "*mosaisch*," polite terminology for "Jewish," a datum utterly missing from the superior court president's 1905 letter. The *Kammergericht* President expressed skepticism that Rosenthal's health could have improved so much in a mere two and a half years, then added: "But even if it can be proved [that his health has improved], I cannot support his reinstatement in consideration of his advanced age of more than 59 years, and in view of his inadequate performance as well as his frequent unsatisfactory conduct during his career, as indicated on pages 116, 131, 161, 183, 193, 232, 233, 258 of Volume 1 of his personnel record, pages 4 and 16 of Volume 2, and pages 85 and 109 of his Disciplinary Case record."[4] Acting upon this recommendation, the Justice Minister declined in late November 1907 to restore Rosenthal to the bench.[5]

Rosenthal, it turns out, was that relative rarity in the German (Second) Empire (*Kaiserreich*): a Jew appointed to the Prussian judiciary. Clearly a talented, intelligent, and able man (having pursued his legal studies beyond the prescribed minimum to earn a Juris Doctor degree, something done only by a minority of all law graduates, including judges), Rosenthal's career was marred not only by personal failings of arrogance and laziness but by the frustrating dilemmas of nineteenth-century German Jews who sought careers in the legal professions.[6] Many talented Jewish lawyers triumphed over these frustrations, but Rosenthal succumbed, and in many ways his story of failure illuminates those other stories of triumph. This essay will return to Rosenthal's personal story as it describes and analyzes the Jewish experience in the German legal professions from the early nineteenth century to the present. Embedded in the larger history of Jewish presence in German culture and society, intertwined with the history of the rise and fall of liberal political, economic, social, and especially legal ideology in Germany in the past two centuries, Jewish lawyers and judges provide a study in microcosm of the emancipation, assimilation, and exclusion or even extermination that all German Jews experienced in Germany's transi-

---

97, Nr. 362, Bl. 44, GStA, Berlin.

[4] Letter from Kammergerichtspräsident to Justice Minister von Beseler, 16 November 1907, I. HA 97, Nr. 362, Bl. 48, GStA, Berlin.

[5] Letter from Justice Minister von Beseler to Rosenthal, 26 November 1907, I. HA 97, Nr. 362, Bl. 50, GStA, Berlin.

[6] Personal- und Qualifikationsnachweisung, 23 May 1904, I. HA 97, Nr. 362, Bl. 16, GStA, Berlin; the president of the *Kammergericht* wrote "Rosenthal has adequate gifts, but he is a careless and superficial judge who labors without professional pride. When he was in Seelow, even repeated admonitions were not sufficient to move him to engage in conscientious work. In Landsberg he was removed on my recommendation from non-contentious jurisdiction because his careless and irrelevant work was damaging in these cases."

tion to modernity and to post-modernity. This essay will argue that Jews in the German legal profession were in many ways the miner's canaries of German liberalism and that their fate cannot be understood apart from an inquiry into the fate of liberalism and its supporting legal ideology in nineteenth- and twentieth-century Germany.

Emancipation of Jews in Germany

Accounts of the history of Jews in the legal professions in Germany fall into two categories: celebratory recitations of Jewish contributions to German legal thought and life since the eighteenth century; and lamentations about the discrimination, exclusion, and ultimate extermination of Jewish jurists after Weimar, to the loss of Germany and the world.[7] But all begin the narrative in the late-eighteenth century years of the Enlightenment and the liberal emancipatory policies of the French Revolution, agreeing with Thomas Nipperdey's framing of the narrative of modern German history: "In the beginning was Napoleon."[8]

The politically fragmented character of eighteenth century Germany had led to a similar fragmentation in the legal regulation of Jewish life. The absolutist regimes of the German kingdoms, duchies, and principalities within the Holy Roman Empire of the German Nation hardly provided guarantees of rights for any Christian subjects before the promulgation of the Prussian General Law Code of 1794, not to mention any guarantees for Jews, who were barely-tolerated residents. Everywhere, Jews lived in Germany subject to significant civil disabilities, as "merely tolerated subjects in the state, who indeed enjoy its protection, but are in no way members of civil society."[9] In such circumstances, the question of Jews studying law and entering into the legal professions was simply not raised.[10]

---

[7] Examples of celebratory accounts include Hans-Peter Benöhr, "Jüdische Rechtsgelehrte in der deutschen Rechtswissenschaft," in *Judentum im deutschen Sprachraum*, ed. Karl E. Grözinger, (Frankfurt a. M.: Suhrkamp, 1991), 280–308 (Frankfurt a. M.: Suhrkamp, 1991); for a contrasting lamentation, see Horst Göppinger, *Juristen jüdischer Abstammung im "Dritten Reich". Entrechtung und Verfolgung*, 2d ed. (Munich: Beck, 1990).

[8] Thomas Nipperdey, *Deutsche Geschichte 1800–1866. Bürgerwelt und starker Staat* (Munich: Beck, 1983), 11, "Am Anfang war Napoleon." Also available in English translation, idem, *Germany from Napoleon to Bismarck, 1800–1866*, trans. Daniel Nolan (Princeton, N.J.: Princeton University Press, 1996), 1.

[9] Reinhard Rürup, "Die Emanzipation der Juden und die verzögerte Öffnung der juristischen Berufe," in *Deutscher Juristen jüdischer Herkunft*, ed. Helmut Heinrichs, Harald Franzki, Klaus Schmalz, and Michael Stolleis, (Munich: Beck, 1993), 1–25. See also the excellent account in English, idem, "The Tortuous and Thorny Path to Legal Equality: 'Jew Laws' and Emancipatory Legislation in Germany from the Late Eighteenth Century," *Yearbook of the Leo Baeck Institute* 31 (1986): 3–33, on the Emancipation Edict, 14–16.

[10] Benöhr, "Jüdische Rechtsgelehrte," 281–82, identifies four barriers to Jews entering the legal professions: 1) admission to university, 2) receipt of the doctoral degree, 3) admission to preparatory training, and 4) admission to the bar because of the fixed number and practice of state appointment.

But in the course of the seventeenth and eighteenth centuries, a small segment of the Jewish population, often under the direct protection of one or another of the German royal or ducal courts as "Hofjuden," emerged as financiers and entrepreneurs and entered life outside of the Jewish community.[11] By the mid-1700s, a group of Jewish intellectuals coalesced in Berlin around the monumental figure of Moses Mendelssohn, perhaps the leading figure of the German Enlightenment, and in conversation with non-Jewish Germans, such as Friedrich Lessing, began to contemplate the civil emancipation of the Jews. All envisioned a period of "civil improvement" for most Jews, meaning the opportunity for poor, insular Jews to attain the benefits of cosmopolitan and German culture before being fully admitted to the rights of citizens. Alongside this emancipatory civil improvement, and as an essential part of it, Jews began, very gradually at first, to pursue both the neo-humanistic classical secondary education at the Gymnasium that was a precondition to admission to university study and to study in small numbers at German universities.[12]

The first four Jewish law students entered the University of Königsberg beginning in 1788, and small numbers followed. The problem was that under the prevailing system, all law-related careers remained closed to Jews, no doubt deterring many who otherwise would have pursued the study of law. Conversion to Christianity immediately opened the door to entry into legal careers, although social discrimination often extended to converts. For example, in 1799, Isaac Elias Itzig, a member of a prominent Berlin banking family who had studied law at university and had himself baptized, sought admission to the period of practical legal training (*Auskultatur*) required before becoming a judge or advocate. The minister of justice objected that Itzig's family connections to his still-Jewish family should disqualify him, but the King of Prussia decided "that a Jew who has converted to the Christian religion, even if he still remains connected to his Jewish family, nevertheless can be admitted to the justice service in accord with his qualifications."[13]

Civil emancipation of Jews in France as a result of the French Revolution in 1789 formed the background against which we should view not only the early stages of legal study by Jews but also legal steps toward emancipation of Jews in the German states. In 1798, France extended the effect of its emancipation to the German regions on the left bank of the Rhine, which had been annexed into France, guaranteeing to Jews there free choice of

---

[11] Horst Fischer, *Judentum, Staat und Heer in Preußen im frühen 19. Jahrhundert. Zur Geschichte der preußischen Judenpolitik* (Tübingen: Mohr [Siebeck], 1968), 8–25.

[12] Reinhard Zimmermann, "'Was Heimat hieß, nun heißt es Hölle': The Emigration of Lawyers from Hitler's Germany: Political Background, Legal Framework, and Cultural context," in *Jurists Uprooted: German-Speaking Émigré Lawyers in Twentieth-Century Britain*, ed. Jack Beatson and Reinhard Zimmermann (Oxford: Oxford University Press, 2004), 1–71, 9–13.

[13] Rürup, "Die Emanzipation der Juden," 7, citing Fischer, Judentum, *Staat und Heer*, 206, documentary appendix, Nr. 2.

careers and eligibility for appointment to all state offices. Under Napoleon, these regulations later extended east of the Rhine, particularly to the model satellite Kingdom of Westphalia (ruled by his brother, Jerome). When German rule returned to these areas after 1815, it proved difficult to roll back the reforms. Even before 1815, major German powers, especially Prussia, had to compete with French emancipation, of Christians and Jews alike, in order to prevail in the great contest for the political loyalties of the people.[14]

The first important piece of German legislation with regard to emancipation for Jews was the Prussian Edict of Emancipation of March 11, 1812.[15] Paragraph 7 of this law made Jews citizens of Prussia "with the same civil rights and liberties as Christians" insofar as the edict did not provide explicitly to the contrary. While §8 opened to Jews all university teaching, school teaching, and local offices, §9 expressly postponed to a later date decision on opening other public posts to them, including judicial posts and the private practice of law. Indeed, the meaningfulness of this edict was decreased further by the fact that in 1812 Prussia, having been defeated in 1807 by the French and deprived by the Treaty of Tilsit of its eastern provinces which had the highest proportion of Jewish population, actually possessed a far smaller Jewish population than it had before the defeat. This reality strictly limited the Emancipation Edict of 1812 in its scope and amounted to a relatively easy gesture, a display of expansive liberalism at very little cost.[16]

The Congress of Vienna in 1814–1815 greatly expanded Prussian territory as a reward for its important role in the final defeat of Napoleon and the French Revolution. Prussia regained its former territories in the Rhineland and new territories that constituted all of the part of Germany that had been absorbed into France for almost 20 years. It regained most of its eastern territories from Poland, particularly West Prussia and Posen, which had a higher proportion of Jews in their population than the western parts of Germany. Prussia's Jewish population returned to the roughly one percent level at which it remained for the rest of the history of the state. Prussia also became a land of plural legal systems, with French civil law (the *Code civil* of 1804) and procedure prevailing in the Rhineland, the General Law Code in some territories, and common or Roman law and procedure elsewhere. Likewise, the regulation of Jews was plural, and the Prussian government never extended the application of the Emancipation Edict of 1812 to the

---

[14] Rürup, "The Tortuous and Thorny Path to Legal Equality," 9–14.

[15] The text of this edict may be found in Ernst Rudolf Huber, *Dokumente zur deutschen Verfassungsgeschichte*, 3 vols. (Stuttgart: W. Kohlhammer, 1961–66), I: 46–47; the best account of the internal deliberations that lay behind proclamation of this edict is Annegret H. Brammer, "Judenpolitik und Judengesetzgebung in Preußen 1812 bis 1847, mit einem Ausblick auf das Gleichberechtigungsgesetz des Norddeutschen Bundes von 1869" (PhD diss., Universität Tübingen, 1986), 34–60.

[16] Rürup, "Die Emanzipation der Juden," 9–13.

regained territories.[17]

Preservation of French law in the Rhineland presented Prussian authorities with a difficult decision with regard to Jews in the legal profession, for three legally-trained Jews had entered the state service under French rule, including one, Heinrich Marx, as a lawyer in private practice in Trier. Despite positive evaluations from the local chief judge and a recommendation that these civil servants be retained, the Minister of Justice in 1816 refused to do so based upon §9 of the Edict of 1812. Heinrich Marx, father of Karl Marx, converted to Christianity and continued to practice law.[18] Although other German states followed more generous policies, Prussia insisted on conversion as a condition for Jews to enter legal professions until after 1848 for private practitioners, and until 1870 for judges.[19]

The period of restoration and reaction in Germany between 1815 and 1848 (known in German history as the *Vormärz*, before the March 1848 revolutions) saw a varied response by Jewish students to their limited career prospects in their choice of whether to study law. Although statistics are fragmentary before 1886, Reinhard Rürup has discerned certain patterns. In the *Vormärz*, Jews made up about ten percent of the population of law students, well above the one percent of total population that was Jewish. Certain universities, among them Heidelberg in the Palatinate and Göttingen in Hannover, proved particularly attractive for Jewish students, both because of their sterling reputations for legal education and because of their relatively liberal regulations with regard to Jewish students. Prussian universities, particularly Berlin, remained especially unreceptive to Jews, with correspondingly smaller numbers of Jewish law students enrolling.[20]

Career options remained limited for Jews. Everywhere the judiciary remained closed to them. Private practice was a state office in Prussia, depending upon appointment by the Minister of Justice, and thus Jews remained excluded. The free city of Frankfurt am Main, with its large Jewish banking and trading community, was in 1837 home to ninety-four practicing attorneys, ten of whom were Jews. Elsewhere than Prussia, in Holstein, Hamburg, and Hannover for example, some Jews admitted during the French era remained in their offices. And policies in the southwest of Ger-

---

[17] Barbara Strenge, *Juden im preußischen Justizdienst 1812–1918. Der Zugang zu den juristischen Berufen als Indikator der gesellschaftlichen Emanzipation* (Munich: Saur, 1996), 20–36.

[18] Ibid., 29–31. A sensitive account of Heinrich Marx's life appears in the definitive new biography, Jonathan Sperber, *Karl Marx: A Nineteenth-Century Life* (New York: W.W. Norton, 2013), 12–24.

[19] Perhaps the most notable nineteenth-century legal and political career of a converted Jew was that of Eduard von Simson, born in 1810 in Königsberg, baptized by his parents at age 13 and later president of the revolutionary Frankfurt National Assembly in 1848, later president of the Reichstag, and first president of the Reichsgericht in Leipzig in 1879; see the biographical sketch, Gerd Pfeiffer, "Eduard von Simson (1810–1899)," in *Deutsche Juristen jüdischer Herkunft*, ed. Heinrichs, Franzki, Schmalz, and Stolleis (Munich: C.H. Beck, 1993), 101–15.

[20] Rürup, "Die Emanzipation der Juden," 13–14.

many, in Württemberg, Baden, and Hesse-Kassel, admitted Jews in small numbers to private practice.[21] Likewise, university professorships, particularly in law, remained closed to Jews before 1850. The most spectacular case of discrimination occurred with the jurist Eduard Gans of Berlin, who completed by all accounts a brilliant university career by winning his doctorate in law in 1819. Upon his application for a position as temporary lecturer at the University of Berlin, he placed into question application of the language of §8 of the Edict of 1812 which explicitly opened to Jews all university teaching posts. By a special order of August 18, 1822, known as the "Lex Gans," the Prussian cabinet suspended this portion of the edict in order to avoid having to appoint Gans. Faced with this explicit step, Gans converted to Christianity in 1825, received immediate appointment as associate professor of law at Berlin in 1826, and from 1828 on enjoyed a very distinguished career as full professor there.[22]

Retreat from emancipation reached its climax in Vormärz Prussia with the so-called "Jew Law" ("*Judengesetz*") of July 23, 1847, whose aim was to unify the manifold laws regulating the rights of Jews in the kingdom. It represented a general retreat from the spirit of the Emancipation Edict of 1812, admitting Jews to state offices only if their powers did not include the exercise of "judicial, police, or executive authority."[23] Although the "*oktroyierte*" or imposed Prussian Constitution of December 1848, as amended in 1850, provided in Article 12 that "the freedom of religious belief ... is guaranteed" and made "the enjoyment of civil and political rights independent from religious belief," Prussian authorities continued to interpret and apply this provision restrictively with respect to appointment of Jews to public offices, including legal and judicial positions.[24] After Prussia's victory over Austria in 1866 led to the political reorganization of Germany in 1867 into the Prussia-dominated North German Confederation, Prussia finally acceded to full emancipation of Jews in the North German Law Concerning the Equality of the Confessions in Civil and Political Relations of July 3, 1869, which provided: "All still-existing restrictions on civil and political rights based on differences in religious belief are hereby removed. In particular, qualification to participate in local and state representative bodies and to occupy public offices shall be independent of religious belief."[25] This Law carried over into the new German Empire in 1871, and it apparently definitively opened all legal professions to Jews as a matter of law; however, as we shall see, even in what can fairly be remembered as the "golden era" of the German Empire for German Jews, the practice of the Prussian Ministry of Justice was far from non-discriminatory.

---

[21] Ibid., 15.

[22] Strenge, *Juden im preußischen Justizdienst*, 38–42.

[23] Fischer, *Judentum, Staat und Heer*, 177–90.

[24] Huber, *Dokumente* I: 401–14, 402, incorporating in primary part the language from Article 11 of the constitution of December 5, 1848.

[25] Huber, *Dokumente* II: 248.

Assimilation and Inclusion

The era of the German Empire (1871–1918) and Weimar Republic (1919–1933) represents the age of success for Jews in the German legal professions. Although Jews had to continue to cope with widespread social discrimination, with the rise in the 1880s, 1900s, and again during Weimar of political antisemitic movements, and with the emergence of racialist thinking that after 1919 radically shifted conceptions of antisemitism from religious to racial, they entered into all aspects of legal life in Germany and seemed to establish solid foundations. Jews played an important role in the thriving German *Rechtsstaat* that ushered in the full flower of industrial capitalism and made the German economy thrive.

Before 1878, the language of "state office" had affected the prospects of German Jews in all aspects of the legal professions because of their historically-close connection, particularly in Prussian law, with the state. This conceptual connection extended even to the private practice of law. By the last half of the nineteenth century, the employment market for law graduates consisted of four roughly equal career-tracks: general state administrative office, judge, state-appointed private practitioner, and business adviser/manager.[26] Obviously, civil service positions in the general administrative bureaucracy and in the judiciary involved state appointment and thus opportunity for preferment or discrimination. Although state administrators (*Beamten*) and judges (*Richter*) required substantially identical preparatory education, legal study at university, and passage of identical first bar examinations, their practical trainings before the second bar examination (*Referendariat*) were separate, and administrators enjoyed higher status and pay than judges. Closely associated with the state and thus with royal prerogative, it was inconceivable that administrators could be practicing Jews (although baptized Jews could rise, and later in less-prestigious ministries such as finance, commerce, and railroads Jews gained access based upon practical competence). But beyond the civil service and judiciary proper, until 1878, the Ministry of Justice held the authority to appoint private practitioners in Prussia and exercised this in such a way as to limit both the total number and the number in any particular locality quite strictly (*numerus clausus*). Thus, even the "free" profession of lawyer (*Rechtsanwalt*) involved appointment by a Ministry often hostile to Jews as a group.[27]

Beginning around 1860, lawyers in Prussia and throughout Germany began to agitate for a new regulation of the practicing bar, using classically liberal language of the "free path for talent." Explicitly liberal economic language about letting the market determine the optimal number of private practitioners shaped the debate past the caesura of unification in 1870–

---

[26] Kenneth F. Ledford, *From General Estate to Special Interest: German Lawyers 1878–1933* (Cambridge and New York: Cambridge University Press, 1996).
[27] Krach, *Jüdische Rechtsanwälte in Preußen*, 8–14.

1871, and led to the adoption in 1878–1879 of a series of Imperial-level laws that created nationally-uniform codes of civil and criminal procedure, required the federal states of the Empire to organize their courts on a uniform basis, and established framework regulations for qualification for appointment to the bench. These laws also "freed" the practicing bar in Prussia and the other states that still filled the profession by means of appointment at the discretion of the Ministry of Justice, eliminating the hated *numerus clausus* and establishing a meaningful system of self-discipline and self-regulation in the hands of a truly free liberal profession.[28]

The opening of the bar to all who were qualified marked an epochal moment in the relationship of Jews and the legal professions in Germany. No longer would the career prospects of a talented young German Jew depend for success upon the favor of a prejudiced Ministry of Justice. Every German who completed six semesters of study at the legal faculty of a German university, passed a first bar examination, completed a four-year period of practical legal training at the offices of various courts, prosecutors, and practitioners, and then passed a second bar examination, accrued the right to practice law at any court in the land (other than the Imperial Supreme Court, whose practitioners still were appointed). Not surprisingly, the number of Jews entering legal study, practical legal education, and the post-second-bar-examination status of "trainee-judge" (*Assessor*), as well as the private legal profession, began to increase dramatically.[29]

The trend of greater acceptance had already begun with the proclamation of the German Empire, based upon the 1869 North German Law Concerning the Equality of the Confessions. The Prussian Ministry of Justice began to appoint Jews not only to posts as practitioners but also to judicial positions as judges at lower courts, the first in 1870. Tillmann Krach records those figures as reproduced in Table 1:

Table 1: Jews in Prussian Legal Professions, 1857–1872[30]

	1857	1861	1872	%
Trainees	68	42	114	7.6
Judges	0	0	9	0.2
Lawyers	0	0	75	3.0

---

[28] Kenneth F. Ledford, "Lawyers, Liberalism, and Procedure: The Imperial Justice Laws of 1877–79," *Central European History* 26 (1993): 165–93.

[29] Hannes Siegrist, *Advokat, Bürger, Staat. Sozialgeschichte der Rechtsanwälte in Deutschland, Italien und der Schweiz (18.–20. Jh.)*, 2 vols. (Frankfurt am Main: Vittorio Klostermann, 1996), Tabelle 13.3, II: 591, provides a sweeping comparison of the growth of the number of practitioners and the number of law students from 1840 to 1940.

[30] Tillmann Krach, *Jüdische Rechtsanwälte in Preußen. Über die Bedeutung der freien Advokatur und ihre Zerstörung durch den Nationalsozialismus* (Munich: Beck, 1991), Tabelle 1, 414.

Thus, even before the major reforms of 1877–1879, Jews had begun to enter the legal professions in significant numbers, well in excess of Jews' proportion in the total Prussian and German population (about one percent) and, most importantly, the rapid increase in the number of trainees (here a total of both categories, Referendare and Assessoren) of Jewish faith indicated that the proportion in the legal professions would continue to increase. Krach's research confirms these expectations as shown in Table 2:

Table 2: Jews in Prussian Legal Professions, 1880–1904[31]

	1880	%	1893	%	1904	%
Trainees	482		427		693	
Judges	99	3.8	168	4.5	191	4.2
Lawyers	146	7.3	885	25.4	1,287	27.4

The growth of the proportion of Jews in the legal professions, however, remained unevenly distributed between the bar and bench. While the reforms of 1877–1879 ensured unfettered access to private practice of the law for Jews, the promise of the emancipatory legislation of mid-century remained unfulfilled, especially in Prussia. As Barbara Strenge has demonstrated at great length, discriminatory appointment policies administered by the Prussian Ministry of Justice, and especially as stringently applied during the tenure of the reactionary Justice Minister Karl Heinrich von Schönstedt between 1894 and 1905, not only limited the number of Jews appointed to judicial posts, as compared to their proportion among law graduates and practitioners, but practically barred unconverted Jews from advancement to higher judicial posts such as court of appeal judges or the supervisory posts at superior courts and courts of appeals.[32] Peter Pulzer demonstrates that the discriminatory policy extended beyond Prussia to states such as Hessen, Bavaria, and Saxony.[33]

Table 3 provides a comparison among the thirteen court of appeal districts in Prussia between 1895 and 1906 regarding Jewish private practitioners. Already twenty-three percent of the total number of lawyers in 1895, the proportion of Jewish lawyers exceeded twenty-seven percent in 1906. Regional differences were significant, varying in relation to the overall Jewish population, but notably the Berlin bar exceeded fifty percent throughout the Kaiserreich.

---

[31] Ibid., Tabelle 2, 415.

[32] Strenge, *Juden im preußischen Justizdienst 1812–1918*, 350–53.

[33] Peter Pulzer, "Religion and Judicial Appointments in Germany, 1869–1918," *Yearbook of the Leo Baeck Institute* 28 (1983): 185–204, 196–99.

Table 3: Percentage of Jewish Private Practitioners in Prussia, 1895 and 1906[34]

Court	1895			1906		
	Total	Jewish	%	Total	Jewish	%
Berlin	655	354	54.05%	1,241	655	52.78%
Breslau	382	137	35.86%	482	184	38.17%
Cassel	78	12	15.38%	85	11	12.94%
Celle	252	39	15.48%	288	34	11.81%
Cologne	586	42	7.17%	613	53	8.65%
Frankfurt/Main	201	54	26.87%	258	92	35.66%
Hamm	298	17	5.70%	455	35	7.69%
Kiel	130	16	12.31%	174	14	8.05%
Königsberg	177	23	12.99%	195	36	18.46%
Marienwerder	135	27	20.00%	148	33	22.30%
Naumburg	279	22	7.89%	318	24	7.55%
Posen	172	43	25.00%	200	70	35.00%
Stettin	154	18	11.69%	166	26	15.66%
TOTAL	3,499	804	22.98%	4,623	1,267	27.41%

---

[34] Strenge, *Juden im preußischen Justizdienst 1812–1918*, 251, Tabelle 19, and 335, Tabelle 22.

Likewise, Table 4 sets out the stricter control exercised by the Ministry of Justice on the proportion of Jews in the Prussian judiciary, clearly establishing the continued discriminatory appointment policy followed by von Schönstedt and continued by his successors.

Table 4: Percentage of Jewish Judges in Prussia, 1898 and 1905[35]

Court	1898			1905		
	Total	Jewish	%	Total	Jewish	%
Berlin	601	40	6.66%	666	40	6.01%
Breslau	519	39	7.51%	575	36	6.26%
Cassel	130	0	0.00%	134	2	1.49%
Celle	288	1	0.35%	308	2	0.65%
Cologne	374	14	3.74%	514	21	4.09%
Frankfurt/Main	173	7	4.05%	189	10	5.29%
Hamm	340	11	3.24%	437	11	2.52%
Kiel	148	4	2.70%	159	5	3.14%
Königsberg	263	19	7.22%	271	23	8.49%
Marienwerder	178	21	11.80%	186	19	10.22%
Naumburg	328	5	1.52%	340	5	1.47%
Posen	239	15	6.28%	246	11	4.47%
Stettin	169	6	3.55%	174	5	2.87%
TOTAL	3,750	182	4.85%	4,199	190	4.52%

The notable case of Albert Mosse serves as a telling illustration of the difficulties that Jews faced in advancing in the Prussian judiciary.[36] A member of a distinguished Jewish family, whose brother Rudolf was one of the leading left-liberal newspaper and book publishers in Berlin and all of

---

[35] Übersicht über die Konfessionsverhältnisse der Beamten im höheren Justizdienst, sowie der Rechtsanwälte, I. HA Rep. 84(a), Nr. 3259, "Konfessionsverhältnisse der höheren Justizbeamten, 1893–1930," Bl. 171–73, 173, GStA, Berlin.

[36] The literature on Albert Mosse and the Mosse family is large. The most accessible account in English is Werner E. Mosse, "Albert Mosse: A Jewish Judge in Imperial Germany," *Yearbook of the Leo Baeck Institute* 28 (1983): 169–84; see also the brief account in Strenge, *Juden im preußischen Justizdienst*, 230–32. For an account of the life of Albert Mosse's father, see Elisabeth Kraus, "Marcus Mosse. A Jew in the Prussian Province of Posen, 1808–1865," *Yearbook of the Leo Baeck Institute* 42 (1997): 1–28, and for a multi-generational study of the Mosse family as a case study in the assimilated German-Jewish bourgeoisie, idem, *Die Familie Mosse. Deutsch-jüdisches Bürgertum im 19. und 20. Jahrhundert* (Munich: Beck, 1999), especially 200–41 on the career of Albert Mosse.

Germany, originally from the eastern province of Posen, but later based in Berlin, Mosse was a brilliant student in the legal faculty at Berlin and became the protégé of one of the leading law professors of the era, Rudolf von Gneist. A veteran of the Franco-Prussian War of 1870–1871, Mosse aimed from the beginning for a career as a judge and received his first judicial appointment in 1876 to the district court in Spandau, just outside of Berlin, transferring to the city court in Berlin in 1879 at the tender age of 33. Though Mosse was widely recognized as a brilliant legal mind, even Gneist's patronage could not bring him advancement beyond promotion to the superior court of Berlin in 1885, when he was only 40, the first Jew so appointed in Prussia.[37]

This meteoric rise for a Jew soon ran into roadblocks. In 1886, convinced in part by advice from Gneist that further promotion was unlikely for him since he was a Jew, Mosse accepted the invitation of the Japanese government to travel to Tokyo as legal adviser to participate in the Meiji-era reform of Japanese administration and law. From 1886 to 1890, Mosse served with distinction, earning upon his return from Japan a sterling evaluation from the German ambassador there, Theodor von Holleben, who recommended Mosse for promotion and distinction in an attempt to ward off the anticipated criticism:

> If I may permit myself in closing to add one final remark, that Herr Mosse's Jewish faith, as well as his family relationships with persons whose political opinions are not favorable to the government—in particular to the Editor of the *Berliner Tageblatt* [Albert's brother, Rudolf Mosse]—are not unknown to me. The first characteristic, however, never manifests itself unpleasantly, and with regard to his political view I can only assure you that he stands politically at a great distance from those of his relatives mentioned above. Herr Mosse has always shown himself to be a good patriot, loyal to the King, and to have a character beyond reproach.[38]

Upon his return to Germany, Mosse received his expected elevation to a Court of Appeal, but not as he had hoped to the prestigious *Kammergericht*

---

[37] The rank system for judges in Prussia between 1878 and 1933 was complex. Courts were arrayed in a hierarchy from district courts at the lowest level to the thirteen courts of appeal in the state, with superior courts as an intermediate instance with original jurisdiction in significant cases and appellate jurisdiction in cases decided at the district courts (Amtsgericht, Landgericht, Oberlandesgericht). Yet for salary and status purposes, district court judges and superior court judges were considered as a single rank. Higher-ranking judges included all court of appeal judges and presidents of superior courts as the next level; followed by senate presidents of the courts of appeal, and finally the presidents of the thirteen courts of appeal. Mosse's appointment to the superior court in Berlin was thus an appointment to a court of greater dignity, but not an advancement in his personal rank. That breakthrough came only when he was appointed to the Königsberg court of appeal.

[38] Letter, Holleben to Chancellor [Caprivi], 13 April 1890, R901/27946, 101, Bundesarchiv-Lichterfelde, Berlin.

in Berlin, but rather to the remote eastern Court of Appeal for East Prussia in the Baltic city of Königsberg. He was the first non-baptized Jew appointed in Prussia to any court of appeal judgeship.

By all accounts, Mosse's service in Königsberg was distinguished. Besides his work as a judge, he wrote a commentary on the German Commercial Code, lectured in commercial law and civil procedure at the University of Königsberg, and served frequently as substitute for judges who presided over the Senates of the Court of Appeal, although he never received promotion to those prestigious posts. The President of the Königsberg Court of Appeal twice recommended Mosse for promotion to a post on the Imperial Supreme Court in Leipzig, in 1896 and 1897, to no avail. Disappointed, Mosse retired in 1907 at the early age of 61, returned to Berlin, and remained active in Berlin municipal government and the affairs of the Jewish community there until his death in 1926. Werner E. Mosse concludes that Albert Mosse's career demonstrates the considerable opportunities open to Jews in the lower ranks of the judiciary, but the seemingly impenetrable barriers that excluded even the ablest and most assimilated from the higher, policy-making and administering, ranks.[39] Indeed, as Table 5 shows, before the First World War only four practicing Jews received appointment to judicial posts above the lowest level.[40]

Table 5: Promoted Judges in Prussia, 1907[41]

Rel. Status	Total	Promoted	%
Christian	3,365	631	18.75%
Jewish	155	4	2.58%
Baptized Jews	108	30	27.78%
TOTAL	3,628	665	18.33%

Despite the obstacles to advancement in judicial careers, and parallel to the significant advancement in the private practice of law, German Jews in the *Kaiserreich* pursued a number of cultural and legal strategies to escape the cultural prejudices that surrounded them. One strategy was conversion to Christianity, which Alan Levenson argues reached a new stage around the turn of the twentieth century.[42] One leading advocate of mass conversion was Adolf Weißler, a private practitioner in Halle an der Saale who was also the leading historian of the bar in private practice in Germany.[43] Conver-

---

[39] Mosse, "Albert Mosse," 182–83.

[40] Strenge, *Juden im preußischen Justizdienst 1812–1918*, 307.

[41] Ibid., 325–26.

[42] Alan Levenson, "The Conversionary Impulse in Fin De Siècle Germany," *Yearbook of the Leo Baeck Institute* 40 (1995): 107–22, 112–13.

[43] See Adolf Weißler, *Geschichte der Rechtsanwaltschaft* (Leipzig: Pfeffer, 1905).

sion, individual or corporate, was the logical extension of the assimilationist impulse so strong in the German Jewish community, which identified profoundly as German patriots and wrapped itself in embrace of neo-humanistic classical education and German high culture.[44] Indeed, although Weißler himself never converted to Christianity, he was so distraught in the face of German defeat in 1918 that he committed suicide in 1919 and prescribed as his epitaph: "He did not wish to survive the humiliation of his people."[45]

German Jews also pursued legal strategies to resist the prejudice that waxed and waned during the German Empire. One strategy was of name change. Prussian Jews, under the terms of §2 of the Emancipation Edict of 1812, for the first time had to adopt, register, and use surnames rather than patronymics by declaring a name before local authorities in their place of residence within six months (§3). In a pathbreaking study on "the stigma of names," Dietz Bering has examined how Prussian officials administered the system to try to continue to identify Jews by virtue of their names, both given names and surnames, and how Jews used the legal processes of name-change and defamation suits to protect their right to assimilate by name into German society.[46] Jews changed their names in order to assimilate and to avoid the burdens of antisemitic discrimination and abuse, and government policy varied over time between freedom of choice in names and policies designed to prevent Jews from escaping the stigma of their names.

Finally, Jews throughout the German Empire and the Weimar Republic invoked legal process to protect themselves by suing antisemites for defamation (*Beleidigung*). Closely connected with widespread notions of honor and the cult of dueling, Jews who felt themselves insulted often were refused when they challenged their persecutors to duels, being viewed as "unworthy of satisfaction" (*Satisfaktionsunfähig*).[47] Civil suits for defama-

---

[44] For a moving description of this assimilated Jewish subculture, see Fritz Stern, "Ancestral Germany," in *Five Germanys I Have Known* (New York: Farrar, Straus and Giroux, 2006), 13–50. Till van Rahden, *Juden und andere Breslauer. Die Beziehungen zwischen Juden, Protestanten und Katholiken in einer deutschen Großstadt von 1860 bis 1925* (Göttingen: Vandenhoeck & Ruprecht, 2000) provides a detailed sociographical study of this second-largest city in Prussia which supports Stern's accounts drawn from the letters of his parents and other relatives. The latest and broadest analysis of the "German-Jewish symbiosis" is Manfred Voigts, *Die deutsch-jüdische Symbiose. Zwischen deutschem Sonderweg und Idee Europa* (Tübingen: Niemeyer, 2006).

[45] Levenson, "The Conversionary Impulse," 113.

[46] Dietz Bering, *Der Name als Stigma. Antisemitismus im deutschen Alltag 1812–1933* (Stuttgart: Klett-Cotta, 1987); translated and abridged as *The Stigma of Names: Antisemitism in German Daily Life, 1812–1933*, trans. by Neville Plaice (Ann Arbor, MI: University of Michigan Press, 1992).

[47] The definitive work on the cult of honor and dueling is Ute Frevert, *Ehrenmänner. Das Duell in der bürgerlichen Gesellschaft* (Munich: Beck, 1991). See also Kevin McAleer, *Dueling: The Cult of Honor in Fin-de-Siècle Germany* (Princeton: Princeton University Press, 1994). For a perceptive analysis of the general culture of honor in Germany as related to actions for defamation in general, see Ann Goldberg, *Honor, Politics, and the*

tion were the alternative, as well as quasi-criminal and criminal prosecutions for defamation, and leading antisemites suffered judgment after judgment against them, notably the antisemitic politician Hermann Ahlwardt.[48] This strategy extended into the Weimar Republic, when Jewish government officials, finally admitted to positions of power and influence, used even the notoriously hostile and reactionary courts of that era to strike back with substantial success at their antisemitic critics.[49]

Franz Rosenthal's disciplinary problems in the 1880s thus had their roots in this very complex mix of prejudice, assimilation, and honor. Early in his career, in 1881–1882, he had been a district court judge in the small Neubrandenburg town of Mittenwalde. There he had run into conflict with a court clerk named Günther, who was clearly an antisemite. In October 1882, the disciplinary panel of the *Kammergericht* convicted Rosenthal of having demonstrated himself, by his conduct in office, unworthy of the respect and honor that ought to be accorded to his post as judge, and sentenced him to punitive transfer to a less-desirable court. Although Rosenthal appealed this decision, the appellate panel confirmed it, and Rosenthal found himself dispatched to Seelow on the Oder in 1883. The facts of the case are telling.[50]

Günther was an unreliable employee, given to drink, but nonetheless under the supervision of Rosenthal who was the only judge in the small court in Mittenwalde. The nature of life in the small town also meant that they could hardly avoid encountering one another in public places such as the local tavern. In the billiard room of that tavern in January 1881, Günther publicly insulted Rosenthal in front of witnesses, and Rosenthal simply walked away. Further, he did not report the matter to his supervisory judge at the superior court until after a second incident came to that judge's attention in March 1882. That second incident took place in the courthouse in Mittenwalde in February 1882, when Rosenthal overheard Günther in his office speaking disrespectfully about Jewish judges and legal trainees, all in the presence of a Jewish Assessor. When Rosenthal remonstrated with Günther, Günther replied: "Mr. Jew-Judge, if you want to get me fired, that is fine with me. Bring me up on charges. It is no honorable occupation to

---

Law in Imperial Germany, 1871–1914 (New York and Cambridge: Cambridge University Press, 2010).

[48] See the impressive recent studies, Barnet Hartston, *Sensationalizing the Jewish Question: Anti-Semitic Trials and the Press in the Early German Empire* (Leiden: Brill Academic Press, 2005), and Christoph Jahr, *Antisemitismus vor Gericht. Debatten über die juristische Ahndung judenfeindlicher Agitation in Deutschland (1879–1960)* (Frankfurt a.M.: Campus, 2011). For an account of efforts by Jews to use defamation actions to defend against antisemitic statements, see Ann Goldberg, *Honor, Politics, and the Law in Imperial Germany, 1871–1914* (Cambridge: Cambridge University Press, 2010), 58–68.

[49] Bering, *The Stigma of Names*, 3-11, particularly the diligent efforts of the Berlin Police President, Albert Grzesinski.

[50] Anschuldigungsschrift [complaint], July 22, 1882, I. HA, Rep. 97, Nr. 363, Akten des Kgl. Kammergericht betreffend die Disziplinar Untersuchung gegen den Amtsrichter Dr. jur. Franz Paul Rosenthal in Mittenwalde, Bl. 67, GStA, Berlin.

work under a Jew district judge." Rosenthal calmly told Günther to behave himself and ordered him out of the courthouse, and Günther left the building. But Rosenthal never brought this second incident to the attention of his supervisory judge, nor did he impose any administrative disciplinary penalty on Günther. The superior court learned of the affair only when Günther himself filed a disciplinary complaint against another court employee and Rosenthal had to provide a detailed statement to the superior court president.[51]

The import of the complaint against Rosenthal was that his unwillingness to discipline the insubordinate Günther, and especially his unwillingness to protect his honor as a Jew, was a breach of the duties that his position as district judge imposed upon him. As a Jew, Rosenthal had sullied the honor of the Prussian judiciary by failing to defend his honor as a Jew in the face of a coarse challenge from an inferior. This was, of course, an instantiation of the double-bind of antisemitism on culturally assimilated Jews: had Rosenthal insisted on the dignity of his office in the face of Günther's insults, he would have been accused of manifesting the touchiness and pushiness ascribed by antisemites as a negative Jewish characteristic; in not reacting, he was adjudged by his peers to have cravenly dishonored the entire judiciary, cowardice also being an antisemitic ascriptive characteristic of Jews.

Although the experiences of Mosse and Rosenthal establish the very real limits under which Jews in the Prussian judiciary operated during the German Empire and Weimar Republic, room for success and prominence for Jews in legal professions was very real. Jews rose to leading positions in German legal faculties, as leaders of the German Bar Association (*Deutscher Anwaltverein*), and made inroads into the judiciary.[52] Despite the persistence of social discrimination, despite the episodic employment of antisemitic political demagoguery by fringe parties and even by "respectable" conservatives both before and after the First World War, Jews continued to experience a firm foothold on their position of respect in the German legal professions.

Table 6 shows that, while the Weimar Republic may have been targeted by its right-wing opponents as a "Jew republic," the Jewish presence in the legal professions certainly enjoyed no great expansion. The proportion of Jews in both the judiciary and private practice remained much the same as it had been in the closing years of the pre-war period in legal professions that felt crowded and stagnant because of the reduced size of Germany and the collapsing economy and resultant state budgetary austerity from 1929 onward.

---

[51] Ibid.

[52] Peter Landau, "Juristen jüdischer Herkunft in Kaiserreich und in der Weimarer Republik. Dem Andenken Ernst Landsbergs," in *Deutsche Juristen Jüdischer Herkunft*, 133-213.

Table 6: Jews in Prussian Legal Professions, 1925–1933[53]

	1925	%	1927	%	1931	%	1933	%
Trainees			192	9.0	161	5.2	174	4.5
Judges			312	5.8	392	6.8	401	7.0
Lawyers	2,208	26.2					3,370	28.5
Berlin	1,179	45.4					1,879	48.3

Jewish lawyers attracted the hostility of antisemites because of their warm embrace of the republican form of government and their continued visibility. Leading figures in the "Republican Judges' Association" included prominent Jewish lawyers such as Hugo Sinzheimer, although by no means were all pro-republic lawyers and judges Jewish.[54] Prominent Jewish practitioners also attracted hostility for their visibility in high-profile political and criminal litigation. Douglas Morris has recently provided an excellent treatment of the practice of Max Hirschberg, the Jewish lawyer in Munich whose pro-republican political practice included a withering and embarrassing cross-examination of Adolf Hitler in a libel action that Hitler himself had brought over accusations that he had betrayed Germandom in the South Tyrol by accepting money from Mussolini.[55] Despite the well-deserved reputation of the Weimar Republic as an era of rampant antisemitism and right-wing political justice, Jewish legal professionals during the republic solidified their position within their fields.

Exclusion and Extermination

The story of the systematic exclusion of Jews from the ranks of the judiciary and the bar after the rise to power of the National Socialists on January 30, 1933, is a sadly familiar one.[56] Both before and after the Reichstag

---

[53] Krach, *Jüdische Rechtsanwälte*, Tabelle 3, 416-17.

[54] Theo Rasehorn, *Justizkritik in der Weimarer Republik. Das Beispiel "Die Justiz"* (Frankfurt am Main: Campus, 1985); see also Birger Schulz, *Der Republikanische Richterbund (1921-1933)* (Frankfurt am Main: Peter Lang, 1982).

[55] Douglas G. Morris, *Justice Imperiled: The Anti-Nazi Lawyer Max Hirschberg in Weimar Germany* (Ann Arbor, MI: University of Michigan Press, 2005).

[56] The most accessible English-language account remains Ingo Müller, *Hitler's Justice: The Courts of the Third Reich*, trans. Deborah Lucas Schneider (Cambridge, MA: Harvard University Press, 1991), 27-119. The definitive account is Krach, *Jüdische Rechtsanwalte*, 165-402.

Fire on February 28, 1933, Jewish lawyers and judges had to endure SA (*Sturmabteilung*, Storm Troopers) organized assaults, harassment, and humiliation. The nation-wide boycott of Jewish businesses on April 1 specifically included Jewish private practitioners. And legislative restriction began on April 7 with the enactment of the "Law for the Restoration of the Professional Civil Service" and the "Law on Admission to the Practicing Bar." The first of these decreed the immediate dismissal of all "non-Aryan" civil servants except for those either already appointed before August 1, 1914, or, at the insistence of President Paul von Hindenburg, who had been Field Marshal and supreme commander during the war, those who had fought for Germany or its allies at the front during the First World War or whose father or son had died at the front in the war.[57] By April 30, 1934, some 574 Jewish judges and prosecutors had lost their jobs under this law. The second of these laws was drawn less restrictively than the first, permitting the denial of admission to the bar or the revocation of admission both to non-Aryan lawyers and to "persons active in a communistic sense." The same exception for those admitted before August 1, 1914, and for veterans or survivors of the First World War further ameliorated the immediate effect of this provision, so that of the 3,370 Jewish lawyers in Prussia, 2,609 remained in practice by summer 1933.[58]

But the institutions of the private bar experienced the same "coordination" (*Gleichschaltung*) that every institution in Germany felt at the hands of the National Socialists, as Nazi administrators over the period after summer 1933 applied ever more restrictive interpretations in these laws of the exceptions that permitted Jewish practitioners to continue in the profession.[59] Nazi officials increasingly excluded Jews from the judiciary, prevented Jews from enrolling in the universities in the legal faculties, purged those faculties of their Jewish professors, and found ways to challenge those lawyers who sought refuge under the two exceptions to the Law on Admission to the Practicing Bar and those judges who claimed them under the Law for the Restoration of the Professional Civil Service.[60] The Nuremberg Laws of September 1935, particularly the Reich Citizenship Law, and the subsequent decrees issued in accordance with it, increasingly restricted the freedom to practice of the remaining Jewish jurists, until the remaining 2,300 practitioners were excluded by the Fifth Supplemental Decree on September 17, 1938, which definitively disbarred all remaining

---

[57] Wolfgang Benz, "Von der Entrechtung zur Verfolgung und Vernichtung. Jüdische Juristen unter dem nationalsozialistischen Regime," in *Deutsche Juristen Jüdischer Herkunft*, 813-52, 823-26. See also Horst Göppinger, *Juristen jüdischer Abstammung im "Dritten Reich". Entrechtung und Verfolgung*, 2d ed. (Munich: Beck, 1990), 45-84.

[58] Benz, "Von der Entrechtung," 825.

[59] For an account of the coordination of the German Bar Association, see Fritz Ostler, *Die deutsche Rechtsanwälte 1871–1971*, 2d ed. (Essen: Juristischer Fachbuchverlag, 1982), 229–37; for an account at the local level of the court of appeal district in Celle (Hannover), see Ledford, *From General Estate to Special Interest*, 291–95.

[60] Göppinger, *Juristen jüdischer Abstammung*, 87–97.

Jews, permitting practice only as representatives of Jewish clients, "*Judenkonsulenten*" ("Jew-counselor").[61]

Those Jewish jurists who remained responded to these developments in a number of ways. A significant number emigrated, early, after the Nuremberg Laws of 1935, or in a final great wave after the *Kristallnacht* pogrom of November 1938.[62] Others remained in Germany and suffered a spectrum of fates. One remarkable outcome is the story of Horst Berkowitz of Hannover. Born in Königsberg in East Prussia, he volunteered for service in the First World War, where he was severely wounded and partially disabled. After the war, he completed university study in law and his practical legal training in the city of Hannover and was admitted to the bar there in 1922. He became a partner of two established lawyers, despite the fact that one was a strident member of the conservative (and antisemitic) German National People's Party, and he enjoyed a remunerative and satisfying practice until 1933. His partners terminated their partnership as of July 1, 1933 (giving three days' notice), but because of his status as a wounded front veteran, he practiced until 1938, representing only Jewish clients in accord with legal and social restrictions. In the midst of *Kristallnacht* on the night of November 9–10, 1938, he was arrested and sent to Buchenwald, only to be released in December. In December 1940, Berkowitz became a forced day-laborer at the concentration camp in the village of Ahlem outside of Hannover. Released after the war, Berkowitz found himself rehabilitated by the British occupation army, and he embarked upon a successful postwar career as a practitioner and then judge, culminating in many honors and distinctions, including the *Bundesverdienstkreuz*.[63]

Sadly, a more typical story is that of Hermann Reis of Marburg. Born in a small village in Hessen outside of Marburg to an observant orthodox Jewish family, Reis studied law in Marburg and Frankfurt, socialized mainly with other Jews and married a relatively well-to-do Jewish woman, but generally shared in the assimilated atmosphere of Imperial and Weimar Republic Germany. A front veteran, Reis set up practice in Marburg with a partner, Willy Wertheim, also Jewish and a front veteran, and he enjoyed a prosperous practice and a comfortable bourgeois existence. The seizure of power by the Nazis had an immediate impact on Reis, however, for despite the front service of Reis and his partner Wertheim, both lawyers lost their admission in 1933 because Wertheim had represented a Communist Party legal aid organization in 1932 and had enclosed a friendly note with his bill for his fee. Reis chose to remain in Marburg rather than emigrate, living

---

[61] Benz, "Von der Entrechtung," 839.

[62] Much of the literature is a listing of those who emigrated, their destinations, and their subsequent careers; see Göppinger, *Juristen jüdischer Abstammung* and the many biographical sketches in *Deutsche Juristen jüdischer Herkunft*.

[63] Ulrich Beer, *Versehrt, verfolgt, versöhnt: Horst Berkowitz, ein jüdisches Anwaltsleben* (Essen: Juristischer Fachbuchverlag, 1979).

from his investments and from his work as a "Jew counselor" representing Jewish clients. When war came, Reis became one of the administrators of the Marburg Jewish community, shrunk now to a hundred members, until he too was deported to the extermination camp at Auschwitz, where he perished.[64]

Jewish judges faced swift exclusion as the two exceptions provided in the Law for the Restoration of the Professional Civil Service suffered rapid erosion. Nationwide studies of the fates of lawyers and judges excluded during the Third Reich are absent, but the Berlin *Kammergericht* has enjoyed particular attention by researchers.[65] After the Nuremberg Laws of 1935, virtually all of the 536 Jewish judges and prosecutors there were excluded from office. Some emigrated, some remained and survived, many perished, as reflected in Table 7.

Table 7: Fate of Jewish Judges in *Kammergericht* District, 1933–1945[66]

	Number	%
Died	169	39.21%
Deported	106	24.59%
Died in custody	6	1.39%
Suicide	13	3.02%
Died in war	5	1.16%
Natural causes	39	9.05%
Survived	262	60.79%
Liberated	7	1.62%
Emigration	173	40.14%
Hid	7	1.62%
Mixed marriage	39	9.05%
Mixed ancestry	35	8.12%
Unknown circumstances	1	0.23%
TOTAL	431	100.00%
Total in 1933	536	

---

[64] John K. Dickinson, *German and Jew: The Life and Death of Sigmund Stein*, 2d ed. with an introduction by Raul Hilberg (Chicago: Ivan Dee, 2001; first ed. 1967); in the first edition, Dickinson used a pseudonym for Hermann Reis and for other identifiable figures in the narrative (and for the town of Marburg) at the request of Reis's surviving brother, a common practice at the time.

[65] Most recently, see Hans Bergemann and Simone Ladwig-Winters, *Jüdische Richter am Kammergericht nach 1933. Eine Dokumentation* (Cologne: Carl Heymanns Verlag, 2004), and idem, *Richter und Staatsanwälte jüdischer Herkunft in Preußen im Nationalsozialismus. Eine Dokumentation* (Cologne: Bundesanzeiger Verlag, 2004).

[66] Bergemann and Ladwig-Winters, *Richter und Staatsanwälte jüdischer Herkunft in Preußen*, 114.

Although some Jewish law professors, judges, and practitioners either remained in Germany and survived or returned after 1945 from emigration, the rich Jewish contribution to the German legal professions, like the rich symbiosis of German-Jewish culture, perished in the murderous catastrophe of the Third Reich.

Conclusion

Although Horst Göppinger bravely lists the names of pre-1933 Jewish law professors, judges, and practitioners who returned to Germany after 1945, the prominent Jewish presence in the German legal professions was at an end.[67] The postwar population of Germany included very few Jews, and even in 2005, there were only 108,000 Jews in a total population of 82.5 million, many of whom have arrived only recently from Russia.[68] Statistics on the number of Jews in legal professions are not available. Indeed, the only study of legal professionals that spans the caesura of the "Zero Hour" or "*Stunde Null*" of 1945 traces the continuity not of the Jewish presence in the German bar but of lawyers in the Federal Republic who had been implicated with the National Socialist party but nevertheless reestablished themselves in the postwar profession.[69]

The relationship of German Jews to the legal professions always had at its core a close connection to liberal politics and liberal notions of meritocracy and the value of individual achievement. The heyday of this connection came in the liberal legal reforms of 1869–1879, which not only emancipated Jews from civil disabilities with greater clarity than before in the century-long emancipation process, but, by opening the private legal profession to market forces, guaranteed Jews an opportunity to claim for themselves a niche in the law determined only by their own hard work and competence. Some Jews pursued legal careers in the judiciary and the academy, but there the process of state control of appointment and advancement limited their opportunity to advance in their fields to the full extent of their talent and hard work. Most Jews entered private practice, where they thrived, advanced, and seemed by the late Empire and Weimar Republic to be fully integrated and respected.

But the values of liberalism had been under assault from the 1890s in Germany, both within and without the legal professions, and by the crisis at the end of Weimar, the liberal value of judgment based on an individual's merit was under widespread assault. Liberalism had reached its limits in

---

[67] Göppinger, *Juristen jüdischer Abstammung*, 325–68.

[68] Federal Statistical Office, "Population, By Age Groups, Marital Status, and Religious Affiliation," 2003–5, http://www.destatis.de/print_e.php. The definitive account of the reconstruction of Jewish communal life in the postwar Germanies is Jay Howard Geller, *Jews in Post-Holocaust Germany, 1945–1953* (New York and Cambridge: Cambridge University Press, 2005).

[69] Eva Douma, *Deutsche Anwälte zwischen Demokratie und Diktatur 1930–1955* (Frankfurt am Main: Fischer, 1998).

political, economic, and social crisis, and as frustrated Germans abandoned liberalism, Jews in the legal professions and elsewhere fell victim to profoundly illiberal schemes that rejected the universalism of emancipation, suspected the aims of and prospects for assimilation, and ultimately sought a solution for crisis by excluding Jews first from state service, then the private legal profession, then the "national community" by law, and finally from the "national community" by persecution and murder.[70] The entire presupposition of the involvement of German Jews in the legal professions was the context of liberalism, and when liberalism lost its support, German Jews irreparably lost their place both in the German legal professions and in German society as a whole.

---

[70] I have explicated my argument about the limits of liberalism elsewhere; Kenneth F. Ledford, "Lawyers and the Limits of Liberalism: The German Bar in the Weimar Republic," in *Lawyers and the Rise of Western Political Liberalism*, ed. Terence C. Halliday and Lucien Karpik (Oxford: Clarendon Press. 1998), 229–64.

Louis Marshall, Julius Henry Cohen, Benjamin Cardozo, and the New York Emergency Rent Laws of 1920: A Case Study in the Role of Jewish Lawyers and Jewish Law in Early Twentieth Century Public Interest Litigation

Samuel J. Levine*

I. Introduction

In 2006, Cardozo Law School hosted a groundbreaking conference on "Jews and the Legal Profession," exploring the impact Jewish lawyers have had on the practice of law in the United States.[1] Scholars from a wide range of disciplines addressed a variety of important and interrelated themes including: sociological issues, such as the connection between the Jewish social and religious experience and areas of law commonly practiced among Jewish lawyers in the United States; historical studies of the role of Jewish lawyers in the evolution of the American legal profession; and the substantive function of Jewish law in the development and conceptualization of American law.[2]

This chapter aims to consider an example of the interplay of these themes through an examination of the litigation surrounding the New York Emergency Rent Laws of 1920. In particular, the chapter focuses upon a series of cases litigated by two of the most prominent Jewish lawyers in United States in the first half of the twentieth century: Louis Marshall and Julius Henry Cohen. Typical of many leading Jewish lawyers at the time, in

---

* Professor and Director of the Jewish Law Institute, Touro College Jacob D. Fuchsberg Law Center. This Chapter originally appeared as an article in *Journal of the Legal Profession* 33 (2008): 1–29. I thank Suzanne Stone and Marc Galanter for inviting me to participate in the conference on Jews and the Legal Profession, and Bob Gordon, Larry Mitchell, Russ Pearce, and Tanina Rostain for helpful conversations. For assistance in historical research, I thank the Law Librarians at Pepperdine University School of Law, in particular Don Buffaloe, Senior Research Services Librarian. Finally, I thank Fraida Liba, Yehudah, Aryeh, Rachel, and Shira for continued encouragement.

[1] See Center for Jewish Law and Contemporary Civilization, http://www.cardozo.yu.edu/cjl/conferences.asp?ids=3948 (the conference was cosponsored by the American Association of Jewish Lawyers and Jurists, Fordham Law School's Institute on Religion, Law, & Lawyer's Work, Harvard Law School's Program on the Legal Profession, and New York Law School's Center for Professional Values and Practice) (last visited Oct. 8, 2008).

[2] See conference invitation, http://www.cardozo.yu.edu/jlis/conference-invitation.pdf (invitation to the Jews and the Legal Profession Conference, October 22–24, 2006) (last visited Oct. 8, 2008).

addition to their other accomplishments, Marshall and Cohen distinguished themselves in their commitment to public service. Moreover, much of Marshall's most important work was dedicated to serving the needs of American Jewish individuals and communities, while Cohen showed a sustained interest in Jewish communal concerns, albeit to a considerably lesser degree than Marshall. In the context of the rent cases, however, Marshall and Cohen found themselves on opposing sides, yet in much of the litigation they each represented Jewish clients.

Among other notable aspects of the litigation, the cases reached the New York Court of Appeals and the United States Supreme Court, which at that time included two of the most eminent jurists in the history of the United States, Judge Benjamin N. Cardozo and Justice Oliver Wendell Holmes, Jr., respectively.[3] One element of the strategy Cohen employed in advocating before these courts adds yet another component to the significance of Jewish lawyers and Jewish law in the context of the Emergency Rent Laws cases. Specifically, in both his briefs and his oral arguments, Cohen relied, in part, on materials from medieval Jewish legal history. In his memoirs, published nearly twenty-five years later, Cohen offers a candid and entertaining reflection on his possible motivations for including these materials, recalling a colorful—if historically questionable—anecdote suggesting that he hoped to influence Cardozo through the references to Jewish law.[4]

Part I of this chapter provides a brief background of the New York Emergency Rent Laws, tracing the enactment of the legislation as well as the course of the ensuing litigation. As illustrated in the names of the parties, many of the cases involved Jewish litigants, in addition to Jewish lawyers. Part II explores the roles of Marshall and Cohen in these cases, placing their contributions in the context of their broader efforts and shared commitments to furthering public and Jewish communal interests. Finally, Part III of the chapter focuses on Cohen's reliance on Jewish legal sources and other historical precedents in his arguments supporting the constitutionality of the New York Emergency Rent Laws. In light of the limited substantive relevance of Jewish law to the legal issues surrounding the Emergency Rent Laws, the chapter looks at alternative motivations for Cohen's inclusion of these materials in his briefs and arguments. In particular, Cohen's memoirs recall the remark of one of the judges on the New York Court of Appeals suggesting that the reference to Jewish law was an effective method for influencing Cardozo.[5]

However, the chapter concludes that this story, even if accurate, was most likely not a reliable reflection of Cohen's reasons for relying on Jewish

---

[3] See, e.g., 810 West End Ave. v. Stern, 130 N.E. 931 (N.Y. 1921); Block v. Hirsh, 256 U.S. 135(1921).

[4] See Julius Henry Cohen, *They Builded Better Than They Knew* (New York: Julian Messner Inc., 1946) (dedicated "To my friends-Portraits within" [dedication page, unnumbered]); the original title of the book was apparently: *They Builded Better Than They Knew, Selective Portraits for an American Gallery 1895–1945.*

[5] See ibid.

law, and indeed, that Cohen may have recounted the colorful story primarily as means of entertainment. This conclusion is reached on the basis of a number of factors, including a consideration of Cardozo's attitude toward the law and toward his Jewish heritage, as well as an examination of the interactions of lawyers and judges involved in the New York Emergency Rent Laws Cases. Ultimately, the chapter suggests, Cohen's anecdote provides a valuable framework for reflection on the interests and interrelationships that might have influenced judicial decision making in the early twentieth century. Moreover, in light of controversies that have arisen regarding the religious beliefs and personal relationships of members of the current Supreme Court, this exercise has abiding relevance and potential application in the early twenty-first century as well.

II. Background—Emergency Rent Laws

A. The Legislation

During World War I and in the years that followed, many large American cities experienced severe housing shortages, resulting from the combination of a precipitous growth in population and a drastic decrease in construction.[6] In New York City, landlords took advantage of the situation, demanding exorbitant rent increases under the threat of eviction.[7] As the New York Court of Appeals later found, "dispossess[ion] proceedings, more than had ever been known before, were pending to the number of upwards of 100,000; each proceeding practically involved a family averaging four or five persons."[8] In response, in April 1920, the New York State Legislature passed a set of housing laws placing a variety of restrictions on landlords.[9] Significantly, however, in practice the April Laws generally allowed landlords to increase rents up to twenty-five percent.[10] Of more urgent concern, leases of unspecified duration were deemed to be set to expire on October 1, enabling landlords to serve eviction notices on tens of thousands of tenants, who would be required to leave their dwellings on September 30.[11]

In the face of the impending crisis, the Legislature convened an extraordinary session and, on September 27, 1920, enacted the Emergency Rent Laws.[12] Among other significant features, with limited exceptions, the

---

[6] See People ex rel. Durham Really Corp. v. La Fetra, 230 N.Y. 429, 437–38 (1921).

[7] See ibid., 438.

[8] Ibid.

[9] April Housing Laws, N.Y. Sess. Laws 1920. chs. 131–38. See Joseph A. Spencer, "New York City Tenant Organizations and the Post World-War I Housing Crisis," in *The Tenant Movement in New York City, 1904–1984*, ed. Ronal Lawson (New Brunswick: Rutgers University Press, 1986), 72; Jared N. Day, *Urban Castles: Tenement Housing and Landlord Activism in New York City, 1890–1943* (New York: Columbia University Press, 1999), 134–36.

[10] See Spencer, "New York City Tenant Organizations," 73; Day, *Urban Castles*, 139–40.

[11] See Spencer, "New York City Tenant Organizations," 73–74.

[12] September Housing Laws, N.Y. Sess. Laws 1920, chs. 942–53.

September housing laws stayed dispossession proceedings until November 1, 1922, and required that rent increases comply with statutory and judicial determinations of reasonableness.[13] Not surprisingly, the September laws engendered strong protests from landlords, leading to a series of cases litigated though the various levels of the New York State court system,[14] reaching the New York Court of Appeals[15] and, ultimately, the United States Supreme Court.[16] A look at the identities and interactions of many of the parties, a number of the lawyers, and some of the judges in these cases provides a window into various aspects of the attitudes and impact of Jewish lawyers in the United States in the early twentieth century.

B. The Cases

Litigation over the Emergency Rent Laws commenced almost immediately after they were enacted and proceeded expeditiously through both the New York State and the United States court systems.[17] One of the earliest decisions on the Emergency Rent Laws was handed down in the New York State Supreme Court in Bronx County on October 19, 1920.[18] The names of the parties, Jacob Guttag and Hyman Shatzkin,[19] as well as the lawyers, Bernard Deutsch and Julius Tobias,[20] present an early illustration of the involvement of Jewish individuals in these cases. Similarly, a number of New York County cases decided shortly thereafter included Jewish parties, as indicated by names such as: Rose Heyman,[21] Mortimer Oster-

---

[13] See People ex rel. Durham Realty Corp. v. La Fetra, 230 N.Y. 429, 438 (1921); Spencer, "New York City Tenant Organizations," 74–75 n. 9. See also Guy McPherson, "Note: It's the End of the World as We Know It (and I Feel Fine): Rent Regulation in New York City and the Unanswered Questions of Market and Society," *Fordham Law Review* 72 (2004): 1131–32; "Note, Residential Rent Control in New York City," *Columbia Journal of Law and Social Problems* 3 (1967): 30–32.

[14] See *infra*, Part I.B.

[15] See Durham Realty Corp. v. La Fetra, 230 N.Y. 429 (1921).

[16] See Edgar A. Levy Leasing Co. v. Siegel, 258 U.S. 242 (1922); Marcus Brown Holding Co. v. Feldman, 256 U.S. 170 (1921).

[17] Edgar A. Levy Leasing Co., 258 U.S. 242; Marcus Brown Holding Co., 256 U.S. 170; Durham Realty Corp., 230 N.Y. 429. Likewise, the Emergency Rent Laws engendered almost immediate scholarly reaction. See Harold G. Aron, "The New York Landlord and Tenant Laws of 1920," *Cornell Law Quarterly* 6 (1920): 1–35. See also George W. Wickersham, "The Police Power and the New York Emergency Rent Laws," *University of Pennsylvania Law Review* 69 (1921): 301–16.

[18] Guttag v. Shatzkin, 113 Misc. 362, 185 N.Y.S. 71 (N.Y. Sup. Ct. 1920), rev'd, 194 A.D. 509 (N.Y. App. Div 1920), rev'd, 230 N.Y. 647 (1921).

[19] *Guttag*, 113 Misc. at 362.

[20] Ibid., 363. Similarly, Clara Wasserman, the plaintiff in a case decided in Kings County on October 16, 1920, was represented by Benjamin Ammerman. See People ex rel. Wasserman v. Fagan, 113 Misc. 255, 185 N.Y.S. 308 (N.Y. Sup. Ct. 1920).

[21] See Heyman v. Osterweis, 113 Misc. 282 (N.Y. Sup. Ct. 1920). The opinion is dated October 1920.

weis,[22] Ellis Hyman,[23] Abraham Gordon,[24] Edgar A. Levy Leasing Company,[25] Jerome Siegel,[26] and Henry Stern.[27]

Notably, of the numerous lawyers who participated in the cases—many of whom were likewise Jewish—two lawyers stand out, both for their central roles in the rent cases and for their broader significance in Jewish and legal communities in the early twentieth century: Louis Marshall and Julius Henry Cohen. Cohen worked on a number of Emergency Rent Laws trial court cases, decided in November[28] and December, 1920,[29] in New York State Supreme Court, New York Special Term, and he continued to litigate many of the cases through the final appeal.[30] Marshall, who rarely served as a trial attorney,[31] became involved at the appellate level.

On December 24, 1920, the New York State Supreme Court, Appellate Division, First Department, issued several opinions relating to the Emergency Rent Laws, all of which list Cohen as counsel arguing in support of the laws.[32] In two of the cases, *Edgar A. Levy Leasing Co. v. Siegel*[33] and

---

[22] See ibid.

[23] See Hyman v. Gordon, 185 N.Y.S. 301 (Mun. Ct. 1920). The opinion is dated October 25, 1920.

[24] See ibid.

[25] See Edgar A. Levy Leasing Co. v. Siegel, 194 A.D. 482 (N.Y. App. Div. 1920). As noted in the appellate court opinion, the trial court judgment was entered on November 26, 1920. Ibid., 483.

[26] See ibid., 482.

[27] See 810 West End Ave. v. Stern, 186 N.Y.S. 56 (N.Y. App. Div. 1920). The appellate court opinion, decided December 24, 1920, does not cite a date for the trial court judgment. See also Versailles Holding Corp. v. Stein (N.Y. Sup. Ct. Nov. 26, 1920) (unpublished opinion, on file with author); Burke v. Hurlbut (N.Y. Sup. Ct. Dec. 17, 1920) (unpublished opinion, on file with author); Sperling v. Barton, 188 N.Y.S. 857 (N.Y. App. Term 1921). Likewise, Jewish parties were named in many of the reported cases litigated pursuant to the April Laws. See, e.g., Kuenzli v. Stone, 182 N.Y.S. 680 (N.Y. App. Div. 1920); Blek v. Davis, 183 N.Y.S. 737 (N.Y. App. Div. 1920); Horn v. Klugman, 183 N.Y.S. 150 (N.Y. Mun. Q. 1920), *rev'd*, 184 N.Y.S. 927 (N.Y. App. Div. 1920); Shanik v. Eckhardt, 183 N.Y.S. 155 (N.Y. App. Div. 1920); Paterno Investing Corp. v. Katz, 184 N.Y.S. 129 (N.Y. Sup. Ct. 1920); Seventy-Eighth St. & Broadway Co. v. Rosenbaum, 182 N.Y.S. 505 (N.Y. Mun. Ct. 1920). See also Spencer, "New York City Tenant Organizations," 70–71 (noting the prevalence of Jewish litigants, lawyers, and communal organizations in the controversy over the Emergency Rent Laws).

[28] See, e.g., William Brandt & Co. v. Weil, 185 N.Y.S. 497 (N.Y. Sup. Ct. 1920).

[29] See, e.g., People ex rel. Durham Realty Corp. v. La Fetra, 185 N.Y.S. 638 (N.Y. Sup. Ct. 1920); People ex. rel. Brixton Operating Corp. v. La Fetra, 185 N.Y.S. 632 (N.Y. Sup. Ct. 1920); Ullmann Realty Co. v. Tamur, 185 N.Y.S. 612 (N.Y. Sup. Ct. 1920). Cohen also participated in an Emergency Rent Laws case that came before a federal court, on the basis of diversity jurisdiction, and was decided in December of 1920. See Marcus Brown Holding Co. v. Feldman, 269 F. 306 (S.D.N.Y. 1920).

[30] See, e.g., Edgar A. Levy Leasing Co. v. Siegel, 258 U.S. 242 (1922).

[31] See Oscar Handlin, "Introduction," in *Louis Marshall: Champion of Liberty, Selected Papers and Addresses* I, ed. Charles Reznikoff (Philadelphia: Jewish Publication Society of America, 1957), xvi [hereafter *Marshall: Papers and Addresses* I].

[32] See Edgar A. Levy Leasing Co. v. Siegel, 186 N.Y.S. 5 (N.Y. App. Div. 1920); 810 West End Ave., Inc. v. Stern, 186 N.Y.S. 56 (N.Y. App. Div. 1920); People ex rel. Durham Realty

810 West End Ave. v. Stern,[34] Cohen and Marshall are listed as lead counsel for the opposing sides. Less than one month later, on January 19, 1921, the New York Court of Appeals heard arguments on many of these cases,[35] with Cohen and Marshall serving as central figures in the proceedings.[36] The Court of Appeals decided these cases in several opinions handed down on March 8, 1921."[37] Finally, less than one year later, the cases of *Levy Leasing*[38] and *810 West End Avenue*[39] reached the United States Supreme Court,[40] argued on January 24 and 25, 1922, with Marshall and Cohen again

---

Corp. v. La Fetra, 186 N.Y.S. 63 (N.Y. App. Div. 1920); People ex rel. Brixton Operating Corp. v. La Fetra, 186 N.Y.S. 58 (N.Y, App. Div. 1920); Guttag v. Shatzkin, 186 N.Y.S 47 (N.Y. App. Div. 1920), *rev'd*, 130 N.E. 929 (N.Y. 1921); Clemilt Realty Co. v. Wood, 186 N.Y.S. 415 (N.Y. App. Div. 1920); People ex rel. H.D.H. Really Corp. v. Murphy, 186 N.Y.S. 38 (N.Y. App. Div. 1920); People ex rel. Ballin v. O'Connell, 186 N.Y.S. 46 (N.Y. App. Div. 1920).

An additional Emergency Rent Laws case was decided in the New York State Supreme Court, Appellate Division, Second Department, on December 7, 1920. See People ex rel. Rayland Realty Co. v. Fagan, 194 A.D. 185 (N.Y. App. Div. 1920). Although Cohen is not listed as counsel on the case, William D. Guthrie, who worked with Cohen on many of these cases, is listed as having submitted an amicus brief. Ibid., 186.

[33] *Edgar A. Levy*, 186 N.Y.S. 5.

[34] *810 W. End Ave.*, 186 N.Y.S. 56.

[35] See, e.g., People ex rel. Durham Realty Corp. v. La Fetra, 230 N.Y. 429, 434 (1921), which also decided the appeal of People ex rel. Brixton Operating Corp. v. La Fetra, 186 N.Y.S 58; Edgar A. Levy Leasing Co. v. Siegel, 230 N.Y. 634 (1921); 810 West End Ave. v. Stern, 230 N.Y. 652 (1921); People ex rel. H.D.H. Realty Corp. v. Murphy, 230 N.Y. 654 (1921); People ex rel. Rayland Realty Co. v. Fagan, 230 N.Y. 653 (1921); People ex rel. Ballin v. O'Connell, 230 N.Y. 655 (1921); Clemilt Really Co. v. Wood, 230 N.Y. 646 (1921); Guttag v. Shatzkin, 230 N.Y. 647 (1921).

[36] Cohen is listed as counsel in People ex rel. Durham Realty Corp. v. La Fetra, 230 N.Y. 429, 434 (1921), the opinion of which served as the majority opinion for the other Emergency Rent Laws cases in the Court of Appeals as well. Cohen was also listed in the cases of: People ex rel. H.D.H. Really Corp. v. Murphy, 230 N.Y. 654 (1921), People ex rel. Rayland Realty Co., Inc. v. Fagan, 230 N.Y. 653 (1921), and People ex rel. Ballin v. O'Connell, 230 N.Y. 655 (1921). Marshall is listed in Edgar A. Levy Leasing Co. v. Siegel, 230 N.Y. 634 (1921), and 810 West End Ave. v. Stern, 230 N.Y. 652 (1921).

[37] The majority opinion for all of these cases was handed down in People ex rel. Durham Realty Corp. v. La Fetra, 130 N.E. 601 (N.Y. 1921). For the concurring opinion in these cases, see Guttag v. Shatzkin, 230 N.Y. 647, 648 (1921) (Crane, J., concurring in result). For the dissenting opinion in these cases, see Edgar A. Levy Leasing Co. v. Siegel, 120 N.E. 923, 924 (N.Y. 1921) (McLaughlin, J. dissenting).

[38] Edgar A. Levy Leasing Co. v. Siegel, 120 N.E. 923 (N.Y. 1921).

[39] 810 West End Ave. v. Stern, 130 N.E. 931 (N.Y. 1921).

[40] In 1921, three other cases involving emergency rent laws reached the Unites States Supreme Court. On April 18, 1921, in a 5-4 decision, the Court upheld a Washington, D.C., emergency rent law. See Block v. Hirsh, 256 U.S. 135 (1921). Justice Homes wrote the majority opinion, while Justice McKenna wrote a dissenting opinion, joined by Chief Justice Taft and Justices Van Devanter and McReynolds. On the same day, divided along the same lines, the Court upheld the New York Emergency Rent Laws, affirming the judgment of the United States District Court for the Southern District of New York. See Marcus Brown Holding Co! v. Feldman, 256 U.S. 170 (1921). In a preview to the Levy Leasing litigation, Cohen and Marshall filed opposing briefs in the case. See *infra* notes 85 and 134 and accompanying text. Finally, on October 10, 1921, deciding a case litigated

serving as lead counsel. On March 20, 1922, in a 6-3 decision, the Court ruled in Cohen's favor, upholding the constitutionality of the Emergency Rent Laws.[41]

III. The Lawyers: Louis Marshall and Julius Henry Cohen

A. Louis Marshall

Marshall's life and work have been well-documented through his own words in letters, papers, and addresses posthumously edited and collected in two large volumes.[42] Tellingly, the subtitle of the collection ascribes to Marshall the appellation "Champion of Liberty,"[43] drawn from a tribute Benjamin N. Cardozo offered on Marshall's seventieth birthday.[44] Succinctly summarizing Marshall's career, Cardozo described him as "a great lawyer; a great champion of ordered liberty; a great leader of his people; a great lover of mankind."[45]

Marshall's reputation as a lawyer grew in part out of his work as a name partner in the prominent corporate law firm, Guggenheimer, Untermyer & Marshall. Complementing his corporate practice, Marshall served as a leading constitutional lawyer, earning Cardozo's praise through his efforts to champion the liberties of numerous minority groups and communities, including: African-Americans, whose housing and voting rights he worked to protect in his capacity as a director of the National Association for the Advancement of Colored People; Native-Americans, whose property rights he defended in serving voluntarily as counsel for the Pueblo nations;[46] Japanese-Americans, who were subjected to discriminatory property laws; and Catholics, whose religious freedoms were infringed upon by a law that was challenged in the landmark United States Supreme Court case of *Pierce v. Society of Sisters*.[47] Indeed, Marshall gained such respect as a lawyer that he was considered in 1911 as a possible nominee to the United States Supreme Court.[48]

Moreover, as Cardozo further observed, as part of his commitment to "liberty" and "mankind," Marshall distinguished himself as a "great leader

---

by Marshall, the Court issued a Memorandum Decision dismissing an appeal of People ex rel. Brixton Operating Co. v. La Fetra, 257 U.S. 665 (1921).

[41] See Edgar A. Levy Leasing Co. v. Siegel, 258 U.S. 242 (1922). The majority opinion was written by Justice Clarke, with Justices McKenna, Van Devanter, and McReynolds dissenting without opinion.

[42] See *Marshall: Papers and Addresses* I & II.

[43] Ibid., I, 42.

[44] See ibid. (Introductory quotation, unnumbered).

[45] Ibid.

[46] See Handlin, "Introduction," xxxix–xl.

[47] Ibid.

[48] Ibid., xvii.

of his people," the Jewish community.[49] Marshall felt a deep and abiding connection to his Jewish heritage, nurtured during his upbringing in a home observant of Orthodox "practice."[50] On a communal level, Marshall was a central figure in various institutions and organizations, serving, for example, as president of Temple Emanu-El and chairman of the Board of Directors of the Jewish Theological Seminary.[51] Most significantly, Marshall helped found the American Jewish Committee and continued to guide it for many years while serving as its president.[52] The broad and ambitious mission of the AJC, "to aid in securing the civil and religious rights of the Jews in all countries where such rights are denied or endangered," reflected the scope of Marshall's efforts and concern for Jewish individual and communal needs.

B. Julius Henry Cohen

Though less prominent a figure than Marshall in both legal and Jewish communities, Julius Henry Cohen played a substantial role in numerous matters of public interest in the first half of the twentieth century. Like Marshall, the most comprehensive source of information about Cohen's life and work is found in his own words.[53] Unlike Marshall, however, whose writings were collected and published by others after his death, Cohen reflected upon his own experiences in a candid, insightful, and highly entertaining memoir, framed largely through a portrayal of Cohen's interactions with important public figures over the course of fifty years.[54]

Cohen demonstrated concern for the public interest through the variety of positions he held and efforts he undertook, including, among many others: assisting in the formation of the Port of New York Authority and serving as its general counsel for more than twenty years; serving as a founding member of the American Arbitration Association and helping to establish its policies and procedures; playing a central role in resolving the 1910 garment workers' strike in New York; and serving as Special Assistant United States Attorney and Special Deputy Attorney General in a number of cases of public importance.[55]

---

[49] Ibid., xiii; see also ibid. (dedication page, unnumbered).

[50] Ibid.

[51] Ibid., xix; see also Jerold S. Auerbach, *Rabbis and Lawyers: The Journey from Torah to Constitution* (Bloomington: Indiana University Press, 1990), 98–100, 109–10.

[52] See Handlin, "Introduction," xxvi. One scholar describes Marshall as "the undisputed leader of Jewish communal affairs until his death in 1929," and concludes: "hardly an issue of consequence in American Jewish life was resolved independently of his contribution." See specifically Auerbach, *Rabbis and Lawyers*, 94, 110–11.

[53] See Auerbach, *Rabbis and Lawyers*, 110.

[54] See Cohen, *They Builded Better*. See also Julius Henry Cohen, "Rent Control After World War 1— Recollections," *N.Y.U. Legal Quarterly Review* 21 (1946): 267.

[55] See "J.H. Cohen Dies; Ex-Counsel to Port Authority," *New York Herald Tribune*, Oct. 7, 1950; "Julius Cohen, 77. Lawyer 53 Years," *New York Times*, Oct. 7, 1950; "Necrological: Julius Henry Cohen," *New York Law Journal*, Oct. 18, 1950. See also Gerald Fetner,

Cohen's connection with his Jewish heritage was far less public than Marshall's and, based on his own reflections, his attitude toward Jewish religious practice may best be characterized as somewhat ambivalent.[56] Nevertheless, in much of his professional life he was closely involved with segments and influential individual members of the Jewish community, through both the substance of his public interest work and the identity of many of his associates and clients. In fact, in some ways Cohen's legal career typified the experience of many leading Jewish lawyers at the time.[57] Indeed, one scholar has cited Cohen and Morris Hillquit as examples of early twentieth-century "Jewish lawyers ... who were deeply involved with new immigrant groups, unionism, the use of arbitration in industrial disputes, and public service as counsel to various administrative agencies."[58]

C. Interactions Between Marshall and Cohen

Thus, although they found themselves on opposing sides in the Emergency Rent Laws cases, Marshall and Cohen shared a number of common goals and principles, reflected in their similar perspectives on other legal issues. Indeed, Marshall and Cohen were two of the primary architects of the agreement that settled the garment workers' strike. Not incidentally, as Cohen later observed, most of the employers and workers in the garment industry were members of a relatively closely-knit Jewish community.[59]

"Public Power and Professional Responsibility. Julius Henry Cohen and The Origins of Public Authority," *American Journal of Legal History* 21 (1977): 15.

[56] See Samuel J. Levine, "Rediscovering Julius Henry Cohen and the Origins of the Business/Profession Dichotomy: A Study in the Discourse of Early Twentieth Century Legal Professionalism," *American Journal of Legal History* 47 (2005): 11–12 n. 52. For further discussions of Cohen's work, see ibid.; idem, "Professionalism Without Parochialism: Julius Henry Cohen: Rabbi Nachman of Breslov, and the Stories of Two Sons," *Fordham Law Review* 71 (2002–03): 1339–56.

[57] See Cohen, *They Builded Better*.

[58] Andrew L. Kaufman, *Cardozo* (Cambridge, MA: Harvard University Press, 1998), 99; Jerold S. Auerbach, *Unequal Justice: Lawyers and Social Change in Modern America* (Oxford: Oxford University Press, 1976) (noting that "during the 1930's ... [minority-group lawyers, especially Jews, flocked into a field of practice where it was possible to merge liberal reform or radical hope with professional fulfillment"); Marc Galanter, "A Vocation for Law? American Jewish Lawyers and Their Antecedents," *Fordham Urban Law Journal* 26 (1999): 1125 (observing that Jewish lawyers in the United States "have contributed disproportionately to many branches of the 'public interest sector,' with particular prominence in public service, public interest law firms and the defense of minorities and unpopular causes, to name a few"); Robert Gordon, "The Independence of Lawyers," *Boston University Law Review* 68 (1988): 33 (stating that "the ideal of independent lawyering ... has found some of its greatest exponents among Jewish lawyers [for example, Louis Brandeis, Louis Marshall, Felix Frankfurter, Jerome Frank], who, excluded from the inner circles of the WASP elite, had the vantage point of marginality to scold that elite for selling out its public service traditions to big business clients"); Russell G. Pearce, "Jewish Lawyering in a Multicultural Society: A Midrash on Levinson," *Cardozo Law Review* 14 (1993): 1616–23.

[59] See Cohen, *They Builded Better*, 183. Cohen quotes at length the view of one historian who observed:

According to Cohen, it was out of familiarity with and concern for the Jewish community that such prominent lawyers as Marshall and Louis D. Brandeis devoted so much of their time,[60] while other lawyers of varying political views worked together,[61] in an effort to find a resolution to the matter. As Cohen put it, "They understood and knew the people in the industry. They had different views on economics and on politics but they had a common background."[62]

Along with their common interests, Marshall and Cohen shared mutual respect. A few years after they worked to resolve the garment industry dispute, Marshall wrote a gracious letter thanking Cohen for sending a copy of the "Protocols of Peace in the Dress and Waist Industry" and congratulating Cohen for "having accomplished the practical adoption of the

---

> The fact that most employers and workers alike long belonged to the relatively compact Jewish community, where the sufferings of one group could not long escape the attention of the other, aided understanding. The more enlightened employers did not want the needle trades, the most distinctively Jewish industries in America, to remain at a sweatshop level. Prominent Jews had used their influence to bring peace to the industries on a basis fair to all. As a result the needle industries, while contributing some stirring chapters to the history of American industrial strife, have been especially noted for experiments in peaceful industrial relations.

Similar sentiments were expressed in Will Herberg, "The Jewish Labor Movement in the United States," *American Jewish Year Book* 53 (1952): 18–20, cited in *Marshall: Paper and Addresses* II, 1128. The author of the article recounts the efforts of Brandeis, Marshall, and others, noting that Marshall and Jacob H. Schiff "felt that the good name of the Jewish community was being imperil[ed] by the conflict, particularly since public opinion was overwhelmingly on the side of the workers...." Moreover, the author concludes that "In the sensitivity to public opinion, the strong tradition of arbitration, and the common ethnic, cultural, and religious background [...] probably contributed very considerably to the achievement of the Protocol of Peace and to the development of industrial relations in the major Jewish unions for some time thereafter."

[60] With respect to the contributions of Brandeis to the resolution of the dispute, it may be worthwhile to note Marshall's remarks in a 1912 letter. *Marshall: Papers and Addresses* II, 1127 (Letter from Louis Marshall to Miss Gertrude Barnum, Nov. 29, 1912). Following a disclaimer, stating that "I am not induced to do so by personal vanity," Marshall emphasizes the "possible historical importance" of his reflections. Although Marshall acknowledges that "Mr. Louis D. Brandeis performed valiant service in the early stages of the general strike of the clockmakers in July, 1910," Marshall declares that "his efforts did not bring about the settlement of the strike...." Ibid. Marshall adds that, "[a]s a matter of fact, the manufacturers and the workmen were unable to agree and drifted entirely apart, to the extent that conditions became well nigh perilous." Ibid. According to Marshall, "[i]t was at that time that I was called in by the representatives of the contending parties, to act as mediator, as a result of conferences covering about two weeks, I personally prepared the protocol of peace, and brought about its adoptions by both parties." Ibid. Nevertheless, Marshall insists that "[t]his is of course merely for your information, as I have no desire to minimize the importance of the contribution of Mr. Brandeis to the settlement of the strike." Ibid., 1128.

[61] In Cohen's view "[t]his explains why Max Meyer and Reuben Sadowsky could work with Morris Hillquit and Meyer London." See Cohen, *They Builded Better*, 183. Cohen dedicated four chapters of his memoirs to his recollections of Meyer, Brandeis, Hillquit, and London, respectively. See Cohen, ibid., 179–89; 190–200; 201–14; 215–22.

[62] Ibid., 183.

now famous protocol of the cloak industry."⁶³ In turn, recalling in his memoirs the difficulty involved in finding an appropriate title for the agreement, Cohen credits Marshall with selecting the inherently "mysterious" term "Protocol."⁶⁴ In a depiction that may tellingly reveal an element of Cohen's perceptions of both Marshall and Jewish religious leaders, Cohen characterizes Marshall as thus "show[ing] his shrewdness, the shrewdness of an old rabbi."⁶⁵

Likewise, despite their disagreement on the merits of the Emergency Rent Laws, Cohen's recollection of the dispute includes words of glowing praise for Marshall, whom he identifies as "very distinctly [the] leading lawyer" for the landlords in these cases.⁶⁶ Cohen describes Marshall as "a great constitutional lawyer of [his] day"⁶⁷ and "one of those extraordinary people who can give you the number of the volume, the page reference and even the year any case was decided."⁶⁸ Moreover, on a more personal level, Cohen admired Marshall as "a great character" who "came here from leadership at the Syracuse bar which he won by clear merit."⁶⁹

Notably, although Marshall and Cohen often shared common legal and social ideals,⁷⁰ Cohen did not fault Marshall for taking the position that the Emergency Rent Laws were unconstitutional. Cohen understood the perspectives and legal arguments offered in support of landlords, acknowledging that "[a]s a matter of fact, these laws did result in considerable hardship in some instances, especially in the cases of widows dependent upon fixed incomes coming from rentals."⁷¹ In fact, Cohen estimated that had a poll been conducted among leaders of the legal establishment consisting of "lawyers on Pine, Wall, Broad Streets and lower Broadway, something like

---

⁶³ *Marshall: Papers and Addresses* II, 1130 (letter from Louis Marshall to Julius Henry Cohen, Jan. 20, 1913). The letter concludes with Marshall's acknowledgment that Cohen is "entirely right in [his] analysis of the situation." Ibid. Specifically, reflecting their commonly shared—if broadly articulated—ideals, the last lines of the letter state: "Reason and justice must be regarded as equally important to labor and capital. It is the golden mean between oppression and anarchy." Likewise, a letter from Marshall to Meyer London in the midst of negotiations expressly credited the drafting of the protocols to the work of Marshall, London, and Cohen. See ibid., 1128 (letter from Louis Marshall to Meyer London, Sept. 1, 1910).

⁶⁴ Cohen, *They Builded Better*, 221.

⁶⁵ Ibid.

⁶⁶ Ibid., 168. Cohen's recollections of the litigation surrounding the Emergency Rent Laws were published separately in an issue of the *New York University Law Quarterly Review* shortly prior to their publication as a chapter in his memoirs. See ibid., *They Builded Better*, 162–75.

⁶⁷ Cohen, *They Builded Better*, 169.

⁶⁸ Ibid.

⁶⁹ Ibid., 172.

⁷⁰ Ibid., 183.

⁷¹ Ibid., 168.

ninety-five percent [sic] would have been for 'unconstitutionality'... of the Emergency Rent Laws."[72]

In light of these impressions, Cohen presents a candid and insightful observation about William D. Guthrie's participation on behalf of tenants in these cases. In Cohen's account, Guthrie agreed to join the litigation at the urging of Bernard Hershkopf, whose "fine social instinct put him in complete sympathy with the [Emergency Rent L]aw[s]," and with whom Guthrie worked on important constitutional cases.[73] A leading member of the elite legal establishment, Guthrie had served for more than two decades as a name partner, and over a decade as senior partner in the law firm that evolved into the Cravath Firm.[74] Indeed, during the last years of his leadership, from 1901 to 1906, the firm was named Guthrie, Cravath & Henderson.[75] Like Marshall, Guthrie argued many important cases before the United States Supreme Court, and at one point Guthrie was considered a possible candidate for the Court.[76] According to Cohen, as a result of Guthrie's professional status, other lawyers found surprising Guthrie's support for the constitutionality of the Emergency Rent Laws. In Cohen's colorful recounting of a lunch meeting he had with Guthrie at the Downtown Club, "after the public announcement" that Guthrie had joined him on the case, "friend after friend of [Guthrie's] came up to him ... and intimated politely that he must be rapidly approaching senility."[77] By the same measure, though, Cohen realized the value of having a lawyer of Guthrie's caliber and reputation as co-counsel on the cases. Given the centrality of the constitutional questions raised by the Emergency Rent Laws, and the formidable opposition posed by Marshall, Cohen attached substantial importance to the fact that "Guthrie was known throughout the country as a great authority on constitutional law."[78]

---

[72] Ibid., 170.

[73] Ibid., 169.

[74] See Robert T. Swaine, *The Cravath Firm and Its Predecessors: 1819–1947*, Volume I (Clark, N.J.: The Lawbook Exchange, 2006), vii, 359–62, 659–65, 767–82.

[75] See ibid., vii, 664–65.

[76] See ibid., 781; Andrew L. Kaufman, "Cardozo's Appointment to the Supreme Court," *Cardozo Law Review* 23 (1979): 24 n. 9. Robert Gordon has identified Guthrie, Marshall, and a number of others as among "perhaps the most prominent" of "superelite" lawyers who entered practice in New York City between 1860 and 1910 and who were also "active in reform politics or law reform." Robert W. Gordon, "The Ideal and the Actual in the Law: Fantasies and Practices of New York City Lawyers. 1870–1910," in *The New High Priests: Lawyers in Post-Civil War America*, ed. Gerard W. Gawalt (Westport: Greenwood Press, 1984), 67 n. 6.

[77] Cohen, *They Builded Better*, 169.

[78] Ibid. Among other distinctions, Guthrie held positions as Storrs Lecturer at Yale University in 1907–08 and as Ruggles Professor of Constitutional Law at Columbia University from 1909 to 1922. See Swaine, *Cravath Firm*, 74, 362. He was also the author of William D. Guthrie, *Lectures on the Fourteenth Article of Amendment to the Constitution of the United States* (New York: Little, Brown & Co., 1898) which "received favorable reviews in the Harvard Law Review and in the Yale Law Journal.'" Ibid. at 660 (citations omitted). Not surprisingly, Marshall and Guthrie often crossed paths in the course of

Perhaps more dramatically, Cohen understood the political significance of Guthrie's willingness to represent tenants against the interests of the real estate industry. Employing characteristic candor, Cohen observed that Guthrie's support "helped us a lot, because if Guthrie came with us, we could not be called a *bunch of radicals*."[79] Though Cohen did not elaborate on this reference to radicals, the self-mocking tone—including the italicized emphasis—unmistakably points to the composition of the lawyers and activists who supported the Emergency Rent Laws. In addition to the legal arguments leveled against the constitutionality of the Emergency Rent Laws, the laws faced a number of challenges in the public arena as well, perhaps most prominently as a result of the combination of the Red Scare and the visibility of Socialist tenant groups.[80] In particular, a number of Jewish union groups, social organizations, and lawyers were closely associated with the efforts of the tenants, often serving in leadership roles, prompting a rising incidence of antisemitism.[81] Thus, Cohen recognized, Guthrie's decision to part ways in this matter with the overwhelming majority of the legal and political elite, allying himself instead with groups and lawyers viewed by many as radicals, helped lend an air of credibility and a prospect of hope to the struggles of a largely unpopular cause.

IV. Cohen's Argument from Jewish law

A. *The Supreme Court Brief*

As lead counsel in Emergency Rent Laws cases before both the New York Court of Appeals[82] and the United States Supreme Court,[83] Cohen and

---

their work, including working together on the landmark Unites States Supreme Court case of Pierce v. Society of Sisters, 268 U.S. 510 (1925). Guthrie and Hershkopf served as counsel for the Society of Sisters, see Brief on Behalf of Appellee, while Marshall filed an amicus brief on behalf of the American Jewish Committee in support of the appellees. See Brief for American Jewish Committee. It is worth noting Marshall's letter to Guthrie, years later, chiding Guthrie for language he used that, in Marshall's estimation, carried antisemitic intonations. See *Marshall: Papers and Addresses* I, 277–80 (Letter from Louis Marshall to William D. Guthrie, Apr. 9, 1926). Although Marshall stated that "[i]t is needless for me to say that I know that you have no prejudices" and "[w]e have fought together on a number of occasions to combat prejudices of this character," he nevertheless declared that "unconsciously, you have permitted yourself to use expressions which are unfortunate, and coming from such as you are apt to contribute to a perverted notion in public mind." Ibid. See also Auerbach, *Rabbis and Lawyers* 121–22; *Marshall: Papers and Addresses*, I, 277 (quoting Guthrie's earlier letter to Marshall that had commended Marshall for voicing a similar protest to an address by Elihu Root: "You have admirably and most eloquently resented an unwarranted attack upon thousands of educated and patriotic Americans").

[79] Cohen, *They Builded Better,* 169 (emphasis in original).

[80] Spencer, "New York City Tenant Organizations," 51–93.

[81] See ibid., 70–71. The antisemitism was exacerbated by the fact that many of the landlords were Jewish as well. See also notes 19–27 and accompanying text.

[82] See People ex rel. Durham Realty Corp. v. La Fetra, 230 N.Y. 429, 434 (1921).

[83] See Brief on Behalf of the Attorney-General and the Joint Legislative Committee on Housing, Edgar A. Levy Leasing Co. v. Siegel, 258 U.S. 242, 243 (1922).

Guthrie were joined on their briefs by Guthrie's colleague, Hershkopf, and by Elmer G. Sammis. In the 117-page brief they submitted to the United States Supreme Court in *Edgar A. Levy Leasing Co. v. Siegel*,[84] they presented a number of arguments in support of the constitutionality of the Emergency Rent Laws, relying primarily upon Supreme Court precedent,[85] the police power of the State,[86] and an examination of the emergency conditions that prompted the enactment of the laws.[87]

The final argument in the brief, authored by Cohen and documenting responses to emergency housing shortages in other countries, referenced both modern and historical remedies, including a relatively esoteric development in Jewish law from sixteenth-century Italy.[88] As Cohen later noted, he cited the example from Jewish law not only in the brief but also in his oral arguments, in both the New York Court of Appeals and the United States Supreme Court.[89] Cohen's reference to Jewish law in the Emergency Rent Laws litigation may prove to be of considerable historical and sociological interest. In light of the central role of Jewish lawyers and parties in these cases, it seems somewhat fitting that Cohen cited Jewish legal precedent. Perhaps more significantly, Cohen's later recollections suggest the strategic value of relying on Jewish law, as well as Irish law, before the New York Court of Appeals in this case.[90] To the extent that Cohen's recollections were both earnest and accurate, they may shed light on some of the strategic calculations lawyers took into account in appearing before early twentieth-century judges.

Cohen's historical argument in the Supreme Court brief is premised on the observation that "Emergencies involving the occupancy of land have arisen and been dealt with in the past, first by communal customs and then by legislation which converted the customs and legally unenforceable obli-

---

[84] See ibid.

[85] See ibid., 10–34. Specifically, they urged the Court to adopt as controlling precedent the rulings decided on April 18, 1921 in Block v. Hirsh, 256 U.S. 135 (1921), and Marcus Brown Holding Co. v. Feldman, 256 U.S. 170 (1921), both of which upheld emergency rent laws. Indeed, as they noted in the brief, in Marcus Brown Holding, the Court decided many of the same issues regarding the constitutionality of New York's Emergency Rent Laws. See Brief, *supra* note 83, at 17. Strikingly, Cohen had filed a brief, by leave of the Court, in Marcus Brown Company, along with the other lawyers who joined him in arguing Levy Leasing. See Brief on Behalf of the Attorney-General and the Joint Legislative Committee on Housing of the State of New York. Likewise, Marshall, who was lead counsel opposing Cohen in Levy Leasing, had filed an opposing amicus brief in Marcus Brown Holding, on behalf of Edgar A. Levy Leasing Company and 810 West End Avenue Incorporated. See Points for Edgar A. Levy Leasing Co. Inc. and 801 West End Avenue Inc. as Amici Curiae on Constitutionality of Chapters 136, 944 and 946 of the New York Laws of 1920.

[86] "Brief," 34–54, *supra* note 83.

[87] See ibid., 54–92.

[88] See ibid., 104–6.

[89] See Cohen, *They Builded Better*, 170–72.

[90] See ibid.

gations into positive law."[91] In particular, "[h]istory has thus again and again evolved as the fair and proper remedy in such cases (1) the restriction of the right to evict, or the recognition of the tenant's right of renewal, and (2) the fixing of reasonable rentals by disinterested authority."[92] As historical evidence for these conclusions, the brief offers a short paragraph documenting equitable protection of tenants' rights in the Roman Empire, followed by more extensive discussions of Jewish law and Irish law.[93]

Cohen introduces the section on Jewish law by asserting that "[i]t is a curious fact that the Jews of the Middle Ages lived through a crisis in many respects similar to that before the court, and dealt with it in a manner analogous to the legislation in suit."[94] Specifically, "[c]onfined to ghettoes and forbidden to own land, they were obliged to rent both dwellings and business places in the limited areas in which they were permitted to stay and do business."[95] Consequently, "[i]t often happened that as soon as the landlord discovered that the tenant was able to make a living in the place where he was settled or was successful in his business, the landlord would raise the rent in the dwelling place or street to a large amount."[96] Finally, "when the tenant was unwilling to pay the rent which the landlord demanded, the landlord would find another Jew to whom he would rent the place."[97] In short, "the first Jew lost his living to the second,"[98] resulting in both "rent profiteering" and "ruinous competition for premises among Jews."[99]

As Cohen's brief details, to remedy these conditions, rabbinic authorities in the Jewish ghetto enacted a form of rent regulation. As Cohen describes it:

> [T]he rabbis deduced from the Talmud the law of Hazakah, which gave the tenant in possession the right to continue, even without a lease, as against another Jew seeking to outbid him, and instituted a regulation excommunicating any Jew who offered an unreasonable rent in order to secure a dwelling place or store over the head of a Jew already in occupancy.[100]

Cohen documents this legal analysis in a footnote, citing a number of scholarly works on Jewish law, including encyclopedic treatises written in

---

[91] See "Brief," 104, *supra* note 83.
[92] Ibid.
[93] Ibid., 104–14.
[94] Ibid., 104.
[95] Ibid.
[96] See "Brief," 104, *supra* note 83.
[97] Ibid., 104–5.
[98] Ibid., 105 (internal quotation omitted).
[99] Ibid.
[100] Ibid.

Hebrew[101] and an article published in *The Menorah Journal,* an American journal on Jewish law.[102] The footnote quotes verbatim an English translation of one such rent regulation, enacted on June 21, 1554, by delegates of the Jewish congregations of Rome, Ferrara, Mantua, Romagna, Bologna, Reggie, Modena and Venice.[103]

Cohen completes the discussion with a quotation from *Jewish Life in the Middle Ages,* by Israel Abrahams:

> The *Jus Casaca* ... gave the Jewish tenant of a Christian's house in the ghetto a right in that house which no other Jew could usurp.... Clement VIII legalized this Jewish arrangement by practically making evictions impossible so long as the rent (also fixed by him) was duly paid.... Similar laws of Chazaka were applicable to Jewish landowners; Duran, for instance, reports a takanah [*i.e.,* a regulation] which

---

[101] See "Brief," 105, *supra* note 83 (citing Eisenstein, *Ozar Haddinim—A Digest of Jewish Law* (1917): 129–30; Eisenstein, *Ozar Yisrael,* Vol. IV (1910): 265). Both of these works were compiled by Judah David Eisenstein, though as published, the title of the former differed from Cohen's citation. The transliterated title page of the 1927 edition reads: "Ozar Dinim u-Minhagim: A Digest of Jewish Laws and Customs, compiled by J. D. Eisenstein." Likewise, the 1917 edition was published with the lengthier title.

[102] See "Brief," 105, *supra* note 83 (citing Nathan Isaacs, "Jewish Law in the Modern World," *The Menorah Journal* 6 (1920): 258). Cohen identifies Isaacs as Professor of Law at the University of Pittsburgh, former Professor of Law and Assistant Dean at the University of Cincinnati Law School, and the 1919–1920 Thayer Teaching Fellow at Harvard Law School. Isaacs later returned to Harvard, and in 1924 was named Professor of Business Law at the Graduate School of Business Administration. He also lectured at Columbia University, the Army Industrial College, the University of Rochester, and Yale Law School. In addition, Isaacs was active in Jewish organizations, and among his extensive scholarly endeavors, he edited the National Law Library along with Roscoe Pound. See "Dr. Nathan Isaacs of Harvard Dead," *New York Times,* Dec. 19, 1941; see also Editor's Introduction to Nathan Isaacs, "Study as a Mode of Worship," *Commentary* 1 (June 1946): 77.

[103] See "Brief," 105, *supra* note 83:

> (v). Whereas there are many who infringe on the tekanah of Rabbenu Gershom, which forbids any Jew from ousting another Jew from a house rented from a Christian landlord, and whereas such offenders claim that when the landlord sells his house the Jewish tenant thereby loses his chazaka (i.e., his rights of preferential tenancy), we therefore decree that though the Christian owner sell his house, the right of the Jewish tenant to retain possession is unchanged, and any Jew who ousts him is disobeying the tekanah of R. Gershom and also this tekanah, now newly enacted.

The quotation is taken from *Jewish Life in the Middle Ages,* by Israel Abrahams, which was published in several editions in the late-nineteenth and early-twentieth centuries, by The Macmillan Company and The Jewish Publication Society of America. In editions published in 1896, 1897, 1911, 1917, and 1920, the quotation is found on pages 70–71. See Israel Abrahams, *Jewish Life in the Middle Ages* (Philadelphia: Jewish Publication Society, 1896), 70–71. The brief does not reference a page number for this quotation. In addition, the brief does not indicate which edition of Abrahams' book Cohen consulted. See note 104.

rendered it unlawful for a Jew to evict a fellow Israelite by raising the rent or by any other device whatsoever.[104]

On a substantive level, Cohen's reliance on sources of Jewish law appears misplaced. After all, notwithstanding some degree of factual similarities, the internal regulations in the Jewish ghetto in sixteenth-century Italy seem largely irrelevant to the Emergency Rent Laws in early twentieth-century New York. Presumably, Cohen did not expect the New York Court of Appeals or the United States Supreme Court to rely upon Jewish legal principles as grounds for upholding the constitutionality of the Emergency Rent Laws.

Not surprisingly, in response to Cohen's historical arguments, Marshall and his co-counsel, Lewis M. Isaacs, emphasized a number of factual and analytical differences between the Jewish legal precedents and the New York Emergency Rent Laws. Indeed, Marshall replies harshly in his Supreme Court brief, in a section under the heading of "The Supposed Precedents in European Countries."[105] Marshall begins with the declaration that "[o]ur opponents have ... referred to alleged *responsa* rendered in mediaeval times, in their capacity as arbitrators."[106] After dismissing the relevance of Cohen's other historical references, Marshall asserts categorically: "Nor are *responsa* rendered in the exercise of an ecclesiastical as distinguished from a judicial function by rabbis, who were intent upon the avoidance of conflict among members of the synagogue, of the slightest moment."[107] Finally, Marshall adds, "[t]he very fact that the Jews, in the days when these arbitraments took place, were not permitted to own real property of itself indicates how far afield these alleged precedents are apt to lead one."[108]

To be sure, some of Marshall's conclusions are open to question and may prove less than fully accurate. For example, Marshall claimed that in enacting medieval decrees, rabbis exercised an "ecclesiastical" rather than "judicial" function.[109] However, while Marshall correctly alluded to the

---

[104] See "Brief," 105–6, *supra* note 83 (ellipsis and brackets in original) (quoting Abrahams, *supra* note 103). Cohen references page 69 of Abrahams' book. In the 1896, 1897, 1911, 1917, and 1920 editions of the book, the quotation is found on pages 71 and 72. For further discussions of these laws, sometimes transliterated as *jus gazaga*, see, e.g., Menachem Elon, *Jewish Law: History, Sources, Principles,* Vol. II, trans. Bernard Auerbach & Melvin J. Sykes (Philadelphia: Jewish Publication Society, 1994), 782–86; Louis Finkelstein, *Jewish Self Government in the Middle Ages* (New York: Feldheim, 1964), 20–35, 111–47, 171, 181; Atlilio Milano, "The Private Life of a Family of Jewish Bankers at Rome in the Sixteenth Century," *Jewish Quarterly Review* 30 (1939): 149; Israel Schepansky, "Takkanot Robbenu Gershom Me'or ha-Golah," *Hadarom* 22 (1966): 103; *The Jewish Encyclopedia*, vol. 7, 395; Meir Tamari, *With All Your Possessions: Jewish Ethics and Economic Life* (Lanham, MD: Jason Aronson, Inc, 1987), 12.

[105] See "Points For Plaintiff-in-Error," 108; Edgar A. Levy Leasing Co. v. Siegel, 258 U.S. 242 (1922).

[106] Ibid.

[107] Ibid.

[108] Ibid.

[109] Ibid.

important distinction in Jewish law between various functions and roles of rabbinic authorities,[110] the enactment of communal decrees falls within the legislative function exercised by legal authorities as part of the Jewish legal system.[111] In fact, not unlike the Emergency Rent Laws, the rabbinic decrees referenced by Cohen, though perhaps serving an "ecclesiastical" purpose of avoiding conflict, constitute a form of communal legislation, with binding legal force.[112] Nevertheless, despite perhaps succumbing to a degree of overstatement, Marshall convincingly demonstrated basic differences between the Jewish legal principles cited by Cohen and the substantive issues in the Emergency Rent Laws cases.[113]

In contrast to the relatively cursory and arguably inapposite comparisons to Jewish law, Cohen dedicated several pages of his brief to a more thorough survey of Irish, English, and Scottish rent laws.[114] Spanning the early eighteenth century through the early twentieth century, these legal systems implemented various rights of renewal to protect tenants from unfair treatment by landlords.[115] As Cohen notes in the brief, eight months earlier, in *Block v. Hirsh*, the United States Supreme Court had upheld a similar emergency rent law in the District of Columbia, in part on the basis of historical precedent in English law.[116] Writing for the majority in *Block*, Justice Oliver Wendell Holmes, Jr., stated that "[t]he preference given to the tenant in possession is an almost necessary incident of the policy and is traditional in English law. If the tenant remained subject to the landlord's power to evict, the attempt to limit the landlord's demands would fail."[117] Thus, Cohen understandably offered similar historical examples from English law in support of the New York Emergency Rent Laws.[118] However,

---

[110] See Samuel J. Levine, "An Introduction to Legislation in Jewish Law, With Reference to the American Legal System," *Seton Hall Law Review* 29 (1999): 916; Samuel J. Levine, "Jewish Legal Theory and American Constitutional Theory: Some Comparisons and Contrasts," *Hastings Constitutional Law Quarterly* 24 (1997): 441.

[111] See Levine, "Legislation in Jewish Law."

[112] See ibid.

[113] Notably, years earlier, Marshall had relied heavily on Jewish law in an argument before the New York Court of Appeals in the case of Riker v. Leo, 133 N.Y. 519 (1892). In fact, Marshall presented a veritable disquisition on the principles of charity in Jewish tradition, through repeated and extensive quotations from the Torah, the Talmud, and the work of Maimonides. See *Marshall: Papers and Addresses* II, 913–23 (excerpting Marshall's argument on behalf of the North American Relief Society). In Riker, however, the Jewish law of charity seemed particularly relevant, as the issue in the case revolved around a Jewish philanthropist's bequest to a Jewish charitable organization. See id. In contrast, although many of the cases relating to the New York Emergency Rent Laws—including the cases that Cohen and Marshall litigated—involved Jewish parties, there existed no substantive nexus between the New York laws and the Jewish laws Cohen cited.

[114] See "Points for Plaintiff-in-Error," 106–14, *supra* note 105.

[115] See ibid.

[116] See "Brief," 114 (citing Block v. Hirsh, 256 U.S. 135 (1921)), *supra* note 83.

[117] See *Block*, 256 U.S. at 157–58.

[118] Nevertheless, in responding to Cohen's historical arguments, Marshall discounted the

such explanation does not account for Cohen's inclusion of Jewish law in the brief in the absence of any substantive relevance to the case.

B. Judge Benjamin N. Cardozo and Jewish Law

Instead, perhaps an alternative—if not more plausible—explanation for Cohen's reliance on Jewish law and, to some degree, his reliance on Irish law, can be found in Cohen's later depictions of the events surrounding the oral arguments in these cases. In his memoirs, published in 1946, Cohen recalls that he raised the historical analogies during the two most important oral arguments he presented in the course of the Emergency Rent Laws litigation: before the New York Court of Appeals and before the United States Supreme Court.[119] In Cohen's account, a day or two after his argument in the New York Court of Appeals, Judge Frederick E. Crane, an Associate Judge of the Court of Appeals, remarked to Judge Luke Stapleton: "They are a clever bunch, Guthrie and Cohen—[they] cite Irish precedents and they get [Judge John W.] Hogan; they cite Jewish precedents and get [Judge Benjamin N.] Cardozo—and so they bag two of the judges before they even begin their argument."[120]

On one level, Judge Crane's reported remark appears indicative of political realities that dominated New York in the early twentieth century.[121] Indeed, among other factors, the religion and ethnicity of candidates played a primary role in the selection of judges for the Court of Appeals at that time.[122] To the extent that Cardozo's Jewish heritage and Hogan's Irish

---

relevance of various European legal systems as well. For example, he wrote that:

> Our opponents have indulged at some length in citations from historians, decisions and statutes dealing with conditions in European countries, as e.g. in Ireland and Scotland.... These passages from the history of other countries, whose organic law differs fundamentally from ours have no application here, where legislation is necessarily governed by our written Constitutions.

See "Points For Plaintiff-in-Error," 108, *supra* note 105. In addition, Marshall borrowed at length from a New York Court of Appeals decision distinguishing between American law and English law. In part, he quoted:

> [W]e are unlike any of the countries whose industrial laws are referred to as models for our guidance. Practically all of these countries are so-called constitutional monarchies in which, as in England, there is no written Constitution and the Parliament or lawmaking power is supreme. In our country the Federal and State Constitutions are the charters which demark the extent and limitations of legislative power...."

Ibid. at 109 (quoting Ives v. South Buffalo Ry. Co., 201 N.Y. 271, 287 (1911)).

[119] See Cohen, *They Builded Better*, 170–72.

[120] Ibid., 170.

[121] Parenthetically, it may be noted that these kinds of political considerations have continued to exert a degree of influence into the early twenty-first century as well.

[122] See, e.g., John T. Noonan, *Persons and Masks of the Law: Cardozo, Holmes, Jefferson, and Wythe as Makers of the Masks* (New York: Farrar, Straus and Giroux, 1976), 132, stating that the New York Court of Appeals that in 1928 decided the case of Palsgraf v. Long Island Railroad Company, 248 N.Y. 339 (1928), "had been composed with that attention to religious affiliation (Protestant, Jewish, Catholic) and regional origin (up-

heritage factored into their successful candidacies,[123] it might be suggested that they accordingly would have responded to arguments that resonated with their religious and ethnic backgrounds.

Upon further analysis, though, it remains highly questionable that Cohen actually believed his reference to Jewish law could have influenced Cardozo's decision in the case. In fact, at various points, Cohen's memoirs—often recalling events that, as this one, had occurred decades earlier—suggest a penchant for colorful and largely impressionistic storytelling, at the possible expense of accuracy or earnestness. Likewise, Cohen's reference to the purported conversation about employing Jewish law as a method of winning over Cardozo may prove to be more entertaining than enlightening.

Indeed, aspects of Cohen's depictions of events surrounding the Emergency Rent Laws litigation include inaccuracies that raise serious questions about the reliability of his recollections. For example, according to Cohen, the conversation about the supposed effect of Jewish law on Cardozo took place between Judge Crane and "Judge Luke Stapleton."[124] However, Stapleton, who served as a New York State Supreme Court Justice on both the trial court and appellate levels, resigned from the bench at the end of 1917,[125] more than three years before Cohen and Guthrie argued the Emergency Rent Laws case in the New York Court of Appeals.[126]

---

state, metropolis) which often has exhausted political wisdom in New York"). Indeed, in one account, Cardozo was considered for appointment to the Court of Appeals in 1914 only after a number of Catholics had declined Governor Martin Glynn's nomination, including William Guthrie, Frederic Coudert, and William Kelley. See Kaufman, *Cardozo*, 615. Kelley declined specifically "when he learned that he was being offered the position because he was a Catholic." Ibid. Although Kaufman, ibid., has questioned the historical precision of some details of this account, the story accurately reflects historical dynamics of appointment to the Court of Appeals in the early twentieth century, including the relevance of the appointee's religious affiliation.

[123] Cardozo did, in fact, receive some—though not universal—support in his New York judicial campaigns from Jewish communal leaders and organizations. See Kaufman, *Cardozo*, 117–29. Perhaps of greater significance in the context of Cohen's reference to Jewish law, by nearly all accounts Cardozo ascribed great value to Jewish religion and tradition. See, e.g., Alan M. Stroock, "Recollections of Four Cardozo Law Clerks," *Cardozo Law Review* 1 (1979): 20-22 (recalling author's clerkship for Cardozo during the 1934 and 1935 Terms of the United States Supreme Court):

> Justice Cardozo's attitude toward his Judaism is difficult to define.... [H]e was proud of his ancestry. But I do not remember his ever going to a Synagogue or his observing any of the religious holidays at home. He was a good friend of Rabbi Stephen Wise and other religious leaders, but he never took an active part in any Jewish organization or Jewish cause such as Zionism.... On the other hand, he preserved in his subconscious memory his recollections of the Jewish ceremonies of his youth.... Moreover, I believe that he thought that his philosophy of life and law was basically Jewish in all its elements....

See also sources cited in note 138.

[124] Cohen, *They Builded Better*, 170.

[125] See "Stapleton Will Retire," *New York Times*, Dec. 15, 1917, at 14.

[126] September Housing Laws, N.Y. Sess. Laws 1920, chs. 942–53.

Of course, Cohen could have correctly recalled that Stapleton was no longer a judge in 1921, but nevertheless decided to use the title as a measure of respect for Stapleton. Alternatively, Cohen might have correctly recalled that the conversation transpired between Crane and Stapleton, despite erroneously believing that Stapleton had still been serving as a judge at the time. In any event, Cohen's error casts further doubt upon an already dubious story regarding an event that had occurred a quarter century prior to the publication of his memoirs.

Similar questions arise over Cohen's recounting of the courts' decisions in the New York Emergency Rent Laws cases. In his recollection of the cases in which he cited Jewish law, Cohen states that Judge Pound and Justice Holmes wrote the prevailing opinions in the New York Court of Appeals and the United States Supreme Court, respectively.[127] In fact, though, while Judge Pound did write the majority opinion for the New York Court of Appeals in the Emergency Rent Laws cases,[128] Justice Clarke wrote the majority opinion for the United States Supreme Court in *Edgar A. Levy Leasing Co. v. Siegel*.[129]

Cohen's error might be explained as nothing more than a matter of confusing *Levy Leasing*, which the United States Supreme Court decided on March 20, 1922,[130] with two other rent laws cases the Court had decided on April 18, 1921, *Block v. Hirsh*[131] and *Marcus Brown Holding Co. v. Feldman*[132] Justice Holmes had, indeed, written the majority opinions in both of the earlier cases.[133] In addition, Cohen and Marshall had both filed briefs in *Marcus Brown*, which involved the New York Emergency Rent Laws, and they had included similar arguments relating to the relevance of Jewish law.[134]

Yet, even this somewhat understandable source of Cohen's confusion would not explain the further error he commits in his references to the supposed opinion of the Supreme Court in the case he litigated against Marshall regarding the New York Emergency Rent Laws. When Cohen quotes the majority opinion of Justice Holmes, the quotations are not from the opinion in *Marcus Brown*, but from the opinion in *Block v. Hirsh*.[135]

---

[127] See Cohen, *They Builded Better*, 170.
[128] See People ex. rel. Durham Realty Corp. v. La Fetra, 230 N.Y. 429 (1921).
[129] See Edgar A. Levy Leasing Co. v. Siegel, 258 U.S. 242 (1922).
[130] See ibid.
[131] *Block v. Hirsh*, 256 U.S. 135 (1921).
[132] Marcus Brown Holding Co. v. Feldman, 256 U.S. 170 (1921).
[133] See ibid.; see also *Block*, 256 U.S. at 135.
[134] See Brief on Behalf of the Attorney-General and the Joint Legislative Committee on Housing of the State of New York, at 68–69; Points for Edgar A. Levy Leasing Co. Inc. and 801 West End Avenue Inc. as Amici Curiae on Constitutionality of Chapters 136, 944 and 946 of the New York Laws of 1920, at 63–64.
[135] See Cohen, *They Builded Better*, 172, 353 nn. 9–10 (citing *Block*, 256 U.S. at 135). See also *Block*, 256 U.S. at 157–58.

Although argued and decided together with *Marcus Brown*, *Block* involved a District of Columbia rent law and therefore was not in any way litigated or argued by Cohen or Marshall.[136] Again, these lapses may not conclusively render unreliable Cohen's account of the conversation between Crane and Stapleton, but they present additional grounds for healthy skepticism.

Perhaps more to the point, it simply seems incredible that a judge of Cardozo's stature and integrity would have arrived at a decision on legislation as important as the Emergency Rent Laws based on a minor reference to Jewish law, rather than through thoughtful analysis of the vital concerns of American law at issue in the case. While Realists might ponder the possible influence of psychological factors related to Cardozo's Jewish background, Cardozo was an outspoken critic of such a theory of the judicial function, self-consciously engaging in faithful adherence to principled consideration of law and public policy.[137]

Furthermore, notwithstanding the importance of Cardozo's Jewish heritage in both his personal and professional conduct and ideals,[138] it remains particularly unlikely that he would have relied on substantive Jewish law to reach a decision. After all, a number of years later, Cardozo specifically criticized Magistrate Louis Brodsky for issuing an opinion that, Cardozo concluded, had been influenced by Brodsky's concern for the Jewish community.[139] In Professor Andrew Kaufman's characterization, Cardozo believed that "Brodsky had no business letting his own personal views as a Jew affect his judicial judgment."[140]

---

[136] See *Block*, 256 U.S. at 135.

[137] See John C.P. Goldberg, "The Life of the Law," *Stanford Law Review* 51 (1999): 1419 (reviewing Kaufman, *Cardozo*). See also Kaufman, *Cardozo*, 458–61 (describing differences and disputes between Cardozo's articulation of his judicial philosophy and Jerome Frank's Realist approach).

[138] Cardozo's relationship to his Jewish heritage has been explored extensively in numerous works. See, e.g., Paul Bricker, "Justice Benjamin N. Cardozo: A Fresh Look at a Great Judge," *Ohio Northern University Law Review* 11 (1984): 30–31; Kaufman, *Cardozo*; George S. Hellman, *Benjamin N. Cardozo: American Judge* (New York: McGraw-Hill Book Co., Inc, 1940), 163–78; Richard Polenberg, *The World of Benjamin Cardozo: Personal Values and the Judicial Process* (Cambridge, MA: Harvard University Press, 1997) 13–18, 174–85, 238–40; Stroock, "Recollections." For other works on Cardozo, see, e.g., Stanley Charles Brubaker, "Benjamin Nathan Cardozo: An Intellectual Biography" (PhD diss., University of Virginia, 1979); Joseph P. Pollard, *Mr. Justice Cardozo: A Liberal Mind in Action* (New York: The Yorktown Press, 1935); Richard A. Posner, *Cardozo: A Study in Reputation* (Chicago: University of Chicago Press, 1990).

[139] Kaufman, *Cardozo*, 487–88.

[140] Ibid., 488. As recounted in Kaufman's biography of Cardozo, the episode, which occurred in 1935, involved Brodsky's dismissal of charges against a group of demonstrators who boarded a German liner and tore down a Nazi flag. See ibid. at 487. Brodsky wrote "an inflammatory opinion in which he set forth what might have been in the minds of the defendants in seeking to tear down the Nazi flag," suggesting that "they might have viewed the flag as emblematic of all the acts, which he listed, of the Nazi regime's destroying human freedom." Ibid. at 488. In response to a letter he received in support of Brodsky's opinion, Cardozo referred sharply to Brodsky's "shameful utterance," adding that "[i]t would have been bad enough if [Brodsky] had been a Gentile; but for a Jew it was unforgivable[,]" because "[n]ow our traducers will say ... that these are the standards

Of course, there is no indication that Cardozo's judgment in the Emergency Rent Laws cases was based on considerations other than the merits of the case. If anything, though, to the extent that outside factors could have exerted some degree of influence on Cardozo's decision, presumably Cardozo's close personal and professional relationship with Louis Marshall, Cohen's adversary in the litigation, would have had more impact than Cohen's references to Jewish law.[141] After all, Marshall had served for many years as a mentor to Cardozo, working with Cardozo on a number of cases and causes, beginning in 1899 when Cardozo was twenty-nine years old.[142]

In addition, Marshall's continuing support had proved instrumental at important stages of Cardozo's career. For example, Marshall had secured publication for Cardozo's first book, published in 1903,[143] and he had played a central role in Cardozo's successful 1913 campaign for the trial division of the New York Supreme Court.[144] Finally, and not incidentally in the context of Cohen's remark about Cardozo's purported interest in Jewish law, Marshall's relationship with Cardozo often reflected a common regard for their shared Jewish heritage,[145] presumably outweighing any perceived advantage Cohen might have gained from a citation to medieval Jewish legal sources.

Likewise, Cohen's co-counsel in the Emergency Rent Laws cases, William D. Guthrie, engaged in a variety of professional activities that would seem more significant and potentially influential in the perspective of judges on the New York Court of Appeals than would Cohen's brief references to Jewish legal history. Like Marshall, Guthrie reportedly played an important role in Cardozo's professional advancement, providing crucial

---

of the race." Ibid. (quoting Letter from Benjamin N. Cardozo to Aline Goldstone, Sept. 14, 1935). Thus, as Kaufman concludes, "Cardozo viewed the matter all the more seriously because Brodsky was a Jew whose performance cast Jews, particularly Jewish judges, in a bad light." Ibid. (quoting Letter from Benjamin N. Cardozo to Aline Goldstone, Sept. 14, 1935).

[141] See ibid., accompanying notes 43–45.

[142] See Kaufman, *Cardozo*, 79, 110.

[143] The title of the book was *The Jurisdiction of the Court of Appeals of the State of New York*. See ibid. at 89. According to Kaufman, Marshall not only wrote letters of introduction and praise to A. Bleecker Banks, an Albany law book publisher, but also served as "negotiator and middleman between Cardozo and Banks[,]" such that "[a]ll matters, including suggestions for changes and even transmission of proofs, went through Marshall's hands." Ibid., 89.

[144] See ibid., 117–26. Marshall wrote "lengthy letters" that were published in a number of Jewish newspapers, describing Cardozo's "extraordinary capacity," "preeminent ability," and "sterling character," and insisting that "because of Cardozo's qualifications, if elected, he would shed luster upon the Jewish name." Ibid., 122 (quoting Letter from Louis Marshall to Editor of the *Jewish Morning Journal*, Oct. 27, 1913). Marshall sent the same letter to the editors of the *Jewish Daily News* and the *Warheit*. Ibid., 612 n. 26. As yet a further indication of Cardozo's close relationship with Marshall and appreciation for his support, Cardozo later adopted Marshall's recommendation and hired Abraham Paley of Marshall's office as "attendant and confidential stenographer." Ibid., 126.

[145] See ibid., 110, 171.

support for his election to the Court of Appeals.[146] Moreover, Guthrie's interactions with two other judges on the court, just months after their decision in the Emergency Rent Laws case, suggest close professional—if not personal—relationships.

For example, amid considerable controversy, Guthrie delivered an important speech at the 1921 Republican State Convention in support of the nomination of Judge William S. Andrews to remain on the court.[147] In addition, as chairman of the executive committee of the 1921 Judicial Constitutional Convention, Guthrie worked closely with Judge Cuthbert W. Pound, who served as chairman of the convention.[148] Furthermore, to the degree that Cohen emphasized the relevance of Jewish law and Irish law to the decisions of Judges Cardozo and Hogan, respectively, Guthrie might have hoped to gain the favor of the Catholic judges on the court as a result of his close connections with the Catholic Church.[149]

Finally, other elements of Cohen's account cast even further doubt on either the seriousness or the historical accuracy of his reflections regarding the strategy of including references to Jewish law for the purpose of targeting Cardozo's decision in the Emergency Rent Laws case. For example, just over a month after arguing the Emergency Rent Laws case before the

---

[146] At least one biographer of Cardozo has cited a letter sent by Guthrie in support of Cardozo's candidacy to the Court of Appeals. See Brubaker, "Benjamin Nathan Cardozo," 106 and n. 29 (citing letter from William D. Guthrie to Judge Abram Elkus, Nov. 17, 1925). See also Hellman, *Benjamin N. Cardozo*, 111. Although at one point Kaufman expressed skepticism regarding the accuracy of some of these accounts, see Kaufman, *Cardozo*, 26 n. 15, he later cited the support of leading members of the New York bar, including Guthrie, for Cardozo's appointment as Chief Judge of the Court of Appeals. See Kaufman, *Cardozo*, 179.

[147] See William H. Manz, *The Palsgraf Case: Courts, Law, and Society* (Newark, N.J.: LexisNexis, 2005), 85–86. Guthrie declared that:

> I can conceive of no more destructive assault upon our rights and liberties or of a more fatal blow at the high traditions of the courts of justice of our State, than to have the Republican Party deny a nomination to an able, upright and fearless judges as a punishment for the conscientious and courageous performance of his plain duty to decide according to his conscience.

Ibid., 86 (quoting "Nominate Andrews; Urge Tariff to Aid Foodstuff Exports," *New York Times*, Sept. 24, 1921, at 1–2).

[148] See Francis Bergan, *The History of the New York Court of Appeals, 1847–1932* (New York: Columbia University Press, 1985), 263–70.

[149] As John W. Davis said of Guthrie in a memorial address:

> Second to no other enthusiasm, surety, was his deep devotion to the religion he professed. He was a devoted son of the Catholic Church, scrupulous in conforming to her requirements and faithful to the obligations of his membership. But his religion went far deeper than mere outward observance. It filled his soul and colored all his life.

Swaine, *Cravath Firm*, 782. Among other activities connected with the Catholic Church, in 1926, Guthrie "wrote a voluminous opinion for Patrick Cardinal Hayes, attacking the Mexican constitutional provisions affecting the Catholic Church ... as violations of international law and of the fundamental principles of liberty and justice." Ibid., 780. See also ibid., 362 (describing honors Guthrie received from the Catholic Church).

New York Court of Appeals,[150] Cohen submitted his United States Supreme Court brief in the case of *Marcus Brown Holding Company v. Feldman*.[151] Although *Marcus Brown* involved the New York Emergency Rent Laws, because the case originated and was litigated exclusively in federal court, it did not come before Cardozo and the New York Court of Appeals. Nevertheless, Cohen included in his brief a similar discussion of Jewish law, apparently aiming to demonstrate historical precedents rather than for the purpose of swaying a particular justice with an interest in Jewish legal principles.[152]

As it turns out, one member of the United States Supreme Court, Justice Louis D. Brandeis, would have been a more likely target than Cardozo for Cohen's citations to Jewish law. Although the precise nature of Brandeis' relationship to his Jewish heritage remains a matter of complexity,[153] unlike Cardozo, he had dedicated substantial efforts to a variety of Jewish communal causes and concerns.[154] Perhaps most notably in the context of Cohen's brief, Brandeis had been a leading supporter of the Intercollegiate Menorah Association, which published *The Menorah Journal*,[155] and Brandeis had contributed a letter of tribute to the inaugural issue of the journal.[156] Therefore, had Cohen actually believed that his references to

---

[150] See Edgar A. Levy Leasing Co. v. Siegel, 230 N.Y. 634 (1921) (argued Jan. 19, 1921).

[151] See Brief on Behalf of the Attorney-General and the Joint Legislative Committee on Housing of the State of New York, Marcus Brown Holding Co., Inc. v. Feldman, 256 U.S. 170 (1921). The brief (on file with author) is stamped as filed with the Supreme Court on Feb. 28, 1921.

[152] See ibid., 68–69.

[153] See, e.g., Auerbach, *Rabbis and Lawyers,* 123–49; Robert A. Burt, *Two Jewish Justices: Outcasts in the Promised Land* (Berkeley: University of California Press, 1988), Galanter, "Vocation for Law," 1131–36; Eben Moglen, "Jewishness and the American Constitutional Tradition: The Cases of Brandeis and Frankfurter," *Columbia Law Review* 89 (1989): 959; Philippa Strum, *Louis D. Brandeis, Justice for the People* (Cambridge, MA: Harvard University Press, 1984), 173–80, 224–90.

[154] See Strum, *Louis D. Brandeis.*

[155] See "Editors' Note," in *Letters of Louis D. Brandeis, Vol. III, 1913–1915: Progressive and Zionist,* eds. Melvin I. Urofsky and David W. Levy (Albany: State University of New York Press, 1973):

> Founded by Henry Hurwitz..., the Menorah movement began at Harvard in 1906 and spread to other American and Canadian universities. In 1913 the Intercollegiate Menorah Association was founded and in 1915 the group began publishing the Menorah Journal under Hurwitz's editorship. The Association, dedicated to fostering Jewish culture, disbanded in 1961 at Hurwitz's death."

Ibid., 193 n. 3.

[156] The letter appeared in *The Menorah Journal* 1 (1915): 4; *Letters of Louis D. Brandeis,* Vol. III:

> The Formation at Harvard University on October 25, 1906, of the first Menorah Society is a landmark in the Jewish Renaissance....
>
> America's fundamental law seeks to make real the brotherhood of man. That brotherhood became the Jews' fundamental law more than twenty-five hundred years ago. America's twentieth century demand is for social justice. That has been the Jews' striving [for] ages-long. Their religion and their afflictions

Jewish law affected judicial decision-making in the Emergency Rent Laws cases, he could have highlighted his citation to the 1920 article in *The Menorah Journal* by Nathan Isaacs,[157] an article that would have had strong resonance for—and may even have been read by—Brandeis. Nevertheless, although Cohen provides in his memoirs a detailed description of the reactions of various Supreme Court Justices to the historical points he raised at oral argument,[158] and although elsewhere he dedicates an entire

---

> have prepared them for effective democracy.... Furthermore, the widespread study of Jewish law developed the intellect and made them less subject to preconceptions and more open to reason.
>
> America requires in her sons and daughters these qualities and attainments, which are our natural heritage. Patriotism to America, as well as loyalty to our past, imposes upon us the obligation of claiming this heritage of the Jewish spirit and of carrying forward noble ideals and traditions through lives and deeds worthy of our ancestors. To this end each new generation should be trained in the knowledge and appreciation of their own great past; and the opportunity should be afforded to the further development of Jewish character and culture.
>
> The Menorah Societies and their Journal deserve most generous support in their efforts to perform this noble task.

Ibid., 398–99 (Letter from Louis D. Brandeis to Editor, Menorah Journal, January, 1915). See also ibid., 505 (Letter from Louis D. Brandeis to Henry Hurwitz, Apr. 7, 1915) (stating that "I am much gratified at receiving the pledge from the various members [of the Menorah Society] who met on April 4, 1915 at 600 Madison Avenue, and who have agreed to volunteer their services to the Zionist cause...."); ibid., 638 (Letter from Louis D. Brandeis to Benjamin F. Levy, Nov. 17, 1915) (referring to "[t]he editorial in the Boston Herald, of which a part is quoted in the October number of the Menorah Journal on page 236").

[157] See "Brief," 105, *supra* note 83 (citing Nathan Isaacs, "Jewish Law in the Modern World," *The Menorah Journal* 6 (1920): 258).

[158] See Cohen, *They Builded Better,* 171–72. Though presumably vulnerable to similar questions regarding accuracy and reliability, Cohen's recollections of the oral argument provide an entertaining and potentially valuable perspective on these justices, and thus may merit being quoted extensively. Cohen begins with an account of Justice Joseph McKenna's reaction to the citations to English, Irish, and Jewish legal history:

> Justice McKenna, who was seated on the right of Chief Justice [William Howard] Taft, and on my left, was quite impatient with my historical presentation. He turned to me and said testily, "I don't think this is a matter of legislative wisdom or experience at all. It is just a matter of power."

Ibid., 171. Cohen then describes his response:

> I assured him, as Guthrie had demonstrated, that the power was there. The real question was whether it was exercised capriciously or arbitrarily and the Court could not say that is was a capricious or arbitrary action of the legislature, unless on the basis of past experience and wisdom, it could find no basis whatever to support it. Accordingly, if we were able to show that at critical points in history, parliaments had resorted to this very method for avoiding riot and disorder, then our point was made. The Supreme Court could not, if it would, strike down the act.

Cohen recalls a challenge from' Justice Oliver Wendell Holmes, Jr.: "At this point, Holmes, on the Chief Justice's left (whom we naturally expected to be going our way) said, 'Mr. Cohen, I am inclined to agree with my brother McKenna. I don't think it is our

chapter to a portrayal of Brandeis,[159] Cohen does not mention Brandeis in the context of the Emergency Rent Laws case.[160]

V. Conclusion

It should not be surprising that following his colorful report of Judge Crane's remark regarding the effectiveness of citing Jewish law to win over Cardozo, Cohen counters with a more plausible reason for including historical references in his brief: his primary litigation strategy in the case was to "get the judges away from the prevailing lawyers' bias against the laws and bring into play the forces of history."[161] Likewise, rather than embracing the notion that he targeted Cardozo through the reference to Jewish law, Cohen instead recalls, more credibly, that "[w]e felt sure of liberal judges like Holmes of the U.S. Supreme Court, Cardozo and Pound of the New York Court of Appeals."[162] Indeed, their strategy proved successful and their

---

function to review the wisdom and experience of the legislature.'" Ibid. Cohen replied at length:

> Review not in the sense of substituting your judgment for that of the legislature, but in the sense of reviewing the record to see if there is arty basis for the exercise of the legislative power. You review in the same way as you examine the record in a negligence case, to see if there is any evidence at all upon which the verdict of the jury can be supported, and if you find that there is such evidence, you do not set the verdict aside, you let it stand. This is not substituting the courts' judgment for the jury's, it is reviewing solely for the purpose of determining whether there is any evidence at all in the case to support the verdict of the jury.

Ibid. Following this explanation, Cohen recalls, "I thought the old skeptic leaned back satisfied." Ibid. Finally, Cohen offers a colorful depiction of Chief Justice Taft:

> Then forward advanced the Chief Justice himself. Now what was he going to do "put me on the spot?" And these are the sententious words which came from the lips of this fun-loving Chief Justice: "My brothers seem to be agreed about that, Mr. Cohen, but you may proceed with your argument upon the assumption that a little wisdom and experience will not hurt this court."

Ibid., 171–72.

[159] See ibid., 190–200.

[160] Notably, Brandeis also had professional or personal relationships with the three principal lawyers who litigated the Emergency Rent Laws cases before the Supreme Court: Cohen, Marshall, and Guthrie. Though Brandeis' connection to Cohen was limited largely to their efforts at settling (he garment workers' strike, Brandeis and Marshall worked on a number of common matters relating to Jewish communal concerns. Nevertheless, "[t]he relations between Marshall and Brandeis] were always formal and courteous but also strained and somewhat uneasy although both men were interested in many of the same projects and programs." See "Editors' Note," in *Letters of Louis D. Brandeis*, Vol. I, 294. For expressions of this strain, as portrayed in Brandeis' letters to a third party, see *Letters of Louis D. Brandeis*, Vol. IV, 354 (Letter from Louis D. Brandeis to Julian William Mack, Aug. 26, 1918); ibid., 507 (Letter from Louis D. Brandeis to Julian William Mack, Nov. 18, 1920). Brandeis' references to Guthrie in his letters evince a more positive tone. See *Letters of Louis D. Brandeis*, Vol. V, 93; ibid., 109 (Letter from Louis D. Brandeis to Felix Frankfurter, Jan. 6, 1924).

[161] Cohen, *They Builded Better*, 170.

[162] Ibid.

expectations accurate, as Cohen and Guthrie prevailed both in the New York Court of Appeals, with Judge Pound writing the majority opinion, which Judge Cardozo joined,[163] and in the United States Supreme Court, with Justice Holmes joining Justice Clarke's majority opinion.[164]

Ultimately, Cohen's participation in and compelling reflections upon the Emergency Rent Laws litigation provide a valuable window into the role of Jewish lawyers in the United States in the early twentieth century. Moreover, among other lessons, Cohen's citation to Jewish legal history in his briefs and oral arguments before the New York Court of Appeals and the United States Supreme Court, in front of such eminent jurists as Judge Benjamin N. Cardozo and Justice Oliver Wendell Holmes, Jr., indicates that Jewish law had achieved a degree of respect and legitimacy within American legal discourse. Finally, though it remains unlikely that Cohen's references to Jewish law, as such, had—or were intended to have—an effect on Cardozo's decision in the Emergency Rent Laws case, Cohen's anecdote opens the door for consideration of the interests and interrelationships that might have impacted judicial decision making in the early twentieth century. In light of controversies that have arisen regarding the religious beliefs[165] and personal relationships[166] of members of the current Supreme Court, this study has abiding relevance and potential application in the early twenty-first century as well.

---

[163] See People ex. rel. Durham Realty Corp. v. La Fetra, 130 N.E. 601 (N.Y. 1921).

[164] See Edgar A. Levy Leasing Co. v. Siegel, 258 U.S. 242 (1922).

[165] See, e.g., Gregory A. Kalscheur, "Catholics in Public Life: Judges, Legislators, and Voters," *Journal of Catholic Legal Studies* 46 (2007): 211; John T. Noonan, Jr., "The Religion of the Justice: Does it Affect Constitutional Decision Making?" *Tulsa Law Review* 42 (2007):761; William H. Pryor, Jr., "The Religious Faith and Judicial Duty of an American Catholic Judge," *Yale Law & Policy Review* 24 (2006): 347; Thomas L. Shaffer, "Roman Catholic Lawyers in the United States of America," *Journal of Law & Religion* 21 (2005–2006): 305; Symposium, "Catholicism and the Court: The Relevance of Faith Traditions to Jurisprudence," *University of St. Thomas Law Journal* 4 (2006).

[166] See, e.g., Cheney v. U.S. District Court for the District of Columbia, 541 U.S. 913 (2004) (Scalia, J.); Debra Lyn Bassett, "Recusal and the Supreme Court," *Hastings Law Journal* 56 (2005): 657; Ross E. Davies, "The Reluctant Recusants," *Green Bag 2d* 10 (2006): 79.

The Jewish Law Firm: Past and Present

Eli Wald[1]

I. Introduction

The rise and growth of large Jewish law firms in New York City during the second half of the twentieth century is nothing short of an astounding success story.[2] As late as 1950, there was not a single large Jewish law firm in town. By the mid-1960s, six of the largest twenty law firms were Jewish, and by 1980, four of the largest ten law firms were Jewish firms.[3] Moreover, the accomplishment of these Jewish firms is especially striking because, while the traditional large White Anglo-Saxon Protestant ("WASP") law firms also grew at a fast rate during this period, the Jewish firms grew twice as fast, and they did so in spite of explicit discrimination.

What happened? This chapter studies the rise and growth of large New York City Jewish law firms. It does so on the basis of the public record, with respect to both the law firms themselves and trends in the legal profession generally, and through more than twenty in-depth interviews with lawyers who either founded and practiced at these successful Jewish firms, attempted and failed to establish such firms, or were in a position to join these firms but decided instead to join WASP firms.[4]

One generic[5] explanation is that Jewish law firms rose as the result of changes in cultural values and market conditions in American society after

---

[1] Charles W. Delaney Jr. Professor of Law, University of Denver Sturm College of Law; B.A., Tel-Aviv University; LL.B., Tel-Aviv University; LL.M., Harvard Law School (waived); S.J.D., Harvard Law School. This chapter is based on an article previously published in Eli Wald, "The Rise of the Jewish Law Firm or Is the Jewish Law Firm Generic?" *UMKC Law Review* 76 (2008): 885–938.

[2] See Part III.A below for a definition of a Jewish law firm.

[3] See Tables 1 and 2 below, Part III.C.

[4] These interviews were conducted on the condition of anonymity; thus, any identifying information is excluded, with interviewees referred to as "informants" and each assigned a number for the purposes of this chapter. The transcripts of the interviews are on file with the author.

[5] The term "generic" here borrows from Thomas Sowell, "Are Jews Generic?" in *Black Rednecks and White Liberals* (New York: Encounter Books, 2005), 76–122. In his usual provocative style, Sowell argues that hatred and persecution of Jews are generic in the sense that they have nothing to do with Jews per se. Rather, Jews are the classic "middleman minorities," despised and discriminated against on account of the intermediary role they play between producers and consumers as well as their distinctive social patterns. Sowell concludes: "While there are characteristics and achievements which are uniquely Jewish, the history of middleman minorities around the world seems to suggest that it has not been these uniquely Jewish characteristics which called forth venomous hatreds but characteristics and achievements common to middleman minorities. Howev-

World War II, which saw a gradual decline in antisemitism and religious-based discrimination against Jews in America and an increased demand for legal services by large corporate clients.[6] This account is generic in the sense that inherently it has nothing to do with Jewish law firms and Jewish lawyers, and, indeed, it intrinsically has nothing to do with Jews or with the legal profession itself. Rather, the decline of discrimination generally benefits minorities and in the context of the legal profession it benefited Jewish law firms and Jewish lawyers. Similarly, increased demand for corporate legal services benefited all law firms and led to the rise and growth of large law firms, including Jewish law firms. The generic explanation thus suggests that the reasons for the rise of the Jewish law firms were non-legal; that is, they were to be found outside of the legal realm, and were not uniquely Jewish. The success of the Jewish law firms was nothing more than an example of the consequences of more general trends—the decline of discrimination and increased demand for legal services.

Yet, according to the informants interviewed in this chapter, Jewish law firms were not generic. While Jewish law firms certainly benefited from the decline in antisemitism and increased demand for legal services, a unique combination of factors explains the incredible rise of Jewish firms. First, white-shoe[7] ethos caused large WASP firms to stay out of "undignified" practice areas and effectively created pockets of "Jewish" practice areas where the Jewish firms encountered little competition for their services. Second, discriminatory hiring and promotion practices by the large WASP firms helped create a large pool of talented Jewish lawyers from which the Jewish firms could easily recruit. Finally, the Jewish firms benefited from a "flip side of bias" phenomenon, that is, they benefited from the positive consequences of stereotyping.[8]

This chapter proceeds in eight parts. Parts II and III set up the discussion. Part II offers a brief history of the practice of law in New York City between the late nineteenth and the mid-twentieth centuries, highlighting the emergence of large WASP law firms and the existence of a lower stratum Jewish bar. Part III defines the notion of the Jewish law firm and documents the rise and growth of these firms. Parts IV and V investigate the

---

er unique [Jews] may be, historically the kind of hostility and hatred they have faced has been generic" (121–22). To be clear, I accept neither Sowell's conclusions regarding Jews in his essay nor the general themes in his book regarding the inferior cultural sensibilities of African-Americans. I do, however, find instructive his use of "generic" and utilize it to draw a distinction between, on the one hand, generic non-legal and non-uniquely Jewish reasons and, on the other hand, legal and uniquely Jewish explanations that account for the rise of the Jewish law firms.

[6] See Parts IV and V below.

[7] The phrase "white-shoe" originally referred to elite college males who wore white buckskin shoes at Ivy League schools in the 1950s, and is used to describe law firms in America that were populated by members of the WASP elite and generally excluded anyone who was not a WASP male. See Elizabeth Chambliss, "The Shoe Still Fits," *Legal Affairs* 10 (2005): 18–19.

[8] See Part VI below.

"generic" trends within American society and the legal market that explain in part the remarkable success of the Jewish law firms. Specifically, Part IV explores the consequences of the decline of antisemitism and religious-based discrimination on Jewish law firms and Part V studies the impact of increased client demand for corporate services. Part VI examines a combination of unique factors that explain the growth of the Jewish firms: the existence of protected Jewish pockets of practice, the surprising consequences of effective WASP discrimination against Jewish lawyers and the effects of the "flip side of bias" phenomenon. Following a conclusion in Part VII, Part VIII is an appendix providing a methodological summary of the interviews that inform the analysis in this chapter.

II. A Brief History of the Practice of Law in New York City

A. Large Law Firms in New York City, 1900–1950

The large law firm emerged as a new unit of law practice around the turn of the twentieth century.[9] This type of firm's organizational structure, often referred to as the Cravath System, featured six characteristics: a hierarchical structure based on two distinct types of attorneys (partners and associates); close working relationships among firm attorneys, emphasizing teamwork as opposed to individual work product; investment in, and development of, candidate recruitment procedures followed by systematic

---

[9] See Magali S. Larson, "On the Nostalgic View of Lawyers' Role," *Stanford Law Review* 37 (1985): 448 ("It is well known that the large law firm was born in the last third of the nineteenth century in a period of institutional reorganization."); Wayne K. Hobson, "Symbol of the New Profession: Emergence of the Large Law Firm, 1870–1915," in *The New High Priests: Lawyers in Post-Civil War America*, ed. Gerald W. Gawalt (Westport, CT: Greenwood Press, 1984), 3 ("The legal profession ... was transformed between the 1870s and the 1920s ... Although most lawyers in 1930 still practiced alone or with one partner, the leaders of the profession were no longer men in such firms; they were now all in large firms."). See, generally, Marc Galanter and Thomas Palay, *Tournament of Lawyers: The Transformation of the Big Law Firm* (Chicago: University of Chicago Press, 1991), 4. "Large" has a dynamic meaning. According to James Willard Hurst, "No firms of large membership appeared, even in the great cities, until the end of the [nineteenth] century. The typical partnership was a two-man affair" (*The Growth of American Law* [Boston: Little Brown, 1950], 306). The benchmark for "large" reached fifty attorneys by the 1950s; see Erwin O. Smigel, "The Impact of Recruitment on the Organization of the Large Law Firm," *American Sociological Review* 25 (1960): 58. By the late 1980s, "a firm of 50 members probably would not be considered large" in major cities (Justin A. Stanley, "Should Lawyers Stick to Their Last?" *Indiana Law Journal* 64 (1989): 473). In August 2007, the largest law firm in the world was Baker & McKenzie, with a total of 3535 attorneys. See Lindsay Fortadoa, "Dewey Ballantine, LeBoeuf Agree to Merge Law Firms," *Washington Post*, August 28, 2007. Since 2008, restructuring in the market for corporate legal services and the Great Recession halted the growth of large American law firms. See Marc Galanter and William Henderson, "The Elastic Tournament: A Second Transformation of the Big Law Firm," *Stanford Law Review* 60 (2008): 1867–1929; Eli Wald, "Foreword: The Great Recession and the Legal Profession," *Fordham Law Review* 78 (2010): 2051–66; Bernard A. Burk and David McGowan, "Big but Brittle: Economic Perspectives on the Future of the Law Firm in the New Economy," *Columbia Business Law Review* (2011): 1–117; Eli Wald, "Smart Growth: The Large Law Firm in the Twenty-First Century," *Fordham Law Review* 80 (2012): 2867–2915.

training programs for associates; a probation period for associates, followed by promotion to partnership for some and an "up-or-out" policy for those not promoted; specialization of individual attorneys' expertise and departmentalization of work within the firm based on groupings of individual attorneys; and utilization of technology.[10] By the 1920s, the Cravath System dominated the expanding world of large law firms,[11] and by the 1960s large firms reached their "Golden Era"[12] in terms of being recognized as the elite of the American legal profession.[13]

Wall Street, New York City was essentially the birth-place of the large law firm.[14] During the first half of the twentieth century Wall Street housed not only Cravath, Swaine & Moore, the paradigmatic large firm, but also a significant number of all large American law firms. In 1948, there were 284 law firms in the United States with eight or more partners, located in fifty-seven different cities, with New York City accounting for seventy-three of them. From 1950 through 1970, at least eight of the ten largest firms in the country were New York City firms.[15] Indeed, until the 1970s, due to the concentration of large law firms in New York City, the terms large "American" and "New York City" law firms could be used interchangeably.[16] Moreover, the impact of New York City on the rise and growth of large law firms was not limited to the mere number of firms it hosted and its role as a key business and financial center, which enabled the Wall Street firms to rise to

---

[10] See Eli Wald, "The Rise and Fall of the WASP and Jewish Law Firms," *Stanford Law Review* 60 (2008): 1806–10. See, generally, Galanter and Palay, *Tournament of Lawyers*, 4–19.

[11] See Wayne K. Hobson, *The American Legal Profession and the Organizational Society 1890–1930* (New York: Garland Publishing, 1986), 201. By the 1920s the system Cravath had initiated was well established and regularized. The managing partners of the leading law firms had even entered into a gentlemen's agreement after World War I to eliminate the practice of competitive bidding for the services of the most promising law school graduates. They established uniform entry-level salaries and agreed not to laterally recruit lawyers away from each other.

[12] Galanter and Palay, *Tournament of Lawyers*, 20.

[13] Robert L. Nelson, *Partners with Power: The Social Transformation of the Large Law Firm* (Berkeley: University of California Press, 1988). Nelson describes the large law firm as sitting "atop the pyramid of prestige and power within the American legal profession. Although comprising but a small fraction of lawyers, through its impact on patterns of recruitment, styles of practice, and the collective institutions of the bar, the large law firm has a significance that far exceeds the number of lawyers it employs" (1).

[14] According to Galanter and Palay, large firms grew in size, first in New York City, then in other large cities, then in smaller cities, then overseas. *Tournament of Lawyers*, 14, 18–19.

[15] Robert L. Nelson, "Practice and Privilege: Social Change and the Structure of Large Law Firms," *American Bar Foundation Research Journal* 6 (1981): 104. For a discussion of the growth of large law firms outside of New York City, see Hobson, *American Legal Profession and the Organizational Society 1890–1930*, 163–88.

[16] By the late 1970s, New York City lost its dominance as large law firms grew nationwide. By 1979, all but Shearman & Sterling had been displaced on the largest law firms list by the largest firms of other cities. See below, note 93.

dominance; rather, Wall Street itself emerged as the symbolic home of the large firms—the new legal elite.[17]

The large law firm reflected a new professional ideology significantly different from the era's prevailing notions of lawyering. It purported to be a meritocracy in which hiring and promotion were based upon performance, replacing traditional notions of nepotism, privilege, and class hierarchies. In 1920 Paul Cravath put this change into words as he advised his hearers that for success at the New York bar "family influence, social friendships and wealth count for little." He further emphasized the large number of successful lawyers who had come to New York from small places and "worked up from the bottom of the ladder without having any advantage of position or acquaintance."[18]

In spite of their claim to meritocracy, however, large New York City law firms recruited and promoted almost exclusively WASP attorneys and featured a white-shoe Protestant culture.[19] Jewish attorneys were rarely recruited and even less commonly promoted to partnership.[20] Thus, the large New York City law firm club circa 1950 consisted entirely of WASP white-shoe law firms.[21]

B. Jewish Lawyers in New York City, 1900–1950

The large law firm rose against a backdrop of a changing legal profession. In 1885 there were about 5,000 lawyers in New York City, about 400 of whom were Jewish.[22] The new century brought waves of immigrants and growth to the New York Bar. The years between 1890 and 1910 witnessed an immense growth in part time and evening programs in law schools, as well as great growth in the number of lawyers born abroad or with foreign-born

---

[17] See, e.g., David T. Bazelon, "Portrait of a Business Generalist," *Comment* 24 (1960): 279 ("There is a nice vignette to be written about the popular displacement in the past few decades of the historic phrase 'Philadelphia lawyer' by the new and more magical 'New York lawyer.'").

[18] Robert T. Swaine, *The Cravath Firm and its Predecessors: 1819–1947* (New York: Ad Press, 1948), 265. Similarly, Arthur Dean of Sullivan & Cromwell opined: "In today's larger legal partnerships advancement is by and large by competence alone. Those who achieve positions of influence and leadership in such firms tend to be those who have manifested their ability to relate into a more comprehensive picture diverse fields of specialization and to view the major problems of clients in a broad social perspective." Arthur H. Dean, *William Nelson Cromwell 1854–1948: An American Pioneer in Corporation, Comparative and International Law* (New York: Ad Press, 1957), 85.

[19] See Wald, "Rise and Fall of the WASP and Jewish Law Firms," 1810–25, which explores the apparent contradiction between the large law firm's meritocratic claim and its religious and cultural identity.

[20] Note, "The Jewish Law Student and New York Jobs: Discriminatory Effects in Law Firm Hiring Practices," *Yale Law Journal* 73 (1964): 626, 635.

[21] See Part VI below.

[22] Henry W. Taft, *Legal Miscellanies: Six Decades of Changes and Progress* (New York: Macmillan, Co., 1941), 77.

parents.[23] The newcomers crowded the lower stratum of the bar, competing fiercely for clients and a livelihood.[24] Top educational credentials served as barriers to exclude these unwelcome newcomers.[25] Indeed, "barriers to access became more formidable as the desirability of access increased ... [and] professional opportunity depended upon ethnic, social, religious, and educational credentials."[26] In this formative era of the New York City legal profession, "Cromwells and Cravaths rose to the top; 'Hebrews' sank to the bottom."[27]

Both trends—the growth of the bar and the increased stratification—continued to dominate the New York City legal profession even after 1950, so much so that "in 1960, there were approximately 26,000 lawyers in Manhattan and the Bronx, about 20,500 of whom were active practitioners," and 17,000 of whom were in private practice.[28] The city's bar was almost all native-born white males, and was slightly over sixty percent Jewish.[29] At the same time, ethnic- and religious-based discrimination (intertwined with socio-economic-cultural bias) in the large law firm segment of the New York City bar became common knowledge.[30] Moreover, "Jewish lawyers [were] less likely than their non-Jewish colleagues to gain access to the high-status position in the bar."[31] While they constituted sixty percent of the New York City Bar, Jewish lawyers were overly represented in individual practice (seventy-seven percent) and small firms (seventy-six percent), and significantly under-represented in large law firms (twenty-five percent).[32]

C. New York, New York

In the first half of the twentieth century Wall Street was the center of corporate law practice and had a larger concentration of large law firms than anywhere else in the country and the world. New York City was also where the large Jewish law firm emerged after 1950.[33] It is important to

---

[23] Jerold S. Auerbach, *Unequal Justice: Lawyers and Social Change in Modern America* (New York: Oxford University Press, 1976), 95–96.

[24] Ibid.

[25] Ibid., 95–101.

[26] Ibid., 25.

[27] Ibid., 26.

[28] Jerome E. Carlin, *Lawyers' Ethics: A Survey of the New York City Bar* (New York: Russell Sage Foundation, 1966), 11.

[29] Ibid., 18–19.

[30] "The Jewish Law Student and New York Jobs," 635 ("Gentiles were more successful than Jews in getting good jobs, and in getting the jobs of their choice.").

[31] Carlin, *Lawyers' Ethics*, 22.

[32] Ibid., 28. Protestant attorneys, on the other hand, who constituted only about eighteen percent of the bar, accounted for forty-three percent of the large law firm pool, and only nine percent of the individual practitioner pool.

[33] See Part III.C below.

note, however, that the rise of the WASP firms, and subsequently the Jewish firms, was not restricted geographically to New York City and took place in other large metropolises; first in Chicago, Washington, D.C., Boston, and Philadelphia, later expanding to the west coast, and eventually spreading to many large cities throughout the United States.[34]

Nonetheless, the informants suggest that both the rise of Jewish law firms and the success of Jewish lawyers were due, at least in part, to the unique professional and cultural conditions present in New York City. For example, describing the ideology and approach of the New York City Bar Association, an informant observed:

> It's sort of like the legal conscience of the world. There is no subject the New York City Bar, a city, local bar association will not comment on, anything, human rights in China. The City Bar has a very expansive notion of its jurisdiction. And I went to the meetings of the House of Delegates for the New York State Bar because it's such an extraordinarily interesting social institution. And New York is almost a microcosm of the country. [On the other hand] I've never been active in the ABA, it's just too big for me, too monolithic.[35]

A partner at a large Jewish firm captured the interplay between cultural and professional conditions in New York City and its impact on the practice of law:

> A Shomer Shabbas [Sabbath observer] attorney will work Saturday night or Sunday to make up the time. In almost all cases, it doesn't upset the work flow at all.... A number of times in my career, I had to impose on other attorneys to take over on a Friday or Yom Tov [a day of religious observance], and it is even more difficult for a day or a few days. I always feel uncomfortable when ... imposing on somebody to do that. Sometimes clients have to understand what's going on, especially if you are not a New Yorker and they don't quite understand what it is all about.[36]

Other informants explored the less obvious impact of New York City and its culture on the rise of Jewish law firms. For instance, one informant said:

> That is partly America, partly New York, which is very polyglot and we hardly realize it, but you accept it and you only recognize it when someone comes from outside of New York and step[s] in a subway

---

[34] See, e.g., Toni M. Massaro, *F. Daniel Frost and the Rise of the Modern American Law Firm* (Tucson: The University of Arizona, 2011) (on the transformation of Gibson, Dunn & Crutcher from a California-based regional to a global law firm).

[35] Informant #12, 17–18.

[36] Informant #6, 13.

and [is] startled by the multiple nationalit[ies] and races and everything, which we take completely for granted.[37]

Another informant described the present impact of New York culture with the following remarks:

> For sure, New York City has always, in my judgment, been more progressive and is more progressive today-liberal or progressive-call it what you will, in accepting ... diversity than places in the Midwest.... I'm sure New York is way ahead. I know, from personal experience, that when it comes to prejudice against women ... there are firms in the Midwest that are back where [New York was] thirty years ago.... Five or ten years ago, one of the major firms [down south] had a "wet t-shirt" contest at their summer outing ... I remember reading about that and saying, "Are they in the Middle Ages?" I mean, there's no way a thing like that could happen at ... any New York City law firm. We're just ahead.[38]

III. The Meaning of a Jewish Firm

A. *The Jewishness of the Jewish Firms*

In this chapter, a Jewish law firm refers to a firm whose majority of lawyers, both partners and associates, between 1950 and 1980 were Jewish. While there is no precise record of the religious affiliation of their attorneys, law firms were commonly known as WASP, Jewish, Catholic, or mixed. For instance, one informant stated, "In those days, I think, there were some Jewish firms—predominant Jewish firms—and non-Jewish firms."[39] Another informant labeled a specific firm "a Jewish firm," adding, "The counsel of the firm was James Marshall, son of Louie Marshall. The make-up was really Jewish. That firm was still ... a Jewish firm. It might have had non Jewish [associates] but all of the partners were Jewish."[40]

By a "Jewish" firm, I do not mean to suggest that such a firm featured a unique Jewish firm culture, any specific Jewish values, professional or otherwise, or any commitment to or knowledge of Jewish law.[41] In fact, the Jewish firms were Jewish by discriminatory default; namely, due to the discriminatory hiring and promotion practices at the elite WASP firms, many Jewish attorneys flocked to the "Jewish" firms, thus constituting these firms as Jewish.[42]

---

[37] Informant #4, 17.

[38] Informant #5, 13.

[39] Informant #6, 6.

[40] Informant #2, 5, 8.

[41] In contrast, WASP firms did have a uniquely Protestant identity, coupled with a white-shoe cultural identity. See Wald, "Rise and Fall of the WASP and Jewish Law Firms," 1810–25.

[42] See Part VI below.

In theory, Jewish law firms could have developed as institutions organized around Jewish themes, values, and culture.⁴³ One can imagine, for example, law firms with a special commitment to the notion of doing mitzvahs (i.e., good deeds) in the form of enhanced pro bono.⁴⁴ An informant postulated that Jewish firms, or at least Jewish partners, could build on the affinity between Jewish law and American law and use the latter to instruct and introduce young Jewish students to the former.⁴⁵ To be clear, however, Jewish law firms did not develop such a Jewish identity. While many Jewish lawyers were actively involved with Jewish causes, their support was usually rendered in their personal capacity outside of their legal practice rather than in their professional capacity as lawyers. Judaism did not emerge as a central organizational theme or underlying professional value. For instance, one informant recalled:

> When I was interviewed [by a large Jewish firm,] I mentioned that I was a Sabbath observer; the person who interviewed me wanted to know what that was although he was Jewish.... I explained it to him [and] ... he said, "Just work your tail off we don't care when it is and that will be that."⁴⁶

Another informant noted:

---

⁴³ On the relationship between faith and professional identity, see, generally, Thomas L. Shaffer, *Faith and the Professions* (Provo, Utah: Brigham Young University, 1987); Marc Galanter, "A Vocation for Law? American Jewish Lawyers and Their Antecedents," *Fordham Urban Law Journal* 26 (1999): 1125–47. On the interplay between religious identity and professional identity, see Sanford Levinson, "Identifying the Jewish Lawyer: Reflections on the Construction of Professional Identity," *Cardozo Law Review* 14 (1993): 1577–1612; Martha Minow, "On Being a Religious Professional: The Religious Turn in Professional Ethics," *University of Pennsylvania Law Review* 150 (2001): 661–68; Russell G. Pearce, "Reflections on the American Jewish Lawyer," *Journal of Law & Religion* 17 (2002): 179–88.

⁴⁴ Indeed, historically, Jewish law firms were known for their commitment to pro bono work. For example, "The Scholarship and Defense Fund for Racial Equality (CORE SCDF) ... was a mixed black and white group ... It fell apart with the rise of Black Power and tensions in New York City between Jews and Blacks.... Both Jews of World War II, and Israel and Blacks were all viewed as underdogs, and still remain to this day. And so that was an outlet" (Informant #2, 10).

⁴⁵ The informant believes that, currently, Jewish law and legal studies inform and enhance each other: "Certainly today it [referring to the synergy between Jewish and legal studies] does ... I think it's a tremendous thing to teach kids [today], to show the roots when you're teaching a high school class because they're smart kids, you know, they're in high school already to teach them that the roots of law in the United States, where law's derived from is fascinating it helps strengthen their belief in the Talmud and in the Jewish tradition and their continuity and also, I think it's just fascinating" (Informant #15, 10). On the affinity between Jews and American law, see generally, Jerold S. Auerbach, *Rabbis and Lawyers: The Journey from Torah to Constitution* (Bloomington: Indiana University Press, 1990).

⁴⁶ Informant #10, 3.

> Being [observant] was much more of a problem in terms of these [Jewish] firms than just the mere fact that you were Jewish or Catholic, from my point of view. I remember being interviewed in well-established Jewish firms. One I can remember now the partner who interviewed me was a Shomer [Sabbath observer] himself and he told me that it would be a mistake for me to come there because of the hard time he had. And then going to another firm the guy said to me, "well, you're going to have to go home early on Friday." Kind of put me in that kind of a corner. And I was interviewed by some big [Jewish] firms. But it was more ... like a courtesy, I think, everybody was just going through the motions.[47]

The informant went as far as to characterize practice realities at the Jewish firms as discriminatory vis-à-vis observant Jewish attorneys, noting:

> I like to think of [an observant Jewish attorney with a large Jewish law firm] as a role model except he came after me [graduating in 1958]. In my view, for whatever it's worth, I think he's the guy who broke the glass ceiling [for observant Jewish attorneys at Jewish firms] so far as many people were concerned. When he made the success that he did make very quickly, it opened the door to Yeshiva graduates who were observant.[48]

Another informant describing the hiring patterns of Jewish law firms noted, "The major Jewish law firms weren't hiring first or second generation Jews."[49] An observant informant, however, had a more pleasant experience interviewing with Jewish firms:

> During the interviewing process [my religious observance] sometimes came up and came up also to the effect that I would not work on Saturday. [At one interview] someone said, 'you're exactly what we want, I hope you'll work on Saturday when we need you,' and I told them, 'no I won't work on Saturday.' He said, 'it won't happen too often.' I said, 'no it won't work.' So that was more of the negative type of interview. In this firm, as in most of the [Jewish] firms, at least the spoken word was that there would be no problem, that they would support the fact that I had to leave early on Friday and not come in on Saturday. But sometimes you never know until you get someplace.[50]

Of course, some Jewish lawyers were not as ignorant of Jewish customs and habits, yet they still chose not to emphasize their Jewish identity, let

---

[47] Informant #7, 1–3. Moreover, the same informant reported, "I'd say the lawyers I knew were kind of single practitioners, kind of more my father's peers. And if they were observant they had to be single practitioners because they couldn't get jobs anywhere else" (6). Another observant Jew, working for a large Jewish firm believed that "I was the first Orthodox hired by a Jewish firm" (Informant #14, 2).

[48] Informant #7, 6.

[49] Informant #17, 17.

[50] Informant #18, 6–7.

alone celebrate it as an important component of their professional identity.[51] One informant witnessed this behavior, stating:

> I know people that are involved heavily in the Jewish federation.... They got involved in the 50's and the 60's and thought [that] to be involved in [the] federation you should take off the Yarmulke when you go into the building.... It's interesting. Every once in a while Clinton used to say to me, "Rabbi ... " I insisted I didn't want to be called Rabbi even though I was [a Rabbi].... I wanted them to know a layman wears a Yarmulke.[52]

In some instances, Jewish interests were outweighed by the desire for professionalism and loyalty to clients' interests. A partner at a large Jewish law firm described his firm's decision to open an office in Germany, despite the legacy of the Holocaust, as follows:

> Frankfurt is the center of business across Europe and if we were going to grow, we had to be there, and our clients insisted that we go. We have clients that are very active in the European markets and, you know, if you don't want to open, that's fine, but we'll go elsewhere.[53]

One can take opposite views regarding the Jewish reaction to post-Holocaust Germany, ranging from opposition to opening an office in Germany to celebrating such an office as a triumph over evil. What is significant about the informant's perspective is that it reflects no Jewish consideration whatsoever.[54] The relevant issues were clients' needs and the firm's competitiveness in global legal markets.[55]

---

[51] That is not to suggest that Jewish identity, values, and experiences did not indirectly influence and shape the professional culture and organization of Jewish firms. One informant, for example, discussing the growth pattern of his firm, noted: "Probably the fundamental thing was, we were never sure where we would be going and so on. When you start out, you can go one of two ways. One, you can sort of gamble and keep expanding and so on. The other you can be very conservative and not take the next step until you're sure you have the right base. All of us were basically very conservative people. We never felt that confident that tomorrow would be there so that was probably fundamental" (Informant #17, 11). The same informant further explained, "Well, keep in mind, we grew up during the Depression, we didn't come from rich families, never sure that we were going to be that successful" (13).

[52] Informant #10, 13–14.

[53] Informant #1, 9.

[54] Ibid.

[55] Ibid. Similarly, another informant recalled a conversation in which he was told about a prominent Jewish attorney representing a Congressional committee. On a Friday evening, a member of the committee asked the attorney, "'Mr. XXX, don't you have to go home?' So I said, 'Well what did Mr. XXX say?' And he said [that Mr. XXX replied,] 'Oh Mr. Senator, for matters of national security I'm permitted to violate the Sabbath'" (Informant #15, 22). Once again, client needs and professional identity took precedence over personal identity and religious observance.

Certainly, Jewish firms employing nearly exclusively Jewish attorneys developed some benefits from the homogeneous religious affiliation of their practitioners. An attorney in a Jewish firm confirmed:

> We had a ... very nice firm. It was congenial. There were never any real problems with rooms. Everybody kind of liked everybody else. I never brought up at a firm meeting any issue unless I had first cleared it with most of the partners. It was worth the time and the aggravation to persuade people, so there was never a hostile vote taken or anything like that.[56]

Moreover, at times, Jewish elements did impact the practice of law at the Jewish firms. For example, an informant said of his Sabbath observance:

> Many times when I leave on Friday, my non-Jewish partners and associates see me leave.... They see that advantage I have by having a strict regimen which can't be violated. I have to say, it probably does give to me a psychological advantage over many of the people who don't have that rest or can't count on the rest.[57]

Similarly, another said of Yom Kippur observance:

> So the joke around here was: there was a relatively senior lawyer, a partner in the corporate department ... a very devout Catholic.... We called him the "house guy" because the question was if he's good what is he doing here, why isn't he downtown or something like that? He would call me every February. I'll never forget, every February he'd say, "Yom Kippur, it's six months from now." I'd say, "Why do you care?" and his answer was, "Well, the trouble is, I'm always setting meetings with Jewish lawyers and they never think of these things and then suddenly we find out—oh, the day before Yom Kippur—[they] can't come to the meeting [because] it's Yom Kippur."[58]

Also affecting the practice of law at the Jewish firms was a particular emphasis on the pro bono commitments and extra-curricular activities of Jewish partners, as is noted in the following:

> At that time, there was no such thing as a program to go to Israel for a year after high school.... In fact, some years later on, I helped to set that up, eventually. That's a whole separate story. Someone now in Israel wanted to go, needed Jewish Agency approval to get the mon-

---

[56] Informant #1, 9.

[57] Informant #6, 15.

[58] Informant #10, 2–3.

ey.... I knew people at the Jewish Agency [who] went to Israel, met with the appropriate people, but that's a different success story.[59]

Another informant said of such extra-curricular involvement: "I got involved in the Jewish Community Relations Council which is a bridge, kind of an umbrella over sixty different organizations and worked on the Committee [in various roles]."[60]

Yet, unlike Black corporate firms,[61] Jewish law firms did not have a mission to create lasting Jewish institutions. The Jewish firms were Jewish by discriminatory default, and Judaism simply did not play a constitutive role in their organization and professional identity. One informant's account of the role of Judaism in his life captures the role Judaism played in many Jewish firms:

> I have been interested in my Jewish roots. I identify and am interested in the Jewish tradition and its scholarship and play with that occasionally. I suppose it was Stendahl who said 'life is love and work.' And I have been very happy in my marriage and my family and have been generally very happy in my work. And I continue to support humanitarian causes with hope if not with optimism.[62]

While certainly mindful of his Jewish roots, Judaism for the informant was separate and distinct from his work, something to "play with" after hours, something that informs, in an indirect fashion, commitment to humanitarian causes.[63] Similarly, in many Jewish firms and for many

---

[59] Informant #4, 2.

[60] Informant #2, 11. Another noted: "when you're a Jewish lawyer, you definitely get approached by, you know, causes, working for legal services they figure will appeal to you, so you have that kind of work, so certainly, you know synagogues" (Informant #15, 31).

[61] See David Wilkins, "'If You Can't Join 'em Beat 'em!' The Rise and Fall of the Black Corporate Law Firm," *Stanford Law Review* 60 (2008): 1733–1801.

[62] Informant #3, 91.

[63] The separation between one's professional identity as an attorney and one's religious identity as a Jew was likewise noted by several informants: "The people of my generation [following WWII and the Holocaust] even if we were not personally touched, we were touched, so that has basically defined my interests; I think that plus the fact that I was ambitious, I wanted to succeed, I worked hard, I did everything I could to advance my position but I always from that time became touched by Jewish issues" (Informant #13, 6). Moreover, the same informant reported, "The religious identity was something that I developed as time went by. My background, training, from schools and professional experiences [was different], religion was not a part of it at all." Another informant explained: "I would say that [my religious identity] was not relevant to [my professional identity]. I mean, I am familiar with Jewish charities and such but I don't think one had anything to do with the other" (Informant #19, 8). But for one informant, his Jewish identity, culture, and experience did inform and shape the practice of law: "[My interest in immigration law] was sparked by my study of Jewish history. I have felt always ... you know if you do a study of what went on in the 1930s, the German quota was open at all times for immigration to the United States and if you go through the correspondence between the American Consul General in Berlin and his superiors in Washington ... you'll

Jewish lawyers both at Jewish and at WASP firms, Judaism was of interest, a source that informed pro bono and extra-curricular activities, and yet it was independent of their "work," the practice of law.

Another informant questioned, "it is hard [for a person] to separate religious identity from other identities" and "I always tried to do the right thing. Is it [doing the right thing] being Jewish?"[64] Similarly he was uncertain about what it would mean for the firm to have a Jewish identity, saying, "People like people they can deal with and feel they know. So religion in that sense was relevant."[65] But beyond such a sense of cultural familiarity, he did not believe Judaism played a role in the organization, structure and practice of the firm.[66]

B. Who is a Jew?

The issue of defining Jewish identity is a highly controversial one. In the context of characterizing law firms, even the basic definition of a Jewish firm as one that employed a majority of Jewish attorneys is not without its challenges because no record lists lawyers by their religious affiliation. That said, for the purposes of this chapter, such a headcount is not necessary, nor is a "definite" list of all Jewish law firms of the era.

Instead, suffice it to note that commonly referred to Jewish law firms included "traditional" Jewish law firms established before 1950 (such as Stroock & Stroock & Lavan; Weil, Gotshal; Kaye, Scholer; Proskauer, Rose; Fried, Frank; and the Rosenman firm) and "start-up" Jewish firms founded in the early 1960s (such as Schulte, Roth & Zabel, and Kramer, Levin).[67] In addition, a group of mixed firms, never known as Jewish law firms, existed with a significant contingency of Jewish attorneys, some "traditional" (Paul, Weiss[68] and Cleary, Gottlieb[69]), and others "start-up" (Wachtell, Lipton, Rosen & Katz[70] and Skadden, Arps[71]).[72]

---

see that these anti-Semites said, 'no Jews.' So I felt that I could help people [in such] circumstances ... and I have had the privilege over the years of doing a lot of such cases" (Informant #20, 12–13).

[64] Informant #14, 2.

[65] Ibid.

[66] Ibid.

[67] A partner at a start-up Jewish firm described his first few years of practice with an established mixed firm as "happy years." Along with colleagues from several other Jewish firms as well as from his own firm, he helped establish a somewhat less "traditional," more "entrepreneurial" firm (Informant #16, 2–3).

[68] The firm was formed in 1945 as Mr. Weiss and Mr. Wharton joined forces with Mr. Paul and Mr. Garrison. Unique not only in the heterogeneous religious affiliation of its named partners and attorneys, Paul, Weiss was the first major Wall Street law firm to move to midtown (in 1949), the first to elect a female partner (in 1946 at its D.C. office) and the first to hire a black associate. Judge Rifkind joined the firm in 1950, and the firm enhanced its reputation as a leading litigation law firm. By 1949, the firm had 13 lawyers; by 1970, the firm had 110 lawyers; and by 1972, it had 138. See Paul Hoffman, *Lions in the Street: The Inside Story of the Great Wall Street Law Firms* (New York: Saturday

C. The Rise and Growth of the Jewish Law Firms

In 1950 the New York City elite corporate bar consisted of only well-established, large law firms. Without exception, every member of the elite club was a WASP law firm. Not a single member of the elite large law firm club was a Jewish firm; in fact, there were no large Jewish firms in New York City.[73] This is not surprising given that five years earlier, in 1945, not a single Jewish firm had more than ten lawyers. As one interviewee confirmed, "[There were no] Jewish firms ... [in] the 50s. [The Jewish firms] were very small firms.... [One] existed with eight lawyers.[74]

Review Press, 1973), 112–21.

[69] Cleary, Gottlieb was formed following a split from Root Carter. "Most Jewish attorneys followed Gottlieb to Cleary," and Gottlieb became the first Jewish named partner in a major Wall Street law firm (Hoffman, *Lions in the Street*, 65). The firm grew rapidly, from 17 attorneys as of December 31, 1946, to 27 lawyers four years later, and to 63 lawyers on December 31, 1960. See Leo Gottlieb, *Cleary, Gottlieb, Steen & Hamilton: The First Thirty Years* (New York: The Firm, 1983), 76–77, 138.

[70] Wachtell, Lipton, Rosen & Katz was formed by four Jewish partners. Like Paul, Weiss, Cleary, and Skadden, Wachtell never developed a reputation as a Jewish firm, quickly earning a reputation as one of the elite law firms in New York City and setting the mark for the highest paid associates and the highest profits-per-partner. See Steven Brill, "Two Tough Lawyers in the Tender Offer Game," *New York Magazine*, June 21, 1976, at 55 (describing Skadden, Arps and Wachtell, Lipton as "younger firms, many of which were started by Jewish lawyers who were not as welcome then at the old-line firms"). Wachtell has maintained its reputation as a leader in profit-per-partner. See http://www.abajournal.com/weekly/skadden_wachtell_top_amlaw_100 (last visited July 10, 2013).

[71] In 1963 Skadden, Arps had ten lawyers. By 1980, it had 205; and, by 2004, it was the second largest law firm in New York City with over 1700 attorneys. Skadden, Arps never developed a reputation as a Jewish firm, although many of its attorneys, including some of its founders, were Jewish. See Brill, "Two Tough Lawyers in the Tender Offer Game," 55. See, generally, Lincoln Caplan, *Skadden: Power, Money, and the Rise of a Legal Empire* (New York: Noonday Press, 1993).

[72] One informant explained that while the "mixed" firms never developed a reputation for being "Jewish," the Jewish firms, defined as recruiting and promoting almost exclusively Jewish attorneys, underwent "Cravathization"; that is, over time they began to regularly recruit and promote the best talent, Jewish and non-Jewish attorneys alike, to overcome and "get outside the characterization of a Jewish firm" (Informant #16, 5). The sentiment is consistent with an account given by another informant, a partner at a mixed firm, who explained that the hiring criteria at his firm were always based on merit: "One of the reasons we thought it was very important to hire out of law school is that we wanted people to sort of grow up with us" (Informant #17, 15). See Part VII below.

[73] In 1950, when the benchmark for a large firm was 50 lawyers, Weil, Gotshal was the largest Jewish law firm with a total of 19 attorneys; Kaye, Scholer had 18; Paul, Weiss had 17; Proskauer, Rose had 15; Stroock & Stroock & Lavan had 13; Fried, Frank had 12; and the Rosenman firm had 7. See the *Martindale-Hubbell Law Directory* (Summit, N.J.: Martindale-Hubbell, 1950).

[74] Informant #8, 7.

Table 1: Jewish Law Firms in New York City, 1932–1950[75]

Firm Name	1932	1935	1940	1945	1950
Fried, Frank, Harris, Shriver, & Jacobson[76]	7[77]	6[78]	8[79]	6[80]	12[81]
Weil, Gotshal & Manges	3	3	9	12 (+1 tax counsel)	18 (+1 in Washington, DC office)
Cleary, Gottlieb, Steen & Hamilton[82]	N/A	N/A	N/A	N/A	6 (+1 in Washington, DC office, +1 in Paris, France office)[83]
Paul, Weiss, Rifkind, Wharton & Garrison[84]	4	4	4	4[85]	16 (+1 counsel)[86]

---

[75] Numbers are based on *Martindale-Hubbell Directories* for the years 1932 (the first year it was published) and 1935 through 1950, at five-year intervals.

[76] Fried, Frank's predecessor was Limburg, Riegelman, Hess & Hirsch. Walter Fried joined the Riegleman firm in the late 1930s or 1940.

[77] Limburg, Riegelman, Hirsch & Hess. Walter Fried was apparently a solo practitioner.

[78] Riegelman, Hirsch & Hess. Walter Fried was still apparently a solo practitioner.

[79] Walter Fried was part of the firm by this time.

[80] Riegelman, Strasser, Schwarz & Spiegelberg.

[81] H.J. Frank had joined the firm by this time. Frank was apparently in solo practice before his association with the Riegelman firm.

[82] See Hoffman, *Lions in the Street*, 62–63 (stating that Cleary, Gottlieb was formed in 1945 when George Cleary and Leo Gottlieb left the well-established Root Clark firm).

[83] Cleary, Gottlieb, Friendly & Fox.

[84] Paul, Weiss grew out of the firm of Cohen, C (name could not be determined), Weiss & Wharton.

[85] 1932, 1935, 1940, and 1945 numbers all reflect Cohen, C, Weiss & Wharton. See Hoffman, *Lions in the Street*, 112 (Paul, Weiss, Wharton & Garrison was formed in 1945 and had 13 lawyers).

Stroock & Stroock & Lavan	1[87]	2	2	3	13
Kaye, Scholer, Fierman, Hays & Handler	N/A	N/A	4	9	18[88]
Proskauer, Rose	8[89]	7	9	11 (+1 counsel)[90]	14 (+1 counsel)
Rosenman, Goldmark[91]	N/A	N/A	N/A	N/A	7

By the mid 1960s, however, this reality had changed significantly. Growing much faster than the WASP firms, the Jewish firms had "caught up" with the WASP firms and penetrated the elite law firm club, constituting six of the twenty largest law firms in New York City. In less than a fifteen-year time span, Jewish law firms grew, as a group, at an average of 200%, with Fried, Frank and Paul, Weiss growing by 400% and Kaye, Scholer by 375%. To be sure, WASP firms also grew at an impressive rate. As a group, however, WASP firms grew at 50% the rate of Jewish firms, averaging about 100%. This trend of faster growth continued between 1963 and 1980, and by 1980 Jewish firms accounted for four of the ten largest firms in New York City. WASP firms also grew at an impressive rate; however, except for Shearman & Sterling, all of the WASP firms grew by less than 100% during this time.[92]

---

[86] By 1958, the firm had grown to fifty lawyers. See Hoffman, *Lions in the Street*, 45.

[87] The firm was known as Stroock & Stroock until the 1940s. Peter I.B. Lavan, a.k.a. Peter I.B. Levine, joined the firm in 1945 according to *Martindale-Hubbell Directory*.

[88] By 1958, the firm had grown to 43 lawyers. See Hoffman, *Lions in the Street*, 45.

[89] Proskauer, Rose & Paskus.

[90] Proskauer, Rose, Goetz & Mendelsohn.

[91] Hoffman indicates this was another of the "Jewish giants" (*Lions in the Street*, 33). Its predecessors were Rosenberg, Goldmark & Colin (*Martindale-Hubbell*, 1932) and Goldmark, Colin & Kaye (*Martindale-Hubbell*, 1945). By 1950, it was known as Rosenman, Goldmark, Colin & Kaye. In 1973, when *Lions in the Street* was published, it was known as Rosenman, Colin, Kaye, Petschek, Freund & Emil.

[92] Information in the preceding paragraph regarding the largest New York City law firms between 1963 and 2006 was collected using the following sources: "Growth of 20 Large Law Firms-1963–1981," *New York Law Journal*, Mar. 16, 1981, 3; "National Law Firm Survey," *National Law Journal*, Sept. 18, 1978, 14–17; "National Law Firm Survey," *National Law Journal*, Oct. 6, 1980, 32–37; "The NLJ 250," *National Law Journal*, Sept. 30, 1985, S4–S18; "The NLJ 250," *National Law Journal*, Sept. 24, 1990, S4–S32;

Table 2: New York City Large Law Firms[93]

Firm Name	1950	1963	1981
Shearman & Sterling	31	134	335
Skadden, Arps, Slate, Meagher & Flom	6	10	240
Cravath, Swaine & Moore	21	124	225
Fried, Frank, Harris, Shriver, & Jacobson	12	61	222
Davis, Polk & Wardwell	25	112	221
Weil, Gotshal & Manges	18 (+1 in Washington, DC office)	42	220
Coudert Brothers	14 (+1 tax counsel)	40	218
Sullivan & Cromwell	24	113	216
Dewey, Ballantine, Bushby, Palmer & Wood	16[94]	121	212
Milbank, Tweed, Hadley & McCloy	26 (+1 Counsel, +1 in Washington, DC office)	120	210
Simpson, Thacher & Bartlett	21 (+1 Counsel)	109	209
Cleary, Gottlieb, Steen & Hamilton	6 (+1 in Washington, DC office, +1 in Paris, France office)	75	206

"The 20 Largest Firms Based in New York City," *New York Law Journal,* Oct. 1, 1990, S3–S4; "The NLJ 250," *National Law Journal,* Oct. 9. 1995, C6–C22; "Top 25 New York City-Based Firms," *New York Law Journal,* Dec. 11, 2000, S20; "The NLJ 250," *National Law Journal,* Nov. 15, 2004, S16–S27; "Top 25 New York City-Based Firms," *New York Law Journal,* Dec. 13, 2004, 34 ("Growth of New York Law Firms").

[93] The 1950 numbers are based on *Martindale-Hubbell Law Directory* (1950). The 1963 and 1981 numbers are based on "Growth of 20 Large Law Firms-1963–1981," *New York Law Journal,* Mar. 16, 1981, 3.

[94] In 1950 Dewey Ballantine was known as Root, Ballantine, Harlan, Bushby & Palmer. The firm had sixteen lawyers.

Cahill, Gordon & Reindel	18	88	202
Paul, Weiss, Rifkind, Wharton & Garrison	16 (+1 Counsel)	83	202
White & Case	27	125	189
Donovan, Leisure, Newton & Irvine	20 (+1 Counsel)	69	182
Rogers & Wells	18[95]	62	176
Cadwalader, Wickersham & Taft	17	70	171
Stroock & Stroock & Lavan	13	N/A	170
Kaye, Scholer, Fierman, Hays & Handler	18	86	164

Two general trends taking place post-World War II explain, in part, the rise and growth of the Jewish law firms: first, a gradual decline in antisemitism and religious-based discrimination that made it easier for Jewish law firms to expand their corporate client base; and second, an increased demand for legal services by corporate clients that exceeded the capacity of the dominant WASP law firms and opened the door for other law firms, including Jewish firms. While generally confirming the existence and consequences of these twin trends, the informants' accounts in Parts IV and V shed light on how they specifically contributed to and shaped the growth pattern of the Jewish firms.

IV. Diminished Discrimination and its Impact on the Growth of the Jewish Firm

A. Overall Decline in Antisemitism and Religious-Based Discrimination

Describing the prevailing discriminatory status quo in America in the years before World War II and immediately after it, one informant recalled, "I went to work as an engineer for a very brief time and I went to work for [a large engineering company] but in those times [late 1940s], they did not hire Jews, and neither did anyone else, engineering was not a Jewish profession."[96] When asked about the decline in antisemitism in American society beginning in the 1950s, one informant stated:

---

[95] In 1950, Rogers & Wells was known as Dwight, Royall, Harris, Koegel & Caskey. It had eighteen lawyers. William Rogers joined in 1950. The firm became known as Rogers & Wells in the early 1970s.

[96] Informant #21, 2.

> Well, it changed; the world changed it in several respects, I guess. People, I think, the whole notion of anti-Semitism, of any ethnic discrimination.... The society has really progressed quite dramatically. Discrimination against Jews certainly in the eastern part of the United States in major cities was dramatically less.[97]

The decline of antisemitism and religious-based discrimination was a slow, gradual process. Beginning in the 1950s and intensifying in the 1960s, the process reached its culmination in the 1970s. One informant described the trend as follows:

> Now remember in the late 60's, the world was beginning to open up with the Vietnam War and so on, all the prejudices began to disappear, and certainly after the Second World War the prejudices began to wear down the dam just broke, because every institution was questioned. Every institution was questioned and the young people, including me were questioning everything. And all the old rules began to disappear. And somehow or other Jews began to be able to get into things, and we got hired by clients.[98]

Another informant opined,

> The 70's was a time where I believe there was great openness generally and people understood the need [for diversity,] whether they verbalized it or [not], ... [and that] they were losing out on talent by [not] exposing themselves to various types of people. I think there was a general cultural change going on in the United States, and I think there was a greater need for lawyers in the 70's and the 80's. That was a time of huge growth in the law firms with [greater] need for lawyers, and I think people recognized that they should be focusing on getting the best possible lawyers.[99]

The decline in discrimination, to be sure, centered on ethnic and religious grounds and did not extend to the same degree to racial and gender considerations. One informant remarked, "I think there is also some change in the country. America generally changed in terms of the kinds of discrimination it was willing to practice, putting race aside."[100]

One informant described how increased religious tolerance altered the practice of law and, in particular, courtroom practices:

---

[97] Informant #5, 12.

[98] Informant #21, 6. The same informant further clarified: "Did I say this country has no discrimination today? No obviously there still is. There are still places you can't go to play golf, places you can't buy a house, but there are many more where you can" (16).

[99] Informant #6, 10–11.

[100] Informant #4, 16–17. See Elizabeth Chambliss, "Organizational Determinants of Law Firm Integration," *American University Law Review* 46 (1997): 739–40. Chambliss cautions against the tendency to treat women and racial minorities as a single, undifferentiated group.

> We were sitting down for the scheduling conference, depositions, Friday meeting or something like that and he assigned the schedule and [the federal judge] said, "Oh well we can't set that up because you need to leave early on Friday." I mean, he knew every Jewish holiday, he knew because he had [a Jewish] law clerk and to me, in 1960, this was like unbelievable. I had judges who would on a Friday afternoon make me sit and wait and not let me go home until 3 o'clock even though the case hadn't started, just to sit and wait. An Italian judge would say to me, "I know when the sun sets!" Like I had to be home when the sun set and ten minutes before would [not be a problem]. And one time I remember it was Friday and it was Chanukah so you had to get home particularly early because you had to light candles before Shabbat. And I said to my client, it was about 3 o'clock "I'm going home. Anything happens, you just say 'he had to leave.'" Today, you go into a judge and there's no issue.[101]

Another informant opined that the slow yet gradual decline of racial-based discrimination also benefited Jewish lawyers.[102]

The impact of a decline in antisemitism and religious-based discrimination on Jewish law firms was significant, making it more likely that corporate clients who previously discriminated against Jewish law firms were subsequently more likely to retain them. "I think it's a combination [of] two things," an informant said, speculating regarding the willingness of entity clients to hire Jewish firms. "I think it's a combination of an overall decline in discrimination [and] a 'rat race' for the best lawyers."[103]

Another informant described the combined effect of diminished discrimination and increased reliance on merit-considerations:

> About 14 years ago my firm was asked to represent a [financial institution] and [a Jewish partner with the firm], who was probably the most respected banking lawyer in the country was concerned that the client might not know that [he] was Jewish. So, he got word to the client, the individual in the institution, that he wanted to know that it was all right, or was he disturbed by the fact that he was Jewish, because there were many other lawyers there. [The client] had been advised that he wanted, that he needed and should have good legal representation. He couldn't get better than [the Jewish partner]. That's what he cared about, to be well represented. I really think that the fo-

---

[101] Informant #7, 9–10.

[102] "Jews had a lot of trouble getting jobs in, I think, the Wall Street firms until the fifties or sixties. I think African-American pride and Black independence in the United States and specifically in New York City really helped the Jews" (Informant #15, 19). Notably, the belief that the decline of ethno-religious and racial discrimination in the 1960s were reinforcing phenomena contrasted with the sentiment of some within the Jewish and Catholic communities following the Civil War who feared that greater racial equality for African-Americans might erode the standing and status of ethno-religious minorities. See Jonathan D. Sarna, *When General Grant Expelled the Jews* (New York: Nextbook Schocken, 2012), 24–49.

[103] Informant #10, 16.

cus on the merits of lawyering, [on] a lawyer's abilities has overcome these stereotypes and prejudices.[104]

One informant, explaining the experience of Jewish lawyers at white-shoe firms concluded that the success was a symptom of a more general, even generic, phenomenon: "I think it's a general social change, I mean there were some people who were older partners at that time in the 50's who just would not consider the idea of having a Jewish partner, and life has changed a lot."[105] To the informant, the key issue was the overall decline in antisemitism and religious-based discrimination. The success of Jewish lawyers and Jewish firms was but the consequence of this general societal trend in the legal profession.[106]

B. The Powerful Interplay of Diminished Discrimination, the Rise of Inside Counsel, High Visibility, and the Existence of a Jewish Client Base

The informants suggest that parallel developments within the legal profession magnified the impact of decreased discrimination, making it even more likely that corporate clients would retain Jewish law firms. The first trend was the rise of inside counsel, and more specifically, the shift in decision-making authority within corporate clients over the engagement of outside counsel from discriminating non-lawyer executives to inside counsel.[107] For example, one informant recalled:

> I was picked up by [a large corporation] and the General Counsel for [that large corporation]. He saw me and formed an attachment to me. He saw all the lecturing and the work I had been doing, and being retained by [that large corporation] brought me into the world of [large entity in another industry] and [large corporation in a third industry] because they were all working together on legislative issues. [When] they brought me in as their counsel ... I was really in the world of the [general counsels] of [these three corporations].... And the relation-

---

[104] Informant #12, 24.

[105] Informant #19, 6.

[106] Informant #19, 6–7.

[107] On the rise of inside counsel, see Jonathan R. Maslow, "The Rise of In-House Counsel," *California Lawyer* 1 (1981): 30; Robert L. Nelson and Laura Beth Nielson, "Cops, Counsel, and Entrepreneurs: Constructing the Role of Inside Counsel in Large Corporations," *Law & Society Review* 34 (2000): 457–94; Robert Eli Rosen, "The Inside Counsel Movement, Professional Judgment and Organizational Representation," *Indiana Law Journal* 64 (1989): 479–553; Ted Schneyer, "Professionalism and Public Policy: The Case of House Counsel," *Georgetown Journal of Legal Ethics* 2 (1988): 449–84; Eli Wald, "In-House Myths," *Wisconsin Law Review* (2012); 407–61. See, generally, George P. Baker and Rachel Parkin, "The Changing Structure of the Legal Services Industry and the Careers of Lawyers," *North Carolina Law Review* 84 (2006): 1635–82; Deborah A. DeMott, "The Discrete Roles of General Counsel," *Fordham Law Review* 74 (2005): 955–81. See also Abram Chayes and Antonia H. Chayes, "Corporate Counsel and the Elite Law Firm," *Stanford Law Review* 37 (1985): 277–300.

ships and the networking just began to expand and expand. And before I knew it I was representing [multiple large corporate entities] ... I just happened to be a good lawyer, and I was doing good work. I got hired by [a fourth corporate client] because they were in a case with [the large corporation who was already a client] and they were going to get into trouble. They saw what I did and they came in and hired me. It was that kind of networking and knowing. And, by the way, around this time, the general counsel began to have a much greater role in hiring outside lawyers. And somehow or another, that too helped break the barrier, because the chairman of the board and the CEO didn't hire any more at country clubs. He turned to his general counsel and said, "Get me the best lawyer you can," and if you [were an] outstanding lawyer in the 60's and the 70's and into the 80's, you got hired.[108]

Another informant explained that, while breaking down antisemitism was more difficult in the corporate world, inside counsel helped sever the long-standing ties between corporate clients and their WASP firms.[109]

The second trend, which helped inside counsel to make the decision to hire Jewish firms, was the high visibility of the practice of the Jewish firms and their prominent attorneys. This trend also benefited from diminished discrimination. As one informant put it:

Law, I think, was easier and medicine was easier, because once we became visible, once we were capable of making ourselves visible, it became clear that we were pretty good. And then one thing leads to another. I think law and medicine are kind of unique because they are individual and you can make a reputation for yourself. You can make a reputation climbing up the ladder in the world of the circumscribed corporation but law, it seems to me, is a more open profession. You have more capacity to be seen in law and medicine than you do in management. If you want a career, you need to be seen so I think visibility is critical.[110]

The informants suggest that Jewish law firms displayed their superstar power at a very opportune time; they began rising after 1945 and achieved

---

[108] Informant #21, 6–7.

[109] Informant #10, 9–10. Another informant noted: "And that was true of a whole range of firms. It was referred to then as client loyalty. Unless you really screwed up, there was a tendency not to move around. Starting in about the 1980s that changed. First, in financial institutions and then moved over to a whole bunch of others and now there is no such channel anymore" (Informant #22, 12). On the transformation of the attorney-client relationship between large law firms and entity clients and the shift from stable long-term and loyal affiliations to shorter competitive relationships see David B. Wilkins, "Team of Rivals? Toward a New Model of the Corporate Attorney-Client Relationship," *Fordham Law Review* 78 (2010): 2067–2136.

[110] Informant #21, 17, 18–19. On the role of visibility within and outside large law firms in informing lawyers' professional success see Eli Wald, "The Visibility of Socioeconomic Status and Class-Based Affirmative Action: A Reply to Professor Sander," *Denver University Law Review* 88 (2011): 861–88.

prominence by the late 1970s and early 1980s. This was the period before continued institutionalization of the large firms rendered personal, individual visibility less apparent and anonymity became the norm of large firm practice. "With increasing specialization and division of labor in the blue-chip bar," said a commentator, "the individual lawyer ... has no opportunity to stand out. The firms become the powers, not the men in them.... In short, the blue-chip bar has become a place for a man to make money, not to make his mark."[111] This legal environment was quite different from that of the early 1950s and 1960s, when attorneys such as Milton Handler of Kaye, Scholer, Ira Millstein of Weil, Gotshal, Marty Lipton of Wachtell, Lipton, and Joe Flom of Skadden, Arps rose to prominence and lent their highly visible careers to their Jewish law firms.[112] In those early days of high visibility, success in one major case could mean a ticket out of low status and an opportunity to establish a large corporate client base.[113]

Finally, the interplay of diminished discrimination, the rise of inside counsel, and the high visibility of the work of prominent attorneys at Jewish firms was particularly important to the growth of Jewish law firms and to their development of a large corporate client base because initially Jewish law firms did not represent large entities, or even large Jewish entities. For example, as one informant recollected: "XXX was a Jewish firm. Its client base consisted of mostly Jewish clients, [but] it generally did not represent industry leaders. Instead of representing the first or second largest garment maker, it typically represented the third biggest. The firm's client base changed in the 1970s [when] New York City became about merit.... The decline of the importance of old style relationships was a big deal, replaced by merit representations."[114] Indeed, one informant at a large Jewish firm, describing the firm's clientele in the late 1960s, explained that while "many of our clients were Jewish," the firm had hardly any Fortune 500 clients.[115] Another informant affirmed, "Interestingly enough, for the so-called gentile law firms, in many cases, the principal business was with the Jewish banks.

---

[111] Hoffman, *Lions in the Street*, 52.

[112] Brill, "Two Tough Lawyers in the Tender Offer Game," 54–55. In an exposé article detailing the rise to prominence of Joe Flom of Skadden, Arps and Marty Lipton of Wachtell, Lipton, Brill describes the high visibility of the careers of Flom and Lipton and explicitly argues that their individual successes played a key role in the rise of their respective law firms. See also Malcolm Gladwell, *Outliers: The Story of Success* (New York: Little, Brown and Company, 2008), 116–58.

[113] Informant #17, 4–5 (describing how the success of one name partner in a notorious case played a significant role in establishing the firm's reputation).

[114] Informant #14, 2. An informant at another firm described the client base of his firm in the mid-1960s as consisting of small businesses and start-ups that could not retain the large established law firms of the day (Informant #17, 3). Over time, as the firm's reputation grew, its client base expanded to include large corporate entities (Informant #17, 6).

[115] Informant #16, 3.

The [large] Jewish law firms weren't representing [large] Jewish corporations."[116] One informant added:

> Now, why did [Jewish clients] go to these big [WASP] law firms? Because people wanted ... their businesses. They thought they needed a fancy bank; they thought they needed a fancy lawyer. They can be impressed with them [the WASP firms] ... I'm serious. I was angry about it.[117]

These circumstances were echoed by another informant:

> When [Jewish] clients started coming in from Brooklyn, somebody once mentioned to me, "Why don't we open up an office in Brooklyn?" So, I told him, "I feel that anybody that can afford our rates wants to come to a Manhattan lawyer; they don't want to stay in Brooklyn." That's true.[118]

One informant recalled his frustration with observant Jewish clients taking their business to non-Jewish or to secular Jewish firms:

> I used to walk around almost resentful when I would see the Hasidic and obviously Orthodox people sitting in offices of lawyers. Well, why weren't they coming to me? I understand them, I know the culture. But no, that wasn't the issue. The issue was they wanted successful lawyers and the lawyers had no problem dealing with them. I think in the fifties I would have been embarrassed to bring one of them to my office.[119]

To the extent that Jewish law firms did benefit from the existence of a Jewish client base, the informants point out that rather than representing large Jewish clients, the Jewish firms relied on a large number of smaller entity Jewish clients. One informant described the client base of his law firm as mostly Jewish: "I think the large number were Jewish, with some exceptions. A lot of the real-estate people were ... Jewish clients.... Today, you couldn't tell."[120] Another informant described the development of his expertise as a function of the large number of small corporate clients represented by his firm:

> The [Jewish] firm I joined was basically a corporate law firm. That's what we did, and when I joined it, unlike today, there weren't many defined departments. Maybe there was a tax department, but beside

---

[116] Informant #17, 17. Another noted, "it [a white-shoe law firm] actually represented old Jewish investment banks" (Informant #15, 18).

[117] Informant #8, 11–12.

[118] Informant #10, 15.

[119] Informant #7, 10–11.

[120] Informant #2, 8.

> that the young lawyers were assigned on an occasional basis to whomever needed help and so my early practice experience was exposure to a very diverse area. It involved lending and borrowing transactions, investment transactions, a lot of small private corporations and organizational development, bankruptcy, litigation, contracts. I mean you worked for a partner and then you went to another partner. That is, there were no assignments so I was luckier than people are today because I had very broad exposure to a wide variety of things and circumstances. I developed [expertise] mostly in corporate, in corporate finance and the securities area and I got involved in public offerings and everything having to do with stocks and bonds.[121]

The experience was shared by the following informant:

> I came here [to a Jewish firm], I worked for I would say five years, doing everything. I mean, we didn't have a very big bunch of clients but work was kind of fun.[122]

Moreover, the informants suggest that not only did large entity Jewish clients fail to patronize the large Jewish firms, they also failed to use their influence to advocate for increased diversity within their WASP law firms. Said one informant, "I have not perceived the entree of Jewish lawyers coming as a result of demands from Jewish clients."[123] And another remarked:

> I am not aware that ... in the 70's clients were saying, "We want to make sure that we have a Jewish lawyer [as] opposed to a non-Jewish lawyer," or [asking that firms be] more diverse.... From my perspective, I don't know if that is correct.... [My] sense at the time was not that clients wanted more diversity.[124]

Drawing a distinction between the conduct of large Jewish clients in the past and contemporary corporate calls for increased diversity, one informant noted:

> Very prominent investment firms had all of their personal business done by a Jewish law firm. But their public business was done by a non-Jewish firm. They made no effort whatsoever to encourage the non-Jewish firm to hire Jews. However, once [Jewish attorneys] started to show up at [white-shoe firms], they did feel a little more comfortable about that. But these [Jews at investment firms] were the German Jewish people exercising their patrimonial rights [with regard to the Jewish attorneys at white-shoe firms]. But I would not credit that point in history any very serious attempt by them to influ-

---

[121] Informant #13, 2–3.
[122] Informant #21, 4.
[123] Informant #10, 15.
[124] Informant #6, 12.

ence the hiring or retention of people. I wouldn't credit it all. Never saw it [referring to "A Call to Action," a demand by large corporations for greater diversity at large law firms[125]].... That is an example of strong arming I have never seen before. But it is the kind of strong arming that is going on now days. Nowadays it is acceptable. If it existed in earlier years, it was a hell of a lot [more] subtle.[126]

V. Increased Client Demand for Corporate Legal Services and the Growth of the Jewish Firm

A. The Growth of Business Law and Increased Demand for Corporate Legal Services

The growth of the large law firm is explained by a complex mix of demand and supply considerations.[127] Increased demand for corporate legal services[128] explains in part the rise and growth of large firms. Indeed, the

---

[125] In 1999, chief executives of about 500 major corporations signed a document entitled "Diversity in the Workplace—A Statement of Principle." The Statement evidenced the commitment of the signatory corporations to diversity in the legal profession. In particular, it was intended to be a mandate for law firms to make immediate and sustained improvements in this area. See http://www.acc.com/vl/public/Article/loader.cfm?csModule=security/getfile&pageid=16074 (last visited July 10, 2013).

[126] Informant #22, 10–11. For analysis of Corporate America's diversity efforts vis-à-vis their outside counsel, see David B. Wilkins, "From 'Separate is Inherently Unequal' to 'Diversity is Good for Business': The Rise of Market-Based Diversity Arguments and the Fate of the Black Corporate Bar," *Harvard Law Review* 117 (2004): 1548–1615; Eli Wald, "A Primer on Diversity, Discrimination, and Equality in the Legal Profession or Who is Responsible for Pursuing Diversity and Why," *Georgetown Journal of Legal Ethics* 24 (2011): 1079–1142.

[127] See, e.g., David B. Wilkins and G. Mitu Gulati, "Why Are There So Few Black Lawyers in Corporate Law Firms? An Institutional Analysis," *California Law Review* 84 (1996): 528 n. 109 ("a variety of factors, including, inter alia, the inherent dynamics of partnership tournaments, the needs of clients, the potential for extracting higher profits through leverage, and status competition among firms for the coveted designation of being a "national"—or increasingly a "global"—leader in the corporate law firm world contributed to the rapid escalation in firm size.").

For a supply side account of the growth of the firm, see Galanter and Palay, *Tournament of Lawyers*, 77–120 (arguing that tournament theory, or the promotion-to-partnership system, is a cause of law firm growth); Kevin A. Kordana, "Law Firms and Associate Careers: Tournament Theory versus the Production-Imperative Model," *Yale Law Journal* 104 (1995): 1923–33 (arguing that law firm growth is better explained by the "production-imperatives" of the work these firms do for their clients). See also George Rutherglen and Kevin A. Kordana, "A Farewell to Tournaments? The Need for an Alternative Explanation of Law Firm Structure and Growth," *Virginia Law Review* 84 (1998): 1705 (growth of firms is explained by the leveraging of partners' human capital and the competition between firms for associates are sufficient); Wald, "Smart Growth" (studying models of organic and strategic large law firm growth).

[128] Ronald Gilson was among the first to distinguish supply side from demand side explanations and stress the importance of the latter. See Ronald J. Gilson, "The Devolution of the Legal Profession: A Demand Side Perspective," *Maryland Law Review* 49 (1990): 916 ("The study of professionalism by lawyers and sociologists has been dominated by a myopic, albeit understandable, focus on the supply side of the traditional market for legal services.").

Cravath blueprint for the organization of the large law firm was, in part, an institutional response on the supply side to the demands of large corporate clients. "It is well known that the large law firm was born ... in a period of institutional reorganization dominated by the rise of the giant business corporation."[129] Thus, the rise of large law firms in the late nineteenth and early twentieth centuries was in response to the growing needs of big corporate clients.[130]

After 1950, increased demand for legal services explains the growth of WASP and Jewish law firms alike. The increase in corporate demand for legal services has been both quantitative and qualitative. Significant growth in the body and scope of statutory and administrative laws regulating the conduct of entity clients shaped the legal needs of large corporate clients and called for a corresponding growth in the size and expertise of the large law firms.[131] Nelson argues that increased government regulation of business, blockbuster litigation involving corporations, and the proliferation of high transaction cost deals,[132] "reflects growing demand for corporate legal services of a type big firms offer."[133] In addition, Nelson asserts that restructuring in the market for corporate legal services further contributes to large firm growth: the shift from continuous, general service relationships between corporate clients and law firms led to firm growth based on highly specialized, often isolated, transactions and lawsuits.[134] Further, "the breakdown of stable regional markets for law firms created a national market in corporate legal services that was unprecedented. The leading firms in New York City and in other major legal centers openly competed for the most lucrative client relationships and projects."[135]

---

[129] Larson, "On the Nostalgic View of Lawyers' Role," 448.

[130] Milton C. Regan, Jr., "Taking Law Firms Seriously," *Georgetown Journal of Legal Ethics* 16 (2002): 155.

[131] Large law firms had "no choice but to grow so rapidly to meet the intense demand created by the flood of business in corporate, litigation and intellectual property practices ... no choice but to staff up to meet torrential increases in the volume of work" (Inst. of Mgmt. & Admin., Inc., "1980s Redux? Large Law Firms Report Record Profits & Revenues," *Law Off. Mgmt. & Admin. Rep.* 98–99 [1998]: 1).

[132] See, e.g., Marc Galanter, "Reading the Landscape of Disputes: What We Know and Don't Know (and Think We Know) about Our Allegedly Contentious and Litigious Society," *UCLA Law Review* 31 (1983): 4–71.

[133] Robert L. Nelson, "Of Tournaments and Transformations: Explaining the Growth of Large Law Firms," *Wisconsin Law Review* (1992): 747.

[134] Ibid., 747–48.

[135] Ibid. On the growth of large firms since 2000, see Bruce E. Aronson, "Elite Law Firm Mergers and Reputational Competition: Is Bigger Really Better? An International Comparison," *Vanderbilt Journal of Transnational Law* 40 (2007): 817–19; James R. Faulconbridge et al., "Global Law Firms: Globalization and Organizational Spaces of Cross-Border Legal Work," *Northwestern Journal of International Law & Business* 28 (2008); 455–88; Carole Silver, "What We Don't Know Can Hurt Us: The Need for Empirical Research in Regulating Lawyers and Legal Services in the Global Economy," *Akron Law Review* 43 (2010): 1009–79.

Jewish law firms were able to take advantage of increased demand for corporate legal services because the dominant WASP corporate bar was fairly small in terms of the absolute number of large firms and their size, as well as in terms of the relative number needed to deal with the increased client demand for corporate legal services.[136] Consequently, after 1945, Jewish firms gained ground on the WASP firms in a relatively short time span. If the WASP firms had been either more numerous or bigger in size, perhaps they would have been better positioned to meet the growing needs of corporate clients and would have crowded out the Jewish firms. But their relatively small number and size did not allow them to eliminate the competition. While the WASP firms grew rapidly and consistently both before and after 1945,[137] their growth after 1945 could not satisfy the even greater growing client demand for corporate legal services.[138]

B. The "Economics of Discrimination"? Increased Demand and the Decline of Religious-Based Discrimination

The increased demand for corporate legal services, which led to the growth of the WASP firms in the first half of the twentieth century, contributed to the rise and growth of the Jewish law firms after WWII. In addition, it led to a significant change in the hiring and promotion practices of the large firms. The WASP law firms could not satisfy their increased need for associates from within the ranks of WASP associates. They began, gradually and hesitantly, to hire and eventually promote Jewish lawyers. One informant affirmed this trend, stating:

> As the ... law business grew, the firms grew, [and] the need for high quality lawyering grew, meaning a) the growth of business, b) the growth of business regulation and the increasing need for lawyers, the need to give both legal and ethical advice to keep these corporations out of trouble.... These law firms needed people, and they couldn't afford to discriminate. Discrimination became a negative business plan—they were shooting themselves in the foot because they had to reject superior lawyers to hire ethnically acceptable inferior lawyers.... [It's] true whether you're discriminating against Jews, ... Catholics, ... Asians, ... Blacks, or ... anybody. Any time you discriminate, you take some guy who's not as good over the person

---

[136] In 1945 there were approximately three dozen elite, large WASP law firms with less than 2,000 attorneys. By 1971, the stable group of large WASP law firms grew in number of lawyers employed to approximately 3,000, but the number of firms stayed stagnant (Hoffman, *Lions in the Street*, 1–14).

[137] Shearman & Sterling grew by 150% between 1963 and 1981 and was still the largest law firm in New York; Cravath grew by 81%, Davis, Polk by 97%, Sullivan & Cromwell by 91% and Simpson, Thatcher by 92%. However, the Jewish firms grew much faster. See above, Table 2.

[138] Fried, Frank grew by 264%, Weil, Gotshal by 424%, Paul, Weiss by 143%, Kaye, Scholer by 91% and Cahill, Gordon (a Catholic firm) by 130%. See above, Table 2.

you're discriminating against, so as a business proposition.... I think those are two factors that changed the world.[139]

Another informant argued:

> What changed? Brain-power needs. The complexity of the world became so great—an explosion in the marketplace, globalization, the growth of the economy.... The coverage is so big that you need manpower.... So, you want to hire. You use them all up, and you need talent, too. So, Harvard has 500 students and 250 are WASPs. [All of the WASPs] get jobs, [and] there is [sic] still plenty of jobs for the other 250 Jews. So, the growth in the economy created a demand. They need more manpower. They need more bodies and they need some talent ... so ... they need the Jews. My view is as simple as that. It's the law of supply and demand.[140]

And a third informant added:

> I think that [the decline of discrimination against Jewish lawyers was] tie[d] into the commercialization of the practice of law. And whether it's corporations or law firms, we're looking simply for merit and for talent, so, [the] old school [discriminatory hiring practices of] the firms in the teens, 20's and 30's wouldn't work anymore.[141]

The informants' accounts, however, caution against too-quickly accepting the theory that competition leads to the decline of discrimination, as is evidenced in the following:

> The firms ultimately had to take in Jewish people because they grew so quickly. But my friend ... in my class tells the story of going to a WASP firm [that was] well known, and being shown around the conference room. They had medallions from the various law schools, including Yale [whose seal includes several Hebrew letters]. And one fellow there who did the interview ... asked what ethnicity [my friend] was. He said, "Czechoslovakian or what?" He said, "Can you read this?" [referring to the Hebrew letters in Yale's seal]. So, there were relatively few Jews who were being taken and that had to change because of the explosions in the law firms and the demand for ... smart

---

[139] Informant #5, 12–13.

[140] Informant #8, 13, 14.

[141] Informant #4, 16. Another informant added: "I would say success in the law depends on a lot of things. Well, you have to have some intelligence and be able to cope with issues, and Jews—many of them are highly qualified in that respect so as the need for lawyers grew, and the number of people able to do the work and to bring something to the table didn't grow particularly by comparison [Jewish lawyers experienced decreased discrimination]. People realize you have to hire the most qualified people ... and there are a lot of very qualified Jews and I think the world, the community came to understand that they were depriving themselves of a whole segment of the population, mainly Jews, who had great ability and why should they do that; why should they exclude them, so they hired them" (Informant #13, 10).

lawyers. And if you were looking for smarts, Jews had the big capital among them.[142]

Another informant pointed out that, while increased client demand was a key factor causing both the growth of large firms and the decline of discrimination, the decline was gradual and slow and took over twenty years to develop into the norm, and added, "I believe in the 70's in some of the non-Jewish firms, they would have had more difficulty accommodating for their needs."[143]

A time-consuming, gradual change in the hiring and promotion practices of the WASP firms meant that many Jewish lawyers in this "transition" period did not succeed in securing a job and struggled to survive professionally. For many lawyers who had been the objects of discrimination, the change came too late. The following account makes explicit the consequence of a prolonged decline in discrimination:

> My first job [was with] a firm called Gold & Bach & Burrell, a small firm [of] about 10 or 11 lawyers. Jeff Gold graduated [from] Yale in 1941, first in his class, then he started his own practice; Marty Burrell [graduated from] Harvard [with a joint] M.B.A. & J.D in those days it took some doing.... The firm eventually went bankrupt, as did many of the firms, and I got fired my first year. I wanted to be a corporate lawyer, and I thought it might be a bit different.... Then I went to work in a storefront in Brooklyn where I eked out a living doing wills and house closings, making $5,000 a year, [and] moved to Court Street in Brooklyn. Then I got a break, I went into the legislature. I rose to the position of chief counsel for the speaker of the New York City senate.... I met a friend of mine who was a member of this firm. And twenty-five years ago, I joined this firm and, little by little, I gradually moved up to Senior Partner.[144]

---

[142] Informant #2, 6–7 (names have been omitted to preserve anonymity). See Gary S. Becker, *The Economics of Discrimination* (Chicago: University of Chicago Press, 1971). Becker's seminal analysis is considered by some to be the "prevailing economic theory of race discrimination" (Richard H. McAdams, "Cooperation and Conflict: The Economics of Group Status Production and Race Discrimination," *Harvard Law Review* 108 [1995]: 1033). See also David Charny and G. Mita Gulati, "Efficiency-Wages, Tournaments, and Discrimination: A Theory of Employment Law for 'High-Level' Jobs," *Harvard Civil Rights-Civil Liberties Law Review* 33 (1998): 62 ("The cornerstone of the modern discussion has been the model developed by Gary Becker."). Cf. Pierre Bourdieu, *Outline of a Theory of Practice,* ed. Earnest Gellnor et al. and trans. Richard Nice (Cambridge: Cambridge University Press, 1977) (advancing a theory of discrimination that centers on human capital, social capital, and cultural capital); Meir Dan-Cohen, *Rights, Persons, and Organizations: A Legal Theory for Bureaucratic Society* (Berkeley: University of California Press, 1986) (advancing an organizational theory of discrimination); Rosabeth Moss Kanter, *Men and Women of the Corporation* (New York: Basic Books, 1977) (same); Kenji Yoshino, *Covering: The Hidden Assault on our Civil Rights* (New York: Random House, 2006) (exploring racial passing and covering).

[143] Informant #6, 7.

[144] Informant #8, 9–10.

No doubt, diminished antisemitism and increased demand for corporate legal services "generically" explain the rise and growth of the Jewish law firms.[145] Indeed, the latter provides a general explanation for the growth of all large law firms, including the old WASP firms, rather than an account of the unique, faster growth of the Jewish firms. The informants suggest, however, that the rise of the Jewish law firm was not generic. Rather, it was also explained by the conduct and practices of the WASP firms.

VI. The Unique Growth of the Jewish Law Firm

A. White-Shoe Ethos and Protected Pockets of "Jewish" Practice Areas

The large WASP firms stayed clear of what they perceived to be "undignified" practice areas, inconsistent with their white-shoe ethos and notions of professionalism, such as real-estate, hostile takeover work, bankruptcy, and litigation.[146] As one informant put it, "In the 1950s Jews were restricted to Jewish firms and Jewish practice areas."[147] Another remarked:

> [A particular attorney] was a real-estate lawyer and litigator and a real-estate investor—a very wealthy man.... And, as you probably know, at the time, the largest firms at the time really had no real-estate partners.... That's not the case today.... Real-estate, like divorce, was viewed as dirty work. And WASP lawyers didn't get involved in real-estate ... until they saw there was something worth happening in the area. So, this fellow was involved in a variety of developments, real-estate developments and otherwise.[148]

This division is emphasized by another informant:

> The specialization or over-specialization that we have now didn't exist then.... Real-estate was not a big thing in those days.... It was almost [unheard of] for the large firms to have a real-estate department, and now that's a big thing ... and bankruptcy is big; when I say that I mean, what I'm trying to say, is that those specialties in the old days were little firms that did only that—you had a bankruptcy firm, you had a real-estate firm.... There is much more specialization now.[149]

---

[145] Malcolm Gladwell offers yet another generic explanation for success in the professional realm—building on one's background conditions, life's circumstances as well as social and cultural capital to distinguish oneself as an outlier. Gladwell, *Outliers*.

[146] One informant at a traditionally white-shoe firm tellingly recalled the transition of the firm into the previously "undignified" real-estate practice area: "I pretty much started the real-estate group here, I started as a corporate lawyer as we were doing mergers and acquisitions, and the head of the M & A group ... said to me ... 'we need real-estate law.' ... Basically it was real-estate that was really hooked into our corporate practice, it was, you know, securitized real-estate" (Informant #15, 14–15).

[147] Informant #14, 2.

[148] Informant #2, 5–6 (names have been omitted to preserve anonymity).

[149] Informant #10, 6–8.

This conduct by the WASP firms created pockets of practice that Jewish law firms occupied and promptly came to dominate. In the hostile takeover market, for example, Skadden, Arps and Wachtell, Lipton took advantage of the reluctance of the white-shoe firms to get involved in a less than dignified practice and in the mid 1970s monopolized this "Jewish pocket." A commentator said of the monopoly:

> Either because they're still snobby about such fighting, or because Flom and Lipton have such a head start on them in experience and reputation, the old-line law firms are still only rarely involved in tender fights. Usually, when a fight starts, a company whom they represent as general counsel brushes them aside because the investment bankers they're using have told them to get Flom or Lipton.[150]

Consequently, Skadden, Arps and Wachtell, Lipton were able to monopolize the hostile takeover pocket of practice:

> There is probably no other major area of law where so small a group of attorneys, and one attorney in particular, enjoys such total domination.... Flom today enjoys unprecedented pre-eminence in the field. My count has him on one side or the other, or working for the investment bankers, in ninety percent of the tender fights of the last three years. Lipton is the only lawyer who seems to share even a portion of the field with him.[151]

Bankruptcy law was another example of an "undignified," Jewish practice area. One informant remembered:

> Years ago it was like bankruptcy because they were collection lawyers. It was like a primate part of the Bar, you weren't proud to be a collection lawyer and do bankruptcy. Now [in the 21st century] the biggest firms have major bankruptcy departments.[152]

Another informant described how practicing in this protected pocket of practice allowed his firm to develop expertise and build its reputation:

> We acted in the XXX Bankruptcy, which, up to that point was the largest bankruptcy that had taken place in the US. And [a partner with the firm] headed the effort on that. It turned out to be a very successful liquidation and established our reputation as creditor's rights lawyers with the major banks. Also in [the same year], we represented [a large corporation] which was on the brink of bankruptcy. We acted as counsel to [that corporation] in working out an agreement with banks and [other parties] to solve its fiscal crisis. That too was a matter of considerable notoriety particularly in the banking

---

[150] Brill, "Two Tough Lawyers in the Tender Offer Game," 54.
[151] Ibid.
[152] Informant #20, 17.

world and on Wall Street. So that [a few years later], we had an established reputation for corporate merger/acquisition/take over matters, major creditor's rights problems, financial issues.[153]

As one informant revealed, the Jewish pockets of practice allowed Jewish firms to establish and develop a loyal client base, with little competition from the WASP firms:

> We had a family; I've known that family for probably ... forty-five years, through thick and through thin, through marriages through divorces, etc. ... They had to do major estate planning, and I am totally capable of that.... I introduced them to the person here that does that, and they put in a lot of time and effort.... The person that did the estate planning [later] left the firm and took with him the list of clients he worked with.... He wrote each of them a ... nice form letter, saying, "If you have any interest in your relationship, here's a release" ... and this guy sent back a little note that said, "[the informant] has been my lawyer for forty years [and] I'm not changing now."[154]

Building on client relationships within the Jewish pockets and establishing their expertise and reputation, the Jewish firms were gradually able to cross over and represent the same clients outside of the "undignified" arenas in "respectable" corporate affairs. One informant described the transformation and expansion of the firm's client base:

> In those days bankruptcy was not such a respectable practice but it smelled to me like a big firm going into bankruptcy may just fit in one of these days and the rest is history, because in the 70's, the real industry started to boom and here we were and that practice just took off, the firm really took off, and of course it grew in other areas too.[155]

Another informant similarly noted:

> In 1969, we represented [a large corporation] in a merger with [another large corporate entity]. That transaction ended up with two relationships that became very important. We met [a banker at a large investment bank] in that transaction and he liked the work that we did and as a result of that we began to do a fair amount of work for [the investment bank], which was one of the leading investment banks. And the company that acquired [our 1969 corporate client] liked what we did and we began to do a significant amount of legal work for [the acquiring entity] which was a major step forward in that we were now representing a leading Wall Street investment bank and

---

[153] Informant #17, 4–5 (names have been omitted to preserve anonymity).
[154] Informant #10, 9–10.
[155] Informant #21, 8.

one of the country's largest corporations. Both were very active clients.[156]

Several years later, a successful representation of one corporate client in conjunction with a takeover attempt saw the client base of the firm grow from one major client, to several clients the following year, to several hundred clients a decade later.[157] Importantly, the firm was able to expand its practice and client base beyond the protected practice areas into mainstream corporate practice, so much so that the informant revealed that "[Today] we're fairly active in what I call the corporate governance area, advising companies as to how to structure their board processes and corporate governance guidelines and so on which has become a major part of our practice."[158]

While the WASP firms were willing to concede "dirty" law practice to the Jewish firms, they were unable to contain the areas of concession. The Jewish firms crossed over to the "dignified" practice areas, as is noted in the following:

> When the tender-offer boom began a few years ago, Flom became a hot commodity, not only to raiders but to the more established target companies who decided they'd rather have him defending them than attacking them. As late as 1970, Skadden, Arps had 29 lawyers.... Now the firm has ninety.... This skyrocketing growth dwarfs the much slower expansion of the old, white-shoe firms on Wall Street.... Joe's done the most magnificent thing anyone's ever done i[n] the law business.... He's broken the link between the old investment-banking firms and blue-chip companies and their Wall Street lawyers.[159]

Moreover, white-shoe ethos not only restricted the growth of WASP firms in terms of practice areas, but also limited their growth in terms of lateral hiring, which was considered rude and unprofessional.[160] As one informant recalled:

> After I'd been [in public service] for five years, I decided I wanted to go back to private practice and I wanted to return to New York I remember looking through the New York Martindale-Hubbell trying to see if there was any firm there that appealed to me and I came to the conclusion that there wasn't. You know there were certain firms that

---

[156] Informant #17, 3.

[157] Informant #17, 5–6.

[158] Informant #17, 7. The same informant further said, "I would say that as you got to the millennium, 2000, we were one of the major established law firms with expertise in securities, corporate law, tax and trusts, executive compensation, real-estate [and litigation]."

[159] Brill, "Two Tough Lawyers in the Tender Offer Game," 54.

[160] Fern S. Sussman, "The Large Law Firm Structure: An Historic Opportunity," *Fordham Law Review* 57 (1989): 969.

100 • JEWS AND THE LAW

> are famous never taking in people that are laterals. In more recent years there have been a few exceptions to that, but basically you know the major firms at that level didn't take in laterals. So it wasn't so hard to exclude those firms. The only firm I went to made me an offer, promised a partnership. [It was] still very definitely a Jewish firm with these two Catholic partners.[161]

The Jewish firms, on the other hand, uninhibited by the weight of white-shoe culture, were aggressive in recruiting laterally. One informant described such hiring patterns at his firm:

> We do a lot of lateral hiring. And, if you look at the economics of it, assuming that you take in thirty or forty kids, how many of them are going to become partners? ... I mean, economics doesn't permit it, which means you have to get rid of people along the way. And ... you have to fill in the gaps at some point. And so you bring people in, while you're getting rid of people. It's a strange dynamic, but it exists. So, we do a great deal of that and more.[162]

Another informant recalled his personal experience when he was laterally cherry-picked to lead the corporate department of a large Jewish firm:

> About twenty-five years ago, in 1981, after eighteen years [elsewhere, with another Jewish firm, which was also growing] I joined [a different large Jewish firm] as head of the corporate department.... We hired nine people ... and they were really first rate people.... We had people from many different firms ... and one of the partners came with me and is with me still, and an associate came with me and eventually became a partner and subsequently led the real-estate department. Also [having] join[ed] was the head of our corporate department.[163]

The contrast between the aggressive recruiting practices of the Jewish firms and the more passive practices of the WASP firms, as well as their consequences in terms of lateral recruitment and retaining talent, are captured in the following account of one informant:

> I think one or two people left, and [a small Jewish firm I was with before being recalled into the army] called and asked me to come down and talk to them, which I did, and they said, "We would like you to come back. We're sorry you left us; it's a year or two later, but we'd like you to come back." And they made me a very substantial salary offer, which was substantially more than I was making [at the new firm], and I was making twenty-five percent more than I had been making there when I left.... Now, we're talking early 1960s, so

---

[161] Informant #11, 7–8.
[162] Informant #1, 10.
[163] Informant #2, 1, 8.

$12,000 a year was a lot of money, and I think I was making $12,000 here and they offered me $16,000 or $18,000, which was a stupendous amount of money, and I told them I really was very comfortable here, that I really like[d] the people here [and] I liked what I was doing. I had a career here, and I was staying.[164]

B. Effective Discrimination by the WASP Firms and its Consequences: The Creation of a Robust Entry-Level and Lateral Pool of Elite Jewish Lawyers to the Benefit of the Jewish Law Firms

In the 1950s and 1960s, WASP law firms effectively discriminated against Jewish lawyers.[165] According to one informant, "There's no question that in 1955 the major New York law firms were not hiring Jews."[166] Echoing the same sentiment, another informant remembered, "I was at the top of the class and very high ranked student. I started interviewing in the downtown law firms, not a chance. There was no way that a Jewish, a young Jewish lawyer was going to get accepted into the big firms. It just wasn't going to happen."[167] A third informant noted, "When I came down to look for a job in 1953 there weren't too many Jews being hired so, it was just beginning. There were then some firms that had no Jews, some major law firms that had some Jews and unless it was a Jewish firm even the ones that had some Jews didn't have many."[168]

The realities of discriminatory practice were clearly perceived by Jewish attorneys. "I suppose it was just generally assumed that Jewish people, or Jewish boys—it was all boys then—wouldn't go to a Sullivan & Cromwell or something else like that," recalled one informant. "There certainly was discrimination ... so that is all true."[169] One of the informants added:

In the fall of 1953, a number of members of my class were elected to the board of editors. And that also coincided with our looking for jobs for the summer of 1954. If you looked at the board of the *Columbia Law Review* from the class of '54, '55 there was a very, very significant Jewish population on that board so going back to the attitudes of myself and my colleagues in the fall of '53, then there were Jewish firms [like] Proskauer, Strauss and Spiegelberg, although frankly, I was unaware of that firm at that time, and I don't know anyone in my class who went to that firm. And there was one firm which was regarded as egalitarian and that was Paul Weiss which had Jewish partners, Catholic partners, and Gentile partners and even the occasional black associate. Many people in my class had a lot of trouble

---

[164] Informant #5, 6–7.
[165] "The Jewish Law Student and New York Jobs: Discriminatory Effects in Law Firm Hiring Practices," 630.
[166] Informant #17, 17.
[167] Informant #21, 2–3.
[168] Informant #13, 9.
[169] Informant #4, 15–16.

getting summer jobs. I don't know what the percentages were but [I have a] clear memory of how discouraged many people were going through the interview process over and over again and not getting any offers. So you know at the end of the summer of 1954, we entered our third year in law school. And except for people who had offers from the summer everybody went through the same process all over again, and also I have the same memory of how discouraged people were.[170]

The same frustration was expressed by another informant:

This would have been early '58, the downtown white-shoe firms were simply not really hiring Jews as they do now.... Certainly, the discrimination was evident to me when I was at ... law school, and none of us had any doubt that it was there. I mean, we all talked about it, and we recognized it and deplored it.[171]

By effective discrimination, I do not mean to suggest that no Jewish lawyers were hired by the WASP firms. For example, one informant noted:

I had, as I started to look in the job market in 1955, had mentally thought that there were two problems I faced. One, [my law school] was not ranked with Harvard or Columbia, and secondly because I am Jewish, and not the least hesitant to say so I thought that I was relegated to firms that were not of size or substance, and in point of fact I literally stumbled into the offices of [a large white-shoe firm]. Literally stumbled in without an appointment, without prearranged anything and asked for an interview. At the end of the very first interview, I had a job offer, but was told that I had to come back for a second round. So I came back for the second round, had the offer and was accepted on the spot.... But it was my impression that life being what it was, my destiny was to be in one of the smaller firms. To my surprise, [a large white-shoe firm], which had no Jewish partners [extended me an offer].[172]

Another informant described his experience interviewing at a large white-shoe firm:

Then in my second year I decided I should try New York ... [a mixed firm] was clearly the place I sort of wanted to go.... I went to [a white-shoe firm] [because] I figured I really would not care for it, and so it would be a good sort of stress interview for me, good thing to subject

---

[170] Informant #11, 2–4. The informant added that: "The other memory I have is, when I was interviewed, interviewing at a firm called ... a very white-shoe firm, the person who interviewed me who I think was not yet a partner ... tried very hard to get me an offer ... and he failed, and he was very apologetic about that" (6) (names have been omitted to preserve anonymity).

[171] Informant #5, 4, 11.

[172] Informant #22, 4–5.

> myself to. And I actually interviewed there first.... So, I go [to the white-shoe firm] first and am interviewed by a man. He was so different than my expectations, that I was just you know.... I left the office and my expectations were ... I went to [the mixed firm].... Somebody there at some point suggested that it was a strike against me that I wasn't on the law review. They sort of didn't care for that. By the way, I have many friends there. I respect the firm immensely.... So, I just sat there not knowing what the hell to do, and I decided finally to go with my heart, and I went with [the white-shoe firm]. I enjoyed the summer and came back and stayed. That's the law firm choice.[173]

Rather, my aim is to convey a professional reality whereby discrimination was the norm at WASP law firms. This discrimination was indicated by the following informants' accounts:

> [I] found a job here. And this was a very small firm at the time. It was a predominantly Jewish firm because, even in those days, it wasn't easy for Jews to break into the large law firms. Although, some of the major firms did have Jewish partners. White & Case had one and Sullivan & Cromwell had a couple. But, it was not the norm.[174]

> Absolutely—there's no question about that now—I cannot give you statistics, [and] I'm sure some of these "pubas" would argue with me, but I was there. I saw it happen. The major firms who were known as the white-shoe firms—the Gentile firms—they hired Jews, but very few. In no way did they hire Jews in proportion to the number of Jews that were at the top of their class and were successful in law school—that simply didn't happen.[175]

In addition, WASP firms that did hire Jewish attorneys as associates tended not to promote them to partnership.[176] Tellingly, one informant recalled:

> I went back to [a large white-shoe firm after a couple of years in public service], and was told that I would have to take my place in line as one option. The other option was to try to get a partnership in [another] firm. I had those offers at the time. [A large Jewish firm] was one of the firms that offered me a partnership. Looking at the opportunities, and even at that point of time—now this in 1968—I had a considerable concern about what the opportunities were for Jews in

---

[173] Informant #12, 5–6.

[174] Informant #1, 5.

[175] Informant #5, 19.

[176] One informant noted: "and actually in our day [the mid-1960s] the Gentile law firms were hiring Jewish associates. The question was whether you became a partner or not" (Informant #17, 17). See also Auerbach, *Unequal Justice,* 25–26.

the field, and opted for [the large Jewish firm] to get that issue out of the way.[177]

Another informant similarly noted, "At the time, we [at a large white-shoe firm] had a lot of associates who were Jewish, probably not in the same proportion as now, but ... many. [There were] many senior associates, but none of them stayed, and none of them made partner."[178]

Importantly, whereas in the decades preceding World War II, elite colleges and law schools discriminated against Jewish students by imposing admission quotas,[179] beginning in the late 1940s and throughout the 1960s, a growing number of Jewish attorneys were top graduates and editors of the Law Review at elite law schools.[180] As one informant remembered:

> What was happening in the early 50's was the opportunity to get into a really top flight law school as graduates of the Hebrew College.... There had been a few exceptions [Jewish graduates of Hebrew College who were admitted to elite law schools before the 1950s].... Suddenly, in our time in 1954 and 1955, the [elite] law school opened up at Harvard for whatever reason. Generally Hebrew College graduates had done very well in graduate school and they gave the school a very much-deserved reputation. And so it was like, "Hey, you know you could really go to a good law school." And I think that was the attraction for me ... and now it seemed like even guys like me could get in.[181]

Still, many Jewish graduates of elite law schools could not find a job with the white-shoe firms. The informants affirmed this fact in the following accounts:

> Because, no, you got into law school and the minorities did well, the Jewish students did well ... [but] they still couldn't get jobs. It wasn't

---

[177] Informant #22, 7.

[178] Informant #4, 8. The informant left the non-Jewish firm after two years to join a small law firm with another former associate at the firm (9).

[179] One informant recalled: "And by then when I went to [an elite] college, talking about discrimination, I had applied at the high school and they made it perfectly clear that I was Jewish and in those days, you had to fill out a form with your name and your religion. I said I was Jewish and I was told that I'd be very lucky to get in because they had to set a quota. I was told 'we take no more than 10% Jews, and if you get in you'll be a very lucky boy'" (Informant #21, 3). See, generally, Jerome Karabel, *The Chosen: The Hidden History of Admission and Exclusion at Harvard, Yale and Princeton* (New York: Houghton Mifflin Company, 2005).

[180] One informant described the discriminatory admission policies of elite colleges and law schools prior to the 1950s as coinciding "with what was happening in the United States: quotas on Jews at Harvard and Columbia and, those places where, starting in the twenties, the United States became, you know, the world moves the same way you know, same spirit that you saw in the fascist countries of Europe, which was true in England, it was true in the United States" (Informant #15, 18).

[181] Informant #7, 4–5.

the law school, so it had to be some other thing.... The Jewish kids at the top of the class had a tougher time ... with the white-shoe law firms.[182]

Getting a job was impossible. It was impossible because the law firms that hired law students were all—with the exception of a couple, which I will tell you about—blatantly anti-Semitic.... They posted—and I remember to this day—on the bulletin board of the Yale Law School—this great liberal bastion of universal love of all creeds—the interviews that were to be given at the Yale Law School campus. Fifty percent of the law school was Jewish, [and] not one single Jewish name—not one single—[was posted], including the editor-in-chief of the Yale Law Journal ... or ... the man who was first in his class.... I complained, so they took this list and they went to the Hotel Taft in New Haven, and they interviewed them down there. A Sabbath[-]observing Jew is like having cancer on top of AIDS—useless. The law firms that hire[d] were few in number.[183]

Graduating Law School in 1958 was tough times for jobs generally.... I don't think I encountered the normal discrimination so to speak because I don't think I had even attempted to get into the white-shoe firms.... So there were plenty of firms to go to that you didn't have to try to break into where you were not wanted.[184]

As a result of these discriminatory hiring and promoting practices, Jewish attorneys tended to flock to the Jewish law firms, sometimes self-selecting out of even applying for a position with the WASP firms. "I wouldn't interview [with] those [WASP] firms," said one informant.[185] And another noted, "I think many of them practiced discrimination not even realizing it was discrimination; plus the fact that there's also self-

---

[182] Informant #5, 18.

[183] Informant #8, 5. Also telling is the account of another informant about his experience seeking a law-related job while attending college:

> Nobody had better credentials than me. I was chief editor of the high school newspaper. Nobody had better criteria, it was irrelevant. It was totally irrelevant. So the lady described the position, and said, "Well, we would expect you to come in at X and you leave at Y, and once every three weeks, you'd be expected to come in to work on Saturday. We rotate that." And I told her, "Well, I can come in and work on Sunday or at night but I am an observant Jew and I cannot work on Saturday." Now you'd think that, today it is not an issue, wrong at that time. "Oh well, we have two or three Hebrews"–that was her expression, Hebrews—"but they all come in and work on Saturday." I said that I'm afraid that I would not be able to. That was it. So it was very satisfying for me to be in an office thirty-five years later with a Jewish client who prevailed, they were a target and won [against a client represented by the law firm with which the informant sought the position as a college student]. And I learned later that one of the founders of the firm was Jewish. But I never knew that until much later that that was the case (Informant #2, 6).

[184] Informant #7, 1.

[185] Informant #1, 6.

discrimination where people don't apply there because they ... don't want to be rejected."[186]

The deeper roots of self-selection were described as follows by an informant who interviewed with WASP firms, but ended up accepting an offer from a Jewish firm:

> And then there is reverse discrimination.... I did not do much interviewing [with WASP firms,] but I do remember ... several years later I met somebody at [a WASP firm] and he said to me, "[W]hy didn't you respond to our offer?" I said "what [offer]?" He said, "We telephoned your home, and I think we spoke to your mother, and we made you an offer. We asked you to call; you never called back." So I said, "I didn't call back because I didn't know that it happened." So, at an appropriate time, I said to my mother, "Mother, do you remember getting a call from [the WASP firm] offering me a job?" She said, "yes." "How come you didn't tell me about it?" [I asked]. She said, "Well, you already had a job offer from a firm that was very." She wouldn't have used this word—"egalitarian"—I don't know what word she used. She said, "And I thought it was a good firm, and I didn't see any reason why you should consider an offer from a Gentile firm." So, the point I'm trying to make ... is that it worked both ways.[187]

Another informant commented about the disapproval of his classmates upon learning of his decision to join a white-shoe firm:

> I remember when I went to [a white-shoe firm] for the summer and came back from the summer, then when I announced I was going to go back there after graduation, a number of my classmates, particularly Jewish classmates, made it clear that they disapproved of my decision. I don't want to say made it clear, there are various ways of making things clear and it just infuriated me that they were drawing upon these stereotypes that get to them and they obviously did, because they are so fixed. [Stereotypes] count, they matter.... There's no question that a stereotype was present. Then it subsisted for a while. I do think it isn't there today, but I could be wrong. It just really got me pretty upset, mostly disappointed in the people who otherwise, had good judgment.[188]

The effective discrimination by the WASP firms resulted in the creation of a large pool of highly qualified attorneys from which the Jewish firms could pick and choose elite talent at their discretion. A partner at a Jewish

---

[186] Informant #10, 16. Informant #16, for example, did not recall experiencing any antisemitism or bias, but conceded that, in spite of graduating in the top of the class and serving on the *Columbia Law Review*, he did not apply for a summer position with any of the white-shoe firms because he believed such firms were only hiring "token" Jewish attorneys and not promoting them subsequently (2).

[187] Informant #11, 4–5. The informant later noted: "I can tell you that I was very reluctant to interview at [a large Jewish firm] because I didn't want to go to a Jewish firm" (6).

[188] Informant #12, 22.

firm recalled, "We hired nine people, of which six had continued into federal clerkships. And they were really scholastically outstanding: we had several editors and editors-in-chief who were authors of the *Harvard Law Review*.... They were really first rate people."[189] One informant concluded, "the Jewish firms' edge was that they were getting the Jewish students at a period when the non-Jewish firms were actually not hiring,"[190] and another opined that [Jewish firms] "benefited from discrimination, [we] recruited a lot of Jewish attorneys."[191] A third informant noted:

> In terms of recruitment I perceived there was, still at that point of time, this is now 1967, 1968, 1969, to 1970, a divide. That younger people who aspired to achieve, who were of the Jewish faith, had less opportunity, except in targeted areas, or targeted firms like [a large Jewish firm], to grow, whereas, non-Jews had no problems. So the opportunity was to get really talented people from that market, and later on from that market of women lawyers trying to achieve who likewise had the same barrier and so we pushed actively in those two areas because the chances of getting a well qualified Law Review graduate in one or another of those markets was greater than getting somebody who was not Jewish because he or she might go to [a particular white-shoe firm] or [another particular white-shoe firm].[192]

Indeed, one informant suggested that some at Jewish law firms saw it as their mission to hire discriminated-against, elite Jewish lawyers: "One outstanding example was [a particular Jewish law firm] [which] ... made its business to hire Jews—particularly Orthodox Jews—that came from law schools and couldn't get jobs otherwise."[193]

The existence of a large, talented pool of Jewish candidates, over-looked by the WASP firms and consequently available to work for the Jewish firms, was also confirmed by an informant recalling his job-hunting days:

> I already had the understanding that the firms I would be looking at would be the Jewish firms, and it was not because I was looking for the Jewish firms, but I was looking for a job, and whether right or wrong, I do not know—all I can give you is personal experience—there was a feeling that the white-shoe firms downtown ... were not interested in Jews. I can't say that [from] firsthand testimony, [but] I do know [that] when I came to [a growing Jewish firm] they hired me ... relatively quickly, [and] I concluded [that] this would be anecdotal ... [to] whatever discrimination or alleged discrimination or the perception of discrimination that was occurring in these large firms.... We were getting, in my opinion, the cream of the crop, and when I

---

[189] Informant #2, 8.
[190] Informant #15, 18.
[191] Informant #16, 4.
[192] Informant #22, 7–8.
[193] Informant #8, 5–6.

> say "cream of the crop," let's face it, there were non-Jews that were cream of the crop too, but many Jews would feel the same [way] that I did and therefore immediately opt for a firm like [ours]. When I came to the firm ... there were fifty-four lawyers, and now there's ... four or five hundred ... with offices all over.[194]

In conclusion, the Jewish firms benefited from near exclusive access to this talented pool of attorneys between the early 1950s and the mid 1960s, and to a lesser, yet still significant, degree between the mid 1960s and the early 1980s—access that allowed them to grow at a pace faster than that of the WASP firms while recruiting and retaining top talent.

Curiously, and seemingly contrary to the basic logic of supply and demand, the pool of elite Jewish candidates throughout the 1950s and 1960s remained large, notwithstanding discrimination by the WASP firms and limited hiring by the growing, but still relatively small, Jewish firms. In other words, in spite of relatively weak demand for their services by discriminatory WASP firms and growing Jewish firms, the supply of talented Jewish lawyers graduating from elite law schools remained robust. The informants suggest a complex interplay of religious, cultural, and socio-economic considerations that drove many Jews to attend elite law schools in spite of grim hiring prospects. Some suggest the affinity between Judaism and Jewish studies and law.[195] One informant affirmed this affinity, stating:

> When I started ... I was in tax law. There are, I think, a greater proportion of people with a religious studies background in tax law than in anything else, because I think there is a parallelism.... Tax has an affinity [with the Talmud in that] you are [dealing with] a multitude of layered interpretations.[196]

Others highlighted the commitment within the Jewish community to education:

> I became a lawyer just because I wanted more education. I didn't have any lawyers in my family. I didn't know any lawyers but I went to law school because I wanted more education and I didn't have a particular career path.[197]

Indeed, the connection between religious upbringing and education, on the one hand, and law, on the other, entailed a commitment not only to

---

[194] Informant #10, 2–3.

[195] Informant #15, 1–3. The informant said later, "And I will say that, oddly enough, Talmudic study is a very similar experience to law" (6). See, generally, Auerbach, *Rabbis and Lawyers*, 42.

[196] Informant #4, 19–20.

[197] Informant #13, 1.

pursuing graduate education but to elite education, status, and credentials as building blocks for a future professional career. An informant confirmed:

> From Ramaz [an orthodox Jewish school] I was admitted both to Columbia and to Harvard, and much to the disappointment of the people at Ramaz, I chose to go to Columbia. They would've liked me to go to Harvard, which says something about that.... I think I wanted to be a lawyer from the time I was ten years old.... There was no one in the family that I knew who was a lawyer ... I think I liked dealing with words and writing.... So ... law seemed like an obvious extension of the kind of things that I was good at.... I could read fast, I could articulate well, and so forth.... The only diversion was the possibility of going to Yeshiva to Rabbinical School.... Then I considered seriously for career reasons maybe I'd rather be a rabbi than a lawyer. [I] decided that while I might like studying to be a rabbi, I would never like the work, [whereas] even if I didn't like studying [the] law, I was sure I was going to like [practicing law], from what I could see.[198]

Other informants describe a cultural background in which graduate school was an obvious extension of their upbringing, if not the only acceptable choice after college.[199] Particularly telling is the following account of an informant who describes his decision to attend law school as his only available option to avoid starvation:

> I went to law school because, like many children of rabbis, it's a form of rebellion to not go into your father's profession. I found [being a rabbi] to be a very difficult profession—great physical and psychological toll.... So, being a rabbi was not for me. I had no scientific skills. Also, many of my classmates were [studying to be doctors]; in those

---

[198] Informant #4, 1, 3.

[199] One informant described the cultural and educational background that led him to attend law school as follows:

> Everybody, all our nephews and relatives were all doctors. My brother's a doctor, my cousins are doctors. I was the first lawyer in the family, I majored in sociology and my brother came in from medical school and said, "What do you do with sociology ... you have to take chemistry." So I put myself through a year of chemistry to satisfy him. And I took calculus and math and said, "I don't want to be a doctor" (Informant #20, 12).

Another informant's account revealed similar influences. "It was, very frankly, it was the choice of being a doctor or being a lawyer. I couldn't stand the sight of blood. I had a large mouth at that time already and thought the law would be an appropriate alternative" (Informant #22, 3). The same informant also discussed the relationship between the Jewish community and a strong educational drive: "From the get-go, education has been a cornerstone of those of the Jewish faith in terms of their religion and in terms of their home life and their experiences and the like. And the same is with Catholics by the way. There is a secondary reason in some areas and that is ... a sense of patrimony about looking after one's own.... There is some unity between Jews among compatriots as there is in Catholics. In terms of scholarship there are some Jews that do exceedingly well and there are some that do terribly. But the cornerstone of educational need and the requirement is beaten into you the first day" (9–10).

days, it was the biggest accomplishment to be a Jewish doctor.... So, I didn't want to compete in the world of doctors. It was hard enough to get into medical school for Jews at the time. There were so many who wanted to be doctors. So, I took up a little art education, having zero money, no capital, [and] no abilities to open a business because there were very few Jews in business, unless they were running their parents['] business.... I learned not to starve to death. The only thing that was available to me was to get a law degree.[200]

While the informant's perception regarding law practice as a possible lucrative occupation was, as we have seen, somewhat mistaken, his reasoning is nonetheless revealing. He subjectively perceived his only career options as a rabbi, a doctor, a scientist, or an attorney.

Other informants identified a poor socio-economic background as the driving force behind attending law school; law school and a career as a lawyer represented not only a natural extension of an educational path, but also a ticket out of poverty.[201] One informant said:

Thompson Harris was a preparatory high school for city college and city college professors taught in the high school. If you wanted to be eligible to go to this high school, you had to pass an examination, and if you passed the exam, you obviously went. If you didn't pass, you went to the regular high schools. I was fortunate enough to go to Thompson Harris, which was a great educational experience.... [After World War II,] I finished at law school and then I got a fellowship at the London School of Economics, by which time ... my wife was at the University of London.[202]

Similarly, another informant recalled:

[I] lived in Brooklyn for virtually all of my childhood in a two-family home. [I w]ent to [the] Horace Mann School [an elite prep school] [and] rode the subway for an hour and twenty minutes each day.... I remember in high school wanting to be a lawyer. I actually am one of those people that said that's what I'm going to be, and that was somewhere around the age of sixteen, so I never had any doubt.[203]

---

[200] Informant #22, 1–3.

[201] A legal career was not uniformly perceived as a means of upward mobility. One informant noted, "We were not 'upwardly mobile' in the common sense. The American dream was not for [my father, a rabbi]. He did not get a benefit from it, and he had no interest in me having the benefit of it.... I don't think [my father] was particularly interested in my becoming a lawyer, but he would have liked me to continue to study Jewish law" (Informant #3, 10).

[202] Informant #1, 3.

[203] Informant #5, 1–2. Another informant recalled:

Then when I finished the sixth grade my parents, and I think it was particularly my mother, thought the Fort Lee public school system is not what she wanted for her child. So she and two other families banded together and they

One informant revealed, "[My parents] were not highly educated people. I have two older brothers. I was very fortunate to be able to have a good education. The schools were quite helpful with the financial drain at that time."[204]

The robust supply of elite Jewish lawyers was thus not as sensitive to weak demand and challenging job prospects because, for many Jewish men, the decision to attend an elite law school was more than a mere cost-benefit analysis. Rather, it was the product of their upbringing, which emphasized education and scholarly pursuits as important and desirable values, commitment to graduate education, a perception that the law was a worthy alternative to a religious career, and a sense of debt to parental sacrifices that demanded a scholarly and thoughtful career path.[205] The unique combination of effective discrimination against Jewish law students and attorneys by white-shoe firms and the commitment of Jewish students to enroll in elite law schools notwithstanding grim job prospects upon graduation thus resulted in the creation of a large talented pool of Jewish lawyers from which the growing Jewish firms recruited nearly exclusively.

C. The Transformation of Professional Ideology and the Flip Side of Bias[206]

The decline of the old, prevailing large law firm professionalism paradigm and the rise of the business paradigm, what Russell Pearce has called a "paradigm shift,"[207] played an important, and unexpected, role in the

---

formed a carpool and enrolled us into a school called Horace Mann in New York City. There were two brothers in one family, one in another and I and we were the only children from New Jersey going to Horace Mann. So I went to school in New York. Most of my friends were from New York, but I still lived in New Jersey. The social scene was a little bit strange for me (Informant #12, 2).

[204] Informant #6, 1.

[205] An upbringing committed to education and excellence as a means of pursuing the American Dream and socioeconomic mobility is, of course, not unique to Jews and is common among other minority groups. See, e.g., Amy Chua, *Battle Hymn of the Tiger Mother* (New York: Penguin Press, 2011); Peter H. Huang, "Tiger Cub Strikes Back: Memories of an Ex-Child Prodigy about Legal Education and Parenting," *British Journal of American Legal Studies* 1 (2012): 297–347, on upbringing and commitment to education among some Asian-American parents.

[206] By the "flip side of bias," I mean to denote the positive consequences of prejudice and contrast them with the usual negative outcomes of bias. See "An Interview with Jennifer Lee: What is Stereotype Promise?" http://www.russellsage.org/blog/interview-jennifer-lee-what-stereotype-promise (last visited July 10, 2013).

[207] See Russell G. Pearce, "The Professionalism Paradigm Shift: Why Discarding Professional Ideology Will Improve the Conduct and Reputation of the Bar," *N.Y.U. Law Review* 70 (1996): 1229–76; Eli Wald, "Glass Ceilings and Dead Ends: Professional Ideologies, Gender Stereotypes, and the Future of Women Lawyers at Large Law Firms," *Fordham Law Review* 78 (2010): 2245, 2264–73. See also Richard A. Posner, *The Problematics of Moral and Legal Theory* (Cambridge, MA: Harvard University Press, 1999), 185–211.

growth of the Jewish firms. As a result of a gradual ideological paradigm shift at large law firms—the decline of white-shoe ethos, paternalistic collegiality and secrecy,[208] and the rise of a more explicitly competitive business ideology emphasizing the financial bottom line, profits-per-partners, an eat-what-you-kill ethos, and around the clock client service—the same prejudices, stereotypes, and bias that fueled and helped sustain effective discrimination against Jewish attorneys under the old ideology made Jewish attorneys and Jewish law firms desirable under the new model. That is, the paradigm shift in the underlying ideology of large law firms that replaced the prevailing white-shoe ethos with a more explicitly business-oriented notion of professionalism resulted in the "flip side of bias"; namely, it rendered the loathed "qualities" of Jewish lawyers under the old model—wealth maximizing, manipulative on behalf of clients, and instrumentalism, not to say conniving—into positive attributes of lawyering under the new one. The very same stereotypes that fueled prejudice against Jewish lawyers and Jewish law firms were now perceived as desirable qualities.[209]

The informants' accounts confirm that the "flip side of bias" was a general phenomenon operating outside of the legal profession. For example, one informant stated, "The medical corps did not qualify for combat service because the general I.Q. was far below army standards. So, they took five Jewish kids from New York and put them in the medical corps so they could raise the general average so it became combat-worthy."[210] Yet, they emphasize the interplay of the "flip side of bias" phenomenon with factors such as the possession of cultural and social capital, especially the notion of high intellectual self-esteem, in explaining their success in law practice.[211]

---

[208] One informant's account of being promoted to partner demonstrates the old paradigm and its approach to disseminating information:

> [A] hint was when I was invited to a lunch with the head of the firm, who invited all of the partners to his home on Long Island for lunch in the fall. And if you were invited there, and you were an associate, it was a pretty good sign.... But I did not know when the partners made these decisions.... I was called out of a deposition in Philadelphia and the head of the firm ... told me I just went to partner. I had a hard time understanding what he was saying. He just sort of dumped it out. I went back into deposition and couldn't tell anybody (Informant #12, 10–11).

[209] See Wald, "The Rise and Fall of the WASP and Jewish Law Firms," Part II.C.3.

[210] Informant #1, 2.

[211] See Pierre Bourdieu, "The Forms of Capital," in *Handbook of Theory and Research for the Sociology of Education*, ed. John G. Richardson (New York: Greenwood, 1986), 241–58; James S. Coleman, "Social Capital in the Creation of Human Capital," *American Journal of Sociology* 94 (1988): 95, 100–101. On the impact of cultural and social capital on lawyers' careers, see, e.g., Fiona M. Kay and John Hagan, "Cultivating Clients in the Competition for Partnership: Gender and the Organizational Restructuring of Law Firms in the 1990s," *Law & Society Review* 33 (1999): 517, 542; Fiona M. Kay and John Hagan, "Raising the Bar: The Gender Stratification of Law-Firm Capital," *American Sociology Review* 63 (1998): 728, 737; Ronit Dinovitzer, "Social Capital and Constraints on Legal Careers," *Law & Society Review* 40 (2006): 445, 445–47, 451–52; Bryant G. Garth and Joyce Sterling, "Exploring Inequality in the Corporate Law Firm Apprenticeship: Doing

The same informant added:

> Probably, in the back of my mind, there was the expectation that I would attend law school at some point. But, since I couldn't afford it, it was a vague hope. But then I got the scholarship at Yale, and that permitted me to participate in Yale activities, and after that, I went into the army, and then the G.I. Bill came along and that provided me with adequate funds.[212]

Describing his experience at Harvard Law School one informant recalled a process of great intellectual growth, "I went to law school very unsophisticated and very ignorant. I did not know anything about law, about Harvard, or about much else related to the legal profession. But I was a pretty good soldier, and I went and did what I was supposed to do."[213] Within a year, however, "All sorts of things happened to me in my second year at law school. I became much more sophisticated and 'worldly.'"[214] Tellingly, the informant never doubted his own capacity to grow so rapidly, to succeed, even excel at law school. Confident in his intellectual abilities, it was only a matter of time until he was to prove his talents. "I had been a young 'hot shot' student when I got out of law school."[215]

Another informant explained his decision to attend law school as follows: "[I] probably [chose law school] because ... I like to read; I like intellectual exercises, and actually the affinity between law and mathematics, although using very different types of ways of the intellectual exercise, the logical exercise[s] are very similar."[216] One informant explained that after graduating from law school he felt socially awkward. It was not merely that he self-selected out of interviewing with the large white-shoe firms because he thought they would not hire a Jew, or with the large Jewish firms because he thought they would not hire an Orthodox Jew. Rather, it was his perception that his lack of people skills would lead to failure in interviewing.[217] But, the informant reasoned, this notion of social awkwardness

---

the Time, Finding the Love," *Georgetown Journal of Legal Ethics* 22 (2009): 1361, 1368; John P. Heinz et al., *Urban Lawyers: The New Social Structure of the Bar* (Chicago: University of Chicago Press, 2005), 69; John Hagan, "The Gender Stratification of Income Inequality Among Lawyers," *Social Forces* 68 (1990): 835, 837; Jo Dixon and Carroll Seron, "Stratification in the Legal Profession: Sex, Sector and Salary," *Law & Society Review* 29 (1995): 381, 382; David B. Wilkins, "Doing Well by Doing Good? The Role of Public Service in the Careers of Black Corporate Lawyers," *Houston Law Review* (2004): 1, 27 (arguing that for black lawyers, a lack of social capital in the form of elite networks maintains or reinforces their disadvantage in the profession); John Hagan et al., "Cultural Capital, Gender and the Structural Transformation of Legal Practice," *Law & Society Review* 25 (1991): 239, 239–44.

[212] Informant #1, 2.
[213] Informant #3, 19.
[214] Informant #3, 20.
[215] Informant #3, 23.
[216] Informant #6, 3.
[217] Informant #14, 1.

explains why he, and possibly other Jews, was interested in law. Many Jews thought that the only obstacle they had to overcome was social awkwardness. They never doubted their own abilities otherwise. Law was an "obvious" choice because "once you overcome the social factor, your mental capacities are there and Jews are confident in their ability to exercise judgment."[218] Law schools, the informant concluded, "made it possible for Jews to play the game."[219]

Indeed, high intellectual self-esteem played a role not only in the success of Jewish law students at elite law schools and of Jewish attorneys at large firms, but it also helps explain the growth and success of Jewish law firms. One informant explained that since there was no legal authority for a position he wanted to take, "I wrote [an] article which provoked the debate. In a way sometimes it's very useful to have the entire academic world take the opposite position because there must be something to your position if everybody in the academic world argues against it."[220] The point is not merely that the informant's position subsequently became the law on the issue; rather, it is that the informant, a practicing attorney, felt completely comfortable doing battle with leading scholars in the academic arena.

The informants highlighted the significance of familial and community support in developing high intellectual self-esteem which, in turn, allowed them to benefit from the flip side of bias and reap the benefits of positive stereotyping. Describing the reaction of his family to his decision to attend law school, one informant noted, "Oh, [they were] very proud. To have a kid go to Yale was beyond their dreams. So, there was nothing but great support. Not that they could afford anything, but they ... approved heartily. And you know, it worked out well for me afterwards."[221] Another reinforced the idea of strong cultural and familial support:

> I was fifteen ... [and] the career paths, I think ... probably would have been either the rabbinate or law. And just sort of looking around, I thought the law was the more socially promoting, reinforcing kind of position.... The family was certainly supportive of me. I think at the time that I started law school, my father was either changing businesses or whatever it was, and at that time I even got a partial stipend or scholarship from Columbia Law, because it was something of a financial difficulty.... I cannot remember what I would call a serious discussion or even dispute over a career choice.[222]

Moreover, another informant noted the importance of an upbringing in a cultural commitment to education to the development of cultural capital, stating, "The opposition [to law school] was only to the extent that people

---

[218] Informant #14, 1–2.
[219] Ibid.
[220] Informant #17, 9–10.
[221] Informant #1, 5.
[222] Informant #4, 12.

didn't think that you should be pursuing secular careers at all. Even in those days, there were rabbis that would have preferred that I would have stayed on."[223]

The stereotype of Jewish attorneys as learned experts, now a desirable quality under the new more competitive professional paradigm, was, according to the informants, consistent with their actual backgrounds. Describing his hobbies and interests as a child, one informant recalled:

> If you mean before I was four and a half, there were no hobbies.... [I was] taught to read, to 'study,' to pray, to carry out religious ritual and to count simple arithmetical operations ... [growing up] I essentially had a five and a half day week; the day was from 8:45 to 6:30, Sunday through Thursday, and 9 to 12 Friday.[224]

Education took clear precedent over work. The same informant remembered, "Mostly, there was no time to work, because we did not work on the Sabbath and on Sunday I was at school all day. There was no real opportunity to work."[225] Further, "I never learned to do things with my hands. I, too, did not learn to do anything menial until I went out on my own, and had to learn to wash dishes and make beds."[226] The account is revealing exactly because the informant hailed from a poor socio-economic background. Not learning to make his bed was not an indication of a privileged background, rather, it was a reflection of commitment and devotion to learning and the intellectual over the mundane.

Another explained that he grew up in a culture in which commitment to education was a foregone conclusion, and graduate school was a default choice when one did not know what to do after college. When asked why he went to law school, the informant responded:

> I have no good answer for you. I'm not so sure that I knew what I was going to do as I went into my last year of college. I really had not pulled up my sleeves.... But what happened was, I took the law school boards and I did very, very well. I can't say I stayed up nights, that I was going to save the world.[227]

Finally, commenting on the powerful interplay of commitment to education within the Jewish community and high intellectual self-esteem exhibited by Jewish lawyers, one informant jokingly noted:

> It seems you have to be an ordained rabbi now to get on the law review. But the reason why, is because we [observant Jews] actually, I

---

[223] Informant #6, 2.
[224] Informant #3, 3, 4.
[225] Informant #3, 6.
[226] Informant #3, 16.
[227] Informant #10, 4–5.

think, have an edge. As people were getting used to abstract thinking, and for legal reasoning, this was something that we had all done for a very long time ... the basis, so much of the basis of law and civil law, whether it's, you know, torts or property law, is derived from the Judaic system and the problem, I think, with the whole method of reasoning and thinking [is] that it is so familiar to us. And [since selection to law review is] based on your first year's performance, I frankly think we had an unfair advantage.[228]

The "flip side of bias" phenomenon helped build the Jewish law firm's reputation. Under the new business model of professionalism, the thin religious identity of the Jewish firm—the product of the religious identity of its lawyers—served as a selling point to its clients. "But it may reflect a tendency that I've heard said rightly or wrongly about the stereotype of Jewish lawyers that they're always pushing to get ahead," said one informant. "If you're pushing to get ahead, you're focusing on what you need to get ahead."[229]

While the Jewish firms never cultivated an explicitly Jewish culture of legal practice, their perceived religious identity, one which "flipped bias" rendered desirable, arguably made law firms with a majority of Jewish lawyers more attractive to entity clients and, ironically, enabled Jewish law firms to actually benefit from bias and prejudice. An informant confirmed this perceived identity, stating:

> You have to understand that most of this is a perception.... [It] is important to be seen by litigators because, how many people have ever seen me in court? That's how you get a reputation. You get a reputation by being seen with litigators. Just tell your clients, your students this one thing: it's a perception.[230]

VII. Conclusion

The interplay of diminished religious-based discrimination and increased client demand for corporate legal services provides the backdrop for the incredible success story of the Jewish law firm in New York City. The chapter identifies several factors, however, that combined to help explain the emergence and unique growth of the Jewish firm: the rise of inside counsel as decision-makers within large corporate entities regarding the engagement of outside counsel replacing discriminating executives; the emergence of Jewish firms at a time when individual visibility of superstar attorneys was still feasible and played a significant role in the building of firm-wide reputations; and the existence of a Jewish client base consisting of a large number of smaller entities. All of these factors, operating in the

---

[228] Informant #15, 6, 8–9.

[229] Informant #15, 29.

[230] Informant #1, 7.

shadow of diminished antisemitism and religious-based discrimination, enabled the growth of Jewish firms.

Moreover, the relatively small number and size of the old WASP firms; their refusal to compete with the Jewish firms over the provision of "undignified" legal services, such as real-estate, bankruptcy and hostile takeovers, resulting in the de facto creation of Jewish pockets of practice in which the Jewish firms could prove their expertise and from which they crossed over to more "dignified" practice areas; effective discriminatory hiring and promotion practices by the old WASP firms against Jewish attorneys, which created a pool of talented entry-level and lateral Jewish lawyers from which Jewish law firms could cherry-pick; and the "flip side of bias" phenomenon all explain the unique growth of Jewish law firms at a rate far exceeding that of the WASP firms.

Current practice realities in New York City and throughout the United States have changed significantly.[231] The informants suggest that Jewish lawyers presently face little to no systematic ethno-religious-based discrimination.[232] For instance, one informant noted, "There's no suggestion of antisemitism at the bar in New York.... [Outside of New York City,] I don't know. I wouldn't like to try a case in Texas. Not because I'm Jewish, but because you can get home-towned."[233] Another opined: "You sort of had no choice, even if at your heart you were racist. You had to understand that the economics of the business could no longer support your racism."[234] One informant noted the current level of religious tolerance and accommodation afforded to Jewish attorneys.[235] Moreover, to the extent it currently persists,

---

[231] While large law firm systematic ethno-religious discrimination against Jews and Catholics is a thing of the past, some previously excluded groups still face significant hurdles and others experience implicit discrimination. On the glass-ceiling effect experienced by many women lawyers at large law firms see Cynthia Fuchs Epstein et al., "Class Ceilings and Open Doors: Women's Advancement in the Legal Profession," *Fordham Law Review* 64 (1995): 291–449; Deborah L. Rhode, "The 'No-Problem' Problem: Feminist Challenges and Cultural Change," *Yale Law Journal* 100 (1991); 1731–93; Wald, "Glass Ceilings and Dead Ends," 2250–64. On the experience of black lawyers at large law firms, see David B. Wilkins and G. Mitu Gulati, "Why Are There So Few Black Lawyers in Corporate Law Firms?" 493–614. See also Maria Chavez, *Everyday Injustice: Latino Professionals and Racism* (Rowman & Littlefield, 2011).

[232] But some informants suggest that religious observers, Jewish or Christian, might still face some hurdles. For example, one observant opined: "And whether that [being a religious observer] would be a draw back in some firms, I don't know. I suspect it probably would. Here it doesn't, but we're not a usual firm" (Informant #1, 12). Another noted: "It's true that Jews today are not suffering heavily the way it had been 50–60 years ago when firms as a practical matter did not hire Jews ... it would be naive to think that [currently] there are not elements of prejudice and discrimination but its level is a lot less than it was" (Informant #10, 9).

[233] Informant #10, 9.

[234] Informant #11, 22.

[235] Informant #15, 4-5. The informant further commented:
> I think that culturally this firm [an old white-shoe firm] has been a super-meritocracy because really we only care about one thing, which is, talent. And if you do a good job, then nothing else matters and, in fact, the courtesy [to

religious discrimination reflects the opinions of the older generation within large firms. As one informant stated:

> I think that when you look at what we would call the very established white-shoe firms, in many of their firms there really is what might be described as the old firm and the new firm ... I remember I had a case, I tried a case ... and one of the important witnesses in that case was a member of the board, who was a [senior] partner [at an old white-shoe firm]. I think it's fair to say that he had not covered himself in the handling of this situation. And I mentioned [to another partner at that firm] that I'd had [contact] with this particular partner and the reaction was, "Well, you have to understand, he's part of the old firm, he's not part of the new firm."[236]

Consequently, as old WASP firms hire and promote Jewish lawyers, and as Jewish firms hire and promote non-Jews, the Jewish firms, which never developed a distinctive professional Jewish culture, are losing their Jewish identity:

> Our law firm is hardly a Jewish law firm anymore ... we have offices all over the world in Germany and [China] and ... and you can be sure the people working for us in Germany and [China] aren't Jewish, they are whoever they are and whatever they are is fine. So the firm, our firm, has expanded into the pluralistic world.[237]

That is, since the Jewish firms were Jewish only by discriminatory default, they gradually lose their Jewishness as they hire and promote non-Jews. An informant affirmed this fact, stating, "There were a number of non-Jewish, and today I would say it was a mixed firm. Largely, I don't know if it's fifty-fifty or two thirds/one third but very, very significant people in the firm are non-Jewish."[238] Similarly, a partner at a non-Jewish firm described the composition of his firm as follows: "You know, the proportion now is probably, if I had to guess, I would say, a third to forty percent of the partners are Jewish, a third to forty percent [are] Catholic, and a third [are an]other [religious affiliation]."[239]

Indeed, contemporary practice realities in New York City nearly render the old divide among large law firms meaningless. One informant noted:

> observant Jewish attorneys] is pretty overwhelming ... the whole thing has changed and the courtesy has been absolutely overwhelming.... And I think it really has to do with the fact that it's a meritocracy and a business that is very, so to speak, color blind (ibid.).

[236] Informant #11, 23–24.

[237] Informant #21, 7.

[238] Informant #2, 8. Another informant with a large Jewish firm estimated that thirty to forty percent of the firm's current partners are not Jewish, describing the change as the "Cravathization" of the Jewish firm (Informant #16, 4).

[239] Informant #4, 8.

> My favorite story [is] about [a particular old WASP firm], where a [a Jewish partner] I know, was head of the tax department. He and I were negotiating part of that deal that you see all bound in volumes. We had a whole group on the phone ... He was trying to persuade me to do something in a different format. He says, "Look ... you have to pay the tax [using a Yiddish phrase]." There was absolute silence, and I said, "Look guys, it's all right. I'll explain it to you." But to me, that one telephone conference call represented how far we had come from 1960 to the year 2000 ... or ... 1998. That year he was—and I was—we were both very comfortable, and could talk in that language. So, it was within a lifetime, it was a big step forward.[240]

And another informant commented:

> Our [Jewish] firm has expanded into the pluralistic world and the white-shoe firms have expanded into the pluralistic world, and we had a very funny experience because, at one point, we were talking to [a particular old WASP firm] about doing an arrangement together and [the old WASP firm], which really used to be one of the white-shoe law firms, sent their executive committee over to meet with our executive committee. Their executive committee was all Jewish, our executive committee was all Christian, and we commented on the fact that the world had really changed. And it has, it has. This is really astonishing.[241]

As Jewish firms decline, has something of value been lost? The informants suggest that Jewish law firms were created because of discriminatory practice realities, and the decline of religious-based discrimination should lead to the decline of "Jewish" firms. One informant pointed out:

> From having dichotomized law firms, Jewish and un-Jewish ... did you make a virtue out of a vice? The vice was anti-Semitism. The virtue was [that] there were some firms who took a few Jews.... The point is, it's like saying, "We'll put you in a concentration camp, but we'll be better, we'll give you bread ... [and] put you out of the system." So, somebody came to the rescue of a few people. There's no virtue; that's the point.[242]

Others echo the sentiment, suggesting that because Jewish law firms were Jewish only by discriminatory default, such firms will disappear as

---

[240] Informant #4, 15.

[241] Informant #21, 7–8. Informants at old white-shoe firms similarly described contemporary realities. For example, one informant opined, "At most of the large professional [law] firms it is true today that [one's religious identity does not constitute a barrier] and clearly it was a different situation back in the 50's and 60's, and after I became an associate here [a white-shoe firm] and they admitted their first Jewish partner, that alleviated the situation somewhat and over the years that's changed quite a bit" (Informant #19, 5–6).

[242] Informant #8, 15–16.

Jewish attorneys become less and less religious.[243] In fact, one informant stated:

> I tend to believe that Jewish lawyers compartmentalize their [Jewishness] from the standpoint of law—they're as hungry as everybody else. What is good for their education, what is good for their practice...? Maybe it shows the narrowness in terms of Jewish lawyers. Don't misunderstand me, they may go to a lecture [about Judaism] ... or something ... [and] they'll jump in and what not, but as a regular course, it's a luxury.[244]

The rise and growth of large Jewish law firms in the second half of the twentieth century is a remarkable success story of overcoming discrimination in the legal profession. Paradoxically, part of the very success of the Jewish firms is reflected in their demise by the early twenty-first century: because systematic large law firm ethno-religious discrimination against Jewish lawyers has become a thing of the past, the very reason for the existence of Jewish law firms has been nullified. As other minority groups, however, continue to struggle for equality within the profession's elite large law firms, can the experience of the Jewish firms serve as a "separate-but-equal" blueprint for overcoming contemporary forms of discrimination for women, racial, and ethnic minority attorneys?

Perhaps not. As this chapter establishes, the success of large Jewish law firms was the result of the coming together of numerous conditions and circumstances between 1945 and 1980, from the general decline of ethno-religious discrimination in American society and increased demand for corporate legal services; to the unique structure of the market for elite corporate legal services including the relatively small number and size of large firms, their anti-competitive conduct, including staying out of undignified practice areas such as real-estate, hostile takeovers, bankruptcy, and even litigation allowing Jewish firms to establish themselves in these pockets of practice and then cross over to more dignified legal arenas, WASP firms' traditional and die-hard organizational habits and their discriminatory hiring and promotion practices; the rise of in-house counsel; the affinity of Jews to American law and the legal profession resulting in their flocking to law schools notwithstanding grim job prospects; and the flip side of bias phenomenon that has elevated the status and perception of Jewish lawyers as the dominant ideology of large law firms became more

---

[243] See, generally, Alan M. Dershowitz, *The Vanishing American Jew: In Search of Jewish Identity for the Next Century* (Boston: Little Brown, 1997) (raising the possibility that, over time, a majority of lawyers in all large law firms will be Christian, if only due to the decline of the number of Jews in America and the corresponding decline in the number of Jewish lawyers). At the same time, with the increased secularization among American professionals, it is equally possible that, to borrow from Dershowitz, the vanishing religious lawyer would render the question of the religious identity of the large law firm meaningless.

[244] Informant #10, 29.

competitive and meritocratic. Such a unique combination of conditions and circumstances may never be replicated again.

To be clear, some of these conditions apply to some minority lawyers, for example, Joan Williams has opined that women lawyers may benefit from the flip side of bias as in-house counsel departments increasingly value stereotypically feminine qualities such as cooperative styles of practice and being a team player.[245] But other key conditions are absent, for example, large law firms have become hyper-competitive and are unlikely to allow any newcomers the benefit of protected pockets of practice. As importantly, even if "separate-but-equal" styled law firms could succeed, the desirability of combating inequality by resorting to "separate-but-equal" institutions is likely to be a complex and controversial issue. Jewish lawyers, after all, did not choose to practice in Jewish law firms, they were forced into them by explicitly discriminatory practice realities. While implicit discrimination is still rampant in BigLaw, many minority lawyers today do have a choice to enter these institutions and some choose to do so hoping that equality can be achieved by and from within large law firms rather than forced upon them by "separate-but-equal" competitors. Assuming other minority lawyers may choose to practice in "separate-but-equal" large law firms if such entities existed, would such institutions be desirable in a "post-gendered," "post-racial" America?[246]

VIII. Appendix

I interviewed twenty-two male Jewish lawyers who graduated from law school between 1945 and 1962, either joined a large New York City firm, WASP, Jewish, or mixed, or established their own, and practiced in New York City throughout their respective careers.[247] I began by identifying a

---

[245] Michelle Coleman Mayes and Kara Sophia Baysinger, *Courageous Counsel— Conversations with Women General Counsel in the Fortune 500* (Leverage Media, 2011), 31 (quoting Joan Williams: "women have traditionally been under the pressure of not putting themselves ahead in the packing order, but rather, assuming a more attentive, helpful, emotionally intelligent role. These are the sort of things they were expected to do, but now, these same qualities are seen as being very effective for corporate legal leadership.").

[246] See, e.g., Anne-Marie Slaughter, "Why Women Still Can't Have It All," *The Atlantic* (July-August 2012), available at http://www.theatlantic.com/magazine/archive/2012/07/why-women-still-cant-have-it-all/309020/; Sheryl Sandberg, *Lean In: Women, Work, and the Will to Lead* (New York: Alfred A. Knopf, 2013); Devon W. Carbado and Mitu Gulati, *Acting White? Rethinking Race in "Post-Racial" America* (Oxford: Oxford University Press, 2013).

[247] Lateral lawyer movement between 1945 and 1962 was uncommon. See Eli Wald, "Lawyer Mobility and Legal Ethics: Resolving the Tension between Confidentiality and Contemporary Lawyers' Career Paths," *Journal of the Legal Profession* 31 (2007): 199. A majority of the interviewees joined a law firm and have practiced with it ever since. Some interviewees did leave their respective firms to assume public positions and returned to the firms thereafter.

universe that consisted of the nineteen largest law firms in New York City in 1963,[248] and excluded from the list one law firm that dissolved.[249]

The study benefited from the assistance of two knowledgeable sources—a New York City law professor who is an advisor to the Center for Jewish History in New York and a New York City law professor who was the director of a program in Jewish law and interdisciplinary studies. These informants were knowledgeable with respect to the experience of the Jewish lawyers who were the object of my inquiry and familiar with the history of New York City Jewish law firms. These sources were asked to review the list of large firms and suggest other New York City firms of which they were aware that were either a white-shoe firm, a Jewish law firm, or a mixed law firm. They confirmed that the list of large law firms included all the firms that are traditionally considered white-shoe firms. Based on their advice, I added to the list three law firms, two Jewish firms and one mixed firm, founded in the late 1960s, but after 1963. The final list of firms consisted of twenty-one of the largest firms in New York City.

My unit of analysis was the Jewish male lawyer who graduated from law school between 1945 and 1962 and was interested in joining a large New York City law firm.[250] My focus in the study was the attorney's interest and decision to apply to law school, his law school experience, his experience with the large law firm job market after law school, and his career path (for example, attempting to join a white-shoe firm as opposed to joining or founding a Jewish firm). I wanted to study the ways and the extent, if any, that ethnic and religious-based considerations played a role or were perceived to have played a role in the career of the attorney, and in his understanding and perception of the organization of the large firm. The purposive universe was limited to partners who have remained with their respective firms and thus experienced not only hiring and promotion with the firm, but also had the perspective of long tenure and the opportunity to observe

---

[248] Large New York City law firms experienced steady growth between 1945 and 1965. While the internal ranking within the largest nineteen firms changed, the list itself was stable. The firms in the initial list were, in order of their size: Shearman & Sterling; White & Case; Cravath, Swaine & Moore; Dewey, Ballantine; Milbank, Tweed; Sullivan & Cromwell; Davis, Polk; Simpson, Thatcher & Bartlett; Cahill, Gordon; Kaye, Scholer; Paul, Weiss, Cleary, Gottlieb; Cadwalader; Donovan, Leisure; Rogers & Wells; Fried Frank; Weil Gotshal; Coudert Brothers; and Skadden, Arps. The largest law firm, Shearman & Sterling, had 134 attorneys, and the smallest, Skadden, Arps, had ten attorneys. Remarkably, the same firms were the largest law firms in New York City in 1981, although the internal ranking within the list changed. See above, Table 2.

[249] Coudert Brothers dissolved in 2005. See Ellen Rosen, "The Complicated End of an Ex-Law Firm," *N.Y. Times*, Feb, 9, 2007, C7.

[250] The number of female attorneys who graduated from law school between 1945 and 1962, joined a large New York City firm, and continued to practice with the firm, was very low, and I decided to exclude them from the universe. Furthermore, I was interested in studying ethnic and religious-based discrimination and decided to avoid the separate and important question of gender discrimination. See generally Chambliss, "Organizational Determinants," 739–40 (asserting that the common tendency to treat women and racial minorities as a single undifferentiated group is misguided).

changes in the firm's employment practices, if any, over time.[251] From December 2004 through July 2005, I conducted twenty-two semi-structured interviews, which were all taped and transcribed verbatim. Page numbers in the informants' citations in this chapter refer to the pages of the transcribed interviews. I spoke with twenty partners at fourteen large law firms. On three occasions, I interviewed more than one partner from a firm, and, thus, I was able to corroborate much of the information.[252] I also spoke with two former partners at two additional law firms who currently hold public office. The respondents were told that their identity would be kept confidential.

Within the list of law firms, I contacted respondents by snowball sampling. After interviewing a partner, I asked him for a list of partners at other firms who would be the most knowledgeable about the experience of the cohort of Jewish lawyers I was studying. I contacted the referrals and continued the process. Snowball sampling can introduce bias into a study in that the sample firms and the respondents within the firms may not be representative of the universe, but rather of a selected group or network within a universe. These potential biases are always a concern.

In this case, I believe bias through snowball sampling is less of a concern. The purpose of the present chapter is not to generalize to a broad universe, but to explore ideas and perceptions about the growth of Jewish law firms in New York City. The qualitative interviews provided in-depth descriptions of the experiences of these lawyers and law firms. It is important to remember that the number of all large New York City law firms was small.[253] Furthermore, within the list of law firms, the universe of study was restricted to Jewish male lawyers who graduated from law school between 1945 and 1962 and were still practicing with their respective firms. Within that small universe, my sample was relatively large, consisting of twenty-two interviews and sixteen law firms.[254] Finally, in exploring the experience of Jewish male lawyers attempting to break into the large law firm sphere between 1945 and 1962, I was interested in the possibility of the existence of a network that possibly facilitated the effort. In any event, I contacted every candidate for interview identified by my snowball sampling.

---

[251] While it would have enriched the study to have the perspective of attorneys from all law firms on the list, time and resource constraints did not allow for this.

[252] Interviewing a second partner at a firm was possible when more than one partner met the criteria: graduation from law school between 1945 and 1962 and continuous practice with the firm.

[253] The universe consisted of twenty-one law firms. The nineteenth "largest" firm in the universe had ten attorneys in 1963.

[254] Snowball sampling resulted in a fairly robust list of twenty-four candidates for interviews. I contacted all twenty-four attorneys referenced by my interviewees. Two declined to participate in the study.

Jewish Lawyers for Causes of the Political Right

Ann Southworth[*]

American Jews have long defied the notion that socio-economic status is the best predictor of Republican Party support.[1] Jews enjoy greater affluence than most other ethno-religious groups,[2] but they are among the most loyal supporters of the Democratic Party.[3] As Milton Himmelfarb famously remarked: "Jews earn like Episcopalians and vote like Puerto Ricans."

Explanations for this apparent anomaly focus on a variety of factors, some relating to Jewish religious values, and others rooted in particular historical circumstances. The most commonly cited reasons include Jews' experience of discrimination and resulting sympathy for marginalized social groups,[4] Judaic culture and its commitment to social justice,[5] Jews' educational achievement, which is correlated with support for liberal causes, and the power of political identity—the influence that Jews' longstanding attachment to the Democratic Party continues to exert on their allegiances.[6] A perception that the Republican Party has harbored antisemitic elements and defended social hierarchies that have impeded Jews' advancement has reinforced Jews' identification with the political left.[7] Observers periodically speculate about whether and when Jews may eventually shift their support to the Republican Party.[8] With the exception of the Orthodox community,

---

[*] Professor of Law, University of California–Irvine School of Law.

[1] Robert Lerner, Althea K. Nagai and Stanley Rothman, "Marginality and Liberalism Among Jewish Elites," *The Public Opinion Quarterly* 53 (1989): 330–52; Nathan Glazer, "The Anomalous Liberalism of American Jews," in *The Americanization of the Jews*, eds. Robert M. Seltzer and Norman J. Cohen (New York: New York University Press, 1995), 133–43.

[2] Pew Research Center, *U.S. Religious Landscape Survey* (Washington, D.C.: Pew Forum, 2008), 58–61.

[3] Steven M. Cohen, Sam Abrams, and Judith Veinstein, "American Jews and the 2008 Presidential Election: As Democratic and Liberal as Ever?" The Berman Jewish Policy Archive at NYU Wagner, New York, New York.

[4] Steven M. Cohen, *The Dimensions of Jewish Liberalism* (New York: American Jewish Committee, 1989).

[5] Michael Walzer, "Is Liberalism (Still) Good for the Jews?" *Moment* (March 1986): 13–16.

[6] Cohen, Abrams, and Veinstein, "American Jews."

[7] Cohen, Dimensions of Jewish Liberalism; Steven M. Cohen and Charles S. Liebman, "American Jewish Liberalism: Unraveling the Strands," *The Public Opinion Quarterly* 61 (1997): 405–30.

[8] See, e.g., Alan M. Fisher, "Realignment of the Jewish Vote?" *Political Science Quarterly* 94 (1979): 97–116; Anna Greenberg and Kenneth D. Wald, "Still Liberal After All These

however, Jews have remained solidly in the Democratic camp.

Given this history, it is unsurprising that the best-known Jewish cause lawyers have served causes associated with the political left, e.g., civil rights, civil liberties, human rights, economic justice, and the women's movement. This essay focuses on a rarer and less noticed phenomenon—Jewish lawyers who serve causes of the American political right. I consider here sixteen Jewish lawyers who were among seventy-two lawyers whom I interviewed in 2001 and 2002 for a book on lawyers for conservative and libertarian causes.[9]

The interviews grew out of a research project that I pursued jointly with John P. Heinz and Anthony Paik.[10] We examined lawyers who serve several strands of the conservative alliance that has coalesced behind the Republican Party during the past few decades, including social conservatives, libertarians, and business interests. Those constituencies pursue competing and sometimes incompatible public policy objectives,[11] but they have formed a successful and enduring coalition in American politics since the late 1960s.

The research was not designed to assess the role of Jewish lawyers in the conservative movement, to explore the relationship between these lawyers' religious beliefs and their political projects, or to generate rigorous statistical comparisons of Jewish and non-Jewish advocates for conservative causes. Moreover, the confidentiality commitments that I made to the interviewed lawyers prevent me from offering detailed profiles. Instead, this essay pursues a modest aim—to offer several observations about these lawyers' characteristics, political values, and positions in conservative lawyer networks, and to suggest how these lawyers' experiences and views might relate to broader trends in Jewish political identity and voting patterns.

The interviews revealed striking differences among lawyers for the core constituencies of the conservative alliance—social conservatives, libertarians, and business interests. Advocates for social conservative groups generally came from more economically modest backgrounds than their business counterparts, attended less elite law schools, and were less likely to work in major metropolitan areas. Many of them said that they looked to God as a

---

Years?" in *Jews in American Politics*, eds. L. Sandy Maisel and Ira N. Forman (Lanham, MD: Rowman & Littlefield, 2001); Norman Podhoretz, *Why Are Jews Liberals?* (New York: Random House, 2009).

[9] Ann Southworth, *Lawyers of the Right: Professionalizing the Conservative Movement* (Chicago: University of Chicago Press, 2008).

[10] John P. Heinz, Anthony Paik, and Ann Southworth, "Lawyers for Conservative Causes: Clients, Ideology, and Social Distance," *Law & Society Review* 37 (2003): 5–50; Anthony Paik, Ann Southworth, and John P. Heinz, "Lawyers of the Right: Networks and Organization," *Law & Social Inquiry* 32 (2007): 883–917.

[11] Jerome L Himmelstein, *To the Right: The Transformation of American Conservativism* (Berkeley: University of California Press, 1990), 14; George H. Nash, *The Conservative Intellectual Movement in America* (Wilmington, DE: Intercollegiate Studies Institute, 1998), xv–xvi.

regular source of inspiration and guidance. Lawyers for libertarian groups also generally came from working and middle-class backgrounds, but the goals they pursued were largely secular. Most of the business representatives came from economically secure backgrounds, and they characterized their advocacy as work rather than activism. Lawyers for the core constituencies appeared to inhabit different social worlds, and they had little contact with one another.

Some lawyers, however, appeared to serve as mediators or brokers among the constituencies. They did so partly through their work for "mediator" organizations, such as the Federalist Society, American Enterprise Institute, and Heritage Foundation, which seek to appeal to all elements of the conservative alliance and to promote communication and cooperation among them.[12] Such organizations attract disproportionate foundation funding and especially elite and prominent lawyers, indicating they may play an important role in integrating the conservative movement.[13] Nevertheless, deep cultural differences among lawyers for the various constituencies make cooperation difficult.[14]

The Jewish lawyers in this sample worked almost exclusively for libertarian, business, and mediator organizations—not social conservative causes. They held more elite credentials than the other religious groups represented in the sample. Most of the Jewish lawyers for libertarian and business interests were not particularly religious, or committed to the Republican Party or the conservative movement, while those who worked for mediator organizations were more observant, more involved in Republican Party activities, and better-integrated into the larger network of conservative lawyers. Overall, the Jewish lawyers appeared to have more in common with the Type I Protestants—a category that includes "mainstream" Protestant denominations: Episcopalian, Methodist, Lutheran, Presbyterian, and Congregationalist[15]—than with any other religious group.

The Research Design

To define the set of lawyers to study, we drew a sample of conservative and libertarian organizations using several complementary methods. We first chose seventeen "issue events"—legislative controversies involving domestic policy issues that were important to the different constituencies of the conservative alliance in the late 1990s. The events included proposals

---

[12] Heinz, Paik, and Southworth, "Lawyers for Conservative Causes."

[13] Research on the communication network among a subset of the interviewed lawyers lends empirical support to the idea that the Federalist Society and Heritage Foundation play important roles in uniting lawyers for the different constituencies (Paik, Southworth, and Heinz, "Lawyers of the Right"; Southworth, *Lawyers of the Right*, 142–45).

[14] Southworth, *Lawyers of the Right*.

[15] See John P. Heinz, Robert L. Nelson, Rebecca L. Sandefur, and Edward Laumann, *Urban Lawyers: The New Social Structure of the Bar* (Chicago: University of Chicago Press, 2005), 60–61.

regarding abortion, affirmative action, school prayer, tort reform, environmental policy, gay rights, civil rights, flag burning, funding for the National Endowment for the Arts, the minimum wage, compulsory union dues, property rights, gun control, criminal procedure, funding for the Legal Services Corporation, and cultural assimilation for immigrants. We then searched for articles about these events in eighteen newspapers and magazines: *Wall Street Journal, New York Times, Washington Post, Los Angeles Times, Chicago Tribune, Dallas Morning News, Atlanta Journal & Constitution, Time, Newsweek, U.S. News & World Report, National Journal, Washington Monthly, Roll Call, Washington Times, National Review, Weekly Standard, American Spectator,* and *Public Interest*. This method produced the names of eighty-one organizations, seventy-one of which used lawyers in some capacity. To compensate for the issue-event method's possible bias in favoring lobbying groups over litigation and research organizations, we supplemented the list with five additional organizations that were particularly active in those policy arenas using two directories: The Conservative Directory, published by RightGuide.com, and the Heritage Foundation's list of "U.S. Policy Organizations."[16] I then identified particularly prominent lawyers for the seventy-six organizations that used lawyers, requested interviews with ninety-eight of them, and interviewed seventy-two. The interviewed lawyers include many leaders of the conservative movement, including prominent representatives of all the major constituencies. They worked for conservative religious groups, abortion opponents, libertarian organizations, groups devoted primarily to business interests, affirmative action opponents, "order-maintenance" groups (organizations concerned with crime and/or preserving the established social and cultural order), and mediator organizations.

Table 1 shows the characteristics of the interviewed lawyers. They are overwhelmingly male. They worked for a large variety of organizations in various roles including as founders, officers, litigators, scholars, and consultants. The religious backgrounds of these lawyers varied, with Catholics, Protestants, and Jews, as well as lawyers who described themselves as not religious, all represented. Their practice settings included advocacy organizations and public interest law firms, think tanks, universities, trade associations, large law firms, and small firms. Roughly half had received degrees from "elite" or "prestige" law schools, defined as the top 20 schools in the U.S. News and World Report rankings.[17] The largest number were located in Washington, D.C., but others practiced in Virginia, New York, California, Arizona, Illinois, and several other Midwestern states.

---

[16] Bridgett G. Wagner, John E. Hilboldt, and Eric T. Korsvall, *Policy Experts 2000: A Guide to Public Policy Experts and Organizations* (Washington, D.C.: Heritage Foundation, 2000), 681–789. For a more complete description of the research design, see Heinz, Paik, and Southworth, "Lawyers for Conservative Causes."

[17] The "elite" category included schools ranked in the top 7 in the 2000 *U.S. News & World Report* rankings, and the "prestige" category included those ranked from 8 to 20.

Table 1: Characteristics of Interviewed Lawyers

	#	%		Practice Setting	#	%
Gender				**Practice Setting**		
Male	67	93		Advocacy Organizations	35	48
Female	5	7		Think tanks	5	7
				Universities	8	11
Constituency				Trade associations	4	6
Religious	16	22		Large firms	7	10
Pro-life	9	12		Small firms & solo	13	18
Order maintenance	4	6				
Libertarian	19	26		**Location**		
Affirmative action	4	6		DC	30	41
Business	11	15		DC suburb	4	6
Mediator	9	12		Other major city	22	31
				elsewhere	16	22
Religion				**Law School**		
Catholic	15	21		Elite	21	29
Protestant II	16	22		Prestige	12	17
Protestant I	19	26		Regional	14	19
Jewish	16	22		Local	25	35
Not religious	4	6				
Other	2	3				

Table 2: Characteristics of Interviewed Lawyers by Religious Categories (Column Percentages)

	Jewish (*n*=16)	Catholic (*n*=15)	Protestant II (*n*=16)	Protestant I (*n*=19)
Law School				
% Elite	63	20	13	32
% Prestige	19	13	25	16
% Regional	6	33	6	26
% Local	13	33	56	26
Federal Clerkship				
% Yes	37	13	6	21
% No	63	87	94	79
Location				
% DC	56	33	19	53
% DC suburb	0	13	12	0
% Major city	44	33	31	21
% Elsewhere	0	20	38	26
Constituency Served				
% Religious	0	33	50	11
% Abortion	6	27	12.5	11
% Order maintenance	0	0	0	5
% Libertarian	50	6	25	21
% Affirmative action	6	13	0	5
% Business	19	6	12.5	26
% Mediator	19	13	0	21
Practice Setting				
% Advocacy organization	25	53	81	26
% Think tank	6	7	6	10.5
% University	19	7	6	16
% Trade association	6	7	0	10.5
% Large firm	19	7	0	16
% Small firm	25	20	6	21

The Jewish Lawyers in the Sample

Sixteen of the seventy-two interviewed lawyers identified themselves as Jewish in response to a question asking about religion.[18] Table 2 compares the characteristics of the interviewed lawyers by religious category. Jews were an especially elite group in terms of professional credentials: eighty-two percent of them had attended law schools in the elite or prestige categories, and thirty-seven percent of them had clerked for federal judges. Those proportions are substantially higher than for any other religious category, including Type I Protestants. Many of them had served at high levels in Republican Administrations. Several of the older lawyers claimed prominent liberals as mentors, while the mentors of the younger lawyers included well-known libertarians and conservatives, such as Milton Friedman, Richard Epstein, Richard Posner, Ronald Coase, Henry Manne, Edwin Meese, Robert Bork, Alex Kozinski, Laurence Silberman, Douglas Ginsburg, Charles Cooper, and Clarence Thomas. More than two-thirds of them were active in the Federalist Society.

The Jewish lawyers were disproportionately affiliated with libertarian, business, and mediator groups: eight served libertarian groups (working on issues such as school choice, property rights, and regulation); one worked for an organization that opposes affirmative action; three served trade groups; and three worked for mediator organizations. One outlier worked for a pro-life group. None of them worked for groups that sought to prohibit flag burning, outlaw same sex marriage, expand opportunities for school prayer, or restrict pornography. In the types of causes they pursued, they differed substantially from Catholic and Type II Protestants (defined as all Protestant denominations except Lutherans, Methodists, Presbyterians, Episcopalians and Congregationalists). More than half of the interviewed Catholic and Type II Protestant lawyers served conservative religious advocacy organizations and pro-life groups. Type I Protestants were much less likely than Catholics or Type II Protestants to serve social conservative groups, but their participation in those causes was still much more substantial than the participation of Jewish lawyers.

Jews were fairly evenly distributed among the different types of practice settings—again, much more like Type 1 Protestants than Catholics or Type II Protestants, who were heavily concentrated in nonprofit advocacy groups. The Jewish lawyers worked exclusively in major urban centers, compared to roughly three-quarters of the overall sample, two-thirds of the Catholic lawyers, and just half of the Type II Protestants.

There appears to be a strong correspondence between the Jewish lawyers' religious identity, the types of causes they served, and the extent to which they identified with the Republican Party and the conservative movement. None of the Jewish lawyers who served business advocacy

---

[18] The question asked, "What is your religion? That is, are you either Protestant, Roman Catholic, Jewish, or something else?" The follow up question asked for greater specificity—e.g., "Orthodox, Conservative, Reform, Other"?

groups described themselves as strong Republicans or observant Jews. These lawyers tended to vote Republican but called themselves Independents. One business advocate said that he is a member of a loose-knit organization of Jews who are uncomfortable with organized religion, and another said that he typically buys a ticket to attend services on High Holy Days. On the other hand, all three of the lawyers associated with mediator organizations reported that they were registered Republicans and observant Jews. One was an Orthodox Jew who called himself "a hard core conservative guy," and another explained that he was part of a tight-knit network of observant Jews who were highly active in the conservative movement. Of the lawyers for libertarian groups, two described themselves as strong Republicans, and both of them attended conservative temples. The other two registered Republicans among the sixteen, both advocates for libertarian causes, were not observant. One attributed his loyalty to the G.O.P. to his experience as the child of immigrants from a repressive Communist regime. He explained that he never had "that much in common with social conservatives," but that "on international points, economic points," the Republican Party mostly got it right. Two prominent lawyers for libertarian organizations said that they identified more with the Libertarian Party than the G.O.P., and neither was an observant Jew. One of those lawyers, who grew up in "Jewish New York" and "always ... had a strong view of autonomy," said that he was "estranged from the political system" and "not active" in his synagogue. The other said, "My party is the Libertarian Party" and reported that he last attended a synagogue two years ago for High Holy Day services—"a Reform service with a very liberal rabbi [and] a female cantor."

Some of the Jewish lawyers commented on their apparently anomalous roles as advocates for causes associated with the conservative movement, although the older lawyers offered such explanations more often than did the younger lawyers. Several of the older lawyers volunteered that they once counted themselves liberal Democrats. A business advocate had participated in the Chicago Freedom Movement and in labor and tenant organizing efforts, and even spent a night in jail in the 1960s. After graduating from law school, he had worked on labor issues in a Democratic administration, remained during the Reagan administration, found that he was able to accomplish what he called "some very progressive stuff" under Reagan that the Carter administration was "too afraid to touch" (because union concessions would be required to reach agreement on the legislation), and eventually switched his registration from Democratic to Independent.[19] A leading

---

[19] Explaining why he entered government service rather than private practice, he observed: "The kinds of law firms that I would have been interested in from a corporate law standpoint really had no room for Jews, and I did not want to go anywhere that, with a little luck and some talent, I couldn't go to the top—have a shot at the top." For an account of discrimination against Jewish lawyers in the first half of the twentieth century, see Jerold S. Auerbach, *Unequal Justice: Lawyers and Social Change in Modern America* (New York: Oxford University Press, 1976). An analysis of current disparities in the

property rights lawyer described himself as a registered Republican who continues to be a liberal Democrat as that label applied in the Kennedy era—before "the Democratic Party was taken over by a bunch of wacko radicals" around the time of the McGovern campaign. He rejected the idea that his property rights work constituted conservative advocacy, arguing this his eminent domain work primarily benefits vulnerable individuals who are wronged by abusive exercises of government power: "Property owners in eminent domain [do not receive] due process of law. The government can come in, seize their property and kick them out and say, 'Sue me.' They had been historically subjected to gross under-compensation.... The city could drive a bulldozer through a building that housed a business worth a lot of money, and you weren't entitled to a nickel for the destruction of the business. I was representing people who [were] being shabbily treated or grossly mistreated ... while courts were averting their eyes." Another property rights lawyer, whose parents were "old Roosevelt Democrats," reported feeling that "the Democratic Party has run away from me." An affirmative action opponent did not consider himself a conservative but strongly resisted the notion that race and ethnicity should influence decision-making in the private and public sectors. The only Jewish pro-life advocate said that his opposition to abortion flowed from Jewish doctrine: "That life is paramount and that you don't snuff it out." In most other respects, he still counted himself a liberal at the time of the interview.[20]

The younger Jewish lawyers generally indicated that their political commitments had not undergone any dramatic transformation from left to right. A school choice advocate said, "I've always had very strong beliefs toward the conservative or libertarian side," and an opponent of regulation claimed to have "been a libertarian since my last year of high school after watching *The Fountainhead* on late-night television." A lawyer for a mediator group recalled that he had "always been skeptical—at least from the time I can remember—skeptical of big government."

The three Jewish lawyers who worked for mediator organizations commented on the relationship between their religious backgrounds and service to conservative causes. A lawyer in his fifties had been deeply involved in conservative movement politics since his days as a graduate student at an elite university, where he worked closely with a leading economist and came to know a cadre of graduate students who eventually became conservative movement leaders. He served in several appointed positions in the Reagan Administration, including an international affairs job that allowed him to observe "Israel bashing" up close and protest against it. Since then, he has been involved in a variety of libertarian and conservative causes, including

---

presence of Jews in the bar and as partners in large law firms appears in Heinz et al., *Urban Lawyers*, 66–68.

[20] The same lawyer reported that he had been very disappointed when the ACLU and Anti-Defamation League decided to take pro-choice stances. He also indicated that he sought to build political alliances on abortion across religious lines, even though he did not agree with the absolutism and radical tactics of some Christian abortion opponents.

service to an organization composed mostly of conservative Jews who seek to "affirm the congruence between Judaism's ethical and social world on the one hand and the traditional norms of American society ... on the other." He said that he sees "a connection between my religious beliefs, my political involvement, the kinds of cases I work on, [and] my appetites for other types of civic involvement."

A lawyer in his sixties had graduated from an elite law school in a class that included an extraordinary number of well-known activists of the political left. He said that his own interest in "fighting segregation" had inspired him to attend law school and thereafter to work on voting issues in the South. He claims still to continue to share his liberal law school classmates' commitment to social justice and "mak[ing] a difference," though he now endorses a starkly different set of policy prescriptions. He recalled "being absolutely rocked out of [his] skull" while reading an op-ed piece by Irving Kristol on the New York City subway; the column "gave all these arguments [for] voting for Nixon, and I thought, 'Oh my God, I'm not alone. There are people who think this way.... There is nothing wrong with me!'" He described the day when he switched his registration from Democrat to Republican because he had concluded that liberals did not share his "most basic assumption" about "the goodness of America and its capacity to achieve social justice." The experience, he said, was profoundly disorienting:

> I'm Jewish. The best man at my wedding was a Democratic member of Congress with 100 percent voting record with the ADA.... [But] in the ... most morally courageous act of my life, I went to get the card—a registration card, checked the box called, gulp, Republican, signed the form and went to the postal box and stuck it in, and became, as I said, at the time, the only Republican I knew, and having done it I didn't feel Jewish for six months.... [Later], of course, I started associating with people who had gone through pretty much the same emotional identity experience I went through.

The same lawyer contrasted his experience with that of a younger generation of Jews whose conservative commitments did not require such a repudiation of their past and attendant "emotional and identity contortions."

One such younger lawyer recalled that his parents, both public school teachers, had struggled financially to enable their children to attend a Jewish day school because they felt that the public schools were failing: "It always struck me as incredibly unfair and inequitable that they had to pay twice; they had to pay their property taxes and they had to pay for our private schools." He recalled then how he came to embrace conservatism while still very young:

> Growing up in New York City in the 1970s ... our taxes were unbearably high. There were no services.... It was hard to have a lot faith in "big" government. My parents were both school teachers. They constantly talked about how they were being ripped off by the unions....

How corrupt the system was, how they weren't rewarded. How awful public schools were. How many welfare cheats there were. How often the welfare families didn't have the same kinds of values as the other families—even poor families that they encountered. And all I did was just listen to them. I listened to them about the dangers of drugs, about the fact that there's right and wrong. And they wonder why I became a Republican? I wonder why they've remained [Democrats]. I know the reasons, two reasons. The first reason is they're from New York and everybody's a Democrat. And because they're Jews. And there was this long tradition of Jews being Democrats. And I used to say that my Grandfather—everything that he said was incredibly rightwing and conservative, even, frankly, Paleo-Con.... But, it's as if he would go in the ballot box intending to vote Republican, and the hand of God would come and move his hand to the left. And my parents—it's not to say my parents have never voted Republican. They have, as opposed to my grandfather, who I'm sure never did. But their identity is pretty much Democratic.... I didn't have any of that baggage.

Lawyers associated with mediator groups play important roles in integrating the conservative coalition by helping to bind together seemingly disparate constituencies. One of the most difficult challenges associated with these groups, and one of the most critical tasks for the Republican Party, is finding common ground between the two core constituencies—social conservatives, on the one hand, and business interests, on the other.[21] Two of the Jewish lawyers who served mediator organizations commented on their efforts to build bridges among those constituencies. One, who said that he was very much involved day-to-day in "coordinating and ... strategizing for the conservative movement as a whole," reported that one of his primary projects is trying to knit diverse groups together by forging some kind of understanding about their common commitment "to pursue traditional values" through means that "do not impinge on liberty." He added, "I personally believe in fusionism"—a term coined by Frank Meyer, who in the 1950s tried to unite libertarians and traditionalism around a synthesis of ideas about freedom and moral authority.[22] Another lawyer for a mediator organization, who has been active on a broad variety of domestic and foreign policy issues, is an outspoken proponent of giving religious faith a more prominent place in the public sphere while at the same time protecting religious institutions from governmental interference.[23] Some of his

---

[21] Heinz, Southworth, and Paik, "Lawyers for Conservative Causes"; Southworth, *Lawyers of the Right*.

[22] George H. Nash, *The Conservative Intellectual Movement in America* (Wilmington, DE: Intercollegiate Studies Institute, 1998), 321–22; Paul Gottfried, *The Conservative Movement* (New York: MacMillan, 1993), 16–17.

[23] He opposed a proposal that would have banned faith-based organizations from evangelizing as a condition of receiving government grants to provide social services. He said that he had urged the leader of a major evangelical group to "get down on his knees and pray that he will do the right thing here—[How can the government] tell a minister that

work focused on "ending the caricature of religious people, particularly Christians." He asserted that there are close parallels between the establishment's disdain for Christian evangelicals today and its past prejudice against Jews: "Christians have become the Jews of the 21st Century—the scapegoats of choice." He also said that his "extraordinary experience as [a] Jew in the evangelical movement" had reinforced his interest in his own faith.[24] Christian evangelicals' firm commitment to Israel's future undoubtedly contributes to the effort to build ties with observant Jews.

Although several of the Jewish lawyers in this research served mediator organizations and may have played important roles in integrating the coalition, previous research on the communication network among a subset of the interviewed lawyers[25] suggests reasons to doubt whether Jewish conservatives are the most central players in the network. In the interviews, I asked lawyers whether and how often they contacted each of fifty prominent conservative lawyers.[26] Twenty-six lawyers were both interviewed and included on the list of notables, and twenty-four of the twenty-six were in contact with at least one of the others during the twelve months prior to the interviews. Figure 1a shows the connections among these lawyers (represented by circles) who were both interviewed and on the list of notables.[27] The overall pattern of the network shows a central core surrounded by a rim of less connected lawyers.

Figure 1b shows the constituencies served and the religious affiliations of the lawyers in Figure 1a. Two distinct clusters flank a tightly knit core. The top of the figure includes only social conservatives, while the lower right side consists exclusively of business interests and the left of libertarians. As indicated in Figure 1a, the lawyers in these distinct parts of the network communicated very little with one another. The "core" of the figure consists of seven lawyers who received ten or more contacts each. One Jewish lawyer is in that core, but the others are all in a row across the bottom of the space. This figure suggests that religion is somehow related to

---

he can't say what is fundamental to his faith?"

[24] He elaborated: "All of this has had a wonderful effect for me personally of rooting me more firmly in my own faith. I never confused Judaism with liberal politics—ever.... But, having grown up in an Orthodox Jewish environment, I backslid terribly. And just becoming involved in [the evangelical movement] has sent me on a search for a synagogue where I could feel comfortable.... There was always this same notion, which says—which makes me innately conservative—Yes, the dead hand of the past can suffocate, but cut yourself off from your roots and you're dead."

[25] Figures 1a and 1b and their analyses come from Paik, Southworth, and Heinz, "Lawyers of the Right."

[26] The names on the list were selected through extensive prior research on the conservative movement (see Heinz, Paik, and Southworth, "Lawyers for Conservative Causes") and through consultation with knowledgeable informants in the field. All of the lawyers on the list worked for one of the eighty-six organizations identified through the methods described above.

[27] The arrows show the connections. Some of the arrows have a point at one end but not the other because not all of the reported ties are reciprocated.

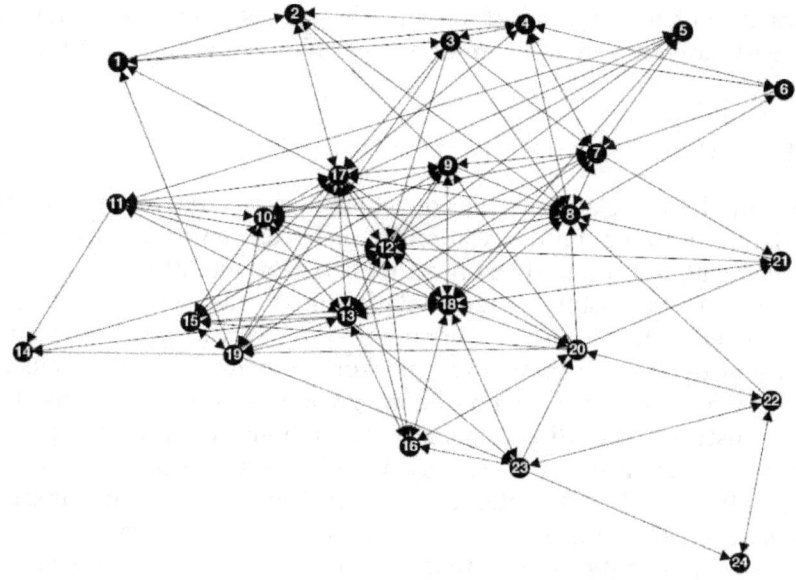

Figure 1a. Contact Links Among Notable Conservative Lawyers (N=24)

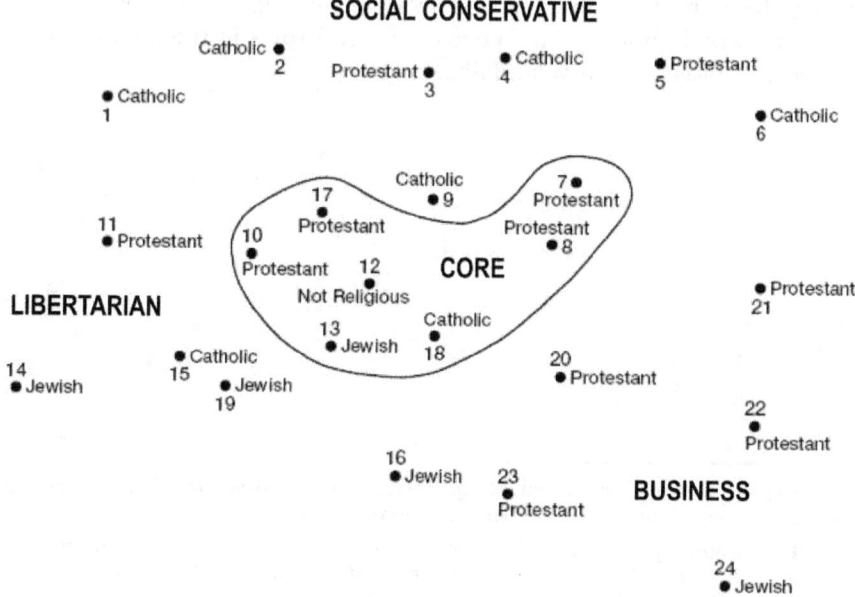

Figure 1b. Religious Affiliations of 24 Notables

the structure of the network of conservative lawyers, but it also indicates that Jewish lawyers generally are on the periphery, not in the core, of that network.[28]

Conclusion

Overall, the views and patterns of activity described here are consistent with a larger literature on the relationship between Jews and the conservative movement and recent data on voting behavior and attitudes. As would be predicted by the history of Jews' relationship to the American conservative movement,[29] the Jewish lawyers in my study were situated primarily in the parts of the conservative lawyer network associated with markets and individualism, not those committed to greater government support for religious institutions or discouraging abortion, homosexuality, and pornography. The Jewish lawyers' characteristics and service to causes were more similar to those of Type I Protestants than to Type II Protestants or Catholics, perhaps reflecting a growing similarity between Jews and liberal Protestant denominations in attitudes about a variety of issues.[30] Moreover, these lawyers' patterns of service are consistent with research finding a link between religiosity and Republican Party support;[31] the lawyers who identified most strongly with the G.O.P. were religiously observant, while those who were more politically independent tended to be secular Jews. Lawyers associated with mediator groups, including some Jewish lawyers, seek to bind together the various constituencies of the Republican coalition. But Jewish lawyers do not appear to occupy central roles in the larger network of advocates for conservative and libertarian causes.

---

[28] For a more detailed discussion of the relationship between religion and network structure, see Paik, Southworth, and Heinz, "Lawyers of the Right."

[29] Edward Shapiro, "Right Turn? Jews and the American Conservative Movement," in *Jews in American Politics*, eds. L. Sandy Maisel and Ira Forman (New York: Rowman & Littlefield, 2001), 195–211; Podhoretz, *Why Are Jews Liberals?*

[30] Cohen and Liebman, "American Jewish Liberalism," 421–22. Summarizing the findings of their research, Cohen and Liebman assert that "with respect to many key issues, [Jews] think like Episcopalians" (ibid., 426).

[31] Cohen and Liebman, "American Jewish Liberalism"; Steven M. Cohen, *American Modernity and Jewish Identity* (New York: Tavistock Publications, 1983).

Jews, Antisemitism, and Legal Development

Gentleman's Agreement: The Antisemitic Origins of Restrictions on Stockholder Litigation

Lawrence E. Mitchell[*]

Introduction

In March 1944, Governor Thomas Dewey signed into law a bill passed after only two days of consideration in the New York State Legislature. That law was section 61-b (now section 627) of the *New York Business Corporations Law*. The statute gave corporations sued derivatively the right to demand that plaintiffs post a bond as security for the corporation's litigation expenses, including legal fees, if they owned less than $50,000 in value (about $619,350 in 2010) or 5% of the corporation's outstanding stock.[1] Lawyers and judges at the time universally acknowledged that the statute effectively eliminated derivative suits by making them far too expensive for a plaintiff to maintain. The statute was the first of its kind and similar statutes now exist in 19 states. Almost every state has some form of statute restricting the standing of derivative suit plaintiffs.[2]

Section 61-b had a highly unusual birth. Most New York legislation originated either within the legislature, in the New York Law Revision Commission, or in the Judicial Council of the State of New York. None of these organizations were involved in the conception of section 61-b, nor were they asked for their opinions.[3] More surprising, the statute was passed despite

---

[*] Professor Lawrence E. Mitchell is the Joseph C. Hostetler–Baker & Hostetler Professor of Law at Case Western Reserve University School of Law. He is co-editor of the SSRN Journal of Multidisciplinary Business Law and the author of a number of law review articles and several books, including *Corporate Irresponsibility: America's Newest Export* (2001) and *The Speculation Economy: How Finance Triumphed Over Industry* (2007), which was awarded *ForeWord Magazine*'s 2007 Gold Medal as Best Book of the Year in Business & Economics and a 2008 "IPPY" Silver Medal in Finance and Economics. Professor Mitchell's areas of expertise include, among others, regulation, fiduciary duty and corporate law, governance, and finance.

[1] At the same time, it passed a related statute requiring that the plaintiffs have held their shares at the time of the wrong complained of. Several years earlier, and under circumstances similar to those under which section 61-b was passed, the legislature passed a statute requiring corporations sued derivatively to indemnify defendants (but not plaintiffs) who were wholly or partly successful for their reasonable expenses, including legal fees. The inflation calculator used is available at *CPI Inflation Calculator*, online: Bureau of Labour Statistics, at http://data.bls.gov.

[2] Deborah DeMott, *Shareholder Derivative Actions: Law and Practice*, loose-leaf (consulted on November 5, 2010) (Eagan, MN: West, 2010), at § 3.01.

[3] Sergei S. Zlinkoff, "The American Investor and the Constitutionality of Section 61-B of the New York General Corporate Law," *Yale Law Journal* 54 (1945): 359.

opposition by almost all of the major bar organizations in New York City.[4] No hearings were held on the statute, and there was barely any legislative debate.[5]

Section 61-b was a product of the efforts of the New York Chamber of Commerce, a non-governmental organization composed primarily of the executives of substantial corporations.[6] The Chamber of Commerce had commissioned a report to study the abuses of derivative actions and to recommend reform a year before the bill's introduction in the legislature. The report, known as the Wood Report, was only released simultaneously with the introduction of the bill it was meant to justify.

Restricting stockholder litigation to those stockholders who demonstrably had a significant financial interest in the corporation appeared to make sense. It was, after all, a way of deterring frivolous suits. In the 1975 case of *Blue Chip Stamps v. Manor Drug Stores*,[7] Justice Rehnquist's only securities law opinion in his thirty years on the United States Supreme Court, he echoed the same concerns about frivolous litigation while imposing important limitations on the ability of plaintiffs to sue corporations for securities fraud once class actions had replaced derivative suits. The case began three decades of Supreme Court jurisprudence that imposed increasingly tight restrictions on plaintiffs.

There are legitimate reasons to be concerned about "strike suits"[8] and abusive litigation. But there is another story behind these doctrinal developments that becomes clear upon close examination of the historical record. The 1944 Act, I argue, was adopted as a proximate result of deeply

---

[4] These included the Committee on State Legislation of the New York County Lawyers' Association; the Federal Bar Association of New York, New Jersey and Connecticut; and the Law Reform Committee of the New York City Chapter of the National Lawyers' Guild. See George Hornstein, "The Death Knell of Stockholders' Derivative Suits in New York," *California Law Review* 32 (1944): 136. The New York County Lawyers' Association was dominated by the small firm and sole practitioner Jewish bar, and the Association of the Bar of the City of New York (ABCNY) was dominated by the large, Protestant "white shoe" firms. Although Hornstein noted ABCNY opposition, another contemporary writer, Victor House, notes that while the ABCNY "appears" to have opposed the legislation, there was no formal record of such opposition. See Victor House, "Stockholders' Suits and the Coudert-Mitchell Laws," *New York University Law Quarterly Review* 20 (1945): 377–401. Moreover, Zlinkoff, in his very careful article, does not mention the ABCNY at all. The lack of formal record is significant because the Association of the Bar was dominated by the very big-firm Protestant lawyers who play the villain in this piece and would have no reason to oppose the legislation. Thus, the lack of formal record calls into question the strength and intensity (and indeed the sincerity) of their opposition.

[5] Zlinkoff, *supra* note 3, at 355; Hornstein, *supra* note 4, at 124. It is worth noting that at this time direct actions by stockholders against directors were rare: see, e.g., *Gordon v. Elliman*, 119 N.E.2d 331 (N.Y. 1954) (broadly holding that derivative suits were the norm and the stockholders' class action was a thing of the future.)

[6] Zlinkoff, *supra* note 3, at 360 n. 34.

[7] 421 U.S. 723 (1975).

[8] The term "strike suit" is generally used to mean litigation brought for the main or sole purpose of forcing a settlement to the profit of plaintiffs' lawyers, rather than for the purpose of redressing an actual wrong and recovering damages for plaintiffs.

ingrained antisemitism in the New York bar and corporate executive suites. This antisemitism was the background for widespread distrust of the plaintiffs' bar. It provided the foundation and structural conditions that made the case for the statute seem persuasive.[9]

I make my argument as follows: Part I analyzes the Wood Report, concluding that it used an empirically suspect small data sample with respect to derivative litigation and, at the same time, ignored readily available comprehensive litigation data demonstrating that derivative litigation was not a serious legal problem in the 1930s and 1940s. It also examines the rhetoric of the Wood Report and its sample set of plaintiffs to conclude that derivative suit plaintiffs overwhelmingly were Jewish and that the Wood Report subtly highlighted this fact. Part II presents empirical evidence from 1937 and 1960, which demonstrates that the plaintiffs' bar was overwhelmingly Jewish and was treated as the bottom of the legal hierarchy. Part III discusses the nature of the social antisemitism that led to the stratification of the bar and to prejudice against the plaintiffs' bar. Part IV concludes.

I. The Wood Report

A. The Problem of Derivative Litigation

The locus of (almost) absolute power in the corporation is the board of directors, a statutorily created body with the function of overseeing the affairs of the corporation. In light of the board's virtually absolute powers, the law has imposed on directors (as well as on corporate officers and other employees), fiduciary duties to the corporation designed to ensure that those powers are exercised in the corporation's best interest, and not for the benefit of corporate insiders or anybody else. In a post-Enron world, it does not require much proof (if it ever did) to establish that directors and officers sometimes violate these fiduciary obligations, either by shirking their responsibilities (governed by a doctrine known as the duty of care) or by enriching themselves at the corporation's expense (governed by a doctrine known as the duty of loyalty).

It is undisputed that the board is the ultimate voice of the corporation. Hence a dilemma. If the board speaks for the corporation, how likely is it that they will sue the corporation (or members of the board or corporate officers) when they violate their fiduciary duties? Equity provided an answer to the dilemma.[10] To permit meaningful enforcement of these duties,

---

[9] See B'nai B'rith Vocational Service, *Law Professors Talk: A Study of Discrimination in the Employment of Jewish Graduates of Law Schools* (Washington, D.C.: B'nai B'rith Vocational Service Bureau, 1949) for an interesting discussion of the possibilities available to Jewish lawyers in the 1940s. That the law professors were too optimistic, even in their pessimism, is borne out by the statistics discussed in Part II.

[10] For a history of the development of derivative litigation, from its very primitive roots in the 1810 English case of *Adley v. The Whitstable Co,* through the 1950s, see Bert S. Prunty Jr, "The Shareholders' Derivative Suit: Notes on its Derivation," *NYU Law Review* 32 (1957): 980–94. See also DeMott, *supra* note 2.

courts created the device of the derivative suit. Put simply, derivative suits permit a stockholder (after making a demand on the board to rectify the situation and having that demand rejected) to bring a suit against the offenders in the name of the corporation.

Derivative litigation was theoretically effective but practically problematic. Except for those who owned very substantial amounts of stock, no one stockholder had much of an incentive to sue the directors or officers. Recovery per share was likely to be minimal except in the very rare case of massive wrongdoing, and such amounts as were recovered went to the corporation as the real party in interest. Thus, even if a stockholder were to recover a judgment in a derivative suit, that recovery would be at best indirect, in the form (theoretically at least) of an increase in share value.

Somebody needed an incentive to sue if the duties were to be enforced at all. The solution was to permit the successful plaintiff's lawyer to recover legal fees from the defendants. Because plaintiffs' lawyers took these cases on a contingent fee basis, the component of recovery reflecting legal fees could be quite substantial. This gave lawyers an incentive to take the risk of representing small stockholders in enforcing fiduciary duties, thus ensuring that these duties would have some meaning.[11] This solution, however, also created the problem of so-called "strike suits." Once lawyers had a financial incentive to sue corporations, the corporations and their lawyers faced the prospect of meretricious litigation, brought solely for the purpose of forcing settlements and enriching lawyers.

The prospect of litigation run amok created the desire for mechanisms that would sort out the legitimate lawsuits from the strike suits. Thus was enacted New York section 61-b.[12] The reasoning is obvious. If the problem was excessive litigation instigated by people who had little financial interest in the corporation (the lawyers and their shareholding clients), and who therefore could be expected to further their own interests at the corporation's expense, discouraging suits by all but the most significant stockholders ensured that only stockholders who were likely to have the corporation's interests in mind would sue. Thus, you will recall, section 61-b required stockholders who owned less than $50,000 in value or 5% of the corporation's stock to post security for expenses, a costly undertaking in the first place, but even more so when one considers that a losing plaintiff would forfeit the bond and be liable for the defendant's expenses. The rule virtually precluded small stockholders from bringing suit.

---

[11] It is unusual for a winning party to collect legal fees in the United States. The origin of the rule is in nineteent- century trust law, in which beneficiaries of a common fund were held to be responsible for the fees of lawyers whose work benefited the fund. By 1939, the rule was universal as to derivative suits. See Hornstein, *supra* note 4, at 143.

[12] This may be the more appropriate place to note that the New York legislature which passed the statute consisted of 51 senators, of whom only five had clearly Jewish surnames, and 150 assemblymen, of whom eleven had clearly Jewish surnames. This was an era when Jews generally did not seek elective office. Irving Howe, *World of our Fathers* (New York: Harcourt Brace Jovanovich, 1976), 360.

The rule makes no sense if its purpose is to limit stockholder litigation only to those suits having merit. In the first place, as noted above, recovery in a derivative action goes to the corporation, not the stockholder. Consequently, a large stockholder would have no incentive to sue. He would have invested his time and effort in litigation that only partly and indirectly brought him benefit, thus posing a classic free-rider problem. Why should a large stockholder bother to sue when so much of the benefit would go (indirectly) to the other stockholders anyway?[13] And why, indeed, when a stockholder with such a large block was typically in a position to negotiate a side deal with management on his own? There was no incentive for large shareholders to sue, and section 61-b made it all but impossible for small shareholders to sue. The ultimate effect of the statute was to prevent litigation altogether, in the absence of a small stockholder or law firm capable of bearing the financial risk of the litigation.[14] Why such a stringent measure? The Wood Report provides an answer.

B. An Analysis of the Wood Report

The *Survey and Report Regarding Stockholders' Derivative Suits* (the Wood Report),[15] written by Franklin S. Wood on behalf of the Special Committee on Corporate Litigation of the Chamber of Commerce of the State of New York, appears to be a serious empirical study of the problems posed by derivative litigation. The report covers 117 pages of text and four substantial appendices, the last of which consists of 18 elaborate charts purportedly detailing every derivative action in New York's First Department (Manhattan and the Bronx), Second Department (Brooklyn, Rockland and Westchester counties) and the United States District Court for the Southern District of New York. The report provided no comparative data with respect to other forms of litigation, analyzing the problem of derivative litigation in a vacuum. Yet in 1934, only two years after the beginning of the ten-year period examined by the report, the Judicial Council of the State of

---

[13] The personal benefits to the large stockholder might outweigh the cost of bringing suit. More likely, however, is that even if the stockholder had a large, illiquid position, which might otherwise make a suit worthwhile, he could use the power that accompanied his position to pressure management (unless he held a large minority block in a close corporation).

[14] The New York Court of Appeals provided relief to plaintiffs in *Baker v. McFadden Publications*, 90 N.E.2d 876 (1950), which held that plaintiffs against whom the statute was invoked, and against whom an order to post security for expenses was levied, could vacate the order if they were able to solicit sufficient additional stockholders to meet the statute's threshold and act as plaintiffs. According to Stanley Nemser, a prominent New York plaintiffs' lawyer at the time, this virtually ended defendants' practice of invoking the statute in order to preclude plaintiffs from circulating serious allegations of wrongdoing by the corporation or its managers among its stockholders. Interview of Stanley Nemser (12 April 2002) at the offices of Wolf Popper, New York, N.Y.

[15] US, Franklin S. Wood for the Special Committee on Corporate Litigation, Chamber of Commerce of the State of New York, *Survey and Report Regarding Stockholders' Derivative Suits* (New York: Chamber of Commerce, 1944).

New York had begun to compile highly detailed records on all litigation in New York State trial courts—records ignored by Wood.[16] Analyses of the Wood Report, both on its own terms and in this broader context, reveal that it was deeply flawed and that it considerably overstated the problem of abusive derivative litigation.[17]

Wood identified 1,400 minority stockholders' actions from 1932 to 1942 (1,266 after eliminating duplication), of which 573 involved public corporations.[18] Of those 573 cases, 13 (2%) resulted in recovery by the corporation, 33 (6%) were settled with court approval, and 215 (37%) were dismissed. Of the other 312 cases, 60 (10%) were "settled privately" (presumably without court approval), 155 (27%) were discontinued, 54 were still pending at the publication of the Wood Report, and there was no identifiable disposition for the remaining 43. The report noted that in the successful actions (actions resulting in a verdict for the corporation), only about 5% of the amount sued for was recovered. In recoveries that were based upon court-approved settlements, 3% of the claimed amount was recovered. From this, the report concluded that most derivative suits were abusive. Its solution to the problem was legislation in the form ultimately passed as section 61-b, which would "largely abate ... the major vices of promiscuous derivative actions...."[19]

But how "promiscuous" were these actions? Does the data support the conclusion that derivative suits presented a crisis so significant that legislation virtually eliminating them was justifiable? To evaluate this claim, it is important to evaluate the situation with respect to all civil litigation in the First Department.[20]

From 1935 through 1942, the average number of civil cases in the First Department ranged from 34,429 to 58,579, with a mean of 51,500 cases a year.[21] Using Wood's numbers (which include, without distinction, suits involving both closely held and public corporations, and leaving aside the U.S. District Court for the Southern District of New York as to which comparable data was unavailable),[22] the number of derivative suits ranged from

---

[16] US, New York State Judicial Council, *Annual Report of the Judicial Council of the State of New York 1937–1955* (Albany, N.Y.: The Council, 1937–1955).

[17] Zlinkoff's analysis, *supra* note 3, is the most thorough and thoughtful, and I will draw upon his critique for one set of data not otherwise readily available.

[18] Wood, *supra* note 15, at 6–7. Derivative suits against close corporations (of which there were 693) are not of interest because they principally involve disputes among shareholders, some if not all of whom are managers, and typically involve questions of distributing corporate wealth among shareholders rather than wrongdoing by officers and directors.

[19] Ibid., 24.

[20] Ibid., Appendix D. All of the following data is taken from the annual tables presented as this summary. I have calculated the proportions. I have also left out the data from the Second Department as it is consistent with that from the First Department.

[21] I have used the mean instead of median simply because they are close enough that I thought the mean to be at least as representative a figure as the median.

[22] The Second Circuit cases were a very small proportion of the total (130 of 1,400).

80 to 139, with a mean of 109. In other words, from 1935 to 1942, derivative suits ranged from 0.22% to 0.41% of all civil cases, or a mean of 0.29%. Put differently, out of a total of 281,423 civil cases in the First Department during this period, a grand total of 815 (or 0.29%) were derivative. Since, on average, 58% of these involved closely held corporations, that means only 342, or 0.12%, involved publicly held corporations.[23]

It seems fair to conclude, then, that as far as the consumption of judicial resources was concerned and despite the very real existence of strike suits, derivative litigation posed no significant burden. At least Wood provided no tangible evidence that the negative aspects of derivative litigation (the strike suit) outweighed the positives. But there are a number of potential objections to this conclusion. First is the possibility that plaintiffs' lawyers made pre-litigation demands on boards to obtain bribes. Next is that derivative suits ought to have been curbed because their success rate (and even their trial rate) was so low in proportion to that of civil suits. Third might be that derivative suits were so generally meretricious that they were overwhelmingly dismissed. Fourth would be that the amount of recovery was so low that they were simply a form of harassment without significant benefit to the corporation.

The first of these potential objections is that even if derivative litigation was not a significant proportion of all litigation, plaintiffs' lawyers may have been using it to "hold up" corporations and their executives. With rare exception, a prerequisite to derivative standing is that the plaintiff make a demand on the board to correct the action complained of. Perhaps, the argument runs, plaintiffs' lawyers engaged in a practice of promiscuous demand making, leading corporations to make payments in the nature of bribes to dissuade them from filing lawsuits. If this were true, plaintiffs' lawyers could well have had a valuable business in derivative litigation that never reached general public view, and the comparative paucity of derivative suits would therefore have had no bearing on the scope of the problem, which could nonetheless have been significant for corporations.

Such a story is implausible. Or rather, it is only plausible if one accepts that plaintiffs' lawyers never talked with one another and that corporations would therefore have been able to keep such payments secret. Otherwise, as Jonathan Macey and Geoffrey Miller noted with respect to strike suits, such payments would be rare.[24] The reason is that corporations that paid such bribes would rapidly become known as suckers and attractive targets for

---

[23] There is no convenient way of backing out the derivative suits brought in the Second Circuit from these numbers, since Wood purported to eliminate duplicative suits without indicating where they were brought. Given the relatively small number of derivative cases brought in the Second Circuit, it seems reasonable to conclude that they would not materially affect the results.

[24] Cf. Jonathan R. Macey & Geoffrey P. Miller, "The Plaintiffs' Attorneys' Role in Class Action and Derivative Litigation Economic Analysis and Recommendations for Reform," *University of Chicago Law Review* 58 (1991): 78 ("[m]ost observers agree that strike suit litigation is relatively uncommon").

plaintiffs' lawyers, resulting in frequent and expensive demands. The only rational response to such demands, as to derivative litigation, is resistance. Thus, the "under the radar screen" argument for the significance of the strike suit problem is quite weak.

The second potential objection is that the success rate of derivative litigation was disproportionately low compared with that of all civil litigation. The numbers do bear this out in percentage terms, but when one looks at the absolute numbers it appears that litigation in general was not a terribly successful plaintiffs' endeavour. (In fact, it appears that civil litigation was rarely pursued to completion). Looking solely at jury trials from 1934 to 1942 (the period under study), the number of cases that resulted in victory for the plaintiff after trial ranged from 458 to 609, or from 0.81% to 1.36% of all civil cases. Those that were settled or discontinued after trial ranged from 619 to 1,158, or from 1.57% to 2.06% of all civil cases. At the same time, verdicts for defendants after trial ranged from 295 to 474, or from 0.50% to 1.00% of the total. Finally, average monetary awards to plaintiffs ranged from $5,407 ($83,602) to $7,800 ($120,602), with a mean of $6,207 ($95,971).[25] Even in light of income levels at the time, these hardly seem like exorbitant judgments.[26]

Data available for completed bench trials is less thorough, but there is enough to round out the picture. From 1934 to 1942, the number of completed bench trials ranged from 1,129 to 1,601, or from 2.11 percent to 4.24 percent. Finally, the number of trials as a percentage of all cases (without regard to disposition) ranged from 1,884 to 2,216, or from 3.5% to 6.44% of all cases on the calendar during the year.

The third potential objection is that derivative suits were so often dismissed because they were meretricious. Sergei Zlinkoff provided some interesting additional analysis to suggest that this was not the case.[27] Noting both that the vast majority of cases never went to trial and the absence of information as to why they were discontinued (settlements, etc.), Zlinkoff argued that "it would seem more proper in evaluating the results of derivative suits to consider the figures for the number of suits in which issue was joined and thereafter either the plaintiff or defendant was successful, eliminating actions that were discontinued."[28] In doing so, he determined that issue was joined in 171 cases, of which 13 resulted in recovery for the plaintiff and 93 in settlements, with victory for the defendant in only 65 suits. In

---

[25] The numbers following each mean in parentheses give the immediately preceding amount in 2010 dollars. These amounts are based on the U.S. Department of Labor on-line inflation adjuster: *CPI Calculator, supra* n. 1. I have used the same source of conversion throughout this chapter. Since data is aggregate, I used the year 1938—the median year of the period under study—as the basis for calculating inflation.

[26] In 1944, median per capita income in the State of New York for heads of households was roughly $1,072 ($13,305). This information was obtained from the staff at the United States Census Library.

[27] Zlinkoff, *supra* note 3, at 362.

[28] Ibid.

other words, 62% of the derivative suits in which issue was joined resulted in stockholder victory.[29] These numbers hardly suggest the prevalence of abusive derivative litigation.

The fourth possible objection is that derivative suit recoveries were too low to significantly benefit the corporation, so the suits were merely a form of harassment. The evidence suggests that the amounts awarded either upon the plaintiff's victory or upon settlement did indeed bring substantial redress for the corporation. Drawing at least in part from cases in which he was involved, Zlinkoff showed that in seven cases from 1935 to 1944, damages ranged from $350,000 ($5,411,621) to $4,000,000 ($61,847,092) with a mean of $1,665,771 ($25,775,773) and a median of $1,800,000 ($27,891,191).[30] While these may seem modest when compared to contemporary judgments today,[31] they hardly seem out of line with the legal fees of which the Wood Report complained. Reporting fees in twelve derivative suits (which, regrettably, are not the same cases reported by Zlinkoff but which do cover roughly the same period), the Wood Report showed individual defendants' legal fees ranging from $4,890 ($75,608) to $135,000 ($2,087,339) with a mean of $38,178 ($590,300) and a median of $16,000 ($247,388).[32] Unfortunately Wood does not give the disposition of any of these actions. Those fees, however, hardly seem disproportionate to the size of the judgments noted by Zlinkoff, and one could see them as a relatively low price to pay to enforce fiduciary obligations, especially in light of the crisis precipitated by corporate America in the 1920s.[33] Thus, when more data is introduced and the data presented in the Wood Report is carefully analyzed in context, it is hard to see derivative suits as the scourge the report makes them out to be.

C. The Rhetorical Posture of the Wood Report

The empirical evidence suggests that derivative suits were relatively rarely brought, and that when they did occur, their frequency was not grossly disproportionate to that of other types of litigation. Judgments awarded in successful or settled derivative suits appear to be reasonably high when compared with the data for all cases. And legal fees, while substantial, seem proportionate to the damages awarded, especially when one

---

[29] Ibid.

[30] Ibid., 362–63 n. 46.

[31] For confirmation see Robert J. Shiller, *Irrational Exuberance*, 2d ed. (Princeton: Princeton University Press, 2005); Lawrence E. Mitchell, *Corporate Irresponsibility: America's Newest Export* (New Haven: Yale University Press, 2001).

[32] Wood, *supra* note 15, at 8. The $135,000 fee was highly aberrant; the next largest fee was $71,490 ($1,105,362), with only two more fees over $50,000, two in the low $30,000s, and the rest in the teens and below.

[33] Hornstein provided the counsel fees awarded to plaintiffs in twelve derivative actions between 1932 and 1939, noting the ratios of fees to amounts awarded to the successful corporation. The median is 31%, with a mean of 30%. George D. Hornstein, "The Counsel Fee in Stockholders' Derivative Suits," *Columbia Law Review* 34 (1939): 814.

considers that the fees reported were for multiple defendants. Why then, one may ask, the effort to prohibit derivative suits?

The rhetoric of the Wood Report begins to provide a clue. Its rhetoric seems overheated: it called derivative suits "vexatious litigation."[34] This very term was used by Justice Rehnquist in *Blue Chip*, despite the fact that it appeared in none of the briefs in that case. And of the relationship between stockholder-plaintiff and lawyer, the Wood Report said: "This shoddy burlesque of a professional relationship to clients makes the ambulance-chaser by comparison a paragon of propriety."[35]

Even more significant was the way the Wood Report discussed derivative plaintiffs. It noted that "an inexhaustible supply of the smallest of small investors have suddenly become masters of the most intricate details of corporate finance, and the most alert of sentinels to employ attorneys and attack corporate management on the slightest suspicion of a big lawsuit." It then went on to note the prominence of women among the plaintiffs and to list suits that featured women plaintiffs, after which it rather sarcastically speculated on their knowledge and financial sophistication. What the report declined to mention is that 21 of the plaintiffs in the 32 listed actions had traditionally Jewish surnames, and seven more had arguably Jewish surnames. It would not have taken much for a reader of the time to substitute "Jews" for "women."[36]

In short, derivative suits were not a problem. The problem, I argue, was white Anglo-Saxon Protestant status panic that produced a particular form of antisemitism and motivated the statute. To support this argument, it is necessary to examine the composition and status of the plaintiffs' bar.

II. The Jewish Bar

The plaintiffs' bar was the Jewish bar. Rich bodies of data collected in 1937 and 1960 sustain the argument that the very structure of the bar was itself a product of antisemitism.

---

[34] Wood, *supra* note 15, at 48. According to the Oxford English Dictionary, the term "vexatious litigation" has been in use since at least the seventeenth century, and refers to lawsuits brought without merit by "evil disposed Persons." See *The Oxford English Dictionary*, 2d ed., s.v. "vexatious." A full etymology of the term is beyond the scope of this chapter, but it is clearly meant to cast aspersions on those who bring such suits.

[35] Wood, *supra* note 15, at 47. The "ambulance chaser," by the way, was an earlier term of epithet for plaintiffs' lawyers coined by elite White Anglo Saxon Protestant (WASP) members of the bar. Of course, they were referring largely to Jewish lawyers: Jerold S. Auerbach, *Unequal Justice: Lawyers and Social Change in Modern America* (London: Oxford University Press, 1976), 40–44.

[36] Comparing the Wood Report's text with its tables, it appears that approximately 20% of plaintiffs were women. It should be noted that women, historically, formed a very substantial proportion of American shareholders. See Lawrence E. Mitchell, *The Speculation Economy: How Finance Triumphed Over Industry* (San Francisco: Berrett-Koehler Publishers, 2007), 203. It is also interesting to note the misrepresentation of the text in light of the data presented in the tables. Given the other flaws in the Wood report, it is at least a legitimate inference that Wood chose the obviously Jewish female plaintiffs from among this 20% to present in his text.

In the 1930s, discrimination by white Anglo-Saxon Protestant lawyers against other lawyers was nothing new. The Association of the Bar of the City of New York (ABCNY) was founded in 1870 as an attempt to stratify the bar, and every president of the ABCNY from 1870 to 1920 was listed in the New York Social Register.[37] Its Grievance Committee spent disproportionate amounts of time investigating ethnic lawyers, who were typically sole practitioners rather than corporate lawyers who were members of firms. The American Bar Association was not much different. J. Clay Smith, Jr., in his study of African-American lawyers, quoted what he described as an "influential" ABA member in the 1920s as noting that "the legal profession was a means by which Jews, immigrants, and city-dwellers might undermine the American way of life."[38] Thus the ABA attempted to shut down law schools catering to these three groups who, as we will see, were largely one and the same in New York: Jews. And while in the very early years these lower reaches of the bar consisted of a more varied group of minorities (some Irish lawyers as well as Jews who were centered at least in part around the Tammany Hall machine), by 1944 the demographics of the bar, but not the attitude of the elite, had changed significantly, leaving Jews as the overwhelming minority group in the bar.

A. 1937

Concrete evidence of the structure of the bar appears in a 1939 report written by Melvin Fagen and based on a study of the Conference on Jewish Relations led by Simon Rifkind.[39] That report described in elaborate empirical detail the plight of Jewish lawyers in New York during the 1930s.[40] It began by quoting one New York Jewish lawyer as describing the practice of law as "a dignified road to starvation."[41] The data revealed in the report suggested that this was far more the rule for Jewish lawyers than the exception. But my interest is not in disparate income levels; it is in the evidence of discrimination which led to that disparity.

---

[37] Lawrence Fleischer, "Association of the Bar of the City of New York: 125 Years 1870–1995: The City Bar: Then and Now," *N.Y.L.J.*, September 11, 1995, p. S1.

[38] J. Clay Smith Jr., *Emancipation: The Making of the Black Lawyer 1844–1944* (Philadelphia: University of Pennsylvania Press, 1993), 42; Robert Stevens, *Law School: Legal Education in America from the 1850s to the 1890s* (Chapel Hill: University of North Carolina Press, 1983), 100–101; Auerbach, *Unequal Justice*, supra note 35.

[39] Melvin M. Fagen, "The Status of Jewish Lawyers in New York City," *Jewish Social Studies* 1 (1939): 73–104. Rifkind later became a named partner of one of New York's premier law firms, a firm that included Lloyd Garrison, Dean of the University of Wisconsin Law School and grandson of the great abolitionist William Lloyd Garrison, and which adopted principles of racial and ethnic equality as well as public service. Paul Weiss traces its roots to 1875 but took its modern form in 1946. Rifkind joined the firm in 1950. In the interests of full disclosure, I spent several happy years as an associate at Paul Weiss Rifkind Wharton and Garrison.

[40] Ibid.

[41] Ibid., 74.

Fagen's report estimated that approximately 22,000 lawyers were practicing in all five boroughs in 1937, of whom 11,400, or a slight majority, were Jewish. (Jews constituted roughly 28% of the population of New York City.)[42] Of the 11,400 Jewish lawyers, 9,467, or 83%, practiced in Manhattan.[43]

More important than the size of the Jewish bar was its distribution over types and areas of practice, because this determined both status and income. The most important indicator of income and status in the bar was the law school one had attended.[44] Fully 66.8% of Jewish lawyers who had attended law school graduated either from Brooklyn Law School (25.8%), New York University (22.7%), New York Law School (12.1%), St. John's Law School (10.7%) or Fordham Law School (6.2%), none of which at the time were among the elite American law schools. The only elite school attended by New York Jewish lawyers in any meaningful numbers was Columbia (11%), a fact that was somewhat of an oddity in light of that university's antisemitic tradition.[45]

Fagen's report identified the principal reasons for Jewish attendance at non-elite law schools as the availability of night programs and cheaper tuition,[46] two factors which were highly important to students from relatively poor families. The report made no mention of antisemitism as a factor.

---

[42] The population of New York City in 1940 was 7,454,995. See Campbell Gibson, "Population of the 100 Largest Cities and Other Urban Places in the United States: 1790 to 1990" (June 1998), online: U.S. Census Bureau, at www.census.gov/population/www/documentation/twps0027/twps0027.html.

[43] The identification of lawyers in New York was based on United States census data. The identification of Jewish lawyers was done by including those lawyers who listed themselves as belonging to Jewish organizations or contributing to Jewish charities, as well as by a search through Martindale-Hubbell for lawyers with obviously Jewish names. Lawyers with obviously non-Jewish names were excluded, and an ambiguous group of about 3,000 lawyers was further reduced by discussion with lawyers familiar with those individuals in question. Fagen conceded the imprecision of this methodology, *supra* note 39, at 75. As my own decidedly non-Jewish name was bestowed upon my unwilling family by an insistent customs official, I am particularly sensitive to this flaw. Nonetheless, based on its methodology, the survey seems more likely to have underestimated rather than overestimated the number of Jewish lawyers. I have no effective way of counting the numbers or ethnicity of commuting lawyers living in suburbs like Bronxville, Greenwich, and Scarsdale. It is well known, however, that Jews had not significantly migrated to the suburbs at the time, and that suburbs like those just mentioned did not welcome Jews (indeed Bronxville positively excluded them). For evidence that significant Jewish migration to the suburbs began only at the end of World War II, see William E. Nelson, *The Legalist Reformation: Law, Politics, and Ideology in New York, 1920–1980* (Chapel Hill: University of North Carolina Press, 2001).

[44] Fagen, *supra* note 39, at 82.

[45] Ibid. Columbia was the first elite university to restrict Jewish admissions; see John Higham, "Social Discrimination Against Jews in America, 1830–1930," in *The Jewish Experience in America*, vol. 5, ed. Abraham J. Karp (Waltham, MA: American Jewish Historical Society, 1969), 369; Marcia Graham Synnott, "Antisemitism and American Universities: Did Quotas Follow the Jews?" in *American Jewish History*, vol. 6, ed. Jeffrey Gurock (New York: Routledge, 1997), 473, 479–80, and 499.

[46] Fagen, *supra* note 39, at 82–83.

This is not terribly surprising in light of the reluctance of Jews to talk about antisemitism, and the fact that the report was written by a Jew. Nevertheless, scholars of the era, including Jerold Auerbach, Irving Howe and Digby Baltzell, all described antisemitism as a major factor limiting Jewish attendance at elite universities.[47]

This educational stratification created a bar structure highly disadvantageous to Jews. In 1937, few Jewish lawyers were in corporate practice, which was by far the most lucrative practice area. Only 11% of Jewish lawyers reported having a corporate practice, with a large plurality dependent upon small merchants (35.28%) and "general" practice (22.15%). Sixty percent of Jewish lawyers reported being sole practitioners, the lowest income level group with a median of $1,874 ($28, 378).[48] Only 6% reported that they were the head of a firm (with a median income of $8,879 ($134, 425), 15% reported being a member of a firm (with a median income of $4,137 [$62,633]) and 14% reported working as an employee of a firm (also with a median income of $4,137). The median income for Jewish lawyers as a group was $2,426 ($36,729), 23% lower than the median $2,990 ($45,268) earned by all New York lawyers.[49]

In 1937, 21% of all New York lawyers with five to ten years' experience were members of firms, as were 35.34% of lawyers with 17–23 years of experience. Similar proportions (in the mid-30% range) were firm members throughout their careers. The proportion of all New York lawyers who headed an office (the most lucrative practice situation) ranged from 14.38% for those with five to ten years experience to a high of 33.38% for those with 24 to 34 years of experience. In their early years of practice, New York lawyers as a whole were employed significantly more in firms than the subset of Jewish lawyers, but the reverse was true for lawyers with the longest experience. Among those with four years of experience or less, the proportion employed in firms was 39.27% for all New York lawyers and 9.74% for Jews. This gap gradually decreased as the number of years of practice increased, to the point where the situation was reversed among lawyers with 35 or more years of experience. In that most senior cohort, only 3.02% of all New York lawyers were employed in firms, as compared to 29.16% of Jewish lawyers.[50] The probable reason for this reversal is that a high proportion of experienced non-Jewish lawyers, but only an insignifi-

---

[47] Auerbach, *supra* note 35, at 126–27; Howe, *supra* note 12, at 411–12; E. Digby Baltzell, *The Protestant Establishment: Aristocracy and Caste in America* (New York: Random House, 1964), 129–35, 209–12. Auerbach, Baltzell, and Howe all were writing after the fact. It may be that the report's reluctance to identify overt antisemitism as a cause is due in part to the traditional Jewish-American fear that claiming the existence of antisemitism will stir up even more of it. See generally Alan M. Dershowitz, *Chutzpah* (Boston: Little, Brown & Company, 1991).

[48] Fagen, *supra* note 39.

[49] The latter larger figure is for all lawyers, including Jews, so it almost certainly understates the income disparity between Jewish and other lawyers.

[50] Fagen, *supra* note 39, at 86–92, 101–3.

cant proportion of experienced Jewish lawyers, became members or heads of the firms of which they had previously been employees. The vast majority of Jewish lawyers did not have jobs in firms early in their careers, which of course is the time when the track to partnership is established, and this most likely accounts for their small proportion of membership in firms. While they may have been more accepted into firms as employees when they gained experience in practice, they were clearly not often accepted as members of those firms.

The inescapable conclusion is that as of 1937, only seven years before the adoption of Section 61-b, the vast majority of Jewish lawyers were marginalized in the New York bar.[51] Nor, as we will now see, had this situation changed in any meaningful way over the two decades that followed.

B. 1960

The next year for which significant data is available is 1960, which was not long before the securities class action supplanted the derivative suit in importance, and the United States Supreme Court began to impose substantial restrictions on securities litigation. The 1960 data comes from a report drafted by Columbia University sociologist Jerome Carlin (the Carlin Report), which examined the "social conditions of moral integrity in the legal profession."[52] Despite its broad ambition, the Carlin Report limited its inquiry to the New York Bar as the nation's most significant. The relevance of Carlin's important conclusion that ethical behaviour is a function of status within the bar will become clear later in this discussion. For now, I want simply to concentrate on the data that more or less parallel those for 1937 set out in Fagen's 1939 report.

In 1960 (the focal year of Carlin's data), there were approximately 26,000 lawyers in Manhattan and the Bronx, of whom 17,000 were active private practitioners. Seventy percent reported receiving at least 50% of their income from business practice, but the vast majority of that group represented small businessmen and closely held corporations. Only 20% reported that most of their work involved representing large corporations.[53]

In describing the hierarchical structure of the New York bar, Carlin noted that "the firm is the significant unit for the system of social stratification of the bar."[54] While 4,300 law offices with from 1 to 100 lawyers were counted in Manhattan and the Bronx, and more than 50% of lawyers re-

---

[51] Stevens, *supra* note 38, at 246 ("In the 1930s to the 1940s, Jewish students were heavily channeled into government service, teaching, and the non-elite or predominantly Jewish law firms. There was still a hint of antisemitism among the large firms in the 1960s.").

[52] Jerome E. Carlin, *Lawyer's Ethics: A Survey of the New York City Bar* (New York: Russell Sage Foundation, 1966), xxvii.

[53] Ibid., 11–13.

[54] Ibid., 18.

ported working in firms, only 21% reported working in firms of 15 or more, a fact which is very significant for bar hierarchy.[55]

In an interesting contrast to the 1937 data, which reported that only 68.6% of Jewish lawyers were native born in comparison to 80.8% of the bar overall,[56] the Carlin Report indicated that "almost all" members of the New York bar were native born. More than 60% of these were Jewish, 18% were Catholic, and 18% were Protestant.[57] Thirty-six percent of all lawyers had graduated from what Carlin described as "high quality university law schools."

Where a lawyer attended law school remained critically important to bar status. Carlin noted that the social status of lawyers really was fixed upon their entry to college, beginning a circular trap. The status of one's undergraduate institution was depended on one's religion and parental socioeconomic status, and the likelihood of admission to an elite law school depended on the status of one's undergraduate institution. The result was that Jewish lawyers, most of whose parents had relatively low socioeconomic status, had little chance of attaining elite status in the bar.[58]

The 1960 data bear this out, but they also tell a more troubling story. Elite colleges and law schools appear to have discriminated significantly against Jews. As to undergraduate education, 70% of Protestants of high socio-economic status, 42% of middle socio-economic status and 28% of low socio-economic status had attended Ivy League or similar quality colleges.[59] By contrast, only 34% of Jews of high socio-economic status, 17% of middle socio-economic status and 9% of low socio-economic status had attended Ivy League colleges or similar institutions. At the top colleges, the ratio between high socio-economic status Protestants and Jews was almost reversed. A high socio-economic status Jew was only 6% more likely to have attended a top college than a low socio-economic Protestant (although the difference was 42 percentage points as between high and low socio-economic status Protestants).[60] To put it differently, a low status Protestant had an almost one in three chance of attending an Ivy League school. For the low status Jew, the chances were slightly less than one in ten.

Seventy-seven percent of large-firm lawyers had attended Ivy League law schools, in contrast to only 20% of small-firm lawyers and sole practi-

---

[55] Ibid.

[56] Fagen, *supra* note 39, at 79.

[57] Carlin, *supra* note 52, at 18–19.

[58] Ibid., 22, 28–32.

[59] Carlin used the term "top quality colleges," and provided a category of "other top quality colleges" in his data. He did not define these, but one suspects he meant Williams, Amherst, Swarthmore, Haverford, Chicago, Stanford and the like. Rankings did not exist at the time, at least not in a form I was able to find.

[60] Carlin, *supra* note 52, at 29. Catholics fared even worse with respect to high-status college admissions, and their presence in the bar was dramatically lower than that of Jews. However, Carlin noted that, adjusting for college and law school attended, Catholics had about the same chance of being in a large firm as Protestant lawyers.

tioners. Protestants and Jews who attended top colleges had more even levels of attendance at Ivy League law schools, although a significant disparity remained. But the dramatic difference in attendance at top colleges meant that a considerably lower proportion of Jews than Protestants attended Ivy League law schools.[61]

Race played a seemingly independent role in bar status. Only 19% of Jews with a top education were members of large firms, compared to 45% of Protestants. Carlin noted that, "a Jewish lawyer who achieved high academic standing (that is, was selected for the staff of law review) in an Ivy League school has no better chance of being in a large firm than a Protestant lawyer who did not 'make law review' and who attended a non-Ivy League law school."[62]

Finally, Carlin demonstrated that there was substantial immobility between strata of the bar throughout a lawyer's career, and that race played an important role in this immobility. It should not be surprising by this point to learn that Jewish lawyers had significantly less upward mobility and more downward mobility than Protestant lawyers. One of the important practical results of all of this, which I will discuss further in Part III, is that lawyers at different levels of the bar had very little contact with one another and very little shared professional experience. It is worth noting that the prestigious Association of the Bar of the City of New York was dominated by Protestant, large-firm lawyers, while the more plebeian New York County Lawyers' Association was populated principally by small firm lawyers and sole practitioners (and hence, Jews).[63]

Needless to say, antisemitic discrimination in the bar mirrored the problem of antisemitism and racial exclusion in the larger society.[64] My hypothesis is that the marginalization of Jews at the lowest levels of the bar (and at the correspondingly lowest income levels), as well as their social exclusion from the circles travelled in by large-firm elite Protestant lawyers, set the stage for the suspicion and hostility that led to restrictions on stockholder litigation and to negative attitudes toward the corporate plaintiffs' bar.

C. A Tale of Two Bars

Combining the above data on the number and practice types of Jewish lawyers in the New York bar with the New York Judicial Council report on

---

[61] Ibid., 29–30.

[62] Of course there was substantial self-selection, but this was due to the common knowledge among law faculties and Jewish law students that their chances of finding jobs at big firms were minimal. My own father (St. John's Law School 1956, law review editor, second in his class) reports that he and other Jewish students were carefully directed by the Dean to those firms that might consider hiring Jewish applicants. See also B'nai B'rith, *Law Professors Talk*, supra note 9.

[63] Carlin, *supra* note 52, at 36.

[64] See Part III A and accompanying text below, and Baltzell, *supra* note 47.

litigation success rates, one might question whether *all* types of litigation were seen to suffer from the same level of abuse that derivative litigation did. This raises the question of why the New York Chamber of Commerce or other groups did not try to restrict civil litigation in general. Conversely, one might wonder why I am attributing antisemitic motives to the fact that there was a drive to stop derivative litigation but not other forms of litigation.

The answer begins to reveal itself when one looks at the practice areas in which the Jewish bar was involved. As noted above, an overwhelming proportion of Jewish lawyers represented small merchants or individual clients. Fagen reported that 42% of Jewish lawyers represented "merchants,"[65] 25% represented a "general" clientele, 14% reported representing corporations,[66] and 8.5% reported representing "wage earners and small shopkeepers." Categories of representation for Jewish lawyers fell off significantly from that point into the single digits. Carlin tells us that 70% of New York lawyers reported deriving at least 50% of their income from business clients, but that "most" lawyers representing corporations worked for closely held corporations.[67] In addition, large law firms reported 68% of their practice as involving business, but small firms and sole practitioners, where Jewish lawyers typically were found, reported only 27% and 36% of their practice as involving business. Moreover, only 14% of large firms and 34% of medium firms (which as we have already seen, were largely white Anglo-Saxon Protestant) reported having a "mainly Jewish" individual clientele, whereas 46% of firms of two to four lawyers and 44% of sole practitioners reported having "mainly Jewish" individual clients.[68] In light of the practice of firms (including large firms) representing the individual affairs of their business clients, and in light of the types of businesses Jews engaged in,[69] one can infer without too much difficulty that much of the

---

[65] Fagen, *supra* note 39, at 99. (I have extracted the proportions from the raw data provided in Fagen's tables.)

[66] Recall that Jewish corporations generally were involved in the retail and wholesale trades, soft goods, entertainment and communication. It is possible that some proportion of these 419 Jewish corporate lawyers represented WASP corporations, but in light of the available evidence, hardly likely. See Baltzell, *supra* note 47. Moreover, in light of Carlin's data that most Jews represented closely-held corporations, the likelihood that they would have represented major corporations seems even less.

[67] Carlin, *supra* note 52, at 13.

[68] Ibid., 24.

[69] Baltzell, *supra* note 47, at 207–8, noted that "the Protestant establishment" in the 1920s (and thereafter) dominated "heavy manufacturing, railroad transportation and public utilities ... (along with commercial banking and insurance)," while Jews were engaged in soft goods, retail and wholesale business, and entertainment and communication business. The German Jewish aristocracy, principally involved in finance but with interests branching into railroads and mining, was exceptional. See Stephen Birmingham, *Our Crowd: The Great Jewish Families of New York* (New York: Harper & Row, 1967). It is especially interesting to note WASP dominance in major industry in the 1920s for, as I shall discuss below, these industries were the principal site of the abuses that led to the 1929 Crash, the Pecora investigations, and passage of the securities laws of the

158 • JEWS AND THE LAW

litigation in New York courts took place between individuals or small businessmen, largely Jewish and represented by Jewish firms on both sides. White Anglo-Saxon Protestant lawyers would be unlikely to notice or care.

Yet, it was the large white Anglo-Saxon Protestant firm that represented large, publicly-held corporate clients, the very types of businesses that were likely to be targeted by derivative suits. It is a reasonable inference, although admittedly an inference, that these firms and their clients would be far more aware of the perils of derivative litigation than of the lawsuits that took up the rest of their trial calendars. Thus, it would be natural for the Wood Report to ignore other types of litigation.[70] Had it not done so, its case, already weak when examined closely, would seem to have fallen apart solely on the numbers.

III. Social Antisemitism

A. The Height of American Antisemitism

The late 1930s through the mid-1940s, the era of the Wood Report and section 61-b, has been described as the "high tide" of antisemitism in America.[71] It was a time when the America First Committee, formed to keep the United States out of the war, attracted as its leaders Henry Ford and Father Coughlin, men who previously had established famously antisemitic reputations. Leaders of this committee insisted that the Roosevelts and "90 percent of the New Dealers" were Jewish, that Jews were in control of the federal government, and that Hollywood producers (who often were Jewish) were making movies designed to lead America into war (an accusation which led to a Senate investigation of Hollywood). This was a time when Charles Lindbergh, fresh from receiving a medal from his hero, Adolf Hitler,

---

1930s. Thus the WASP suspicion of plaintiffs' lawyers (and the continuing contemporary suspicion of plaintiffs but not defendants) seems wholly unwarranted and, in the earlier period, can likely only be explained in terms of class. Given the structure of the bar, class meant race.

70 One might expect small-practice Jewish lawyers to have heavily engaged in personal injury litigation, often against WASP-controlled insurance companies, and that this too would be viewed with offence by the WASP establishment. Note first that it is virtually impossible to bring a personal injury "strike suit"; typically, the injury will be apparent. Moreover, a random sampling of 200 personal injury cases between 1900 and 1945 revealed obviously Jewish lawyers in fewer than 10% of cases, although Jews did appear more often for the plaintiff than for the defendant.

71 Leonard Dinnerstein, *Antisemitism in America* (Oxford: Oxford University Press, 1994), 128. It is worth noting that while statistics show a peak of antisemitism during this period, there was an enormous amount before that. The earlier antisemitism seems to have been more violent and more populist in nature, led by demagogues like Georgia's Tom Watson and Henry Ford's *Dearborn Independent*. The class of WASP about which I am speaking would never have engaged in this crude, largely lower-class and middle-class, form of antisemitism. For an interesting story of the deep racial antisemitism that ran through the American military in the years after World War I, see Joseph W Bendersky, *The "Jewish Threat": Anti-Semitic Politics of the U.S. Army* (New York: Basic Books, 2000).

spoke against the Jews who he claimed controlled the press, the media, Hollywood, and the federal government. While Lindbergh was so heavily criticized that the America First Committee virtually disappeared, antisemitism during this period continued to increase.[72] Dinnerstein quoted Jewish actor Kirk Douglas, who easily "passed" (passed for a non-Jew), as saying during this period: "The things that in their nightmares Jews speculate non-Jews say.... I found out they do."[73]

Regularly kept polling data demonstrate increasing antisemitism during this period.[74] In May 1938, 36% of respondents polled agreed that Jews had too much power in America; by 1945 (when Hitler had essentially annihilated European Jewry and Jewish migration to America had long been stemmed by restrictive immigration laws) that number had risen to 58%.[75] When Lindbergh made his famous Des Moines speech on behalf of the America First Committee, he named three groups he believed were drawing America into the war: Jews, the Roosevelt administration, and pro-British groups. In a survey conducted in 1941, 40% remembered the accusation against Jews, compared with 31% as to the Roosevelt administration and 21% as to pro-British groups.[76]

Despite the fairly widespread belief that Jews were agitating to involve America in the war, once the war had begun at least one-third of the American population believed that Jews were less willing to serve in the armed forces and less patriotic than even German and Japanese Americans.[77] In June 1944, only a year before the European war ended and Jewry had been virtually wiped out in Europe, 24% of survey respondents identified Jews as the greatest menace to Americans, with only 9% identifying Japanese and 6% identifying Germans.[78]

In short, antisemitism simply was pervasive throughout America during the era in which the Wood Report was drafted and section 61-b was passed. Dinnerstein noted a 1942 poll which asked high school students who would be their last choice as a roommate. The only double-digit negatives were African-Americans at 78% and Jews at 45%. A contemporaneous report by *Fortune* asked factory workers who they would least like to have move into

---

[72] Ibid., 129.

[73] Ibid., 131.

[74] See the rich empirical data contained in Charles Herbert Stember et al., *Jews in the Mind of America*, 2d ed. (New York: Basic Books, 1966). See especially ch. 5, "Reactions to Anti-Semitic Appeals before and during the War" (dealing with the World War II era).

[75] Ibid., 114.

[76] Ibid., 121.

[77] Ibid., 116–17.

[78] Ibid., 128. Two years earlier, the results were almost the reverse in direction, if not in magnitude, with 24% identifying Japanese, 18% identifying Germans, and a still significant 15% identifying Jews. Since all of this polling data explores self-professed attitudes, there might be an underreporting bias in antisemitic attitudes. Given the general public acceptance of antisemitism during this period it is hard to imagine that there is an overreporting bias.

their neighbourhoods, and this time African-Americans and Jews were joined by the Chinese (who interestingly scored only 9% on the student survey) with 72%, 42% and 28%, respectively.[79] Finally, a poll asking the respondents whether they had heard any negative comments about Jews during the preceding six months led to 46% affirmative responses in 1940, growing steadily to 64% affirmative in 1946, the year after the war ended and the reality of the Holocaust had been widely reported.[80]

Nativism and general anti-immigrant sentiment, as well as class and economic conflict, added to the cruder and more virulent forms of antisemitism. Despite its popular peak in the 1940s, it had become deeply embedded in the consciousness of the eastern, urban, Protestant elite.

B. Status Panic

The kind of discrimination that led to the Wood Report could well have been overt and intentional, or it could have been (and likely was) more subtle. Laura Z. Hobson's wonderful period novel, *Gentleman's Agreement*,[81] described antisemitism in New York among "the better sort" at its height in 1940s America. Dramatizing the same psychological forces that Charles Lawrence described as unconscious racism,[82] Hobson showed the socially unacceptable status of even assimilated Eastern European Jews, and the psychologically subtle, subconscious defences of discriminatory practices even among those who would have been horrified to be called antisemitic.[83]

Sociologist Digby Baltzell, the leading scholar on white Anglo-Saxon Protestants in America, reported that the relatively quick transformation of mass Jewish poverty into Jewish economic success led antisemitic attitudes within the Protestant elite to become so ingrained that they became

---

[79] Ibid., 96.

[80] Ibid., 60–61. The horror stories of antisemitism during this era, from citizens' groups organized to criticize Jews to Coughlinites to the deep antisemitism embedded in textbooks as well as in the military, from ordinary soldiers threatening their Jewish colleagues to government training manuals, are sufficient to fill volumes. It seems adequate to establish the environment in which the Wood Report was drafted to provide the evidence in the text and refer the interested reader to other sources. See, e.g., Steven Alan Carr, *Hollywood and Anti-Semitism: A Cultural History* (Cambridge, UK: Cambridge University Press, 2001); Jerome A. Chanes, ed., *Antisemitism in America Today: Outspoken Experts Explode the Myths* (Secaucus, N.J.: Carol Publishing Group, 1995); Robert S. Wistrich, *Antisemitism: The Longest Hatred* (New York: Pantheon Books, 1991).

[81] Laura Z. Hobson, *Gentleman's Agreement* (New York: Simon and Schuster, 1947). The novel was made into an Academy Award winning movie starring Gregory Peck, Celeste Holm, and John Garfield.

[82] Charles R Lawrence III, "The Id, the Ego, and Equal Protection: Reckoning with Unconscious Racism," *Stanford Law Review* 39 (1987): 317–88.

[83] For an earlier and cruder depiction of the exclusion of even upper-class Jewry in the character of the Princeton—educated Robert Cohn, see Ernest Hemingway, *The Sun Also Rises* (1926).

intuitive.[84] From their hegemony in the 1920s, a period referred to by Baltzell as "the Anglo-Saxon decade," WASPs had, by the 1940s, begun to withdraw significantly from the public arena, defeated by the liberalism of the New Deal, by the loss of their power in Washington, and by the booming economic success of immigrant groups.[85] What had principally been for them a matter of class,[86] now became a matter of caste, as their increasing loss of power to Jews led them to retreat into private and exclusive clubs, resorts, suburban enclaves such as Bronxville and Tuxedo Park, and the closed urban society of the Upper East Side. In so doing, they ultimately relinquished the role of ruling aristocracy for the more comfortable and less challenging role of social elite. As they saw their power wane, they fully internalized the antisemitic stance that had become pervasive throughout America.[87] Clubs, exclusive neighbourhoods and tightly drawn social circles provided safety and affirmation. As they did in the face of the Progressive onslaught of the Gilded Age, the "decent people," as Baltzell quoted Edith Wharton as having said, "fell back on sport and culture."[88]

Yet the new class of immigrant Jews was improving its lot through hard work and education, and in fact, this was precisely why antisemitism among the Protestant elite became so pervasive. Certain kinds of businesses remained relatively open,[89] perhaps because commercial transactions did not require the sustained social interaction common in other kinds of business-

---

[84] Batzell, *supra* note 47. This book, in which Baltzell, who is credited (evidently wrongly) with coining the acronym WASP, spends more time on antisemitism than any other social attitude of the WASP elite, arguing that antisemitism largely defined the WASP caste. See Eric Pace, "E. Digby Baltzell Dies at 80; Studied WASP's," *New York Times* (20 August 1996), B6 (in which Baltzell's widow is quoted as saying that he did not coin the term), http://www.nytimes.com/1996/08/20/us/e-digby-baltzell-dies-at-80-studied-wasp-s.html.

[85] Such withdrawal in the face of adversity characterized the predecessors of the WASP caste in the Gilded Age, as so wonderfully detailed in the whinings of Henry Adams. See Ernest Samuels, ed., *The Education of Henry Adams* (Boston: Houghton Mifflin, 1973). See also Baltzell, *supra* note 47, at 112–13.

[86] One might be tempted to think that the story I tell is one based on class rather than antisemitism. I shall do my best to demonstrate otherwise (see *infra* note 90). It does appear that the easier social acceptance of German Jews in contrast to Eastern European Jews supports antisemitism as a hybrid form of racism. For an argument suggesting the grounding of at least some strain of American antisemitism in racism, see Jack Wertheimer, "Antisemitism in the United States: A Historical Perspective," in Chanes, *supra* note 80, at 33–54. Bendersky comes down clearly on the side of biology and race in explaining military antisemitism, with frightening echoes of Nazi ideology. See Bendersky, *supra* note 71, at 15–25, 34–35.

[87] Baltzell, *supra* note 47; Dinnerstein, *supra* note 71, at ch. 7: "Antisemitism at High Tide: World War II (1939–1945)." It is interesting to note some of the parallels between the behaviour of the WASP aristocracy and that of non-slaveholding Southern whites in the antebellum period. In each case, the existence of a lower class facilitated the maintenance of caste, regardless of personal or individual economic achievement.

[88] Baltzell, *supra* note 47, at 112–13.

[89] Principally in the soft-goods and retail trades, and of course entertainment. Heavy manufacturing, commercial banking, finance, transportation, and insurance were still the province of the WASP elite. Baltzell, ibid., 207–8.

es. But the professions were different, and the state of the bar, especially in New York, illustrates the severe limitations on Jewish advancement within the elite ranks of the legal profession, limitations which persisted at least through the 1960s. Jews were excluded from much of industry, engineering, medicine (for the most part) and while not from law, certainly from the elite corporate bar. Jewish lawyers turned instead to other forms of legal practice, including challenging corporations through derivative litigation. In so doing, they refused to accept their second-class status quietly and strived for economic success in the only ways available to them, and they hit the Protestant elite (which controlled American industry and the corporate bar) exactly where it lived.

The Carlin Report provided evidence of this internalized social antisemitism, an antisemitism that was not virulent but did affect elite attitudes toward Jews. A 1955 article in *Look* magazine, entitled *The Position of the Jews in America Today*, pretty much sums things up.[90] The author, highly sympathetic to American Jews and critical of antisemitism, could still ask such questions as "Why are there so many Jewish organizations?" and "What makes Jews so clannish?" He could still make such affirmative statements as "Jews do tend to be clannish..."; "For centuries, the Jews were misfits..."; "some Jews ... tend to be over aggressive"; "a great many are hypersensitive in their relations with Gentiles"; and perhaps most astonishing of all, "They seem to have a special exposed nerve that registers every tremor of prejudice like a seismograph: Let a Gentile use an idiomatic phrase like 'He jewed me down,' and every Jew within earshot will mark him as a bigot."[91]

More concretely, perhaps, the author could point to the continued discrimination against Jewish students in "the majority" of fraternities and sororities, to quotas on Jews at medical schools and their virtual exclusion from engineering schools, to the persistence of overt employment discrimination against Jews, and the fact that, "among real estate brokers in certain areas, there is a tacit agreement not to sell to Jews."

It is hard to prove crude antisemitism as the direct cause of any discrimination against Jews, something Hobson illustrated nicely in her book (although the author of the *Look* article unintentionally does a good job). Few people of the level of sophistication and education that characterized the eastern white Anglo-Saxon Protestant upper classes would have been so ill-mannered as to proclaim outright their dislike of Jews and their attribution to them of unpleasant characteristics. (One of the ironies in Hobson's novel is that the protagonist, Phil Green, is a Stanford-educated, California-raised white Anglo-Saxon Protestant reporter who poses as a Jew in New York society for the purpose of understanding, and writing about, anti-

---

[90] Recall that this was five years before the data reported by Carlin. William Attwood, "The Position of the Jews in America Today," *Look* 19:24 (29 November 1955).

[91] It is worth noting that language, even metaphorical, that describes Jews as having a "special exposed nerve" reinforces the idea of antisemitism as rooted in race or biology.

semitism. He is tarred with precisely the same brush, and has precisely the same characteristics attributed to him, as other "Jews," simply as a result of identifying himself as Jewish). It was the Jewishness of the plaintiffs' bar, I argue, that caused concerns about derivative suits to assume crisis proportions during a status panic among the white Anglo-Saxon Protestant corporate and legal elite.

C. A View from the Plaintiffs' Bar

The truth of the conclusion that the push to restrict derivative litigation was motivated by antisemitism is poignantly brought home by a 1937 article written by Harris Berlack, a Jewish member of the New York bar.[92] The article acknowledged both the paucity of studies on methods of enforcing shareholders' rights and the general disrepute in which the derivative suit was held, despite the fact that it was the only significant process available for the enforcement of shareholder rights. As Berlack put it: "the stockholders' suit is universally reviled."[93] Why? Not because it was easy for plaintiffs. Berlack discussed the hurdles faced by a stockholder plaintiff and his lawyer, detailing the expense, risk and difficulty of succeeding. Having done so, he then comes to the point which, while coded, smacks undeniably of the taint of antisemitism underlying the "universal" hostility to shareholder litigation. Using Berlack's own words to illustrate:

> In the sort of case under consideration, however, the labor involved is so great and the outcome so uncertain that *the leaders of the bar* are seldom inclined to take the gamble. This leaves the field to the younger and less experienced *or to the less successful* and sometimes less scrupulous members of the profession. Plaintiffs, as a consequence, find it difficult to obtain proper representation; *and defendants must oppose tactics which are not always the most ethical, or, at the least, are subjected to an attack which is unnecessarily and unpleasantly belligerent.*[94]

> For the abuse heaped upon the "strikers" there may be ample justification. Unfortunately, those constantly affiliated with large corporate interests *have developed the habit of placing all complaining stockholders in the same category.*[95]

> So intensified has become the rancor of this attitude, that the *upstart* who dares to question the conduct of corporate affairs is cast *outside the pale* of common decency.[96]

---

[92] Harris Berlack, "Stockholders' Suits: A Possible Substitute," *Michigan Law Review* 35 (1937): 597–614. By giving Berlack the benefit of the doubt, as I do, one can see this piece as poignant. One can also see it as a classic example of Uncle-Tomism.
[93] Ibid., 599.
[94] Ibid., 603 (emphasis added).
[95] Ibid., 605 (emphasis added).
[96] Ibid. (emphasis added).

> The viciousness of such attacks [of plaintiffs and their counsel] militates against their very purpose; it insures that stockholders' suits will be instituted and conducted, as a rule, only by those *who are most impervious to abuse—and hence capable of the most objectionable conduct*.[97]

The coding in these passages is thin. Berlack, a Jew and a New York plaintiffs' lawyer, did not want to be tarred with the same brush as his colleagues, and used the very language of coded antisemitism to insist on his own innocence. We already know who the "leaders of the bar" and the "less successful" lawyers were. Why should the fact that the latter were the ones willing to take on these suits lead to their revilement? "Unnecessarily and unpleasantly belligerent attacks"? An "unpleasantly belligerent" nature is one of the classic antisemitic saws. "Placing all complaining stockholders in the same category"? That sounds awfully like stereotyping, and given the facts as we know them, the "category" into which all of these lawyers were put is obvious. "Upstart"? Of course these would be people who impertinently attempted to rise above their station or interfere with the activities of their betters.[98] "Cast outside the pale"? The term has special meaning as Berlack used it. The original pale was the protected English settlement around Dublin. To be cast outside the pale was to be thrown into uncivilized and unprotected territory. The Pale of Settlement meant the areas at the western edges of Russia in which Jews were permitted to live. The term connects Berlack's fear of being ostracized with a perhaps subconscious desire to be separated from his own people. "Those who are most impervious to abuse"? Why? Because the contempt in which they are already held makes the marginal pain of further abuse insignificant, especially for the starving lawyer trying to make a living.

Read together with Berlack's (perhaps unintentional) self-revelation, the rhetoric of the Wood Report tells us exactly why derivative suits were considered to be such a significant problem, despite the reality of their

---

[97] Ibid., 606 (emphasis added).

[98] Upstart indeed. John Higham illustrates this nicely: "And discrimination reflected, as it had for fifty years, a conjunction of two factors: the great *but insecure* inequalities of a middle class society in which men striving for distinction feared inundation; and the urgent pressure which the Jews, as an exceptionally ambitious immigrant people, put upon some of the more crowded rungs of the social ladder." John Higham, "Social Discrimination Against Jews in America, 1830–1930," in *The Jewish Experience in America*, vol. 5, ed. Abraham J. Karp (Waltham, MA: American Jewish Historical Society, 1969), 371. And Higham went on, describing discrimination in the period immediately before that of the Wood Report as caused by "status panic," (ibid.), and seeing the very success of the Jews as the cause of social antisemitism. "Whereas other European groups generally gained respect as assimilation improved their stature, the Jews reaped more and more dislike as they bettered themselves," (ibid., 376), and "unfavorable stereotypes have pictured an overbearing Jewish ability to gain advantage in American life. Only one other important immigrant group—the Japanese—has normally been disliked for its strength rather than its weakness" (ibid.). It was the temerity of Jews to challenge their betters that led to the "universal revilement" of derivative litigation.

relative innocence and the lack of serious scholarly concern about this. I argue that the reason was the irritation and vexation felt by white Anglo-Saxon Protestant lawyers and their clients at having to defend themselves against low life "upstart" Jews who were demanding an equality which the elite was unwilling to grant them. Had the challenge of derivative litigation come from Protestant—or at least Christian—lawyers, the empirical evidence suggests that it would not have been so "universally despised" and that any problems could have been worked out through a "gentleman's agreement."[99] Recall the substantially better educational opportunities for low-status Protestants than for Jews and the fact that career opportunities for low-achieving Protestants were equivalent to that for high-achieving Jews.[100]

D. The Composition of the Wood Committee

The composition of the Committee that supported Wood further supports the suspicion that antisemitism motivated its Report. The committee consisted of three members in addition to Wood: Richard Lawrence, Thomas Parkinson and Arthur Reis.

Wood was a prominent New York lawyer who, several years after graduating from Cornell and Cornell Law School, began his own practice in New York and later joined what became Hawkins, Delafield & Wood in 1945. The most interesting aspect of his life for our purposes is the fact that he lived in Bronxville, a town known for its exclusion of Jews, and that he was a member of the Bronxville Board of Zoning Appeals from 1948 to 1958. Not only as a resident, but also as a public official, he was undoubtedly quite conscious, and presumably supportive, of the "gentleman's agreement" to exclude Jews from the town.[101] Wood was a member of the University Club (described by Birmingham as "for years, the most steadfastly anti-Jewish club in New York"),[102] as well as several other clubs.[103]

---

[99] Or it could have been that poorer WASP lawyers were reluctant to take on such suits because they had a very real opportunity to rise in status within the bar, which Jewish lawyers did not.

[100] *Supra* note 60 and accompanying text.

[101] Bronxville's discriminatory history is well known in the New York area. Like the antisemitism implicit in section 61-b itself, it is only circumstantially demonstrable (evidently Bronxville builders were not so crude as to include restrictive covenants in their deeds), but those circumstances are rather powerful. See, e.g., Harry Gersh, "Gentlemen's Agreement in Bronxville: The 'Holy Square Mile'," *Commentary* 27 (1959): 109; Marilynn Wood Hill, "Bronxville: From Country Hamlet to Suburb," in *Building a Suburban Village: Bronxville, New York, 1898–1998*, ed. Eloise L. Morgan (Bronxville: Bronxville Centennial Celebration, 1998), 17–19.

[102] Birmingham, *supra* note 69, at 261.

[103] Like antisemitism itself, Wood evidently was a complex man. He served as plaintiffs' counsel in at least one derivative suit in 1934, and was defense counsel in two others. As plaintiffs' counsel, he worked with a Jewish firm. I do not quite know what to make of this, other than what I have already said—that Wood, like antisemitism, was complex.

Lawrence was a member of the Union League of New York, and Parkinson was a member of the Century Association, both clubs identified by Baltzell as high in the ranks of the WASP aristocracy.[104] Parkinson was also a member of the Washington, D.C. Cosmos Club, itself highly exclusive (and co-founded by the antisemitic Henry Adams).

Arthur Reis was a Jew, an unsurprising fact given the long historical presence of the token (or "Court") Jew in most non-Jewish establishment organizations. In America, the Court Jew's role was to lend validity to the decisions of the powerful by providing "the" Jewish perspective.[105] Nor is it surprising that Reis was of German-Jewish descent, which meant that he was likely to have been socially acceptable at one level and was largely capable of "passing." While we know relatively little about him, he probably shared the prejudices of his class with respect to his Eastern European brethren.[106] Reis' father Robert was a German-born Jew who established Robert Reis & Company in 1885,[107] which became one of the larger mens' underwear manufacturers. Arthur Reis joined that company after receiving his undergraduate degree from Columbia in 1903 and eventually succeeded his father as president of the company.[108] His wife, Claire Raphael Reis, was

---

[104] Baltzell, *supra* note 47, at 368–71.

[105] The Court Jew has actually existed throughout history. The term comes from Germany, where the Hofjude, or Court Jew, became an official position in the courts of many nobles. The original function of the Court Jew was as a financial advisor, and often a financier as well, since many of the Court Jews were chosen from among the wealthy and because of their excellent business connections. They often formed family allegiances with other Court Jews which created a kind of upper class among European Jewry, and they were often subjected to the contempt of other Jews because of their strong desire and often successful attempts to assimilate into mainstream society. At the same time, because of their high positions, they often were able to, and did, intercede with governing authorities on behalf of the Jewish community. There were no Court Jews as such in America. However, the term came to be used as an epithet to describe obsequious Jews who attached themselves to powerful politicians or businessmen and who were highly discreet and deferential on matters of Jewish concern, thus foregoing the opportunity to help other Jews that was taken advantage of by European Court Jews. See generally Ze'ev Glicenstein, "The Era of the Court Jew," *The Canadian Jewish News* 32:11 (14 March 2002): 34; Philologos, *Court Jews: Our Man in Vienna*, online: *Forward*, at http://web.archive.org/web/20020822092454/www.forward.com/issues/2002/02.02.01/arts5.html; David E. Lipman, "The Court Jews," online: Gates to Jewish Heritage, at http://web.archive.org/web/20011016093434/www.jewishgates.org/main.asp; Vivian B. Mann & Richard I. Cohen, eds., *From Court Jews to the Rothschilds: Art, Patronage, Power, 1600–1800* (Munich: Prestel-Verlag, 1996); Salma Stern, *The Court Jew: A Contribution to the History of Absolutism in Europe*, trans. Ralph Weiman (New Brunswick, N.J.: Transaction Books, 1985).

[106] I have been able to find out relatively little about Reis other than his background and principal activities. Thus I cannot be sure that his attitude towards the class of Jewish lawyers with which we are concerned was negative. The circumstances alone suggest that it was likely that he shared the prejudices of the German-Jewish class, and would have been unlikely to have raised, even if he had seen, the antisemitism implicit in the statute and the Wood Report.

[107] "Arthur M. Reis, 64, A Manufacturer," *New York Times* (24 December 1947), 21.

[108] Ibid.

also from an unusually privileged Jewish background, having been educated in Germany, France and the United States.[109] She was very active in promoting and teaching classical music in New York City, became a well-known authority on the subject, received numerous awards, published many articles, and was even invited by Franklin D. Roosevelt to serve on the Committee on the Use of Leisure Time.[110] Notwithstanding Reis' privileged background and status, it is unlikely that his underwear business would, at an earlier time, have put him at the very highest levels of German-Jewish aristocracy. He was, however, a member of the Century Club, which was at the apex of German-Jewish Society, having supplanted the Harmonie club in that position.[111]

E. Race or Class?

There is another possible argument that transcends antisemitism as an explanation for why derivative suits were viewed as so threatening, an argument which is highlighted by Carlin's conclusions that ethical behavior was a function of status within the bar. This argument would suggest that the animosity to derivative suits was less driven by dislike of Jews than by class differences. But this is difficult, if not impossible, to sustain. Had it been the case that the plaintiffs' bar was made up largely of Irish and Italian lawyers, the class story might be plausible, but it was not. Of course there was elite discrimination against those ethnic groups. But it never came close to reaching the extent of antisemitism,[112] and those groups were themselves participants in the antisemitism which was so pervasive during the era of the Wood Report. For the most part, the Irish and Italians at that time had their own defined economic roles in the trades: the police, politics, civil service, and shop-keeping sectors which were never the province of the Protestant elite and therefore did not bring the groups in competition with it.[113]

More importantly, if class were the issue, it should have been the case that lower-class Protestant lawyers were treated as poorly as Jewish lawyers from their entry into college through to their admission to the bar and their employment in firms. But the evidence we have already examined suggests just the opposite. Lower-class Protestants, and particularly academically unsuccessful lower-class Protestants, had almost the same chances to attain elite legal status as did wealthy and academically successful Jews, whereas

---

[109] Donna P Parker, *Reis, Claire Raphael*, online: The Handbook of Texas Online, at http://tshaonline.org/handbook/online/articles/RR/fre51_print.html.

[110] Ibid.

[111] Birmingham, *supra* note 69, at 345.

[112] John Higham, "Social Discrimination Against Jews in America, 1830–1930," *Publications of the American Jewish Historical Society* 47:1 (Sept. 1957): 27–28.

[113] The Irish control of New York City politics through the Tammany machine, from the last quarter of the nineteenth century until the Second World War, is well known. Howe, *supra* note 12, at 363.

poor and academically unsuccessful Jews had almost no chance at all. Finally, it is worth repeating that, as Baltzell saw it, the white Anglo-Saxon Protestant elite largely defined itself in opposition to Eastern European Jewry, in contrast to the negligible notice it took of other ethnic minorities. The class argument falls apart on the facts.

F. Ethical Issues

It is possible that the Jewish plaintiffs' bar behaved unethically as a class, and that it was this lack of ethics rather than antisemitism that motivated the Wood Report and Section 61-b. Again, there is empirical evidence. As I noted earlier, the purpose of the Carlin report was to examine the ethical behaviour of New York lawyers. We have already seen the stratification of the bar, which remained consistent between 1939 and the time of Carlin's work. Carlin concluded in his study that understanding the stratification of the bar was "essential" to understanding the forces that determined a lawyer's ethical behaviour.[114]

Here Jewish lawyers fared less well. Carlin concluded that in general, large-firm lawyers, who were mostly WASP, were more likely to conform to explicit ethical norms than smaller firm lawyers, who were more likely to be Jewish. From this one might conclude that it was indeed rational to distrust the plaintiffs' bar. But the conclusion is not obvious. In Carlin's words:

> Viewed alone, ... [the data] suggests a direct connection between cultural or religious characteristics and conformity with ethical norms. However, further analysis of the data indicates that the significance of ethnicity is largely confined to the role it plays in allocating lawyers to different status positions in the bar and in exposing them to different pressures.[115]

In other words, Carlin found that when lawyers of different ethnicity were of equal status in the bar, ethnicity was "virtually eliminated" as a factor in ethical compliance.[116] The extent to which Jewish lawyers were more likely than Protestant lawyers to violate explicit ethical norms was a clear function of the stratification of the bar based on antisemitism.

Even if Jews were more likely to violate explicit ethical norms, can we conclude that they were intrinsically less trustworthy? Two aspects of the ethical dimension suggest not, and further suggest that the ethical violations by Jewish lawyers were, for the most part, far more innocuous than the social and economic damage wrought by corporate managers and their counsel. The first of these aspects is the type of ethical rules that lower-status lawyers tended to violate, none of which were related to the issues raised in the Wood Report or were likely to be relevant in a sophisticated,

---

[114] Carlin, *supra* note 52, at 23.
[115] Ibid., 126.
[116] Ibid.

large firm corporate practice. The second is the fact that the rules of ethics themselves were drafted against a rather explicit background of antisemitism, and that many of those rules (such as the prohibition on advertising) were clearly designed to damage the prospects of struggling Jewish lawyers and thereby discourage them from becoming members of the bar in the first place.

First let us look at the types of ethical violations considered in Carlin's report. Before doing so, however, it is worth remembering that the rules of ethics we are dealing with are not rules of morality, but are positive rules that were constructed and adopted by the bar. As every law student comes to understand, the rules of legal ethics are sometimes counterintuitive, and are designed to permit consistent self-regulation of the bar. As I will shortly explain, some of the ethical violations Carlin referred to were clearly wrong and indefensible under any system of ethics, but others were more ambiguous, obviously arising from the need to make a living under the difficult circumstances I described above. Still others, including the prohibition on advertising, had little if any moral content and may have been based on indefensible policies such as the creation of barriers to entry in order to limit competition.

A brief listing of Carlin's categories[117] will indicate the nature of the ethical violations he focused on. Recited like the ten plagues visited upon Egypt at the Passover Seder, they were: kickbacks to clients for referral of other clients; conflicts of interest; purchasing stock in a corporation to which the assets of a bankrupt client corporation were to be transferred; sending Christmas cards to all clients; overlooking a client's bribe of a tax or other governmental official; accepting ordinary commissions from title insurance companies without informing the client; recommending an "almost fair" settlement offer to a client in exchange for future concessions from the insurance adjuster; accepting a referral fee from another lawyer; misinforming a client as to the weakness of the state's case against him in order to ensure continued installments on fees; taking a divorce case where the parties had agreed to a consent decree on the basis of adultery that had not been committed (adultery being the only ground for divorce in New York); following a client's instructions to disregard an oral agreement with the other lawyer in order to take a better deal; bribing police to get a charge of homosexuality against a "promising youth" removed from the records; and insider trading.[118]

As one can readily see, some of these actions (having the records purged of charges of a dubious crime for a "promising youth," referral fees, the divorce consent decree, and sending Christmas cards to clients) were at least morally defensible. Some of these are also based on ethical restrictions that are downright anticompetitive (referral fees, Christmas cards). Others, while violations of a client's trust, were not necessarily damaging to a client

---

[117] For a detailed explanation, see ibid., 44–45.
[118] Ibid.

(accepting a normal title insurance commission without disclosure). Most of the others were unambiguously wrong, but one can see their clear relationship to a lawyer's ability to survive. One can also see that the situations in which most of these violations occurred would never come up in the large-firm corporate context. And it should be quite clear that none of them had anything to do with the kinds of issues that come up in derivative litigation. Thus the implication that plaintiff's lawyers were somehow less trustworthy than corporate managers seems unfounded, especially when the serious national economic damage caused by those corporate managers during the first thirty years of the previous century and the beginning of this one is compared with the relatively petty nature of most of the ethical offences listed above.

Conclusion

One can seldom identify with certainty the motivations of actors in law or in society. Even self-expressed motivations are open to question. Nonetheless, the correlation between the enactment of section 61-b and the pervasive antisemitism in the New York bar is undeniable in light of the facts. Although the drafters of the Wood Report were responsible and sophisticated lawyers, careful analysis of that report makes it clear that such lawyers would never have presented it to their clients as high-quality legal work. This dimension of my study alone provides strong evidence that antisemitism was, if not the sole motivating force, at least a powerful force behind the enactment of Section 61-b. When the data on the structure and stratification of the New York bar are taken into account, along with the additional evidence collected at the time by the New York courts and by Judge Rifkin, and when all of that material is examined against the backdrop of the pervasiveness of social antisemitism and its presence in higher education, it would appear to be established on a balance of probabilities that the mid-century attempt to eliminate derivative litigation as a practical means of enforcing shareholder rights was motivated by antisemitism in the New York bar and among its white Anglo-Saxon Protestant clients.

While it is commonly accepted among intellectuals today that things are seldom what they seem, the story I have told is a potent reminder that even the most reasonably presented legal initiatives can conceal depths of discrimination and bigotry against which we must be ever vigilant. Although the restrictions on shareholder litigation that I have discussed remain in force, and even greater restrictions have been added, a sophisticated understanding of their origins ought to make us more cautious in taking even well-considered moves to limit recourses to a variety of legal actions. Sometimes those actions, even if they are subject to abuse, are the best tools we have for enforcing legal obligations and vindicating legal rights.

From Emancipation to Assimilation: Is Secular Liberalism Still Good for Jewish Lawyers?

Russell G. Pearce[1] and Adam Winer[2]

The old, iconic Jewish query of distrust and apprehension—"Is it good for the Jews?"—is thought to have originated in the nineteenth century among the anxious inhabitants of the Russian Empire's Pale of Settlement. Though American Jews enjoy a level of freedom that far eclipses that of their ancestors, they nonetheless continue the custom of asking whether political and social developments are good for the Jews. While this question once pertained to the physical survival of the Jews, today one can meaningfully ask whether a given trend will help or hinder the communal vitality of American Jewry, and whether a political culture is or is not conducive to the flourishing of Jewish identity and practice.

This chapter addresses the question to secular liberalism—the philosophical perspective that served as the ideological catalyst for Jewish success in the United States generally and the legal profession in particular. Secular liberalism, committed to the equal treatment of each member of society, was the dominant jurisprudence of the civil rights movement, and became the reigning ideology of the legal profession as Jewish lawyers moved from the margins to the mainstream. Secular liberalism's claim that all individuals merit equal status means that the factors that differentiate them from one another (such as religion, ethnicity, and worldview) are simply irrelevant and ought to be excluded from public discourse. This stance, though remarkably effective in combating overt discrimination against minority groups, also presents them with a unique set of challenges.

This chapter will argue that secular liberalism limits lawyers in general, and Jewish lawyers in particular. According to secular liberalism, the central goal of public life is to maximize the freedom of the individual, allowing each person to pursue their own vision of the "good life" without the interference of others. This means that institutions operating within the public sphere, such as the legal profession, must maintain neutrality towards the various conceptions of the "good life" by adopting no particular moral or religious outlook. The legal profession, once dedicated to the public good in word and in deed, has accordingly abandoned this aspira-

---

[1] Edward & Marilyn Bellett Chair in Legal Ethics, Morality & Religion, Fordham University School of Law. Thanks to research assistants Rachard Kemp, Jere Keys, Jonathan Kret, and Joseph Tartakovsky.

[2] Adam Winer received his B.A. in Philosophy from McGill University in 2013.

tion. Law has become a business in its own right, with lawyers selling themselves as "hired guns" to the highest bidder. Consequently, lawyers have experienced a tremendous loss of meaning in their work, reporting disproportionately high rates of depression, substance abuse, and dissatisfaction with their choice of career. One reason for this of particular relevance to Jewish lawyers is that secular liberalism bifurcates the personal and professional lives of lawyers, asking them to check their values at the office door. This paradigm runs directly contrary to the teaching of the four major streams of Judaism—Reform, Reconstructionist, Conservative, and Orthodox—that our obligations as Jews persist in all parts of our lives, including our public work. Leaders of all four movements have argued that practice of the Jewish religion is not restricted to the performance of specific commandments, but entails a spiritual awareness that ought to inform or guide all of one's decisions and actions, including professional ones. By rejecting this central tenet of Judaism, secular liberalism weakens Jewish identity in a way that denies Jewish lawyers—and American Jews generally—a valuable resource for finding meaning in their lives, for maintaining their Jewish identity, and for continuing their commitments to equal justice under law.

I. From Governing Elite to Hired Guns: The Impact of Secular Liberalism on the Legal Profession

We emphasize at the outset that this project is very different than that of, say, Norman Podhoretz, whose much-publicized book, *Why Are Jews Liberals?*, focuses on the Jewish tendency to support politically liberal positions, as opposed to the relationship between modern American Jewry and the philosophical underpinnings of liberalism.[3] The primary goal of philosophical liberalism is to maximize individual freedom.[4] It assumes that all individuals are politically equal, that they all possess a unique set of preferences and beliefs, and that they all do not necessarily share the normative vision of "the good life" held by others.[5] Given this diversity of preferences and beliefs, philosophical liberalism presumes that the goal of maximizing individual freedom requires that "no person or group has the right deliberately to impose personal ethical values ... on anyone else."[6]

In the philosophical liberal paradigm, therefore, equal opportunity and peaceful coexistence between discrete individuals and groups can only be achieved when society treats each person on his or her merits, as atomized individuals blind to particular differences. To achieve its end of maximizing individual freedom, liberalism demands that the public sphere, and not just

---

[3] Norman Podhoretz, *Why Are Jews Liberals?* (New York: Doubleday, 2009).

[4] Ronald Dworkin, "Who Should Shape Our Culture?" *The Law School*, Autumn 2005, 20–21.

[5] Ronald Dworkin, "What is a Good Life?" *New York Review of Books*, February 2011.

[6] Dworkin, "Who Should Shape Our Culture?" 21.

the public square, be radically universal.[7] Since the only proper public considerations are those readily shared by individuals, differences like religion or race must be restricted to the private sphere. For purposes of this chapter, we use the term "secular liberalism" to describe the brand of liberalism that advocates for the exclusion of religion from the public sphere.[8]

Implicit in secular liberalism are two core assumptions. First, society can only achieve equality of opportunity if people ignore difference. Even the acknowledgement of inherent difference prepares the way for discrimination against minorities or women (who, although a majority, may be culturally and politically subordinate).[9] Second, to paraphrase Richard Rorty, secular liberalism takes the position that differences grounded in identity, like religion, are "conversation stoppers."[10] That is, religious and other identity-based perspectives are impossible to resolve through public debate, however well-reasoned or thoughtful. Therefore, the only way for disparate people to coexist is to privatize those elements of our identities that differentiate us from one another.[11]

This chapter traces the ascendance of secular liberalism as the guiding ethos of the American legal profession. Applying the framework proposed in the article "The Legal Profession as a Blue State," we use the term "Blue State" to describe the secular liberal construction of the lawyer's role.[12] The term, of course, draws from common parlance, in which Blue State voters are allied with the Democratic Party, while Red State voters are Republican supporters. This choice of terminology serves to highlight the influence exercised upon legal ethics by public discourse: law is a "Blue State" profession because it reflects the philosophical commitments common to Blue State voters.

Recent polls suggest that Blue and Red State voting blocs have correspondent philosophical standpoints regarding the relationship between the

---

[7] See Russell G. Pearce, "The Jewish Lawyer's Question," *Texas Tech Law Review* 27 (1996): 1261.

[8] This, at least, is its pure form. In the Jewish community, secular liberalism also appears in hybrid or syncretistic forms, including coexistence with a strong or thick Jewish nationalism that is logically inconsistent with secular liberalism's commitment to privatizing identity.

[9] For a fuller exposition of the position that race should be disregarded, see Anthony Appiah, "The Uncompleted Argument: Du Bois and the Illusion of Race," *Critical Inquiry* 12 (1985): 35.

[10] See Richard Rorty, *Philosophy and Social Hope* (New York: Penguin Books, 1999), 168–74.

[11] See Russell G. Pearce and Amelia J. Uelmen, "Religious Lawyering in a Liberal Democracy: A Challenge and an Invitation," *Case Western Reserve Law Review* 55 (2004): 142–45 (on the general consensus on the issue of religion and lawyering is that it is "unprofessional"). They cite Levinson's explanation of "professionalism" which requires "the exclusion of ... aspects of self" and the "conception that the professional's conduct [be] governed by the morality dictated by the profession and not from outside the profession." See Pearce, "The Jewish Lawyer's Question," 1261.

[12] Russell G. Pearce, "The Legal Profession as a Blue State: Reflections on Public Philosophy, Jurisprudence, and Legal Ethics," *Fordham Law Review* 75 (2006): 1340–41.

individual and the political community.[13] Blue State voters, comprising liberals and libertarians, generally hold the view that government has no business imposing moral principles upon its citizens.[14] This position casts individuals as distinct from one another and from society at large: both liberal and libertarian theorists "deny that there exists any social entity above or beyond the individuals who comprise it."[15] Accordingly, the role of government is not to embody or administer any particular moral vision but merely to protect the freedom of each individual.[16]

Red State voters, in stark contrast, view the political community as just that: a community, whose members bear moral responsibility toward one another and in which the proper moral values ought to guide the conduct of the community as a whole.[17] Although Red State voters are typically social conservatives, many progressives share their dedication, whether grounded in religion or philosophy, to communal responsibility and moral governance.[18] To the chagrin of Red State commentators, the legal profession is widely regarded as being ruled by a Blue State ideology that does not permit lawyers to inject moral or religious considerations into their work.[19] This development, however, is a relatively recent one, and a radical departure from the conception of the legal profession articulated by the framers of America's Constitution and the founding fathers of America's legal system.

The early American elite subscribed to a hybrid model of governance, combining elements of liberalism and republicanism. In this understanding of political life, the government (as in republican thought) was tasked with pursuing the public good—something prohibited to hands-off liberal gov-

---

[13] Ibid. These findings have drawn controversy: Barack Obama wrote them off as somewhat "overstated." Barack Obama, *The Audacity of Hope: Thoughts on Reclaiming the American Dream* (New York: Crown Publishers, 2006), 52. This chapter does not assert that liberals lack values; rather, they perceive their "own policy prescriptions as neutral with regard to values at the same time that they believe that politically conservative perspectives wrongly impose values on the public sphere in ways that are intolerant and impermissibly limit individual freedom." Pearce, "Blue State," 1341 n. 13.

[14] Pearce, "Blue State," 1340–41.

[15] Michael J. Sandel, *Liberalism and the Limits of Justice* (Cambridge: Cambridge University Press, 1998), 67, in reference to liberal John Rawls and right-wing libertarian Robert Nozick.

[16] Liberalism and libertarianism differ as to whether regulating business and redistributing wealth are a part of the appropriate role of government; see Sandel, *Liberalism*, 66, and Pearce, "Blue State," 1340–41.

[17] Pearce, "Blue State," 1340–41.

[18] Ibid. See also Martin Luther King's dismissal of the liberal ideal of procedural justice, and support for a conception of substantive justice rooted in natural law: Martin Luther King, "Letter from Birmingham City Jail," in *A Testament of Hope: The Essential Writings and Speeches of Martin Luther King, Jr.*, ed. James Melvin Washington (San Francisco: HarperSanFrancisco, 1986), 289–302; also see Network of Spiritual Progressives, "Our Vision and Mission," http://spiritualprogressives.org/newsite/?page_id=303 (in praise of political communities of solidarity and moral kinship, as opposed to the liberal, atomistic model of societal life) (accessed August 8, 2013).

[19] See sources listed in Pearce, "Blue State," 1339–40.

ernments.[20] The government's concern with the public good can be seen in the exhortation to "promote the general Welfare" in the Preamble to the Constitution.[21] On the other hand, aspects of the public good which the government strove to maximize were decidedly liberal, consisting of "the Blessings of Liberty."[22] The framers promoted majority rule, so long as it was tempered by a morally upright elite class.[23] Alexander Hamilton pinpointed professions as the virtuous class that could ensure the smooth functioning of the fledgling state, writing that the "learned professions," such as law, "form no distinct interest in society, and according to their situation and talents, will be indiscriminately the objects of confidence and choice of each other and of other parts of the community."[24] Lawyers' fitness to rule was an inherent feature of their profession: since their sole interest was thought to be the public interest, they could sidestep the selfish tendencies that rendered the landed interests and merchant class less capable of responsible governance.[25] Lawyers exercised a significant degree of control over the institutions of American government through their command of the judicial branch and leadership of the legislative and executive branches. Outside of their official positions of leadership, lawyers linked citizenry to government policy in numerous ways: they dispensed legal advice, represented clients in court, were active in civil discourse, and ensured that business and family relationships were in accord with government policy. Lawyers, described by Alexis de Tocqueville as the "American aristocracy," functioned as, and were lauded as, the governing class of antebellum America.[26]

---

[20] Jennifer Nedelsky, *Private Property and the Limits of American Constitutionalism* (Chicago: University of Chicago Press, 1990), 170–83. See also Pearce, "Blue State," 1347, and Gordon Wood, *The Radicalism of the American Revolution* (New York: A.A. Knopf, 1992), 253–58.

[21] "The United States Constitution," http://usconstitution.net/const.html#Preamble (accessed August 8, 2013).

[22] Ibid. See also Nedelsky, *Private Property*, 170-83, Pearce, "Blue State," 1347, and Wood, *Radicalism*, 253–58.

[23] Nedelsky, *Private Property*, 170–83, Pearce, "Blue State," 1347, and Wood, *Radicalism*, 253–58.

[24] Alexander Hamilton, "The Federalist 35," in *The Federalist Papers* (New York: Penguin Books, 1987), 234. See the following for explanations of the role of lawyers in this period: David Hoffman, *A Course of Legal Study, Addressed to Students and the Profession Generally*, 2d ed. (Baltimore: J. Neal, 1836), 26–27; George Sharswood, *An Essay on Professional Ethics*, 5th ed. (Philadelphia: T & J.W. Johnson, 1896), 25, 30–31, 53–54; Wood, *Radicalism*, 254, 325; Russell Pearce, "Rediscovering the Republican Origins of the Legal Ethics Codes," *Georgetown Journal of Legal Ethics* 6 (1992): 252–56.

[25] See sources *supra* note 23. This unmitigated faith in the virtue of lawyers rested upon a natural law jurisprudence: see Pearce, "Blue State," 1348.

[26] Alexis de Tocqueville, *Democracy in America*, 1835, trans. Arthur Goldhammer (New York: The Library of America, 2004), 309. See also Pearce, "Blue State," 1348 and idem, "Lawyers as America's Governing Class: The Formation and Dissolution of the Original Understanding of the American Lawyer's Role," *University of Chicago Law School Roundtable* 8 (2001): 387–92.

A key theme of this chapter is the intimate connection between the role of lawyers and the philosophical attitudes held by Americans regarding the political community. This relationship has maintained itself at various stages of American history, from the age of the inception of America's governing institutions to the present. In the postbellum period, the nature of the legal profession shifted along with the public philosophy of the times: as republicanism and its natural law foundations lost credibility, the stricter version of liberalism was embraced.[27] As talk of a public good waned, and as majority rule eclipsed the trust invested in a small elite, the mandate of lawyers was correspondingly tightened. Lawyers lost their lofty directive to discern and promote the public good, and took up the more modest task of stabilizing the relationship between the interests of the rich and the poor.[28] Though the broad empirical knowledge and rigorous training of lawyers were held in high regard, public confidence in the capacity of lawyers to govern society in a virtuous manner had crumbled.[29]

This trend intensified in the twentieth century, with the loyalty of lawyers to the public good devolving into mere rhetoric.[30] During the 1960s, philosophical liberals of all political stripes became thoroughly convinced that no public good could be spoken of, and that human beings naturally inclined to the pursuit of their own material interests.[31] The claim of any person or profession to represent the public good was met with nothing but suspicion. Similarly, lawyers took pride in their concern for the public good until the 1960s, when this self-conception shattered. Surveys indicated that lawyers saw their work as largely disconnected from the general welfare.[32]

Lawyers began to adhere to notions of professional conduct more coherent with Blue State liberalism. David Luban identifies two principles that guide the comportment of today's lawyers. First, lawyers exercise "extreme partisan zeal on behalf of the client."[33] Second, "lawyer[s] bear[] no moral responsibility for the client's goals or the means."[34] Moral considerations

---

[27] Pearce, "Blue State," 1351–53. See sources cited.

[28] Louis Brandeis, *Business—A Profession* (Buffalo, N.Y.: William S. Hein & Co., 1996), 337.

[29] Pearce, "Blue State," 1355–57.

[30] Ibid., 1358–61.

[31] Ibid., 1359–60.

[32] See Robert A. Kagan and Robert Eli Rosen, "On the Social Significance of Large Law Firm Practice," *Stanford Law Review* 37 (1985): 431–32; Robert L. Nelson, "Ideology, Practice, and Professional Autonomy: Social Values and Client Relationships in the Large Law Firm," *Stanford Law Review* 37 (1985): 539–40; Margaret Cronin Fisk, "Lawyers Give Thumbs Up," *National Law Journal* 38 (1990). See also Pearce, "Governing Class," 407–10, for a summary of survey data as well as reactions to this data.

[33] David Luban, *Lawyers and Justice: An Ethical Study* (Princeton: Princeton University Press, 1988), xx.

[34] Ibid. See also Murray Schwartz, "The Zeal of the Civil Advocate," in *The Good Lawyer: Lawyers' Roles and Lawyers' Ethics*, ed. David Luban (Totowa, N.J.: Rowman & Allanheld, 1983), and William H. Simon, "The Ideology of Advocacy: Procedural Justice and Professional Ethics," *Wisconsin Law Review* 29 (1978): 115–16. While Luban argues

have become so cleanly detached from the practice of law that even to discuss moral considerations with one's client is a severe breach of professional conduct. To Luban, lawyers are expected to "remain morally neutral toward lawful client ends, refraining from wagging a censorious finger at the client or pulling their punches out of moral squeamishness."[35] In the Blue-State dominated practice of law, the role of the lawyer is simply to further the self-interested ends of his or her client, within the bounds of the law.

To make to these two principles work lawyers must separate their personal identify from their professional role. Professor Sanford Levinson has explained that the "professional project" requires that lawyers attempt to make themselves "almost purely fungible.... Such apparent aspects of the self as one's race, gender, religion, or ethnic background ... become irrelevant to defining one's capacities as a lawyer."[36] The professional project is grounded in a particular understanding of rule of law, which aims to make justice equally accessible to all individuals and dictates that justice is best served when the group identity of lawyers is irrelevant to their work in the courtroom. For the system to work correctly, "all parties [must] receive equal representation," and for that to happen lawyers must "function as extreme partisans who should not bring their own [identity] to bear on their representation."[37] When lawyers put aside their own identities, they sideline any ethical concerns that may arise in their work, and allow a strict sense of role morality to govern their conduct.

The divorce of legal practice from the public good has given rise to the troubling self-perception of lawyers, not as public servants or members of a responsible governing class, but as "hired guns"—as morally disinterested businesspeople who happen to practice law. The past two centuries have witnessed the breakdown of the conceptual gap between business and the legal profession. Even in the early nineteenth century, when most leaders of the legal profession so strongly articulated the need for this gap, some lawyers already championed the notion that lawyers work as hired guns, carrying out the wishes of their clients with no regard for ethics.[38] This approach failed to gain traction, however, as lawyers were firmly en-

---

against this approach, he and other scholars mistakenly view it as rooted in the ethical rules governing the work of lawyers. Model Rule 2.1, conversely, explicitly states that lawyers may give moral counseling to clients. American Bar Association, "Model Rules of Professional Conduct" (Chicago: American Bar Association, 2013), at http://www.americanbar.org/groups/professional_responsibility/publications/model_rules_of_professional_conduct/model_rules_of_professional_conduct_table_of_contents.html, at "Rule 2.1" (accessed August 8, 2013). For a broader discussion on this issue, see Pearce, "Republican Origins," 280.

[35] David Luban, *Legal Ethics and Human Dignity* (Cambridge: Cambridge University Press, 2007), 9.

[36] Sanford Levinson, "Identifying the Jewish Lawyer: Reflections on the Construction of Professional Identity," *Cardozo Law Review* 14 (1993): 1578–79.

[37] Pearce and Uelmen, "Religious Lawyering," 143.

[38] Pearce, "Governing Class," 385.

trenched in their role as a governing class.[39] But this state of affairs changed by the late 1800s, when both lawyers and non-lawyers lamented a sorry state of affairs in which lawyers began to resemble businessmen (describing some lawyers as "hangers-on of police courts" and "ambulance chasers," and law firms as "a money-making mechanism") rather than a learned profession.[40] America's bar associations were born as a result of this turbulent shift in the role of lawyers. The bar associations allowed law's "best men" to be the normative voice of the profession: the bar imposed stricter regulations upon entry into the practice of law, compiled codes of ethical conduct, and cracked down on violations of the above.[41]

The bar associations developed a triple-pronged approach to legal professionalism, claiming that these three principles effectively separated their reputable profession from business.[42] First, lawyers laid claim to unique modes of knowledge and experience that could not be obtained by non-lawyers. Second, the associations insisted emphatically that law, in contrast to business, did strive to further the public good. Finally, the associations argued that lawyers could be relied upon to regulate themselves, while other, profit-seeking businesses required the watchful eye of government.[43] This understanding of professionalism kept its currency until the 1960s, when Wall Street lawyers still considered themselves "guardians of the public good."[44] Whether or not this self-perception was an accurate one, professionalism lent meaning to legal work, giving lawyers a gratifying standard to which they could aspire. The late 1960s marked a "crisis" in professionalism, with more lawyers beginning to question openly the very distinction between law and business, and to deny the orientation of the legal practice toward the public interest.[45] Non-lawyers also challenged the hallowed status of the bar; given the dominant philosophical liberal view that all humans were at bottom self-interested, lawyers could no longer claim to be altruistic agents who rose above selfish materialism.[46]

---

[39] Ibid.

[40] Ibid., 395–99.

[41] Ibid., 399. See also John A. Matzko, "'The Best Men of the Bar': The Founding of the American Bar Association," in *The New High Priests: Lawyers in Post-Civil War America,* ed. Gerald W. Gewalt (Westport: Greenwood Press, 1984), 75–96.

[42] Russell G. Pearce, "The Professionalism Paradigm Shift: Why Discarding Professional Ideology Will Improve the Conduct and Reputation of the Bar," *New York University Law Review* 70 (1995): 1239–40.

[43] Pearce, "Governing Class," 399–400.

[44] Erwin O. Smigel, *The Wall Street Lawyer: Professional Organization Man?* (New York: The Free Press, 1964); Pearce and Uelmen, "Religious Lawyering," 147.

[45] Russell G. Pearce, "Revitalizing the Lawyer Poet: What Lawyers Can Learn from Rock and Roll," *Widener Law Journal* 14 (2005): 913 n. 32. See also Eugene R. Gaetke, "Renewed Introspection and the Legal Profession," *Kentucky Law Journal* 87 (1999): 903–18.

[46] See sources in Pearce, "Lawyer Poet," 910–11.

In short, some lawyers readily accepted, and even celebrated, the paradigm of lawyer as mercenary. However, even those lawyers who did subscribe to more noble ideals were unable to deflect the accusation that lawyers had simply become hired guns. Accordingly, the public reputation of lawyers took a permanent nosedive. The bar, in defiance of these developments, continued to employ the rhetoric of professionalism for more practical purposes: if the strict division between law and business could be sustained, at least on rhetorical terms, then the bar could more easily prevent accounting firms and other businesses from encroaching upon the legal services market traditionally cornered by lawyers.47

The decline of professionalism, even if embraced by some, has taken a drastic toll upon lawyers. First, lawyers now lack a substantive ideal to live up to; if representation of clients is solely an income-generating venture, then the public good, or religious or ethical values, must be tossed aside as a hindrance to this goal. A lawyer responding to public and private challenges to this amoral role may appeal only to the adversarial system, which requires that each client have the ability to hire counsel who would unswervingly champion his or her interests.48 Most lawyers who seek to achieve substantive rather than procedural justice are stuck; with the exception of the small cadre of cause lawyers, they cannot act upon their values, as these have no place in law, and they cannot take recourse in the adversarial system. For these lawyers, the hired gun model of lawyering is often unfulfilling. Of course, not all lawyers share these qualms with the adversarial system. Nonetheless, even those who endorse the ideal of procedural justice are often disillusioned with today's adversarial system, which is intended to dispense equal justice to all. This goal is subverted by the enormous disparity in access to legal services among Americans.49 Finally, the legal profession suffers from a distinct lack of definition. Although the rhetoric of professionalism is still present, it rings increasingly hollow. Lawyers feel a pronounced sense of fragmentation: on the one hand, they are chastised for seeking to promote the general welfare within a liberal public sphere supposedly impervious to values, and on the other hand, those who do simply seek profit in their work are humiliated when confronted with the rhetoric of a more robust professionalism.50

---

47 Russell G. Pearce, "How Law Firms Can Do Good While Doing Well (and the Answer is Not Pro Bono)," *Fordham Urban Law Journal* 33 (2005): 214. See also Deborah L. Rhode, "Law, Lawyers and the Pursuit of Justice," *Fordham Law Review* 70 (2002): 1543–62; Susan Daicoff, "Lawyer, Know Thyself: A Review of Empirical Research on Attorney Attributes Bearing on Professionalism," *American University Law Review* 46 (1997): 1337–1427.

48 See *supra* notes 33–35.

49 See generally Deborah L. Rhode, *Access to Justice* (New York: Oxford University Press, 2004).

50 See generally Pearce, "Paradigm Shift"; Mary Ann Glendon, *A Nation Under Lawyers: How the Crisis in the Legal Profession is Transforming American Society* (New York: Farra, Straus and Giroux, 1994); Anthony T. Kronman, *The Lost Lawyer: Falling Ideals of the Legal Profession* (Cambridge, MA: Belknap Press, 1993); Sol M. Linowitz and

The rhetorical usage of the now-suspect ideal of professionalism, coupled with the expectation that lawyers conduct themselves as mercenaries, renders a career in the legal profession deeply disappointing for many lawyers. Relative to other professions, lawyers enjoy a very low rate of workplace satisfaction. Many lawyers express regret over their choice of profession, and go so far as to warn potential lawyers to think twice.[51] After all, to become a lawyer means to enter the American profession with a high rate of depression, and to risk other forms of emotional distress at a rate fifteen times higher than the average American. Needless to say, alcohol abuse among lawyers also tops the American average by a large margin.[52] The practice of law, in short, is in need of renewed direction.[53]

But while this dilemma results from the influence of secular liberalism on professional ideology, secular liberalism has had a positive effect that merits closer examination: it once helped to promote civil rights and civil liberties, and to open the door to the legal profession for minority groups, including Jews.

II. How Secular Liberalism was Good for Jewish Lawyers

Jewish legal thinkers played an important role in developing the ideology of secular liberalism and in applying it, in particular, to civil rights and the separation of religion and state. Many of America's most renowned Jewish lawyers, including Louis Brandeis, Felix Frankfurter, and Louis Marshall, were guided by a strong orientation toward social justice in choosing to advocate for these causes. It was no coincidence that these Jewish lawyers exhibited a commitment to both social justice and the American legal system: steeped in the Jewish obligation to pursue justice, they found the same imperative within the practice of American law. Indeed, legal historian Jerold Auerbach highlights their "identification of Judaism with Americanism": the conviction that being a good Jew meant contributing to American society, which shared with Judaism "a common tradition that emphasized the rule of law and the quest for social justice."[54] Since both discourses were centered on constitutionalism, the two could

---

Martin Mayer, *The Betrayed Profession: Lawyering at the End of the Twentieth Century* (New York: C. Scribner's Sons, 1994); for a critique of this debate, see Samuel J. Levine, "Faith in Legal Professionalism: Believers and Heretics," *Maryland Law Review* 61 (2002): 217–42.

[51] Glendon, *A Nation Under Lawyers*, 85.

[52] Ibid., 87. See also Patrick J. Schiltz, "On Being a Happy, Healthy, and Ethical Member of an Unhappy, Unhealthy, and Unethical Profession," *Vanderbilt Law Review* 52 (1999): 871–951; Lawrence S. Krieger, "What We're Not Telling Law Students—and Lawyers—That They Really Need to Know," *Journal of Health and Law* 13 (1998–1999): 3–4.

[53] Pearce and Uelmen, "Religious Lawyering," 142–45.

[54] Jerold S. Auerbach, *Rabbis and Lawyers: The Journey from Torah to Constitution* (Bloomington: Indiana University Press, 1990), 17. We note, however, that Auerbach rejects this approach as inauthentic.

easily be equated: the features that Brandeis, Frankfurter, and Marshall saw as characteristic of Judaism were also operative in Americanism.

Each of these three eminent Jewish lawyers acted upon his deep loyalty to the Jewish people by devoting great effort toward securing equal status for Jews, both within America and internationally.[55] But their commitment to social justice extended beyond their allegiance to the Jewish people: each fought for non-Jewish causes as well. While Brandeis' driving pursuit was economic justice, Marshall represented Catholics in Oregon who wished to keep parochial schools open, and sought civil rights for African-Americans.[56] Frankfurter also focused upon economic issues, and spoke out on behalf of Sacco and Vanzetti, alleging that their conviction for murder was unfairly based upon their anarchist views and status as immigrants.[57]

Despite their evident commitment to their fellow Jews, the question remains as to whether or not any of these three would have considered their dedication to social justice to be a direct consequence of their being a part of the Jewish people, or an obligation imposed upon them by their Jewish faith or Jewish moral worldview. It is likely, in fact, that only Marshall would have considered himself a religious Jew, while Brandeis and Frankfurter (though certainly not observant) may have felt an affinity with the ethical principles of Judaism.[58] What is clear is that all three considered themselves members of the Jewish people.[59]

They had great reason to do so. Not only did Jews play an important role in promoting the secular liberal project, Jews benefited greatly from its success.[60] Today, Jews are well represented at the highest levels of the legal profession.[61] In the United States, antisemitism has diminished significantly to the point where it is not a significant stumbling block to Jews individually or collectively, and has minimal impact upon Jews wishing to enter the legal profession.[62] The participation of past and present Jewish lawyers in

---

[55] Ibid., 17–18, 117–18, 123–49, and 154–67; Albert Vorspan, *Giants of Justice* (New York: Union of American Hebrew Congregations, 1960), 22–39, 40–57.

[56] Vorspan, *Giants of Justice*, 25–27 (regarding Brandeis) and 55 (regarding Marshall).

[57] Robert A. Burt, *Two Jewish Justices: Outcasts in the Promised Land* (Berkeley: University of California Press, 1988), 56–58.

[58] Vorspan, *Giants of Justice*, 46, and Auerbach, *Rabbis and Lawyers*, 124–26, 154, 164.

[59] Vorspan, *Giants of Justice*, 39, and Auerbach, *Rabbis and Lawyers*, 17, 147, 162–67, 186.

[60] See Noah Feldman, *Divided by God: America's Church-State Problem and What We Should Do About It* (New York: Farrar, Straus and Giroux, 2005), 164–85 (recounting the American Jewish community's role in the development of legal secularism in the post-WWII era); Naomi Weiner Cohen, *Jews in Christian America: The Pursuit of Religious Equality* (New York: Oxford University Press, 1992), 85–87.

[61] See Russell G. Pearce, "Reflections on the American Jewish Lawyer," *Journal of Law and Religion* 17 (2002): 179 n. 1 (citing *Encyclopedia Judaica*'s entry on "Lawyers," which states that "by the late 1960s 20% of America's 350,000 lawyers were Jewish"). See also Eli Wald, "The Rise of the Jewish Law Firm or is the Jewish Law Firm Generic?" *University of Missouri-Kansas City Law Review* 76 (2008): 885–938.

[62] See Pearce, "Reflections on the American Jewish Lawyer," 183–84 (stating that the

the secular liberal project,[63] both in the United States as a whole and in the American legal profession particularly,[64] is well documented. Political scientist Gregg Ivers has argued that "organized Jewish interests were among the first to understand litigation as an effective method of collective action to advance communal interests and to instigate constitutional reform."[65] The Jewish community's legal activism began shortly after the turn of the century, but intensified tremendously in the late 1940s, spearheaded by different organizations and different strategies with shared goals. Jewish leaders, such as Louis Marshall at the American Jewish Committee and Leo Pfeffer at the American Jewish Congress, shaped the role of Jewish groups in promoting law reform efforts that would succeed in transforming.[66] They had two aims, which they saw as complementary, resisting discrimination and ensuring church-state separation.

A. Leo Pfeffer and Separation of Church and State

Nothing in the realm of church-state law better exemplifies the Jewish role than Leo Pfeffer of the American Jewish Congress.[67] Pfeffer (1909–1993) was born in Austria-Hungary, but arrived in the Lower East Side at a very young age. His lifelong career at the American Jewish Congress began when he was hired, in October 1945, as a staff member on the Congress' Commission on Law and Social Action. Pfeffer had a hand in half of the establishment clause cases that came before the Supreme Court during his career. Samuel Krislov, a professor of legal history, has written that "Leo Pfeffer is probably sui generis.... No one comes to mind ... to rival Pfeffer's intellectual dominance over so vital an area of constitutional law for so extensive a period."[68] In one early case, *Friedman v. New York*, 341 U.S.

---

legal profession itself is evidence of the decrease in antisemitism in America and that Jews have overall "gained greater acceptance"). See generally Auerbach, *Rabbis and Lawyers*.

[63] See Philip Hamburger, *Separation of Church and State* (Cambridge: Harvard University Press, 2002), 351. Hamburger cites an 1889 speech by Rabbi J. Bloch presented before the Secular Union Convention where he states, "and speaking of the prophets of old... all of these from Moses to Samuel, and from Samuel to Malachi, all were the strongest advocates of the separation of church and state."

[64] See Feldman, *Divided by God*, 170, describing the significant role American Jews played in the promotion of legal secularism in the post-WWII era: "The best strategy for American Jews was not, however, strong secularism, with its open hostility toward organized religion; such a stance would have been perceived as anti-Christian and would have been risky for American Jews eager to avoid open confrontation with the majority. Legal secularism offered a more attractive option of saying that religion was just fine, but that the law must draw a sharp line between religion and government."

[65] Gregg Ivers, *To Build A Wall: American Jews and the Separation of Church and State* (Charlottesville: University Press of Virginia, 1995), 2.

[66] Ibid., 34–65.

[67] For a helpful discussion of his efforts and successes, see Marc D. Stern, "The Rise and Fall of Jewish Interest in Religion Clause Litigation," on file with the authors.

[68] John R. Vile, ed., *Great American Lawyers: An Encyclopedia*, vol. 2 (Santa Barbara,

907 (1951), Pfeffer argued that a New York law requiring the closure of stores on Sundays clashed with the First Amendment's prohibition on laws regarding an establishment of religion: it effectively made the Christian day of rest everyone's day of rest, and, as one consequence, disadvantaged Jewish shopkeepers who then were required to close both Saturday and Sunday. The case was dismissed as lacking in merit. So, too, was the appeal in *Heisler v. Board of Review*, 343 U.S. 939 (1952), in which a woman was denied unemployment benefits for refusing to accept an offered job that required work on Saturdays. But the same argument that denial of benefits for refusal by reason of religious conscience was unlawful won the day, twelve years later, in *Sherbert v. Verner*, 374 U.S. 398 (1963). And the Sunday closing laws were eventually overturned. This pattern of progress, in which arguments dismissed would later prevail and become the settled law of the land, was characteristic of the change in church-state law.[69]

Pfeffer wrote the brief for the AJC in what would become the landmark case of *McCollum v. Board of Education*, 333 U.S. 203 (1948). There, Pfeffer argued that allowing "released time," i.e., setting aside class time for religious instruction in public schools—a staple of American public education—violated the First Amendment by, in Pfeffer's words, "aiding religion, preferring some religions over others, influencing or compelling children to attend religious instruction, rendering financial aid to religious instruction by allowing public school classrooms to be used for that purpose, and by implicitly, if not expressly, participating in the instruction."[70] The petitioners prevailed. Justice Black wrote "the First Amendment's language, properly interpreted, had erected a wall of separation between Church and State."[71] This case was crucial in establishing Jefferson's metaphor as a national rule of law.[72]

Pfeffer would write of the balancing act that the organizations had to perform, between fighting to ensure religious liberty and avoiding the appearance of anti-Christian or anti-religious motivation. Jewish groups feared a backlash.[73] This fear became particularly acute as the AJC prepared to litigate *Zorach v. Clauson*, 343 U.S. 306 (1952), in which New York's released time was challenged, not with regard to public schools but in churches and parochial schools. Pfeffer would recall that the AJC would only agree to sponsor the suit if the lead attorney and lead plaintiff were

---

Calif.: ABC-CLIO, 2001), 561.

[69] Leo Pfeffer, "An Autobiographical Sketch," in *Religion and the State: Essays in Honor of Leo Pfeffer*, ed. James E. Wood, Jr. (Waco, TX: Baylor University Press, 1985), 490–92.

[70] Ibid., 493–94.

[71] *McCollum v. Board of Education*, 333 U.S. 203, 211 (1948).

[72] See Hamburger, *Separation of Church and State*, 472–78.

[73] Pfeffer, "Religion and the State," 492–93.

non-Jews.[74] The plaintiffs argued that the Free Exercise and Establishment Clauses were violated by the effects of the released time program, which worked to force students to attend sessions of religious instruction, or stigmatized Jewish students who remained at school during the released time hours.[75]

Pfeffer lost the case. But it was a display of what Pfeffer described as his "absolutism" in church-state separation. Absolutism was necessary, he believed, because "any compromise becomes too often the starting point for further compromises."[76] In this view, the government must make no foray into the sphere of religion. For example, in *Committee for Public Education and Religious Liberty v. Nyquist*, 413 U.S. 756 (1973), Pfeffer led the challenge against a New York law that provided reimbursements and grants to non-public schools for their upkeep. But because the money could be used to repair not only classrooms but chapels, the Supreme Court ruled with Pfeffer, and held the law's effect would be to advance the religious mission of sectarian schools. In this and in similar litigation, Pfeffer recommended a six-part test in order to determine whether a particular school was "pervasively sectarian," considering, *inter alia*, its stated purpose, the place of religion in its curriculum, and the image of the institution in the community. This would become the "pervasively sectarian" rule, the standard by which courts for years judged constitutionality of government programs to aid religiously affiliated education. (It was overruled by *Mitchell v. Helms* in 2001.) As the *Nyquist* court held, "In the absence of an effective means of guaranteeing that the state aid derived from public funds will be used exclusively for secular, neutral, and nonideological purposes, it is clear from our cases that direct aid in whatever form is invalid."[77] This reflected Pfeffer's absolutism—and this was no accident.

The American Jewish Congress participated in nearly a third of the appellate cases on religion and state between 1951 and 1971; in early years they limited themselves to amicus briefs, and then progressed to sponsorship and oversight, choosing plaintiffs, selecting courts and remedies, and devising legal strategies.[78] Pfeffer's work has been continued today by scholars like Aryeh Neier, the former national executive director of the ACLU, Marc D. Stern, the AJC's general counsel and co-director of its Commission on Law and Social Action (the same commission that first hired Pfeffer), and Rabbi David Saperstein, the longtime director and chief legal counsel at the Union for Reform Judaism's Religious Action Center.[79]

---

[74] Ibid.

[75] Ibid., 500.

[76] Ibid., 529.

[77] *Committee for Public Education & Religious Liberty v. Nyquist*, 413 U.S. 756, 780 (1973).

[78] Frank J. Sorauf, *The Wall of Separation: The Constitutional Politics of Church and State* (Princeton: Princeton University Press, 1976), 59–68.

[79] For more on Aryeh Neier, see Open Society Foundations, "Aryeh Neir, President

Impressive as this history is, it requires context. Marc Stern cautions against exaggerating the role of Jewish groups in church-state litigation. Explaining that the notion that "church-state litigation is a Jewish invention" is a "myth,"[80] he observes that the Jewish community's contribution was mostly in the second half of the twentieth century. He explains that in earlier periods Catholics contested Protestantism in public schools and Protestants opposed funding of Catholic social welfare agencies and schools.[81] Mormons were also active litigants.[82]

B. Jack Greenberg and Civil Rights

Jewish organizations and lawyers were also engines of the civil rights movement. The National Association for the Advancement of Colored People was founded in 1909, only three years after the American Jewish Committee, with the aid of Jewish leaders. From the outset Louis Marshall litigated cases and served as general counsel for the NAACP. He went on to serve on the organization's board from 1923 to 1929.[83] Jewish and black lawyers collaborated through the 1930s and 1940s to litigate throughout the South, paving the way for Thurgood Marshall's landmark 1954 victory in *Brown v. Board of Education of Topeka*, 347 U.S. 483.[84] Joseph Rauh, a protégé of and clerk to Justice Cardozo, assisted the NAACP beginning in the late 1950s and also served on its board for many years. Louis Marshall and Rauh are only a few among the many Jewish lawyers for whom civil-rights successes brought renown.

The struggles against anti-Jewish discrimination and anti-black discrimination were often seen as one and the same. This is illustrated in the career of Jack Greenberg, who played a key role in the legal battle for African-American equal rights during his service at the NAACP Legal Defense and Education Fund. Although he denied that "religion had anything to do with his becoming a civil rights lawyer," he claimed that Jewish peoplehood

---

Emeritus," http://www.opensocietyfoundations.org/people/aryeh-neier (accessed August 8, 2013); for Rabbi David Saperstein, see Religious Action Center, "Rabbi David Saperstein, Director and Counsel," http://rac.org/aboutrac/leadershipandstaff/rds/ (accessed August 8, 2013); for Marc D. Stern, see "AJC Leadership and Staff," http://www.ajc.org/atf/cf/%7B42d75369-d582-4380-8395-d25925b85eaf%7D/AJC_STAFF_JUNE_2012_1.PDF (accessed August 8, 2013).

[80] See Stern, "Rise and Fall," 1.

[81] Ibid. For more on the limited Jewish role in the nineteenth century, see Arthur Gilbert, "Jewish Commitments in Relations of Church and State," in *Church-State Relations in Ecumenical Perspective*, ed. Elwyn A. Smith (Pittsburgh: Duquesne University Press, 1966), 58.

[82] Stern, "Rise and Fall," 1.

[83] Ivers, *To Build a Wall*, 40.

[84] Ronald Smothers, "Jews and Blacks Recall the Decades of Partnership," *The New York Times*, November 30, 1988, http://www.nytimes.com/1988/11/30/us/jews-and-blacks-recall-the-decades-of-partnership.html?n=Top%2FReference%2FTimes%20Topics%2FSubjects%2FR%2FReligion%20and%20Belief, (accessed August 8, 2013).

influenced him.[85] He described himself as "an ethical, secular Jew,"[86] and attributed the heavy involvement of Jews in the civil rights movement to two factors: first, to the influence of labor Zionism and socialist ideals upon Jews involved in American public life between the 1940s and 60s, and second, that the changes sought by blacks would also bolster the position of Jews in America.[87] According to Jonathan Kaufman, Greenberg believed that:

> [B]y fighting segregation of blacks, he was also fighting discrimination against Jews. You could not compare the treatment of blacks and Jews in this country.... Jews were far better off. But it was also true that blacks and Jews were often beaten with the same stick, that housing rules that kept one out kept out the other, that people who didn't like one usually didn't like the other. A society in which someone's color or creed didn't matter meant a climate that would benefit both blacks and Jews.[88]

C. Jews in the Legal Profession, Especially in New York

Despite their influence in shaping legal change, the "entry of Jews into the legal profession," writes Jerold Auerbach, "was prolonged and painful, strewn with obstacles of exclusion and discrimination set by law schools and law firms."[89] Louis Marshall remarked (around 1895) of the Association of the Bar of the City of New York that, "few Jews were admitted to membership, that men of the highest character and ideals had been ostracized, that others who would have been very glad to have become members shrank from having their names proposed because of similar indignities ... [and] that it was only in exceptional cases that men of my faith were appointed on committees of the organization."[90] It often took the form of outright antisemitism, but more frequently, it was couched in the language of snobbery, nativism, and elitism. A New York delegate to the ABA emphasized (as if it were in doubt) that it was "absolutely necessary" for members of the bar to be "able to read, write and talk the English language—not Bohemian, not

---

[85] Jonathan Kaufman, *Broken Alliance: The Turbulent Times Between Blacks and Jews in America* (New York: Scribner, 1988), 87.

[86] Ibid.

[87] Ibid., 106.

[88] Ibid., 95–96.

[89] Auerbach, *Rabbis and Lawyers*, 150.

[90] Jerold S. Auerbach, *Unequal Justice: Lawyers and Social Change in Modern America* (New York: Oxford University Press, 1976), 122. One of the "few Jews" to not only gain membership to the New York Bar but to also attain a high level of influence—even "superelite" status—within the Bar and the professionalism movement was Julius Henry Cohen. See Samuel J. Levine, "Rediscovering Julius Henry Cohen and the Origins of the Business/Profession Dichotomy: A Study in the Discourse of Early Twentieth Century Legal Professionalism," *American Journal of Legal History* 41 (2005): 11–13.

Gaelic, not Yiddish, but English."[91] The college requirement for entry was a hotly disputed issue, and legitimate concerns about the fitness of lawyers mixed with xenophobia and an elite's attempt to protect its privileges.[92] Other restrictions were also raised to check the entrance of ethnic minorities; the Illinois state board of bar examiners in 1922 urged higher standards in response to a rise in successful foreign-born applicants.[93] The views of George W. Wickersham—the name made famous by the firm Cadwalader, Wickersham, and Taft, still the oldest continuously operated corporate law firm in America—typified the perspective of the City Bar's gatekeepers. He found it "appalling" that men without college degrees, untutored in the "full realization of the meaning of our law historically," would enter the ranks of judges and legislators. He lamented that, "[t]o think that those men, with their imperfect conception of our institutions, should have an influence upon the development of our constitution, and upon the growth of American institutions, is something that I shudder when I think of."[94] In such statements, bigotry could hide behind legitimate concerns.

During the pre–WWI period, Joseph Proskauer recalled, the "doors of most New York law offices were closed, with rare exceptions, to young Jewish lawyers."[95] It took a mind as powerful as Felix Frankfurter's to persuade one New York firm to hire its first Jew—but only after the hiring partner advised Frankfurter to change his name.[96] Even when Jews, as a community, made significant strides, the community met the successes with caution. The confirmation battle in 1916 over Brandeis' seat was bitter and laced with antisemitism, but Frankfurter urged that, upon the fact of confirmation, there be "no boisterous Jewish celebration."[97]

"Post–World War I American society," writes Victoria Saker Woeste, "was a wasp's nest of xenophobia, restrictive immigration policies, and racial divisions. Yet in some ways it was possible to avoid the sting: American Jews were attaining higher levels of professional prominence and accomplishment than ever before and becoming increasingly active in

---

[91] Auerbach, *Unequal Justice*, 115. Cohen, however, rejected such notions of prejudice, classism, and elitism from his contemporaries, arguing that professionalism demanded the dismantling of such barriers to admission in favor of a system where individuals could succeed based on hard work and strong morals. See Samuel J. Levine, "Conference: The Law: Business or Profession? The Continuing Relevance of Julius Henry Cohen for the Practice of Law in the Twenty-First Century: Foreword," *Fordham Urban Law Journal* 40 (2012): 4–5.

[92] See generally Auerbach, *Unequal Justice*, ch. 4, entitled "Cleaning the Bar." It is an amusing historical fact that the dean of Fordham Law School opposed the proposal to require a college degree, but for this reason: "radicalism and socialism were very widespread" on campuses. Ibid., 116.

[93] Auerbach, *Unequal Justice*, 123.

[94] Ibid., 115–16.

[95] Auerbach, *Rabbis and Lawyers*, 151.

[96] Ibid.

[97] Ibid., 155.

politics and philanthropy."[98] In 1932, Cardozo was approved, unanimously, as the second Supreme Court Justice of Jewish descent. Like many others, lawyers and judges alike, he was constantly conscious of his position as an exemplar, willing or not, of the Jewish people. Reprimanding a friend who spoke approvingly of the actions of a New York judge who had leniently let off a number of anti-Nazi protesters who had boarded a German ship, he wrote, "What is the use of striving for standards of judicial propriety if you ... condone such lapses! It would have been bad enough if [the judge] had been a Gentile; but for a Jew it was unforgivable. Now our traducers will say—and with some right...that these are the standards of the race."[99]

It is also worth recalling that Jewish lawyers faced express antisemitism. Alan Stroock, a Jew serving as one of Cardozo's law clerks, once had a D.C. home purchase revoked because of a restrictive covenant against Jews. Cardozo was so infuriated—especially after learning that this happened despite knowledge that Stroock was his clerk—that Cardozo urged Stroock to bring a suit and said that he, a sitting Justice, would issue a public statement of support.[100] In Spring 1936, it happened that eight Jewish editors of the *Harvard Law Review* were still not hired for the coming year, provoking Frankfurter to growl: "I wonder whether this School shouldn't tell Jewish students that they go through ... at their own risk of ever having opportunity of entering the best law offices."[101] A New York attorney named Morris Ernst even implored Justice Harlan Stone to meet with Wall Street law firm partners in an effort to persuade them to lift their restrictions.[102]

As the years went by and American antisemitism declined, the law was one of the last fields of breakthrough. Names, even after WWII, remained a problem. Ezra G. Levin, co-chair of Kramer Levin Naftalis & Frankel, recalls a story from the 1950s, when a fellow Columbia classmate interviewed at a white-shoe New York law firm. The student's name did not disclose his Jewish background. The partner led the student into a room that had on its wall Yale's insignia, which includes an inscription in Hebrew. Levin reported that, "The partner wanted to know if he could read it."[103] In 1960, Jewish lawyers, although comprising 60 percent of New York City's bar membership, were represented in much smaller numbers (25%) at larger firms. Protestants, though constituting only 18% of the bar, made up 50% of the city's large firm lawyers.[104] Yet it was later in this decade that things rapidly

---

[98] Victoria Saker Woeste, "Insecure Equality: Louis Marshall, Henry Ford, and the Problem of Defamatory Antisemitism, 1920–1929," *Journal of American History* 91 (2004): 881.

[99] Andrew L. Kaufman, *Cardozo* (Cambridge: Harvard University Press, 1998), 488.

[100] Ibid., 489.

[101] Auerbach, *Unequal Justice*, 186.

[102] Ibid.

[103] Anthony Lin, "Can the 'Jewish Law Firm' Success Story Be Duplicated?" *New York Law Journal,* May 16, 2006.

[104] Ibid.

began to change. According to Eli Wald, "[although] as late as 1950 there was not a single large Jewish law firm in New York, by the mid-1960s six of the largest twenty law firms were Jewish, and by 1980 four of the ten largest law firms were Jewish firms."[105] Wachtell, Lipton, Rosen & Katz was founded in 1965 by four young Jewish lawyers who, it was said, had doors at other firms closed to them. At the same time, barriers at historically antisemitic law firms declined and eventually disappeared. By the year 2007, Jewish lawyers had become leaders of both Cravath, Swaine & Moore and Sullivan & Cromwell; the latter's Jewish chair had even been an ordained rabbi.[106] Wald observes that "[t]he accomplishment of the Jewish firms is especially striking because while the traditional large WASP law firms grew at a fast rate during this period, the Jewish firms grew twice as fast and did so in spite of explicit discrimination."[107]

Wald notices another interesting phenomenon. Despite their successes, firms dominated by Jewish partners played

> a significant role in overcoming discrimination. They provided a platform on which Jewish attorneys could perform and excel, disprove biases and prove their worth. They offered, not unlike their black counterparts, an oasis of comfort and security in what was correctly perceived to be a hostile and anti-Semitic legal environment. Nonetheless, because religious discrimination and an exclusionary ethos against Jewish attorneys, at least in large urban areas, seem to be a thing of the past, to the extent that the Jewish firm played an important role in undermining discrimination, its time, and the need for it, has passed.[108]

The last part of this quote is especially significant. It describes a real and not inevitable consequence of Jewish success in the legal profession. The larger question, of which this particular observation is only a symptom, is that of assimilation and the waning of Jewish self-identity, or the Jewish continuity as a distinct community.[109] It is what Alan Dershowitz describes as "the vanishing American Jew" and the "vanishing American Jewish

---

[105] Eli Wald, "The Rise and Fall of the WASP and Jewish Law Firms," *Stanford Law Review* 60 (2008): 1805.

[106] See Lin, "Can the 'Jewish Law Firm' Success Story Be Duplicated?" for a discussion of the recent emergence of Jewish partners in top leadership positions at these traditionally Protestant firms. Evan Chesler became the first Jewish chair of Cravath, Swaine & Moore in 2013. "Evan R. Chesler," http://www.cravath.com/echesler/ (accessed August 8, 2013). Joseph Shenker was elected vice-chair of Sullivan & Cromwell in 2006 and chair in 2010. "Joseph C. Shenker," http://www.sullcrom.com/lawyers/JosephC-Shenker/ (accessed August 8, 2013).

[107] Wald, "Rise and Fall," 1805.

[108] Ibid., 1865.

[109] Marc Stern observes, for instance: "It is worth noting in this connection that so-called Jewish law firms are now religiously diverse and cannot be counted on as formerly to carry the cudgels for the Jewish community on many controversial church-state issues." Stern, " Rise and Fall," 26–27 n. 75.

lawyer."[110] Perhaps it is only natural that the push for emancipation, reaching and then surpassing its old arbitrary limits, would eventually become a pull toward assimilation. In any event, assimilation and the related problem of the weakening of faith are very different matters from the problems of a previous generation, and they demand a very different solution. Eli Wald has written that the "rise and success of large law firms with distinctive [Jewish] religious and cultural identities [was] surprising because the large firm was purportedly a-religious and meritocratic," but over time we have seen the "decline of the overt religious identity of Jewish law firms."[111] Wald raises doubts about the "ability of the large [religiously identified] law firm to sustain a credible claim for elite professional status in the post-religious twenty-first century."[112]

Nonetheless, it is precisely the decline of religion that removed barriers. Although Wald does not use the terminology of "secular liberalism" to describe this shift, he does employ an analogous concept. Regarding formalism, which was the "dominant American jurisprudential school of thought until the 1920s and 1930s,"[113] Wald asserts that it:

> celebrated law as an independent science, a body of esoteric knowledge based on and derived from general self-contained principles. In particular, law was to be independent of religion, the practice of law was to be free of religious influences, the professional identity of attorneys was to be separate and distinct from their religious identity, and the religious identity of a firm was to be non-existent. For the new law firm to formally adopt a religious identity would have amounted to a rejection of formalism and its claim for the law's independence from religion."[114]

Wald explains as well that a complete understanding of the shift also requires examination of other important factors, such as the need for experienced lawyers in areas that the white-shoe firms had traditionally avoided like litigation, bankruptcy, and real estate. Even when prejudice remained, it redounded to the benefit of Jewish applicants: as law became more of a business, stereotypes of money-grubbing and aggression were helpful.[115]

---

[110] Alan M. Dershowitz, "The Vanishing Jewish Lawyer: Will the Assimilation of Jews Affect the Social Conscience of the Legal Profession?" *California Law Review* 14 (1997); see also Alan M. Dershowitz, *The Vanishing American Jew: In Search of Jewish Identity for the Next Century* (Boston: Little, Brown and Company, 1997), 1, who summarizes the issue: "The good news is that American Jews—as *individuals*—have never been more secure, more accepted, more affluent, and less victimized by discrimination or anti-Semitism. The bad news is that American Jews—as a *people*—have never been in greater danger of disappearing through assimilation, intermarriage, and low birthrates."

[111] Wald, "Rise and Fall," 1804–6.

[112] Ibid., 1806.

[113] Ibid., 1809.

[114] Ibid., 1809–10.

[115] See Lin, "Can the 'Jewish Law Firm' Success Story Be Duplicated?"

The project of secular liberalism, on the whole, has been a decidedly ambiguous one for Jewish lawyers. Secular liberalism exuded great appeal to Jewish lawyers in the 20th century because it promised to banish anti-semitic discrimination from public life. While it was undeniably successful in this regard, it came with an unexpected and hefty price tag: where Jewish lawyers themselves were once banned from the public sphere, it is now their Jewish identities and value systems that are excluded.

III. How Secular Liberalism Limits Jewish Lawyers Today

Today, Jewish lawyers and the Jewish community face a different set of challenges. Many practitioners of law, Jewish and otherwise, are unable to find meaning and satisfaction in their work. In addition, American Jews find their numbers declining as Jewish identity becomes less important to increasing numbers of Jews. The erosion of professionalism among lawyers, the subsequent loss of meaning in practicing law, and the notable slide in Jewish identity can be linked to the unabashedly individualistic culture of secular liberalism. Ironically, a strong religious or moral identity might be of great assistance to many lawyers in overcoming the difficulties posed by the hired gun ideal. However, the same brand of secular liberalism that dismantled the wall between law and business demands that particularities such as religion be hidden from the public eye. Indeed, secular liberalism's hostility toward importing values into the public sphere undermines any attempt to bring the public good into sharper focus within the legal profession, especially for religious Jews (from all movements) and other religious people who find meaning in their faith. The privatized Judaism of secular liberalism offers no help to Jewish lawyers seeking to find meaning in their work and offers a fairly uncompelling ground for non-Orthodox Jews to retain a Jewish identity. Moreover, in promoting the exclusion of religion from the public sphere, secular liberalism can sometimes minimize (and sometimes even justify) discrimination against Orthodox Jews in the legal profession.

The basic problem for a Jewishness seduced by secular liberalism is that it offers no particularly persuasive reason for an individual, lawyer or not, to be Jewish. If it makes no difference in the public sphere whether I am Jewish or not, why bother? Why be Jewish as opposed to any other faith—or why have any faith at all? To willingly inhabit a particular and limited identity seems an arcane and needless deviation from one's universal status as an American. There are compelling answers to these questions, of course, but they are not found within the logic of secular liberalism.

A. Finding Meaning in Being a Jew: Declining Numbers

The facts show that as the number of Jews in America declines, the most vital segment of the community is its most traditionally religious demographic, namely, the Orthodox community.[116] By contrast, Reform, Conservative, and Reconstructionist communities fail to exhibit the same levels of growth.[117] They work toward self-revitalization, to be sure, but not with the confidence and vigor of the Orthodox.

Most agree that the Jewish population is declining. But this does not mean that *all* segments of Judaism are on the wane. According to University of Florida professor Joshua Comenetz, today's Hasidic population is about 180,000, or 3% of the approximately 6 million American Jews.[118] The total Orthodox population has been estimated (see below) at 9% of the total Jewish population, or 540,000, with 24% of the Jewish population as Conservative/Reconstructionist, 30% as Reform, 22% as "Just Jewish/Secular," and 14% as unknown.[119] While the non-Orthodox population falls due to intermarriage and loss of identity, the Hasidic population doubles every 20 years. Hasidic and other Orthodox Jews tend to have many children and these groups also tend to resist intermarriage—in other words, the many children are highly likely to be raised Orthodox, and to remain within the Orthodox fold as adults. If these trends continue, Comenetz predicts that Hasidic and other growing Orthodox Jewish groups will constitute a majority of U.S. Jews sometime in the second half of this century.[120] It is worth observing that intermarriage may be a result, and not a cause, of declining Jewish identification. If Judaism were compelling people to stay Jewish, making Jews feel it was essential that their spouses and children remained Jewish, intermarriage would not have the effect it does. Compelling faiths maintain themselves. This explains why the rise of Orthodox as a percentage of the Jewish population mirrors the rise of evangelicals in the American population.

---

[116] Jacob B. Ukeles, Ron Miller, and Pearl Beck, *Young Jewish Adults in the United States Today: Harbingers of the American Jewish Community of Tomorrow?* (Washington, D.C.: American Jewish Committee, 2006), http://www.ajc.org/site/apps/nlnet/content3.aspx?c=7oJILSPwFfJSG&b=8479755&ct=12481325 (accessed August 12, 2013). In this publication, prepared for the American Jewish Committee, the authors claim "by almost every measure of Jewish connection, the Orthodox are the most highly engaged, at times, much more Jewishly engaged than all other young Jews." They note that the "percentage of young Jewish adults between the ages of 18 and 29 who are Orthodox (16%) is nearly double the percentage of Orthodox among Jewish adults ages 30 to 39 (9%). Thus, while a small group today, young Orthodox Jewish adults are likely to be a much larger group in the future."

[117] American Jewish Committee, "American Jewish Committee Publishes Synagogue Census," August 7, 2002, http://www.ajc.org/site/apps/nlnet/content2.aspx?c=ijITI2PHKoG&b=1531911&ct=867941 (accessed August 12, 2013). In the Synagogue Census, published by the American Jewish Committee in 2001, it is reported that "Orthodox congregations represent a full 40 percent of U.S. synagogues, followed by Reform with 26 percent and Conservative with 23 percent."

[118] Joshua Comenetz, "Census-Based Estimates of the Hasidic Jewish Population," *Contemporary Jewry* 26 (2006): 35–74.

[119] Benjamin Phillips, "Numbering the Jews: Evaluating and Improving Surveys of American Jews" (PhD diss., Brandeis University, 2007), 197. (Numbers adapted from a survey conducted in 2005.)

[120] Comenetz, "Census-Based Estimates."

At one time in America, "cultural Judaism"—the members of the Jewish population who are aware of their Jewish lineage, but who consider themselves unaffiliated with a religious community or undertake no religious observance—was similarly confident. But this was also in a time of exclusion and discrimination. Cultural Judaism has withered, and for today's adherents it appears to be the last stop before leaving Judaism altogether.[121] Absent the genuine experience of discrimination, this faithless brand of faith generally provides very little impulse in support of Jewish continuity. While cultural Judaism will likely persist in areas like New York and Chicago which have large Jewish populations, its decline will probably continue.[122]

B. Discrimination against the Orthodox

The Orthodox, in both the legal and organized Jewish communities, are still considered undesirable in some measure. Taking Saturday off, for instance, may offend secular liberalism, in that one refuses to work on a day that colleagues normally do. Other employees might see this as an unfair benefit. Similarly, a kippah, for its wearer a sign of respect, may be misinterpreted as sign of disrespect, or at least of intentional differentiation, in the office or courtroom. According to Avi Schick, "workplace discrimination" against those who wear kippot is a reality, even if the evidence remains anecdotal.[123] He writes:

> A few years ago, at a Columbia Law School forum, a partner at one of the country's largest law firms candidly observed that wearing a yarmulke to an interview will diminish one's job prospects. An informal study at Fordham Law School concluded that Jewish students on the Law Review who wore yarmulkes to their job interviews were far less likely than their classmates to be called back for a second interview. And New York law firms are far more progressive—and accommodating—than most.[124]

Many firms have made great strides in this respect—witness *mincha* (afternoon prayer) groups at many top firms and the increased employment of

---

[121] See Ukeles, Miller, and Beck, *Young Jewish Adults*, 18. The statistics suggest that "intermarried and the non-orthodox Jewish singles/married-but-childless counterparts are the least engaged and the most numerous."

[122] The "American Jewish Committee Publishes Synagogue Census" found that "the 50 metropolitan areas with the largest Jewish populations contain 82 percent of all U.S. synagogues, a total of 3,075. The New York-Northern New Jersey-Long Island area alone accounts for one-third of the synagogues."

[123] Avi Schick, "French Dressing: Lessons for America from the Proposed French Ban on Religious Garb," *Slate*, December 30, 2003.

[124] Ibid. In this small informal study, it was found that when men wore kippot to interviews, thirty percent got callbacks. When men did not wear kippot, ninety percent got callbacks.

Orthodox Jews[125]—but, as Schick notes, reports suggest something like an informal quota.

Secular liberalism does a disservice in creating ambivalence regarding this discrimination. Orthodox Jews violate, even if only on a symbolic level, the commitment to a secular public sphere. Secular liberalism, therefore, fails to provide a strong condemnation of bias against Orthodox Jews who violate secular liberalism's prohibition of bringing one's religious identity into the public sphere.

IV. The Way Forward: Jewish Lawyering

The religious lawyering movement urges lawyers of faith to integrate their religious commitments into their work. It has been growing in popularity, spurred in large part by the crisis of professionalism.[126] Chief Justice Warren Burger brought this development to the public's attention in his 1984 Report to the American Bar Association on the State of Justice, where he lamented the abandonment of the public good by the legal profession in favor of self-interest, and called for a return to "the great ideals that distinguish our profession from the actors in the marketplace."[127] Burger's call, though, has not been heeded: today, the legal profession is typically described as "lost" and "betrayed," in "decline," requiring "redemption," without which it risks "demise" and "death."[128]

The growth of the religious lawyering movement has been motivated by the inability of the legal profession to provide lawyers with a cohesive and meaningful ethos. This failure forces lawyers to look outside of the discourse of contemporary professionalism. For lawyers who are religious people, religious texts, practices and communities are an obvious place to look for resources to help find meaning in their life. Through religion, lawyers can seek direction in making the right decision in complex dilemmas or can examine broader questions such as the need to act ethically in the first place.[129] Rooted in an ethos of responsibility and accountability to

---

[125] See Lin, "Can the 'Jewish Law Firm' Success Story Be Duplicated?"

[126] See, e.g., Samuel J. Levine, "Introductory Note: Symposium on Lawyering and Personal Values—Responding to the Problems of Ethical Schizophrenia," *Catholic Lawyer* 38 (1998):148 ("Religious values, in particular, have gained increasing prominence in the arena of legal ethics, as they present a comprehensive system of ethics for lawyers seeking to integrate their personal and professional lives"). See also Nancy B. Rapoport, "Living 'Top Down' in a 'Bottom Up' World: Musings on the Relationship Between Jewish Ethics and Legal Ethics," *Nebraska Law Review* 75 (1999): 18–36 (describing a legal ethics analysis which unites "my Jewish world and my academic world," 20).

[127] Warren Burger, "The State of Justice," *American Bar Association Journal* 70 (April 1984): 66.

[128] Pearce, "Paradigm Shift," 1257.

[129] See David Luban, ed., *The Good Lawyer: Lawyers' Roles And Lawyers' Ethics* (Totowa, N.J.: Rowman & Allanheld, 1984); Stephen Gillers, "Can a Good Lawyer Be a Bad Person?" *Michigan Law Review* 84 (1986): 1011–29 (reviewing Luban collection). See also Robert P. Lawry, "The Central Moral Tradition of Lawyering," *Hofstra Law Review* 19 (1990): 311–63; James L. Nolan, "To Engage in Civil Practice as a Religious

society at large, the religious lawyer is in a better position to avoid the hazards of corruption and autonomous self-interest.[130] Indeed, religion offers lawyers an alternative paradigm of self-interest in which individual happiness is attained through dedication to the welfare of others. Many religions endorse the idea that each person has a unique calling, which can lend a deep sense of meaning to all work.[131]

From the inception of the American republic until the present day, lawyers have maintained their dominant role in American government, through their rule of the judiciary and leadership of the legislative and executive, and they continue to mediate between government and citizenry on an informal basis.[132] Despite the normative conception of lawyers as hired guns, the legal profession retains its status as an elite class with enormous power and influence.[133] Religious lawyering has much to offer this profession, as it can instill in lawyers a profound sense of responsibility for the pursuit of justice and the good of society. It not only impresses upon lawyers the imperative to protect the public good, but gives them a language in which to articulate it. Of course, religious lawyering does not spell the

---

Lawyer," *Fordham Urban Law Journal* 26 (1999): 1111–23.

[130] Russell G. Pearce and Eli Wald, "The Obligation of Lawyers to Heal Civic Culture: Confronting the Ordeal of Incivility in the Practice of Law," *University of Arkansas Little Rock Law Review* 34 (2011): 1–52 (describing autonomous self-interest). See also, e.g., Amelia J. Uelmen, "Can a Religious Person Be a Big Firm Litigator?" *Fordham Urban Law Journal* 26 (1999): 1079, in which she discusses issues that emerge when religious values are integrated into practice in a large firm corporate and litigation context:

> Religious reflection brings me to a sense of obligation—not because of an external command, but rather out of an internal conviction about the essence of my nature as a person and the consequent relationships with God and with others. Listening to God within, I understand who I am as a person and feel the desire to correspond to that reality in my daily life. It is not a burden, but a joyous and grateful response in the context of a relationship. Based on religious reflection, I arrive at the conclusion that if I would like to be a person, to be fully human, I *must* keep before me a vision of the common good, I *must* live according to the implications of this vision in every aspect of my life.

[131] See, e.g., Judith L. Maute, "Changing Conceptions of Lawyers' Pro Bono Responsibilities: From Chance Noblesse Oblige to Stated Expectations," *Tulane Law Review* 77 (2002): 147, in which she writes, "The contemporary 'religious lawyering movement' has renewed interest in the concept of vocation as a faith-based command to serve the common good. Being 'called' to serve in a vocation is rooted in Judeo-Christian, Islam, and Baha'i traditions." See also Martin Luther King Jr., "Facing the Challenge of a New Age," Address delivered at the First Annual Institute on Nonviolence and Social Change (December 3, 1956), in *The Papers of Martin Luther King Jr., Volume II: Rediscovering Precious Values, July 1951–November 1955*, ed. Clayborne Carson et al. (Berkeley, CA: University of California Press, 1994), 457.

[132] Bruce Green and Russell G. Pearce, "Public Service Must Begin at Home': The Lawyer as Civics Teacher in Everyday Practice," *William & Mary Law Review* 50 (2009): 1223–27.

[133] See Pearce, "Governing Class," 419–20 ("the development of the *pro bono* duty encouraged elite lawyers to exclude consideration of the public good from their representation of clients.").

end of the association between lawyer and client; clients need not fear that their moralistic attorneys will cease to advocate for them. Religious lawyering seeks to uphold the lawyer-client relationship, but reminds lawyers that procedural justice does not absolve them of moral concerns and that in certain situations lawyers ought to engage in dialogue with their clients regarding the moral ramifications of various courses of action.

A. Objections to Religious Lawyering

The religious lawyering movement is often presented with three objections. First, even commentators who concede that standards of professionalism should be reevaluated question the inclusion of religion in this project. After all, there is no incontrovertible link between being religious and being ethical.[134] These commentators argue that the religious lawyering movement would do well to focus upon the promotion of universal ethical values and shed its assumption that the religious are somehow more ethical than everyone else.[135] Religion is not the world's exclusive source of morality and even religious ethics are underwritten by general, transcendent principles.

Of course, this objection is on target in one key sense: religious faith is not necessarily an indicator of higher moral development, and certainly does not guarantee ethical conduct. Religious lawyering, though, does not rely upon this crude equation of religion and ethics. Indeed, there are numerous bases and motivations for ethical behavior, including the emotional tendency to empathize with the suffering of others, the desire to please others and make them happy, the political stance that basic rights ought to be respected, various religious worldviews, and the philosophical and psychological standpoint that the social nature of human life collapses any neat distinction between the good of the individual and the good of the community.[136] Many reasons, whether conscious or unconscious, can

---

[134] In John Gross, *The New Oxford Book of Literary Anecdotes* (New York: Oxford University Press, 2006), 86.

[135] Bruce A. Green, "The Role of Personal Values in Professional Decisionmaking," *Georgetown Journal of Legal Ethics* 11 (1997): 46–47.

[136] For a philosophical account of empathy with others, see David Hume, *A Treatise of Human Nature: Being an Attempt to Introduce the Experimental Method of Reasoning into Moral Subjects* (Oxford: Oxford University Press, 1978), 574–91, 602–21. Most political theorists endorse, for different reasons, the notion that individuals bear moral obligations toward one another: to social contract theorists, for instance, membership in a society imposes upon each individual the duty to forgo any actions which others might reasonably object to; see T. M. Scanlon, "Contractualism and Utilitarianism," in *Ethical Theory: An Anthology*, ed. Russ Shafer-Landau (Malden, MA: Blackwell, 2007) 644–60, and see generally John Rawls, *A Theory of Justice* (Cambridge, MA: Belknap, 1971). The psychological factors that underlie morality are an increasingly popular topic of scholarly research: see, for example, Darcia Narvaez and Daniel K. Lapsley, eds., *Personality, Identity and Character: Explorations in Moral Psychology* (Cambridge, MA: Harvard University Press, 2009). See generally Luigino Bruni, *The Wound and the Blessing: Economics, Relationships and Happiness* (Hyde Park, N.Y.: New City Press, 2012) for an account of the social nature of human happiness.

compel one to act ethically, and religion is only one of these reasons. The fact remains, though, that many lawyers lack a basis for ethical behavior, and that religion can plug them in to the conversation about ethics. We need not view religion as competing with these other reasons. Religion can also bridge the gap between private and professional life for those who hold values but hesitate to act upon them in their role as lawyer. Prominent 20th-century Jewish philosophers and rabbinic leaders across the denominational spectrum have emphasized the Jew's obligation to serve God in each and every part of his or her life, including the workplace.[137] Rabbi Leo Baeck, one of the foremost intellectual influences of the Reform movement, was quoted as saying that a Jew "directs him [- or her-] self towards God in such a way that no part of his [or her] life is without this center, without this contact."[138] The Jewish Reconstructionist Movement holds that Jews should embody the ideal of "Godliness," and cultivate "those hopes, beliefs, and values within us that impel us to work for a better world, that give us strength and solace in times of need, that challenge us to grow, and that deepen our joy in moments of celebration."[139] The 20th-century Orthodox leader and philosopher Rabbi Joseph B. Soloveitchik wrote that Jewish law "penetrates into every nook and cranny of life. The marketplace, the street, the factory, the house, the meeting place, the banquet hall, all constitute the backdrop for the religious life."[140] The famed Jewish philosopher Abraham Heschel, who taught at the Conservative movement's Jewish Theological Seminary, also believed that Judaism ought to be present in every part of one's life, noting that the "meaning of redemption is to reveal the holy that is concealed, to disclose the divine that is suppressed. Every [individual] is called upon to be a redeemer, and redemption takes place every moment, every day."[141]

Certainly, the virtues embodied by a religious lawyer might correspond with secular values such as equal justice, concern for the poor, and honesty. But the fact that values may be derived from a plurality of vantage points does not make religion irrelevant to the legal profession. Religion allows lawyers to unify their professional and personal lives within a holistic framework, and "offers [lawyers who are religious] an often more compelling reason to adopt [ethical] values"[142] than do ethical discourses which

---

[137] See sources in Pearce, "The Jewish Lawyer's Question," 1266–67.

[138] Ibid. (drawing from Rabbi Alexander Schindler, *Sermon on the Installation of Rabbi Sharon Kleinbaum at Congregation Beth Simchat Torah* (Sept. 11, 1992), 9 (quoting Rabbi Leo Baeck)).

[139] "Is Reconstructionist Judaism for You?" *Jewish Reconstructionist Movement*, http://www.jewishrecon.org/resource/reconstructionist-judaism-you (accessed August 12, 2013).

[140] Rabbi Joseph B. Soloveitchik, *Halakhic Man*, trans. Lawrence Kaplan (Philadelphia: Jewish Publication Society, 1983), 94.

[141] Rabbi Abraham Joshua Heschel, *Between God and Man: An Interpretation of Judaism* (New York: The Free Press, 1965), 80.

[142] Pearce and Uelmen, "Religious Lawyering," 153.

hold less normative sway over the religious lawyer.[143]

The second objection to religious lawyering stems from a concern for the lawyer-client relationship. Religious lawyering aims to open up the public sphere so that lawyers will feel more comfortable discussing their faith, and will not hesitate to introduce ethical considerations into their advocacy. Might not these lawyers place an undue amount of pressure upon their clients to act in accord with religious values that the clients may not share? This fear has been widely discussed in the field of legal ethics. In a noteworthy 1996 case, the Tennessee Supreme Court's Board of Professional Responsibility considered the situation of a Catholic lawyer who represented a minor seeking to obtain an abortion without parental consent. The Board opined that the lawyer could not, as he wished, suggest to his clients that they consider alternatives to abortion or that they discuss their predicament with their parents or legal guardians before making a decision.[144] This conclusion can be seen as a resounding rejection of any lawyer's desire to insert his or her religious convictions into a professional setting.

The Tennessee Board's judgment, however, is nowhere near universally accepted. Legal ethicists are quick to point out that it contrasts with the Model Rules of Professional Conduct. Rule 2.1 states that, "in rendering advice, a lawyer may refer not only to law but to other considerations, such as moral, economic, social, and political factors, that may be relevant to the client's situation."[145] Of course, lawyers must exercise their discretion in bringing up non-legal considerations: the Comment to Rule 2.1 elaborates that a lawyer may refer only to "relevant moral and ethical considerations in giving advice."[146] All lawyers ought to employ sensitivity when dealing with

---

[143] Robert K. Vischer, "Heretics in the Temple of Law: The Promise and Peril of the Religious Lawyering Movement," *Journal of Law and Religion* 19 (2003–2004): 430 (the religious lawyering movement "directly challenges the notion ... that a lawyer's personal allegiances and affiliations should be irrelevant to her representation of clients"). See also Robert F. Cochran, Jr., "Professionalism in the Postmodern Age: Its Death, Attempts at Resuscitation, and Alternative Sources of Virtue," *Notre Dame Journal of Law, Ethics, and Public Policy* 14 (2000): 316, in which he discusses how for Christians the conclusion of Matthew 25—"Just as you did it to one of the least of these who are members of my family, you did it to me"—is more likely to inspire aid to the poor than the ABA Model Rule 6.1 guideline to give fifty hours of *pro bono publico* legal services on an annual basis:

> [Religious] communities are more likely than the profession to inspire lawyers to go beyond the requirements of professional codes and against the incentives of the market. Their teachings are the kind which are likely to wake you up in the middle of the night with questions about the direction of your life. They can change the way a person lives.

[144] Board of Professional Responsibility of the Supreme Court of Tennessee, Formal Op. 96-F-140 (1996), http://www.tbpr.org/Attorneys/EthicsOpinions/pdfs/96-f-140.pdf (accessed August 12, 2013).

[145] American Bar Association, "Model Rules of Professional Conduct" at Rule 2.1.

[146] Ibid. at Rule 2.1, comment 2 (2004). See also American Bar Association, "Model Code of Professional Responsibilities" (1983), http://www.americanbar.org/content/dam/aba/migrated/cpr/mrpc/mcpr.authcheckdam.pdf, at Ethical Consideration 7–8 (accessed August 12, 2013) ("In assisting his client to reach a proper decision, it is often

their clients, but this should not in any way prevent them from laying out the full range of options available, and explaining the moral implications of each one.

This form of counseling only becomes inappropriate if the lawyer projects his or her own preferences upon the client and pressures them to select that particular option. Lawyers often, but not always, find themselves in a position of power over vulnerable clients.[147] For a lawyer to coerce his or her client to act in accordance with the lawyer's belief system is a violation of the client's trust, even when it is not strictly forbidden by the Model Rules. Based upon this understanding, the Model Rules forbid numerous forms of potentially coercive behavior from the lawyer-client relationship, including requesting substantial gifts and engaging in consensual sexual activity.[148]

To the extent that lawyers are permitted by the Model Rules to introduce any relevant considerations into their advocacy, one could read Rule 2.1 to discourage lawyers from bringing in any considerations, religious or otherwise, which have no bearing upon the situation of their clients. Nonetheless, the framework of the Model Rules suggests otherwise. For example, Model Rule 1.8 indicates that these discussions are not prohibited outright: while it carefully delineates the nature of business transactions between lawyer and client, and expressly warns lawyers against requesting gifts from their clients, the Rule does not bar lawyers from suggesting to their clients that they support a given cause or political candidate, or adopt a given religious belief.[149] Still, legal ethicists maintain that lawyers should not charge their clients for time spent discussing such topics.

Some scholars have also argued that religious lawyers should be up front with clients about their beliefs from the outset of their relationship.[150]

---

desirable for a lawyer to point out those factors which may lead to a decision that is morally just as well as legally permissible").

[147] Of course, this is irrelevant in practice contexts where the client holds greater authority over the lawyer. See Uelmen, "Can a Religious Person Be a Big Firm Litigator?" 1092 ("in the relationship between a corporate client and its outside counsel, it may be the client who dominates the relationship or manipulates the lawyer. Concerns about the lawyer 'imposing' personal values may be out of context").

[148] American Bar Association, "Model Rules of Professional Conduct" at Rule 1.8(j), 1.8(c); see John M. O'Connell, "Keeping Sex Out of the Attorney-Client Relationship: A Proposed Rule," *Columbia Law Review* 92 (1992): 909. See also Roger C. Cramton, "Delivery of Legal Services to Ordinary Americans," *Case Western Law Review* 44 (1994): 560.

[149] American Bar Association, "Model Rules of Professional Conduct" at Rule 1.8(a) and Rule 1.8(c).

[150] See B. Carl Buice, "Practicing Law to the Glory of God," *Texas Tech Law Review* 27 (1996): 1033 (arguing that lawyers should disclose their beliefs when taking on divorce cases); Harold S. Lewis, Jr., "Shaffer's Suffering Client, Freedman's Suffering Lawyer," *Catholic University Law Review* 38 (1988): 131 ("unfair surprise to the client about possible outcomes could be mitigated substantially if a lawyer holding Shaffer's view were to disclose the moral limits of her advocacy when the relationship is formed"). For a contrasting view, see Green, "The Role of Personal Values," 55 (claiming that, in some cases, there is an unavoidable tension between standards of professionalism and the

The Model Rules offer further clarification here, stating that in cases where the "personal interest" of a lawyer poses "a significant risk" of "materially" hindering their advocacy on behalf of a client, then the lawyer must disclose this fact.[151] Under this rubric, a lawyer would be required to disclose his or her religious beliefs to a potential client only if these beliefs would prevent the lawyer from providing full representation to the client. For example, the Catholic lawyer in the Tennessee case mentioned above would be required to disclose a conflict of interest only if his religious beliefs would prevent him from seeking court permission for her to obtain an abortion. If the lawyer intended only to discuss all options with his client—as any competent lawyer should—and to act upon the client's wishes even if she elected to seek an abortion, then he would not be obligated to disclose his religious beliefs to her at the outset. This standard does not apply only to religious beliefs: lawyers should disclose any aspects of their identity (ranging from their religious or moral views to their financial interests) that may seriously impact their ability to represent a client. In addition, lawyers should be receptive to the needs of their clients, and should not cajole them to adopt religious or moral viewpoints when they know that this is unwanted.[152]

A third objection is centered on the political ramifications of religious lawyering. According to this objection, religious lawyering threatens to upset the delicate balance achieved by America's liberal democratic system of government. American democracy hinges upon a majority rule with safeguards for the rights of individuals as well as minority groups. Some commentators think that the very reason that majority rule in overwhelmingly Christian America can coexist with individual and minority rights is that religious beliefs are sealed firmly within the private sphere, such that Christian norms may not be imposed upon secular individuals, as well as members of other religions.[153] They argue that religious lawyering, with its attempt to push the private identities of lawyers into the public sphere, might open the floodgates of religious intolerance within the courtroom.[154]

---

values of individual lawyers which cannot be reconciled, even if the lawyer in question fully discloses his or her values to the client).

[151] American Bar Association, "Model Rules of Professional Conduct" at Rule 1.7(a)(2).

[152] Robert Cochran argues that non-religious lawyers also impose their values upon clients. See Robert F. Cochran, "Crime, Confession, and the Counselor-at-Law: Lessons from Dostoyevsky," *Houston Law Review* 35 (1998): 328 ("Moral influence occurs almost every time a client enters a law office"). See also Thomas L. Shaffer and Robert F. Cochran, Jr., *Lawyers, Clients, and Moral Responsibility* (St. Paul, MN: West Pub. Co. 1994), 50–54.

[153] David Lyons, *Ethics and The Rule of Law* (New York: Cambridge University Press, 1984), 191 (to appeal to the authority of religious belief, rather than to reasons which are compelling to all citizens, is "to deny the essential spirit of democracy"). This sentiment is echoed in Richard Rorty's essay, "Religion as a Conversation Stopper," in *Philosophy and Social Hope*, 171 ("The main reason that religion needs to be privatized is that, in political discussion with those outside the relevant religious community, it is a conversation-stopper").

[154] See Martha Minow, "On Being a Religious Professional: The Religious Turn in Professional Ethics," *University of Pennsylvania Law Review* 150 (2001): 672 ("As a member

They think that this result would give rise to a more fragmented and combative public sphere, in which all rational and civil means of cooperative decision-making have been exhausted. Two groups in particular might shudder in anticipation of the unequal and discriminatory treatment they would receive: members of religious minority groups and non-believers.

In fact, religious lawyering coheres fully with American liberal democracy. While the American government may not force any individual to accept religious authority, all individuals are free to base their own actions, not to mention their votes, upon religious belief.[155] The majority of liberal political theorists concur that government has no business regulating, or even passing judgment upon, the reasons that individuals employ in making decisions. One person's religious convictions, of course, may not be convincing to others: to John Rawls, the goal of public discourse is for individuals with discrete belief systems to construct a common mechanism for decision-making. In order to do so, individuals must present their views in a way that is compelling to others. An atheist, for instance, is not likely to endorse a given policy because of an appeal to the authority of religious tradition, but might well be convinced to support the same policy by a different argument.[156] It is perfectly consistent with the modus operandi of liberal democratic institutions, then, for a lawyer's professional practice to be informed by his or her religious identity.[157] Religious values do not undermine those of a liberal democratic system of government: given that 83% of Americans identify themselves as members of a religion,[158] America's liberal democratic institutions would not enjoy the stability that they do if most Americans found them incompatible with their religious identities.[159] Accordingly, religious lawyering is congruous with liberal democracy even if religious lawyering is not consistent with philosophical liberalism.

Skepticism about the political consequences of religious lawyering may be animated by commonly held stereotypes about religious people. One

---

of a religious minority group, I am reminded of the risk of second-class status, exclusion, and worse").

[155] U.S. Constitution, Amendment I.

[156] This analysis of Rawls is found in Kathleen A. Brady, "Religious Organizations and Mandatory Collective Bargaining Under Federal and State Labor Laws: Freedom From and Freedom For," *Villanova Law Review* 49 (2004): 163–64 ("Rawls would permit comprehensive religious and moral doctrines to be introduced into public discourse about fundamental political principles provided that those who make these arguments also give public reasons to support their position"). See John Rawls, *Political Liberalism* (New York: Columbia University Press, 1993), 224–25.

[157] Another matter entirely, and one which is the subject of heated public debate, is *how* lawyers should discuss their religious identity with clients (see second objection above).

[158] Pew Forum on Religion & Public Life, "U.S. Religious Landscape Survey: Religious Affiliation: Diverse and Dynamic" (February 2008), http://religions.pewforum.org/pdf/report-religious-landscape-study-full.pdf, 20 (accessed August 12, 2013).

[159] John A. Coleman, S.J., "Public Religion and Religion in Public," *Wake Forest Law Review* 36 (2001): 281. Coleman explores the role played by religion in liberal democracies in engaging citizens in political life, and in sustaining democratic institutions.

such misunderstanding is that the inclusion of religion in the public sphere will necessarily foster conflict, as the gaps between various religions, and between religious people and non-believers, cannot be bridged. This view rests upon the assumption that each religion (or atheism) is a uniform and inflexible entity, whose members follow ardently a rigid and intractable belief system. In truth, religious groups admit of tremendous internal diversity, and tend to feature a lively culture of debate and scholarship as well as highly developed mechanisms for conflict resolution.[160] The worldviews of religious communities are hardly detached from the secular world, both drawing from and inspiring secular intellectual developments. Religious individuals are not as a rule closed to dialogue with those outside of their community of faith.[161] Even those with strongly defined identities and beliefs, whether religious or secular, have much to gain from and contribute to a healthy public discourse.[162]

Just as practitioners of religion make sense of the world through a communal commitment to sacred texts and practices, even the staunchest secularist has a framework through which he or she makes sense of the world: factors as diverse as emotional and genetic makeup, childhood experiences, culture, and education inform one's belief system. The proponents of a more extreme variant of secular liberalism demand that we discard our belief systems when we participate in political life and employ only reason. Charles Taylor calls this the myth of "disengaged reason," which is an "ideal picture of a human thinking that has disengaged from its messy embedding in our bodily constitution, our dialogical situation, our emotions, and our traditional life forms in order to be pure, self-verifying rationality."[163] Not one of us is capable of making a truly objective judgment about the world, abstracted from our own experience. Religious lawyering allows one to participate in civic life without aspiring to a fictional rationality. To the contrary, the religious lawyer is encouraged to act upon his or her

---

[160] See Stephen L. Carter, *God's Name in Vain: The Wrongs and Rights of Religion in Politics* (New York: Basic Books, 2000), charting the contribution of religion to political culture.

[161] Jeremy Waldron, "Religious Contributions in Public Deliberation," *San Diego Law Review* 30 (1993): 841–42:

> Even if people are exposed in argument to ideas over which they are bound to disagree ... it does not follow that such exposure is pointless or oppressive. For one thing, it is important for people to be acquainted with the views that others hold. Even more important, however, is the possibility that my own view may be improved, in its subtlety and depth, by exposure to a religion or a metaphysics that I am initially inclined to reject.

[162] Michael J. Perry, *Religion In Politics: Constitutional and Moral Perspectives* (New York: Oxford University Press, 1997), 46 ("We probably need reminding that, at its best, religious discourse in public culture is not less dialogic—not less open-minded, not less deliberative—than is, at its best, secular discourse in public culture").

[163] Charles Taylor, *The Ethics of Authenticity* (Cambridge, MA: Harvard University Press, 1991), 101–2.

beliefs in a manner respectful of the diverse and pluralistic character of the American public sphere.

This approach does not give lawyers carte blanche to invite bigotry and closed-mindedness into the legal profession, flatly dismissing all views apart from their own. This behavior, like any conduct that encroaches upon the dignity of others, merits "professional and social critique, and discipline where appropriate."[164] What religious lawyering does propose is that lawyers who wish to integrate their religious identities into their work establish functional lines of communication with clients and colleagues who may not share their views.[165] Religious lawyering does not seek to upend liberal democratic institutions, but to carve out a space for multiple visions of societal life within America's system of governance. Values such as the rule of law will be best served if we place identity and difference out in the open and celebrate them rather than engage in a futile attempt to paper them over.

On a fundamental level, religious lawyering is an expression of the desire of many lawyers to inject new life and meaning into their once-proud profession, and to renew the commitment of lawyers to the public good. This shift can take place in the spirit of pluralism and mutual respect, without infringing upon the rights of minority groups, including non-believers.

B. Jewish Lawyering

So how does this apply to Jewish lawyers specifically? Religious lawyering rose to prominence with Christian scholars in the early 1980s, and found adherents in the Jewish community in the 1990s. Since that time, one now finds a significant number of Jewish-themed articles[166] and—within the last fifteen years—the movement has been the subject of hundreds of law review articles and increased attention by law schools and bar associations.[167] Many cities have active groups of interfaith lawyers and of same-faith law groups. Jewish organizations as disparate as Chabad, Agudah, and Reform Judaism have also become involved. In doing so, they succeeded in

---

[164] Pearce and Uelmen, "Religious Lawyering," 159; Vischer, "Heretics in the Temple of Law," 478–85.

[165] To the *Guardian*'s Julian Baggini, liberal governance "requires ... that articles of faith, or other substantive conceptions of the good life, do not carry any weight simply because they are matters of faith. The requirement to justify your position in terms that are not exclusive to your specific comprehensive world view is not an excessive or impossible one." Julian Baggini, "'A secular state must be neutral'—what does that mean exactly?" *The Guardian*, February 16, 2012, http://www.theguardian.com/commentisfree/2012/feb/16/what-mean-secular-state-neutral (accessed August 12, 2013).

[166] See, generally, Jerome Hornblass, "The Jewish Lawyer," *Cardozo Law Review* 14 (1993): 1639–55.

[167] Russell G. Pearce and Amelia J. Uelmen, "Religious Lawyering's Second Wave," *Journal of Law and Religion* 21 (2005–2006): 272–73. In 2001, the Institute of Religion, Law & Lawyer's Work opened at Fordham University School of Law. Pepperdine University School of Law opened its Institute on Law, Religion and Ethics in 2003. Religious lawyering has become a topic of conferences and CLE programs nationwide.

actualizing Jewish identity within the legal sphere. As Eli Wald explains with regard to Jewish law firms, "While [they] did not explicitly build on Jewish values and culture to define its professional identity, religious and cultural considerations did play an important part in its rise to dominance."[168]

What are the advantages of a specifically Jewish approach to lawyering?[169] First, consistent with the approaches that we know work in addressing continuity, religious lawyering provides those lawyers who remain committed to the Jewish community's vitality with the tools to find meaning in their work. Second, we suggest, Judaism has much to teach Jewish lawyers. The Jewish tradition shows how one can ground a commitment to universal justice in an openly particularistic commitment. Moreover, Judaism can help lawyers work through the crisis of professionalism by transcending an ethical dichotomy between businesspeople and professionals.[170] The study of Jewish lawyering can help us reconcile our identities as both Jews and lawyers. It is to acknowledge that the profession of lawyering is a part, and only a part, of one's life—and it need not be the dominant part. Lawyers do not need to always vote and act with lawyers. As Leon Wieseltier has observed in decrying the notion that Jews ought to vote in ways that correspond to their economic class: "It is not a delusion, not a treason, to vote against your own economic interest. It is a recognition of the multiplicity of interests, the many purposes, that make up a citizen's life."[171]

An insight common to most religious traditions, and one which we fully endorse, is that all individuals ought to behave morally in both their professional and personal lives. Moreover, we call into question any conception of self-interest that is autonomous in nature, and which (like Milton Friedman) casts the individual and public 'goods' as antithetical to one another. Lawyers in particular should take this message to heart. As the chief conduit between the American people and America's political institutions, a great deal of power has been invested in the legal profession. Accordingly, the legal profession must develop a professional ethos that instills in lawyers a sense of responsibility for the well-being of the legal system as well as society at large. This ethos would encourage lawyers to act upon their

---

[168] Wald, "Rise and Fall," 1833.

[169] For more discussion see, e.g., Pearce and Uelmen, "Religious Lawyering's Second Wave," 269–81; Pearce, "How Law Firms Can Do Good While Doing Well," 211–16; idem, "White Lawyering: Rethinking Race, Lawyer Identity, and Rule of Law," *Fordham Law Review* 73 (2005): 2081–99; Pearce and Uelmen, "Religious Lawyering," 127–60; Pearce, "Reflections on the American Jewish Lawyer," 179–88; idem, "Faith and the Lawyer's Practice," *St. John's Law Review* 75 (2001): 277–81; idem, "Foreword: The Religious Lawyering Movement: An Emerging Force in Legal Ethics and Professionalism," *Fordham Law Review* 66 (1998): 1075–82; idem, "The Jewish Lawyer's Question," 1259–1270; idem, "Jewish Lawyering in a Multicultural Society: A Midrash on Levinson," *Cardozo Law Review* 14 (1993): 1613–37.

[170] See Pearce and Uelmen, "Religious Lawyering," 142–45.

[171] Leon Wieseltier, "Because They Believe," *New York Times Book Review*, September 8, 2009, 9.

"private" moral worldviews in their public role as lawyers. As emphasized throughout this chapter, such behavior need not destroy the lawyer-client relationship and must be conducted in a spirit of respect and openness.

In 1993, Professor Sanford Levinson came to Fordham Law School to workshop a paper that offered the first thorough academic analysis of Jewish lawyering.[172] Professor Levinson told the story of how Sandy Koufax refused to play during the World Series when the game fell on Yom Kippur.[173] It is a wonderful metaphor for the aesthetic of secular liberalism: Koufax brought his faith into the public sphere by taking a day off. But he took *only* a day off. His religious identity, as the story is told, did not influence in any substantive way the way he played baseball, whether his understanding of how to play with integrity or how to respect teammates and opponents. This chapter offers a different story. As a young man, the Magid of Mezeritch asked to study with the Baal Shem Tov. As a test, the Baal Shem Tov asked the Magid to read for him. The Magid did. "No, no, no," said the Baal Shem Tov. "Technically, you're proficient. But your reading lacks soul." The Magid began to read again. And this time the room was filled with light, and it was as if they were back at Sinai.[174] So our answer to the Jewish lawyer's question for the future is this: if there is a Jewish way to read, then surely there are Jewish ways to play baseball—and to be a lawyer.[175]

---

[172] See Levinson, "Identifying the Jewish Lawyer," 1577–1612.

[173] Ibid., 1579–83.

[174] The "Baal Shem Tov" is Rabbi Israel Baal Shem Tov, the "master of the good name," and the founder of the Hasidic movement in Judaism. See Elie Wiesel, *Souls on Fire: Portraits and Legends of Hasidic Masters*, trans. Marion Wiesel (New York: Vintage Books, 1972), 3–39; see also Louis Jacobs, *Hasidic Prayer* (New York: Schocken Books, 1973), 1–16.

[175] Pearce, "Jewish Lawyering."

Hating the Law for Christian Reasons: The Religious Roots of American Antinomianism

Jay Michaelson[1]

Introduction

What explains the curious American ambivalence about law? On the one hand, our nation loudly proclaims the "rule of law," and venerates its founding documents and founding fathers.[2] On the other hand, an increasing chorus of public figures (especially conservative ones) have decried the death of common sense in an age of bureaucracy and legalism,[3] a "litigation explosion" that is destroying our nation's economy,[4] and, in general, an obsession with legalism, codes, and rules instead of authentic human

---

[1] Ph.D., Hebrew University of Jerusalem, 2013; J.D., Yale, 1997. The author wishes to thank Nathaniel Persily, Suzanne Last Stone, William Nelson, Jonathan Boyarin, John Witt, Kenneth Ehrenberg, Andrew Novak, and Daniel Boyarin for their comments on earlier drafts of this chapter. Some of the research for this chapter was undertaken while the author was a Golieb Fellow in legal history at NYU Law School, and was greatly aided by the review and feedback of the legal history colloquium there. Research was also supported by the Weinig traveling fellowship at the Hebrew University of Jerusalem.

[2] On the religious quality to this veneration, see Sanford Levinson, *Constitutional Faith* (Princeton: Princeton University Press, 1988), 9–53; Thomas Grey, "The Constitution as Scripture," *Stanford Law Review* 37 (1984): 1–25.

[3] See, e.g., Philip Howard, *The Death of Common Sense: How Law is Suffocating America* (New York: Grand Central Publishing, 1994), 171–87; Eugene Bardach and Robert Kagan, *Going by the Book: The Problem of Regulatory Unreasonableness* (Piscataway, N.J.: Transaction Publishers, 1982).

[4] See Walter Olson, *The Litigation Explosion* (New York: Dutton Publishing, 1990); Patrick Garry, *A Nation of Adversaries: How the Litigation Explosion is Reshaping America* (New York: Insight Books, 1994); Thomas Burke, *Lawyers, Lawsuits and Legal Rights: The Battle over Litigation in American Society* (Berkeley: University of California Press, 2004); Jethro K. Lieberman, *The Litigious Society* (New York: Basic Books, 1981). On the factual inaccuracy of *The Litigation Explosion* and similar works, see William Haltom and Michael McCann, *Distorting the Law: Politics, Media, and the Litigation Crisis* (Chicago: University of Chicago Press, 2004); Marc Galanter, "An Oil Strike in Hell; Contemporary Legends About the Civil Justice System," *Arizona Law Review* 40 (1998): 717–52; Carl T. Bogus, *Why Lawsuits are Good for America* (New York: New York University Press, 2003); Peter W. Huber, *Liability: The Legal Revolution and Its Consequences* (New York: Basic Books, 1988). See also Andrew Blum, "Studies Clash on the Litigation Explosion's Myths and Realities," *National Law Journal* (Nov. 16, 1992): 1 (analyzing studies of Marc Galanter, Michael Saks, and others); Austin Sarat, "The Litigation Explosion, Access to Justice, and Court Reform: Examining the Critical Assumptions," *Rutgers Law Review* 37 (1985): 319–36; Robert C. Post, "On the Popular Image of the Lawyer: Reflections in a Dark Glass," *California Law Review* 75 (1987): 379–89.

decency. Lawyers are routinely the butt of jokes, and simultaneously feared and despised by the American public. Do we love law, or hate it? And what are we really talking about when we talk about the law?

This chapter argues that our popular American legal discourse[5] is essentially a religious one, a Protestant antinomianism which can be traced to the New Testament. Beginning with Paul, and amplified by the Protestant Reformation, this religious ideology echoes throughout centuries of Anglo-American legal thought. Its radical anti-legalism simultaneously praises "Law," usually the law inscribed on the heart or spirit, and denigrates written laws, which govern bodies with words. True law, in the anti-legalist tradition, is that which enables "common sense" and "basic human decency" to prevail over codes, rules, and letters. True law nourishes the soul; written law undermines it.

As with other antinomianisms, from the view criticized by Luther, who coined the term in 1539, to that of Anne Hutchinson in 17th-century Massachusetts, the question of law is a fundamentally religious one.[6] For Paul, as for today's critics of legalism, it is not merely that the letter of the law matters less than its spirit, or that formalism is bad but discretionary standards are good. Rather, the letter of the law corrupts the souls of people who adhere to it, by dragging them down into the world of the flesh. Adherence to the (written) law is at best unnecessary, at worst an obstacle to grace.[7]

In Part One, I provide a brief description of Anglo-American anti-legalism, with three very different examples from different historical time periods. I begin with relatively recent sources, including anti-legalist writers and the discourse surrounding the 1998 impeachment of President Clinton; perhaps because of Clinton's own legalistic evasions, or because the ascendant Christian Right was on the offensive, the Clinton impeachment is a useful site for capturing the (relatively) contemporary tone of American anti-legalism. Next, Part One observes a strikingly similar "flight from the

---

[5] As will become clear in the sources that follow, I am more interested in popular, often unreflective assessments of the legal system than the informed views of lawyers and legal academics. My subject here is not legalism as it *is* but legalism as it is *perceived*; not Judaism as it *is* but Judaism as it is *perceived*; and not the actual merits or traits of any particular legal or religious system.

[6] See sources cited *infra*, Part II, Section D. In his discussion of the Antinomian Controversy in Massachusetts, David Hall defines antinomianism as the view that "the moral law is not binding upon Christians, who are under the law of grace." David D. Hall, ed., *The Antinomian Controversy, 1636–1638: A Documentary History* (Durham, N.C.: Duke University Press, 1990), 3. This definition does capture the specific controversy in 1636–38, but is too narrow as a general definition, even for Christian antinomianism, which also negates the value of the ritual law (circumcision, dietary law), as well as for non-Western and secular antinomianisms. See Duncan Kennedy, "A Semiotics of Critique," *Cardozo Law Review* 22 (2001): 1158. A systematic study of antinomianisms is presently underway by the present author.

[7] See Gal 3:6 ("Christ redeemed us from the curse of the law"); 5:7 ("You who want to be justified by the law have cut yourselves off from Christ; you have fallen away from grace."); 2 Cor 3:6 ("for the letter kills, but the Spirit gives life"); Rom 2:15, 28–29; 7:5. See generally sources cited *infra*, Part II.

law" in ancient rhetoric surrounding the jury, and how the jury's conscience and common sense was initially seen not as aids to legal fact-finding, but as stand-ins for Divine revelation; the early jury, we shall see, did not apply the written law so much as displace it. (This same role, I note in passing, was played by the early writ system and the Court of Chancery.) Finally, Part One examines the debates around the adoption of the British Common Law in the early nineteenth century, in which the written law is troped as that which subverts grace, undermines basic human decency, and reduces us all to soulless automatons. In all these cases, both ancient and contemporary, "Law" may be valorized, but laws are not; people are valued over "codes"; and the objective of good law is not to provide clear rules for conduct, but to create better people.

Having sketched the outlines of anti-legalism in Part One, I move to its religious roots in Part Two, which engages in an extended fashion with Pauline texts of the New Testament. The critiques are virtually identical: law undermines humanity, the letter matters less than the spirit. But the larger context is clearer: the carnality or spirituality of humanity, and in terms of the old and new covenants with God. Focusing on circumcision as a primary site of debate, Part Two shows how concerns about the law are really concerns about the body and soul. For Pauline Christianity, influenced by Platonic dualism, the essence of the human being is the non-corporeal—and thus immortal—soul.[8] Part Two also observes that for biblical and early talmudic Judaism, there was no such dualism: the body, rather than the spirit, was the site of religious significance.[9] Thus "old" Judaism required circumcision of the flesh, because it is the body that is important; the "new" covenant demanded only the circumcision of the heart, because it is the soul that matters. "Old" law focused on actions (e.g., how one must treat one's enemies); "new" law on intent (e.g., that one must love one's enemies). And most importantly, "old" interpretations of scripture were literal, but "new" ones were spiritual. Finally, Part Two surveys how the Pauline concerns about the letter and spirit become amplified over the years, through Augustine, Aquinas, and most importantly during the Protestant Reformation. The ancient question—that if we are essentially souls, not bodies, what is the significance of literal, body-centered law—did not go away over the centuries. On the contrary, it grew so important, and so central, that we have come to take it for granted.

If it is true that our popular rhetoric about law is essentially a religious rhetoric, then we should expect to find many religious themes, not merely the letter/spirit-flesh/spirit one, in popular legal imagination. Indeed, this

---

[8] See, e.g., 1 Cor 15:50 ("Flesh and blood cannot inherit the kingdom of God, nor does the perishable inherit the imperishable."); Daniel Boyarin, *Carnal Israel: Reading Sex in Talmudic Culture* (Berkeley: University of California Press, 1993), 233–35.

[9] See Boyarin, *Carnal Israel*, 30–33, 230–33; Ephraim Urbach, *The Sages* (Cambridge, MA: Harvard University Press, 1987), 248–50; Jerold S. Auerbach, *Rabbis and Lawyers: The Journey from Torah to Constitution* (Bloomington: Indiana University Press, 1990), 34–44.

is the case—and surprisingly so. In the concluding part of this chapter, I observe the curious coincidence that just as American anti-legalism suspiciously resembles Christian anti-Judaism, so too does American anti-lawyerism—by which I mean the vast, hyperbolic, and often fictitious set of stereotypes, jokes, and opinions about contemporary lawyers[10]—suspiciously resemble antisemitism. The case for this phenomenological similarity will be made in a subsequent study. Here, I provide only a sketch—but one eerily familiar either to those familiar with the history of antisemitism, or to anyone who watches a courtroom drama today: that lawyers are "bloodsuckers"; that they exaggerate the letter of the law, subverting its spirit; that they harm the economy; that they lie, cheat, and steal; in short, that they are Shylock—the great villain of Shakespeare's *The Merchant of Venice*. These stereotypes, applied to lawyers who are "obviously" not Jewish (such as the late Johnny Cochran)[11] and to the legal profession before Jews were even admitted to it, is not about Jews per se. Rather, it is that law itself is somehow conceived as "Jewish." The chapter concludes with some wider observations about the potential blind spots in a religiously constructed anti-legalism.

To be clear, I am not arguing that people who dislike legalism or lawyers are antisemitic. We are not speaking here of actual Jews and actual Judaism, or of actual antisemitism or bigotry.[12] Rather, we are speaking of the

---

[10] See Marc Galanter, *Lowering the Bar: Lawyer Jokes and Legal Culture* (Madison: University of Wisconsin Press, 2005), 31–195; idem, "An Oil Strike in Hell," 735; idem, "Predators and Parasites," *Georgia Law Review* 28 (1994): 654; The Gallup Poll (1993) (ranking lawyers next to used-car salesmen in public opinion of professions); Randall Samborn, "Anti-Lawyer Attitude Up," *National Law Journal* (Aug. 9, 1993) (hereinafter Samborn, "Anti-Lawyer"): 1, 20 (noting 75% of those polled in 1993 believed that lawyers are hampering the nation's economy); Olson, *The Litigation Explosion*, 2 (saying that the lawyer "clogs and jams the gears of commerce, sowing friction and distrust between the productive enterprises on which material progress depends and all who buy their products, work at their plants and offices, join in their undertakings") and 339 (alleging civil lawsuits have "reduced valuable enterprise to ruin, made miserable the practice of honorable professions, and brought needless pain to broken families"); Dan Quayle, "Address to American Bar Association," Aug. 16, 1991, reported in David S. Broder and Saundra Torry, "ABA President Disputes Quayle on Litigation Proposals," *Washington Post*, Aug. 14, 1991 (alleging that "too many lawyers and too many lawsuits [are] forcing the nation to lose its edge in the world marketplace"); Alfred Adask, "Daddy, Why Doesn't the Vice President Like You?" *Anti-Shyster* (Jan. 1992): 12–13, quoted in Galanter, "Predators and Parasites," 660 n. 105 ("Our entire judicial system has become an extortion racket designed to enrich lawyers at the expense of productive members of society. Almost every licensed, practicing lawyer is a beneficiary and co-conspirator in that extortion racket ... [Lawyers are] 98% bad people, lousy Americans, ethical cowards, professional sociopaths who are almost certainly the primary cause of the social and economic decline of this nation."). On the factual inaccuracy of anti-lawyer jeremiads, see Charles R. Epp, "Do Lawyers Impair Economic Growth?" *Law & Social Inquiry* 17 (1992): 585–623; Frank B. Cross, "The First Thing We Do, Let's Kill all the Economists: An Empirical Evaluation of the Effect of Lawyers on the United States Economy and Political System," *Texas Law Review* 70 (1992): 645–83; Galanter, "Predators & Parasites," 647–51.

[11] On Jewish lawyer jokes, see Galanter, *Lowering the Bar*, 148–51.

[12] There are, of course, a large number of Jews in the legal profession. Law school facul-

law *typed as* Jewish. Obviously, many people without any bigotry whatsoever (including, of course, Jewish people themselves) hold anti-legalistic and anti-lawyer opinions, while many racists and antisemites do not. Indeed, critiques of legalism may be well-founded, and I do not take any position on litigation, the regulatory state, or formalist/anti-formalist debates within jurisprudential thinking—although I have remarked elsewhere that legalism, much maligned, may hold more promise for a multicultural democracy than an anti-legalist privileging of "common sense" over arcane rules and standards.[13] My argument here is descriptive, not normative: that popular anti-legalism is religious in origin and form.

When we Americans speak of the law, we are speaking about much more than the law. We are, often unconsciously, re-enacting a religious dispute that has existed for millennia about the essence of the human being and the role of law in interacting with it. What we are talking about, when we talk about the law, is the soul.

I. "Quirks of Law or Common Sense": Anti-Legalism

What do Americans mean when they speak of the "Rule of Law"? Obviously, it is, rhetorically if not substantively, a foundational principle of the American Republic, and means, essentially, that one is subject to written laws, rather than the whims of those in power; in *Marbury*'s famous locution, it is "the rule of law, not men," the principle that power is not all, but that, in some way, law is autonomous from political action and force.[14] The

---

ties, for example, are 27% Jewish, though Jews are only 4% of the U.S. population. Survey by James Lindgren, *Measuring Diversity*, quoted in Daniel A. Farber and Suzanna Sherry, "Is the Radical Critique of Merit Anti-Semitic?" *California Law Review* 83 (1995): 865 n. 80. The National Jewish Population Survey (1995) (measuring U.S. Jewish population at 5.5 million in U.S. population of about 270 million). See also Donna E. Arzt, "The People's Lawyers: The Predominance of Jews in Public Interest Law," *Judaism* 35 (1986): 47–62. However, the argument here is not that the number of Jews in the legal profession somehow promotes legalism as a "Jewish" value—most are probably unaware that it is one. But see Jerold S. Auerbach, *Rabbis and Lawyers: The Journey from Torah to Constitution* (Bloomington: Indiana University Press, 1990), 22 (noting Jewish lawyers' "dynamic view of law" reinforced by their "Talmudic style of inquiry"); Jerome Hornblass, "The Jewish Lawyer," *Cardozo Law Review* 14 (1993): 1639. Similarly, though there is obviously antisemitism within the legal profession and directed towards it, see Charles Silberman, *A Certain People: American Jews and Their Lives Today* (New York: Simon and Schuster, 1985), 95–100 (discussing dislike of Jewish lawyers by, inter alia, future chief justices Harlan Stone and William Howard Taft); Alan Dershowitz, *Chutzpah* (New York: Little Brown, 1991), 71–74 (tracing antisemitism in the bar, particularly in opposition to the nomination of Louis Brandeis to the Supreme Court), the sources we will examine *infra* rarely mention Jews, and are largely from a time in which Jews were excluded from the bar.

[13] Jay Michaelson, "In Praise of the Pound of Flesh: Legalism, Multiculturalism, and the Letter of the Law," *Journal of Law in Society* 6 (2005): 98–153.

[14] Marbury v. Madison, 5 U.S. (1 Cranch) 137, 163 (1803). See, generally, Ian Shapiro, ed., *The Rule of Law* (New York: NYU Press, 1992); John Rawls, *A Theory of Justice* (Cambridge, MA: Belknap Press, 1986), 235–42; Joseph Raz, "The Rule of Law and its Virtue," *Law Quarterly Review* 93 (1977): 195–202; Ronald Dworkin, *Taking Rights Seriously* (Cambridge, MA: Harvard University Press, 1978), 14–44; Richard H. Fallon, Jr., "The

phrase has an almost religious, talismanic quality; it is a touchstone, pregnant with meanings that shift over time.[15] During the Clinton impeachment, of course, it was a shibboleth for the Right. But it may also be cited by the Left, as in critiques of the "War on Terror."[16]

As is well known, however, there is a sharp distinction, in Justice Scalia's felicitous phrasing, between the Rule of Law and a law of rules.[17] The gap between the two is the subject of this part. By looking at three very different instances of Anglo-American wrestling with the law—the Clinton impeachment, the growth of the jury, and the adoption of British Common Law in America—we shall see a recurring pattern: that the "law" being talked about here is not a set of normative rules that bind conduct, but rather a kind of quasi Natural Law, the essence of which lies not in casebooks or the United States Code but in the consciences of the accuser and the accused. Indeed, particularly as troped by Clinton's impeachers (and some of his defenders) the "rule of law" is actually a curiously antinomian concept—antilogonomian, to be more precise—which valorizes 'common

---

Rule of Law' as a Concept in Constitutional Discourse," *Columbia Law Review* 97 (1997): 1–56; Lon Fuller, *The Morality of Law* (New Haven: Yale University Press, 1967), 80–85; Robin West, "Law, Rights, and Other Totemic Illusions: Legal Liberalism and Freud's Theory of the Rule of Law," *University of Pennsylvania Law Review* 134 (1986): 817, 818, 838–41 (discussing Owen Fiss, Laurence Tribe, Charles Fried, Ronald Dworkin, and others who "regard the Rule of Law as the key to moral governance and civilized progress").

[15] See Jessie Allen, "Blind Faith and Reasonable Doubts: Investigating Belief in the Rule of Law," *Seattle University Law Review* 24 (2001): 692, citing Sanford Levinson, *Constitutional Faith* (Princeton: Princeton University Press, 1988); Thomas C. Grey, "The Constitution as Scripture," *Stanford Law Review* 37 (1984): 1–25; Bowman, "Falling out of Love," 22–23 (describing rule of law as part of American liberal myth).

[16] See, e.g., Kim Lane Scheppele, "Law in a Time of Emergency: States of Exception and the Temptations of 9/11," *University of Pennsylvania Journal of Constitutional Law* 6 (2003): 1001–83 (finding the rule of law in the United States to be eroded in the political response to September 11); Heinz Klug, "The Rule of Law, War, or Terror," *Wisconsin Law Review* (2003): 365–84 (reviewing the Bush administration's undermining of international law). It may be that the "War on Terror" is a victory for the rule of law, however; legal challenges to the erosions of civil rights under the War on Terror have fared fairly well. See David Cole, "Judging the Next Emergency: Judicial Review and Individual Rights in Times of Crisis," *Michigan Law Review* 101 (2002): 2565–95 (finding that courts have generally been protective of civil liberties and dismissive of "national security" claims in times of crisis; in addition, courts have been more willing, not less, to stand up to the government in the post-September 11 United States than in earlier crises); Rosa Brooks, "Protecting Rights in the Age of Terrorism: Challenges and Opportunities," *Georgetown Journal of International Law* 36 (2005): 677; Christiane Wilke, "War v. Justice: Terrorism Cases, Enemy Combatants, and Political Justice in U.S. Courts," *Politics & Society* 33 (2005): 637–69; Anne Gearan, "Bush's War on Terror Runs Afoul of the Rule of Law: Despite Popular Support, It Has Suffered Mostly Defeat in Court," *Seattle Post Intelligencer* (Aug. 28, 2002), B7.

[17] See Antonin Scalia, "The Rule of Law as a Law of Rules," *University of Chicago Law Review* 56 (1989): 1175–81; H.L.A. Hart, *The Concept of Law* (Oxford: Oxford University Press, 1972), 132ff. (discussing role of "rule-scepticism" in law); Ronald Dworkin, "Is Law a System of Rules?" in *Essays in Legal Philosophy*, ed. Robert S. Summers (Berkeley: University of California Press, 1976), 25–60.

sense' and the good heart over Pharisaic legalism and Shylockian evasion. This form of law depends not on rules and codes of conduct, not on legalistic defenses and particular precepts, but rather on commonly-accessible moral certainties and on a judge (or jury) of honest and good people. It is, in some ways, anti-law, at least insofar as it does an end-run around the legal text and toward the virtues of the decision maker. President Clinton was not called upon to defend himself against the charge of perjury; he was called to defend *himself*, William J. Clinton, and make his case for forgiveness and absolution.

As we will see in the next part, this special, theologized notion of spiritual law/conscience as opposed to written law/legalism is virtually identical to the antinomian (more precisely, antilogonomian) writings of Saint Paul. It is a religious doctrine, and remains so. But first let's turn the clock back to a more innocent time of blue dresses, cigars, and Monica Lewinsky.

A. *"The Rule of Law" without Laws: Clinton's Cigar*

In the opening statements of the Impeachment Trial of President William Jefferson Clinton, the phrase "rule of law" appeared twenty-three times.[18] A contemporary editorial called it "the central magic of the American governmental experience."[19] One commentator argued that "the impeachment trial of President Clinton made 'rule of law' a household phrase."[20] Indeed, for some, it was the very subject of the impeachment itself; in large part because the President was accused of perjury and obstruction of justice, crimes that interfere with the judicial process, the Senate was told by one of the House Managers that "[w]hat is on trial here is the truth and the rule of law."[21] "The vote that all of us are asked to cast is in the final analysis a vote on the rule of law," said House Judiciary Committee Chair Henry Hyde prior to the House vote, calling it one of the great achievements of our civilization, for the alternative is the rule of raw power."[22] Elsewhere, Hyde linked the rule of law to equality, asking, "Do we still have a government of laws and not of men? Does the law apply to some people with force and ferocity while the powerful are immune? Do we have one set of laws for the officers and another for the enlisted? Should we?"[23]

---

[18] 1999 WL 14067 (FDCH) (Jan. 15, 1999) *passim*; 1999 WL 14071 (FDCH) (Jan. 16, 1999) *passim* (Westlaw).

[19] Editorial, "Fairness for Ken Starr," *New York Times* (April 5, 1998), D14.

[20] Allen, "Blind Faith," 694. See also Deborah L. Rhode, "Conflicts of Commitment: Legal Ethics in the Impeachment Context," *Stanford Law Review* 52 (2000): 270.

[21] Opening Statement of Impeachment Trial, Jan. 14, 1999, 1999 WL 12853, at 59 (Westlaw).

[22] 144 Cong. Rec. H11, 776–77 (daily ed. Dec. 18, 1998) (statement of Rep. Hyde).

[23] Statement of Rep. Henry Hyde (R-NY), House Judiciary Committee, Nov. 19, 1998, 1998 WL 801030, at 41 (Westlaw).

Another time, he suggested that American veterans died for the rule of law, and that the impeachment trial honored their memory.[24]

Hyde was not alone in his high-flown rhetoric. One congressman called the rule of law "our nation's most fundamental value."[25] (Given the phrase's prominence in the Watergate hearing, there was likely a more familiar echo in the context of presidential inquiries as well.[26]) And indeed, the first article of impeachment charged the President with acting "in a manner subversive to the rule of law and justice, to the manifest injury of the people of the United States."[27]

Yet the rule of law is not synonymous with the practice of lawyers; indeed, as used in this discourse, it is the opposite of what lawyers do. Well before Monica Lewinsky's dress appeared on the evening news, President Clinton had already been seen by conservatives as guilty of "lawyerly evasions" of the truth and as running a "lawyer-filled White House."[28] By the time the impeachment hit full swing, the gloves were off. The president's 'legal' responses—as opposed to 'factual' ones—and the overall 'legalistic' tone of his defense were continual targets of attack.[29] Consider pundit William Safire's words in an opinion piece entitled *Kill All the Lawyers*. Safire suggested that Clinton should, "as Shakespeare suggested, first, kill all his lawyers. They now plan two days of argument about why lying under oath isn't really perjury, or why perjury about sex doesn't count, or why Monica wasn't given a Miranda warning."[30] These legal arguments, with the exception of the last one, might actually seem to be very relevant ones to

---

[24] Hyde's statement, in part, was: "The families of executed dissidents know that this is about the rule of law, the great alternative to the lethal abuse of power by the state. Those yearning for freedom know this is about the rule of law ... If they know this, can we not know it? If across the river in Arlington Cemetery, there are American heroes who died in defense of the rule of law, can we give less than the full measure of our devotion to that great cause?" Impeachment Trial of President Clinton, at 1193 (statement of Rep. Hyde).

[25] Statement of U.S. Rep. Stephen Buyer (R-IN) at the Senate Impeachment Trial, Jan. 16, 1999. 1999 WL 14071 (FDCH) at 16 (Westlaw).

[26] See Joel K. Goldstein, "The Presidency and the Rule of Law: Some Preliminary Explorations," *Saint Louis University Law Journal* 43 (1999): 791–94.

[27] Impeachment Article No. 1, as presented by Rep. Hyde to the Senate. 1999 WL 4876 (Westlaw).

[28] See, e.g., Garry, *Nation of Adversaries*, 155–60 (calling the Clinton White House, in 1997, a "lawyer-filled White House" and accusing First Lady Hillary Rodham Clinton of "'I-am-a-litigator' evasiveness"). Garry makes these points to show that law is an inadequate social regulator, and actually helps scoundrels like the Clintons evade the truth.

[29] See Rhode, "Conflicts of Commitment," 315–16 (citing surveys showing distaste both for "forced disclosure of a consensual sexual relationship unconnected to the president's performance in office" and "the legalistic defenses that the president and his lawyers" put on).

[30] William Safire, "Kill All the Lawyers," *New York Times* (Dec. 7, 1998), A25. That a writer with the erudition of Safire is unaware of the irony of this quote is impossible. Safire certainly knows that the words in question were uttered by a tyrant, and were a prelude to the destruction of order in Shakespeare's play *The Second Part of King Henry the Sixth*. I discuss this quote in section III of this chapter, p. 270.

make in a trial (or proto-trial) about perjury and the impeachability thereof. But this is not what Safire and others had in mind. In the words of Rep. James Sensenbrenner, such arguments were "legalistic hair splitting," when what the case was *really* about was "basic questions of right and wrong."[31]

How bizarre: the Clinton legal defenses—that there must be more than lying under oath to constitute the crime of perjury, or that more than an ordinary crime is required for the constitutional standard of impeachment—were not particularly obscure exercises in hair-splitting, even if the President's famous (and oft-misquoted) evasions such as "It depends on what the meaning of 'is' is" were just that. Really, these defenses were standard legal practice: my client did not commit a crime; even if he did, the crime doesn't merit the punishment.[32] As White House Special Counsel Gregory Craig said:

> Allegations of legal crimes invite, indeed they call out, for legal defenses.... So, to accuse us of using legalisms to defend the President when he's being accused of perjury is only to accuse us of defending the President.... We plead guilty to that charge, and the truth is that an attorney who failed to raise these defenses might well be guilty of malpractice.[33]

Yet in a trial about legal questions, recourses to law were mocked, if not condemned. As Deborah Rhode points out, the fact that Clinton's lawyers were behaving like lawyers was precisely the problem.[34] Similarly, Representative Vic Fazio (D-CA), in his last speech before retiring, bewailed the impeachment proceedings as "a moment where legalism reigned over human understanding and acknowledgment that we are all sinners before our Lord."[35]

---

[31] Opening Statement of Impeachment Trial, Jan. 14, 1999, 1999 WL 12853 (Westlaw).

[32] One observer suggested that Clinton's legalism was the appropriate response to a trap being laid for him. See "Counseling Clinton," C1 (quoting defense attorney Roy Black: "I don't think that half of the commentators who are criticizing ... [Clinton] for being evasive know what goes on in a courtroom. Clearly, in the grand jury he was being set up to take a fall for perjury. That is why he was being hypertechnical and he evaded all the minefields ... a lawyer advising the president has to tell him to do what he has been doing."). Defense attorney Johnnie Cochran agreed the grand jury process was "a perjury trap." Ibid. Interestingly, one commentator has suggested that President Clinton was himself a victim of legalism because "the post-Watergate reforms have substituted ethical perfectionism enforceable through criminal penalties—a sort of utopian legalism—for the constitutional scheme of controlling both public corruption and factional excesses through political interactions between, and factional conflict within, governmental branches." Frank O. Bowman III, "Falling Out of Love With America: The Clinton Impeachment and the Madisonian Constitutions," *Maryland Law Review* 60 (2001): 5, 14.

[33] Transcript: White House Special Counsel Craig's Statement, *CNN* (Jan. 20, 1999), accessible at http://cnn.com/ALLPOLITICS/stories/1999/01/02/transcripts/craig.html (statement of Gregory Craig, White House Special Counsel at the Senate Impeachment Trial), quoted in Rhode, "Conflicts of Commitment," 321.

[34] Rhode, "Conflicts of Commitment," 321. Rhode reports Kenneth Starr as suggesting, outrageously, that a lawyer should pursue the truth, not defend his client. Ibid., 325–26.

[35] Statement of U.S. Rep. Vic Fazio (D-CA), House Floor Debate, Dec. 18, 1998, 1998 WL

Importantly, hyperbolic statements and critiques of lawyers and "legalism" were not confined to one side of the aisle. Charles Schumer, then the ranking Democrat on the House Judiciary committee, rebuked Kenneth Starr thus:

> The innate and sound wisdom of the American people, that lying about an extramarital affair should not lead to the removal of a duly elected President from office, is far more in keeping with the founding fathers' visions of impeachment than your legalistic arguments, Mr. Starr.[36]

As with Clinton's accusers, the dichotomy in Schumer's statement is clear: innate and sound wisdom on the one hand, legalistic arguments on the other. Similarly, Representative Richard A. Gephardt of Missouri, the House minority leader, said that "the considered judgment of the American people is not going to rise or fall on the fine distinctions of a legal argument."[37] Once again we have the dichotomy of considered judgment on one side, fine distinctions of a legal argument on the other.

The attacks on lawyers also crossed party lines outside of Congress. Liberal columnist Maureen Dowd, not to be outdone by Safire, wrote that "it was inevitable, of course, that lawyers would destroy civilization. Shakespeare warned us to kill them all. We didn't."[38] Dowd went on to blame every attorney involved in the impeachment—both of Clinton's, David Kendall, Kenneth Starr, and others—for "a titanic twilight struggle between armies of lawyers." One former prosecutor opined that bad lawyering on all sides was responsible for the impeachment debacle: "Pick the easiest targets. Blame it on the lawyers ... all these players are lawyers, playing their roles way, way over the top. Legally permissible, maybe, but neither smart nor sensible. They have done their profession, which has an image problem anyway, immeasurable harm, all for their own selfish interests."[39] And legal commentator David Margolick ascribed "the President's highly legalistic defense, using a tortured definition of sex that has earned him great ridicule," to "the training elite lawyers are now likely to get, which can blind them to what matters most."[40] Robert Gordon attacked "the notion of a very narrow technical specialty in which what the lawyer does is simply advise

---

883527, at 33 (Westlaw).

36 Statement of Rep. Charles Schumer (D-NY), House Judiciary Committee, Nov. 19, 1998, 1998 WL 804603 (FDCH), at 4 (Westlaw).

37 Quoted in William Glaberson, "The Testing of a President: The Lawyers; Legal Gamesmanship May Take Toll," *New York Times*, Sept. 24, 1998, A20.

38 Maureen Dowd, "Power of Attorney," *New York Times*, Sept. 20, 1998, sec. 4, p. 2.

39 Benjamin L. Bailey, "There's a Way Out of This Mess: Bad Lawyering Set Us to Wallering in All This Sleaze," *Charleston Daily Mail*, Dec. 12, 1998, A4.

40 David Margolick, "Like Sex Acts, Lawyer's Job is Matter of Definition," *New York Times*, Sept. 26, 1998, A15.

on the available legal strategy."[41] William Simon said that "we try to teach lawyers to make value judgments, to weigh principles, but the professional culture of technicality and literalism is even stronger."[42] Throughout, the dichotomy between values and technicality, spirit and literalism, was maintained.

What defenses, exactly, were his lawyers supposed to make instead of "legal" ones? The answer was clear: contrition.[43] Time and again, in the House and the Senate, the President's critics (and many of his friends) stated that what the President really needed to do was to confess his sin—constitutional, sexual, or otherwise—admit that he lied, and throw himself on the mercy of his accusers. Safire again:

> Dissociate yourself dramatically from all past legalistic hair-splitting. Admit that it's fair to say you lied under oath—not 'misled' but lied—and show that you are unafraid to face prosecution later. Say that you are ashamed not just of your behavior but of your cover-up.[44]

Sometimes the religious context of this drama of contrition and forgiveness was overt, as when Rep. Bob Ney (R-Ohio) explained that, "as a Christian country," America should forgive President Clinton, "for no one is perfect in this life."[45] (Rep. Ney subsequently voted for impeachment.) Other times, however, the "rule of law" itself functioned as the religious touchstone, providing not a framework for adjudication but a standard for grace and forgiveness.[46] Judge Richard Posner, in his nearly instantaneous analysis of the legal and moral issues surrounding the impeachment, saw the impeachment primarily as political drama rather than as a trial really about

---

[41] Ibid. (quoting Gordon, then a professor of law and history at Yale Law School).

[42] Ibid. (quoting William Simon, a Stanford law professor).

[43] See statement of Rep. Charles Schumer (D-NY), House Judiciary Committee, Dec. 7, 1998, 1998 WL 846818, at 110–12 (discussing role of contrition in House members' considerations). But see "Counseling Clinton: Free Legal Advice for an Accused Leader," *Boston Globe*, Sept. 27, 1998, C1 (quoting Steven Duke: "Disregard advice that you confess to perjury and obstruction of justice. Those who want you to do that are the same folks who said if you would only confess to an intimate relationship with Monica Lewinsky all would be forgiven. They are the same people who want you to testify before the House Judiciary Committee. They are not your friends.").

[44] Safire, "Kill all the Lawyers," A25.

[45] Michael Grunwald, "Fence-Sitters Can't Get Past Clinton's Words," *Washington Post*, Dec. 17, 1998, A1. But see statement of Rep. Jerrold Nadler (D-NY), House Judiciary Committee, Dec. 10, 1998, 1998 WL 854485 (FDCH), at 107 (Westlaw) ("Contrition is a remedy for sin and is certainly appropriate here. But while insufficiency of contrition may leave the soul still scarred, unexpiated sin proves no crimes and justifies no impeachments.") Give Rep. Ney credit for consistency: in 2006, Rep. Ney pled guilty to accepting thousands of dollars of bribes, stating, "I accept responsibility for my actions and am prepared to face the consequences of what I have done." *New York Times*, Oct. 14, 2006, A8. Perhaps hoping for forgiveness himself, Rep. Ney did not immediately resign from Congress, despite facing up to ten years in prison.

[46] On the religious tone of the Clinton impeachment, see Allen, "Blind Faith," 691–92.

the rule of law.[47] Posner marshals considerable evidence from the Starr referral that the President both perjured himself and obstructed justice, and suggests that these crimes may well be impeachable within the (vague) constitutional standards. He suggests, however, that following the shaming of impeachment, "All that remained was for Clinton to make a full and frank confession that he had lied and broken the law."[48] Posner's reasons are political, not theological; in his view, impeachment itself was sufficient punishment, and the resulting senate trial (which, viewers will recall, culminated in later-disgraced Senator Trent Lott presenting Chief Justice William Rehnquist with a wood-paneled plaque honoring his service) was a mockery of justice, which Clinton could have spared the nation by confessing.[49] (Interestingly, this was precisely the pattern expected in seventeenth century prosecutions of sin; initially, the defendant would be expected to press his case, but eventually, he was to confess his sin and profess contrition.)[50] Yet is it not ironic that in a public trial ostensibly about the rule of law—which Posner calls "essential to the freedom and wealth that distinguish the United States from most other nations"[51]—that a law of rules seems so utterly inadequate?[52] Perhaps contrition would have been the better political move. But is this really the "rule of law"? Apologize, confess, and throw yourself on the mercy of your judges?

What the House Managers seem to have meant by "rule of law" is what Margaret Radin and others have called a "substantive" view: that it is "the institutional embodiment of a moral system centered on fairness."[53] The question, then, is not whether perjury is an impeachable defense, and certainly not what the meaning of 'is' is, and not even the autonomy of the law from political processes and power, but rather the moral fairness and moral worth of the legal actors. In such a view, written, codified, proceduralized law is totally inadequate, and actually destructive to the "rule of law's" higher purpose. That this is precisely what Paul said about the written law is the subject of the next part, but, for now, the trajectory of the

---

[47] Richard Posner, *An Affair of State: The Investigation, Impeachment, and Trial of President Clinton* (Cambridge, MA: Harvard University Press, 1999), 34–58.

[48] Ibid., 195.

[49] Ibid.

[50] Peter Charles Hoffer, *Law and People in Colonial America* (Baltimore: Johns Hopkins University Press, 1992), 48.

[51] Ibid., 155.

[52] Rhode points out a further irony: that the impeachment process itself "frequently offended fundamental concepts of due process and procedural fairness." Rhode, "Conflict of Commitment," 344 ("Majority leaders announced and altered hearing ground rules at will. Charges against the president came and went; wide disparities persisted among the grounds for impeachment in Starr's referral, Majority Counsel David Shipper's presentation, the House Articles of Impeachment, the House Committee Report, and the House Managers' Senate trial materials.").

[53] Allen, "Blind Faith," 695; Margaret Radin, "Reconsidering the Rule of Law," *Boston University Law Review* 69 (1989): 783–91.

argument is clear: that we are seeing here a particular ideology of law that simultaneously encodes an ethos of moral guilt and innocence but simultaneously insists that the legal system, if it is limited by rules, laws, and procedures, is an inadequate forum for real adjudication.

What President Clinton needed to do was not recite the correct legal words but admit his sin and hope for grace. He needed sincerity, not subtlety; a confessor, not a lawyer. Consider the remarks of later-disgraced Congressman Tom DeLay (R-TX), the fiery Evangelical who as House Majority Whip led the crusade to impeach the president. For DeLay, the impeachment process was really about "relativism versus absolute values," and that he would not allow the president to "use legalese and lawyerese to do two-steps around the questions."[54] Notice how "legalese and lawyerese" is equivalent with "relativism," i.e., the opposite of "substantive rule of law" and morality.

My point here is not to debate the legal realists as to whether the rule of law exists, or enter the substantive debates about whether the House Managers (many of whom were later convicted of crimes themselves) sincerely meant what they said or not. Rather, it is to show that this rhetoric, far from being mere partisan zealotry, reveals a deep ambivalence over the capacity for written law to adequately judge the human soul. There are at least five good reasons to take the impeachers' rhetoric seriously. First, even if members of Congress did not really mean what they said as a matter of jurisprudence, they still chose this rhetoric over other available options, inviting the question of why they did so. Second, as already noted, anti-legalist discourse found homes on both sides of the aisle. Third, the G.O.P. stayed "on message" even after the message had led it to electoral Waterloo; if this is dissembling, it is at the very least a very earnest, principled, and determined dissembling. Fourth, it is not a new discourse, as the next two sections will show.

Finally, we should take this rhetoric seriously because we may believe it ourselves. Does anyone seriously dispute the value of "getting away from lawyer-talk and ... talking about things that the American public would understand," as one Congressman suggested during the proceedings?[55] Do we really believe that the President's guilt or innocence hangs on the language of a perjury statute or the precise definition of "sexual relations"? Whatever our opinion about the impeachment, do we not agree with then-dean of the Yale Law School, Anthony T. Kronman, when he spoke of the perception that "the gulf between the law and common sense has opened up in this crisis to a considerable degree. And that has caused people to lose confidence in the law"?[56] Surely anyone with such "common sense"—and to

---

[54] Quoted in Ann Louise Bardach, "Delayed Justice," *The New Republic*, Feb. 15, 1999, 11–12.

[55] Statement of U.S. Rep. William Jenkins (R-TN), House Judiciary Committee Hearings, Dec. 9, 1998, 1998 WL 849446, at 216.

[56] Quoted in Glaberson, "Testing of a President," A20.

this topic we shall turn in the next part—recognizes that written legal definitions do not get at what is most important about justice. Right?

B. Juries without Laws: Ordeals, Juries, and Equity

Flash back to more than two centuries ago. In the mid-1780s, a New Hampshire jury was instructed as follows: "[D]o justice between the parties not by any quirks of the law ... but by common sense as between man and man."[57] The conceptual analogy to the Clinton impeachment in such an instruction, though from an utterly different historical context, is clear. But its significance is greater when we remember that eighteenth century juries were generally empowered to find law as well as fact,[58] and that these juries are made up of "peers," non-lawyers, ordinary folk who can weigh the facts and apply, or perhaps ignore, the law. The jury, in a sense, is the polar opposite of the lawyer, or the judge with his law books. The jury, as we shall see, encodes a certain modality of suspicion of the law into the legal process, returning criminal law, and occasionally civil law as well, to the theological role it once played: determining true guilt or true innocence, sin or salvation.

Obviously, in America, the jury's success is largely a matter of its constitutionalization. But surely the "trial by an impartial jury" in the Sixth and Seventh Amendments is more than a parchment-writ clause; it is an American ideal. Reflecting the democratic ideals of the nation, the jury was seen as among the most important political right—of the jurors, not only the accused—at the time of the Founding, particularly by Anti-Federalists, who saw jury participation as a means to change the nature of government, and to make laws.[59] And it resonates with a popular American conception of what the law is, a conception that runs deeper than the text of the Constitution. Today, even as the percentage of cases actually tried by jury declines year after year, and even as the jury's power to resolve legal questions has disappeared,[60] eighty percent of all jury trials worldwide take place in the United States.[61] What explains this lofty and anomalous status?

---

[57] Eighteenth-century New Hampshire jury instruction, quoted in William Nelson, "The Eighteenth-Century Background of John Marshall's Constitutional Jurisprudence," *Michigan Law Review* 76 (1978): 910.

[58] William Nelson, *The Americanization of the Common Law: The Impact of Legal Change on Massachusetts Society, 1760–1830* (Athens: University of Georgia Press, 1994), 3.

[59] See Akhil Amar, "The Bill of Rights as a Constitution," *Yale Law Journal* 100 (1991): 1187–89; idem, "Reinventing Juries: Ten Suggested Reforms," *University of California-Davis Law Review* 28 (1995): 1169–70; Kenneth Klein, "Unpacking the Jury Box," *Hastings Law Journal* 47 (1996): 1336–38.

[60] On the diminution of the power and range of the jury in the last two hundred years, see Jeffrey Abramson, *We, the Jury* (New York: Basic Books, 1994), 36–37; John Langbein, "On the Myth of Written Constitutions: The Disappearance of the Criminal Jury Trial," *Harvard Journal of Law and Public Policy* 15 (1992): 119–27.

[61] Valerie P. Hans and Neil Vidmar, *Judging the Jury* (New York: Plenum Publishing, 1986), 31.

My claim is that the jury represents the rule of man, not laws. A jury, but not a law book, can determine the "real" guilt or innocence of a human being, just as the Clinton Impeachment Congress seemed to want to do, and just as a Pharisaic legalism can never do.

As John Langbein has shown, the jury's initial rise to prominence in the English legal system was not inevitable; rather, it was a tale of coincidence and incompetence of alternative procedures that seemed about to fail at any number of occasions.[62] Indeed, one of the salient features of the modern jury—that the jurors not know anything about the case or parties beforehand—is the antithesis of the institution's original purpose, which was to put people who knew the details of the alleged crime, and the character of the accused, in charge of dispensing justice. Even the catchphrase of "judgment of his peers," transmuted into "a jury of his peers," is an anachronistic interpretation of the Magna Carta—there were no criminal trial juries in 1215.

The historical origin of the jury is the ordeal process, which the jury was explicitly seen as replacing. Though today associated with superstition and irrationality, the torture and ordeal processes were actually a coherent, albeit desperate, means of ascertaining factual guilt or innocence, given the theistic worldview of the medieval Church and the unavailability of conventional legal procedures.[63] Recall that few medieval legal systems had developed rules of evidence, procedures by which the testimony of witnesses could be taken into account by a decisionmaker, or formulas for when such evidence could be thought to be valid and when it could not.[64] As such, only two forms of 'evidence' were acceptable for certain crimes: confessions and the testimony of God, the infallible Fact-finder, as expressed in signs and wonders. Torture was seen as acceptable to obtain the former, ordeals the latter.

Torture and ordeals are not, then, a superstitious flight into unreliable methods of proof. Quite the contrary, for medieval Europeans, they were the only reliable methods of proof. Confession under physical torture was seen as a mere corporeal extension of the confession under "spiritual torture" of mental anguish.[65] Torture helped break the will to lie and, like the internal workings of conscience, prod the defendant to admit what he (or she) knows all along to be true. Ordeals are even more reliable a method for

---

[62] See John Langbein, *Torture and the Law of Proof: Europe and England in the Ancien Regime* (Chicago: University of Chicago Press, 2005), 74ff. See also John Langbein, ed., *History of the Common Law: Procedure and Institutions* (unpublished, on file with author, 1997 ed.), ch. 2.

[63] See Langbein, *Torture*; Talal Asad, *Genealogies of Religion: Discipline and Reasons of Power in Christianity and Islam* (Baltimore: Johns Hopkins University Press, 1993), 83–97 (tracing history of torture in inquisitorial procedure and its implicit conceptions of truth and reason); Michel Foucault, *Discipline and Punish* (New York: Vintage, 1979), 40ff. (likening torture of the accused to "torture of truth").

[64] Langbein, *Torture*.

[65] Ibid.; Asad, *Genealogies*, 118–19.

ascertaining guilt or innocence, because the decision maker is omniscient. God, who determines (to take one example) whether burns inflicted by an inquisitor develop sores or not,[66] is a more effective judge than any human being weighing evidence. God knows what happened, and He is unlikely to lie.[67]

Briefly, as a point of comparison, contemporaneous Jewish law, lacking the Christian ambivalence about the status of law to adequately judge people—since, as we will see in the next part, law was divine and legal process divinely mandated—developed complex laws of evidence, standards for testimony in capital and non-capital crimes, and a detailed judicial procedure.[68] And yet, Jewish law also had recourse to a heavenly fact-finder when earthly ones were not available: the "court of heaven," which had jurisdiction in cases of indirect tort causation, acts of omission, unforeseeable damages, and other instances where the limitations of legal theory and procedure precluded earthly judgments.[69] Importantly, the 'heavenly judgments' rendered by this court were never implemented by a human court. Yet they filled in gaps similar to those filled by the ordeals and torture processes, except, here, the assumption was that ordinary cases could be decided by human beings according to rules; only exceptions were handled by God.

Torture and ordeals were like the "court of heaven," only with far greater jurisdiction. By the end of the twelfth century, however, ordeals had come to be seen as an impious 'tempting' of God, and were increasingly at odds with the developing rationalism. They were finally proscribed by Canon 18 of the Fourth Lateran Council of 1215.[70] Torture continued to be extensively used. Talal Asad suggests that the move from ordeals to torture signifies an incipient, proto-humanistic shift away from God as the producer of evidence and towards the human, itself resulting from the study of Roman law and its penetration into canon law.[71] But it, too, eventually fell into greater and greater disrepute.

The jury was understood to take the place of torture and ordeals in rendering verdicts of fundamental guilt or innocence. This analogy was explic-

---

[66] Obviously, the details of the ordeals procedures are quite gory and involve the use of a wide variety of media. See T.F.T. Plucknett, *A Concise History of the Common Law* (New York: Little Brown, 1956), 113–18.

[67] See Asad, *Genealogies*, 90–95.

[68] See Menachem Elon, *Jewish Law: History, Sources, Principles* (Philadelphia: Jewish Publication Society, 1994).

[69] On *dinei shamayim*, see Aaron Kirschenbaum, *Beyond Equity: Halakhic Aspirationism in Jewish Civil Law* (Jersey City, N.J.: Ktav Publishing, 1991), 137–78.

[70] Canon 18 of the Fourth Lateran Council reads, "Neither shall anyone in judicial tests by hot or cold water or hot iron bestow any blessing ...." (reprinted in H.J. Schroeder, ed. and trans., *Disciplinary Decrees of the General Councils* (St. Louis: Herder, 1937)). See also Asad, *Genealogies*, 95.

[71] See Asad, *Genealogies*, 84–90.

itly recognized in the thirteenth century, as the English jury began its ascent.[72] Plucknett writes:

> A jury was just a newer sort of ordeal ... the jury states a simple verdict of guilty or not guilty and the court accepts it, as unquestioningly as it used to accept the pronouncements of the hot iron or the cold water.... At first, the jury was no more regarded as 'rational' than the ordeals which it replaced, and just as one did not question the judgments of God as shown by the ordeal, so the verdict of a jury was equally inscrutable. It is but slowly that the jury was rationalised and regarded as a judicial body.[73]

The early jury worked because it, like God, could weigh the soul of the accused and determine guilt, and, without explanation, could pronounce guilt or innocence. Because it relied on the soul, it was reliable, but because it relied on people, it had a degree of rationality greater than that of the ordeal process. In its early forms, following the Assize of Clarendon (1166), the presenting jury was comprised of villagers who, while lacking divine omniscience, knew something about the accused and the facts of the case and could pursue arrests, combining investigative and prosecutorial functions. It made sense in a social structure where order was already maintained by posses of citizens organized under the frankpledge system. And, in the jury's later forms, it did not require law, or even explanation; English juries were never asked to explain their reasoning until the seventeenth century,[74] and, even today, it is somewhat bizarre that of all the various controls imposed on the jury over the course of several centuries of experimentation,[75] juries are still instructed to keep quiet about why they reached the decision that they did.

The silence of the jury is particularly striking when we recall that for much of the period in which the institution was in use, legal questions now thought to be 'questions of law' for the judge to decide were often within the jury's purview. One reason we possess relatively little doctrine in tort or contract prior to Blackstone, for example, is that disputes in these areas of law were often considered best resolved by twelve men, good and true, than the complexities of property law, trusts, and estates, which were more befitting the attention of judges.[76] One suspects that much of the explanation for this phenomenon is economic—property and estate law affected the most monied and powerful classes, whereas ordinary tort and contract

---

[72] Plucknett, *Common Law*, 118ff.

[73] Ibid., 124–25. See also Langbein, *Torture*, 74.

[74] John Langbein, "The Criminal Trial Before the Lawyers," *University of Chicago Law Review* 45 (1978): 287ff.

[75] See Langbein, *Common Law*, ch. 8; Nelson, "Eighteenth-Century Background," 904–17.

[76] See J.H. Baker, *The Law's Two Bodies: Some Evidential Problems in English Legal History* (New York: Oxford University Press, 2000).

disputes were not of such concern. But for whatever reason, the fact remains that legal questions we now consider part of the 'science of law' were considered, until the beginning of the nineteenth century, within the provenance of the jury's conscience and common sense.

Likewise, in the early American context, it was assumed that jurors need not even be instructed as to the law, even though juries often decided questions of law as well as fact in the pre-revolutionary period, and immediately thereafter.[77] The pre-revolutionary jury instructions discussed by William Nelson are instructive here—though some have heavily critiqued Nelson's selection criteria.[78] One such instruction from 1759 Massachusetts informs jurors that they "need no Explanation [since] your Good Sence & understanding will Direct ye" to the right outcome.[79] Jurors with no legal training were thought to be "good judges of the common law of the land."[80] Standards of evaluating evidence were often matters of conscience; Nelson elsewhere quotes a 1741 Connecticut jury charge as informing jurors that prosecution evidence was "satisfactory if you have no particular reasons in your own breast, in your consciences to discredit them,"[81] a means of evaluating credibility still essentially in place today. If Nelson's sources are indicative, then as with doing justice "not by any quirks of the law ... but by common sense as between man and man,"[82] the jury's methodology in these instructions is inscrutable, but reliable, unwritten, but providential.

In other words, the essence of the jury's appeal remains the same implicit theory of the Clinton impeachment: that justice is done by common sense between man and man—soul to soul—not by quirks of law. Even after

---

[77] See William Nelson, *Marbury v. Madison: The Origins and Legacy of Judicial Review* (Lawrence, KS: University Press of Kansas, 2000), 26–33 (quoting, inter alia, John Adams, Thomas Jefferson, and John Jay). But see Hiller B. Zobel, "Some Agonies and Misuses of Legal History," *New England Quarterly* 50 (1977): 145 (quoting pre-revolutionary Massachusetts Chief Justice [later Governor] Hutchinson, who complains that "I have found Juries taking upon them to judge of the Wholesomeness of the Laws, and thereby subverting the very End of their Institution.") Compare F. Thornton Miller, *Juries and Judges versus the Law: Virginia's Provincial Legal Perspective, 1783–1828* (Charlottesville, VA: University of Virginia Press, 1994).

[78] Critiques of Nelson include Zobel, "Agonies and Misuses" (charging that Nelson "repeatedly misread, misstated, or misapplied manuscript evidence" and committed "serious scholarly negligence"); David H. Flaherty, Review of *Americanization of the Common Law: The Impact of Legal Change on Massachusetts Society, 1760–1830*, by William E. Nelson, in *University of Toronto Law Journal* 26 (1976): 108–11 (stating that Nelson "paints too black and white a picture" though agreeing with his analysis of the jury's evolution). But see Herbert A. Johnson, Review of *Americanization of the Common Law: The Impact of Legal Change on Massachusetts Society, 1760–1830*, by William E. Nelson, in *Columbia Law Review* 76 (1976): 713–19 (calling the book "one of those exceptional first books that with the passage of time may become a classic of historical literature").

[79] Massachusetts court jury instruction, quoted in Nelson, "Eighteenth-Century Background," 904.

[80] James Sullivan, 1779 letter to Elbridge Gerry, in Nelson, *Marbury v. Madison*, 25.

[81] Quoted in Nelson, *Marbury v. Madison*, 26.

[82] Quoted in Nelson, "Eighteenth-Century Background," 904.

the American Revolution, as the jury's power to find law was curbed, it retained "the role of the people in the administration of government" and offered a bulwark against tyranny, particularly for Anti-Federalists.[83] All of this was to be achieved without explaining, without formal legal training, and without the supposedly obtuse details of common law precedent.

Nor is the jury the only Anglo-American legal institution that was conceived of as, essentially, anti-legal. Equitable courts, such as the early writ system and the Court of Chancery, were seen in very similar ways. First, the English writ "system," from which much of our common law is ultimately descended, played a similar role; in the first centuries following 1066, writs were not really a "system" at all but rather a series of appeals for a royal decree.[84] One petitioned the king for a redress of a specific action, a petition that sought to cast the injustice in question into a formulaic mold so that it could be addressed by the Monarch and his agents,[85] and appealed to royal *voluntas* instead of the *judicium* of a local court.[86] It is, not to belabor the point, a move from the rule of law to the rule of man. The very nature of writ procedure is, at its heart, asking the King to write a wrong by whatever reasoning he chooses.

Second, when writs themselves became so acutely legalistic (even spelling counted) two equitable systems of deciding cases, the church and the Court of Chancery, came to supplant the Common Bench from without, while a single writ (trespass) came to dominate it from within.[87] Like the jury, Chancery was seen as an alternative to abstruse doctrines and legal formalism, and petitioners appealed to the Chancellor to do "as good faith and conscience require."[88] Equity was an explicit move away from laws and towards "faith and conscience" as the Court of Chancery gradually grew in the fourteenth and fifteenth centuries to dominate the English legal system. As Keeton puts it, "the court of chancery is a court of conscience."[89]

---

[83] Kenneth Klein, "Unpacking," 1338–39 (quoting Herbert J. Storing, ed., *The Complete Anti-Federalist* (Chicago: University of Chicago Press, 1981), 1:19).

[84] See Raoul C. Van Caenegem, *Royal Writs in England from the Conquest to Glanvill* (London: Quaritch, 1959), 177–79.

[85] The classic, though now heavily critiqued, treatment of the writ system is F.W. Maitland, *The Forms of Action at Common Law* (Cambridge: Cambridge University Press, 1909). See also S.F.C. Milson, *Historical Foundations of the Common Law* (London: Butterworths, 1981), 33–36.

[86] Van Caenegem, *Royal Writs*, 177ff. Much of the writ system's success may be attributed to the increasing power of the English monarchy in the twelfth century (in contrast with the waning power of local courts), to its precedents in Germanic dispensations of justice, and to its power struggle with canon law. But the flight from the law and to the king is, I suggest, an important modality of anti-legalism that appears right from the very beginning of post-Hastings English history.

[87] See G.W. Keeton, *An Introduction to Equity* (London: Pitman & Sons, 1965), 11–17; Milson, *Common Law*, 60ff.

[88] A.W.B. Simpson, *A History of the Common Law of Contract: The Rise of the Action of Assumpsit* (Oxford: Oxford University Press, 1975), 397 (spelling modernized).

[89] Keeton, *Equity*, 17. Hoffer notes that the King's Bench, Court of Common Pleas, and Court of Chancery occupied the same large hall in Westminster Hall. The choice of venue

In all these instances, the religious character of equity is explicit. Chancery took over equitable roles gradually being ceded by ecclesiastical courts, and was staffed by ecclesiastical personnel.[90] From the eleventh century (following the revolution led by Pope Gregory VII renouncing secular control of ecclesiastical institutions) to the sixteenth century, equity was highly influenced, in form and substance, by the Church of Rome.[91] Chancellors often saw themselves as concerned with the respondents' souls.[92] Formally, the real prosecutor was God, not the petitioner; it was the ecclesiastical Chancellor's task to ensure that the respondent's soul would not be damned for his deeds. And, tellingly, the exercise of Chancery was conscience, not rules: "[E]quity is according to the conscience of him that is Chancellor, and as that is larger or narrower, so is equity."[93]

In general, appealing to conscience and to the spirit is about justice, not law. The jury, the king, the Chancellor, and the court of equity (which stayed separate from the court of law until 1875) were not parts of "law," but apart from it.[94] Moreover, in America, it is notable that throughout most of the eighteenth century, equity courts were the only courts where judges decided cases. Juries did the rest.[95] Thus, we might say that equity, in some form, was the *only* option. And when these systems decay, as with Chancery in the nineteenth century,[96] and, arguably, the "litigation explosion" jury of today, they are accused of becoming overly formalistic and unconcerned with actual guilt and innocent. Consider Dickens' famous depiction of Chancery in *Bleak House*, which might be written about lawyers today:

---

was thus quite stark. Hoffer, *Law and People*, 2–3.

[90] See Harold Berman, *Faith and Order: The Reconciliation of Law and Religion* (Grand Rapids: Eerdmans, 1993), 71; R.H. Helmholz, "The Early Enforcement of Uses," *Columbia Law Review* 79 (1979): 1503–13 (noting a continuity between canon law and common law, as Chancery courts directly took over for ecclesiastical courts in certain jurisdictional areas while applying both canon law and common law to cases at bar).

[91] Berman, *Faith and Order*, 56–58; Charles J. Reid, and John Witte, "In the Steps of Gratian: Writing the History of Canon Law in the 1990s," *Emory Law Journal* 48 (1999): 647–88.

[92] Simpson, *Common Law of Contract*, 399. See also Larry DiMatteo, "The History of Natural Law Theory: Transforming Embedded Influence into a Fuller Understanding of Modern Contract Law," *University of Pittsburgh Law Review* 60 (1999): 862–65.

[93] *Gee v. Pritchard*, 36 Eng. Rep. 670, 679 n.1 (Ch. 1818) (quoting John Selden's *Table Talk*). The remainder of the quote is the familiar adage against forum shopping amongst venues with subjective measures: "'Tis all one, as if they should make his food the standard for the measure we call a Chancellor's foot; what an uncertain measure would this be! One Chancellor has a long food, another a short foot, a third an indifferent foot; 'tis the same thing in the Chancellor's conscience."

[94] There was, to be sure, considerable cooperation between the courts—procedures migrate back and forth, questions of law were referred between the fora, and so on. See Plucknett, *Common Law*, 210.

[95] Nelson, *Marbury v. Madison*, 25.

[96] See John Langbein, "Fact-finding in the English Court of Chancery: A Rebuttal," *Yale Law Journal* 83 (1974): 1628ff.

Tripping one another up on slippery precedents, groping knee-deep in technicalities, running their goat-hair and horsehair warded heads against walls of words and making a pretense of equity with serious faces, as players might.[97]

Common sense, not precedent, and justice, not technicalities is a dichotomy that shall reappear in the next section, and that, of course, is familiar today.

To be sure, the symbolic meaning of the American jury has evolved dramatically in the last two centuries.[98] By the end of the nineteenth century, after the 'golden age' of American law had wrought its changes in judges' self-perceptions as the ones making law (and, to some extent, policy) as opposed to only assisting in the uncovering of universal principles, the "jury of one's peers" became seen less as a populist-political body ensuring sound lawmaking, and more as a protector of the individual rights of the accused.[99] And by the end of the twentieth century, trial rules, jury instructions, and other devices curtailed the jury's power still further as the institution came under pressure from both elite and popular sides. Yet the democratic ideal of the jury, and its essential function as men honest and true has not disappeared; nor has, as we shall see in the context of substantive law, the opposition of those men to the soulless men of law.

C. Judges without Laws: The Common Law in America

A third instance of the conflict between legalism and the law of "common sense" is the debate surrounding the adoption of the common law in early nineteenth century America. The status of British common law in the colonies was the subject of arguably the first large-scale jurisprudential debate in the American experience. American colonies did not import English common law and its attendant debates and tensions wholesale and without debate. In fact, patterns of adoption varied considerably from jurisdiction to jurisdiction,[100] and, until a few decades preceding the founding of the Republic, legal regimes varied widely from state to state, reflecting everything from theocratic to mercantile laissez-faire principles.[101] Local

---

[97] Charles Dickens, *Bleak House* (New York: Chelsea House, 1987), ch. 1. On the veracity of Dickens' representation of Chancery, see W.S. Holdsworth, *Charles Dickens as a Legal Historian* (New Haven: Yale University Press, 1929), 79–81 ("I am sure that it would be possible to produce an edition of Bleak House, in which all Dickens's statements could be verified by the statements of the witnesses who gave evidence before the Chancery Commission, which reported in 1826.")

[98] See Nelson, *Marbury v. Madison*, 36–40.

[99] See Klein, "Unpacking," 1344–46.

[100] George Athan Billias, ed., *Law and Authority in Colonial America* (Mineola, N.Y.: Dover Publications, 1965) contains a number of treatments of how common law doctrines and procedures were imported, adapted, or rejected in varying American colonies. On the nexus between the legal profession and the common law, see J.H. Baker, ed., *Legal Profession and the Common Law: Historical Essays* (London: Hambledon Press, 1986).

[101] Erwin Griswold, *Law and Lawyers in the United States: The Common Law Under*

courts often had enormously wide discretion and little legislative control.[102] The initial Anglicization of colonial law, which began in the 1690s and continued throughout the first half of the eighteenth century, was the first attempt to unify "American law," and involved considerable integration of English common law, at first more procedurally than substantively.[103] For the next hundred years, debates raged as to how much common law to import, how much to allow juries to find law as well as fact, and how unified American law was to become. These debates comprise the formative period of an "American" jurisprudence, and are part and parcel of the dramatic economic, political, ideological, and religious changes that took place over the period. Yet as we will see, they are also marked by the now-familiar dichotomies between true law and written law, soul and body. They are, in large part, debates framed by the categories of religion.

Now, it is undoubtedly true that much of the debate over the adoption of the common law was primarily political, and only secondarily jurisprudential. The perceived excesses of English imperialism had frequently been characterized by Massachusetts colonists, for example, as excesses of law, and as mis-locations of the source of law's authority in the crown rather than in local law-dispensing institutions.[104] Decisions regarding jury nullification were often made for political interests, rather than philosophical ones.[105] However, even in such cases, the rhetoric of early-Republic debates repeatedly revolved around whether judges or legislatures were better equipped to avoid the same universally-agreed-upon pitfalls: legalism, obscurantism, and mechanism.

Stress (London: Stevens, 1964), 7–8. For the earlier history of the British common law, see generally J.H. Baker, *Introduction to English Legal History*, 3d ed. (London: Butterworths, 1990); Milson, *Common Law*.

[102] See generally Hendrik Hartog, "The Public Law of a County Court: Judicial Government in Eighteenth Century Massachusetts," *American Journal of Legal History* 20 (1976): 282–329. American law and legal procedure had always varied widely from jurisdiction to jurisdiction; in the seventeenth century, it varied widely from town to town. Nelson, *Americanization*, x–xi.

[103] See Bruce Mann, "The Evolutionary Revolution in American Law: A Comment on J.R. Pole's 'Reflections,'" *William and Mary Quarterly* (1993): 168–75; and Eben Moglen, "Settling the Law: Legal Development in New York, 1664–1776" (PhD diss., Yale University, 1993), cited in Nelson, *Americanization*, xi–xiii.

[104] See John Reid, *In a Defiant Stance: The Conditions of Law in Massachusetts Bay, the Irish Comparison, and the Coming of the American Revolution* (University Park: Penn State University Press, 1977), 161–73. To Professor Reid, even the use of the mob could be characterized as constitutional and legal in nature by Whig colonists. See also Peter Teachout, "Light in Ashes: The Problem of 'Respect for the Rule of Law' in American Legal History," in *Law in the American Revolution*, ed. Hendrik Hartog (New York: NYU Press, 1981), 192–93 (reviewing Reid and noting the "protean" character of legal institutions).

[105] See Nelson, *Americanization*, xiv. But see ibid., xvi–xvii (arguing that ideological and philosophical values associated with the American Revolution played a central role in legal and procedural change).

1. Law and Lawyers: Moses, or Shylock?

As a threshold matter, let us recall that in the Revolutionary period, crime was as much a religious as a "secular" legal matter. William Nelson points out that before the American Revolution, half of all prosecutions were for immorality, and were seen as cases of "a sinner against God;" such prosecutions were generally resolved without a high degree of recourse to formal institutions.[106] By 1800, however, only 7% of prosecutions were for immorality, legal institutions grew considerably, and the criminal came to be seen as "one who preyed on the property of his fellow citizens."[107] During this period of evolution, then, we must understand that an essentially religious law is being secularized, but not without objection or debate. This secularization, part of what Nelson characterizes as a "gradual breakdown of ethical unity," moved more generally in a direction of law that favored commercial life.[108] My claim is that law has always been theologized in the American experience, and thus to read these debates in the way proposed here is to read them in their original, religious context.

Revolutionary and early American-Republican attitudes regarding law and lawyers generally varied wildly. On the one hand, the rule of law in principle and practice was valorized, primarily by elites who were often themselves legal practitioners.[109] Lawyers played an integral part in the Founding—lawyers of one type or another comprised 25 of the 56 signers of the Declaration of Independence, 32 of the 55 members of the 1787 Constitutional Convention, and four of the first five presidents[110]—and the cooption of the rule of law, it has been argued, allowed the Revolution itself to take the form it did.[111] Elite discourse often depicted law in religious terms, often related to divine or natural law, as the foundation of American culture—in one engraving, law is portrayed as a sublime gift to America, with George Washington in the Mosaic role.[112] Thomas Paine waxed poetic about the rule of law:

> [L]et a crown be placed thereon, by which the world may now, that so far as we approve of monarchy, that in America *the law is king*. For

---

[106] William Nelson, *Dispute & Conflict Resolution in Plymouth County, Mass, 1725–1825* (Chapel Hill: University of North Carolina Press, 1981), 133–35; see also Hoffer, *Law and People*, 40–41.

[107] Nelson, *Americanization*, 118.

[108] Ibid., 37–48, 109–17.

[109] See Robert Ferguson, *Law and Letters in American Culture* (Cambridge, MA: Harvard University Press, 1984), 11–34.

[110] Fred Barash, *The Founding: A Dramatic Account of the Writing of the Constitution* (New York: Linden Press, 1987), 43–45; Griswold, *Law and Lawyers*, 12.

[111] See Reid, *In a Defiant Stance*, 173.

[112] J.P. Elven, "Washington Giving the Laws to America" (engraving), in Robert A. Ferguson, *Law and Letters in American Culture* (Cambridge, MA: Harvard University Press, 1984), 13.

as in absolute governments the king is law, so in free countries the law ought to be king; and there ought to be no other.[113]

Even in less grandiose terms, it should strike any reader how saturated with the rhetoric of law—fundamental constitutional rights, natural law, inalienable rights, and so on—the political acts of the American revolution were, even if scholarship remains divided on exactly which source of law (natural law, constitutional law, custom) carried the most weight for the revolutionaries.[114] For John Adams, law was the tool against tyranny, even as tyranny itself manifested itself in outmoded canon law, feudal law, and royal acts such as the Stamp Act.[115] The power of the lawyer was to understand and critique the fallacies inherent in bad law, and to crystallize the issues and injustices at stake for the population.[116] Foreshadowing Toqueville's famous observations of an American legal aristocracy, law was routinely elevated above the natural sciences and religious service as being the most important and honorable profession in America.[117] By the time the fragile Republic was established, lawyers saw themselves as *"ex officio* natural guardians of the law" (Chancellor Kent's phrase) and as performing essential roles for the maintenance of the state and, indeed, human happiness.[118]

And yet, contrary to today's idealized images of the eighteenth century lawyer-statesman, early-Republic-era lawyers were sometimes held in deep suspicion, and were the frequent objects, in Morton Horwitz's words, of "lower class hatred" of professional elites. Lawyers—many of whom wore the formal wigs and costumes and used distinguishing titles—were seen as suspiciously English, because, though many revolutionaries were lawyers,

---

[113] Thomas Paine, "Common Sense," in *The Basic Writings of Thomas Paine*, ed. Richard Huett (Hoboken, N.J.: Wiley, 1942), 40.

[114] See Ferguson, *Law and Letters*, 12–15. On the sources of law as conceived by the Founders, see John Reid, "The Irrelevance of the Declaration," in Hartog, *Law in the American Revolution and the Revolution in the Law*, 46, 49–69 (arguing that the Declaration of Independence was primarily a claim of constitutional rights, not natural rights); John Reid, *Constitutional History of the American Revolution: The Authority of Law* (Madison: University of Wisconsin Press, 1993) (characterizing American revolution as oriented toward a basically conservative reading of the English constitution); James Q. Whitman, "Why Did the Revolutionary Lawyers Confuse Custom and Reason?" *University of Chicago Law Review* 58 (1991): 1327–29 (tracing evolution of scholarly opinion); Thomas C. Grey, "Origins of the Unwritten Constitution: Fundamental Law in American Revolutionary Thought," *Stanford Law Review* 30 (1978): 843–93.

[115] Ferguson, *Law and Letters*, 16–19.

[116] John Adams, "A Dissertation on the Canon and Feudal Law (1765)," in *The Life and Works of John Adams*, ed. Charles Francis Adams (Boston: Little, Brown, 1854), 3:445. See also Ferguson, *Law and Letters*, 18–19.

[117] Ferguson, *Law and Letters*, 12, 25.

[118] Ibid., 24–26 (quoting James Kent, "Address Delivered Before the Law Association of New York City," Oct. 21, 1839, in William Kent, ed., *Memoirs and Letters of Chancellor James Kent* (Boston: Little, Brown, 1898), 235–36).

more elite lawyers were royalists.[119] Much anti-lawyer sentiment, consequently, divided along political lines. In general, Hamiltonian Federalists viewed the legal profession more favorably than Jeffersonian democrats,[120] although Jefferson himself was regarded as a kind of ideal lawyer-statesman by his admirers.[121]

The common law, comprised as it was of mostly English precedent with the musty whiff of the Old Country in the leaves of the law books, was sometimes seen as importing "monarchical and aristocratical institutions of England" into the new Republic.[122] Critics also accused the common law of advancing more prosaic, earthly ends, such as increasing the power of lawyers themselves. "The numerous precedents brought from 'old English authorities,'" wrote one pamphleteer, "answer no other purpose than to increase the influence of lawyers."[123] Citizens of Delaware and Massachusetts raised popular protests to abolish the legal profession entirely; citizens of Vermont burnt courthouses; Shays' rebellion poured out its wrath on the judicial system.[124] Prior to the Founding, two colonies banned the pleading of cases for compensation.[125] One census report from 1770 New Hampshire informed George III that "Grafton County ... contains 6,489 souls, most of whom are engaged in agriculture, but included in that number are 69 wheelwrights, 8 doctors, 29 blacksmiths, 87 preachers, 20 slaves and 90 students at the new college. There is not one lawyer, for which fact we take no personal credit, but thank an Almighty and Merciful God."[126]

Some rhetoric took a stronger tone. At one extreme (and it is an extreme), consider John Dudley, the New Hampshire Supreme Court justice (from 1785–1797), renowned for boasting that he had never read Blackstone or Littleton and never would, once charged a jury as follows:

---

[119] Morton Horwitz, *The Transformation of American Law 1780–1860* (Cambridge, MA: Harvard University Press, 1977), 145–46. See also Gerard W. Gawalt, "Sources of Anti-Lawyer Sentiment in Massachusetts, 1740–1840," *American Journal of Legal History* 14 (1970): 283–307; Milton M. Klein, "From Community to Status: The Development of the Legal Profession in Colonial New York," in Baker, *Legal Profession*, 380 (discussing the rise of the legal profession as such and the attendant resentment of it); Alfred S. Konefsky, "Law and Culture in Antebellum Boston," *Stanford Law Review* 40 (1988): 1119–59 (critiquing narratives of lawyer ascendancy and relating legal profession to other elites).

[120] Miller, *Legal Mind in America*, 41, 119–20.

[121] See Ferguson, *Law and Letters*, 34ff.

[122] Honestus (Benjamin Austin), "Observations on the Pernicious Practice of the Law," in Griswold, *Law and Lawyers*, 12–13.

[123] Ibid., 12.

[124] Charles Warren, *A History of the American Bar* (Boston: Little Brown, 1912), 214–17.

[125] Frank R. Rosiny, "Despair Not," *New York State Bar Journal* 65 (1993): 42–43; Kenneth Lasson, "Lawyering Askew: Excesses in the Pursuit of Fees and Justice," *Boston University Law Review* 74 (1994): 729.

[126] Quoted in Deborah Rhode, "Too Much Law, Too Little Justice: Too Much Rhetoric, Too Little Reform," *Georgetown Journal of Legal Ethics* 11 (1988): 989.

> Gentlemen, you have heard what has been said in this case by the lawyers, the rascals! ... They talk of law. Why, gentlemen, it is not law that we want, but justice! They would govern us by the common law of England. Common-sense is a much safer guide.... A clear head and an honest heart are worth more than all the law of all the lawyers.[127]

Such subversions of the common law were abundant in the first half-century of the Republic's independence, as juries often decided cases on the basis of community tradition or a sort of watered-down version of natural law, in contrast to the English rules of anglophile lawyer elites.[128] And as we shall see, even figures at the opposite extreme from Dudley's suspicion of the common law—George Wythe, for instance, or even John Marshall himself—believed in a sort of Americanized natural law which undermines the common law even as it rationalizes it.

Moreover, Dudley's infusion of American values (common-sense, clear-headed) into dichotomies between law and justice is absolutely central to the antinomian, or antilogonomian, tendency in American thought. And the contrast between an 'honest heart' and 'the law of all the lawyers' is a reinscription of the Pauline rhetoric to which we will turn in the next part, which becomes clear when such jurisprudential statements are explicitly theologized. For example, Jesse Higgins writes in 1805 that

> God never intended his creature man, should be under the necessity to carry a written book in his pocket, or a lawyer by his side, to tell him what is just and lawful; he wrote it on his mind.[129]

This is explicitly theological language (the law 'written on his mind' echoing Paul's law 'written on the table of his heart,' discussed in the next part) used to make a theological-anthropological point. These debates are about the soul.

2. Common Law: Old England, or Old Testament?

In this context, debates regarding the common law provide a useful insight into the dynamic of letter and spirit in the period of the Founding and the fifty years after it, a time that saw considerable changes in the self-conception of American law and society and, as a whole, comprised a period of dramatic American jurisgenesis.[130] They also further undermine the

---

[127] Jury charge given by John Dudley, judge on the New Hampshire Supreme Court, quoted in Griswold, *Law and Lawyers*, 13.

[128] On the "Anglicization" of the bar, and Massachusetts more widely, in the years prior to the Revolutionary War, see John Murrin, "The Legal Transformation: The Bench and Bar of Eighteenth Century Massachusetts," in *Colonial America: Essays in Politics and Social Development*, ed. Stanley Katz (Boston: Little Brown, 1971), 415ff.

[129] Jesse Higgins, *Sampson against the Philistines* 92 in Maxwell H. Bloomfield, *American Lawyers in a Changing Society, 1776–1876* (Cambridge, MA: Harvard University Press, 1976), 48.

[130] The claim that the early nineteenth century, in contrast to the eighteenth century, was

claim that today's theologized legal rhetoric discussed above is merely partisan posturing—it is not. Instead it is a recurring theme in American popular-jurisprudential discourse.

The debate tended to hew to ideological lines. Republicans favored the codification of existing law and, to varying degrees, a move to a quasi-civil law regime; they mistrusted the legal elites who would import English artificiality, technicality, and elitism to the new states.[131] Federalists, however, tended to resist codification because it destroyed the essence of the common law—namely, its flexibility, "naturalness" (contra 'mechanistic'), and democratic potential.[132] Notice, however, how each side of the adoption debate praises the same virtues. Federalists want to preserve the "natural" common law; Anti-Federalists want to remove its "technicality." The common law may once have been a fixed set of divinely inspired principles, but, to its critics, it was already becoming a stagnant set of talmudic rules.[133] Consider the 1824 complaint of Henry Dwight Sedgwick that the English common law was too filled with "artificialness and technicality."[134] Or that of Anti-Federalist William Sampson, who explicitly Judaized the common law, calling it "mystical and cabalistic ... oral tradition opposed to written law; it was written law, but presuming the writing lost."[135]

Now, the reality of the common law's operation was not nearly so Pharisaic as polemicists depicted it; although *stare decisis* did render the common law as written, precedential, and complex, skilled lawyers could easily find their way around unwanted precedents and navigate through the case law to find supporting authorities, and juries were not so deferential that they could not be selective in applying, or ignoring, common law precedent

---

a time of unprecedented judicial creativity has been made for decades. See Roscoe Pound, *The Formative Era of American Law* (Boston: Little Brown, 1938); Grant Gilmore, *The Ages of American Law* (New Haven: Yale University Press, 1977). It has also been critiqued, see, e.g., Peter Teachout, "Book Review," *Vermont Law Review* 2 (1977): 239–49. The analysis here does not intend to enter into the scholarly debate on this question but to locate a more fundamental, theological grounding for the common law and law more generally. On the common law prior to the Founding, including antinomian disputes surrounding it, see William E. Nelson, *The Common Law in Colonial America, Vol. 1* (Oxford: Oxford University Press, 2008).

[131] Anti-Federalists believed the common law was anti-democratic because it vested power in elite judges rather than "take its doctrines from the people." Charles Jared Ingersoll, "A Discourse Concerning the Influence of America on the Mind (1823)," in Miller, ed., *The Legal Mind in America*, 78.

[132] Jesse Root, "The Origin of Government and Laws in Connecticut (1798)" and James Madison Porter, "Review of Cases (1827)," in Miller, ed., *The Legal Mind in America*, 161 (arguing that common law promotes liberty).

[133] On this transformation in American views of the common law, see the first chapter of Horwitz, *The Transformation of American Law 1780–1860*.

[134] Henry Dwight Sedgwick, "On an Anniversary Discourse (1824)," in Miller, ed., *The Legal Mind in America*, 121, 124.

[135] William Sampson, "An Anniversary Discourse (1824)," in Miller, ed., *The Legal Mind in America*, 121, 124.

in the context of policy struggles and interests of justice.[136] But of course, it would be rather awkward for Federalists favoring the common law's adoption to point out that, really, all the old precedent does not matter because lawyers can work around it anyway. Instead, what Federalists tended to say was that the Common Law was not Pharisaic at all, in origin or in application. Jesse Root, for example, in a polemical 1798 study of the Connecticut law, argued that the foundation of the common law comes not from any particular set of principles but from, essentially, natural law, a topic to which we will return in the next part. For Root, the common law comes from "the law of nature and of revelation—those rules and maxims of immutable truth and justice, which arise from the eternal fitness of things."[137]

This fictive trans-temporality allies the common law not with old English precedent but rather with natural law of "nature and of revelation," which, of course, is of essentially religious origin. Those immutable principles, in turn, are part of the larger Federalist project of immutable laws contrasted with contingent politics. Those elements of the common law which were intrinsically English could be weeded out, as in Nathaniel Chipman's proposal that Blackstone's Commentaries be used as a repository of principles which "accord with the principles of the American democracy and governments, and which are founded in the universal principles of jurisprudence," with the remainder to be discarded.[138]

In other words, common law's defenders shared the same fundamental principles as its attackers: what is wanted is not Pharisaic rules, not byzantine legal precedents, but—Chipman again—"the perfection of reason, arising from the nature of God, of man, and of things."[139] The only question was how best to implement those divine imperatives. As one might expect, Federalists were inclined to trust (elite) judges, rather than popular representatives, only here the conceptual theory is that judges were trained to exercise the right faculties to discover immutable law, while legislatures created only the law of man. Rather like the theologized natural law discussed in the next part, Federalist 'law' was, like the Pauline spirit of the law and like the modalities of guilt and innocence in play in the Clinton impeachment, "written upon the table of our hearts"[140]

In this view the common law was fixed, permanent, and perfect,[141] because it was a reflection of reason—or, in the characterization of Bernard

---

[136] See J.H. Baker, *The Law's Two Bodies* (New York: Oxford University Press, 2000); Teachout, "Light in Ashes," 188–90.

[137] See Root, "Origin of Government," in Miller, ed., *The Legal Mind in America*.

[138] Nathaniel Chipman, "Sketches of the Principles of Government (1793 ed.)," in Miller, ed., *The Legal Mind in America*, 35. The revised, enlarged edition of "Sketches" was printed in 1833 (Burlington: Edward Smith, 1833 ed.). Quotes in the text are from the 1793 edition.

[139] Ibid., 34–35.

[140] Ibid.

[141] See Horwitz, *Transformation*, 1; Nelson, *Americanization*, 19ff.

Bailyn, a "repository of experience in human dealings embodying the principles of justice equity, and rights" that "stood side by side with Enlightenment rationalism in the minds of the Revolutionary generation."[142] Thus even judges who only applied the law—what Nelson calls "automatons who mechanically applied immutable rules of law to the facts of each case"[143]— were applying a law very different from the legislatively-derived or Model Code-encoded law of today. If they were mechanical instruments at all, they were instruments of reason and eternal verities—not of codes, statutes, and C.F.R.s.

For this reason, Nelson's characterization of revolutionary-era common law judges as 'automatons' may be somewhat misleading; they may have been expected to be automatons, but they were automatons dispensing reason and wisdom; it is only that the wisdom is deferred from the decision maker himself to a prior source. Without entering into the scholarly debate on how much or how little revolutionary judges and lawyers really did alter inherited legal thought and doctrine,[144] my claim is that even for those who favored what we today might see as increased legalism, the sort of law (or Law) they favored was in fact quite different from a Shylockian legalism. To the extent it was rhetorically glossed as embodying eternal truths, as opposed to humanly-created contingent rules that bind parties in their literal terms, it was still Portia's law, not Shylock's; natural law, not talmudic legalism; and, as I shall suggest below, the New Testament, not the Old.

Indeed, this helps explain why lawyers and jurists at the time saw it as their duty to educate themselves not only in the law, but (in Rufus Choate's words) in "admiration of the beautiful, the good, the true in art, in poetry, in thought."[145] The lawyer was no automaton; Joseph Story admonished Harvard law students in 1829 to "addict [themselves] to the study of philosophy, or rhetoric, of history, and of human nature."[146] Thomas Jefferson prescribed fourteen hours of reading a day in physical science, natural law, ethics, politics, history, poetry, and other subjects.[147] In this pre-expertise age, the lawyer's development of his soul, at least in these aspirational forms, paralleled the soul of the law—even as Story's own work contributed to the settling, codification and technical-ization of American law. For Kent, lecturing in 1794, the linkage was clear: one must be "well read in the whole circle of the arts and sciences" in order to develop "an accurate acquaint-

---

[142] Bernard Bailyn, *Pamphlets of the American Revolution 1750–1776* (Cambridge, MA: Belknap Press, 1965), 26–27.

[143] Nelson, *Americanization*, 19.

[144] For an arbitration of the dispute, see Teachout, "Light in Ashes," 167–75.

[145] Rufus Choate, "The Power of a State Developed by Mental Culture: A Lecture Delivered Before the Mercantile Library Association, Nov. 18, 1844," in Ferguson, *Law and Letters*, 26.

[146] Quoted in Ferguson, *Law and Letters*, 26.

[147] Ibid., 28–31.

ance with the general principles of Universal Law."[148]

In the end, the results of these debates varied. Some states banned any citation or exposition of common law after 1776, while others adopted it nearly wholesale.[149] But both sides of the common law debate promoted the same sets of ideals—non-technicality, non-legalism, human reason (or common sense) properly applied, and so on. They just disagreed as to whether common law espouses these ideals. They argued not the merits of legalism or non-legalism but rather what variety of law can achieve the universally-desired aims—what may be less mechanistic, more full of "naturalness" and democratic potential. Whether the common law is favorable or not was adjudicated on the grounds of its proximity to the human heart and its distance from legalism.

As in the Clinton impeachment, and the genealogy of the jury, religion was never far from the stage. In fact, the Christianization and theologization of American law was a commonplace through the end of the nineteenth century. Courts held that "Christianity [was] part and parcel of the common law."[150] In the words of Justice Kent, now Chief Justice of the Court of Appeals of New York in 1811,

> [W]e are a Christian people, and the morality of the country is deeply engrafted upon Christianity.[151]

Consequently, "enlarged Christianity"—Justice Kent's words again[152]—was presumed to be the basis of the common law itself. Indeed, the context of Justice Kent's utterances is *People v. Ruggles*, a case upholding the conviction of a man for 'blasphemously' defaming the name of Jesus Christ. In the reasoning of *Ruggles*, an offense against Christ was an offense against

> the people of this state [who], in common with the people of this country, profess the general doctrines of Christianity, as the rule of their faith and practice; and to scandalize the author of these doctrines is not only, in a religious point of view, extremely impious, but, even in respect to the obligations due to society, is a gross violation of decency and good order.[153]

---

[148] James Kent, "An Introductory Lecture to a Course of Law Lectures: Delivered November 17, 1794," *Columbia Law Review* 3 (1903): 330–43.

[149] Griswold, *Law and Lawyers*, 13.

[150] *In re Granger*, 7 Phila. Rep. 350, 355 (1870), quoted in Stuart Banner, "When Christianity was Part of the Common Law," *Law & History Review* 16 (1998): 27–62. Accord William Blackstone, *Commentaries on the Laws of England* (London: Dawsons, 1966), 4:59 ("Christianity is part of the laws of England").

[151] *People v. Ruggles*, 8 Johns. 290, 295 (1811), available at 1811 WL 1329 (N.Y. Sup.) (Westlaw).

[152] *Ruggles*, 8 Johns. at 297.

[153] Ibid. at 293. See also Banner, "Christianity," 32–38 (discussing blasphemy prosecu-

Blasphemy constituted a violation of "good order" not (only) because it was offensive, but because to strike against Christianity was to "strike at the root of moral obligation, and weaken the security of the social ties."[154] Today such statements may be the province only of the Christian Right, but not two hundred years ago. Christian moral and religious teaching was expressly and unashamedly held to be the foundation of numerous laws in the first century of the Republic, ranging from Sunday closing laws to the requirement of oaths to be sworn on the Bible[155] to laws against "cursing and swearing ... incestuous marriages ... *et peccatum illud horribile non nominandum inter Christianos.*"[156] One court called Christianity "the purest system of morality, the firmest auxiliary and the only stable support of all human laws."[157]

To be sure, the premise that Christianity is part of the common law attracted criticism, most notably from Thomas Jefferson and his supporters,[158] and it was last invoked in 1927.[159] But I would not want to minimize the extent to which the grounding of law in Christianity—or reason, or conscience—legitimizes the law and rescues it from positive, formalist mechanism. Like the natural law, Christian morality provides an antipositivist foundation for the eternal principles of justice.

---

tions and noting that New York made blasphemy a statutory crime). Banner suggests that the "Christianity is part and parcel of the common law" maxim was irrelevant for blasphemy and obscenity cases, because they were framed in terms of breaching the peace (ibid., 37). But this quasi-utilitarian reason is not what Justice Kent says. The fusion between Christianity and common law, as quoted above, is more than just breaching the peace; it is that a statement against Christianity is a statement against Christian society itself. True, later cases do away with the Christian element, but insofar as those cases rely on precedent or formal legal-constitutional grounds (*Commonwealth v. Kneeland*, 37 Mass. [20 Pick.] 206 (1838), for example, rests on the conclusion that the Massachusetts Constitution could not be read as intending to prohibit the legislature from reenacting a law that had "been deemed essential to the peace and safety of society"), they only postpone what the original rationales for such laws were. More generally, Banner's conclusion that the maxim was of little importance generally, and was really only a meta-issue, seems to overly minimize the extent to which rhetoric may legitimize or foundationalize that which lacks foundation and which had been criticized as lacking precisely the moral qualities Christianity could impart. See Banner, "Christianity," 60–63.

[154] *Ruggles*, 8 Johns. at 294.

[155] Ibid. at 297–98.

[156] *Updegraph v. The Commonwealth*, 11 Serge. & Rawl. 394, 399 (Pa. 1824). See Banner, "Christianity," 38–43.

[157] *Commonwealth v. Shipley*, 35 Pa. C. 132, 134 (1908), quoted in Banner, "Christianity," 46. Justice Joseph Story was among the most prominent proponents of this view, and one of the critics of Jefferson's opposition to it. See James McClellan, *Joseph Story and the American Constitution: A Study in Political and Legal Thought* (Norman, OK: Oklahoma University Press, 1971), 118–59.

[158] See Banner, "Christianity," 53–54. Banner's view is that Jefferson's opposition to the maxim is connected to his belief that common law was a set of traditions and practices encoded in law, rather than quasi-natural law as filtered through the wisdom of judges.

[159] See Banner, "Christianity," 27.

D. Law without Laws: Summary and Contemporary Echoes

Consider the remark made in 1846 by James Jackson (later Justice Jackson):

> The intricacy of the law, arising from its technicalities, has been and still is the cause of much censure upon the profession of the advocate. Some men seem to regard the law as a mere piece of mechanism; a form without spirit; words destitute alike of philosophy and meaning.[160]

Without context, Justice Jackson's remark may seem devoid of theological meaning. But as we have seen, and will show in the next part, the terms of this popular perception are quintessentially theological, and derive from the biblical critique of the dehumanizing effect of the Pharisaic law on the spiritual Christian soul. And this antinomian theoretical matrix remains in place today, even as social and economic change have cemented a legalization of culture to an extent unimagined by those who rued the growth of law in the first fifty years of the Republic.

Today, few believe that judges or legislatures "discover" the law,[161] and, while torture has lately reappeared in American legal procedure, its contemporary rationales are different. Yet we are still replaying the same scripts of legalism versus common sense, letter versus spirit. If anything, our own moment is even more anxious about technicality than the earlier ones. The shift in the late nineteenth and early twentieth century away from a Toquevillian-Jeffersonian ideal of the lawyer as an elite, schooled guardian against majoritarian whims to a Holmesian and post-Holmesian instrumentalism, which views law and lawyers (and even judges) basically as tools, is, as Holmes' metaphor implies, a shift toward antihumanism and toward law as mechanism.[162] It is also a shift from the kind of fixed-principles, natural law reasoning discussed above toward a kind of Holmesian moral non-absolutism (relativism is too strong a word).[163] And,

---

[160] James Jackson, "Law and Lawyers: Is the Profession of the Advocate Consistent with Perfect Integrity?" *The Knickerbocker Magazine* (Nov. 1846), 378, reprinted in Miller, ed., *The Legal Mind in America*, 275, 281.

[161] Justice Holmes' important positivist dissents on this point are bellwethers, see, e.g., *Southern Pacific Co. v. Jensen*, 244 U.S. 205, 222 (1917) (Holmes, J., dissenting); *Black & White Taxicab & Trans. Co. v. Brown & Yellow Taxicab & Trans. Co.*, 276 U.S. 518, 533 (1928) (Holmes, J., dissenting). On the erosion of the belief in legislatures to act according to divine will after the 1770s and 1780s, see Nelson, *Marbury v. Madison*, 53–60.

[162] On instrumentalism as an explanation for antilawyerism, see Michael P. Schutt, "Oliver Wendell Holmes and the Decline of the American Lawyer: Social Engineering, Religion, and the Search for Professional Identity," *Rutgers Law Journal* 30 (1998): 177–200. Schutt's theory is not that Holmesian instrumentalism was dehumanizing, but rather that it proposed a set of impossible ideals for the lawyer as social engineer, the unattainability of which caused widespread dislike of and "professional schizophrenia" among lawyers (ibid., 177–91).

[163] See Schutt, "Oliver Wendell Holmes," 171–74.

as Nelson shows, there was a deliberate "legalist reformation" that took place in the first half of the twentieth century, moving toward increased legal redistribution of wealth, support of entrepreneurialism, promotion of a nascent idea of liberty and equality—and often led by progressive Jews and Catholics.[164]

If anxieties about a law divorced from humanity and religion were present even in the context of a lawyer-statesman rhetoric, imagine their strength when the lawyers fulfilled their worst nightmares. This is precisely the picture painted by contemporary jeremiads about the "litigation explosion."[165] This literature, studies have shown, is factually inaccurate, based on a handful of mythically overblown case studies, and sponsored by business groups with financial interests in limiting tort liability.[166] But my claim is that they succeed for an ideological, ultimately religious reason, especially as the tales' outrageous lawyers are consistently contrasted with the "common sense" and "individual responsibility" that are posited in opposition.[167]

Of course, the same conservative parties behind the anti-legalist attacks on President Clinton are more recently behind the anti-legalist attacks on the legal system and the bar, anti-legalist attacks on civil liberties and "political correctness," and anti-legalist attacks on "activist judges." This discourse is largely politically motivated. But not entirely. First, some have written thoughtfully of the costs of "adversarial legalism" as a way of creating social policy, and on the American legal system's "inefficient, complex, costly, punitive and unpredictable method of governance and dispute resolution."[168] And, of course, even the most brutish critiques are not en-

---

[164] William Nelson, *The Legalist Reformation: Law, Politics, and Ideology in New York, 1920–1980* (Chapel Hill: University of North Carolina Press, 2001), 26–54.

[165] See note 4 above.

[166] William Haltom & Michael McCann, *Distorting the Law: Politics, Media, and the Litigation Crisis* (Chicago: University of Chicago Press, 2004), 1–49; Galanter, "Oil Strike in Hell"; Michael Saks, "Malpractice Misconceptions," *Justice System Journal* 16 (1993): 7–19; Michael Saks, "Do We Really Know Anything About the Behavior of the Tort Litigation System?" *University of Pennsylvania Law Review* 140 (1992): 1147–1292. Haltom and McCann convincingly show how the American Tort Reform Association, a heavily-funded umbrella group of trade and business groups, has influenced public opinion and legislation through "pop tort reform" and a rhetoric of individual responsibility masking corporate greed. Haltom and McCann, *Distorting the Law*, 40–43. These efforts have borne fruit: in the last twenty years, a majority of states have enacted meaningful tort reforms. Ibid, 51–52; F. Patrick Hubbard, "The Nature and Impact of the 'Tort Reform' Movement," *Hofstra Law Review* 35 (2006): 437–538 (describing how tort reform movement has shifted from judicial development of doctrine based on common law to legislation). Contrary to the myths, most injured parties do not seek compensation at all—over 87% in a scholarly study of automobile accidents. Halton and McCann, *Distorting the Law*, 81–87. Saks shows that lawyers are usually gate-keepers, not enablers, of would-be litigants; in one study, of 2500 medical malpractice inquiries, a law firm proceeded with 40. Saks, "Do We Really Know Anything?" 1178–80.

[167] Here, I agree with Haltom and McCann that while ideology is not the reason for such tales' existence, it is one of the primary reasons for their success. Haltom and McCann, *Distorting the Law*, 21–22.

[168] Robert A. Kagan, *Adversarial Legalism: The American Way of Law* (Cambridge, MA:

tirely without basis in fact. The operation of 'mechanical' law *has* spread in the century and a half since Justice Jackson observed that Paul's critique of the Pharisees was still applicable to his society. We now have more rules, forms, regulations, and threats of legal action, than at any time in the past. Insurance policies are written so that "ordinary people" cannot understand them; environmental laws are so byzantine that "ordinary farmers" cannot comply with or even pronounce them; even the Paperwork Reduction Act stretches on for pages and pages. The last hundred years have witnessed an explosion of bureaucratic law, bar membership, and, of course, lawyers featured as talking heads, heroes, and villains on television shows; between 1880 and 1980, the number of lawyers increased nine-fold, compared with a fourfold increase in population.[169] Without even mentioning Court TV, Law and Order, Miranda warnings, *Roe v. Wade*, lawyers in movies, lawyers telling boys that kissing girls is sexual harassment, we have seen a lot more lawyers, and a lot more technical law. And such technical law is reviled in the same, religiously loaded terms as ever. It is still feared as enabling, in Horwitz's words, "the shrewd, the calculating, and the wealthy to manipulate its forms to their own advantage."[170] Given that "it ratifies and legitimates an adversarial, competitive, and atomistic conception of human relations,"[171] it is mechanical, where justice should be organic; literal, where justice resides in the soul.

More generally, I think that for most of us, as for Clinton's accusers, the *nomos* is not the *ethos*. Surely none of us really believes that the technicalities of legal procedure *are* the operations of justice, especially not moral justice. As Thane Rosenbaum has argued, moral justice and efficient, legally just results are often entirely at odds.[172] Indeed, as Rosenbaum himself proposes, the written *nomos* is at times replaced by an unwritten, spiritual-moral *ethos* set up in deliberate opposition to it. Antinomian, common sense jurisprudence ultimately is a displacement of significance from law to something that transcends written law, and from bodies to souls. What, after all, does it mean to say, "He was guilty, but he got off on a technicality?" It means that our system of justice allowed him to go free, but some other, unspecified system of justice—in our hearts? our souls?—knows that he is guilty. Yet within a system of justice, the priority of the soul sets up law's undoing, because there must be some arbiter of what 'spirit' is, of what the 'intent' of a law is, and that arbiter will exist ethically prior to the

---

Harvard University Press, 2001), 4. Its title notwithstanding, Kagan's book is less about legalism per se than the recourse to the court system to address social or political issues. See ibid., 3–4.

[169] Richard L. Abel, *American Lawyers* (New York: Oxford University Press, 1989), 6.

[170] Morton Horwitz, "Book Review," *Yale Law Journal* 86 (1977): 565–66.

[171] Ibid.

[172] Thane Rosenbaum, *The Myth of Moral Justice: How our Legal System Fails to Do What's Right* (New York: Harper Perennial, 2004), 19–29. I discuss Rosenbaum's anti-legalism in section II.D.

written law itself. Law becomes a schizoid sort of tool: it is both moral, insofar as it implicates our moral obligations and our conscience, yet amoral or even immoral, because it cannot fully accommodate them. No system of law can exist as a matter of practice without some technicality. But where the legal system itself must judge *people*, and not criminal acts, technicality is problematic, because it cannot capture the soul. A crime is defined in substantive and procedural terms. But a guilty *person*? Now the terms may do more harm than good.

Moreover, inasmuch as we retain the religious notion that, to some extent, a crime is an offense against God—or, in secularized parlance, an offense against "decency" and "values"—a mechanism for uncovering and punishing crime fails insofar as it does not attack the real nature of that sin, i.e., the human soul. Something more is needed: grace, access to conscience, a moral X-Ray machine to discover the content of a man's character. Perhaps the truth of the law is, after all, 'engraved on our hearts' rather than in impeachment articles or on tablets of stone. The letter of the law, then, is a shadow of the true law, a Pharisaic reification of something that is utterly ineffable and beyond iterability. Or, in explicitly theological terms, "The letter kills, but the Spirit gives life."

II. "The letter kills, but the Spirit gives life":[173] Anti-Judaism

"You who want to be justified by the law have cut yourselves off from Christ; you have fallen away from grace."[174]

Where does all this anti-legalism come from? From religion—Christianity specifically, and Paul more specifically.

John Lightfoot once said, "No idea is more familiar to us than the distinction between the spirit and the letter.... Yet, so far as I am aware, it occurs in St. Paul for the first time. No doubt the idea was floating in the air before. But he fixed it, he made it current coin."[175] Lightfoot is right on all counts. Yet while Paul did not invent this distinction, he did more than make it "common coin"—he gave it theological urgency, because only the spirit saves; the law only corrupts. To introduce the doctrine that law undermines the soul, I want to pose a specific religious question that was, at one time, central to the distinction between Christianity and Judaism. Which matters more: circumcision of the flesh or circumcision of the heart? Circumcision of the flesh adheres to the letter of the law, sealing in material

---

[173] 2 Cor 3:6. There is some uncertainty among scholars as to which of the Pauline epistles were actually written by Paul. There is virtual consensus that Romans and Galatians, my two main sources here, are authentically Pauline in origin. Corinthians is widely, though not unanimously, believed by critics to be of Paul's hand as well.

[174] Gal 5:4. This and all translations from the Hebrew Bible and the New Testament are of the New Revised Standard Version (1989).

[175] John Lightfoot, quoted in Boaz Cohen, *Jewish and Roman Law*, Vol. 1 (New York: Jewish Theological Seminary of America, 1966), 31.

form the covenant with God as legislated in the book of Genesis.[176] The latter is devotion to the spirit of the law—and the spirit of the human being—turning the heart and the spirit to the new covenant announced by Christ. Bodily circumcision implies that the site of salvation is not the inner soul and its yearnings but the fleshly, external body being in conformity with a set of laws that govern the way the world should look. Literal adherence to the divine mandate is the sign of salvation; circumcision "makes a Jew," a body that is part of the (bodily) chosen people not because it has any spiritual benefit, or philosophical/allegorical explanation, or rational point, but because it inscribes the covenant with God onto the body.[177]

Not so with the circumcision of the heart. Though the phrase is actually found in Deuteronomy 30:6—"And the Lord thy God shall circumcise thine heart, and the heart of thy seed, to love the Lord thy God with all thine heart, and with all thy soul, that thou mayest live"—it became central to how the early Jewish-Christians, and Paul, came to understand their emerging faith. 'Inner circumcision,' or inner covenant, denies that arbitrary physical actions have any meaning in themselves, and insists instead that intention and spirit are the loci of religious value. "Real circumcision is a matter of the heart—it is spiritual and not literal," says Paul in Romans 2:29. Moreover, for Paul, the spiritual essence of the law allows to some extent the discarding of the outward, literal shell: "Now we are discharged from the law, dead to that which held us captive, so that we are slaves not under the old written code but in the new life of the Spirit" (Romans 7:6).

Today, we are so much Paul's heirs that it is perhaps difficult to imagine preferring the letter, the surface, and the body over the spirit, the inner self, and the soul, especially in matters of religion. How can an (at best) arbitrary inscription on the flesh matter more, in terms of ultimate concern, than reorienting the heart? What is a "religion,"[178] if not that aspect of human life that is concerned with the "spirit?" Surely, without some inner dimension, the ritualistic adherence to the external law makes one like, in the words ascribed to Christ in Matthew 23:27, "whitewashed tombs, which on the outside are beautiful, but inside ... full of the bones of the dead and of all kinds of filth."[179] Surely, one who does this may, like a dissembling lawyer

---

[176] Gen 17:11 ("You shall circumcise the flesh of your foreskins, and it shall be a sign of the covenant between me and you.").

[177] Not that these were absent in non-Pharisaic Jewish sources, of course. See Philo Judaeus, *The Migration of Abraham* (Cambridge: Loeb Classical Library, 1932), 185 (stating that physical circumcision "does indeed portray the excision of pleasure and all passions"). Note, however, that Philo maintained the need for physical circumcision: "Exactly as we have to take thought for the body, because it is the abode of the soul, so we must pay heed to the letter of the laws" (ibid.). On Philo's hermeneutic, see Boyarin, *Carnal Israel*, 7–9, 37–39.

[178] *Religio* as a zone distinct from everyday living itself is, in fact, a Christian concept, which may explain the tension here. See Joseph Dan, *Al haKedusha* (Jerusalem: Magnes, 1997), 12ff.; Asad, *Genealogies*, 27ff. (commenting on how the religious/other distinction insulates religion from questions of power).

[179] Matt 23:27.

or politician, "look righteous to others, but inside [be] full of hypocrisy and lawlessness."[180]

But these "common sense" views are not inevitable; they are historically constructed, they have Paul as their source, and there were, and are, alternatives to them. The intention of this Part is to show that our "common sense" about the meanings of law and religion are tied to a specifically Pauline program of spirit over letter and spirit over flesh. Our rhetoric about law is actually rhetoric about the soul.

A. Flesh and Spirit: Paul's Circumcision

In the beginning, there is the body. We all have bodies, we can all see them, and we all see that they pass away. This, for many classical philosophers, is precisely the problem—if we pass away, what *are* we? How do we understand life in the face of change? Salt dissolves, buildings crumble, and people metamorphose from embryos to children to adults to corpses. If all of the molecules in my body have changed in the years that I have been alive, and if they will all disappear one day, in what way am I the same person I was when I was born? And in what way, if any, can this "I" survive my death?

Pre-Socratic philosophers proposed a wide range of possible answers to this most human problem: that everything was in flux, that there were certain core elements (e.g., water, fire) that remain constant throughout change, and so on. But Plato, who is the beginning of the story here, argued neither that everything changed nor that some one 'thing' always stayed the same, but rather that the essence of every thing was its form, and that while a thing may undergo changes in its substance, it always continued to participate in form. An olive tree grows from a seed to a sapling to a tree, but always in some way reflects or embodies the form of the olive tree. And a human, though the body originates from a humunculus and grows through childhood to old age, and finally dies, also has some essence that does not change in this way: the intellect, or the soul: "In this life itself, what constitutes our self in each of us is nothing other than the soul."[181]

Paul adopts this Platonic dualism to his religious, social, hermeneutic, and legal program, changing it from a philosophical position to a theological one. For example: "If you live according to the flesh, you will die; but if by the Spirit you put to death the deeds of the body, you will live."[182] Or: "Flesh and blood cannot inherit the kingdom of God, nor does the perisha-

---

[180] Matt 23:28.

[181] Plato, *Laws* 110 (New York: Penguin, 2005). See also Josephus, *Wars of the Jews* 7.8.7 ("For it is death which gives liberty to the soul and permits it to depart to its own pure abode ... but so long as it is imprisoned in a mortal body and tainted with all its miseries, it is, in sober truth, dead....").

[182] Rom 8:13. See also Col 3:5—not believed by scholars to be authentically Pauline in origin—"Put to death, therefore, whatever in you is earthly: fornication, impurity, evil desire, and greed."

ble inherit the imperishable."[183] Over and over, Paul emphasizes the dichotomy between "this mortal flesh" and the immortality of the spirit.[184]

This disembodiment of ultimate value also had political import, and was deliberately constructed in opposition to Jewish claims of particularism. As the physical body is devalued, so too the physical race or people to which a person belongs. Differences are effaced; the 'universal soul,' not tribe or clan, are of concern to a universal God. Thus, when faith is a matter of what one feels and what one believes, rather than what one "is" ethnically, it does not matter—as Paul himself emphasizes—whether one is born a Jew or gentile. "God shows no partiality" among peoples.[185] From the perspective of the deity, "[t]here is no longer Jew or Greek, there is no longer slave or free, there is no longer male and female; for all of you are one in Christ Jesus."[186] As Daniel Boyarin has put it:

> In one stroke, by interpreting circumcision as referring to a spiritual and not corporeal reality, Paul made it possible for Judaism to become a world religion. By substituting a spiritual interpretation for a physical ritual, Paul was saying that the genealogical Israel "according to the Flesh" is not the ultimate Israel; there is an "Israel in the Spirit."[187]

B. Letter and Spirit: Saving the Soul

As with ontology, so with jurisprudence and hermeneutics. Just as Paul values the spirit of the human over the flesh, he privileges the spirit of the law over its letter. We are familiar, of course, with the dualist conception of law just as we are with the dualist conception of the self, and Paul drew on existing Greek and Roman conceptions of it. For Paul, God "has made us competent to be ministers of a new covenant, not of letter but of spirit; for the letter kills, but the Spirit gives life."[188] Only the spirit of the law is appropriate for the spirit of the Christian.

As noted above, the "spirit of the law" did not originate with Paul; the concept has been traced to Protagoras[189] and Aristotle,[190] and Greek philosophers and rhetoricians often interpreted the laws—which, being of divine

---

[183] 1 Cor 15:50.

[184] 1 Cor 15:54. Paul never "crosses the line" into pure Platonism or, more pressingly for him, Gnosticism; he maintains some notion of the body, as in his account of the resurrection of the dead, which posits a "spiritual body" rather than a Platonic disembodied soul. See Daniel Boyarin, *A Radical Jew: Paul and the Politics of Identity* (Berkeley: University of California Press, 1997), 60–62.

[185] Rom 2:11.

[186] Gal 3:28.

[187] Boyarin, *Carnal Israel*, 233.

[188] 2 Cor 3:6; see Urbach, *Sages*, 293–95.

[189] See Cohen, *Jewish and Roman Law*, 38–41.

[190] Nicomachean Ethics V.10; On Rhetoric I.13–15, quoted in Cohen, *Jewish and Roman Law*, 39.

origin, were not easily changeable—in accord with their "spirit," which gave wide latitude to those seeking to make large changes in the law.[191] Roman and Greek law had conceptions of a law's "body" and "soul," with the latter given priority in interpretation (including, suggestively, in the case of wills and testaments).[192] Nor was Paul alone; Philo records that the extreme allegorists in Alexandria who had a similar project of creating a "religion of the spirit" were against Judaism's legalism.[193] And within Judaism, the tension between *mishpat* (law) and *tzedek* (justice) was well observed by the biblical prophets,[194] and, as we will see below, even the talmudic rabbis had a clear notion of going beyond the letter of the law. Even the phrase *ruach mishpat*, "the spirit of the law," is used in Isaiah 28:5, although it is used not in its hermeneutical sense but rather to describe divine inspiration.[195] Though we do not know to what extent Paul was familiar with each of these different sources, surely he was influenced by them as much as by Platonic dualism. (Interestingly, jurisprudential dualism need not flow from ontological dualism; Philo was quite dualistic regarding body and soul, but upheld the letter of the law: "Exactly as we have to take thought for the body, because it is the abode of the soul, so we must pay heed to the letter of the laws."[196])

Paul was also influenced, of course, by the teachings of Jesus. However, the evidence is inconclusive as to Jesus' views on the merits of law.[197] On the one hand, Jesus states that the law is to remain in place:

---

[191] Cohen, *Jewish and Roman Law*, 39–40 (discussing criticism of Sextus Empiricus, and the writings of Cicero, Hermagoras and Aristeas).

[192] Ibid., 34; Boyarin, *Radical Jew*, 79.

[193] See Urbach, *Sages*, 289.

[194] See, e.g., Isa 11:3–4; 2 Sam 8:15; Aaron Kirschenbaum, *Beyond Equity: Halakhic Aspirationism in Jewish Civil Law* (Jersey City, N.J.: Ktav, 1991), 10ff.

[195] Isa 28:5–6 ("In that day the Lord of hosts will be a garland of glory, and a diadem of beauty, to the remnant of his people; and a spirit of law [*ruach mishpat*] to the one who sits in judgment, and strength to those who turn back the battle at the gate."). Obviously, the fusion of the spirit of the law and the messianic ideal supports the concept of a "new covenant" generally.

[196] Philo, *Migration of Abraham*, 185. Philo's dualism was quite pronounced: "The chief cause of ignorance and our affinity for it... Nothing so thwarts [wisdom's] growth as our fleshly nature." See Philo, "The Giants," in *Philo of Alexandria: The Contemplative Life, the Giants and Selections*, trans. David Winston (Mahwah: N.J.: Paulist Press, 1981), 65.

[197] See James D.G. Dunn, *Jesus, Paul and the Law: Studies in Mark and Galatians* (Louisville: Westminster John Knox, 1990), 10ff. (arguing that Paul's view on the law was primarily a rejection of legal particularism, not of law as such, and that this can be traced to Jesus); Alan Watson, *Jesus and the Law* (Athens: University of Georgia Press, 1996) (arguing that Jesus claims not to change the law, but does act against law and custom); E.P. Sanders, *Paul and Palestinian Judaism* (Philadelphia: Fortress, 1977), 84–106 (noting that Judaic concepts of justification through works and law themselves depend on a covenant-salvation relationship between God and Israel, and that Jesus often acted in general conformity with some laws).

> Do not think that I have come to abolish the law or the prophets; I have come not to abolish but to fulfill. For truly I tell you, until heaven and earth pass away, not one letter, not one stroke of a letter, will pass from the law until all is accomplished. Anyone who breaks one of the least of these commandments and teaches others to do the same will be called least in the kingdom of heaven, but whoever practices and teaches these commands will be called great in the kingdom of heaven. For I tell you that unless your righteousness surpasses that of the Pharisees and the teachers of the law, you will certainly not enter the kingdom of heaven.[198]

Read on its own, this portion of the Sermon on the Mount seems like a starkly anti-Pauline statement: the coming of Christ does not void the letter of the law, and reward and punishment remain in place. On the other hand, it is immediately followed by a long list of apparent changes in the law regarding the punishment for murder, adultery, divorce, oaths, and *lex talionis*.[199] And the language of "fulfillment" can be taken to mean that Christ fulfills the law by means of his sacrifice and, thus, exempts us from having to do so (this is Paul's interpretation, discussed below). Elsewhere, Jesus inveighs against the Pharisaic-Talmudic "experts in the law" (in some new biblical translations, rendered as "lawyers"[200]) who "load people down with burdens they can hardly carry, and ... will not lift one finger to help them."[201] And Jesus' many statements against the hypocrisy of the Pharisees can oftentimes be read as specifically attacking the outward observance of a ritual performance without the inward transformation (or justice) that God truly wishes. At the very least, Paul was working within a religious framework that was receptive to dualism.

Let us now turn to a few Pauline texts that express this dualism clearly. In the Epistle to the Romans, Paul explains that the true meaning of the law is its spirit, a spirit that may exist apart from the *nomos* as encoded in the Old Testament, and that resides in the heart:

> When Gentiles, who do not possess the law, do instinctively what the law requires ... they show that what the law requires is written on their hearts, to which their own conscience also bears witness.[202]

Paul develops this idea by setting up in Romans a set of oppositions between the outer meaning and the inner meaning; law according to the letter

---

[198] Matt 5:17–20.

[199] Matt 5:21–42. See Watson, *Jesus and the Law*, 98ff.

[200] E.g., *The New English Bible* (Oxford: Oxford University Press, 1961).

[201] Luke 11:46.

[202] Rom 2:15. On Paul's shifting ideas about the law, see generally Heikki Räisänen, *Paul and the Law* (Tübingen: Mohr Siebeck, 1987); Dunn, *Jesus, Paul, and the Law*, 183ff.; 215–16.

and law according to the spirit; and, as we have already seen, circumcision in the flesh and circumcision in the heart.[203] For Paul:

> [T]hose who are physically uncircumcised but keep the law will condemn you who have the written code and circumcision but break the law. For he is not a Jew who is one outwardly, nor is circumcision something external and physical. He is a Jew who is one inwardly, and circumcision is a matter of the heart, spiritual and not literal.[204]

Circumcision is the sign of the "old" Jew, and suggests that the law may still be a viable path to salvation.[205] But for Paul, physical circumcision is subordinate to faith, which is universal and not dependent on obedience to fleshly law:

> Is God the God of Jews only? Is he not the God of Gentiles also? Yes, of Gentiles also, since God is one; and he will justify the circumcised on the grounds of faith and the uncircumcised through that same faith.[206]

Wrongly valuing circumcision was the error of the Galatians, who "astonished" Paul by wanting "to pervert the gospel of Christ" by being circumcised as Jews after having already accepted Christ.[207] The Galatians have it all backwards, prompting Paul to ask, "Are you so foolish? Having started with the Spirit, are you now ending with the flesh?"[208] In Galatians, Paul argues that the law has become obsolete—"Christ redeemed us from the curse of the law"[209]—and analogizes it to the terms of enslavement and to guardianship of a child awaiting majority.[210] ("All who rely on works of the law are under a curse," he says.[211]) Unlike in Romans, circumcision in Galatians is only a substitute for true grace, part of the law that "imprisoned and guarded" the Jews "until faith would be revealed."[212] Once again,

---

[203] Boyarin, *Radical Jew*, 78ff.

[204] Rom 2:28–29.

[205] This is John Gager's view: see his *The Origins of Anti-Semitism: Attitudes Toward Judaism in Pagan and Christian Antiquity* (Oxford: Oxford University Press, 1983), 207; but not Boyarin's: see his *Radical Jew*, 32ff.

[206] Rom 3:29–30.

[207] Gal 1:6–7.

[208] Gal 3:3.

[209] Gal 3:6.

[210] Gal 4:1–3. Compare with 1 Cor 3:1–2, which reads, "And so, brothers, I could not speak to you as spiritual people, but rather as people of the flesh, as infants in Christ. I fed you with milk, not solid food, for you were not ready for solid food."

[211] Gal 3:10.

[212] Gal 3:23.

neither circumcision nor uncircumcision counts for anything; the only thing that counts is faith working through love.[213]

In these texts on circumcision, the law seems irrelevant. However, in other texts, it is worse than that, it is harmful. First, the erroneous reliance on law can cut one off from the true source of grace, i.e., Christ. The law itself is empty: "a person is justified not by the works of the law but by faith in Jesus Christ."[214] Thus to the Galatians, Paul writes, "you who want to be justified by the law have cut yourselves off from Christ."[215]

Second, law keeps one enmeshed with sinfulness and fleshliness. Law's function is to define sin.[216] Ultimately, however, it is to be transcended:

> Live by the Spirit, I say, and do not gratify the desires of the flesh. For what the flesh desires is opposed to the Spirit ... if you are led by the Spirit, you are not subject to the law.[217]

Whereas, if one remains subject to the law, one remains trapped in sinfulness:

> When we were living in the flesh, our sinful passions aroused by the law, were at work in our members to bear fruit for death. But now we are discharged from the law, dead to that which held us captive, so that we are slaves not under the old written code but in the new life of the Spirit.[218]

In this view, the law, with its demarcation of right and wrong, "arouses sinful passions" in an almost proto-Foucaultian sense.[219] And to live by it is to live constantly enslaved by the flesh, whose works include "fornication, impurity, licentiousness, idolatry, sorcery, enmities, strife, jealousy, anger, quarrels, dissensions, factions, envy, drunkenness, carousing, and things like these."[220] Law constantly draws the mind into matters of the flesh and, thus, sin.

Finally, and, perhaps most seriously, this is a matter of life and death: "If you live according to the flesh, you will die; but if by the Spirit you put to death the deeds of the body, you will live."[221] Or elsewhere, "For the Lord is

---

[213] Gal 5:6.

[214] Gal 2:16. Compare with Rom 3:28, which reads, "We hold that a person is justified by faith apart from works prescribed by law."

[215] Gal 5:7–8.

[216] Rom 7:7–11; 1 Cor 15:56.

[217] Gal 5:16–17.

[218] Rom 7:5–6.

[219] See Jeremy Waldron, "Dead to the Law: Paul's Antinomianism," *Cardozo Law Review* 28 (2006): 311–12.

[220] Gal 5:19–21. The fruits of the spirit are "love, joy, peace, patience, kindness, generosity, faithfulness, gentleness, and self-control." See also Gal 5:22–23.

[221] Rom 8:13.

the Spirit, and where the Spirit of the Lord is, there is freedom."[222] These are not, then, merely jurisprudential concerns; they are the essence of salvation.[223]

So far, we have seen that (1) the spirit of the law is its essence, (2) that the spirit of the law maps onto the spirit of the person, and thus connects that person to grace, (3) the letter of the law is, at best, irrelevant, and (4) relying on the letter of the law cuts oneself off from Christ and causes one to live in sin. These are religious claims, different from the ostensibly secular ones we saw in Part One. But their structure and values are almost identical: the letter of the law is disconnected from what really matters, and only the s/Spirit can save us.

For Paul and his heirs, these religious concerns had consequences in the domains of law and litigation. In a passage in 1 Corinthians 6, Paul inveighs against those who have recourse to secular, rather than religious courts:

> If any of you has a dispute with another, dare he take it before the ungodly for judgment instead of before the saints? Do you not know that the saints will judge the world? And if you are to judge the world, are you not competent to judge trivial cases? Do you not know that we will judge angels? How much more the things of this life! Therefore, if you have disputes about such matters, appoint as judges even men of little account in the church! I say this to shame you. Is it possible that there is nobody among you wise enough to judge a dispute between believers? But instead, one brother goes to law against another—and this in front of unbelievers! The very fact that you have lawsuits among you means you have been completely defeated already. Why not rather be wronged? Why not rather be cheated? Instead, you yourselves cheat and do wrong, and you do this to your brothers.[224]

Here, perhaps, we complete the circle to the materials explored in the previous part. The saints, i.e., those who are free from the law, are the most competent to judge cases. The very filing of a lawsuit is a sign of defeat, for

---

[222] 2 Cor 3:17, quoted in Urbach, *Sages*, 295. Of course, whether Urbach is right or not on Paul's intentions does not change the text, which is rigorously anti-law and pro-spirit throughout.

[223] Some New Testament texts are more nuanced. See, e.g., 1 Tim 1:8–10 ("But we know that the Law is good, if one uses it lawfully, realizing the fact that law is not made for a righteous person, but for those who are lawless and rebellious, for the ungodly and sinners, for the unholy and profane, for those who kill their fathers or mothers, for murderers and immoral men and homosexuals and kidnappers and liars and perjurers, and whatever else is contrary to sound teaching."). On the variations within early Christian conceptions of the law, see Räisänen, *Paul and the Law*, 203–29. On Paul's own multivocality, see Räisänen, *Paul and the Law*, 4, who argues, "On the one hand, the clarity, profundity, and cogency of Paul's theological thinking is universally praised. On the other hand, it does not seem possible to reach any unanimity whatsoever as to what his message really was."

[224] 1 Cor 6:1–7.

love, rather than contentiousness, and hortatory principles, rather than rules, are the marks of understanding.[225] And ultimately, it would be better to accept being wronged than to seek legal redress. The domain of law is the domain of bodies, sin, and death. This is why, even today, we are uncomfortable with legalism and why critiques of legalism resonate so effectively—not because it is inefficient, not because it leads to bad results, but because it betrays our very souls.

C. Judaism: A Jurisprudence of the Flesh?

Paul did not innovate his religious-legal ideology in a vacuum. He both projected and rejected a Jewish-Pharisaic jurisprudence of literalism and "fleshliness." Before moving on, it is essential to trace the contours of this historical struggle, both to envision an alternative to Pauline dualism and to recognize its roots.

While Paul did misread and exaggerate talmudic legalism,[226] the Pharisees in turn deliberately reacted against the dualistic ontology and hermeneutics of the new Judeo-Christians, creating a parallel "new covenant" (the Mishna, or "second" body of law) whose laws governed the body, not the soul. As Howard Eilberg-Schwartz observes, "the government of the body has always been a central preoccupation within Judaism,"[227] and, as Mary Douglas suggested, the body likely served as a metonym for society as a whole in Biblical Judaism.[228] Yet the talmudic sages amplified these concerns, deliberately staking out territory in opposition to the nascent Christianity.[229] The myth of "Carnal Israel" is, largely, for real.

First, regarding the soul, the talmudic rabbis—at least in the tannaitic and early amoraic period—believed the soul to be within the body, rather than beyond it.[230] (The terms themselves are generally *nefesh*, life-blood, or

---

[225] See Waldron, "Dead to the Law," 307–10.

[226] See Urbach, *Sages*, 288; Judith N. Shklar, "Legalism," *Journal of Legal Education* 19 (1964): 54; Sanders, *Paul*, 33–75.

[227] Howard Eilberg-Schwartz, "The Problem of the Body for the People of the Book," in *People of the Body: Jews & Judaism from an Embodied Perspective*, ed. Howard Eilberg-Schwartz (Albany: SUNY Press, 1992), 20.

[228] Mary Douglas, *Purity and Danger* (New York: Routledge, 1966), 141–59. See Jay Michaelson, *God in Your Body: Kabbalah, Mindfulness, and Embodied Spiritual Practice* (Woodstock, VT: Jewish Lights, 2007), 77–95, 137–40; idem, "Chaos, Law, and God: The Religious Meanings of Homosexuality," *Michigan Journal of Law and Gender* 15 (2008): 41–119.

[229] Israel Yuval's work on Passover and Easter convincingly shows the talmudic rabbis were well aware of the Christian sect and created ritual, ideology, and liturgy in deliberate response to it. Israel Yuval, "The Haggadah of Passover and Easter," *Tarbiz* 65 (1996): 5–28 (Hebrew); idem, "Easter and Passover As Early Jewish-Christian Dialogue," in *Passover and Easter: Origin and History to Modern Time*, ed. Paul Bradshaw and Lawrence Hoffman (South Bend: University of Notre Dame Press, 1999), 98–124.

[230] Urbach, *Sages*, 220ff. Eventually, more dualistic conceptions of the soul came to prevail. See *Berachot* 10a (discussing nature of the soul and the world in Stoic terms); Boyarin, *Carnal Israel*, 32ff.; Urbach, *Sages*, 248ff.

neshamah, etymologically related to the word for breath.) One midrash quoted by Urbach demonstrates the interrelationship of the soul and the body, "Let the soul, which permeates the body, come and praise the Holy One ... Let the soul, which bears the body, come and praise the Holy One."[231] As Alon Goshen-Gottstein puts it, "there is much talk of soul and body in the rabbinic sources.... However, there is not a fundamental metaphysical opposition between these two aspects.... The soul is the vitalizing agent, whose proper place is in the body, not out of it."[232] Thus it is not surprising that we find in the Talmud recurrent reiterations that the body is the site of holiness or unholiness, good or evil, purity or impurity. The human is defined in terms of the body, whose material design is evidence of divine wisdom and reflects the structure of the cosmos.[233] Sexual renunciation, for example, is likened to murder and blasphemy, and somewhat startling accounts of rabbinic sexuality exist in legendary and midrashic literature.[234] Both good and evil impulses reside in the embodied soul, or the ensouled body.[235]

Second (and again), as with ontology, so with jurisprudence and hermeneutics, in which act is generally privileged over intent, and literal ritual action over spiritualization. Throughout, even the ethical literature, the law, in its external form, appears to be of foremost religious priority.[236] Sometimes the results are shocking; for example, *Pesachim* 8a–b holds that one who gives money to charity only in order to obtain a reward is considered on the same moral level as one who gives money for the sake of doing the good deed itself.[237] Other times, what is missing is surprising; there are

---

[231] Urbach, *Sages*, 249.

[232] Alon Goshen-Gottstein, "The Body as Image of God in Rabbinic Literature," *Harvard Theological Review* 87 (1994): 171–95; Boyarin, *Carnal Israel*, 33; see also Boyarin, *Carnal Israel*, 230–33; Urbach, *Sages*, 224ff.

[233] Boyarin, *Carnal Israel*, 34, 42–46 (comparing rabbinic midrash of the corporeal androgyne with Philo's spiritual androgyne and Plato's *Symposium*); Michaelson, *God in Your Body*, 18–19, 77–85.

[234] Boyarin, *Carnal Israel*, 35 (citing *Tosefta Yevamot* 8:7 and Babylonian Talmud *Yevamot* 63b).

[235] Ibid., 61–70. Boyarin contrasts rabbinic sources with Hellenistic Jewish texts that saw good and evil as "two mind-sets, two lines of action, two models, and two goals" and crucially, "two dispositions within our breasts." Ibid., 68 (quoting Howard Clark Kee, trans., "Testaments of the Twelve Patriarchs," in *Old Testament Pseudepigrapha* vol. 1, ed. James Charlesworth (Garden City, N.Y.: Doubleday, 1983), 775–828). Eventually, the Hellenistic view became dominant in subsequent Jewish psychology and folklore.

[236] The *reductio ad absurdum* of this Jewish position is presented by Paul: the opinion that merely "hearing" and possessing the law, not even fulfilling it in its external manifestation, counted for righteousness. See Rom 2:12–24. Though rejected by the Pharisees, who saw the law not as a set of pre-awarded merits but of ongoing obligations, Boyarin suggests it was present enough in Jewish self-conceptions of chosenness that it provided Paul with an entry point to develop his conception of the "new Jew" in Romans 2. Boyarin, *Radical Jew*, 86–95.

[237] *Pesachim* 8a–b. Contrast this view with that of Kant, who held that an action done for the sake of obeying a law, a fortiori to obtain a reward, is not a moral action at all. Of course, Kant's opinion of "legalistic" Judaism was notoriously negative.

pages of rules governing business transactions, and relatively very few conventionally "religious" discussions of them. Even the talmudic version of the Golden Rule reveals the emphasis on action rather than intent, "surface" rather than depth. The talmudic Sage Hillel, asked to summarize Jewish teaching while standing on one foot, did not choose Leviticus 19:18's "Love your neighbor as yourself," which has to do with a disposition of the heart, and which was called by Jesus as the most important commandment save for love of God.[238] Rather, Hillel said, "What is hateful to you do not *do* to your neighbor."[239] Not the character of one's heart; the quality of one's actions.

As for hermeneutics, in contrast with Paul's 'spiritual' interpretation of Scripture, talmudic rabbis claimed to interpret the law, and Scripture generally, according to the letter, and only in exceptional cases according to the spirit.[240] *Ein HaMikra Yotze Midei Pshuto*—the Bible does not depart from its literal meaning[241]—is the general rule, even as the 'literal meaning' is subject to wide-ranging interpretive techniques and seemingly fantastic departures into myth, midrash, and moral teaching. Indeed, despite at least six terms for "interpretation according to the letter," there is no one term for "interpretation according to the spirit" in the Talmud.[242] In terms of interpretive theory, if not practice, talmudic law only expounds what is meant by the commandment—what is necessary to perform it properly, what fences need to be erected around the core rule, what implications may be derived from a given law, or the phrasing of that law, or the repetition of that law throughout a text. One talmudic-era midrash states *b'otioteha nittenah torah*, meaning that Torah was given in its letters, and must be interpreted according to them.[243] (Parenthetically, this comes at the same time that Jewish theology and mysticism developed a rigorously linguistic ontology, which at its extreme reifies the letters themselves into the physical constituent elements of creation.[244]) Not only does the letter give life for the rabbis, but, for contemporary theologians and mystics, the letter *is* life.

---

[238] Matt 22.36–40: "Teacher, which is the great commandment in the law? Jesus said to him, You shall love the Lord your God with all your heart, and with all your soul, and with all your mind. This is the great and first commandment. And a second is like it, You shall love your neighbor as yourself." We should note that Jesus is also quoted as embracing a Hillel-esque "action-based" Golden Rule, though phrased in the positive, not the negative: "All things whatsoever ye would that men should do to you, do ye even so to them: for this is the law and the prophets" (Matt 7:12, Luke 6:31).

[239] Babylonian Talmud *Shabbat* 31a (emphasis added).

[240] See Cohen, *Jewish and Roman Law*, 62.

[241] Babylonian Talmud *Shabbat* 63a.

[242] Cohen, *Jewish and Roman Law*, 51.

[243] *Midrash Tannaim* at 60; see Cohen, *Jewish and Roman Law*, 36.

[244] I refer here to the *Sefer Yetzirah*, among the oldest texts of Jewish mysticism, believed to date to the mishnaic period. See Gershom Scholem, *Major Trends in Jewish Mysticism* (New York: Schocken, 1941), ch. 2.

It should be no surprise, then, that discarding the letter is disdained in matters of interpretation. The rabbis saw one who discarded the literal meaning in favor of the spiritual one as "like one who says, 'Break the jug but keep the wine.'"[245] Indeed, several statements in the Talmud suggest that the Rabbis were well aware of Paul's more radical project of annulling the written law, and responded directly to it. For example, although the meaning of the passage is debatable, the mishnaic Ethics of the Fathers 3:15 states that "one who profanes the sacred, and despises the festivals, and shames another person publicly, and annuls the covenant of Abraham, and reveals faces of the Torah [against Halakha][246] even if he has learned Torah and done good deeds, he has no portion in the world to come."[247] The selection of the transgressions, and some of the specific language in the Hebrew, suggests that this passage was in all likelihood a polemic against Jewish Christians, as Urbach and others have shown.[248] Another example of the rabbis' explicit rejection of Pauline hermeneutics, as discussed by Boaz Cohen, is found in the midrash recounted at *Exodus Rabba* VI.1 and elsewhere, which uses the word "testament" (*di'atiki*) to condemn King Solomon's annulment of the prohibitions regarding a king marrying many wives.[249] Cohen notes that the Midrash's use of the unusual word for "testament" and rejection of the "spiritual" interpretation of Solomon, the wisest of men, suggests an explicit rejoinder to Paul.[250]

Even when the rabbis circumvent a commandment, they do so in the consummate lawyerly way by finding a way within the letter of the law to effectively short-circuit its spirit. One well-known example is the transfer writ known as the *prozbul*, which effectively nullified the debt-cancellation provisions of the Sabbatical Year; by signing such a document, a creditor effectively transfers debts he holds to a court, which could enforce collection even during the Sabbatical.[251] Surely this does undermine the "spirit of the law," but the rabbis saw themselves as possessing the authority "to interpret and expand the norms of Judaism to cover all aspects of life."[252] Such efforts

---

[245] Babylonian Talmud *Bava Batra* 16a (*shevor he-havit ushmor et yena*).

[246] These words are not in all manuscripts, and appear to be a later addition that underscores the specifically antinomian meaning of the preceding phrase.

[247] Mishna *Avot* 3:15 (translation mine).

[248] See Urbach, *Sages*, 295–96; Cohen, *Jewish and Roman Law*, 35.

[249] *Exodus Rabba* 6.1, quoted in Cohen, *Jewish and Roman Law*, 35.

[250] Cohen, *Jewish and Roman Law*, 34–36. On Jewish-Christian interpenetration and imbrication during their formative periods, see Yuval, "Easter and Passover"; Daniel Boyarin, *Dying for God: Martyrdom and the Making of Christianity and Judaism* (Palo Alto: Stanford University Press, 1999).

[251] On the *prozbul*, see Louis E. Newman, *The Sanctity of the Seventh Year: A Study of Mishnah Tractate Sheviit* (Chico, CA: Scholars Press, 1983).

[252] David Hartman, *A Living Covenant: The Innovative Spirit of Traditional Judaism* (Woodstock, VT: Jewish Lights, 1998), 98. See also Eliezer Berkovits, *Not in Heaven: The Nature and Function of Jewish Law* (Jerusalem: Shalem Center, 2010), 75–82. But see Roger Brooks, *The Spirit of the Ten Commandments: Shattering the Myth of Rabbinic Literalism* (New York: HarperCollins, 1990) (arguing that such efforts preserve the

were not undertaken shamefully, or rarely. Rather, the talmudic rabbis seemed resolute on maintaining the letter of the law, even while nullifying its practical application.

This is not to suggest that the Talmud is univocal in its espousal of the 'letter of the law.' Paul's critiques were necessarily exaggerations.[253] First, several passages in the Talmud rail against excessive legalism.[254] Second, there are many instances in which *svara*, or logical reasoning, was used to "interpret" a Scriptural passage in ways that seem diametrically opposed to its literal meaning.[255] In these cases, general principles—the welfare of society, for example—dictated the outcome of a particular legal case more than the apparent literal meaning of a law.[256] Third, and most importantly, the Talmud has a clear theory of equity. *Bava Metzia* 30b states that "one must go beyond the letter of the law (*lifnim mishurat ha-din*) ... Jerusalem was destroyed because the lawmakers and judges based their judgments on the letter of the law alone and did not seek to go beyond the letter of the law."[257] Now, *lifnim mishurat ha-din*[258] is complex. First, there almost always must be a particular principle, rather than simply the spirit of the law, to justify its use,[259] such as more important legal values trumping less important ones,[260] or scriptural interpretation, or even linguistic meaning.[261] Second, there is no single talmudic term for "equity"; usually *shalom* (peace) and *tzedek* (justice) are used.[262] (Aristotle's formulation of equity—a rectification of law where law is defective because of its generality—enters *halakhic* thought only in the Medieval period.[263]) Indeed, Kirschenbaum argues that *shurat ha-din* actually refers to technicalities only,[264] and the decision to act beyond it is an act "performed in accordance with a general obligation in preference to a limitation therein where the former would

---

"spirit" of the original rules).

[253] On rabbinic interpretations of the law "according to its spirit," see Urbach, *Sages*; Cohen, *Jewish and Roman Law*, 50–56; Berkovits, *Not in Heaven*, 19–31. Of course, just as the Pharisees did not unequivocally embrace literalism, so Paul did not entirely reject it. See Cohen, *Jewish and Roman Law*, 34–36; Gager, *Origins*, 165–67.

[254] See Kirschenbaum, *Beyond Equity*, 22–23.

[255] Berkovits, *Not in Heaven*, 3–8; Kirschenbaum, *Equity*, 27–34. See also Eliezer Berkovits, *Crisis and Faith* (New York: Sanhedrin, 1976), 91–92; David Hazony, "Eliezer Berkovits and the Revival of Jewish Moral Thought," *Azure* 11 (Summer, 2001): 26–36.

[256] See Cohen, *Jewish and Roman Law*, 52–53.

[257] Babylonian Talmud *Bava Metzia* 30b.

[258] See Kirschenbaum, *Equity*, 37–41.

[259] Kirschenbaum, *Equity*, 17–18, 21–23; 37 (the talmudic rabbis "regarded all modifications ... of the traditional law that tend to bring it in line with these hallowed values [of the Torah] as nothing more than the fulfillment of the sacred Torah itself").

[260] See ibid., 109ff.

[261] Ibid., 213 (discussing Babylonian Talmud *Bava Kamma* 99b).

[262] Kirschenbaum, *Equity*, 7–8.

[263] Ibid., xxiv–xxv.

[264] Ibid., 116–17.

produce a result more beneficial to the other party. Thus, such conduct is anchored in the law itself."[265] Finally, some of what we might consider to be cases ripe for equitable decision making were, in fact, deferred to "Heavenly Judgments," or *dinei shamayim*. talmudic law recognized that, because of its theory of torts and its evidentiary requirements, some cases could not be decided by a human court—acts of omission, unforeseeable damage, and indirect causation are three examples.[266] But, in the eyes of God, the tortfeasor is either liable or not liable. The solution imposed by the Talmud was that these cases are decided by the "Court of Heaven," because only that Court could know the right moral result.[267]

Such is the dilemma of Talmud study, familiar to any student of it—for every proposition there is at least one source that contradicts it. Still, it is fair to say that legalism and literalism predominate in the Talmud to a degree that would be surprising to contemporary legal readers. Sometimes this literalism becomes almost absurd; the talmudic sages are famed for their tendency to expound entire laws from single letters, or from duplications of letters, or even, in a proto-Kabbalistic reification of the 'letter of the law', from the decorative crowns written on top of letters.[268] Legal reasoning may even overturn divine decree.[269] Literalism, and legalism, pervades talmudic learning itself, even as practiced today. It is sometimes difficult to convey the view of the world one gets from intensive study of the laws of the Mishna and the endless debates of the Gemara. Questions such as the precise hour when a certain benediction may be recited[270] or why the tithe is applicable to carobs but not to figs[271] are debated back and forth— with digressions into history, myth, magic, and seemingly unrelated law—for amounts of text that equal days if not weeks of study time. The Talmud entrances the student not with lofty prose that uplifts the heart, but with a *weltanschauung* in which duty towards God and one's fellow human being extends into all of the minutiae of physical human experience. To spend

---

[265] Ibid., 117.

[266] Ibid., 137ff.

[267] *Dinei shamayim* do become the grounds for legal sanctions in post-talmudic literature, but not in the Talmud itself. Kirschenbaum, *Equity*, 147–69. In fact, Kirschenbaum suggests that *dinei shamayim* are actually a kind of affirmative defense, since pleading that an act falls under one of the *dinei shamayim* effectively asks that it be removed from the jurisdiction of the human court. Ibid., 151–52.

[268] See, e.g., Babylonian Talmud *Sanhedrin* 51a (Rabbi Akiva deriving an entire rule from the use of the letter *vav*); Cohen, *Jewish and Roman Law*, 37; Kirschenbaum, *Equity*, 14.

[269] On the story of "the oven of Achnai," in which the rabbinic assembly refuses to heed a divine voice telling them to rule a certain way on a case of ritual purity, see Suzanne Last Stone, "In Pursuit of the Counter-Text: The Turn to the Jewish Legal Model in Contemporary American Legal Theory," *Harvard Law Review* 106 (1993): 841; Robert A. Burt, "Precedent and Authority in Antonin Scalia's Jurisprudence," *Cardozo Law Review* 12 (1991): 1691; Berkovits, *Not in Heaven*, 47ff. The narrative itself is at Babylonian Talmud *Bava Metzia* 59b.

[270] This topic is the first one discussed in the Babylonian Talmud; see *Berachot* 2a.

[271] Babylonian Talmud *Bava Metzia* 21a.

days or years poring over these minutiae, engaging in legalistic *pilpul*, or dialectical legal reasoning, is seen not as "analyzing a text to death" but bringing it to life.

Indeed, we might say that the very purpose of religious law is different for the talmudic rabbis than for Paul. For Paul, religion expresses the harmony of human life, personal autonomic excellence. For the rabbis, Jewish laws are about expressions of the harmony of human interaction, and of communal heteronomic excellence.[272] Yes, heteronomy may allow individuals to be knaves at heart, but the site of holiness for the rabbis was the communal, earthly, and material. For the Talmud, every existential situation invites not a reflection in conscience, but a specific way to discharge one's duty. The imaginative enterprise of talmudic law, still with us today, attempts to transform the world into the kingdom of God not by turning to a realm that transcends the material, but by shaping the material in the form of the ineffable.[273]

D. Christianity: Law in a Religion of Spirit

> [T]he insertion of a Pauline discourse against the shackles of the Law into a Roman imperial framework guarantees a regime of perpetual Western disease that can be characterized as the pathetic search for a law without Law ... combined with the suspicion that any Law is illegitimate.[274]

How is Pauline anti-legalism connected to American anti-legalism?

My argument thus far has been ideological, not historical. It goes without saying that the New Testament is the most important, most widely read book in America. Thus to the extent an idea is prevalent in that book, it is likely to have an influence on American culture. And, as I have tried to show, the values of Pauline anti-legalism are strikingly similar to those of American anti-legalism. Beyond these conceptual and phenomenological points, however, can a true historical link be shown? Too what extent, given the importance of Pauline/Protestant Christianity to American identity, is it reasonable to suppose that a fundamental Pauline doctrine about the nature of sacred law influenced American thinking about secular law?

As stated in the introduction, it is impossible to prove, over centuries of history and dozens of doctrinal shifts, a simple historical link from St. Paul to William Safire. Even 'smoking guns,' such as the statement that Clinton should be forgiven because this is a Christian country, do not prove the

---

[272] See H. Wheeler Robinson, "Law and Religion in Israel," in *Judaism and Christianity*, vol. 3, *Law and Religion*, ed. Erwin I. Rosenthal (London: Sheldon Press, 1938), 58.

[273] The contemporary period's classic reaffirmation of Jewish legalism is Joseph Soloveitchik, *Halakhic Man*, trans. Lawrence Kaplan (Philadelphia: Jewish Publication Society of America, 1984). See Michaelson, "In Praise of the Pound of Flesh," 148–51; idem, *God in Your Body*, 16–19.

[274] Jonathan Boyarin, "Another Abraham: Jewishness and the Law of the Father," *Yale Journal of Law and Humanities* 9 (1997): 368.

genealogy. We can, however, supplement the reasonable inference that the most important ideology and the most important book in America has had some influence on American legal thought by tracing some of the impact of Pauline dualism on the aspects of subsequent religious thought most important to American Protestantism. Our treatment will necessarily be attenuated, but as we will see, the problem of the letter and spirit of the law is articulated in Christian thought well beyond Paul, and is most important in precisely those streams of thought most relevant to the American milieu.

Throughout this history, the specter that haunts Christian thinking about the law are the poles of Jewish legalism, at one extreme, and antinomianism, on the other. Legalism, as we have seen already and as we shall now explore in more depth, became identified with Judaism as Christianity separated from Judaism and became its own religious, and eventually political, community. Paul's anti-Judaism was a polemical argument with religious authorities who insisted that the governance of the body, the letter of the law, and the physical people Israel were of import. As Christianity became the dominant, rather than the upstart, religion, subsequent anti-Judaism became intertwined with antisemitism and with pointing out the errors of the Jews. The valence of legalism thus shifted, from the default assumption of religious life to an erroneous interpretation of it.

Antinomianism in the Christian context is the view that Christ discharged us from the need to obey the law; it is the polar opposite of legalism. Though, as we have seen, this current was already present in Paul, the term itself was first used by Martin Luther in the 1530s, culminating in his 1539 treatise *Against the Antinomians*,[275] in response to more radical reformers who sought to disparage religious law (both as expressed in the Old Testament and, the reformers believed, by the contemporary Catholic church) even more than Luther himself had done. The radicals thought themselves in agreement with Luther; after all, it was Luther who heightened the Pauline focus on the distinction between law and grace, the letter of the law and the spirit of the law, materialism and spirituality. Luther, however, responded that the law had three purposes, 'curb, mirror, and guide,' and that only the first had been obviated by Christ. This has led to the somewhat contradictory position of subsequent Protestant theology, summarized as "We are justified by faith alone but not by a faith that *is* alone."[276]

---

[275] Martin Luther, "Against the Antinomians," in *Luther's Works, American Edition*, vol. 47, ed. Jaroslav Pelikan and Helmut T. Lehmann (Philadelphia: Muehlenberg and Fortress, and St. Louis: Concordia, 1955–86), 107–19. See Francis Aveling, "Antinomianism," in *The Catholic Encyclopedia*, ed. Charles George Herbermann et al. (New York: Appleton, 1907), and R.D. Linder, "Antinomianism," in *Elwell's Evangelical Dictionary of Theology*, ed. Walter A. Elwell (Grand Rapids: Baker Books, 2001), both available at http://www.mb-soft.com/believe/txn/antinomi.htm.

[276] See R.C. Sproul, *Essential Truths of the Christian Faith* (Carol Stream, IL: Tyndal House, 1992), 3.

Antinomianism was a feature of numerous heretical movements, from the medieval Brethren of the Free Spirit[277] to the Antinomian Controversy centered on Anne Hutchinson in seventeenth-century Massachusetts.[278] Eventually, the term became a general description of the belief that "you can never rely on the law," and is widely used today in that more general sense in the scholarly literature,[279] as well as to refer to Non-Western anti-legal ideologies such as Left-Hand Tantra in India.[280] Antinomianism may be non-Christian or even non-religious in nature—but as the sources we are now to explore make clear, American antinomianism is a distinctly Christian, and Protestant, phenomenon.

1. Augustine

We begin with St. Augustine, who, in the first two decades of the fifth century, elucidated his views on law and grace during the Pelagian controversy.[281] The law, for Augustine, adds nothing and, on the contrary, by its literality can lead towards error and sin. Expounding on Paul, Augustine writes in *On the Spirit and the Letter*:

> [T]hat teaching which brings to us the command to live in chastity and righteousness is 'the letter that killeth,' unless accompanied with 'the spirit that giveth life.' ... signifies nourishing the inner man by our spiritual intelligence, since 'being carnally minded is death, while to be spiritually-minded is life and peace.'[282]

---

[277] See Robert Lerner, *The Heresy of the Free Spirit in the Later Middle Ages* (Notre Dame: University of Notre Dame Press, 1972), 10–34.

[278] On Hutchinson, see Hall, *Antinomian Controversy*; Emery Battis, *Saints and Sectaries: Anne Hutchinson and the Antinomian Controversy in the Massachusetts Bay Colony* (Chapel Hill: University of North Carolina Press, 1962); Michael P. Winship, *Making Heretics: Militant Protestantism and Free Grace in Massachusetts, 1636–1641* (Princeton: Princeton University Press, 2002). On other Christian antinomians, see J. Wayne Baker, "*Sola Fide, Sola Gratia*: The Battle for Luther in Seventeenth-Century England," *The Sixteenth Century Journal* 16 (1985): 115–33. In a subsequent study, I hope to provide an ideological comparison of multiple antinomian ideologies, including Jewish/Christian Frankism, Hindu Tantra, and antinomian Christianity.

[279] Kennedy, "Semiotics of Critique," 1158. See, e.g., Emily Albrink Hartigan, "Unlaw," *Buffalo Law Review* 55 (2007): 841–61; Marc Galanter, "The Three-Legged Pig: Risk Redistribution and Antinomianism in American Legal Culture," *Mississippi College Law Review* 22 (2002): 47–55.

[280] See Anagarika Govinda, "Principles of Tantric Buddhism," in *2500 Years of Buddhism*, ed. P.V. Bapat (New Delhi: Government of India, 1959), 357–58; Hugh Urban, "The Omnipotent OOM: Tantra and Its Impact on Modern Western Esotericism," *Esoterica* 3 (2001): 218–59.

[281] See Augustine, "On the Spirit and the Letter," in *Basic Writings of Saint Augustine*, trans. P. Holmes and ed. Whitney J. Oates (New York: Random House, 1948), 1:463.

[282] Augustine, *Spirit and Letter*, chap. 6, 463–64 (quoting 2 Cor 3:6 and Rom 8:6).

Later, Augustine explains that the "letter and spirit" phrase from Paul refers directly to "the law, which forbids whatever is evil,"[283] and spends considerable amounts of time in the same treatise explaining how the law defines sin and grace erases it, with generous quotations of the passages of Paul we examined above. Again, consider the reflection of the following ethos in the dramas of law and 'real' innocence related earlier:

> [W]hoever did even what the law commanded, without the assistance of the Spirit of grace, acted through fear of punishment, not from love of righteousness ... [Paul] calls, however, the 'circumcision of the heart' the will that is pure from all unlawful desire; which comes not from the letter, inculcating and threatening, but from the Spirit, assisting and healing.[284]

The law, in other words, "merely shows what one ought to do, and what one ought to guard against;"[285] real salvation arrives not from following the law for the law's sake but rather by filling the heart with love, which is the spirit of the law. No one, then, can be justified by works, because works do not fill the heart with love—indeed, they may well fill the heart with "boasting" instead.[286] Obeying the carnal law is, according to Augustine, a sort of vicious cycle of carnality and misapprehension that both mistakes the true source of salvation and blocks it out.

In contrast, the true law is the Holy Spirit itself:

> What then is God's law written by God Himself in the hearts of men, but the very presence of the Holy Spirit, who is 'the finger of God' and by whose presence is shed abroad in our hearts the love which is the fulfilling of the law, and the end of the commandment?[287]

If it was Sidney who says, "Look in thy heart, and write,"[288] then it is Augustine who counters, "Look in thy heart, and obey." The internalization and spiritualization of the law is, for Augustine, its fulfillment, because it is in the spirit that the ground for salvation lies.[289]

---

[283] Ibid., ch. 7, 465.
[284] Ibid., ch. 13, 470.
[285] Ibid., ch. 15, 471.
[286] Ibid., ch. 21, 476.
[287] Ibid., ch. 36, 488.
[288] Sir Philip Sidney, "Astrophil and Stella," in *The Oxford Authors: Sir Philip Sidney*, ed. Katherine Duncan-Jones (New York: Oxford University Press, 1989), sonnet 1, line 14, p.153.
[289] It is worth noting parenthetically that just as the Pelagian heresy threatened Christianity on the materialist side, so too the various Gnostic heresies threatened it on the anti-materialist side. For most Gnostic schools, all materiality was evil, a creation of the evil creator god. Thus early Church fathers such as Irenaeus actually constructed highly complex ontologies of matter and spirit. See Irenaeus, *Against Heresies*, book 5, para-

2. Aquinas and Natural Law

If the juxtaposition of Pauline antilogonomianism and temporal power strained the rhetoric of law to its breaking point, then natural law was perhaps the most successful resolution of the tension.[290] As we shall see, natural law functions as a sort of "law without law," an internalized law in harmony with conscience (Luther) or reason (Aquinas), in contrast with the positive law made by humans, which is not necessarily in harmony with either.

In its most concise form, the basic theory of natural law as it pertains to our questions of *logos, nomos,* and dualism is as follows. The universe operates according to various physical laws. Just as the laws of physics govern the proper operation of objects (say, a bridge), the laws of morality and human nature govern the proper operation of people. This "natural law" is as real as Newton's laws; though positive laws may differ, and humans may disobey, societies and persons that do so are no more stable than bridges constructed without regard to the laws of physics.[291] 'Goodness,' which may be maximized or minimized, is as much a property of things as color and shape. In the words of Pastor Elizur Goodrich (1734–1797):

> The principles of society are the laws, which Almighty God has established in the moral world, and made necessary to be observed by mankind; in order to promote their true happiness, in their transactions and intercourse. These laws may be considered as principles, in respect of their fixedness and operation; and as maxims, since by knowledge of them, we discover those rules of conduct, which direct mankind to the highest perfection, and supreme happiness of their nature. They are as fixed and unchangeable as the laws which operate in the natural world.[292]

---

graph 1.1. Irenaeus links the fleshliness of the Incarnation with the God-created-ness of the flesh, and the fleshliness of the Eucharist itself. Ibid., paragraph 2.3. Bodily resurrection was often the site of these debates. See Carolyn Walker Bynum, *The Resurrection of the Body in Western Christianity* (New York: Columbia University Press, 1996), 200–336.

[290] See generally Robert George, ed., *Natural Law Theory: Contemporary Essays* (New York: Oxford University Press, 1995); Knud Haakonssen, *Natural Law and Moral Philosophy: From Grotius to the Scottish Enlightenment* (Cambridge: Cambridge University Press, 1996). For twentieth-century discussions of natural law, see, e.g., Fuller, *The Morality of Law*; John Finnis, *Natural Law and Natural Rights* (New York: Oxford University Press, 1980); Hart, *The Concept of Law,* 8–9; Joseph Fuchs, *Natural Law* (New York: Sheed & Ward, 1965). On natural law in American law, see Robert P. George, "Natural Law, the Constitution, and the Theory and Practice of Judicial Review," *Fordham Law Review* 69 (2001): 2269–83. On natural law's relationship to Paul, see Thurston Howard Reynolds II, "Natural Law Jurisprudence of the Sermon on the Law," *Ohio Northern University Law Review* 31 (2005): 231–70.

[291] This metaphor is indebted to Randy E. Barnett, "A Law Professor's Guide to Natural Law and Natural Rights," *Harvard Journal of Law and Public Policy* 20 (1997): 656.

[292] Elizur Goodrich, "The Principles of Civil Union and Happiness Considered and Recommended: A Sermon (1787)," quoted in Barnett, "Guide to Natural Law," 658.

Although there is some debate regarding the genesis of natural law—some trace it to Plato and Aristotle[293]—all agree that it is essential for the thought of Aquinas, who develops the idea into the form it took from the thirteenth century on.[294] (The larger theoretical question behind these debates is whether natural law is irremediably theological[295] or whether it may have potential for a secular democracy.[296]) Natural law is, for Aquinas, both the implicit, non-codified "Law of Christ"[297] or "the Law of the Spirit of Christ,"[298] and the principles of law that may be deduced from reason ("the rational creature's participation of the eternal law"):[299]

> [T]he light of reason, whereby we discern what is good and what is evil, which pertains to the natural law, is nothing else than an imprint on us of the divine light. It is therefore evident that the natural law is nothing else than the rational creature's participation of the eternal law.[300]

For Aquinas, reason is the conduit between the divine intellect and the human; there can be no contradiction, then, between the teachings of reason and the will of God.[301] Natural moral law, like the ordinary laws of nature, inheres in the human condition itself, and is implicit in transcendent principles of justice or rightness, discoverable by humans. Natural law will be the same for all humans, since all humans are rational and have the

---

[293] See, e.g., Heinrich A. Rommen, *The Natural Law: A Study in Legal and Social History and Philosophy*, trans. Thomas R. Hanley (London: Herder, 1948), 15–35.

[294] See Daniel J. O'Connor, *Aquinas and Natural Law* (New York: St. Martin's Press, 1968), 19–21; Anthony J. Lisska, *Aquinas's Theory of Natural Law: An Analytic Reconstruction* (New York: Clarendon Press, 1996), 82–90; Vincent McNabb, "The Scholastic Attitude Toward the Law," in Rosenthal, *Judaism and Christianity*, 209. It is fairly well-established that Aquinas drew heavily on Maimonides, the medieval Jewish Aristotelian who sought to syncretize Jewish law and thought with Aristotelian philosophy. For Maimonides, almost (but not quite) all of Jewish law could be deduced from natural law, which reason itself could comprehend if it was untainted by imagination or error. See David Novak, "Judaism and Natural Law," *American Journal of Jurisprudence* 43 (1998): 117, 119, 123.

[295] See Novak, *Judaism and Natural Law*, 117, 118 (discussing, and rejecting, the view of Leo Strauss); Pauline Westerman, *The Disintegration of Natural Law Theory: Aquinas to Finnis* (Boston: Brill Academic, 1998).

[296] This appears to be the view of Alasdair MacIntyre. See Alasdair MacIntyre, *Whose Justice? Which Rationality?* (South Bend: University of Notre Dame Press, 1988), 164–82. See also O'Connor, *Aquinas*, 57–59.

[297] Gal 6:2. See Franz Bockle, *Law and Conscience* (New York: Sheed and Ward, 1966), 43ff.

[298] Rom 8:2.

[299] Thomas Aquinas, "Summa Theologiae I-II, Question 91, Art. 2," in *Saint Thomas Aquinas on Law, Morality, and Politics*, ed. William E. Baumgarth and trans. Richard J. Regan (Indianapolis: Hackett, 1988) (hereinafter Aquinas, *S.T.*), 19.

[300] Aquinas, *S.T.* I–II: Q. 91, A. 3 (20).

[301] See Lisska, *Aquinas's Theory*, 89; Rommen, *Natural Law*, 45.

same essential ends.[302] As we might expect, natural law's 'first principles' tend to be quite general in nature—one should act in accordance with reason, one should not offend those with whom he lives, etc.[303] The point is that, for Aquinas, positive law may be derived from, and checked against, natural law. As Aquinas says in the *Summa Theologiae*:

> Every human law has just so much of the nature of law as it is derived from the law of nature. But if, in any point, it deflects from the law of nature it is no longer a law but a perversion of law.[304]

Positive law is thus rescued from Pharisaic nomianism, because even its details may be derived from larger principles, and perhaps overruled by them, and those principles are divine in nature. At the same time, the dictates of human law, to which Aquinas devotes as much attention in the *Summa* as he does to natural law, do not "bind a man in conscience" the way natural law does, because human laws may be just or unjust, and unjust laws are not binding in conscience.[305] Yet Aquinas is careful to point out that the law must be "first and chiefly an ordering to the common good."[306] Here, not only are the stirrings of conscience converted into the dictates of reason and defined as essential, natural law, but the autonomy of the subject to act outside the dictates even of positive law is denied. Natural law is necessary because "man is ordained to an end of eternal happiness which is inproportionate to man's natural faculty" to deduce laws devoted toward that end,[307] and because "man is not competent to judge of interior movements that are hidden but only of exterior acts which appear, and yet, for the perfection of virtue, it is necessary for man to conduct himself aright in both kinds of acts."[308]

Natural law is thus an evolution from the Pauline notion that law exists only to demarcate sin. Natural law governs those internal movements of the heart which for Paul were so essential, and so beyond the reach of law; it is precisely the law beyond law which Paul said could only be inscribed on the heart. And yet natural law ideas, or variations on them, indeed legitimize exceedingly legalistic practical systems of law, such as the precedent-rich English common law, defended by Federalists as trans-political and transhistorical iterations for basically Aquinian reasons. Natural law does not dictate a single substantive position. To take but one example, capital punishment has been justified by such figures as Kant and Hegel as re-

---

[302] See Bockle, "Law and Conscience," 48–52; O'Connor, *Aquinas*, 60–62.
[303] See Aquinas, *S.T.* I–II, Q. 94, A. 2 (46); Daniel Westberg, "The Relation Between Positive and Natural Law in Aquinas," *Journal of Law and Religion* 11 (1994–95): 3–6.
[304] Aquinas, *S.T.* I–II, Q. 95, A. 3 (59). See O'Connor, *Aquinas*, 73–79.
[305] Aquinas, *S.T.* I–II, Q. 96, A. 4 (70–71).
[306] Aquinas, *S.T.* I–II, Q. 90, A. 1 (15).
[307] Aquinas, *S.T.* I–II, Q. 93, A. 4 (23).
[308] Ibid.

quired by natural justice, but many contemporary figures have made equally cogent arguments against capital punishment on natural law grounds.[309] And, of course, natural law theorists long defended the institution of slavery, even as others attacked it.[310] What natural law theory constructs is a subordination of particular law to general reason, even as it supports the promulgation of law precisely through that subordination.

As surveyed in the last part, canon law and natural Law created English equity jurisprudence, and natural law in particular continued to inform the theory and practice of Anglo-American common law through until the beginning of the last century.[311] Nor should we underestimate natural law's conceptual shift in evaluating the subsequent development of church and secular law; running a city, even the City of God, takes rules, and while Jews believed the administration of law to be a divine decree ("Appoint judges and police in all the dwelling places that God has given to your tribes, and be certain to administer honest judgment for your people," said Deuteronomy 16:18), both the antinomian momentum in Paul and the anti-establishment spirit of the Gospels made such administration problematic for the Church, as it gained temporal power. Eventually, canon law developed into a vast edifice of legal structure,[312] with enormously sophisticated substantive and procedural rules, vast subject matter jurisdiction throughout most of Europe, and an influence that we have only begun to recognize.[313] But this law could be justified—as the Catholic Church attempted to do in response to Luther's polemics that it had out-Pharisized the Pharisees—by recourse to the general natural law principles from which it was at least theoretically derived, and from the divine order to rule. In Catholic teaching, Christ gave to Peter two "keys" in the passage related at Matthew 16:19—one of knowledge of God, the other of power to enforce it.[314]

As the mode of access to the divine shifts from Aquinian reason to a more general notion of "conscience," we can see how the same basic move animates the legal sentiments and institutions (such as the jury) which we discussed in the previous part. Natural law was conceived as law, it is true, but it is law of an unusual genesis: the operation of the human conscience and intellect. As such, this internalized 'law' is both *nomos* and *anti-nomos*; in contrast to human, technical law and its anti-divine, mechanical exposi-

---

[309] See Westberg, "Relationship," 19ff. (citing sources).

[310] See ibid., n. 38.

[311] See DiMatteo, "History of Natural Law Theory," 861–69; Berman, *Faith and Order*, 56–71; Reid & Witte, "In the Steps of Gratian," 647–49.

[312] James Brundage, *Medieval Canon Law* (London: Longman, 1995), 6–10, 120–53; Reid & Witte, "In the Steps of Gratian," 650–55.

[313] See generally Brundage, *Medieval Canon Law*; R.H. Helmholz, *The Spirit of the Classical Canon Law* (Athens: University of Georgia Press, 1996). For a comparison of Jewish and canon law, see Zeev Falk, "Jewish Law and Medieval Canon Law," in *Jewish Law in Legal History and the Modern World*, ed. Bernard Jackson (Boston: Brill, 1980), 78.

[314] Reid & Witte, "In the Steps of Gratian," 653–54.

3. The Protestant Reformation

The last site of continued Pauline *agon* that we will explore is the most important one for the American milieu: the Protestant Reformation. In some ways, Martin Luther is a starkly antinomian figure, even though he is the one who coined the term and set himself starkly against it. Luther amplified Pauline suspicion of the letter of the law, and reemphasized the primacy of the spirit, as we shall discuss below. He railed against the byzantine nature of the canon law, accusing the Catholic Church of Judaizing (an insult the Church was happy to reciprocate[315]) and burning books of canon law. Luther's attacks on the literal, carnal interpretation of the Eucharist ritual reveal a strong tendency to allegorize what for the Catholic church was a literal reality.[316] And Luther believed that distinguishing between the law and the gospel—between a religion of law and of grace—was "the highest art in Christendom."[317]

For Luther, to rely on external law—and the concomitant belief in the efficacy of ritual—implies justification by works instead of by faith; if one acts in accord with the laws, one suggests that acts and laws can in some way bring about salvation. This, Luther believed, was the essence of the Pharisaic error[318] and the aforementioned Pelagian heresy.[319] (By the time of Luther's later writings, circumcision becomes for him, as for Paul, the emblem of this literal-carnal misunderstanding of the salvation process.[320]) So in contrast to the Judaizing (i.e. legal-izing) Catholics, Luther (and Calvin, who took the idea of grace to its logical conclusion) saw the human relationship to God as only possible through grace.[321] "Justification by faith," perhaps the Lutheran catchphrase, is really "Justification by grace

---

[315] See Sander L. Gilman, *Jewish Self-Hatred: Anti-Semitism and the Hidden Language of the Jews* (Baltimore: Johns Hopkins University Press, 1986), 64 (discussing Luther's analogies of Judaism and Catholicism); Adam Shear, *Luther's Jewish Problem* (unpublished manuscript, on file with author).

[316] On Protestant denigration of "superstitious ritual" as carrying, at most, an allegorical significance, see Jonathan Z. Smith, *To Take Place: Toward Theory in Ritual* (Chicago: University of Chicago Press, 1987), 100.

[317] Quoted in Bockle, *Law and Conscience*, 24.

[318] Martin Luther, "The Freedom of a Christian (1520)," in *Martin Luther's Basic Theological Writings*, ed. and trans. Timothy Lull (Minneapolis: Augsburg Fortress, 1989), 599.

[319] See Alister McGrath, *Reformation Thought* (Oxford: Blackwell, 1993), 73–75.

[320] See Martin Luther, "On the Jews and their Lies (1543)," in *Luther's Works*, vol. 47, 149ff.

[321] See McGrath, *Reformation*, 88ff. Luther's views in fact evolved over time, but by October, 1517, the components of grace and justification by faith were secure. Ibid., 97.

through faith." As McGrath puts it, "The justification of the sinner is based upon the grace of God, and is received through faith."[322]

Luther also amplifies considerably the Pauline emphasis on the 'spirit' of the text. Drawing on various sixteenth century sources of hermeneutical theory, and rejecting the Church's exclusive right to read and interpret Scripture, Luther eventually develops eight "senses" of biblical language, four according to the "killing letter" (*litera occidens*) and four according to "the life giving spirit" (*spiritus vivificans*).[323] Importantly, Luther in his new interpretive schema shifts the literal meaning of the text from one of four valid methods of reading (literal, allegorical, moral, anagogical-eschatological) to a category of fallen, historical understandings of what is really a spiritual, prophetic text. Luther's hermeneutic has the effect of reinforcing and greatly amplifying Paul's understanding of the letter and the spirit, and directly allies literalism with a lack of perception of Christ's salvation.

The result is often a radical antinomianism, notwithstanding Luther's subsequent disavowals:

> A Christian has no need of any work or law in order to be saved since through faith he is free from every law and does everything out of pure liberty and freely.[324]

Elsewhere he expresses a similar perspective:

> The Law, that slave, no longer has a right to accuse and condemn us because of our sin; for this has been forgiven, and we have become free by the deliverance of the Son. Therefore the entire Law has been abrogated for believers in Christ.[325]

Yet despite statements like these, Luther maintained that the law had religious value. Against his antinomian opponents, Luther "affirmed that the law must be preached to bring repentance, which in turn would lead to justification."[326] Like Paul, Luther saw the divine law as essential to help us recognize our sin:

---

[322] McGrath, *Reformation*, 100.

[323] McGrath, *Reformation*, 147–49. See also Gillian Evans, *The Language and Logic of the Bible: The Road to Reformation* (Cambridge: Cambridge University Press, 1985).

[324] Luther, "The Freedom of a Christian," in *Luther's Works*, vol. 31, 361.

[325] Luther, "Lectures on Galatians," in *Luther's Works*, vol. 26, 446.

[326] Luther, "Against the Antinomians," in *Luther's Works*, vol. 3–4. See also Luther, "On the Councils and the Church," in *Luther's Works*, vol. 41, 147. See Baker, "Sola Fide," 117.

> The terrifying of the conscience must proceed from the preaching of the Law, to the end we may know that we have offended against the Laws of God.[327]

But Luther also incorporates natural law reasoning:

> For what God has given the Jews from heaven, he has also written in the hearts of all men. Thus, I keep the commandments which Moses has given, not because Moses gave commandment, but because they have been implanted in me by nature.[328]

This conscience-driven mode of theologized natural law is the necessary conceptual backdrop to the drama of the Clinton impeachment, the debates over common law, the jury, the rhetoric against legalism and litigation, and the other examples in the previous part. Such moves are not antinomian *per se*, but they are antinomian to the extent that the *nomos* is external as opposed to the inner demands of the heart. For Luther, these demands are themselves the true law. Even if we are to see this internalization of law—and of superego-like structures of control—as essentially neurotic in nature,[329] Luther's position is not simply "anti-law." This is too simple. Rather, Luther viewed the external law as necessary to create the internal law of the conscience.

As to external law itself, Luther does suggest in *Temporal Authority* that secular law is at best irrelevant to Christian practice. Echoing 1 Corinthians, he writes:

> A Christian should be so disposed that he will suffer every evil and injustice without avenging himself; neither will he seek redress in the courts but have utterly no need of temporal authority and law for his own sake.[330]

For Luther, as for Paul, not only the law but the court system as well is best when internalized. What takes place 'out there' is, in ritual and in law, at best irrelevant and at worst damning. Law is useful insofar as it can demarcate the boundaries that are subsequently internalized by the conscience/superego—but that is all.

---

[327] Christopher Hill, *The World Turned Upside Down* (New York: Viking, 1972), 125, quoted in Jonathan Boyarin, "Another Abraham," 354.

[328] Luther, "How Christians should regard Moses (1525)," in Lull, *Martin Luther's Basic Theological Writings*, 138.

[329] See Jonathan Boyarin, "Another Abraham," 353–55.

[330] Martin Luther, "Temporal Authority: To What Extent Should it be Obeyed? (1523)," in Lull, *Martin Luther's Basic Theological Writings*, 675.

4. Summary and Contemporary Echoes

These anti-legalistic and arguably antinomian ideas are with us today, in the mainstream of contemporary Protestantism, in which legalism is seen as an evil to be avoided at all costs. As Robert Tuttle has shown, the opposition to legalism is at the heart of Paul Ramsey's classic *Basic Christian Ethics*,[331] which has been read by millions and taught in Protestant seminaries for decades.[332] Indeed, the second chapter of the book is titled "Christian Liberty: An Ethic without Rules," and Ramsey extols Paul's epistle to the Galatians as his "great declaration of Christian independence from legalism."[333] Arguably going farther even than Paul, Ramsey explicitly denies even natural law or the "law written upon our hearts" when he declares, "no law, not even an inner one, has positive moralizing power."[334] He continues with his denial of law, proclaiming, "all things are lawful for me, all things are now permitted, which Christian love permits."[335] None of this was unintentional; Ramsey, arguably among the most influential Protestant thinkers of the last century, set as his project the adaptation of Christian ethics to a dynamic social context, which necessitated abandoning the artificial fixities of legalism for the adaptable human spirit.[336]

Nor was Ramsey an outlier; similar views were voiced by the leading Protestant theologians of the period.[337] For Niebuhr, for example, "no rule of justice, no particular method of arbitrating the interests of the other with those of the self, can leave the self with the feeling that it has done all that it could."[338] And for Tillich:

> Love is above law, also above the natural law in Stoicism and the supra-natural law in Catholicism. You can express it as a law, you can say as Jesus and the apostles did: "Thou shalt love"; but in doing so you know that this is a paradoxical way of speaking, indicating that

---

[331] Paul Ramsey, *Basic Christian Ethics* (Chicago: University of Chicago Press, 1977). The book was originally published in 1950.

[332] See Robert W. Tuttle, "All You Need is Love: Paul Ramsey's Basic Christian Ethics and the Dilemma of Protestant Antilegalism," *Journal of Law and Religion* 18 (2002–3): 429–35.

[333] Ramsey, *Basic Christian Ethics*, 75.

[334] Ibid., 87. See Tuttle, "All You Need is Love," 433–34.

[335] Ramsey, *Basic Christian Ethics*, 77 (citing 1 Cor 10:23, 24).

[336] Tuttle, "All You Need is Love," 435–36.

[337] Ibid., 437–38. See also Boyarin, *Radical Jew*, 209–19; Kennedy, "Semiotics of Critique," 1158–59. Catholic thought is less extreme than Protestant thought on this subject, though it does reaffirm the Pauline distinction between letter and spirit. See Andrea van Dulmen, *Die Theologie des Gesetzes bei Paulus* (Stuttgart: Verlag Katholisches Bibelwerk,1968), 220 (as quoted in Charlotte Klein, *Anti-Judaism in Christian Theology* (Minneapolis: Fortress, 1978), 47; Romano Guardini, *The Lord* (Washington, D.C.: Regnery, 1956), 169 (as quoted in Klein, *Anti-Judaism*, 50).

[338] Reinhold Niebuhr, *The Nature and Destiny of Man: A Christian Interpretation. I. Human Nature* (New York: Charles Scribner's Sons, 1941), 295 (as quoted in Tuttle, "All You Need is Love," 438).

the ultimate principle of ethics, which, on the one hand, is an unconditional command, is, on the other hand, the power breaking through all commands.... Law is not able because law is the attempt to impose something which belonged to a special time on all times.[339]

The anti-legalism that appeared in secular form in Part One here appears in its original, religious form. Law is fixed, the heart is adaptable. Law is constrictive, the heart expansive. But unlike the secular materials we explored earlier, these religious materials provide the ontological and theological bases for their preferences.

Of course, contemporary Christian thought on the secular law does not conform to the theories of Protestant theologians, who after all are talking about religious law, not "law" in general.[340] In fact, there is a spectrum of contemporary Christian thinking about the nature of secular law and lawyering, ranging from disapproval to embrace.[341] My point is not that this is the sole Christian philosophy of law—but rather that the secular material in Part One is an ideological and historical outgrowth of the religious material in Part Two. Indeed, over two thousand years, Pauline antinomian ideology has become such a part of our own conceptions of both religious and secular law that it is the essence of "common sense."

Today, as Duncan Kennedy has observed, antinomianism is not (or no longer) a particularly Protestant, or even Christian, ideology;[342] it is present whenever we believe intuition to be more reliable than reasoning (what Kennedy calls "irrationalist antinomianism"[343]), which we do all the time. And this is something that all of us share, or are supposed to. To be sure, there are numerous other sources for the general suspicion of law and the recourse to the non-rational—Holmesian skepticism,[344] legal theory, even just a bad lawsuit or two. But the structural forms of American anti-legalism are more than mere grievances; they replicate ancient debates to the letter, and to the spirit.

Interestingly, the religious anti-legalist critique has recently found secular voice in the work of a noted Jewish writer, Thane Rosenbaum's *The Myth of Moral Justice*, which explicitly and self-consciously argues for the

---

[339] Paul Tillich, *The Protestant Era*, trans. James Luther Adams (Chicago: University of Chicago Press, 1948, abr. 1957) 154–56 (as quoted in Tuttle, "All You Need is Love," 440).

[340] See Waldron, "Dead to the Law," 302–4.

[341] See Joseph C. Allegretti, *The Lawyer's Calling: Christian Faith and Legal Practice* (Mahwah, N.J.: Paulist Press, 1996), 10–23; Michael McConnell, Robert Cochran, and Angela Carmells, eds., *Christian Perspectives on Legal Thought* (New Haven: Yale University Press, 2001).

[342] Kennedy, "Semiotics of Critique," 1159 (discussing Pascal, Dostoevsky, and Kierkegaard).

[343] Ibid.

[344] See Witte, "Between Sanctity and Depravity," 727 (quoting Grant Gilmore's description of the Holmesian worldview: "The better the society, the less law there will be. In Heaven there will be no law, and the lion will lie down with the lamb.... In Hell there will be nothing but law, and due process will be meticulously observed.").

incorporation of the non-literal spirit of morality within the legal system.[345] Rosenbaum's critique is fascinating for its maintenance of the law-body/morality-spirit dichotomy.[346] "The law hides behind the body,"[347] he says. It has an "obsessive focus on the body and neglect of the soul."[348] And in so doing, law fails to provide what most non-lawyers expect from it: "a steadying force in our lives."[349] To take but one example, Rosenbaum would replace the reasonable person test with the "conscience-stricken" person test,[350] providing an opportunity for "acknowledging the hurt, telling and retelling the full story,"[351] and offering remedies for "indignity and disrespect."[352] In its full form, Rosenbaum's moral-legal system is a terrifying one in which judges and legal actors inquire into the inner workings of conscience, and there is no place off limits from legal-moral surveillance; it is a combination of a Judaic justice system with a Christian moral one, and while Rosenbaum's particular values are liberal, his ideology fits just as cleanly with conservative, even fundamentalist ones. Rosenbaum occasionally defends himself against the charge of religiosity, but, for our purposes, what is most interesting is the degree to which Rosenbaum attempts to detach his critique from religion, yet replicates the Pauline anti-Jewish argument, without acknowledging it as such, piece for piece. That an outspoken Jewish writer and intellectual can so thoroughly adopt an anti-Jewish, anti-legalist structure of thought is perhaps the strongest evidence that it has, after two thousand years, become part of our collective common sense.

But common sense is not common to all. In the concluding part, I will offer some brief remarks about the anti-Judaic heritage of anti-legalism, its curious juxtaposition with anti-lawyer rhetoric that resembles antisemitic rhetoric, and some of its blind spots. Fundamentally, though, our project thus far has been to trace the genealogy of a particular idea: that law, because it deals with the body, is fallen, corrosive, even deadly. Reading closely the anti-legalistic arguments of key moments in Anglo-American legal history, and placing the New Testament alongside them, one cannot help but notice the affinities. Sometimes the link is acknowledged, other times not. But the core assumptions that law governs only the surface of human life, and that there is a deeper, immaterial spirit that it cannot touch are religious, not secular, in origin. We may see these ideas in our contemporary political rhetoric, without a trace of their lineage. But Paul, Augustine, Aquinas, Luther, and others understood them as religious principles.

---

[345] Rosenbaum, *The Myth of Moral Justice*, 16–29, 35–54.
[346] See ibid., 266–84.
[347] Ibid., 271.
[348] Ibid., 268.
[349] Ibid., 3.
[350] Ibid., 29.
[351] Ibid., 35.
[352] Ibid., 54.

Legalism is not merely inefficient or irritating. It is the antithesis of conscience, the negation of grace, and the rejection of the path to God.

III. "Let's Kill All the Lawyers":[353] Context and Conclusions

A. Anti-Legalism/Anti-Judaism, Antilawyerism/Antisemitism

Arguments regarding legalism and law, which appear to be secular, are in fact religious in nature. They replicate ancient Christian critiques of the law, sometimes overtly and sometimes not, and they are grounded in a specific religious soteriology that sees the literal law and the physical body as obstacles to the salvation of the spirit. Our talk of law is primarily a religious conversation about the soul.

Throughout, the ghosts of anti-Judaism and antisemitism have haunted our analysis. Paul's ideology is anti-Judaic, but not antisemitic, and the difference is significant. Anti-Judaism is an ideological opposition to something that was, more or less, true about Judaism: its legal (even legalistic) orientation. Antisemitism, in contrast, is a hatred of things that were never true about Jews or Judaism: the blood libel, for example.[354] True, anti-Judaism can lead to violence, as in the riots provoked by John Chrysostom in the fourth century. And it can be intertwined with theological doctrines with no historical truth to them—e.g., that the Jews killed Christ. Yet there is still a fundamental difference between hating Jews for what they are (more or less) and hating them for what they are not. Likewise, anti-legalism is an ideology of law, not hatred. Its memes are of letter and spirit, of technicality and human nature—not of Jews poisoning wells.

Yet there is, alongside the anti-Judaic anti-legalism, a discourse of antisemitic anti-lawyerism that replicates, in striking similarity, the memes of classical antisemitism. This phenomenological similarity will be discussed in detail in a future study. Here, I wish only to sketch the barest outlines of that argument.

---

[353] William Shakespeare, *The Second Part of King Henry the Sixth*, act 4, scene 2.

[354] See Gavin Langmuir, *Toward a Definition of Antisemitism* (Berkeley: University of California Press, 1996), 301–16; Alan T. Davies, *Anti-Semitism and the Christian Mind: The Crisis of Conscience after Auschwitz* (New York: Herder & Herder, 1969), 24–28. For example, Langmuir argues that the Jews martyred in the 1096 massacres were victims of anti-Judaism, since they died rather than convert to Christianity. By the end of the thirteenth century, Jews were being killed in Europe because they were thought to commit ritual crucifixion and cannibalism. See also Katz, *Colonial America*, 51ff. (noting radically different forms of antisemitism even within eighteenth-century Europe); Robert Chazan, *Medieval Stereotypes and Modern Antisemitism* (Berkeley: University of California Press, 1997), 129–30. But see Davies, *Anti-Semitism*, 59–71 (arguing that anti-Judaism and antisemitism are intertwined). It is for this reason that most scholars of antisemitism prefer the dehyphenated spelling, rather than the popular "Anti-Semitism." "Anti-Semitism" was a term coined by an antisemite in the nineteenth century in order to elevate hatred of Jews to the level of race science. It has nothing really to do with the Jews qua Semites, and is not directed against other Semitic peoples. See Yehuda Bauer, *A History of the Holocaust* (London: Watts, 1982), 52.

Today's anti-lawyer culture paints a remarkable picture of the lawyer: a greedy, parasitic, and, yes, legalistic figure who is, in a word, Shylock.[355] Today's lawyer-villain is just like what scholar Leonard Dinnerstein calls the "composite portrait" of the antisemite's Jew:

> As a vastly powerful, manipulative, corrupt, devious, cunning, greedy, tricky, materialistic, dishonest, shrewd, grasping and close-fisted man.[356]

Indeed, as Marc Galanter has shown, many of today's lawyer jokes were originally jokes about Jews.[357] The Jew/lawyer is not simply a villain, however; that would be uninteresting. What is interesting is the *type* of villain that each of them is, specifically:

- A "bloodsucker" — a term that echoes both the medieval stories about Jews drinking Christian blood and the meme about usurious Jews/lawyers sucking the blood out of the economy.[358] (One joke asks: What's the difference between a flea and a lawyer? Answer: One is a parasite that sucks the living blood out of you and is linked with the Black Death. The other is a small insect.)

- Greedy — Long a stereotype about Jews, and now of lawyers as well.[359]

- Parasitic — Unlike real workers, Jews and lawyers don't make anything, but are "economic cannibals"[360] who "leech" off of the work of others.[361]

---

[355] For a survey of legal writing on the *Merchant of Venice* from 1863 to the 1960s, see O. Hood Phillips, *Shakespeare and the Lawyers* (London: Metheun, 1972), 92–118. On Shylock, see Harold Bloom, *Shakespeare: The Invention of the Human* (New York: Riverhead, 1998), 181–86; James Shapiro, *Shakespeare and the Jews* (New York: Columbia University Press, 1996); John Gross, *Shylock: A Legend and its Legacy* (New York: Touchstone, 1992); Daniel J. Kornstein, *Kill All the Lawyers?* (Princeton: Princeton University Press, 1994), 65–89; Jerome Hornblass, "The Jewish Lawyer," *Cardozo Law Review* 14 (1993): 1639–56; Richard H. Weisberg, *Poethics: And Other Strategies of Law and Literature* (New York: Columbia University Press, 1992), 93–104; Richard Posner, *Law and Literature: A Misunderstood Relation* (Cambridge, MA: Harvard University Press, 1988), 90–115; Kenji Yoshino, "The Lawyer of Belmont," *Yale Journal of Law and Humanities* 9 (1997): 183–216; Symposium, "The Merchant of Venice," *Cardozo Studies in Law and Literature* 5 (1993): 1–202.

[356] Leonard Dinnerstein, *Anti-Semitism in America* (New York: Oxford University Press, 1994), 19.

[357] Galanter, *Lowering the Bar*, 24, 54–55, 128–29, 166, 172, 187–88. See also the following chapter in this volume.

[358] Moneylending was in fact practiced more by Christians in Europe than by Jews. See Chazan, *Medieval Stereotypes*, 21–34; Langmuir, *Definition*, 305ff.

[359] See, e.g., Samborn, "Anti-Lawyer," 1 (reporting survey results that 31% said lawyers are too interested in money, 27% said they file too many unnecessary lawsuits, and 26% said they manipulate the legal system without regard for right or wrong.); Letter from Benjamin Franklin to the New Jersey Assembly Committee of Correspondence (June 11, 1770), quoted in Jay Alexander, "Legal Careers in Eighteenth Century America," *Duquesne Law Review* 23 (1985): 645 ("the Fees of Practising Attorneys ... had long been complain'd of as a grevious Oppression on the People.").

- Corrosive/destructive — In 1895, one antisemitic writer asked whether "the money lenders of London, the magnificent, titled Shylocks of our modern world may have purposely wrought the ruin of many American banks?"[362] Compare that complaint to the 1992 statement by Walter Olson that litigation "clogs and jams the gears of commerce, sowing friction and distrust between the productive enterprises on which material progress depends and all who buy their products, work at their plants and offices, join in their undertakings"[363] and has "reduced valuable enterprise to ruin, made miserable the practice of honorable professions, and brought needless pain to broken families.[364] Even Dan Quayle once told the American Bar Association that "too many lawyers and too many lawsuits [are] forcing the nation to lose its edge in the world marketplace."[365] Nor is this a complaint only of ideologues and politicians. In a 1993 poll, over three quarters of respondents said that "lawyers are hampering the nation's economy."[366]

- Deceitful — Like Shylock, lawyers don't talk straight, they lie whenever they want, they are not to be trusted, and they sow mistrust among others.[367] "How can you tell that an attorney is about to lie?" asks one lawyer joke. "His lips begin to move." It was Ambrose Bierce who jokingly remarked in the second decade of the last century that a liar is but "a lawyer with a roving commission."[368] A Gallup public opinion poll conducted in the mid- and late- 1990s found 41% of respondents to believe the "honesty and ethical standards" of lawyers to

---

[360] Adask, "Daddy, Why Doesn't the Vice President Like You?" 12–13 (as quoted in Galanter, "Predators and Parasites," 660 n. 105).

[361] See Galanter, "Predators and Parasites," 636 (lawyers criticized as "parasitic rent-seekers who do not really produce anything, but merely batten on the productive members of society, often in alliance with the undeserving-opportunistic malingerers in some versions, the privileged and powerful in others"); Warren, *A History of the American Bar*, 217 (quoting H. St. John Crevecouer, from 1776: "Lawyers are plants that will grow in any soil that is cultivated by the hands of others, and when once they have taken root they will extinguish every vegetable that grows around them."); Galanter, "Oil Strike in Hell," 735 (Quoting Ross Perot: "I wish more of these lawyers would become engineers and make something").

[362] *Illustrated America* (July 27, 1895), as quoted in Dinnerstein, *Anti-Semitism*, 18.

[363] Olson, *The Litigation Explosion*, 2.

[364] Ibid., 339.

[365] Dan Quayle, Address to American Bar Association, Aug. 16, 1991, reported in David S. Broder and Saundra Torry, "ABA President Disputes Quayle on Litigation Proposals," *Washington Post*, Aug. 14, 1991. See Adask, "Daddy, Why Doesn't the Vice President Like You?" 12–13, quoted in Galanter, "Predators and Parasites," 660 n. 105 ("Our entire judicial system has become an extortion racket designed to enrich lawyers at the expense of productive members of society. Almost every licensed, practicing lawyer is a beneficiary and co-conspirator in that extortion racket ... [Lawyers are] 98% bad people, lousy Americans, ethical cowards, professional sociopaths who are almost certainly the primary cause of the social and economic decline of this nation.").

[366] Samborn, "Anti-Lawyer," 1.

[367] Marc Galanter, "The Faces of Mistrust: The Image of Lawyers in Public Opinion, Jokes, and Political Discourse," *University of Cincinnati Law Review* 66 (1998): 806–7.

[368] Ambrose Bierce, *The Devil's Dictionary* (New York: Doubleday Page, 1911). A "lawyer," incidentally, is defined as "one skilled in circumvention of the law."

be "low" or "very low."[369] (39% answered 'Average.') Only 22% of those polled by the ABA during the same period responded that the phrase "honest and ethical" described lawyers.[370]

- Heartless/Soulless — Like Shylock and his Jewish co-religionists, whose cruelty and ruthlessness have no bounds (one popular American myth portrayed Jews selling their children for money[371]), lawyers are insensitive to the suffering of others, using emotional language merely to manipulate. Litigation "seizes on former love and intimacy as raw materials to be transmuted into hatred and estrangement."[372] Lawyers are often depicted as heartless or soulless, as in the popular film *The Devil's Advocate*, in which the Devil himself takes the guise of a lawyer, and for which the slogan was, "The newest attorney at the world's most powerful law firm has never lost a case. But he's about to lose his soul."

All of this is, as I have said, merely a sketch; I shall develop the portrait more fully in a subsequent study. However, as a sketch, the general contours should be clear: Shylock is alive and well, and he just made partner. Three features of this curious coincidence—anti-legalism resembling anti-Judaism together with anti-lawyerism resembling antisemitism—are important to highlight.

First, there is no correlation between these antisemitic memes and actual Jews in the legal profession. The stereotypes predate the entry of Jews into the bar (the "Philadelphia Lawyer," who bore almost all of the foregoing character flaws, was a type when few Jews practiced law at all), and are applied equally to Jewish and "obviously" non-Jewish attorneys. And these memes are notably absent in other professions where Jews are disproportionately represented—medicine most obviously. People may complain about their doctor, or the health care system, but few call doctors, as a general group, parasitic blood suckers without conscience or soul. No, these stories are not really about Jews. Rather, there is something about the law that is "Jewish." This is how perfectly non-bigoted people can voice "antisemitic" opinions about lawyers. It is not that these people are secretly, or unconsciously, antisemitic. Rather, as members of our culture, they—we—have all imbibed a thousand invisible ideologies, and antilawyerism is one of them.

---

[369] The Gallup Poll (Jan. 2, 1997), 2, quoted in *Sourcebook of Criminal Justice Statistics 1996* (Baton Rouge: Claitors, 1997), 125. A plurality of people polled in 1993 said that lawyers should "be more honest" or "ethical" if they wanted to improve their image. Randall Samborn, "Poll: Image of Lawyers around the Country Grows Worse," *New York Law Journal* (Aug. 2, 1993): 1.

[370] Gary Hengstler, "Vox Populi: The Public Perception of Lawyers: ABA Poll," *American Bar Association Journal* (Sept. 1993): 60–65.

[371] See Kate Pickard, "The Kidnapped and the Ransomed," *American Jewish Archives* 9 (1957): 16.

[372] Olson, *Litigation Explosion*, 2.

Second, antilawyerism is a mythic, not realistic, system.[373] There are, to be sure, plenty of reasons to dislike lawyers: the cost, the pain of litigation, advertising, television, and many, many more. But these do not explain antilawyerism. In the first place, there are fewer lawsuits today, per capita, than in Puritan Massachusetts, and America has fewer lawyers per capita than most of the developed world,[374] although there are a lot more lawyers now than in the recent past.[375] The claims that lawyers harm the economy are, at best, uncertain, and are undermined by comparisons with countries with more lawyers that perform better in leading economic indicators, and those with fewer that perform worse.[376] And, of course, the sweeping generalizations about greedy, parasitic shysters are, at best, just that—sweeping generalizations, often motivated by political, ideological, or even emotional agendas. What is important for our purposes is not the truth or falsity of anti-lawyerism, though, but the fact that anti-lawyer animus is expressed in the way it is, as opposed to some other way. Given that there is little connection between anti-lawyer rhetoric and reality, we must ask why *these* memes? Why these images, as opposed to other ones? What is it about lawyers that elicit such strong, and such defined, responses?

Third, it is striking how neatly the antilawyerism/antisemitism phenomenon coexists with the anti-legalism/anti-Judaism one. Scholars have debated for years whether there is any connection between the fantastic memes of antisemitism and the "realistic" ones of anti-Judaism. On the surface, such a link is hard to discern; what does poisoning wells have to do with hyperliteralism? Yes, Shylock is both a legalist and a parasite, but is there really a substantive connection? The correlation (or at least juxtaposition) of anti-Judaic anti-legalism with antisemitic antilawyerism suggests that there is. It is, at least, a very curious coincidence that these disparate rhetorics against Jewishness happen to coexist alongside one another; that

---

[373] See Galanter, "Oil Strike in Hell"; Charles R. Epp, "Do Lawyers Impair Economic Growth?" *Law & Social Inquiry* 17 (1992): 585–623; Frank B. Cross; "The First Thing We Do, Let's Kill all the Economists: An Empirical Evaluation of the Effect of Lawyers on the United States Economy and Political System," *Texas Law Review* 70 (1992) 645–83; Galanter, "Predators and Parasites," 647–51.

[374] Neil Sugarman, "What's Really Important?" *Massachusetts Lawyers Weekly* (Oct. 11, 1993): 1; Robert L. Haig, "Lawyer-Bashing: Have We Earned It?" *New York Law Journal* (Nov. 19, 1993): 2.

[375] According to ABA statistics, there were 257,403 lawyers in America in 1963 — .141% of the population (184 million); 448,000 or .204% of the population in 1977; and 880,000 or .331% of the population in 1996. Laurence H. Silberman, "Will Lawyering Strangle Democratic Capitalism?: A Retrospective," *Harvard Journal of Law and Public Policy* 21 (1998): 610; According to Bureau of Labor Statistics, U.S. Dept of Labor (1994), as quoted in Lasson, "Lawyering Askew," 723, 724; Lincoln Caplan, *Skadden: Power, Money and the Rise of Legal Empire* (New York: Farrar, Straus, and Giroux, 1993), 19 (reporting statistics of administrative office of U.S. courts). The growth in the legal profession has outpaced that of the medical profession, and of the gross national product. Silberman, "Lawyering," 610.

[376] See Cross, "The First Thing We Do"; Galanter, "Oil Strike in Hell."

it just so happens that Americans read law as "Jewish" in the sense of legalism, and lawyers as "Jewish" in the sense of parasitic and cruel.

The mystery is lessened somewhat if we return to the central theme of this study, which is that secular rhetorics of law are really religious rhetorics of the soul. What is Shylock's cruelty, if not a deficiency of soul? What is the lawyer's parasitism, if not a lack of the basic human (manly, really) desire to produce, to "make something of himself"? Antilawyerism, like anti-legalism, is really an ideology of soul and soullessness. It is a claim about the essence of humanity—that we are not merely machines, not merely our bodies, but are unique souls, separate selves, each with our own immaterial, spiritual reality. Take that away, and we're merely Shylocks, counting pennies and twisting the letters of the law. Law-talk is soul-talk in drag.

B. In Praise of the Pound of Flesh

The purpose of this chapter has been to demonstrate a phenomenological similarity between forms of antinomianism, and describe some of their history. It has not been to suggest that legalism is in any way superior to non-legalism, that Jewish law is superior to other forms of law,[377] or that the flotsam and jetsam of our legalistic age is good for the world. In a separate study,[378] I have addressed these questions in some depth, and suggested that, at the very least, our biases surrounding legalism do prevent us from seeing the multicultural and democratic potential of clear rules as opposed to discretionary standards. I think we can see Shylock's demands in his "Merchant of Venice" trial as a kind of multiculturalist "stand for justice" that uses the literal law as a way to resist the hegemonic "spirit" of his interlocutors. Shylock's accusers, recall, argue from universals—but they, too, have their particular aims in mind. Likewise, if we contrast Shylock's law with a jurisprudence that values the 'human' or 'common sense' element, I think that taking the letter of the law seriously provides us with a text for debate and reasoning, and moves the locus for debate away from the inner consciousness of the judge and onto the shared text of the law. And I think that to rely on the 'spirit of the law' brings into play all sorts of philosophical problems of the self, identity, and culture that are better suited to academic discussion than the domain of law and violence.

Consider, "I know it when I see it."[379] Is Justice Potter Stewart's famous statement one of law, or fiat? The phrase was used in a concurring opinion

---

[377] On the phenomenon of Jewish law being a stand-in for whatever policy an academic seeks to espouse, see Stone, "In Pursuit of the Counter-Text," 817–19.

[378] Michaelson, "In Praise of the Pound of Flesh," 148–51.

[379] *Jacobellis v. Ohio*, 378 U.S. 184, 197 (1964) (Stewart, J., concurring) ("I shall not today attempt further to define the kinds of material I understand to be embraced within that shorthand description ['hard-core pornography']; and perhaps I could never succeed in intelligibly doing so. But I know it when I see it, and the motion picture involved in this case is not that."). See Michaelson, "In Praise of the Pound of Flesh," 114–25. Paul Gewirtz has noted that "in addition to the millions of people who have incorporated it into their daily speech," the phrase has been quoted in over 150 federal court decisions,

about the obscenity (or lack thereof) of a Louis Malle film, and Justice Stewart was expressing a frustration with obscenity law, which all of us must feel at one time or another—we all know that obscenity isn't about how many millimeters of nipple are visible, or how an image fits into a three-part test.[380] Surely, this is what *really* goes on behind the distracting veils of prong A and test number two: judging, not merely according to rational and conceptual categories, but in full cooperation with those non-rational faculties of the human mind that distinguish wisdom from dexterity. As jurisprudential theory, it suggests that the ground of determination is ultimately the judge (or the fact finder), and that further explanation or elucidation is either impossible or undesirable. I cannot put it into words, Justice Stewart seems to be saying, but I don't have to: the film before us is not pornography. And perhaps to codify what "it" is misses the point.

The "I know it when I see it" ethos, the anti-legal rants of the Tea Party, the Clinton Impeachment, and all the flights from the law we have seen in this part have much in common: a mistrust of rules, a belief that fundamental guilt or innocence is best accessed by the penetrating reflection of the decision maker, a conception of an inner law of innate wisdom and reasonableness. As I have suggested elsewhere, though, this ethos is problematic from a number of perspectives. For multiculturalists, who know that what you see is not what I see, it raises questions of bias.[381] For formalists, it fails to provide regularity, publicity, and generality.[382] And for participants in a liberal democracy, it fails to provide any text for debate, progress, or change. A legalistic approach offers more possibility for change than an anti-legalistic one. The mechanism for change in an "I know it when I see it"

---

several scholarly treatments, and at least one Stephen Sondheim tune. Paul Gewirtz, "On 'I Know it when I See it,'" *Yale Law Journal* 105 (1996): 1025.

[380] Pornography regulations today are still reviewed according to that Holy Trinity of legalism, the three-part test. Though its terms have been stretched to curious lengths over the years, *Miller v. California*, 413 U.S. 15 (1973), still governs. According to *Miller* and its progeny, courts must decide "(a) whether 'the average person, applying contemporary community standards' would find that the work, taken as a whole, appeals to the prurient interest ... (b) whether the work depicts or describes, in a patently offensive way, sexual conduct specifically defined by the applicable state law; and (c) whether the work, taken as a whole, lacks serious literary, artistic, political, or scientific value." 413 U.S. at 24. The *Miller* test rejected the earlier "utterly without redeeming social value" standard of *Memoirs v. Massachusetts*, 383 U.S. 413, 418 (1966), and itself is a synthesis of several earlier cases' holdings. The third prong has been modified somewhat by the 1987 case of *Pope v. Illinois*, 481 U.S. 497 (1987), which tried to define the term "serious value" in terms of how the "Reasonable Person" would understand it. When Justice Stewart was writing, *Miller* had not yet been decided, Justice Stewart's concurrence reflected a certain frustration with the state of the law at the time.

[381] See Gewirtz, "On 'I Know it when I See it,'" 1037–38 (discussing Catharine A. MacKinnon, "Not a Moral Issue," *Yale Law and Policy Review* 2 (1984): 321–45). For a treatment of this issue in the area of obscenity law, see Anne L. Clark, Note, "As Nasty as They Wanna Be: Popular Music on Trial," *New York University Law Review* 65 (1990): 1481–1531.

[382] See Lawrence B. Solum, "Equity and the Rule of Law," in *The Rule of Law*, ed. Ian Shapiro (New York: New York University Press, 1992), 145; Scalia, *Rule of Law*, 1177–80.

framework is only a change in the "I"—perhaps in a change of personnel on the court, or some form of personal growth—but not democratic process, and not, really, the rule of law.[383]

At the very least, being more aware of the theologized assumptions and religious grammar that undergird familiar turns of phrase such as Justice Stewart's allows a more reflective discussion of their unstated assumptions—not only in jurisprudential terms, but in psychological and political ones as well. First, contrary to the assumption that our well-being is best served by a metaphysics of separate souls, there are many today who have found liberating the discoveries of scientific materialism, such as the insight that consciousness, the "soul," is an illusion of the well-functioning brain, and that we are embodied, impermanent beings. Escaping from dualism need not result in Weberian alienation. Quite the contrary, for many people it provides a release from the prison of ego. For what is the "soul" but the self's projections inscribed upon metaphysics? And what is enlightenment but the release from the tyranny of that self's dominion?

Second, our assumptions about legalism have political ramifications. With the rise of the Tea Party and the attendant conjoining of economic libertarianism with Christian populism, we have seen the convergence of two previously disparate strands of anti-legalist critique. On the one hand, the libertarian seeks to be free from the law to maximize profits and, supposedly, grow the economy as a result. On the other hand, the populist seeks to be free from the law to preserve liberty in a deeper, and I have suggested more religious, sense. A world without lawyers is both a world with less regulation of business, and a world in which "real" people exercise their consciences away from political correctness codes, product warning labels, click-through disclaimers, and other constraining legalisms. It is not at all coincidental that the political correctness codes protect racial, sexual, and other minorities, and that the warning labels and disclaimers are the results of attempts to hold corporations accountable. In the present decade's unlikely convergence of radical populism and radical libertarianism, majorities rule, because the rule of law yields no rules but those of the stirrings of conscience.

Anti-legalism may, in the end, be anti-liberalism. In asserting a universal conscience which, conveniently, reflects the consciences of those doing the asserting, it reinscribes an ancient theological argument in a new political context. And it so often beneath our notice. We hate the law for

---

[383] On tensions between the role of judicial virtues and the rule of law, see Solum, "Equity and the Rule of Law," 129–45. Solum's argument is quite compelling, although it ultimately rests on a set of ideas about the nature of the human subject that, while anecdotally appealing, may not be entirely coherent. See ibid., 142ff. (analogizing *phronesis*, or practical wisdom, to the inarticulate mental processes involved in riding a bicycle). Even Solum, however, acknowledges that there must be some public justification for judicial decisions beyond recourse to *phronesis* (ibid., 144), a justification not offered by the *Jacobellis* concurrence. Were this some small flaw in Justice Stewart's approach, we might all then agree, but my opinion is that *Jacobellis* is attractive to many precisely because it lacks the legalistic 'public justification' that Solum advocates.

Christian reasons, not aware that the reasons are religious, Christian, or particular in any way. Yet ironically, they may be more particular even than the jots and tittles of the law Christianity came to supplant. When Paul prioritized the universal Christian spirit over the particular Jewish text and particular Jewish body, he promised grace to all those capable of love. But only his kind of love. For the rest, for those without the power or privilege to assume that all hearts are universal, there is little recourse when the text of the law has been erased. The spirit, not the letter; the conscience, not the law; the spirit, not the body—this, we have been told for two millennia, is how we are to live in accord with the plan of God. But it was not always thus.

Lawyer Jokes and the Jewish Question: Jews, Lawyers, and Legalism in American Life

Marc Galanter*

I have always liked jokes. The earliest memory I have of hearing a joke is more than 70 years ago when I was visiting a small clothing factory with my father and listening to the owner tell him a story about the great International Scientific Congress on the Elephant. The German delegate delivered a learned paper on the chemical composition of the elephant's toenail; the French representative spoke on the love life of the elephant; and the Jewish delegate spoke on the elephant and the Jewish Question.

I propose to write about lawyer jokes, which became markedly more numerous, more prominent, and more hostile during the last quarter of the twentieth century, the very period in which Jews multiplied and flourished in the higher echelons of the American legal world. Both the Jews and the jokes arrived in conjunction with a pair of profound changes in the relation of lawyers to American society. On the one hand, it was a period of increasing resort to and dependence on lawyers, who emerged as the dominant profession in American life.[1] At the same time regard for lawyers diminished: they became the target of waves of attacks and esteem for them plummeted, amid a collapse of confidence in law and government generally.[2] How, if at all, are these changes connected to the presence and prominence of Jews? This conjunction brings me, after all these years, to the subject of lawyer jokes and the Jewish question.

What do jokes tell us about Jews and the law? If we look for direct evidence in the form of jokes about Jewish lawyers, the answer is nothing or very little. Although there are lots of jokes about Jews and in recent years even more about lawyers, there are hardly any jokes about Jewish lawyers in circulation. I checked this impression by googling "lawyer joke" and came up with 107,000 results; I then googled "Jewish lawyer joke" and came up with three results, none of which led me to a genuine specimen.[3] So, at most

---

* John and Rylla Bosshard Professor Emeritus of Law and South Asian Studies, University of Wisconsin-Madison.

[1] George Gawalt, ed., *The New High Priests: Lawyers in Post-Civil War America* (Westport: Greenwood Press, 1984), vii.

[2] Seymour Martin Lipset and William Schneider, *The Confidence Gap: Business, Labor and Government in the Public Mind* (Baltimore: Johns Hopkins University Press, 1987).

[3] Googled on Aug. 16, 2006. Variations like "joke about a Jewish lawyer" were equally unavailing. I went back to Google on Jun. 24, 2013; this time there were 186,000 hits for "lawyer joke," roughly three times the 65,300 hits for "Jewish joke."

there are a few and they are neither high visibility nor, so far as I can tell, particularly anti-Jewish. If we extend the inquiry back over the past century, there are a few more, some nastier, but none of them have survived. But if we widen our inquiry, we find that there are a rich set of indirect connections between Jews, lawyer jokes, and contemporary attacks on the legal system.[4]

I. From Exclusion to Inclusion

The paucity of jokes about Jewish lawyers, and other ethnic lawyers as well, does not mean that the presence of such outsiders in the real world of law went unremarked or uncontested. African American lawyers, shouldering a crippling burden of handicaps, were simply excluded from the higher echelons of law practice.[5] Although there was lingering prejudice against Irish (and other Catholic) lawyers, Jews were the first minority to join the legal profession in numbers that provoked unease in the legal establishment.[6] Warnings against "the great flood of foreign blood ... sweeping into the bar" and immigrants with "little inherited sense of fairness, justice and honor as we understand them" were followed by sustained campaigns to stem the entry of these undesirables.[7] The reigning authority on legal ethics during the interwar years affirmed the necessity of protecting the bar against the menace of "Russian Jew boys" who had "come up out of the gutter ... and were merely following the methods their fathers had been using in selling shoe-strings and other merchandise...."[8]

The image of Jewish lawyers was two-sided. Jews figured both as heroic civil liberties lawyers in Progressive era fiction and as the archetypical shyster in Samuel B. Ornitz's *Haunch, Paunch and Jowl* (1923).[9] Although

---

[4] On the course of those attacks, see Marc Galanter, "News from Nowhere: The Debased Debate on Civil Justice," *Denver University Law Review* 71 (1993): 77–113; idem, "The Assault on Civil Justice: The Anti-Lawyer Dimension," in *Legal Culture and the Legal Profession,* ed. Lawrence M. Friedman and Harry N. Scheiber (Boulder, CO: Westview Press, 1996), 79–118; idem, "The Turn Against Law: The Recoil Against Expanding Accountability," *Texas Law Review* 81 (2002): 285–304.

[5] Jerold S. Auerbach, *Unequal Justice: Lawyers and Social Change in Modern America* (New York: Oxford University Press, 1976), 210. On the exclusion from the American Bar Association until the World War II era, see ibid., 65–66, 216.

[6] Erwin O. Smigel, *The Wall Street Lawyer: Professional Organization Man* (Bloomington: Indiana University Press 1969), 45. Compare the account by Milton Gould of the obstacles to the rise of an Irish Catholic lawyer in a large New York firm in the late 1930s. Milton S. Gould, *The Witness Who Spoke with God and Other Tales from the Courthouse* (New York: Viking Press, 1979), xxiv–xviii.

[7] The quote is from William V. Rowe, "Legal Clinics and Better Trained Lawyers—A Necessity," *Illinois Law Review* 11 (1917): 591, 602. The campaigns are described in Auerbach, *Unequal Justice,* ch. 4.

[8] Henry S. Drinker, quoted at Auerbach, *Unequal Justice,* 127.

[9] Maxwell Bloomfield, "Law and Lawyers in American Popular Culture," in *Law and American Literature: A Collection of Essays* (Chicago: American Bar Association, Commission on Undergraduate Education in Law and Humanities, 1980), 54. Curiously

excluded from the higher echelons of the profession, Jews became a major segment of the lawyer population in many larger cities. In New York, Jews comprised half of the bar by the 1930s, although *Fortune* reassured its readers that

> 50 per cent of New York lawyers does not mean 50 per cent of New York's lawyer *power*. The most important office law business in America such as the law business incidental to banking, insurance, trust-company operation, investment work, railroading, patents, admiralty, and large corporation matters in general is in the hands of non-Jewish firms. Jewish legal activity will be found most commonly in litigation. In other words, Jews are largely to be found in those branches of law which do not interest non-Jewish lawyers ... [who] tend to prefer the fat fees and regular hours and routine, solicitor-like labors of their office to the active, combative professional service of the law courts.[10]

Barriers to Jewish entry into elite law firms began to give way in the 1950s. I can't resist a personal story here: in 1956 when I was a third year law student at the University of Chicago Law School, I had a job interview there with a well-known Wall Street firm. I should confess that I was not a serious candidate, but had been encouraged to sign up for the interview to offset an embarrassing shortage of applicants. As the interview drew to a close, I asked the interviewer whether, if I were to join that firm, I could realistically expect to be considered for a partnership in light of the fact that I was Jewish. "Oh, you're Jewish," he said. "On both sides?"[11] With the

---

the term "shyster," which has been around since the 1850s, hardly appears in the lawyer joke corpus. See note 51 below.

[10] "Jews in America," *Fortune* (February 1936): 9–10 (published as a book of the same name by Random House (New York, 1936)). Thirty years later, Jerome Carlin found that Jews made up 60% of the New York City bar, but a far smaller portion of elite law practice. Jerome E. Carlin, *Lawyers' Ethics: A Survey of the New York City Bar* (New York: Russell Sage Foundation, 1966), 19, 28. In Chicago, Jews made up a third of the bar in 1975, but were disproportionately present in small practices and low status specialties. John P. Heinz & Edward O. Laumann, *Chicago Lawyers: The Social Structure of the Bar* (New York: Russell Sage Foundation/Chicago: American Bar Foundation, 1982), 12. The authors note that 'percentage Jewish' had a stronger negative correlation with prestige than did any of the other religious and ethnic categories. Ibid., 112. By 1995, Jews were just a quarter of the Chicago bar, but were represented proportionately in large firms and most other practice settings. Robert Nelson et al., "Professional Dominance to Organizational Dominance," in *Reorganization and Resistance: Legal Professions Confront a Changing World* ed. William L.F. Felstiner (Oxford: Hart, 2005), 323.

[11] I had always thought of his response as a spontaneous quick-on-his-feet lawyer's attempt to whittle down a principle or carve out an exception. But as with much legal creativity, it turns out to have a long pedigree. Back in 1929, Emory Buckner, a legendary mentor figure, wrote to Robert M. Huchins, then the new dean of the Yale Law School, about academic opportunities for an outstanding young lawyer who he described as "fifty per cent Jew." Martin Mayer, *Emory Buckner* (New York: Harper & Row, 1968), 139. A few years later, in 1936, the Dean of Northwestern Law School responded to a recommendation by Thurman Arnold that "[a]lthough his faculty had appointed a half-Jew as a librarian, any attempt to appoint a Jew to the faculty would be an 'idle gesture.' (Arnold's

wisdom of hindsight, I can see that his attempt to "kasher" me as acceptably half-Jewish was a sign that we were on the cusp of change. Just a few years later, in 1959, Cravath promoted its first Jewish partner at a meeting marked by an ugly outburst by aging name partner Hoyt Moore.[12] In 1961, Davis Polk elected its first Jewish partner. As the 1960s progressed, exclusion from elite law practice softened into concern about having "too many" Jews.[13] In 1968, Erwin Smigel, whose detailed examination of Wall Street lawyers remains a landmark, reported the "tremendous lessening of discrimination—especially toward Jews" since he had gathered data a decade earlier.[14] That same year Bernard Segal was elected the first Jewish president of the American Bar Association.

There is no data from which to gauge the numerical presence of Jewish lawyers nationwide, but more than one in six law students was Jewish around 1960.[15] As law school enrollments expanded dramatically (and Jewish population remained static), the proportion of Jews in the profession has fallen.[16] At the same time, the collapse of discrimination has increased the presence of Jews in the higher echelons of the profession.[17] A 1995 survey of partners in the highest-billing law firms (in New York and Washington) found that 22% were Jews.[18]

---

unsuccessful candidate was a recent graduate named Abe Fortas.)" See Jerold Auerbach, *Unequal Justice*, 187.

[12] Paul Hoffman reports, "[Edward] Benjamin's case touched off a furious fight in the Cravath councils. At one point in the discussions, Hoyt Moore, well in his eighties and set in the ways of an earlier era, reportedly called a colleague into the corridor and whispered, "All right, who's the first guy who's going to go in and yell, 'Jew! Jew!?'" When no one else would, Moore did, only to be outvoted, a rare rebellion against authority at Cravath." Paul Hoffman, *Lions in the Street: The Inside Story of the Great Wall Street Law Firms* (New York: Saturday Review Press, 1973), 12. Moore was not only a name partner, but an indicted and admitted bag man who had bribed a federal judge on behalf of a client and escaped via the statute of limitations. Ibid., 9; Joseph Borkin, *The Corrupt Judge* (New York: Clarkson & Potter, Inc., 1962), 175, 183, 185.

[13] Yale Law Journal, "The Jewish Law Student and New York Jobs—Discriminatory Effects in Law Firm Hiring Practices," *Yale Law Journal* 73 (1964): 650.

[14] Erwin O. Smigel, *The Wall Street Lawyer: Professional Organization Man?* (Bloomington: Indiana University Press, 1969), 370. The subsequent flourishing of Jews in the upper echelons of the New York bar is described in Eli Wald, "The Rise and Fall of the WASP and Jewish Law Firms," *Stanford Law Review* 60 (2008): 1803.

[15] In a National Opinion Research Center survey of the career plans of seniors graduating from American colleges in 1961, Jews made up nearly 20% of those aiming to be lawyers and 17.5% of those planning to attend law school. Andrew M. Greeley, *Religion and Career: A Study of College Graduates* (New York: Sheed & Ward, 1963), Tables 3.16, 6.2. At this time Jews were just over 3% of the total population of the United States.

[16] In Carnegie Commission surveys of graduate study, Jews were nearly one-fifth of all law students in 1969 (and one-third of students in the twenty top-rated law schools). By 1975 "the proportion of students of Jewish origin dropped to twelve percent." Carl A. Auerbach, "Legal Education and Some of Its Discontents," *Journal of Legal Education* 34 (1984): 50.

[17] John P. Heinz et al., *Urban Lawyers: The New Social Structure of the Bar* (Chicago: University of Chicago Press, 2005), 95.

[18] Amy E. Black and Stanley Rothman, "Shall We Kill All the Lawyers First?: Insider and

In any event it would not be surprising if the public overestimated the portion of lawyers who are Jewish, since perceptions of the Jewish population run about 10 times the actual percentage.[19] It is particularly striking, then, how faint an impression the intersection of Jews and lawyers leaves in the popular imagination, apart from a minority within the minority that cultivates conspiratorial fantasies about Jewish domination.[20] Within this minority there is something of a tradition of seeing Jewish involvement in the law as part of plots to "de-Christianiz[e] America"[21] or achieve world domination.[22]

II. Jews as Over-Users of Legal Remedies

Popular understanding has often attributed to Jews a proclivity to invoke the law more frequently and less appropriately. One example is a set of jokes about conniving claimants that flourished from the late nineteenth

---

Outsider Views of the Legal Profession," *Harvard Journal of Law and Public Policy* 21 (1998): 841.

[19] This overestimation is present for all minorities, but while the overestimate of African Americans and Hispanics is about three times the census numbers, that of Asians is about six times the census, and that of Jews is ten times (26% vs. 2.5% estimate of actual). Elizabeth Theiss-Morse, "Characterizations and Consequences: How Americans Envision the American People" (presentation, Midwest Political Science Association, Chicago, IL, April 3–6, 2003). Jewish respondents are not exempt from such misperceptions but their overestimates of the Jewish population are more modest. However, 42% thought Jews were more than 6% of the population, including 18% who thought they were more than 15%. "L.A. Times/Yedioth Ahronoth Poll," *Los Angeles Times*, March/April 1998, http://www.latimesinteractive.com/pdfarchive/nationalworld/la-980419jewishpoll-407pa2da.pdf.

[20] "...Jews have contributed to ... the general decay of our nation through their obvious perversion of our legal system. Jewish lawyers, judges and other liberals have used our courts to tie the hands of law enforcement personnel, giving criminals more rights than victims of crime. ... [Our] modern laws were not written by ordinary people of common sense and honest integrity. They were written by Jewish lawyers, passed by Jewish-bribed legislators and presided over by Jewish judges. There is no other way to explain a legal system that actually encourages crime and protects criminals as do the laws that we have today, laws that could only be conceived in the twisted, perverted minds of either a criminal, a psychiatrist or a lawyer." (William Forrest, "Innocent by Insanity," *Chinese Swastika Newsletter*, Vol. 1, No. 9 (October 17, 2002), at http://bamboo-delight.com/Newsletter_archives/csn_20021017.

[21] "As a lever for directing society, the law is, of course, perfectly suited to Jewish needs and temperament. It enables the Jews to advance their Talmudic objectives by sure, unimpedable strides, and at the same time lets them remain safely secure from the scrutiny of the public." Father Leonard Feeney, "Catholic Power and the Plots of the Jews," *The Point*, Sept. 1955. (Father Feeney was excommunicated from the Roman Catholic church in 1953.)

[22] An antisemitic and anti-Masonic crusader regards the disproportionate presence of Jewish lawyers in the twentieth century as a manifestation of a policy communicated by "the World Jewish leader, to Chamor, the main Rabbi in France" on Nov. 21, 1389, to "arrange that your sons become advocates and lawyers, and see that you mix yourselves in the affairs of State in order that by putting Christians under your yoke, you may dominate the world and be avenged of them." Col Jack Mohr, "Woe Unto Ye Fundamentalists!" at http://www.scripturesforamerica.org/html2/jm0073.htm.

century past the mid-twentieth century; there are a few survivors in circulation today, but jokes on this theme have largely disappeared. Not all of these jokes targeted Jews, but a significant portion identified Jews as more combative, more ready to resort to the legal system, and prone to invent or magnify injuries.[23]

> #1. Ikey came upon a crowd at the crossing, the wreckage of an automobile and two men gasping on the ground.
>
> "Vat was it; an engine?" he asked one of the victims.
>
> "Yes," he answered feebly.
>
> "Did they blow der whistle?"
>
> "No."
>
> "Did dey ring the bell?"
>
> "No."
>
> "Has der claim-agent been here yet?"
>
> "No."
>
> "Do you mind if I lie down here mit you?"[24]

Faking of accidents to collect compensation, a distinctively American contribution to the annals of fraud, arose in the last quarter of the nineteenth century. When faking flourished in the early years of the twentieth century, it was often associated in the public mind with Jews.[25] The heavy Jewish presence in these conniving claimant jokes reflects a once widespread (and perhaps persisting in some quarters) belief that, overeager to pursue legal remedies and to obstruct remedy for others, Jews used the legal system instrumentally without adhering to its values.

---

[23] I have numbered the joke texts to facilitate cross-reference. With rare exceptions these jokes exist in many versions, sometimes with significant variation. When presenting jokes that are discussed in my book, *Lowering the Bar: Lawyer Jokes and Legal Culture* (Madison: University of Wisconsin Press, 2005), I have provided only a few examples of the joke's sources and variants; more complete documentation can be found there.

[24] James Schermerhorn, *Schermerhorn's Stories: 1500 Anecdotes from Forty Years of After Dinner Speaking* (New York: George Sully & Co., 1928), 218. The first version known to me in which the joke figure is Jewish dates from 1923. A similar opportunism in making claims is often attributed to Scots (collision of two taxis leads to a score of injuries); e.g., James Ferguson, *The Table in a Roar, If You've Heard It, Try and Stop Me* (London: Methuen & Co., 1933), 129.

[25] Joke #1 depicts what Ken Dornstein describes as a prevalent type of fraud involving professional accident fakers or just random passersby who would insert themselves into genuine trolley accidents and then pretend to be injured. Ken Dornstein, *Accidently, on Purpose: The Making of a Personal Injury Underworld in America* (New York: St. Martin's Press, 1996), 60–62, 93, 107–8.

#2.   Two Jewish gentlemen were playing golf. They had wagered a dollar a hole on the contest and the battle was waxing fast and furious. One saw the other pick his ball up out of a bad lie and throw it out on the fairway.

"Moe," he yelled, "you can't do that."

"Vy can't I?"

"It gives in the rulebook that you can't pick your ball up."

"Vell, I did it, didn't I?"

"But vat if you should win this match and my money by such actions.

Vat would I do then?"

"Sue me."[26]

In the first half of the twentieth century Jews were widely regarded as only partly within the moral community,[27] unconstrained by a common morality and with an inappropriate affinity for opportunistic use of formal legal controls. Whether there was a basis for the perception of Jewish readiness to sue,[28] its shadow lives on in items such as:

#3.   What's a Jewish car accident?

No damage to the automobile, but everyone inside has whiplash.[29]

---

[26] J.H. Johnson, Jerry Sheridan, and Ruth Lawrence, *The Laughter Library* (Indianapolis: Maxwell Droke, 1936), 171. The earliest version known to me is found in Irvin S. Cobb, *A Laugh A Day Keeps the Doctor Away* (Garden City: Garden City Publishing Co., 1923), 187.

[27] "As much as American Jews believed that they had fully embraced American civil ideals ... the dominant culture regarded them as 'the white other,' neither clearly marked by color as a subordinate class nor fully welcomed as citizens." Victoria Saker Woeste, "Insecure Equality: Louis Marshall, Henry Ford, and the Problem of Defamatory Antisemitism, 1920–1929," *Journal of American History* 91 (2004): 878.

[28] When Douglas Rosenthal studied personal injury claimants in New York City, he found no religious difference in activity/passivity as clients. Douglas E. Rosenthal, *Lawyer and Client: Who's in Charge?* (New York: Russell Sage Foundation, 1974), 189. However, this does not speak directly to the propensity to bring claims. Nor does Matthew Silberman's finding that Jewish residents of the Detroit metropolitan area in 1967 were more likely to use lawyers, but their small numbers in the sample did not support any firm conclusions. Matthew Silverman, *The Civil Justice Process: A Sequential Model of the Mobilization of Law* (Orlando: Academic Press, 1985), 101. Silberman attributed greater Jewish involvement with the legal system to greater wealth and social integration rather than to religious or ethnic reasons. (These factors would not have been present during the period in which the conniving claimant jokes arose.) So far as I am aware, none of the studies of proclivity to claim has tested the religious/ethnic variable. Ibid.

[29] Jay Allen, *500 Great Jewish Jokes* (New York: Signet Books, 1990), 89.

#4. *How can you tell if someone is half Catholic and half Jewish?*

When he goes to confession, he takes a lawyer with him.[30]

The most pervasive and enduring of these Jewish claimant jokes alleged a propensity to set fires to commercial premises in order to collect insurance.[31] The accusation is one with a long history.[32] In the early twentieth century jokes about insurance fires started by Jewish businessmen were common in both England and the United States, reflecting what many regarded as a "notorious fact."[33]

#5. *Ikey saw his friend Jakey in the smoking-car when he entered, and sat down in the same seat.*

"How was that fire in your place last week, Jakey?" he inquired.

Jakey started nervously.

"Sh!" he whispered. "It vas next week."[34]

While the jokes about conniving claimants have faded into obscurity,[35] the cultural concern with unfounded and exploitative claiming has intensified. The notion that some people have inappropriate recourse to legal remedies has not disappeared. Instead it has been de-ethnicized into a generalized worry about frivolous cases and the "litigation explosion." By the 1980s it was a commonplace that "we are all suffering a progressively debilitating disease, the disease of hyperlexis, too much litigation," as

---

[30] Bernard Saper, "Joking in the Context of Political Correctness," *Humor* 8 (1995): 1.

[31] On these Jewish fire stories, see Christie Davies, "Jewish Jokes, Anti-Semitic Jokes, and Hebredonian Jokes," in *Jewish Humor*, ed. Abner Ziv (Tel Aviv: Papyrus Publishing House, 1986), 85–87; Christie Davies, "Exploring the Thesis of the Self-Deprecating Jewish Sense of Humor," *Humor* 4 (1991): 197–201.

[32] On the lethal association of Jews with fires in medieval Europe, see Joshua Trachtenberg, *The Devil and the Jews: The Medieval Conception of the Jews and Its Relation to Modern Anti-Semitism*, 2d ed. (Philadelphia: Jewish Publication Society, 1983), 89–90.

[33] An insurance publication advised that "There are honorable Jews and there are honorable Gentiles, but that the evil disposed among the race gravitate to incendiarism is a notorious fact. . . ." *Insurance Monitor* 55 (1907): 23, quoted at Tom Baker, "On the Genealogy of Moral Hazard," *Texas Law Review* 75 (1996): 256 n. 79.

[34] *Jokes for All Occasions: Selected and Edited by One of America's Foremost Public Speakers* (New York: Edward J. Clode, 1922), 190. The earliest version known to me is found in Henry Martyn Kieffer, *It is to Laugh* (New York: Dodge Publishing Co., 1907), 105. Long gone in the United States, the story survives in England: Peter Mason, *Next Please (A Judge's Daybook)* (Chichester: Barry Rose Law, 2001), 126 (told of West Riding businessman); Lionel Blue, *Blue's Jokes: Ancient and Modern, Sacred and Profane* (London: Hodder & Stoughton, 2001), 15.

[35] To the extent that they remain, the provenance of these stories suggests that their currency is now largely intra-ethnic, among Jews themselves.

Senator Mitch McConnell put it. Americans, he observed, had developed a "mad romance ... with the civil litigation process." "[Q]uite simply, everyone is suing everyone and most are getting big money."[36] Columnist Jack Anderson reported that "[a]cross the country, people are suing one another with abandon: courts are clogged with litigation; lawyers are burdening the populace with legal bills."[37]

Not only was overuse of the legal system no longer confined to ethnic outsiders, but observations about it had shifted from jokes, which rely on depictions of deviance, to legends which portray the expected rather than the surprising.[38]

III. Jokes about Jewish Lawyers

The conniving claimant jokes were about Jewish litigants, not Jewish lawyers. In the course of the last thirty years, jokes about lawyers have become more numerous, more hostile, and more visible. The lawyers in lawyer jokes tend to be generic, undifferentiated by ethnicity, location, firm size, or specialty. In the world of lawyer jokes, there is no reflection of the changing composition of the increasingly diverse profession; lawyers in jokes are almost always white male private practitioners of no discernible ethnicity. There are no government lawyers (apart from judges and an occasional prosecutor), no in-house corporate lawyers, no legal services or public interest lawyers.[39] Almost without exception, the lawyers in the jokes are in small practices, not large law firms, and represent individual clients, not large impersonal corporations. In contrast, most of what real world lawyers do is supply services to these organizational clients rather than to individuals and increasingly they practice in large aggregations. In the jokes, there is little discernible hierarchy among lawyers who (with few exceptions) relate to one another as peers. Differentials in prosperity and prestige are invisible.

The jokes pay little heed to ethnic identity. There are no jokes (known to me) about African American or Hispanic lawyers (although the older jokes are full of African American clients, usually criminal defendants, and wit-

---

[36] 132 Cong. Rec. S948 (daily ed., February 4, 1986) (statement made on previous day).

[37] Jack Anderson, "U.S. Has Become a Nation of Lawsuits," *Washington Post*, January 25, 1985, B8.

[38] On legends, see Marc Galanter, "An Oil Strike in Hell: Contemporary Legends about the Civil Justice System," *Arizona Law Review* 40 (1988): 717–52; William Haltom and Michael McCann, *Distorting the Law: Politics, Media, and the Litigation Crisis* (Chicago: University of Chicago Press, 2004).

[39] In 2005, under 10% of American lawyers worked for some governmental body (this includes judges); under 9% worked for private entities. Less than 2% were public defenders, legal aid or public interest lawyers. More than three quarters of active lawyers were in private practice, up from about 68% a quarter century earlier. Clara Carson, ed., *The Lawyer Statistical Report: The U.S. Legal Profession in 2005* (Chicago: American Bar Foundation, 2012), 5.

nesses).⁴⁰ In older versions of some jokes, lawyers were occasionally identified by obviously Jewish or Irish surnames, but jokes in which the point turns on ethnic identity are extremely rare.

In my research on the history of lawyer jokes, I turned up only a handful of jokes that turn on the lawyer's Jewish identity, none of them in circulation today. The earliest depicts professional collaboration between two of the country's most prominent lawyers. This version was published in 1905.

> #6. *A story is told at the expense of Joseph Choate, the great lawyer, now ambassador to the Court of St. James.*⁴¹ *On a very important case, Edward Lauterbach, an eminent Jewish attorney, was associated with him. They won their case and when it came to deciding upon the fee, Mr. Choate, the Christian, asked Mr. Lauterbach, the Jew, what he thought they ought to charge. Mr. Lauterbach said he thought $5,000 would be a fair charge. Mr. Choate replied that it shouldn't be less than $15,000. Said Mr. Lauterbach: "Almost thou persuadest me to be a Christian."*⁴²

The mocking reference to the Jew tempted to abandon his religion to enjoy the greater fees of a Christian lawyer is obvious, but the Jewish lawyer's response is ironic—as if to say you guys say we are out for a buck and drive a hard bargain, but behind your cloak of respectability you outdo us.⁴³ Note that the compiler read the joke contemporaneously as "at the expense of . . . Choate."

Another joke, that appears in print only once, as part of a famous 1928 "underground" collection, is worth noting:

---

⁴⁰ Google searches for "Black lawyer joke," "Hispanic lawyer joke," and "Irish lawyer joke" produced zero responses; "Italian lawyer joke" found only an Italian version of a joke well known in the English-speaking world in which the lawyer butt has no discernible ethnic identity.

⁴¹ Joseph H. Choate (1832–1917), prominent lawyer and after-dinner speaker, was the U.S. Ambassador to Great Britain from 1899 to 1905, when this joke was first recorded, and subsequently President of the New York County Lawyers Association He was the cousin of Rufus Choate (1799–1859), an equally famous lawyer of an earlier day. Edward Lauterbach (1844–1923) was prominent as a lawyer for railroads and street railway companies and as a figure in public life and Jewish affairs. He was a vice-president of the Ethical Culture Society.

⁴² *Wit and Humor of the American Bar* (Philadelphia: George W. Jacobs & Co., 1905), 144.

⁴³ The famous original of the punchline is the response of Agrippa (i.e., Marcus Julius Agrippa, 28–92 C.E., grandson of Herod) to Paul's account of his conversion (Acts 26:28), which was the fount of innumerable sermons about "The Almost Christian" (e.g., by John Wesley). To a Jewish source contemporaneous with the first appearance of the joke "the utterance attributed to... [Agrippa] is evidently to be taken as a jest." "Agrippa II," *Jewish Encyclopedia* (1901), 1:271–72.

> #7. Cohen and Murphy had been partners for twenty years when suddenly Cohen got it into his head that he wanted to be in business by himself.
>
> "I don't know, Murph," he said. "I ain't got nottin' against you, but I'd like to try for myself. So I made up my mind we should split."
>
> Murphy accepted his decision gracefully.
>
> "Of course," he said, "we'll part friends."
>
> "Positively the best," said Cohen. "And now let's call in Feldman, our lawyer, and have him draw up the dissolution papers."
>
> Feldman, when he heard the news, was grief-stricken. "After twenty years," he moaned. "Of course, I'm getting paid for doing this, but nothing hurts me so much as to have to draw up these papers breaking up this fine partnership. But, Cohen, since you made up your mind, as the Latin phrase has it, yens de goy [screw the gentile]."[44]

Although it admits of various readings, one that is close to the surface is the classical canard about Jews as clannish outsiders who will betray others and favor their own. Realizing the worst nightmares of those elite lawyers who scorned Jews as incapable of disinterested professionalism, the lawyer here subverts professional norms in favor of narrow ethnic loyalty. We don't know who told this joke or with what intent. All we know is that it did not survive and was not replaced by other jokes about "clannish" or unethical Jewish lawyers.

Although such images haunted the bar worthies who decried Jewish entry to the profession, curiously these images did not spawn jokes about Jewish lawyers. The animus against Jews in the profession projected by their rivals at the establishment bar was not matched by the wider public who might admire or even seek out "a smart Jewish lawyer."

These are literally the only jokes about Jewish lawyers that I found dating from before World War II. As lawyer jokes multiplied in the latter part of the century, jokes about Jewish lawyers were even less abundant. Two of those reflect surprised reactions to Jewish and Gentile lawyers practicing together.

---

[44] *Anecdota Americana* (1928), item 361 (the original "dirty" Anecdota, republished "in slightly different form" as *The Classic Book of Dirty Jokes: Anecdota American* (New York: Bell Publishing Co., 1981)). The original *Anecdota Americana* is available online at http://www.immortalia.com/html/books-and-manuscripts/1920s/1927-anecdota-americana/index.htm (visited Aug. 28, 2006). "Yens" (or "yentz" or "yents") carries the same double meaning of "to copulate" and "to cheat or exploit" as the English "screw" and "fuck." See Leo Rosten, *The Joys of Yinglish* (New York: Penguin Books, 1989), 551.

> #8.   Algernon Montmorency needed a reliable law firm to represent him in a case he had pending. So he went to look for one and soon saw a firm — O'Brien, O'Ryan, O'Hara and Finkelman. He went in to see one of the firm. He was shown to O'Ryan's office and there he had a long talk with him. Finally Algernon arose and said, "O'Ryan before I give you the case there is one thing I'd like to ask. How did Finkelman get into this firm?"
>
> "Oh," said O'Ryan, "he represents the finance company. That's the only way we could keep the furniture."

This curious story, which surfaced in print in 1956, before the era of "integration," combines a suggestion of Jewish intrusiveness and economic blackmail with a hint of Gentile or Irish incompetence or mismanagement.[45]

A story of Jewish provenance, contemporaneous with integration, suggests that Jewish lawyers are underappreciated in the firm hierarchy although they are more proficient and their efforts may be "carrying" their Gentile colleagues:

> #9.   Jackson, Waybrook, Buchanan and Isaacs was one of the finest law firms in the city. One day a friend of Eli Isaacs asked, "Why does your name appear last, Eli? Everyone knows that Jackson is ga-ga. Waybrook spends most of his time in the country, and Buchanan never won a case in court. Your name should be first."
>
> "You forget something," Isaacs smiled.
>
> "What's that?"
>
> "My clients read from right to left."[46]

A more recent appearance by a Jewish lawyer provides no sense that the Jewish dimension is particularly salient in the animus against lawyers. Even where the Jewish lawyer appears in a lawyer joke, not much is made of his Jewish identity.[47]

---

[45] Jerry Lieberman, *Off the Cuff ... From the Private Collection of Joe Laurie, Jr.* (New York: Pocket Books, Inc., 1956), 91. The only subsequent publication I have found is an Indian publication that appropriates this verbatim almost 40 years later in Gratian Vas, *A Consignment of Business Jokes* (New Delhi: Sterling Publishers, 1994).

[46] Leo Rosten, *Leo Rosten's Giant Book of Laughter* (New York: Crown Publishers, 1985), 298; *Topol's Treasure of Jewish Humor, Wit and Wisdom* (New York: Barricade Books, 1995), 165.

[47] I do not regard #10 as a joke about a "Jewish lawyer," for the Jewishness enters through the attribution of thoroughness to Jewish communal fundraising; the qualities displayed by the lawyer (rich, clever, self-serving) are exactly those attributed to lawyers in general and derive nothing from the lawyer's Jewishness.

#10. A local Jewish Federation office realized that it had never received a donation from the town's most successful lawyer. The campaign director called the lawyer to persuade him to contribute: "Our research shows that out of a yearly income of at least $500,000, you give not a penny to tzedaka [charity]. Wouldn't you like to give back to the community in some way?"

The lawyer mulled this over for a moment and replied: "First, did your research also show that my mother is dying after a long illness, and has medical bills that are several times her annual income?"

Embarrassed, the Federation person mumbled, "Um.... No."

The lawyer continued: "Or that my brother, a disabled veteran, is blind and confined to a wheelchair?"

The stricken Federation worker began to stammer out an apology.

The lawyer interrupted her apology, saying: "or that my sister's husband died in a traffic accident," the lawyer's voice rising in indignation, "leaving her penniless with three children?!"

The humiliated Campaign director, completely beaten, said simply, "I had no idea...."

On a roll, the lawyer cut her off once again: "So, if I don't give any money to them, why should I give any money to you?"[48]

This is actually an old Jewish joke about a rich man that migrated from its old country setting, underwent Americanization, and finally had the Jewish element effaced entirely. The switch to a lawyer comes in 1991, just when lawyers (or at least the upper echelons of the profession) were becoming increasingly and visibly affluent—a condition noted with displeasure by many.[49] In this 1997 version it is re-Judaized from the United Way to the Jewish Federation. The lawyer reveals his appalling indifference to family, but this is less an accusation that lawyers or Jews neglect their families than

---

[48] Jhumor List, December 8, 1997.

[49] Peter D. Hart Research Associates, *A Survey of Attitudes Nationwide Towards Lawyers and the Legal System* (1993), 14. In 1993, the Hart survey found that 63% of respondents thought that lawyers make too much money. Only 14% disagreed and 23% were neutral. 59% thought lawyers were greedy and only 19% disagreed. Ibid. (Curiously, the pollsters found "no relationship between unfavorable opinions of lawyers and perceptions of how much lawyers earn." Ibid., 15.) Although there was wide variation in respondents' estimates of lawyers' earnings, the median guess of the public fell very close to the median revealed by a concurrent 1992 survey of ABA members' income (about $90,000). Ibid.

a convenient conventional measure of moral callousness.[50] The story also affords a showcase for the lawyer to display his rhetorical skill and turn the tables on the intrusive fundraiser. Does this tell us anything about perceptions of the Jewish lawyer—that Jewish lawyers are regarded as less charitable than Gentile lawyers? I don't think so.

Of course it is possible that the animus against Jewish lawyers is codified in stories about "shysters" and "ambulance chasers." (A false etymology links the term "shyster" to Jewish lawyers. In fact, the term, which goes back to the 1850s, antedates the visible presence of Jews in the American bar—which of course does not exclude the possibility that some users or hearers may make the association).[51] The campaigns against the evils of ambulance-chasing were dominated by "concern about names" and often focused on exposing Jewish attorneys as the chief perpetrators of unethical practices.[52] There is hardly a trace of this in contemporary "ambulance" jokes,[53] but some "Jewish" jokes use the ambulance-chasing script:

#11. *What's a Jewish Nativity scene?*
       Seven lawyers surrounding a car crash.[54]

The current campaigns to delegitimize "trial lawyers" and "contingency fee lawyers" never invoke the ethnic motif, but it is possible that some in the audience find sufficient cues to awaken the older stereotypes.

The absence of animus against Jewish lawyers in the jokes reflects wider public perceptions. A survey conducted in 2002 presented respondents with eight statements about negative Jewish behavior or influence (Jews killed Christ, have too much influence on Wall Street, care only about themselves, etc.).[55] The statement that "Jewish lawyers are more unscrupulous" elicited agreement from 14% of respondents and disagreement from 76%.[56] This

---

[50] This joke echoes the themes present in a prominent set of jokes that emphasize betrayal of those to whom there are special obligations. See Galanter, *Lowering the Bar,* ch. 7.

[51] On the derivation of the term from the German *Scheisser,* and the shift from its original meaning of bumbling incompetent to sleazy trickster, see Gerald Leonard Cohen, *The Origins of the Term "Shyster"* (Frankfurt am Main: Peter Lang, 1982); James Clapp, Elizabeth Thornburg, Marc Galanter, and Fred Shapiro, *Lawtalk: The Unknown Stories Behind Familiar Legal Expressions* (New Haven: Yale University Press, 2011), 236–42. In any event, the term shyster rarely appears in jokes.

[52] Dornstein, *Accidentally on Purpose,* 142, 146.

[53] E.g., "My lawyer had a bad accident./An ambulance backed over him," in Michael Rafferty, *Skid Marks: Common Jokes About Lawyers* (Bolinas, CA: Shelter, 1988), 86. For other specimens, see Galanter, *Lowering the Bar,* 119.

[54] Julius Alvin, *Excruciatingly Gross Jokes: Vol. X* (New York: Zebra Books, 1993), 1.

[55] Gary A. Tobin and Sid Groeneman, *Anti-Semitic Beliefs in the United States* (San Francisco: Institute for Jewish and Community Research, 2003).

[56] Ibid., 16. The authors point out that "The wording of the statement affected the results: While 10% agree that Jewish lawyers are a little more dishonest and unscrupulous, nearly twice as many (19%) disagreed with the converse of that wording—that Jewish lawyers are no more dishonest or unscrupulous. The results average out to 14%." Ibid., 16 n. 2.

was tied (with "Jewish media executives cause immorality") for the lowest score of the eight statements. "Too much influence on Wall Street," for example, commanded 34% agreement.[57] Among those who harbor hostile images of Jews, Jewish lawyers are not a prominent part of their repertoire of grievances.

The few expressions that single out Jewish lawyers for special condemnation tend to be part of larger webs of conspiratorial beliefs that Jews not only promoted Hitler, but foisted social security and racial integration on Americans. The contention that makes America "an extremely litigious society ... stems directly from all of the 'diversity' and multiculturalism foisted on us by our Hebrew friends." For this writer "...the American legal system, including our courts and our law schools, is thoroughly dominated by the tribe of Judah."[58] He clearly identifies Jewish lawyers as the source of evil in the legal profession[59] and suggests that contemporary "'lawyer' jokes started out as a code word for 'Jew jokes.'"[60] I cite him at such length because he gives full expression to a literal equation of lawyers with Jews for which there is very little evidence in the wider popular or folk culture.

IV. The Migration of Jewish Jokes

Although ethnic characters appear in jokes about clients, defendants, and witnesses, the stories about lawyers are ethnically undifferentiated. There are no visible jokes about Irish, Polish, African American, Hispanic, or Asian lawyers. It is the traits of the lawyer per se, not the differences among lawyers, that engage the tellers and listeners. At the same time the

---

There was little variance by demographic categories, except that those with the least formal education were more inclined to be negative (17%) about Jewish lawyers. Ibid., 16–17.

[57] The authors cite a comparable (16%) response to a similar item on another survey ("Jews are more willing than others to use shady practices to get what they want") as suggesting the reliability of this measure of "the stereotype of the deceptive, cunning Jew." Ibid., at 17.

[58] Richard Brooks, "Ten Truths, Part III," *Whitealert.com*, June 18, 2004, at www.whitealert.com/ten_truths3.htm. These fantasies of domination entail an exaggerated version of the overestimate of Jewish presence: Brooks thinks that most law textbook authors are Jewish and that "roughly fifty percent of both students and faculty" in American law schools are Jews; "this Jewish percentage is skewed even higher at the more prestigious law schools...."

[59] Ibid. He would emend the famous Shakespeare line to say "'Kill all the Jewish lawyers!' *No Jews. Just right!* is a slogan particularly appropriate for the legal profession. Who knows? If we first got rid of all the Jewish lawyers, maybe we wouldn't have to kill any more Jews!" At the same time he says "If you excluded all the Jews from it, the legal profession would be accorded the highest respect and esteem by our citizenry."

[60] Ibid.: "Everyone routinely laughs at jokes which compare lawyers unfavorably to sharks and dead rattlesnakes and this is one area of public discourse where a little bit of anti-semitism is quietly tolerated. You can say 'shyster' or even 'jew lawyer' without raising too many eyebrows, because the public instinctively recognizes the heavy Jewish influence in the law. In fact, I suspect that 'lawyer jokes' started out as a code word for 'Jew jokes.'"

world of lawyer jokes has expanded by absorbing jokes that were earlier told about different ethnic groups. There are also numerous switches from jokes about groups that are stereotyped as dumb (Irish, Poles) or undesirable (Mexicans, African Americans), as well as from politicians, spouses, and mothers-in-law.

The Jewish connection in the great surge of lawyer jokes is not from the now dried-up stream of conniving claimant jokes, nor from the extremely rare (and almost entirely defunct) jokes about Jewish lawyers. Instead it is from a migration of large numbers of "Jewish jokes," i.e., jokes that had been told largely about Jews, into the lawyer joke corpus.

Jokes for the most part do not belong exclusively to a single group or topic. They are constantly being switched to new targets. A joke about politicians, Texans, Jews, or mothers-in-law may be revamped into a joke about lawyers. It should be emphasized that switching is selective rather than indiscriminate. Some attempted switches just don't "take" and disappear from view; others flourish and may grow more prominent than the original version. But what "takes" is not controlled by the teller or writer; it has to strike a responsive chord in the listeners/readers. So just which items negotiate the transition from their original subjects to new ones tells us something about social perceptions. For example, jokes about Jews as devious and untrustworthy partners have been readily revamped as jokes about lawyers, but none of the many Jewish jokes about extended and precarious chains of "talmudic" reasoning has made a successful transition, even though we might suppose they would fit with the many jokes about lawyers' peculiarities of discourse.[61] But once a joke has been successfully switched, those who encounter it in its new raiment may be unaware of its origin and perceive it as native to, and emblematic of, its new setting.

The largest cluster of Jew-to-lawyer switches is in a series of jokes depicting betrayal.

> #12. *An ancient, nearly blind old woman retained the local lawyer to draft her last will and testament, for which he charged her two hundred dollars. As she rose to leave, she took the money out of her purse and handed it over, enclosing a third hundred-dollar bill by mistake. Immediately the attorney realized he was faced with a crushing ethical question: Should he tell his partner?*[62]

---

[61] For the partner switches, see Galanter, *Lowering the Bar*, ch. 6. In the course of a discussion of the limits of "switchability," Davies, "Jewish Jokes, Anti-Semitic Jokes, and Hebridonian Jokes," in *Jewish Humor*, ed. Abner Ziv (New Brunswick: Transaction Books, 1986), 76, observes that "[t]here is . . . a significant stock of Jewish jokes, particularly those deriving their humor from a distinctively Jewish use of indirect and elliptical but relentlessly consistent reasoning that perhaps could be adapted to fit the circumstances of another group but in practice rarely are."

[62] Blanche Knott, *Truly Tasteless Lawyer Jokes* (New York: St. Martin's Paperbacks, 1990), 73.

This widely-circulated story depicts the lawyer's unhesitating victimization of the trusting client, here one specified as particularly vulnerable, an old, nearly blind woman. The neat twist is that he completely misses the ethical violation against the client while sensing an ethical problem in concealing this rip-off from his partner—implying that the latter, as a fellow vulture, would happily share these ill-gotten gains.

This became a lawyer joke only in 1990 after a long career as a joke about the (usually Jewish) merchant instructing his son in business ethics.[63] But where the merchant's advice was hypothetical (i.e., suppose a customer overpaid) the lawyer joke from the start has been a narrative of past events; what is depicted is not just a larcenous inclination but a history of betrayal of the vulnerable.

As *The Extra $100 Bill* suggests, it is touch-and-go whether the bonds of partnership can restrain the lawyer's proclivity to take advantage of the vulnerable. Once this trait is acknowledged, fellowship is tinged with suspicion:

> #13. *The two partners in a law firm were having lunch when suddenly one of them jumped up and said, "I have to go back to the office - I forgot to lock the safe!" The other partner replied, "What are you worried about? We're both here."*[64]

Again, this is an old joke, recorded as early as 1922, about (usually Jewish) business partners that first appears as a lawyer joke in 1989.[65]

Even where there is generosity and sharing, it cannot withstand the imperative of self-interest:

> #14. *John and Joe had been law partners for many years, sharing everything, most especially the affections of their libidinous secretary, Rose. One morning, an agitated*

---

[63] Starting no later than Schermerhorn, *Schermerhorn's Stories*, 144, this story is overwhelmingly told about Jewish characters, although there are some non-denominational clothiers, and an occasional Scot.

[64] *Unnamed Collection of Lawyer Jokes from Internet* (1994), No. 80 [on file with author]. Other lawyer versions are found in Wallace O. Chariton, *Texas Wit & Wisdom* (Plano: Wordware Publishing, Inc., 1989), 201; *Nolo's Favorite Lawyer Jokes CD-ROM* (Berkeley, CA: Nolo Press, 1993); Jess M. Brallier, *Lawyers and Other Reptiles II: The Appeal* (Chicago: Contemporary Books, 1996), 8; *The Lawyer Joke-A-Day Calendar* [for 1997], Sept. 5; Lowell D. Streiker, *An Encyclopedia of Humor* (Peabody: Hendrickson Publishers, 1998), 264; *Lawyer Jokes, Quotes and Anecdotes 2002 Calendar* (Kansas City: Andrews McMeel Publishing, 2001), July 29.

[65] The first appearances refer to partners in a well-known Stock Exchange house (Thomas L. Masson, ed., *The Best Stories in the World* (s.l.: Doubleday, Page & Co., 1922 (original publication, 1913)), 96; Marion Dix Mosher, ed., *More Toasts: Jokes Stories and Quotations* (New York: H. W. Wilson Co., 1922), 374; *Laughter* (New York: Theodore R. Ernst, 1925), 57, but starting with Schermerhorn, *Schermerhorn's Stories*, 276, the characters are almost invariably Jewish and continue to be so. Once the lawyers arrive, almost no other new identities are specified.

> *John came to Joe with the bad news, "Rose is pregnant! We're going to be a father!" Joe, the more reserved of the two, calmed his partner and reminded him that things could be much worse. They were both well-off, and could easily afford the costs of raising the child. Rose would have the best care available, her child would attend only the finest schools, and neither would want for anything. The child would have the benefit of having two fathers, both of which [sic] were caring and well-educated. Gradually, John got used to the idea of fatherhood. When the big day came, both were at the hospital awaiting the news of their offspring's birth. Finally, John could take no more and went outside to take a walk. When he returned an hour later, Joe had the news. "We had twins," said Joe, "and mine died."*[66]

This first appears as a lawyer joke in 1988 after at least sixty years as a story about business partners (once again often Jewish).[67] This version is distinctive in its buildup of the generosity and sharing of the lawyers which is rudely punctured by the individualistic shift from "we" to "mine." The bonds of partnership and intimacy fail to constrain the lawyer's selfishness and opportunism.

Many jokes are built around the rule of three, involving characters who represent a sequence of three occupations, nationalities, or religions. Frequently the lawyer in the occupational triad replaces the Jew or rabbi in the ethnic or religious triad.[68] An excellent example is a story that I regard as the most interesting of all lawyer jokes.

> *#15. A very wealthy man, old and desperately ill, summons to his bedside his three closest advisors: his doctor, his priest, and his lawyer. "I know," he says, "they say 'you can't take it with you.' But who knows? Suppose they're mistaken. I'd like to have something, just in case. So I am giving each of you an envelope containing one*

---

[66] *Lawyer Jokes from Internet 1994*, no. 139 (on file with author; substantially identical to Sid Behrman, *The Lawyer Joke Book* (New York: Dorset Press, 1991), 16).

[67] The first version, about jewelry partners (*Anecdota Americana*, item 269) had none of the amity and cooperation of this version ("In their fright each tried to lay the onus of parenthood on the other."). Of course, there has been a dramatic reduction in the "onus" of out-of-wedlock birth in the past seventy years, so that the element of danger and shame is less salient. Versions about partners in stereotypically Jewish businesses or with stereotypically Jewish names remain current: Milton Berle, *Milton Berle's Private Joke File* (New York: Crown Trade Paperbacks, 1989), 285, 495; Phillip Adams and Patrice Newall, *The Penguin Book of Australian Jokes* (Ringwood: Penguin Books Australia, 1995), 87; Julius Alvin, *Savagely Gross Jokes: Vol. X-XI* (New York: Zebra Books, 1995), 9. Again, no new protagonists have emerged other than lawyers.

[68] See generally Alan Dundes, "The Number Three in American Culture," in *Every Man His Way: Readings in Cultural Anthropology*, ed. Alan Dundes (Englewood Cliffs, N.J.: Prentice-Hall, 1968).

hundred thousand dollars and I would be grateful if at my funeral you would put the envelope in my coffin, so that if it turns out that it's useful, I'll have something." They each agree to carry out his wish.

Sure enough, after just a few weeks, the old man passes away. At his funeral, each of the three advisors is seen slipping something into the coffin. After the burial, as the three are walking away together, the doctor turns to the other two and says, "Friends, I have a confession to make. As you know, at the hospital we are desperate because of the cutbacks in funding. Our CATSCAN machine broke down and we haven't been able to get a new one. So, I took $20,000 of our friend's money for a new CATSCAN and put the rest of it in the coffin as he asked."

At this the priest says, "I, too, have a confession to make. As you know, our church is simply overwhelmed by the problem of the homeless. The needs keep increasing and we have nowhere to turn. So I took $50,000 from the envelope for our homeless fund and put the rest in the coffin as our friend requested."

Fixing the other two in his gaze, the lawyer says, "I am astonished and deeply disappointed that you would treat so casually our solemn undertaking to our friend. I want you to know that I placed in his coffin my personal check for the full one hundred thousand dollars.[69]

The Check in the Coffin in something like this form has been circulating since at least 1876, often but not exclusively as a joke about Jews.[70] The first lawyer version appeared in 1964, and only in the 1980s did lawyer versions

---

[69] Oral tradition (collected by the author, Madison, WI, 1990).

[70] The earliest version I have found is in "Facetiae," *Harper's Bazaar* 9 (1876): 352, reprinted in Rudolf Glanz, *The Jew in Early American Wit and Graphic Humor* (New York: KTAV Publishing House, 1973), 246–47. The trail breaks off at this point, but many features of the story are anticipated by a medieval exemplum about a miser who wants to take his gold with him:

> "A certain usurer of Metz, drawing near unto his death, bound his Friends by oath, that in his grave they should put a purse full of Money, under his head; which [was] done accordingly. His sepulcher [being] afterwards opened, that it might be taken out, there was seen a Devil pouring melting gold down his throat with a ladle." (*The Philosopher's Banquet*, 1614, reprinted in Carew W. Hazlitt, *Shakespeare Jest-Books: Reprints of the Early and Very Rare Jest-Books Supposed to have been Used by Shakespeare*, 3 vols. (London, 1864), vol. 3, item 21. I have modernized the spelling.)

Here it is the deceased that is the object of derision, not one of the survivors. But it displays many of the same elements: the refusal to leave wealth to others and insistence on taking it with; the enlistment of friends to carry out the scheme; the means of deposit in the grave; the result of torment by the devil is replaced by frustration/betrayal by the clever Jew and then by the lawyer, both figures long associated with the devil in the popular imagination.

outnumber Jewish ones.[71] The lawyer combines greed, formalism, manipulation, and betrayal. He is a too-clever deceiver who betrays his client and outdoes his friends by a kind of crazy literalness. The betrayal is done in good form, but form is employed to undermine substance. On the surface the lawyer complies fully with the request. But his compliance is achieved by a daring extension of the conventional equation of check with cash that sabotages the intent of the promise—at the same time that it confirms and extends the zany logic of the deceased, for why should an afterlife where U.S. dollars are honored lack facilities for negotiating a check?

The lawyer's abysmal performance as a trustee is combined with adroit gamesmanship and moral pretension. The doctor and the priest divert part of the money for unimpeachably good causes, but they are guilt-stricken and apologetic. The lawyer appropriates it *all*, and for himself rather than for charitable purposes, and he makes no apologies—in fact, he reproaches them for betrayal and presents himself as the one who faithfully honored the old man's trust. Ironically, the arch deviant uses his formal but empty compliance to claim the most complete fulfillment of duty.

Still, I think this joke is permeated by admiration for the lawyer. The doctor and the priest are hesitant, inhibited do-gooders who end up wasting a lot of human treasure. If they believe the deceased's crazy premise, they are perpetrating an awful betrayal. If they don't believe it, they are foolish, wasteful, crippled by their conscientiousness. In contrast with their hesitant virtue, we have the lawyer's clear, decisive assertion of self-interest. He doesn't believe it and he is free of the inhibiting sentimentality of the others. They really don't believe it either, but they can't face up to the virtue of betrayal. It is the lawyer's unblinking rationality, beneath the guise of compliance, that stuns us. As David Riesman observed, lawyers "are feared and disliked—but needed—because of their matter-of-factness, their sense of relevance, their refusal to be impressed by magical 'solutions' to people's problems."[72]

So, the lawyer is at once a disastrous failure as a trustee, an adroit con artist—and a model of how to deal with irrational demands, in contrast to the megalomania of the deceased and the sentimental paralysis of the other advisors.[73] The deceased, by denying death, would destroy resources that

---

[71] Rabbis remained the protagonists of this escalating altruism version: Hugh Cruikshank, Jr., *The Alaska Book of Jokes* (Bird Creek, AK: Fourth and Feather Productions, 1987), 91; David C. Gross, *Laughing Through the Years: A New Treasury of Jewish Humor* (New York: Walker & Co., 1991), 63; Henry Eilbirt, *What is a Jewish Joke? An Excursion Into Jewish Humor* (Northvale, N.J.: Jason Aronson), 109; Brian Keelan, *The Joy of the Joke* (Toronto: KAV Publishing, 1999), 182.

[72] David Riesman, "Toward an Anthropological Science of Law and the Legal Profession," in *Individualism Reconsidered and Other Essays* (Glencoe, IL: Free Press, 1954), 450.

[73] The analysis that follows is inspired by Richard Raskin's wonderful *Life is Like a Glass of Tea: Studies of Classic Jewish Jokes* (Philadelphia: Jewish Publication Society, 1992), in which he develops three "interpretive frameworks" that he finds "useful for understanding many classical Jewish jokes." The first is *role fiasco* in which a character displays outrageous incompetence in: (a) performing or sustaining a given role; (b)

should be left to the living. Where the doctor and the priest "balance" the claims of the deceased and of the living, the lawyer embraces the claims of the living. But ironically his unabashed assertion of the claims of the living benefits only himself, while the hesitant assertions of the doctor and the priest do benefit deserving others.

The verdict on the lawyer here is complex: it is the lawyer that has the wit to see through sham, the courage to ignore it, and the resourcefulness to figure a way to do it adroitly. At the same time, he lacks a saving common sentimentality, ignores obligations to others, and acts solely to his own advantage. The lawyer is someone with qualities we would want on our side. He is a very desirable ally, but one with a dangerous propensity to abandon those who rely upon him.

I regard *The Check in the Coffin* as the most complex and sophisticated of current jokes about lawyers. Driven by the dying man's heroic denial of death, its basic premise is one that is engaging, immediately recognizable, that has a long historic pedigree, and that, at some level, tempts us into wishing there was something to it. The other friends' diversion of some of the funds to altruistic uses introduces the possibility that there may be some virtue in betrayal. The lawyer then outdoes them in diversion but makes no attempt to match their rationale of an offsetting obligation. The theme of escalating altruistic diversion provides the perfect foil for the depiction of the lawyer as supplied with an excess of penetrating rationality and a deficiency of fellow feeling. We are presented with two competing but incomplete forms of exemplary deviance: the friends act on a vision of higher uses for the treasure, but stumble because they are sentimental; the lawyer fully surmounts the irrationality of the deceased and the sentimentality of the friends, but disappoints because his clear-sighted rationality is entirely devoid of the benevolence that makes the friends endearing. We are shown a world in which the components of an exemplary response to the megalomania of the deceased—rationality and benevolence—are separately embodied in flawed carriers. All the needed pieces are present, but an

---

assessing what behavior or attitude a given situation calls for; or (c) thinking logically and realistically (ibid., 23). A second comic perspective is *tactical manoeuvre* in which the character is essentially a player who is out to get away with something, to pull something off, to evade a responsibility, to get more than his share of something he wants, to get the better of, or turn the tables on, someone else, to get around a prohibition, etc. (ibid., 24). The third framework is *exemplary deviance* in which the comic behavior on display in the punch-line is seen as a positive model we are implicitly invited to admire and emulate, even though it marks a break with conventional codes (ibid., 24). Thus we have outrageous failure to perform, crafty gamesmanship, and admirable deviance. Many lawyer jokes invoke one of these directly or indirectly. Raskin thinks that jokes that can be "understood in two (or three) of [these] perspectives . . . are the very best of the classic ... [Jewish jokes]" because they generate an experience of 'oscillation' between two (or more) interpretive options" (ibid., 29). For those who embrace such experiences, jokes that have this "open-endedness or reversibility ... have an inexhaustible richness..." (ibid., 30). This *Take it With You* version of *The Check in the Coffin* is the only lawyer joke I have encountered that invites analysis in all three of these perspectives.

optimum solution eludes us because of the deformation attendant to each specialized virtue. The lawyer embodies part of what we want, but he brings it to us fused with a self-centeredness we disdain (and embrace).

V. Changing Places

In *The Check in the Coffin* (#15) and many other jokes we see the lawyer replace the Jew as the canny fellow using calculation, formality, and clever interpretation to undermine the shared understanding of others. Lawyer jokes like this one have a Jewish resonance not because they are about Jewish lawyers or about Jews but because in important respects the Jew and the lawyer are the same figure—canny, learned, calculating, set apart from the moral consensus of others, and able to examine its accepted understandings with a skeptical eye. The contemporary anti-lawyerism that resents the pervasive presence of bureaucracy and regulation is a cousin to the rejection of Jews because of their adherence to a worldly legalism. Both violate the Pauline condemnation of earthly technical law (i.e., Pharisaism) as a violation of our humanity. The Jew is condemned for legalism and when the lawyer steps into his place, some of the same grievances and anxieties are mobilized. The scripts and tropes with a long history of service in disparaging Jews can readily be conscripted for attacks on lawyers. It is not that anti-lawyerism is antisemitism in disguise; it is that they have a deep-seated ideological affinity. In a brilliant analysis, Jay Michaelson concludes that "antilawyerism is like antisemitism without Jews."[74] It is not about Jewish lawyers, "it is about the Jewishness of the law itself."[75]

The jokes confirm the affinity of the figures of lawyer and Jew, but they also suggest that although they are kindred, their careers in popular consciousness have different trajectories. Joke scholarship documents the near universal occurrence of "dumb" jokes in which members of an ethnic or regional group (e.g., Poles, hillbillies, Newfies in Canada, Irish in Britain, Belgians in France and Holland, etc.) are depicted as stupid, slow-witted, incapable of coping with the complexities of modern life.[76] Most joke traditions also include jokes about groups that are "canny," smart, tricky, calculating, resourceful. Jews and Scots are the subject of "canny" jokes throughout much of the world, but they are joined by New England Yankees in the U.S., Catalans in Spain, Armenians in Greece and Iran, Gujaratis in India, Ibos in Nigeria, and many others.[77] Many lawyer jokes, like *The Check in the*

---

[74] Jay Michaelson, "The Religious Mistrust of Law: Anti-Legalism, Anti-Judaism, and the Problem of the Soul" (manuscript on file with the author). See also the previous chapter of this volume.

[75] Ibid.

[76] The classic account is Christie Davies, *Ethnic Humor Around the World: A Comparative Analysis* (Bloomington: Indiana University Press, 1990).

[77] For an extended list of the targets of stupid and canny jokes in dozens of locations, see Christie Davies, *The Mirth of Nations* (New Brunswick, N.J.: Transaction Publishers, 2002).

Coffin, are 'canny' jokes. In fact, most of the jokes presented above fit into that category. I noted above that jokes are often switched from one sort of protagonist to another and many current lawyer jokes had long pre-histories as jokes about Jews. Lawyers can be readily substituted in many Jewish jokes. And there is some backwash in which contemporary lawyer jokes are switched into jokes about Jews.[78]

So our analysis might suggest that lawyers and Jews are converging. But I believe the pattern is more complex. Not all canny figures are the same. Scots, for example, are typically depicted as tight, clever, and calculating, but not as malign or threatening or alien—they are an amusing part of the local tapestry. The Jew, on the other hand, is often a different type of canny figure—clever and calculating, but a stranger, an alien in the midst of a host population. This kind of canny figure is what Christie Davies calls the "excluded enterpriser," not part of a benign indigenous canny group but a stranger whose cleverness is associated with deceit, cowardice, and disloyalty.[79]

Over the past half century, the Jews who populate American jokes have moved away from the excluded enterpriser category to become a canny group more akin to Scots and Yankees, different but not outside the imagined moral community. Lawyers, on the other hand, have lost moral standing—they are frequently portrayed not only as tricky and clever but as malign and destructive. So, in effect, lawyers and Jews have exchanged places; Jews are less envisioned as the "other" and have moved toward becoming a tolerated domestic group.[80] Lawyers, from being a familiar presence whose peccadillos were an object of fun, have become more alien and threatening, more akin to Davies' excluded entrepreneurs.

VI. The Arrival of the Future

Of course, this is not the final chapter. Jokes, legends, reputations, and perceptions are labile, and changing, but there are continuities and recurrences, too. Here is a (nearly) 500 year old woodcut that illustrates both the affinity of lawyers and Jews and anticipates the kaleidoscopic rearrangement of the filaments that connect them.

---

[78] Harry Leichter's *Jewish Humor, Jewish Humor Thirteen,* http://www.haruth.com/Jhumor13.htm1#Jewish%20Lawyer (downloaded August 16, 2006) contains several examples.

[79] Davies, *Ethnic Humor,* 115ff.

[80] Of course there is some resistance at the margins to the domestication of Jews (see pages 292-93 above). But for the most part the fascinated over-attention to Jews has shifted to the international stage, fueled by the Arab-Israel conflict and by end-of-the-world fantasies.

302 • JEWS AND THE LAW

Hans Wandereisen, *Der Jurist, Der Jude und Die Frau ...* Nürnberg 1520[81]

---

[81] Einblattdruck von Hans Wandereisen, *Der Jurist, Der Jude und Die Frau ...* Nürnberg um 1520. Reprinted in Cornelis Veth, *Der Advokat in Der Karikatur* (Berlin, 1927); reprinted and discussed in Petra Schöner, *Judenbilder im Deutschen Einblattdruck der Renaissance: Ein Beitrag zur Imagologie* (Baden-Baden: Valentin Koerner, 2002), 219–22.

The verse tells us:[82]

> The lawyer with his book
>
> The Jew with his searching (meddling)
>
> and that (which is) under a woman's apron
>
> These three things (types of equipment)
>
> drive the entire world crazy.

So we have a catalog of disturbing types: lawyer, Jew, and woman. We have already noted the affinity of the figures of the lawyer and the Jew. Although there has been much speculation about the Jew as a feminine figure[83] it is difficult to discern that in the presentation of the Jew here. Instead, it is the smaller, soft-featured lawyer who appears more feminine. With her apron and spoon, the woman seems clearly domestic and the verse suggests that it is her sexuality that makes her a candidate for inclusion in the fellowship of the disturbing. (I wonder what is signified by the woman placing her hand on the arm of the Jew, presumably an unusual gesture at the time.) Curiously, this triad prophetically anticipates the latest twist in the career of the *Check in the Coffin* joke (#15). As noted earlier, in the 1980s the previously predominant Jewish protagonist was displaced by the lawyer. Lawyer versions proliferated as the great surge of joking about lawyers was fueled by the recoil against what seemed to many the unwelcome lawyerization of American life.

But in the new century a new protagonist rose to prominence.

> #16.   *There was a man who had worked all of his life and had saved all of his money. He was a real miser when it came to his money. He loved money more than just about anything, and just before he died, he said to his wife, "Now listen, when I die I want you to take all my money and place it in the casket with me. I wanna take my money to the after-life."* So he got his wife to promise him with all her heart that when he died, she would put all the money in the casket with him.
>
> *Well one day he died. He was stretched out in the casket* [and] *the wife was sitting there in black next to her closest friend. When they finished the ceremony, just before the undertakers got ready to close the casket, the wife said, "Wait just a minute!" She had a shoebox with her* [and] *she*

---

[82] The translation was kindly supplied to me by Prof. Wolfgang Mieder of the University of Vermont.

[83] See Richie Robertson, "Historicising Weininger: The Nineteenth Century German Image of the Feminized Jew," in *Modernity, Culture and "the Jew,"* ed. Bryan Cheyette and Laura Marcus (Stanford: Stanford University Press, 1998).

> came over with the box and placed it in the casket. Then the undertakers locked he casket down and rolled it away.
>
> Her friend said, "I hope you weren't crazy enough to put all that money in there with that stingy old man." She said, "Yes, I promised. I'm a good Christian, I can't lie. I promised him that I was going to put that money in that casket with him."
>
> "You mean to tell me you put every cent of his money in the casket with him?"
>
> "I sure did," said the wife. "I got it all together, put it into my account and I wrote him a check."[84]

This "wife" version had surfaced more than a decade earlier, in the form of a 1989 letter to Ann Landers in which a reader from Bismarck, North Dakota tells it as a true story about her warmhearted Aunt Emma.[85] Thirteen years later it reappeared in an elaborate rendition, embedded in a sermon delivered at the largest church in Oakland. California. Within a few years the "wife" story became the most prevalent version of the joke. Of the 69 post-2000 specimens of the joke that I have collected, only 5 are about Jews, 24 are about lawyers, 34 are about wives, and 6 are about others.[86] (Of my 144 specimens from before 2000, only the 1989 Ann Landers story contains a woman protagonist.) This joke, which had migrated dramatically to lawyers in the last two decades of the twentieth century, has shifted decisively toward the wife protagonist while still flourishing as a lawyer joke.

The woman who gains admission to the ranks of the disturbing is not the career woman or feminist but the dutiful wife (perhaps descended from the one depicted, spoon in hand, five centuries earlier) now outwitting the domestic counterpart of the miserly usurer of the Middle Ages.[87] Unlike the tricky Jew or the deceitful lawyer, the wife is presented as a sympathetic figure, deploying common sense. She is a claimant to Christian virtue but experiences no difficulty fusing it with the strategic gamesmanship that once was the province of the Jew/lawyer. Perhaps the slogan "we are all Jews now" will be replaced or accompanied by "we are all lawyers now."[88] In the joke's new version we celebrate the domestication of legalism, of

---

[84] GlobalSpot.com, January 2, 2006.

[85] "Who Says You Can't Take it with You," *Chicago Tribune*, March 20, 1989. The next appearance known to me is an elaborate version, embedded in a sermon delivered at the largest church in Oakland, CA in 2002. Chris Thompson, "Preaching Prosperity," *East Bay Express*, April 24, 2002.

[86] As of July 7, 2013. My Nexis search had picked up "wife" versions from Australia, South Africa, the Philippines, Ireland, India, and the United Kingdom, as well as various parts of the United States.

[87] See note 70 above.

[88] E.g., James Woolsey, "We Are All Jews," *Jerusalem Post*, October 3, 2003. Mr. Woolsey was director of the Central Intelligence Agency from 1993 to 1995.

lawyer/Jewish canniness, of the use of empty but powerful legal forms to achieve self-interested (and rational) results while paying lip service to principles that we can neither forsake nor embrace without qualification.

The use of legal form by the widow to reach a pragmatic rational result points to the absorption of legalism into domestic life, enabling ordinary people to become equipped with the tools of canniness. Well, it's a joke, so this development is presented as deviance. But it is "exemplary deviance," the trickiness, formalism, calculation, cunning, artifice that we see all about us. It is not a startling intrusion imported by the outsider but the resource and resort of the ultimate insider. So while we hear much grumbling and fretting about the legalization of society, it seems to be proceeding apace; the animus against lawyers registers not only resentment of its discomforts, but resistance to their waning monopoly on the traits that enable one to prosper in a legalized world.

Legalism and the Jews

Jews and Legal Realism

Morton J. Horwitz*

I would like to discuss the influence of Jews on the development of American Legal Realism. Legal Realism, as I argue in my 1992 book, *The Transformation of American Law 1870–1960*, should be defined expansively to include not only the critical jurisprudence of the inter-War years but also the Progressive or Sociological Jurisprudence of the pre-War period.[1] Jews were among the prominent proponents of this critical jurisprudence. In the earlier group were Brandeis and Cardozo, Nathan Isaacs, and Harold Laski.[2] Spanning both periods are Morris Cohen and Felix Frankfurter.[3] In the later period, we need to include Jerome Frank and Felix Cohen.[4] The *Encyclopedia of the Social Sciences*, published between 1930 and 1935, contained articles by perhaps two dozen Realists, including Isaacs and Laski as well as Morris and Felix Cohen. Other Jews who might be called Realists who published in the *Encyclopedia* were Ernst Freund, Sheldon Glueck, Max Lerner, and Max Radin.[5]

---

* Charles Warren Professor of American Legal History, Emeritus, Harvard Law School.

[1] Morton J. Horwitz, *The Transformation of American Law 1870–1960* (New York: Oxford University Press, 1992), 169–70.

[2] Isaacs, a torts and contracts professor at Harvard, Columbia, and Yale, authored, among other articles, "'The Law' and the Law of Change" (pts. 1 & 2), *University of Pennsylvania Law Review* 65 (1917): 665, 748. British political theorist Harold Laski's importance in American Legal Realism stemmed from his teaching at Harvard from 1916–1920 and his close association with both Holmes and Brandeis. See Horwitz, *Transformation*, 183; 318.

[3] Philosopher and legal scholar Morris Cohen authored "Property and Sovereignty" (*Cornell Law Quarterly* 13 (1927): 8–30), one of the masterpieces of legal realist thought, which was "a major contribution to the disintegration of the ... distinction between public and private life." Horwitz, *Transformation*, 165.

[4] New Dealer and federal appeals court judge, Jerome Frank, was an ardent legal realist. He, along with Karl Llewellyn, was a founder of the movement. Frank's controversial and brilliant book, *Law and the Modern Mind* (New York: Brentano's, 1930), critiqued and undermined legal formalism. See Horwitz, *Transformation*, 175–80. Felix Cohen, like Jerome Frank, was a representative of the critical strand of legal realism. Cohen's important article, "Transcendental Nonsense and the Functional Approach," *Columbia Law Review* 35 (1935): 809–49, was a biting critique of legal formalism.

[5] University of Chicago professor Ernst Freund authored *The Legal Nature of Corporations* (Chicago: University of Chicago Press, 1897). "Running through Freund's argument is the effort to overcome the traditional private law emphasis on the individual character of legal rights" (Horwitz, *Transformation*, 102). Harvard Law School professor Sheldon Glueck, with his wife Eleanor, published path-breaking studies in criminology. See, e.g., Sheldon and Eleanore Glueck, *Unraveling Juvenile Delinquency* (Cambridge: Harvard University Press, 1950). Lerner was a professor at Brandeis University and a syndicated

Some Legal Realists turned to value-free social science and, as expressed by Karl Llewellyn, wished to postpone temporarily the question of values.[6] They saw Realism, in Llewellyn's words, as a "methodology" having no connection to moral or political questions.[7] Other Realists, including all of the Jews on the list, were critical of the turn to value-free social science, and saw the move as endangering the critical perspective that Realism had produced.

The critical perspective on law was derived from Progressive politics and, in particular, from Pound's statement that the "law in books" had lost touch with the "law in action."[8] Progressives believed that the connection of law to social justice had been severed by the enormous social dislocations produced by industrialization and corporate concentration. They felt that the Lochner court and its system of Classical Legal Thought was oblivious to the emergence of European-style class struggle in America. The sharp conflict between labor and capital was triggered by an uncontrollable business cycle that had produced three major depressions in the twenty year period between 1873 and 1893. Immigration and urbanization contributed to a sense of dislocation as those small, decentralized 19th century "island communities" were giving way to large, centralized, impersonal, and uncontrollable institutions.[9]

I wish to argue that the critical strand of Realism advanced by those Realists who did not succumb to value-free social science was the first and most prominent example in America of what Peter Novick has called "cognitive relativism," that is, the view that categories of thought and frames of reference are socially and historically contingent.[10] In law, cognitive relativism was devoted to undermining the claim of late nineteenth century Classical Legal Thought that legal categories are neutral, natural, and necessary, and that it is possible to have an "objective" system of legal reasoning that could sharply distinguish between law and politics. Both Felix Cohen's denunciation of "the heaven of legal concepts" as "transcendental nonsense" and Jerome Frank's Freudian effort to link the formalism and essentialism

---

columnist. He wrote, among other articles, "The Supreme Court and American Capitalism," *Yale Law Journal* 42 (1933): 668, reprinted in Robert G. McCloskey, *Essays in Constitutional Law* (New York: Alfred A. Knopf, 1957), 107. Radin was a law professor at the University of California–Berkeley who, as G. Edward White tells us, held "a Realist jurisprudential perspective." Radin stated, for example, that all "all judges ... are influenced by unconscious and implicit premises created by their own temperament." G. Edward White, *Earl Warren: A Public Life* (New York: Oxford University Press, 1982), 59 (quoting Radin).

[6] Karl Llewellyn, "Some Realism about Realism," *Harvard Law Review* 44 (1931): 1226 n. 18.

[7] Karl Llewellyn, *The Common Law Tradition* (New York: Little Brown, 1960), 509–10.

[8] Roscoe Pound, "Law in Books and Law in Action," *American Law Review* 44 (1910): 12.

[9] Robert H. Wiebe, *The Search For Order, 1877–1920* (New York: Hill and Wang, 1967), 44.

[10] Peter Novick, *That Noble Dream: The "Objectivity Question" and the American Historical Profession* (Cambridge: Cambridge University Press, 1999), 145–50.

of "legal fundamentalism" to the psychology of "religious fundamentalism" were prominent examples of cognitive relativism.[11] This critical strand of Realism blended into the emerging sociology of knowledge, which itself is one of the forerunners of modern interpretavist and hermeneutic theories of knowledge.[12] In Europe and America, Jews were prominent in advancing and elaborating theories that Peter Berger has labeled "the social construction of reality."[13] Legal realism was the earliest version of this movement in America.

What was the relationship between critical realism and the experience of post-Emancipation Jewish intellectuals? In Western Europe, cognitive relativism emerged among secular Jews during the late nineteenth century as a reaction to the failed universalist and assimilationist hopes generated by the French Revolution.[14] With the upsurge of nationalism and antisemitism, the Jews of Freud's, Herzl's, and Wittgenstein's Vienna devoted themselves to demonstrating the gap between appearance and reality, and to undermining what they had come to regard as a false picture of social homogeneity presented by universal social theories that submerged the particular in the general.[15] Writing in the aftermath of the Dreyfus Affair, Émile Durkheim also reacted against Enlightenment universalism and rationalism by emphasizing particularism—conventional or customary group or guild norms as a source of values that might restrain the reign of unmitigated greed and self interest.[16] Through their emphasis on the transparency of culture and the contingency of social consciousness, the great Jewish social theorists of the turn of the century joined Kafka, Proust, and Sartre as the prophets of cultural modernism.

In the same year as Vienna elected an antisemitic mayor (1881), the pogroms that followed the assassination of the Czar also catapulted the Jews of the East into modernity.[17] As Irving Howe puts it, they discovered history in place of those timeless religious truths that had been the basis of shtetl Jewish culture.[18] The development of Zionist theory over the next generation, though it protested against Enlightenment universalism, was deeply rooted not only in the historicism of Hegel and Marx but also in the

---

[11] Cohen, "Transcendental Nonsense and the Functional Approach," Frank, *Law and the Modern Mind*.

[12] See Karl Mannheim, *Ideology and Utopia: An Introduction to the Sociology of Knowledge* (London: Routledge, 1991).

[13] Peter L. Berger and Thomas Luckmann, *The Social Construction of Reality: A Treatise on the Sociology of Knowledge* (New York: Irvington, 1980).

[14] See Carl E. Schorske, *Fin-de-siecle Vienna: Politics and Culture* (New York: Knopf, 1980), 146–75.

[15] Ibid. See also Allan Janik and Stephen Toulmin, *Wittgenstein's Vienna* (New York: Simon and Schuster, 1973), 58–61.

[16] Émile Durkheim, *Professional Ethics and Civic Morals*, trans. Cornelia Brookfield (Glencoe, IL: The Free Press, 1958).

[17] Irving Howe, *World of our Fathers* (New York: Simon and Schuster, 1976), 5–7.

[18] Ibid., 11.

modernist view that human nature is socially constructed. Zionist theory sought to transform the degraded Jew of the shtetl by creating a new society in which Jewish alienation and the division of the Jewish soul into public and private realms could be overcome.[19] For the first time in two thousand years, Zionists projected a secular vision of cultural wholeness that might be realized by creating a Jewish state.

In both West and East at the turn of the century, the failures of Emancipation led Jews to emphasize the differences between appearance and reality, between thought and action. Jews became expert at seeing through ideologies to reveal their "real" or latent content, at seeing through institutions to see how they "really" worked, at revealing the conventional nature of manners and the hidden forces behind sexual mores or market capitalism.[20] In Europe, at least, cognitive relativism should not be associated with assimilation but with its failure; not with opportunism and apology but with resistance to and criticism of the existing order. No one more admired this strand of Jewish culture than the non-Jewish institutional economist and sociologist Thorstein Veblen. In his essay, "The Intellectual Pre-eminence of Jews in Modern Europe," written in the immediate glow of the Balfour Declaration, Veblen linked Jewish achievement with Jewish estrangement.[21] He writes:

> Among all the clamorous projects of national self-determination which surround the return of peace, the proposal of the Zionists is notable for sobriety, good will and a poise of self-assurance. More confidently and perspicuously than all the others, the Zionists propose a rehabilitation of their national integrity under a regime of live and let live .... Yet it is always a project for withdrawal upon themselves, a scheme of national demarcation between Jew and gentile; indeed, it is a scheme of territorial demarcation and national frontiers of the conventional sort, within which Jews and Jewish traits, traditions and aspirations are to find scope and breathing space for a home-bred culture and a free unfolding of all that is best and most characteristic in the endowment of the race. There runs through it all a dominant bias of isolation and in-breeding, and a confident persuasion that this isolation and in-breeding will bring great and good results for all concerned. The Zionists aspire to bring to full fruition all that massive endowment of spiritual and intellectual capacities of which their people have given evidence throughout their troubled history, and not least during these concluding centuries of their exile. ... [A] disinterested bystander will be greatly moved to wish them godspeed. ... [But] ... to any disinterested bystander there will [also] come the question: What is the use of it all? It is not so much a ques-

---

[19] Shlomo Avineri, *The Making of Modern Zionism* (New York: Basic Books, 1981).

[20] John Murray Cuddihy, *The Ordeal of Civility: Freud, Marx, Levi-Strauss, and the Jewish Struggle with Modernity* (New York: Basic Books, 1974).

[21] Thorstein Veblen, "The Intellectual Pre-eminence of Jews in Modern Europe," *Political Science Quarterly* 34 (1919): 33–42.

tion of what is aimed at, as of the chances of its working-out. The logic of the Zionist project plainly runs to the effect that, whereas this people have achieved great things while living under conditions of great adversity, scattered piecemeal among the gentiles of Europe, they are due to achieve much greater things and to reach an unexampled prosperity so soon as they shall have a chance to follow their own devices untroubled within the shelter of their own frontiers.[22]

Veblen continues: "It is a fact which must strike any dispassionate observer that the Jewish people have contributed much more than an even share to the intellectual life of modern Europe.... [T]his intellectual pre-eminence of the Jews has come into bearing within the gentile community of peoples, not from the outside; that the men who have been its bearers have been men immersed in this gentile culture in which they have played their part of guidance and incitement.... It is on this ... point that a question is raised here as to the nature and causes of Jewish achievement in gentile Europe...."[23] Veblen answered:

> It appears to be only when the gifted Jew escapes from the cultural environment created and fed by the particular genius of his own people, only when he falls into the alien lines of gentile inquiry and becomes a naturalized, though hyphenate, citizen in the gentile republic of learning, that he comes into his own as a creative leader in the world's intellectual enterprise. It is by loss of allegiance, or at the best by force of a divided allegiance to the people of his origin, that he finds himself in the vanguard of modern inquiry.[24]

> [T]hat pioneering and engineering work of guidance, design and theoretical correlation ... in the modern sciences and in the field of scholarship at large ... presupposes a degree of exemption from hard-and-fast preconceptions, a skeptical animus, ... release from the dead hand of conventional finality.[25]

> The intellectually gifted Jew is in a peculiarly fortunate position in respect of this requisite immunity from the inhibitions of intellectual quietism. But he can come in for such immunity only at the cost of losing his secure place in the scheme of conventions into which he has been born, and at the cost, also, of finding no similarly secure place in that scheme of gentile conventions into which he is thrown. For him as for other men in the like case, the skepticism that goes to make him an effectual factor in the increase and diffusion of knowledge among men involves a loss of that peace of mind that is the birthright of the safe and sane quietist. He becomes a disturber of the intellectual peace, but only at the cost of becoming an intellectual wayfaring man, a wanderer in the intellectual no-man's-land, seeking

---

[22] Ibid., 33–34.
[23] Ibid., 34, 37.
[24] Ibid., 38.
[25] Ibid., 39.

another place to rest, farther along the road, somewhere over the horizon. They are neither a complaisant nor a contented lot, these aliens of the uneasy feet; but that is, after all, not the point in question.[26]

What was the basis of the Jewish attraction to cognitive relativism in America? Did Jewish Progressives see it as advancing a universalist or assimilationist program or did they, like their European cousins, experience it as a form of resistance to the dominant culture?

Here we need to examine briefly the significance of positivism in the development of post-Enlightenment culture. In Europe, by the end of the nineteenth century, the post-revolutionary struggle between church and state, and religion and science had culminated in a system of thought that underlined the separation between facts and values and between law and morals or religion. The development of legal positivism and value-free social science was offered as an "objective" alternative to religious superstition or feudal, local or tribal attachments. The effort to find universal laws of society or of historical development modeled on the laws of the natural sciences expressed this generalizing, universalizing mode of consciousness.[27]

In America, by contrast, positivism only began to emerge in social thought around the turn of the twentieth century.[28] While religious establishment died a slow, non-revolutionary death during the half century after the American Revolution, Protestant religion continued to exercise a powerful hold over American culture. Even secular American social thought remained highly moralistic due to the influence of Scottish common sense philosophy as well as natural rights theory. The struggle between religion and Darwinism after 1870 also postponed the emergence of positivism since Darwinism held out the hope of merging the 'is' and the 'ought,' the descriptive and the prescriptive, the customary and the valuable. If what survives under the "survival of the fittest" is also more evolved and therefore more valuable, then the 'is' also contains its own 'ought.'

Unlike Europe, where rationalism, universalism, and positivism united against the Old Order, in America moralism was not automatically associated with religious superstition or traditional social hierarchy.[29] Only in America were Progressive social thinkers, many of them Jews, able to combine a pre-modern, prophetic, and essentialist moralistic passion for social justice with a critical modernist sense of the socially constructed character of social categories and institutions. If they were "cognitive rela-

---

[26] Ibid.

[27] See Auguste Comte, *Introduction to Positive Philosophy*, trans. Frederick Ferre (Indianapolis: Bobbs-Merrill, 1970).

[28] See Edward A. Purcell Jr., *The Crisis of Democratic Theory: Scientific Naturalism and the Problem of Value* (Lexington: University Press of Kentucky, 1973), 21–22.

[29] See Richard Hofstadter, *Social Darwinism in American Thought*, rev. ed. (New York: George Braziller, 1959).

tivists" they were certainly not "moral relativists." Rather, by challenging the claim of social institutions to be neutral, natural, and necessary, they sought to underline, as Felix Cohen put it in 1931, "[t]hat all valuations of law are moral judgments, ... that the problem which the judge faces is, in the strictest sense, a moral problem, and that the law has no valid end or purpose other than the maintenance of the good life...."[30]

They projected their Jewish moral perspectives onto American Pragmatism, which itself was drawing away from static universalism to emphasize contextualism and consequentialism. They frequently invoked Holmes' aphorism that "general propositions do not decide concrete cases."[31] They were drawn to Dewey's dynamic and experimental conception of the formation of morals through the dialectic interaction between theory and practice and the general and the particular.[32] The famous Brandeis Brief in *Muller v. Oregon* (1908)[33] expresses not commitment to value-free social science but the reformist urge to bring theory and practice, fact and value, into confrontation. As Philippa Strum put it: "Holmes was the detached, cynical observer; Brandeis, the deeply involved reformer."[34] If Holmes argued for the separation between law and morals, Cardozo, like Brandeis, would insist that it "really matters" that "the judge is under a duty ... to maintain a relation between law and morals, between the precepts of jurisprudence and those of reason and good conscience.... The constant insistence that morality and justice are not law, has tended to breed distrust and contempt of law as something to which morality and justice are not merely alien, but hostile.... Not for us the barren logomachy that dwells upon the contrasts between law and justice, and forgets their deeper harmonies."[35] Yet, Cardozo could also proclaim the modernist slogan that law "is not found, but made" because "[e]verywhere there is growing emphasis on the analogy between the function of the judge and the function of the legislator."[36] In the end, however, he brought his Jewish moralism to the fore. "[T]he force which in our day and generation is becoming the greatest [influence] of them all, [is] the power of social justice...."[37]

If the push to value-free social science within Progressivism emerged out of an urban, secularizing and professionalizing effort to distinguish

---

[30] Felix Cohen, "The Ethical Basis of Legal Criticism," *Yale Law Journal* 41 (1931): 201.

[31] *Lochner v. New York*, 198 U.S. 45 (1905), 76 (Holmes, J., dissenting).

[32] See James T. Kloppenberg, *Uncertain Victory: Social Democracy and Progressivism in European and American Thought, 1870–1920* (New York: Oxford University Press, 1986), 55 (discussing the experimentalism at the core of John Dewey's pragmatism).

[33] 208 U.S. 412 (1908).

[34] Philippa Strum, *Louis D. Brandeis: Justice for the People* (Cambridge, MA: Harvard University Press, 1984), 311.

[35] Benjamin N. Cardozo, *The Nature of the Judicial Process* (New Haven: Yale University Press, 1921), 133–34.

[36] Ibid., 119.

[37] Ibid., 65–66.

itself from a rural and religiously-based populism, Jewish Progressives, by contrast, seemed unwilling to abandon their moralistic encounters with law and social life. None of the Jews I have mentioned lost their critical moralism to positivism. Jewish moralism, we need to see, was not assimilationist when set in the background of the emergence of positivism in American social thought. It was highly distinctive—passionate, emotional, and ultimately critical of the existing order. In Legal Realism, moralism combined with the subversive thrust of cognitive relativism.

What is Jewish about these Jewish Progressives? The answer to this question is deeply bound up with controversies over the meaning of Jewish history, and, in particular, with one's understanding of the meaning of Zionism. Does there remain a secular conception of diaspora Jewishness, one that defines the Jew independently both of traditional religious Jewish culture and of the Zionist promise of overcoming the alienated state of *galut* through the wholeness of life in a Jewish state? With the erosion of the Zionist transformative project, what do we now believe about the alienated diaspora Jew who once was to be eliminated through the "negation of *galut*?" After Hitler, does the alienated, cosmopolitan Jewish intellectual any longer offer a creative Jewish alternative to assimilation in diaspora culture?

Let us turn to the case of Morris Cohen, whose opposition to Zionism at the time of the Balfour Declaration presents the strongest case for Progressive American Jews as simply unalienated assimilationists. Because of his constant attacks on the value-free positivism of a major strand of Legal Realism, Cohen has not often been thought of as a Realist. But once we realize that there was in fact a major debate within Realism over its tendencies towards ethical positivism, we not only are able to place Cohen directly within the Realist tradition, we also come to see that among the major opponents of positivism, Jews clearly dominated the intellectual agenda. There were no Jews among the group that defined Legal Realism in terms of behavioral social sciences.[38]

---

[38] Harvard Law School professor Sheldon Glueck's research in criminology, conducted with his wife Eleanor, relied heavily on social science data. However, as with the Brandeis Brief, the social science data served, for the Gluecks, as a vehicle for moral reform. Like Louis Brandeis, they used social science as a means to help achieve their progressive vision of a just society. Sheldon Glueck stated:

> The most creative ... judicial opinions have come from scholars whose disciplined learning in the law has not blinded them to the possibilities of infusion therein of wisdom from other arts and sciences. The twentieth century sociological school of jurisprudence expresses the movement to interrelate the social sciences, of which the law is but one. Law is no longer regarded as a self-sufficient, cabalistic discipline, isolated from the general stream of culture.... We can no longer be content with the use of exclusively legal materials in the critique of the law.... [W]e set down some tentative principles for a penal code that, in the light of modern ethical, psychological-psychiatric, and sociological views give some promise of being more rational and just than the procedure under which we are ineffectively laboring.... In [the] basic work of self-protection, society should utilize every available scientific instrumentality.

In 1919, in the pages of *The New Republic*, Cohen attacked Zionism on Enlightenment universalist grounds. "A national Jewish Palestine must necessarily mean a state founded on a peculiar race, a tribal religion and a mystic belief in a peculiar soil," he wrote, "whereas liberal America stands for separation of church and state, the free mixing of races, and the fact that men can change their habitation and language and still advance the process of civilization."³⁹ "He was convinced that 'no great civilization was ever achieved except by a mixed people freely borrowing from others in religion, language, law and manners.'"⁴⁰ "The policy of assimilation was clearly expressed by Spinoza, who pointed out that Jews like other groups are held together by the bond of common suffering; and that as the nations became enlightened and removed their restrictions against the Jews, the latter would adopt the habits of western civilization and the problem would thus be eliminated."⁴¹ Unfortunately, he conceded, "restrictions against Jews ha[d] nowhere been completely removed...."⁴² "This, in turn, made 'the intellectual Jews particularly susceptible to the mystic and romantic nationalism which began in Germany as a reaction against the liberalism of the French Revolution, against the old faith in the power of cosmopolitan reason and enlightenment which overthrew medievalism. ... Incidentally, the idealistic Zionists are quite willing to ignore the rights of the vast majority of the non-Jewish population of Palestine, quite like the Teutonic idealists with their superior kultur.'"⁴³

As Susanne Klingenstein concludes in her excellent book, *Jews in the American Academy 1900–1940*: "Cohen's faith in the Enlightenment as a means of 'salvation,' in its power to solve the 'Jewish problem' though its 'policy of assimilation,' was absolute."⁴⁴ She contrasts Cohen's position with that of the Zionist Jewish philosopher Horace Kallen, who claimed that "the nationalist philosophy of Zionism is an extension of the assumptions of

---

> This is dictated both by the principle of justice and that of economy. ... [society] has an interest in the welfare of the individual life, and a duty to use every reasonable instrumentality for the rehabilitation of its anti-social members. Even a socially harmful criminal has a right, in justice, to be treated with those instrumentalities that give him the greatest promise of self-improvement and rehabilitation. Justice demands also that, in its work of self-protection, society interfere as little as possible with the free life of its members.

Sheldon Glueck, "Principles of a Rational Penal Code," *Harvard Law Review* 41 (1928): 454–55. See also Sheldon Glueck, "Predictive Devices and the Individualization of Justice," *Law and Contemporary Problems* 23 (1958): 461–62, 476.

³⁹ Susanne Klingenstein, *Jews in the American Academy 1900–1940: The Dynamics of Intellectual Assimilation* (New Haven: Yale University Press, 1991), 51 (quoting Cohen).

⁴⁰ Ibid.

⁴¹ Ibid., 52.

⁴² Ibid.

⁴³ Ibid.

⁴⁴ Ibid., 53.

liberalism from the individual to the group. ... The nationalism which is only another name for [the rights of freedom of thought and of association] was a development of, not a reaction against, the spirit of the French Revolution."[45] Kallen's arguments were important in persuading Louis Brandeis to join the Zionist cause.[46] "Only late in life," Klingenstein concludes, did Cohen soften his hostility to Jewish particularism, though "until the day of his death" he opposed "political Zionism as a form of tribalism."[47]

Yet, Klingenstein continues, "closer examination of Cohen's philosophy reveals the amazing (though upon further reflection not too surprising) fact that his reasoning was governed by the same concern as that of his two colleagues," Horace Kallen and Harry Wolfson, Jewish philosophers who did not retreat into the kind of abstract universalism that Morris Cohen's son, Felix, denounced as "transcendental nonsense."[48] Like them, she concludes, Morris Cohen's thought was characterized "by an almost anxious attempt to strike and keep the balance between extremes."[49] Wolfson and Kallen, "in their endeavors to find a balance between apparent polarities, created new, third units, such as the community of philosophers or the consent community of America."[50] But Cohen's "solution to the problem of being Jewish in America consisted in nothing but the precise philosophical formulation of the problem itself, in his 'principle of polarity.'"[51] In a word, the principle of polarity structured Cohen's effort "to find and defend the virtuous middle way," which Klingenstein calls "cosmopolitanism."[52]

Cohen, she tells us, had never "'belonged' anywhere for a sustained period of time during his childhood and youth. Using a familiar strategy, he appears to have made a virtue of such detachment. As an adult he intensely 'distrusted the concrete, the sensual and the active' .... The means for gaining equipoise and keeping the balance between polar extremes were logic and reason."[53] In this final formulation, I believe, Klingenstein has not carried her insight about Cohen's alienation far enough.

"The present wave of nominalism in juristic science," Cohen wrote in 1931, "is a reaction by younger men against the abuse of abstract principles by an older generation that neglected the adequate factual analysis neces-

---

[45] Ibid., 49 (quoting Kallen). See the discussion of Kallen's work in Dalia Tsuk Mitchell's excellent biography of Felix Cohen, *Architect of Justice: Felix S. Cohen and the Founding of American Legal Pluralism* (Ithaca, N.Y.: Cornell University Press, 2007), 15–16, 52–53, 58–59.

[46] Klingenstein, *Jews in the American Academy*, 49.

[47] Ibid., 51.

[48] Ibid., 54.

[49] Ibid.

[50] Ibid.

[51] Ibid.

[52] Ibid., 64 (quoting David A. Hollinger, *Morris R. Cohen and the Scientific Ideal* (Cambridge, MA: MIT Press, 1975), 6, 7).

[53] Ibid.

sary to make principles properly applicable."⁵⁴ In this observation, Cohen reveals his sympathy with the criticism of reification of concepts that his son Felix was to formulate so brilliantly in "Transcendental Nonsense" four years later.⁵⁵ It reveals his own recognition of the tension between the general and the particular, the abstract and the concrete, the universal and the particular, that was one of the driving forces of Realist criticism. Indeed, Cohen's two greatest contributions to Realist thought, his essays "Property and Sovereignty" (1927) and "The Basis of Contract" (1933), were each studies in the problem of the general and the particular.⁵⁶ Both essays sought to "deconstruct" the sharp separation between public and private law, between a public realm of sovereignty and coercion and a private realm of the voluntary exercise of rights. Cohen sought to show, in typical Realist fashion, that these distinctions were differences of degree not of kind. It was equally possible, he wrote in "The Basis of Contract," to conceive of contract as a delegation of public power to private individuals to use in the public interest. It was also equally possible to think of property in terms of power and coercion instead of voluntariness and natural rights and to conceive of sovereignty either as consent or the vindication of natural rights. But, above all, the institution of property was not a mirror of Lockean pre-political rights; it was a social creation designed to achieve social purposes. Here Cohen was drawn into the cognitive relativist critique of categories as socially constructed.

In Europe, it would seem, the conflict between universalism and particularism in social thought unfolded as a conflict between, on the one hand, the claims, first of religion, and second of value-free social science, to universalism, and, on the other, the particularizing, deconstructive strategies of cognitive relativism. In America, by contrast, where moralism was never associated with the old regime, the conflict between the general and the particular took place around efforts to mediate between the essentialist claims of moralism and the anti-essentialist method implicit in cognitive relativism. If we are to understand the place of the diaspora Jewish intellectuals, we need to understand the structure of the conflict and the specific ways in which they sought to wrestle with the problem. One of the most fertile areas for studying this conflict is the efforts of Jewish legal realists, who were also the first generation of American cognitive relativists, to confront this problem.

---

⁵⁴ Morris R. Cohen, "Justice Holmes and the Nature of Law," *Columbia Law Review* 31 (1931): 352, 363.

⁵⁵ Cohen, "Transcendental Nonsense and the Functional Approach," 809.

⁵⁶ Cohen, "Property and Sovereignty," 8–30; Morris R. Cohen, "The Basis of Contract," *Harvard Law Review* 46 (1933): 553–92.

Jews and American Legal Pluralism

Dalia Tsuk Mitchell*

Introduction

In 1949, shortly after he left the Department of the Interior after fourteen years of service, Felix Solomon Cohen wrote the following about his experience defending the rights of Indian tribes:

> The issue we face is not the issue merely of whether Indians will regain their independence of spirit. Our interest in Indian self-government today is not the interest of sentimentalists or antiquarians. We have a vital concern with Indian self-government because the Indian is to America what the Jew was to the Russian Czars and Hitler's Germany. For us, the Indian tribe is the miners' canary and when it flutters and droops we know that the poison gasses of intolerance threaten all other minorities in our land. And who of us is not a member of some minority?[1]

In recent years, Cohen's canary has been associated with minority groups' struggles for equal rights.[2] Yet, despite the strong ties between Cohen's, and his colleagues', fight for Indian self-government and more recent efforts to extend the guarantees of equal protection to historically marginalized or underprivileged groups, these endeavors reflect rather different understandings of the relationship between individuals, groups, and the state. While contemporary scholars focus on the individual, and individual rights, as the foundation for legal and political analysis, the attention of Cohen and his generation centered on groups and associations. Theirs was a legal pluralist vision. Its insight was that groups and other associations were political, social, and cultural centers in American life. Therefore, the success of American democracy demanded that they be given a place within its political and legal structures. In their scholarship and legal work, legal pluralists tried to define the boundaries both of group autonomy and of group power.

---

* Professor of Law, The George Washington University Law School. I am grateful to Suzanne Stone and Marc Galanter for organizing this conference and for inviting me to participate, and to the participants for their comments.

[1] Felix S. Cohen, "Indian Self-Government," in *The Legal Conscience: Selected Papers by Felix S. Cohen*, ed. Lucy Kramer Cohen (New Haven: Yale University Press, 1960), 305, 313–14. Originally published in *American Indian* 5 (1949): 3–12.

[2] See, for example, *The Miner's Canary: Enlisting Race, Resisting Power, Transforming Democracy*, ed. Lani Guinier and Gerald Torres (Cambridge, MA: Harvard University Press, 2002).

The legal pluralist vision, which was rooted in a substantive understanding of the state's role in protecting groups and associations, had a profound influence on the transformation of law. It influenced labor law as well as corporate law in the first decades of the century, federal Indian law in the 1930s, and debates about minority rights in the 1940s. But legal pluralism did not survive the backlash against collectivism and the fixation on individuals beginning in the 1940s. The prominence of interest group pluralism during the 1950s helped obscure the legacy of earlier interpretations of pluralism, while the decisions of the Warren Court in the 1950s and 1960s made individual rights and liberties, and thus individuals, the center of American liberalism. Still, concerns about the accommodation of diverse interests account for inexhaustible debates as contemporary political theorists, legal scholars, and philosophers struggle to understand the American state in the twenty-first century. The story of early-twentieth century legal pluralism—its rise in the 1920s and 1930s and its demise in the 1940s and 1950s—is thus the story of the origins of the multiculturalism of the 1980s and 1990s.[3]

This chapter examines the roots of the legal pluralist vision, as well as its transformation in the postwar years, through particular lenses, those of Jewish scholars whose work and scholarship brought their own concerns about their place in American society to bear upon their legal pluralist vision. Part I explores Jewish scholars' personal fascination with different theories of pluralism—cultural, political, as well as legal pluralism—in the first decades of the twentieth century. Part II traces the interplay between the personal and the political (or legal) in the work and scholarship of Felix Cohen, whom I have previously described as the voice of legal pluralism.[4] The paper concludes with the demise of legal pluralism in the postwar years and the rise of multiculturalism, a different legal pluralism, a few decades later.

I. The Pluralist Appeal

Ethnicity

American Jewish scholars' fascination with theories of pluralism reaches back at least as far as the turn of the twentieth century. As millions of Jews immigrated to "the golden land" (*di goldeneh medina*),[5] Jewish scholars struggled to mediate the tensions between particularism and assimilation. Advocates of assimilation, memorialized in Israel Zangwill's play *The Melting Pot* (1909), urged immigrants to divest themselves of every vestige of their native culture and merge into the presumably homogenous Ameri-

---

[3] Dalia Tsuk Mitchell, *Architect of Justice: Felix S. Cohen and the Founding of American Legal Pluralism* (Ithaca, N.Y.: Cornell University Press, 2007).

[4] Ibid.

[5] *How We Lived: A Documentary History of Immigrant Jews in America 1880–1940*, ed. Irving Howe and Kenneth Libo (New York: Richard Marek Publishers, 1979), 17–26.

can culture. In response, cultural pluralists, most notably Horace Kallen in his "Democracy versus the Melting Pot" (1915), used a metaphor of "multiplicity in unity" to argue that America ought to remain a nation composed of many cultural or ethnic nations and to urge harmonious cooperation between different cultures.[6] As Kallen most memorably put it, American society was like an orchestra, with "each ethnic group ... the natural instrument, its temper and culture ... its theme and melody and the harmony and dissonances and discords of them all ... the symphony of civilization."[7]

The American Jewish community moved beyond words, using cultural pluralist ideas to protect their cultural sovereignty and to confront anti-semitism. In 1909, Reform Rabbi Judah Magnes and several other New York Jewish leaders established a Jewish organization, the Kehillah, to represent the Jews of New York and to defend their rights and liberties. As if foreshadowing Kallen's cultural pluralism, Magnes, who was afraid that assimilation would be detrimental to the Jewish community, stressed that "the symphony of America ... must be written by the various nationalities which keep their individual and characteristic note, and which sound this note in harmony with their sister nationalities. Then it will be a symphony of color, of picturesqueness, of character, of distinction—not the harmony of the Melting Pot, but rather the harmony of sturdiness and loyalty and joyous struggle."[8]

Two years before Magnes and his colleagues created the Kehillah, a group of New York Jews turned to cultural pluralist ideas to fight discriminatory and exclusionary laws. In 1907, Mrs. Bertha Rayner Frank, "a leading Jewish citizen of Baltimore and the sister of U.S. Senator Isidor

---

[6] Werner Sollors, *Beyond Ethnicity: Consent and Descent in American Culture* (New York: Oxford University Press, 1986), 66, 97; David A. Hollinger, "Ethnic Diversity, Cosmopolitanism and the Emergence of the American Liberal Intelligentsia," *American Quarterly* 27 (1975): 133, 142; Elmer N. Lear, "On the Unity of the Kallen Perspective," in *The Legacy of Horace M. Kallen*, ed. Milton R. Konvitz (London: Associated University Press, 1987), 116; Sidney Ratner, "Horace M. Kallen and Cultural Pluralism," in *The Legacy of Horace M. Kallen*, ed. Konvitz, ibid., 50.

[7] Horace M. Kallen, "Democracy versus the Melting-Pot," in *Culture and Democracy in the United States* (New York: Boni and Liveright, 1924), 125. Originally published in *The Nation*, February 18 and 25, 1915. Kallen, whose family immigrated to the United States from Germany when he was five and whose father was a rabbi in Boston, wanted to be identified as an American, not as a Jew. But at the influence of his professors at Harvard, especially Barrett Wendell and William James, Kallen accepted that being a Jew was not inconsistent with being an American. Interestingly, Kallen's concept of cultural pluralism was traceable to the scientific, even racist, assumptions of anti-immigrationists and their racial determinism. "Men," Kallen wrote, "may change their clothes, their politics, their wives, their religions, their philosophies, to greater or lesser extents, but they cannot change their grandfathers." Yet, even with such assumptions, Kallen wanted to make race and ethnicity positive elements of the American experience. Louis Menand, *The Metaphysical Club: The Story of Ideas in America* (New York: Farrar Straus and Giroux, 2001), 388–93.

[8] Nomi Maya Stolzenberg and David N. Myers, "Community, Constitution, and Culture: The Case of the Jewish Kehillah," *University of Michigan Journal of Law Reform* 25 (1992): 633, 645–46.

Rayner," was excluded from the Blenheim-Marlborough Hotel in Atlantic City, N.J. Responding to this incident, Louis Marshall and other leaders of the Jewish community of New York formed "an ad-hoc committee 'for the enforcement of the rights of Jews in New York State.'" This committee drafted a bill to amend the New York State Civil Rights Act to prohibit "the advertising of discriminatory or exclusionary practices in places of public accommodation or amusement." New York Senator Martin Saxe introduced the bill in the State Senate.[9]

The bill did not receive universal support from "all sections of American Jewish society." Some were concerned that legislation calling attention to ethnicity would hinder, rather than further, the social acceptance of Jews. Others accused Marshall and his colleagues of attempting to protect the rights of the Jewish elite. Cincinnati Reform Rabbi Julian Morgenstern proclaimed that it was the Jew, "not the negro [sic], nor the Chinese, nor the Indian, who seeks his way into summer hotels where he is not wanted." Morgenstern pointedly noted that for these "Jewish social climbers," especially in New York, "the mere fact of their exclusion makes the particular resort more desirable and whets their ambition to force their way, into the forbidden circle."[10]

The amendment to the New York Civil Rights Act was not passed in 1907. But in 1913, Assemblyman A.J. Levy and Senator Robert F. Wagner introduced a similar measure. Both houses passed it immediately and unanimously and, in April 1913, Governor William Sulzer signed it into law.[11] By 1926, seven states had adopted similar statutes at the urging of the Anti-Defamation League and the American Jewish Congress.[12]

These laws were not effective. Hotel owners circumvented them by using phrases such as "restricted clientele" or "churches nearby" to signal to Jews and Gentiles alike who would be permitted on the premises.[13] Moreover, as the promise of assimilation became real for many Jewish Americans, despite waves of antisemitism, legislation focusing on ethnicity rapidly ran into disrepute. In the 1920s, a similar campaign to enact group libel laws failed, leading the American Jewish Congress, by 1935, to oppose such legislation.[14]

Magnes' Kehillah was also not successful. As early as 1918, Magnes recognized that the place of Jews in American society was dramatically different from the role they had in European societies. "The European notion of a

---

[9] Jeffrey Gurock, "The 1913 New York State Civil Rights Act," *American Jewish Studies Review* 1 (1976): 93–94.

[10] Ibid., 107.

[11] Ibid., 93–102.

[12] Evan P. Schultz, "Group Rights, American Jews, and the Failure of Group Libel Laws, 1913–1952," *Brooklyn Law Review* 66 (2000): 71–146.

[13] Gurock, "The 1913 New York State Civil Rights Act," 111.

[14] Schultz, "Group Rights, American Jews, and the Failure of Group Libel Laws, 1913–1952," 99–115.

uniform, ... all controlling ... kehillah," Magnes noted, "cannot strike root in American soil ... because it is not in consonance with the free and voluntary character of American religious, social, educational, and philanthropic enterprises."[15]

Given the heterogeneity of the Jewish community, the Kehillah had very little chance of succeeding. German Jews, who began to arrive in the mid-nineteenth century, as well as Jews of Spanish or Portuguese ancestry who arrived even earlier, were for the most part assimilated and viewed their Judaism as a religious, not a cultural matter. In turn, East European Jews, who maintained a strong Jewish cultural identity, were more likely to denounce ethnicity for the sake of economic solidarity.[16]

Indeed, it was Russian-born Morris Cohen, the renowned Jewish philosopher at City College (and Felix Cohen's father), who offered an acute critique of cultural pluralism. While sharing the cultural pluralists' understanding of the immigrants' experiences, Cohen accused Kallen of cultural determinism, of embracing the "very popular racial philosophy of history," that is, "the constant tendency to emphasize the consciousness of race." Instead of cultural pluralism, Cohen offered a fluid understanding of ethnic relations and argued that particular cultures were repositories for insights that, when brought together, would allow the development of a more comprehensive conception of national identity. According to Cohen, great civilizations could only be achieved when "a mixed people freely [borrowed] from others in religion, language, laws, and manners."[17]

Outside the Jewish community, American thinkers and writers like John Dewey and Randolph Bourne saw in Morris Cohen the fulfillment of their belief that a cosmopolitan approach, unlike cultural pluralism or assimilation, would help individuals attain a more complete human experience and a better understanding of it. Writing on the eve of Wilson's decision to enter the war in Europe, Bourne described immigration as giving Americans a way "to liberate themselves from 'parochialism,' and to develop in themselves a truly 'cosmopolitan spirit.'" Bourne believed that Jewish immigrants were the most useful to the cause. Like their liberal contempo-

---

[15] Stolzenberg and Myers, "Community, Constitution, and Culture: The Case of the Jewish Kehillah," 647.

[16] These differences also affected the attitudes of the American Jewish community regarding the claim that Jews were a national minority, a claim that was typically made with respect to European, not American, Jews. These attitudes were forcefully expressed by different Jewish groups participating at the 1919 Paris Peace Conference. See generally Oscar I. Janowsky, *The Jews and Minority Rights (1898–1919)* (New York: Columbia University Press, 1933).

[17] Morris R. Cohen, "Zionism: Tribalism or Liberalism?" in *The Faith of a Liberal: Selected Essays by Morris Cohen* (New York: Henry Holt, 1946), 327–29. The article was published in the *New Republic* in 1919 as a critique of Zionism, which Cohen associated with Kallen's pluralism. See also Susanne Klingenstein, *Jews in the American Academy 1900–1940: The Dynamics of Intellectual Assimilation* (New Haven: Yale University Press, 1991), 50–51; Hollinger, "Ethnic Diversity," 142, 155.

raries, Jewish intellectuals were impatient with the constraints of particularism.[18]

With this in mind, it is perhaps not surprising that early twentieth century American Jewish scholars gradually turned their back on cultural determinism. While embracing the League of Nations' minority treaties as a solution to the plight of European Jews (and other European minorities),[19] they refused to endorse a similar solution for American Jewry. They simply did not think it was needed. They did not abandon the pluralist emphasis on the role of groups in modern American society, but they focused their attention on the role of economic and political groups. As the following section explains, moving away from ethnicity, Jewish scholars found political pluralism an appealing substitute.[20]

Politics

New political theories—from populism to socialism—proliferated in the early twentieth century. Yet one approach characterized Progressive political discourse. Resisting both the radical collectivist vision of Marxists and socialists and the traditional liberal view of the state as a night watchman, Progressives turned their attention to groups, specifically functional groups, as the fora where individuals found meaning for their ideas and actions. As farmers, workers, professionals, consumers, women, and ethno-cultural groups formed a variety of associations to protect and advance their interests, political scientists argued in favor of adding groups, organizations, and associations to the existing array of local and state governments as the bases of the modern American state.[21]

---

[18] Hollinger, "Ethnic Diversity," 133–40. As Hollinger further indicates, "The concept of the 'cosmopolitan Jew' has long been a stereotype of adulation and of anti-Semitism." Ibid., 138 n. 21.

[19] Philip Gleason notes that the minority treaties "first alerted Americans to the sociological possibilities of the word." According to Gleason, "Jews, a classical minority in several European lands, played a leading role in urging protection for minorities at the peace conference, and American Jews were particularly influential in their councils." Philip Gleason, "Minorities (Almost) All: The Minority Concept in American Social Thought," *American Quarterly* 43 (1991): 392–93.

[20] The discussion in the following two sections draws upon Tsuk Mitchell, *Architect of Justice*; Dalia Tsuk, "Corporations without Labor: The Politics of Progressive Corporate Law," *The University of Pennsylvania Law Review* 151 (2003): 1861–1912; idem, "From Pluralism to Individualism: Berle and Means and 20th Century American Legal Thought," *Law and Social Inquiry* 30 (2005): 179–225; and Dalia Tsuk Mitchell, "Transformations: Pluralism, Individualism, and Democracy," in *Transformations in American Legal History: Essays in Honor of Professor Morton J. Horwitz*, ed. Daniel W. Hamilton and Alfred L. Brophy (Cambridge, MA: Harvard Law School, 2009), 185–210.

[21] See, for example, *The Pluralist Theory of the State: Selected Writings of G. D. H. Cole, J. N. Figgis, and H. J. Laski*, ed. Paul Q. Hirst (New York: Routledge, 1989). For a critique of these theories, see W. Y. Elliott, *The Pragmatic Revolt in Politics: Syndicalism, Fascism, and the Constitutional State* (New York: The Macmillan Co., 1928). For a more recent analysis of theories of political pluralism, see Avigail I. Eisenberg, *Reconstructing Political Pluralism* (Albany: State University of New York Press, 1995).

Some political theorists, such as Arthur Bentley, argued that because individuals organized themselves into groups to pursue their interests, groups and organizations were loci of participation and representation. They believed that by exploring the role of groups in society they could offer a more realistic description of liberal democratic politics and the limited role of the liberal state.[22] Other political theorists, among them John Dewey, Mary Parker Follett, and Harold Laski, not only recognized the existence of a multiplicity of centers of self-government in society, but also embraced it as a constitutive element of democracy. These theorists argued that the state was too broad and abstract a body to command loyalty and allegiance from individuals, who associated more easily with diverse groups and organizations than with a unified state entity. By conceiving of sovereignty as distributive or multiple and by encouraging the growth of organizations such as labor unions, these political theorists sought to guarantee the flourishing of diverse and valuable forms of identities, ways of life, experiences, and viewpoints.[23]

Because these theories, collectively labeled theories of political pluralism, offered a middle ground between conservative individualism and radical collectivism, they provided many Progressive Jews a means of reconciling their socialist background with their own desires to assimilate into liberal American society. The ethnic identity they developed in Jewish neighborhoods, especially in New York, had a socialist-pluralist character. It envisioned human fraternity as a means of ending "the exploitativeness, the inhumane competitiveness, the moral frigidity associated with capitalism." Young men and women read not only Marx and Tolstoy but also Mark Twain, and Theodore Dreiser. They aspired to organize unions and to immerse themselves in the cultural heritage from which they were traditionally excluded. It was their way into American society.[24]

Like socialism, political pluralism, which was blind to ethnic differences and instead celebrated solidarity and the improvement of economic conditions, provided Jews a sense of inclusion, of belonging with others in a struggle against injustice. It allowed them to maintain a unique political identity while rejecting the particularity of ethnic differences. Even as the socialist movement that focused on organizing workers was, in the 1920s, losing its grip on Jewish communities in New York City, second- and third-generation Jewish Americans drew upon the traditions of "radical politics and working-class organization" to articulate a left-liberal alternative to

---

[22] Arthur Bentley, *The Process of Government* (Bloomington, IN: Principia Press, 1908), 465–80. See also Earl Latham, *The Group Basis of Politics* (Ithaca, N.Y.: Cornell University Press, 1952), 12–13.

[23] See John Dewey, *The Public and Its Problems* (New York: H. Holt and Co., 1927); Mary P. Follett, *The New State: Group Organization, The Solution of Popular Government* (New York: Longmans, Green 1918); Harold J. Laski, *Studies in the Problem of Sovereignty* (New Haven: Yale University Press, 1917).

[24] *How We Lived: A Documentary History of Immigrant Jews in America 1880–1940*, ed. Howe and Libo, 161, 174.

what they saw as the structural impediments of liberal capitalism. Their early exposure to socialism and other forms of European radical thought allowed them to dissociate themselves from the exclusionary mainstream of American political culture and to articulate other, more inclusive alternatives.[25] Political pluralism provided the tool.

Take, similarly, the British pluralist Harold Laski. Born in 1893 to a wealthy religious Jewish family in England, Laski was intent on shedding any vestige of his religion. (Against his parents' wishes, he eloped with a Gentile woman.[26]) While some suggest that until World War II Laski never identified as a Jew,[27] it is perhaps more accurate to describe him as belonging to a new group of "non-observant Jews who were intensely conscious and proud of their Jewishness."[28] Laski's political pluralism, which aimed to protect a wide variety of groups, seemed to have grown out of this pride.

Informed by John N. Figgis' works,[29] Laski described the Catholic revival and the growth of nationalism as the two fundamental facts in the history of the nineteenth century. As he saw it, "the church and the state had changed places since the Reformation ... [hence] the evils of unified ecclesiastical control had become the tactics of the modern state."[30] Drawing on church history, Laski argued that the state could not demand "the admission that its conscience [was] supreme," because such demand went "beyond the due bounds of righteous claim." Such a state, he declared, attained "a theoretic unity," by expulsion of those who doubted its rectitude.[31] He proclaimed that, like the divine rights of kings, "the sovereignty of the State"—"the modern Baal to which the citizen must bow a heedless knee"—"will pass."[32]

Laski thought that by focusing on the unity of the state, traditional absolutist (or monist) visions of sovereignty obliterated differences of class,

---

[25] Robert Cohen, *When the Old Left was Young: Student Radicals and America's First Mass Student Movement, 1929–1941* (New York: Oxford University Press, 1993), 24; *How We Lived: A Documentary History of Immigrant Jews in America 1880–1940*, ed. Howe and Libo, at 188; Deborah Dash Moore, *At Home in America: Second Generation New York Jews* (New York: Columbia University Press, 1981), 201–30.

[26] George Egerton, "Review of Isaac Kramnick and Barry Sheerman, *Harold Laski: A Life on the Left* (New York: 1993)," *The American Historical Review* 100 (1995): 902–3.

[27] Jeffrey O'Connell and Thomas E. O'Connell, "From Doctor Johnson to Justice Holmes to Professor Laski," *Maryland Law Review* 46 (1987): 320, 334.

[28] Isaac Kramnick and Barry Sheerman, *Harold Laski: A Life on the Left* (New York: Allen Lane, Penguin Press, 1993), 109.

[29] Figgis examined the relationship between sovereignty, papal supremacy, and monarchal authority during the middle ages. See Franklin G. Snyder, "Sharing Sovereignty: Non-State Associations and the Limits of State Power," *American University Law Review* 54 (2004): 365–99.

[30] Kramnick and Sheerman, *Harold Laski: A Life on the Left*, 101.

[31] Harold J. Laski, "The Political Theory of Disruption," in *Studies in the Problem of Sovereignty*, 66–68.

[32] Harold J. Laski, "The Political Theory of Catholic Revival," in *Studies in the Problem of Sovereignty*, 121, 208–9.

politics, and religion. There were "no rich or poor, Protestants or Catholics, Republicans or Democrats." There were only "members of the States." All groups—"trade unionist and capitalists alike"—surrendered their interests to the state.[33] Laski rejected such a universalist approach. Instead, he announced that sovereignty was "distributive" and not "collective." Attacking the all-absorptive state, he asserted the "inherent worthiness of group associations."[34] "[W]e do not proceed from the State to the parts of the State on the ground that the State is more fundamentally unified than its parts," Laski stressed, "but we, on the contrary, admit that the parts are as *real* and as *self-sufficient* as the whole."[35]

So described, Laski's political pluralism was an attempt to secularize sovereignty. Secular, pluralist, and progressive goals were, for Laski, the antitheses of religious, exclusive, and conservative ideas,[36] while the federal structure of the United States became the ultimate symbol of pluralism. As his biographers conclude, "European repressiveness must have been crystallized for him in the domineering Nathan Laski, demanding he keep to the ways of his father; in contrast, democratic America—the land of opportunity and independence from fathers—and its most prestigious institutions welcomed and rewarded this Jewish foreigner with recognition and influence."[37]

Unlike Laski, American legal scholars were reluctant to accept the idea that the state was equivalent to any other form of association. While they recognized the significance of groups in social and political life, Jewish legal scholars in particular wanted some form of government planning. For one thing, Morris Cohen, who, as already noted, opposed any attempt to prioritize the bonds of groups over the individual will, noted the dangers that "small groups or communities may be far more oppressive to the individual than larger ones," and that "if the state gives up its sovereignty over any group there will be nothing to prevent that group from oppressing the rest of the community." Cohen fully recognized the "wisdom of large measures

---

[33] Harold J. Laski, "The Sovereignty of the State," in *Studies in the Problem of Sovereignty*, 1, 5.

[34] David Schneiderman, "Harold Laski, Viscount Haldane, and the Law of the Canadian Constitution in the Early Twentieth Century," *University of Toronto Law Journal* 48 (1998): 521, 529.

[35] Laski, "The Sovereignty of the State," 9. See also Bernard Zylstra, *From Pluralism to Collectivism—The Development of Harold Laski's Political Thought* (Assen: Van Gorcum, 1968), 34.

[36] Compare Susanne Klingenstein, "Review of David A. Hollinger, *Science, Jews, and Secular Culture: Studies in Mid-Twentieth Century American Intellectual History* (Princeton: Princeton University Press, 1996)," *The Journal of American History* 83 (1997): 1462. It is also important to note the confusion that Laski's analysis revealed. On the one hand, he equated the rise of the national state with the rise of the church, while on the other hand, he praised Catholic and medieval theory for embracing the multiplicity of "autonomous and overlapping communities." Kramnick and Sheerman, *Harold Laski: A Life on the Left*, 102.

[37] Kramnick and Sheerman, *Harold Laski: A Life on the Left*, 104.

of home rule or autonomy to be accorded to various local, vocational, and religious organizations." But he remained concerned about allowing associations and groups freely to exercise their power. Cohen wanted the community at large to regulate the activities of groups.[38] His were the concerns of a first-generation Jewish American, fearing discrimination or oppression from other groups as well as from his own group—the Jewish community. Cohen believed that government planning or control could eliminate the potential for such oppression. His critique of Laski's political pluralism laid the foundation for yet another pluralist variant, which I previously labeled legal pluralism, a theory recognizing the need both to encourage the growth of certain groups and to limit the power of others. As the following section suggests, legal pluralism held a special appeal to Jewish scholars because it was grounded in a particular Progressive vision. Morris Cohen's son, Felix, was among legal pluralism's leading advocates.

Law

The law's treatment of diverse interests had received a renewed and changed attention at the turn of the twentieth century. In the nineteenth century, the recognition of diversity in society was tied to a belief in progress and the assignment of subordinated positions to certain social and cultural groups.[39] At the turn of the twentieth century, the critique of absolutism led to growing skepticism toward existing social norms and values (what historians have described as cultural and ethical relativism, respectively) and toward "traditional foundations of thought and structures of understanding" (what Peter Novick labeled cognitive relativism).[40] This was the core of the legal realists' critique of classical legal thought, which dominated American legal institutions from the 1880s to the 1930s.[41]

Classical legal thinkers described law as a body of axioms from which judges deduced rules in particular cases. Legal realists argued that this vision obscured the connections between law and social, economic, and political concerns and, instead, described law as the outcome of concealed battles over the social utility of diverse activities in a rapidly changing society. Yet, when realists tried to describe ways to improve the legal system, they were confronted with the normative implications of their skepti-

---

[38] Morris R. Cohen, "Communal Ghosts and Other Perils in Social Philosophy," *The Journal of Philosophy* 16 (1919): 673, 687–89.

[39] Lynn Dumenil, *The Modern Temper: American Culture and Society in the 1920s* (New York: Hill and Wang, 1995), 145.

[40] Peter Novick, *That Noble Dream: The "Objectivity Question" and the American Historical Profession* (New York: Cambridge University Press, 1988). See also Morton J. Horwitz, *The Transformation of American Law 1870–1960: The Crisis of Legal Orthodoxy* (New York: Oxford University Press, 1992), 180–82; Richard H. Pells, *Radical Visions and American Dreams: Culture and Social Thought in the Depression Years* (Urbana: University of Illinois Press, 1998), 4.

[41] On legal realism see Horwitz, *Transformation of American Law*.

cism: does skepticism toward one's own legal system and ideals implicate a nonjudgmental attitude toward all customs and values?

Legal realists argued that the law should aim to accommodate the different visions, interests, and experiences of modern American society. This was the essence of the realists' argument that law had to be brought in touch with society. Yet no legal realist embraced a nonjudgmental attitude toward all cultures, values, and structures of understanding. Without dwelling on it, they simply refused to accept that skepticism necessarily implied a relativist stance toward all aspects of life. That which was intellectually possible, and maybe inevitable, was not only practically impossible but also personally destabilizing to most of them. A nonjudgmental view of all customs, values, and forms of knowledge involved a level of uncertainty about law and the world that very few could endure. It produced an existential crisis. Still, to recognize a degree of absolutism in the cultural, ethical, or cognitive realm undermined the critique of classical legal thought. Recognizing the tension, legal scholars struggled to find a middle ground—to avoid an emotional and intellectual crisis (maybe even nihilism) on the one hand and absolutism on the other.[42]

The social scientists among the realists (especially the hard-core social scientists who moved from Columbia Law School to Johns Hopkins and Yale) set out to collect data about the diverse interests, customs, and viewpoints that characterized society. They endorsed cultural and ethical relativism but trusted empirical studies (or social science) to point to the appropriate system of values. They overcame the uncertainties produced by relativism in part by postponing the normative and in part by departing from cognitive relativism. They put their trust in science as the ultimate form of knowledge and in empiricism as an objective way to verify facts and learn about the world.

Other legal realists, including the Jewish legal philosophers Morris Cohen and Felix Cohen, held on to a stronger cognitive relativist approach but continued to believe in the power of certain norms and customs and the disadvantages of others. As Morton Horwitz writes, they sought "to combine a pre-modern, prophetic, and essentialist moralistic passion for social justice with a critical modernist sense of the socially constructed character of social categories and institutions."[43] Their legal realism was a combination of skepticism toward traditional structures of knowledge (or cognitive relativism) and a degree of ethical absolutism. It breathed life into the Progressive origins of the social sciences.

Legal pluralism, which emerged out of this latter, Progressive strand of legal realism, offered a different way out of the dilemma of modernism. It recognized diversity but limited the uncertainties associated with cultural,

---

[42] This argument is developed in Tsuk Mitchell, *Architect of Justice*, ch. 2.

[43] Morton J. Horwitz, "Jews and Legal Realism," in this volume as the previous chapter, p. 314." Compare idem, "Why is Anglo-American Jurisprudence Unhistorical?" *Oxford Journal of Legal Studies* 17 (1997): 551, 581.

cognitive, or ethical relativism. Groups and associations were fora where individuals could pursue particular values, subject only to a general economic and political scheme. The role of the state and the legal system was to guarantee that individuals could associate with others to pursue their needs and that no one association or collective entity could use its power to oppress individuals who belonged to other groups (oppression being defined, at least initially, as economic oppression). Law had little role beyond administering the allocation of power among groups. In short, by focusing on the diversity of groups, scholars were able to endorse a certain amount of skepticism toward the prevailing legal system and ideals. Yet by viewing self-government as a means to the general goal of political and economic equality, legal pluralists were able to embrace skepticism without also sanctioning a nonjudgmental attitude toward all customs and values. Rather than choosing between relativism and absolutism, legal pluralists saw their task as defining the appropriate balance between group autonomy and the limits of group power—the normative limits of their celebration of diversity.

In this vein, legal pluralists expanded upon theories of political pluralism to formulate new legal doctrines. Advocates of the workers' right to organize and corporate law scholars drew on theories of pluralism to portray labor unions and corporations, respectively, as real entities whose existence was both real and distinct from their individual members.[44] But while for the most part political pluralists were not concerned about the power that collective entities might exercise (trusting labor unions and corporations to self-regulate their activities), legal pluralists exposed organizations, associations, and corporations as loci not only of individual self-government but also of coercive power over their members, nonmembers, and other associations, power that liberal legal thought cloaked as free contractual arrangements between individuals.[45] Fearing the power that labor unions or corporations could amass, legal pluralists argued that, in principle, collective entities should be allowed to exercise their powers freely but that courts should tame potential abuses of power by imposing on organizations limitations resembling the constraints on sovereign power. They wanted collective entities to exercise their power to benefit the community at large.

The Depression and the New Deal gave legal pluralists a chance to try out their ideas in practice. Recast as New Dealers in Franklin Roosevelt's administration, they sought to combine decentralized economic and political power with national planning. By legitimating the activities of collective entities, New Dealers hoped both to endorse the multiplicity of interests

---

[44] Mark M. Hager, "Bodies Politic: The Progressive History of Organizational 'Real Entity' Theory," *University of Pittsburgh Law Review* 50 (1989): 575, 579–80.

[45] The classic critique of the distinction between public and private power remains Robert L. Hale, "Coercion and Distribution in a Supposedly Non-Coercive State," *Political Science Quarterly* 38 (1923): 470–94.

and viewpoints that characterized modern society and to promote economic progress while entrusting national planning to limit the destructive potential of capitalism. The securities acts of 1933 and 1934 were based on cooperation between government and big business, the Tennessee Valley Authority combined centralized government planning with regional bureaucracy, and the National Industrial Recovery Act of 1933 created the National Recovery Administration to oversee cooperative programs among business, labor, and government (this scheme was declared unconstitutional in 1935).[46]

Legal pluralists never fully resolved the tension between their commitment to group autonomy or self-government and their concerns about inequities of group power. In the 1930s, they struggled, many of them in government positions, to mediate this tension. Over time, the attention of legal pluralists shifted from political and economic groups to cultural and ethnic ones. But the premise of their argument remained the same: groups and collective entities were the basic units for legal and political analysis. It is with this in mind that we can explore Felix Cohen's attempt to use a legal pluralist vision to shape federal Indian law and the treatment of minorities, more broadly.

II. Felix S. Cohen, a Jewish Legal Pluralist[47]

From Norman Thomas to the Indian New Deal

A second-generation Jewish American on his father's side, and a third generation on his mother's side, Felix Cohen was born and raised in upper Manhattan. He earned a B.A. from City College, a Ph.D. in philosophy from Harvard University, and an LL.B. degree from Columbia University. In the 1930s, when he took his first steps as a practicing lawyer, Cohen followed many Progressive-era Jews, including his father, by rejecting ethnic particularism and emphasizing economic improvement through solidarity and collaboration among groups like labor unions and corporations. A supporter of Norman Thomas, whose socialism did not focus on the power of the working class to bring about change but rather on the civic responsibility of a well-bred elite class toward society, Cohen believed that the future "belong[ed] to labor" and to the lawyers who represented labor unions as well as other organizations: "trade unions, industrial unions, consumer organizations, farm organizations, semi-governmental corporations, and forms of associations that have not yet been invented."[48]

---

[46] Michael J. Sandel, *Democracy's Discontent: America in Search of a Public Philosophy* (Cambridge, MA: Belknap Press, 1996), 252–55. On collectivism in the New Deal, see also Gary Dean Best, *The Retreat from Liberalism: Collectivists versus Progressives in the New Deal Years* (Westport, CT: Praeger, 2002).

[47] This part is drawn from different chapters in Tsuk Mitchell, *Architect of Justice*.

[48] Felix S. Cohen, "What City College will Contribute to the Development of the Law," *The Barrister* (City College of New York) 2 (1938): 4, 8.

While Cohen envisioned individuals coming together to create collective institutions he, like other pluralists, emphasized that the group remained the unit of legal and political analysis. He encouraged lawyers interested in Progressive reform to focus "on the social interests, the social groups, the social values" that would benefit from social change and to work to "bring the entire organized force of these groups and the entire weight of these values" into the processes of government formation.[49]

In 1933 Cohen accepted the invitation of a family friend, Nathan Margold, the new solicitor of the Department of the Interior, to help draft the Indian Reorganization Act. The act was meant to end the late-nineteenth-century federal policy of allotting tribal lands to individual Indians and forcing the assimilation of Indians. The New Dealers wanted to recast Indian tribes as groups with political and economic autonomy over their reservations and worked to grant them more authority over their economic, social, cultural, and political affairs. This endeavor became known as the "Indian New Deal."

Cohen knew little of Indian affairs when he joined the Department of the Interior as assistant solicitor. Influenced by Norman Thomas socialism on the one hand and pluralism on the other, he saw Indian tribes as one of many political and economic groups that would form the foundation of the modern pluralist state. He used his work on Indian reservations to create a model for other groups. This model was based upon group self-government and the collective ownership of property. Cohen wanted to empower tribes by advocating tribal self-government and incorporation for the purpose of running their economic affairs.

Here was the tension inherent in pluralism between an endorsement of group autonomy and a commitment to particular economic and political reforms. While encouraging self-government, early twentieth century legal pluralists also described bureaucratic expertise as a foundation of the modern state. In this vein, Cohen hoped that tribes would organize around an important economic enterprise and believed that, without community enterprises, the tribes would derive little if anything from the new policy.[50] What he failed to realize was how foreign that model was to Indian tribes.

In retrospect, it is perhaps not surprising that the Indian Reorganization Act fell short of most of its political and economic ambitions. It stopped the allotment of Indian lands, but political compromises made it ineffective in consolidating lands for Indian groups. More devastating was the fact that Cohen and his colleagues, ambivalent about the appropriate balance between pluralism and national planning, ended up rushing tribes (sometimes even coercing them) into a system of organization with which many Indians

---

[49] Felix S. Cohen, "Government and the Social Contract: Ethical Evaluations in the Law," in *The Legal Conscience: Selected Papers of Felix S. Cohen*, ed. Lucy Kramer Cohen (New Haven: Yale University Press, 1960), 362.

[50] Assistant Solicitor, Memorandum for Felix S. Cohen, July 20, 1937, Felix S. Cohen Papers Box 8 / Folder 119, Beinecke Rare Book and Manuscript Library, Yale University, New Haven, CT.

were unfamiliar. Tribal governments never became what the New Dealers envisioned them to be. Some commentators go as far as to suggest that tribal governments became "nothing more than adjuncts to the local administration, placidly rubber-stamping the decisions made by the Bureau of Indian Affairs."[51]

Despite its failure to create autonomous communities on Indian reservations, the Indian Reorganization Act aroused "a remarkable degree of Indian political activism." Councils engaged in heated debates with the Bureau of Indian Affairs over the scope of their powers, specifically over the "hiring and firing of agency employees, determination of tribal membership, salaries and perquisites of council members, and the handling of restricted tribal funds." And while tribal councils were, like other governments, often self-centered and self-serving, and while many of their efforts proved futile, they began to create a model for modern tribal leadership.[52]

This political activism also helped transform Cohen's legal pluralist vision. As much as he wanted to view Indian tribes as yet another group with economic and political powers, just like corporations and labor unions, Cohen quickly realized that in order for the pluralist model to be effective, it would have to pay attention to Indian tribes' unique cultures. He was thus in the right place at the right time to bring theories of legal pluralism to bear not only upon the treatment of economic and political groups but also upon the federal government's dealings with cultural and ethnic groups. Other early twentieth century legal pluralists may have been able to evade the issue of ethnic and cultural differences but Cohen was forced to address it.[53] Gradually, his legal pluralist vision and his understanding of his place as a Jew in American society changed. As the following sections elaborate, in the 1940s, just as other intellectuals shifted their attention from groups to individuals as the foundation of political and legal analysis, Cohen turned to the task of articulating a normative theory that would recognize the right of some groups to cultural sovereignty while at the same time limit the power of certain groups to discriminate, exclude, or receive priority in the distribution of natural resources.

Transitions

The 1940s were a crucial decade in the development of the modern discourse of civil rights. In the early half of the twentieth century, legal scholars associated rights with economic and social needs, specifically the rights of individuals to work, to livelihood, to social insurance, and to economic

---

[51] Graham D. Taylor, *The New Deal and American Indian Tribalism: The Administration of the Indian Reorganization Act, 1934–45* (Lincoln: University of Nebraska Press, 1980), 94.

[52] Ibid., 94. See also Paul C. Rosier, *Rebirth of the Blackfeet Nation, 1912–1954* (Lincoln: University of Nebraska Press, 2001), 96–97.

[53] On legal realism and ethnicity, see "Note: Legal Realism and the Race Question: Some Realism about Realism on Race Relations," *Harvard Law Review* 108 (1995): 1607–24.

independence. The "cultural politics of the 1920s," including the rebirth of the Ku Klux Klan and the passage of restrictive immigration laws, turned American intellectuals away from direct engagement with racial problems. Race and culture were seen as divisive issues, especially after racial and cultural battles almost destroyed the Democratic Party in 1924. But in the second half of the twentieth century, the concept of civil rights became associated with the rights of ethnic and religious minorities, specifically the right to be different.[54] For the most part, the shift from class to ethnicity took place in the 1940s.

Several factors helped turn the attention of lawyers, legal scholars, and government officials from the rights of labor to the rights of ethnic and racial minorities. Most dominant among them were apprehension about the potential spread of European totalitarianism, fears of Japanese propaganda directed at African Americans, and increased African American organization and protest. Despite the combined ascendance of both racial and labor related rights during the 1940s and the strong correlation between racial discrimination and economic inequality, the concept of liberty in the postwar years became associated with the right not to suffer racial and ethnic discrimination. The concept of social and economic citizenship gradually lost its primacy.[55]

The shift from social and economic rights to racial and ethnic equality was paralleled by a change in the perception of the role of the three branches of government in protecting civil rights. In the early twentieth century and during the New Deal, legal scholars emphasized the role of the executive and legislative branches in promoting social and economic rights. With totalitarianism in Europe, legal scholars grew concerned about the relationship between statism and tyranny.[56] Limiting the power of the legislative and executive branches became the underlying theme of scholarly writings about rights.

Moreover, if the state could become overpowering, so could groups and institutions. The early twentieth-century pluralist image of the state, with its collectivist undertones, rapidly came into disrepute, and legal scholars and political theorists turned their attention to the defense of the individual. Thus, the 1940s also witnessed a shift of intellectual and political focus

---

[54] Alan Brinkley, *The End of Reform: New Deal Liberalism in Recession and War* (New York: Vintage, 1995), 165; Risa L. Goluboff, *The Lost Promise of Civil Rights* (Cambridge, MA: Harvard University Press, 2007).

[55] John T. Elliff, *The United States Department of Justice and Individual Rights, 1937–1962* (New York: Taylor & Francis, 1987); William E. Forbath, "Civil Rights and Economic Citizenship: Notes on the Past and Future of the Civil Rights and Labor Movements," *University of Pennsylvania Journal of Labor and Employment Law* 2 (2000): 697–718; Risa L. Goluboff, "The Thirteenth Amendment and the Lost Origins of Civil Rights," *Duke Law Journal* 50 (2001): 1609–85; Herbert Hovenkamp, "The Political Economy of Substantive Due Process," *Stanford Law Review* 40 (1988): 379–447.

[56] See, for example, Brinkley, *The End of Reform: New Deal Liberalism in Recession and War*, 154–65.

from collective rights, specifically the workers' right to organize, to individual rights.

By the postwar years these transformations—from class to ethnicity, from civil rights as an affirmative obligation of the state to civil rights as constraints on the government, from collectivism to individualism—were complete. The concept of civil rights no longer was associated with an affirmative obligation of the government to protect individuals and groups; it was now associated with the (liberal) judicial role of imposing constitutional constraints on the government to prevent it from violating individual liberties. The Warren Court is remembered as the champion of this vision of democracy that focused on individual rights and liberties.[57]

Many Jewish scholars seemed to find the new discourse, with its emphasis on equality and social acceptance, appealing.[58] But some, like Cohen, continued to emphasize the substantive role of the state in protecting group rights. Viewing Jewish and American interests as joined in the fight against totalitarianism, Cohen celebrated the vision of legal pluralism as the ultimate American ideal of democracy.

Protecting Groups and Individuals

As early as his famous "Transcendental Nonsense and the Functional Approach" (1935), Cohen described law as a system of group (class, ethnic, religious) violence.[59] Cohen's realist critique of abstract concepts reflected the idea that "the law is itself a system of violence ... concealed or justified by a social ritual and ideology, a set of forms or phrases, a system of constantly reiterated ideals, which portrays the law as a moral force."[60] Cohen's functional approach was an attempt to replace such systematic violence with a theory of law that saw the role of the legal system as facilitating interactions between autonomous groups. Cohen realized that different societies, and different groups within a single society, reacted to similar social conditions in diverse ways. More important, he recognized that similar social conditions could generate different legal rules. For him, functionalism was the recognition that modern phenomena were composed of a multiplicity of facts and effects and should be studied as such.[61]

---

[57] Morton J. Horwitz, *The Warren Court and the Pursuit of Justice* (New York: Hill and Wang, 1998).

[58] See generally Edward S. Shapiro, "World War II and American Jewish Identity," *Modern Judaism* 10 (1990): 65–84.

[59] See Felix S. Cohen, "Transcendental Nonsense and the Functional Approach," in *The Legal Conscience: Selected Papers of Felix S. Cohen*, ed. Lucy Kramer Cohen (New Haven: Yale University Press, 1960). Originally published in *Columbia Law Review* 35 (1935): 809–49.

[60] Felix S. Cohen, "Socialism and the Myth of Legality," *American Socialist Quarterly* 4 (1935): 8.

[61] See Tsuk Mitchell, *Architect of Justice*, ch. 5.

Then, in the late 1930s, as Cohen witnessed the increasingly horrifying treatment of Jews in Europe and the absence of a serious American response, his belief in America's role in protecting diverse groups was shaken. When his plans to bring European refugees to American territories (Alaska and the Virgin Island) did not receive congressional or public support, Cohen came to realize, rather abruptly, that the pluralist description of the modern state as composed of many collective political institutions was insufficient. It could not protect the interests of groups and individuals outside American society. To support the idea that the outsider had a place in modern American society, he had to develop a theory about America's role in protecting human needs within and beyond its borders.

In his efforts to find a place for the outsider in American society, Cohen was forced to reassess the legal pluralist vision of the modern state. Stressing the role of groups and organizations in American society or the importance of social integration was not a justification for opening the borders to strangers or for protecting those strangers' interests. Cohen had to turn to the normative argument underlying pluralism—to the role of diversity in individual and social life. He began to describe the diversity of groups (social, cultural, religious, economic, political) that characterized American society, not only as a means of reconciling the tensions created by relativism or a source of a comforting sense of belonging, but also as the ground for the strength of the American democratic tradition and institutions. In Cohen's writings in the early 1940s tolerance bred freedom.

Here was Cohen's normative argument: pluralism rested on the assumption that diversity was important to individual and social life. Allowing individuals to come together in diverse groups was not enough. To embrace pluralism meant to protect the rights of individuals and groups both within and outside America's borders. As Cohen put it, "The human rights of the citizen are safe only when the rights of the foreigner are protected." Furthermore, the pluralist state would not thrive unless it protected the needs of all human beings. "Hatred of the alien," he announced, was "the mark of a declining civilization, that has lost its capacity to grow and is no longer able to assimilate what is of value in other cultures."[62]

According to Cohen, liberty was born of tolerance. Yet, Cohen's new pluralist interpretation was predicated not only upon an ideal of constitutionally protected individual rights, as the selected quotes might suggest, but also, more essentially, upon an ideal of constitutionally protected group rights. This was indeed the premise of his famous *Handbook of Federal Indian Law*, originally published in 1941. It proclaimed the longtime recognition by the federal government of tribal rights.

Given the typical Jewish scholars' rejection of moral relativism, Cohen did not hold that all group values were equally valid. For legal pluralists in the 1940s, protecting the rights of certain groups also meant limiting the

---

[62] Felix S. Cohen, "The Social and Economic Consequences of Exclusionary Immigration Laws," *National Lawyers Guild Quarterly* 2 (1939): 171, 191–92.

rights of others. As they saw it, in order to protect the rights of minority groups, one had to curtail the rights of oppressive groups. For one thing, Cohen and colleagues who shared his views worked throughout the early 1940s to limit or rebut the impact of literature seeking to foster racial, ethnic, and religious divisions, literature attacking the American way of life or American democratic traditions and institutions, and literature seeking to incite individuals and groups to acts of espionage and sabotage. Labeling such literature "totalitarian propaganda,"[63] they wanted to expose the promulgators of propagandist claims and to engage in a campaign of enlightenment to expose the fallacies of such claims.[64]

Totalitarian propaganda, as Cohen and his colleagues saw it, challenged the idea that the strength of American democracy was its diverse society. By focusing on the divisions in American society propagandists hoped to create "a maze of mutually suspicious and antagonistic racial and religious groups" and undermine national unity.[65] For one thing, Cohen stressed that cleavages based upon ancestry and race could potentially overpower "a nation founded upon the ideal of tolerance and having within it the blood of all races and all nations on earth."[66]

Cohen and his colleagues refused to accept that embracing pluralism could be a double-edged sword. Recognizing that American society also exhibited racist attitudes, they wanted to believe that the diversity of cultural, religious, and social interests characterizing American society was the source of its strength not weakness.[67] For the Jews among them the issue was personal: totalitarianism and antisemitism seemed joined at the root. In a speech delivered a few days after the attack on Pearl Harbor, Cohen criticized American Jews who downplayed the antisemitic nature of totali-

---

[63] Remarks of Senator Guy M. Gillette in the Senate, prepared by the Institute of Living Law, Thursday March 6, 1941, Felix S. Cohen Papers Box 79 / Folder 1243, Beinecke Rare Book and Manuscript Library, Yale University, New Haven, CT; Summary of Memorandum on Nazi Activities in the United States, May 14, 1940, Felix S. Cohen Papers Box 42 / Folder 627, Ibid.; Felix S. Cohen and Edith Lowenstein (for the Institute of Living Law), "Combating Totalitarian Propaganda: The Method of Suppression," *Illinois Law Review* 37 (1942–43): 193, 194.

[64] In 1942, David Reisman proclaimed that the government could suppress speech that threatened the democratic principles embodied in the Constitution. According to Reisman, the government could suppress speech if in so doing it promoted group participation, which, in turn, would advance democracy. See Mark A. Graber, "Old Wine in New Bottles: The Constitutional Status of Unconstitutional Speech," *Vanderbilt Law Review* 48 (1995): 349, 370–71 (discussing David Reisman, "Democracy and Defamation: Control of Group Libel," *Columbia Law Review* 42 (1942): 727).

[65] Transcript for Radio Program (WEVD), March 20, 1942, Felix S. Cohen Papers Box 79 / Folder 1244, Beinecke Rare Book and Manuscript Library, Yale University, New Haven, CT.

[66] Cohen and Lowenstein, "Combating Totalitarian Propaganda: The Method of Suppression," 196.

[67] On cultural attitudes portraying racism as un-American and on racism in America during World War II, see Mary L. Dudziak, "Desegregation as a Cold War Imperative," *Stanford Law Review* 41 (1988): 61, 68–73.

tarian regimes as well as those who urged American Jews not to call attention to themselves in discussions about totalitarianism. He wanted Jews to act. As he pointedly put it,

> No nation crushes the Jews in its midst until it has come to despise reason and morality and the dignity of the human soul, and no nation has yet found a way to live in peace and secure prosperity without these moral qualities.... And so I think that we have a special responsibility to help safeguard our country against the forces that would destroy our Republic by undermining the moral principles of liberty and tolerance on which the Republic is based.[68]

A similar faith in the moral ideals of liberty and tolerance, and a commitment to group rights, characterized Cohen's work in the 1940s to protect the rights of Alaska Natives to use their lands and waters. Applying his pluralist vision to property law, Cohen endeavored to accommodate the meanings that Alaska Natives attributed to ownership and occupancy. He wanted American law to embrace different legal ideals, specifically to recognize the property claims of Alaska Natives. In 1946, such ideas informed Cohen's draft of the Indian Claims Commission Act.

Fully cognizant of the fact that lands would not be returned to Indians, and that only limited compensation might be offered, Cohen stressed the need to establish a commission, not a court, to resolve Indian land claims. Because the proof of aboriginal title or the existence of treaties would require the testimony of Indians and their experts, Cohen wanted the commission to provide a forum for Indian tribes and individual Indians to tell their stories of American history. Accordingly, he suggested that the commission operate not "on a purely legal level" but rather "as an administrative agency empowered to reach a just solution within broad limits established by law."[69] If the Indian Reorganization Act set out to refute the antiquated policy of assimilation, Cohen wanted the commission to rewrite the future by telling a different narrative. He wanted it to offer Indian tribes a forum to voice their versions of American history.

In short, Cohen wanted the commission's proceedings to become exercises in hearing and learning from the testimony of the Indians. He wanted the commission to investigate "the entire field of Indian claims, even for those tribes which may be too poor to hire their own lawyers, and bring in within a reasonable period of time a report which will conclude once and for all this chapter of ... national history."[70] The legal remedy was meant to bring closure. It was also intended to call attention to and memorialize a

---

[68] Felix S. Cohen Papers Box 90 / Folder 1451, Beinecke Rare Book and Manuscript Library, Yale University, New Haven, CT.

[69] Felix S. Cohen, "Indian Claims," in *The Legal Conscience: Selected Papers of Felix S. Cohen*, ed. Lucy Kramer Cohen (New Haven: Yale University Press, 1960), 266–72. Originally published in *The American Indian* 2 (1945): 3–11.

[70] Ibid., 272.

different historical narrative. For Cohen, the Indian Claims Commission Act was a genuine attempt to use law as a tool of reconciliation and commemoration. He hoped that the commission would settle historical acts of political and cultural violence between particular groups while reconstructing new memories upon which they could build a pluralistic present.[71] The federal government's obligation toward Native Americans, anchored in treaties with Indian tribes, became an obligation toward all minority groups and society at large.

Cohen embraced the possibility of dialogue as an alternative to totalitarianism in Europe and changing federal Indian policy in the United States. His work throughout the 1940s aimed to establish new American standards through dialogue. Amidst a world war, Cohen thought that the only alternative to total annihilation was the preservation of diverse cultures. But by the late 1940s, the Department of the Interior had become less responsive to Cohen's pluralist agenda. Postwar discussions of civil rights and liberties in the United States failed to address the special status of minority groups. For one thing, in postwar American legal thought, especially after the rights revolution produced by the Warren Court, all individuals were considered equal and all were to be similarly treated. Special treatment of a group (such as Indian tribes) was associated with discriminatory practices.[72] Furthermore, as the attention of legal scholars and political theorists turned to the protection of individual rights, "American tolerance for different cultural values, such as community responsibility and tribalism," rapidly diminished. A concept of collective rights was envisioned as being in direct opposition to the idea of individual liberty.[73] In this atmosphere, Cohen's work (in the mid-1940s and early 1950s) to protect the property claims of Native Americans and Alaska Natives failed. American legal institutions resisted any attempt to remap the terrain of legal definitions, especially the definition of property, along collectivist assumptions. But, as the following section elaborates, Cohen's vision of legal pluralism survived the postwar backlash.

The Turn to Cultural Pluralism

By the 1950s, instead of using law as a means of promoting a particular vision of the state, Cohen wanted to use law as a means of promoting toler-

---

[71] Ironically, in practice, government attorneys transferred the Court of Claims' procedures to the commission, transforming it into a court and eliminating the flexibility that Cohen hoped to achieve by creating an investigatory commission. Vine Deloria Jr., *Behind the Trail of Broken Treaties: An Indian Declaration of Independence* (Austin, TX: University of Texas Press, 1985), 222–26.

[72] See similarly Moses Moskowitz to Felix S. Cohen, December 6, 1948, Felix S. Cohen Papers Box 50 / Folder 764, Beinecke Rare Book and Manuscript Library, Yale University, New Haven, CT.

[73] Rebecca Tsosie, "Separate Sovereigns, Civil Rights, and the Sacred Text: The Legacy of Thurgood Marshall's Indian Law Jurisprudence," *Arizona State University Law Journal* 26 (1994): 495, 530.

ance. After fourteen years in government service, Cohen no longer trusted policymakers to create a plural polity. He also no longer believed that cultural and ethnic tensions would disappear once groups gained economic and political autonomy. Indians had taught Cohen the need to cherish cultural pluralism both because they were most discriminated against and because Indian philosophy was predicated upon respect for diverse opinions. The Holocaust had crystallized the need. "The Indian tribe is the miner's canary," Cohen concluded his piece on Indian self-government, "and when it flutters and droops we know that the poison gasses of intolerance threaten all other minorities in our land. And who of us is not a member of some minority?"[74]

Cohen's question was meant to invoke empathy. Cohen wanted to believe that once individuals became aware of the experiences and cultures of those different from them, they would be able to see the similarities between themselves and others. Indeed, Cohen's jurisprudential theory in the 1950s aimed to help judges and lawyers become more tolerant. It was intended to uncover hidden assumptions and visions of judges and policymakers so that they could see through their biases and prejudices.

Cohen's hopes and aspirations in the 1930s focused on promoting certain political and economic goals. His legal pluralism was predicated upon the idea that self-governing collectivities would become the foundation of the modern state. In the early 1940s, Cohen emphasized the need to protect diverse groups. His pluralism rested on the assumption that group rights, whether the rights of Native Americans or Jewish refugees, were constitutionally protected. By the 1950s, Cohen seemed to have lost faith in the ability of law to bring about change. He used law as a tool to analyze prejudice so that individuals and groups might learn to be more tolerant of others. His pluralism became predicated upon the possibility of translation and dialogue between different value systems. Group autonomy and group rights became means to an end; they were tools that could be used to encourage and promote tolerance. In a world where racial attitudes often dominated law and policymaking, Cohen made tolerance of different ethnic, racial, and religious values the end of law, politics, and society.

Other Jewish scholars shared Cohen's legal pluralist vision. In the postwar years, as Jews became more assimilated and socially accepted, Horace Kallen's ideal of cultural pluralism rapidly gained prominence among Jewish scholars. They rejected the idea of a color-blind constitution and instead emphasized the right to be culturally different. Writing in 1950, Oscar Handlin, for example, celebrated the hyphenated Jewish-American, reassuring American Jews that "their support of Israel did not imply disloyalty to America." According to Handlin, the American ideal was one of

---

[74] Cohen, "Indian Self-Government," 313–14. See also Felix S. Cohen, Testimony before the Senate Sub-Committee on Labor and Labor Management (March 1952), Felix S. Cohen Papers Box 52 / Folder 795, Beinecke Rare Book and Manuscript Library, Yale University, New Haven, CT; Richard Drinnon, *Keeper of Concentration Camps: Dillon S. Myer and American Racism* (Berkeley: University of California Press, 1987), 268–69.

multiple loyalties, of expansive national identity.[75] In 1956, Kallen himself, while reassessing his cultural pluralist ideal, labeled it "the American idea." As Kallen saw it, this idea "was embodied in four revolutionary theses set forth in the Declaration of Independence": "that all men are created equal; ... that 'life, liberty, and the pursuit of happiness' are every man's unalienable rights"; that the government has a duty to "secure these rights"; and "that when government neglects or fails to perform the services for which it was devised, the people who instituted the government may 'alter or abolish it' and replace it with a 'new government.'" While Kallen clearly recognized that these ideals were not always fulfilled, the successes of the civil rights and women's rights movements sustained his belief that they would eventually be realized. As he saw it, the International Declaration of Human Rights was also "in harmony with his philosophy of cultural pluralism."[76]

Cultural pluralism, as a variant of his legal pluralism, was ultimately Felix Cohen's ideal. In an address he gave at CCNY on March 12, 1953, Cohen described what he labeled the American faith—"a faith different from the Catholic faith, the Protestant faith, the Jewish faith, different from all these, and yet somehow inclusive of them, inclusive too of the faith of good Americans who have been Mormons, Buddhists, Theosophists, Pagans, Atheists and Agnostics." According to Cohen, the core of the American faith was tolerance. Emphasizing the importance of cherishing different cultural identities, including his own, Cohen, who in the early 1930s rejected ethnic particularities, in 1953 endorsed Horace Kallen's ideal of cultural pluralism. His address concluded with the following:

> When the Fathers of our country sought to put what I am trying to say into a few words, they selected the motto, E Pluribus Unum, one out of many. I venture to think that they were not trying to describe an historical incident, the vanishing of the many and the appearance of the one, but rather were trying to describe an ideal of symbiosis. They were describing not the lifelessness of the melting pot in which every metal with its distinctive use sinks into a vast, monotonous, useless amalgam. That we can leave to Nazis and communists and other totalitarians. I venture to think that in this motto, far-seeing statement sought to describe the entity of the symphony. The symphony orchestra plays and every man in it remains an individual human being, more than individual and more human because he is a part of the great orchestra. Here in this great orchestra that is America, every creed, every culture, every people, every skill can make its great contribution. And that, I submit, is the meaning of the American flag, 13 stripes and 48 stars, soon I hope, 49, and perhaps 50 and more. Where else in the world will one find this glorification of diversity, set as the seal upon the life of a people?[77]

---

[75] Shapiro, "World War II and American Jewish Identity," 80.
[76] Ratner, "Horace M. Kallen and Cultural Pluralism," 53–54.
[77] Felix S. Cohen, "The Making of Americanism," Felix S. Cohen Papers Box 71 / Folder

In focusing on cultural diversity, rather than the multiplicity of sovereigns in society, cultural pluralism was a less radical alternative to political or legal pluralism. In acknowledging diversity, it offered a more realistic picture of American society than interest group pluralism, which was also articulated during the 1950s.[78] It is thus not surprising that in the 1960s and 1970s, growing numbers of scholars endorsed cultural pluralism, albeit under a different label: ethnicity. As Nathan Glazer and Daniel Moynihan put it in their book *Beyond the Melting Pot*, "common concerns about employment, economic opportunity, housing, and other important social questions lead members of an ethnic group to act together as pressure groups and live together as social groups."[79] Indeed, while the prominence of interest group pluralism during the 1950s helped obscure the legacy of earlier interpretations of pluralism, multiculturalism reinvented them in the 1980s.

Epilogue

In 1983, as if reiterating Felix Cohen's life lessons—from "Transcendental Nonsense" to the Indian Claims Commission Act—Robert M. Cover wrote:

> A legal tradition is hence part and parcel of a complex normative language and a mythos—narratives in which the corpus juris is located by those whose wills act upon it.... Law is a force, like gravity, through which our worlds exercise an influence upon one another, a force that affects the courses of these worlds through normative space.... The intelligibility of normative behavior inheres in the communal character of the narratives that provide the context of that behavior.[80]

Like the work of the early legal pluralists, Cover's famous "Nomos and Narrative" reminded his audience that groups shared legal understandings that were likely to clash with those of other groups or the national legal

---

1140, Beinecke Rare Book and Manuscript Library, Yale University, New Haven, CT.

[78] Interest group pluralism was a descriptive social theory, purportedly with no ethical conviction. It was inspired by a rejection of all absolutism, including any morally based pleas for social reform. Drawing on models of equilibrium derived from economics, theories of interest group pluralism rested on the assumption that society was composed of multiple interest groups interacting, competing, and trading ends in neutral economic and political markets. Political compromises between diverse pressure groups were presumed to produce shared public goods. Robert Dahl's interest group pluralism was the ultimate example. See Robert A. Dahl, *A Preface to Democratic Theory* (Chicago: University of Chicago Press, 1956); idem, *Pluralist Democracy in the United States: Conflict and Consent* (Chicago: University of Chicago Press, 1967).

[79] Ratner, "Horace M. Kallen and Cultural Pluralism," 59.

[80] Robert M. Cover, "Nomos and Narrative," in *Narrative, Violence, and the Law: The Essays of Robert Cover*, eds. Martha Minow, Michael Ryan, and Austin Sarat (Ann Arbor: University of Michigan Press, 1995), 95–103. Originally published in *Harvard Law Review* 97 (1983): 4–68.

order. Like Cohen, Cover did not envision simple solutions, but he wanted his audience, especially judges, to understand the multiplicity of legal orders in society and to work to allow them mutually to coexist. Cover, however, was more explicit than Cohen about the Jewish origins of his solution.

According to Cover, while the American liberal jurisprudence of rights emerged to counter the centralized force of the Western nation-state, the Jewish legal system, which having had "no centralized power and little in the way of coercive violence" for more than 1,900 years, used a discourse of obligations to reinforce the bonds of solidarity. Lacking a "hierarchically determined authoritative voice," it developed a jurisprudence grounded in the possibility of multiple meanings. Authority was diffuse, but such diffusion reinforced the significance of obligations. "The word 'mitzvah' which literally means commandment but has a general meaning closer to 'incumbent obligation'" occupied in Jewish law "a place equivalent in evocative force to the American legal system's 'rights.'"[81]

Cohen's pluralist vision of the modern state was imbued with a notion of incumbent obligations. While emphasizing the federal government's obligations toward Indians as a group, not merely as individuals, Cohen also stressed that the government's failure to fulfill its obligations was not a problem of contract law. Rather, it was an act of oppression, banned by the U.S. Constitution. "Racial oppression," he cautioned, had "seldom destroyed the people that was oppressed, [but] it has always in the end destroyed the oppressor."[82] Pushing the envelope further, Cover, while stressing the significance of the discourse of individual and group rights, concluded that realization of such rights was not only the obligation of the government, but rather the obligation of every individual.[83]

For Cover as it was for Cohen, the pluralist vision was born both in hope and in doubt. Both viewed law as a means of remedying historical wrongs against minority groups. Yet both also understood the violence inherent in the law, specifically in a national legal system. For both Cohen and Cover, mediating the tension between law's protection and its harm was the task of the modern, pluralist state. Both offered solutions grounded in Jewish norms, which were developed on the margins of a centralized state. It is through their work that we can begin to see the role that Jewish legal scholars played in developing and sustaining the legal pluralist image of the modern American state as well as the significance of this vision to the twenty-first century.

---

[81] Robert M. Cover, "Obligations: A Jewish Jurisprudence of the Social Order," in *Narrative, Violence, and the Law*, eds. Minow, Ryan, and Sarat, 239–48. Originally published in *Journal of Law and Religion* 5 (1987): 65–74.

[82] Felix S. Cohen, "Indians are Citizens," in *The Legal Conscience: Selected Papers of Felix S. Cohen*, ed. Lucy Kramer Cohen (New Haven: Yale University Press, 1960), 257. Originally published in *The American Indian* 1 (1944): 12–22.

[83] Cover, "Obligations: A Jewish Jurisprudence of the Social Order," 248.

Texts, Values, and Historical Change: Reflections on the Dynamics of Jewish Law

David Berger*

The image of Jewish law as a self-contained fortress impervious to the slings and arrows of external fortunes or extra-legal ideologies and values has been nurtured by two very different forces. For centuries, even millennia, Christian authors depicted Judaism as a legalistic religion indifferent to considerations of loving-kindness and grace. As Paul succinctly puts it, "The letter kills, but the spirit gives life" (2 Cor 3:6). An early Protestant joke told of a Catholic priest who mistakenly placed an inedible object in the mouth of a communicant; after waiting an intolerably long time for it to melt on his tongue, the parishioner exclaimed, "Father! You have made a mistake. You have given me God the Father. He is so hard and tough He will never dissolve."

Under the impact of religious and intellectual transformations in the late nineteenth and early twentieth centuries, Christian scholars contrasted the legalism and ethical backwardness of rabbinic Judaism with the spiritually refreshing and ethically sensitive message of Jesus. Jews from across the religious spectrum denounced these assertions, contending that they were rooted in both ignorance and anti-Jewish bias.[1] As I have noted in earlier essays, some of these denunciations were not without their irony, since Reform Jews, who had abandoned many of the rituals of Judaism for reasons by no means alien to the rhetoric of Christian critics, now composed paeans of praise to the spiritually uplifting character of the minutiae of rabbinic law.[2] Now, however, we confront a very different irony. Some

---

* Ruth & I. Lewis Gordon Professor of Jewish History and Dean, Bernard Revel Graduate School of Jewish Studies, Yeshiva University. After the Cardozo School of Law conference where the first version of this chapter was presented, Daniel Sperber published two books of considerable relevance to this theme: *Darkah shel halakhah* (Jerusalem: Reuben Mass, 2007), and *Netivot pesikah* (Jerusalem: Reuben Mass, 2008). While I have not incorporated material from these works into the chapter, readers will profit from consulting them and some of the literature that they cite.

[1] I have discussed the latter development along with the responses of Jewish apologists in David Berger, "'The Jewish Contribution' to Christianity," in *The Jewish Contribution to Civilization: Reassessing an Idea*, ed. Jeremy Cohen and Richard I. Cohen (Oxford: Littman Library of Jewish Civilization, 2007), 80–97, repr. in Berger, *Persecution, Polemic and Dialogue: Essays in Jewish-Christian Relations* (Boston: Academic Studies Press, 2010), 312–32.

[2] David Berger, "Religion, Nationalism, and Historiography: Yehezkel Kaufmann's Account of Jesus and Early Christianity," in *Scholars and Scholarship: The Interaction Between Judaism and Other Cultures,* ed. Leo Landman (New York: Yeshiva University Press, 1990),

Orthodox Jews, acting out of the deepest loyalty to Jewish law and angrily rejecting hostile evaluations of Jewish ethics, respond to what they see as the utter abandonment of legal discipline advocated by Reform and even Conservative Judaism by reinforcing the view that halakhah is marked by a self-contained analysis of texts allowing for very little consideration of changed historical circumstances, external pressures, ideological concerns, and human sensitivities.

To a large degree, the debate about halakhic flexibility is carried out on both sides by recourse to straw men. On the one hand, a legal system whose practitioners have sincerely believed in its divine origin cannot reasonably be expected to have treated it as potters treat their clay; on the other, no legal system could have remained viable from the period of the Talmud to the contemporary age had it not responded to human needs and even ideological transformations in ways that looked beyond the straightforward meaning of its inherited texts.

In this overview, I will attempt to depict certain patterns of halakhic re-evaluation that emerged in response to new economic, humanitarian, and religious concerns. The significant variables determining such re-evaluation include, inter alia, the seriousness of the need, ideological convictions, the susceptibility of the text to reasonable reinterpretation, the severity of the prohibition in question, popular instincts regarding that prohibition, and the attitude of the decisor and his community to the likelihood that popular practice may be in error.

At the risk of classifying myself as the *golem*, or boor, of *Avot* 5:7, who does not proceed in order but addresses the last point first, let me begin with the final variable. Practices of a purely ritual nature developed in various Jewish communities and sub-communities that stand in stark contrast to the apparently unambiguous requirements of Jewish law. Thus, Rabbi Moses Isserles testified that, in sixteenth-century Poland, only exceptionally pious Jews slept in a sukkah.[3] Similarly, most hasidic and many non-hasidic Jews in the diaspora do not eat in a sukkah on the festival of Shemini Atzeret even though the standard major authorities ruled that one must.[4] In the months preceding Passover, a large majority of observant Jews eat grain that should presumably be classified as newly grown and hence prohibited; a generation ago, the vast majority of observant Jews in the United States were not even aware of the prohibition despite its explicit appearance in Leviticus. In these and similar cases, no broader issues are at stake; rather, the assumption that extensive sectors of pious and learned

---

154 (repr. in Berger, *Persecution, Polemic, and Dialogue*, 296); and Berger, "'The Jewish Contribution' to Christianity." See also Christian Wiese, *Wissenschaft des Judentums und protestantische Theologie in wilhelminischen Deutschland: Ein Schrei ins Leere?* (Tübingen: Mohr-Siebeck, 1999), 162.

3 Gloss on *Shulhan 'Arukh*, "Orah Hayyim" 639:2.

4 See Aaron M. Schreiber, *Yesodot ha-Nohag Lehimmana' mi-Yeshivah be-Sukkah bi-Shemini 'Atzeret be-hutz la-'Aretz* (Jerusalem: Netiv ha-Berakhah, 2004).

Jews would be engaging in blatant violations of the Torah was so unacceptable to rabbinic authorities that justifications were sought and found.

Haym Soloveitchik has argued that in the Middle Ages the self-image of a community was a central factor in determining whether or not popular custom would be maintained or overridden. Ashkenazi authorities were more likely to defend prevailing practice because they perceived their communities favorably, while Sephardi rabbis were more willing to assume that their fellow Jews were sinners out of either ignorance or indifference.[5] In a celebrated article, Soloveitchik applies this insight to contemporary Jewry, arguing that in the last few generations Orthodox Jews have lost confidence in the traditions that they learned from their parents, so that they have replaced a mimetic society with one that tests all prevailing practices against the standards established by texts.[6]

Ideological considerations have played an interesting and sometimes ironic role in the reception of that article. Many Modern Orthodox Jews have expressed satisfaction with its thesis because Soloveitchik's examples of deviation from traditional behaviors tend to involve text-based stringencies such as the increased size of the required measure of matzah, and such innovations are ideal grist for mockery directed at the Orthodoxies of the right. Modernist ideology, however, can also trump mimesis. Thus, some of those who lionize the mimetic society as they savor the anti-haredi uses of Soloveitchik's analysis are simultaneously impelled by feminist convictions to change generations of synagogue practice on the basis of textual analysis far more tenuous than the considerations that lead the traditionalist Orthodox to their usually more stringent deviations from the practices of the past. Affirmation or rejection of a mimetic ideal can depend very much on whose ox is being gored.

I shall soon return to women's issues in even more sensitive contexts, but let me first make some observations about the much-studied reactions of rabbinic decisors to serious economic pressures that beset Jews in the Middle Ages. When facing a prohibition of rabbinic rather than biblical status, the difficulties of ruling leniently in the face of economic necessity were substantially mitigated. Thus, in a particularly striking illustration of this point, Rabbi Yom Tov ben Avraham of Seville (Ritva, 1250–1330) made the frontal assertion that the rabbinic prohibition against business dealings with idolaters on pagan holidays lest they thank their gods was never in-

---

[5] Soloveitchik formulates this point vigorously in his *Halakhah, Kalkalah ve-Dimmuy 'Atzmi: ha-Mashkona'ut bi-Yemei ha-Beinayim* (Jerusalem: Magnes Press, 1985), 111–12, 116–19, seeing it as so central that he incorporates it into the book's title. Nonetheless, a key chapter (pp. 59–81) establishes and analyzes a significant distinction between 12th-century French and German authorities, where the argument about contrasting communal self-perceptions does not appear to apply. Recently, Soloveitchik has expressed reservations about the universality of the medieval Ashkenazi inclination to defend problematic popular practice. See his *Ha-Yayin bi-Yemei ha-Beinayim* (Jerusalem: Zalman Shazar Center for Jewish History, 2009), 369.

[6] Haym Soloveitchik, "Rupture and Reconstruction: The Transformation of Contemporary Orthodoxy," *Tradition* 28/4 (1994): 64–130.

tended to apply in cases where economic survival was at stake.⁷ The Tosafists appealed to a principle that can sometimes overcome even a biblical prohibition, to wit, that observing this restriction could generate hatred toward Jews. In this instance they were able to cite compelling talmudic evidence that such a concern is decisive. Rabbenu Tam (1100–1171) dealt with the challenge by restricting the prohibition to ritual objects.

Even more strikingly—and with consequences the medieval authorities are not likely to have foreseen—new assertions about the Jewish evaluation of Christianity, which has legal ramifications beyond its theological significance, emerged out of the crucible of these medieval economic realities. Thus the Tosafists made the modest assertion that their Christian contemporaries, not being particularly pious, are unlikely to respond to a business arrangement with a thanksgiving prayer to their deity. When they formulated this point as "contemporary Gentiles do not worship idolatry," the potential was created for interesting conclusions to be drawn in subsequent generations. Rabbenu Gershom of Mainz allowed transactions on Christian holidays on the basis of a cryptic line in the Talmud affirming that "Gentiles outside the land of Israel are not idolaters; rather, they follow the custom of their ancestors." Here too the potential for a reading broader than the one intended by Rabbenu Gershom is self-evident.⁸ When Tosafot permitted another sort of business arrangement on the grounds that *shituf*, "association" (of other powers with God, which probably applied only to an oath) is not forbidden to Noahides, the seeds were sown for the later affirmation that Judaism considers the worship of Jesus along with God entirely permissible for non-Jews.⁹ In other words, when straightforward law is leavened by other considerations, it is not just the law in question that can be affected; despite what Soloveitchik once called "halakhic federalism," a position initially intended to apply to a focused, restricted context cannot always be expected to know its place.¹⁰ *Bush v. Gore*, the Supreme Court decision that effectively resolved the 2000 presidential election in favor of

---

⁷ *Ve-tu she-'anu tzerikhim latet ve-laset 'immahem mi-shum hayyei nefesh*. To be sure, this point appears as the third in a series of four arguments for a permissive position. See *Hiddushei ha-Ritva le-Rabbenu Yom Tov be-Rav Avraham alIishbili: Massekhet Avodah Zarah*, ed. R. Moshe Goldstein (Jerusalem: Mosad Harav Kook, 1978), col. 16 (on *Avodah Zarah* 6b).

⁸ A *locus classicus* presenting and evaluating these arguments is Tosafot *AZ* 2a, s.v. *asur*.

⁹ For a discussion of the various interpretations of the relevant Tosafot (*San.* 63b s.v. *asur*), see Appendix III of my *The Rebbe, the Messiah, and the Scandal of Orthodox Indifference* (London: Littman Library of Jewish Civilization, 2001); Hebrew version, *Ha-Rebbe Melekh ha-Mashiah, Sha'aruriyyat ha-'Adishut, ve-ha-'Iyyum 'al Emunat Yisra'el* (Jerusalem: Urim, 2005).

¹⁰ I made this point in Berger, "Jacob Katz on Jews and Christians in the Middle Ages," in *The Pride of Jacob: Essays on Jacob Katz and his Work*, ed. Jay M. Harris (Cambridge, MA: Harvard University Press, 2002), 60–61, repr. in Berger, *Persecution, Polemic, and Dialogue*, 72.

George W. Bush, is, or at least may soon become, an instructive case in point.[11]

All, or virtually all, of these medieval arguments for permitting problematic economic activity are perfectly plausible. The underlying question is whether, as Jacob Katz and others have taken for granted, the permissibility of such business dealings was absolutely predetermined by the economic realities that faced medieval Jews. Despite the instincts of historians, one cannot be utterly certain that the answer to this question is affirmative. Rabbi Yehiel of Paris told his interlocutors during the Paris disputation of 1240 that if Jews did not sincerely believe that contemporary Christians were different from ancient pagans in legally relevant ways, they would not suspend talmudic law affecting economic matters; after all, he said, we have provided abundant evidence that we are willing to die for our faith.[12] As it happens, the grounds for suspending those laws did not require the far-reaching re-evaluation of the status of Christians that Rabbi Yehiel proffered in the disputation; moreover, the embrace of martyrdom in moments of religious ecstasy may well be more probable than the willingness of an entire community to commit slow economic suicide. Still, the observation that Jews would not provide knowingly insincere excuses for violating the Torah is surely correct. Israel Ta-Shma, the distinguished scholar who dealt with some of these issues, once told me that one's initial inclination is to assume that rabbinic decisors would conjure up any available interpretation, however flimsy, to justify a conclusion required for economic survival. Nonetheless, he added, as one reads the arguments of a figure like Rabbenu Tam in detail, an unexpected reaction begins to develop, to wit, "This conclusion is actually correct." While this may be a tribute to Rabbenu Tam's genius, it says something important about the subtlety and complexity of the interplay between communal need and textual analysis.

Rabbenu Tam himself famously asserted in a related context that it is a mitzvah to provide Jews with sustenance,[13] and this leads us to a key element in this discussion, to wit, the overt consideration of concerns that are not part of the narrow textual discourse. I call these competing religious values, by which I mean that they compete with the legal conclusion that would follow from a simple reading of the directly relevant texts, and we shall encounter them in various guises in the course of our discussion. It is, moreover, important to note what Rabbenu Tam's formulation affirms, namely, that the recognition of economic needs is itself a religious value, so that it may legitimately be considered in choosing a plausible halakhic position over a competing one that would be more compelling in a world without real people and critical human needs.

---

[11] See "Editorial Notebook," *New York Times*, Aug. 15, 2006 (discussing *Bush v. Gore*, 531 U.S. 98 (2000)).

[12] *Vikkuah Rabbenu Yehi'el mi-Paris*, ed. Reuven Margaliyot (Lvov: 1928), 21.

[13] R. Isaac b. Moses, *Or Zarua'*, no. 202. The passage is reproduced in Soloveitchik, *Halakhah, Kalkalah, ve-Dimmuy 'Atzmi*, 136, document 21. (Note 26 on page 66 mistakenly refers the reader to document 22.)

Despite Katz's emphasis on the role of economic pressures in driving halakhic decision-making, he was not only cognizant of the role of texts but also emphasized the intuitively less obvious impact of what he called ritual instinct. Such an instinct can sometimes overcome dire economic needs to the point where pious laypeople will not even ask their rabbis if a particular act might be permitted given exigent circumstances. If the forbidden act has been avoided since childhood to the point where the prohibition is embedded in the deepest layers of the individual's psyche, it becomes almost unthinkable, especially if it requires an unmediated physical action.[14]

In examining this complex matrix of texts, instincts, needs, values, and convictions, let me now turn to competing religious values of two major sorts: ideological and humanitarian. These are independent categories, but they can interact in a striking fashion.

With the rise of both the Reform movement and general estrangement from all forms of Judaism, Orthodox rabbinic authorities reacted in diverse and sometimes contradictory ways. Here, the religious value was the protection of the traditional community from deviation, a value with the potential for conflict with straightforward law. In some cases, this value extended to the need to establish a *modus vivendi* with a deviationist movement that could not be vanquished. To accomplish these ends, some authorities endorsed mild innovations like a vernacular sermon or a male choir. More significantly, there were rabbis in Central Europe who were prepared to classify Reform Jews under a talmudic rubric that exempted children brought up among non-Jews from the harsh sanctions applicable to heretics.[15] In the twentieth century, no less a figure than the Hazon Ish (Rabbi Avraham Yeshayahu Karelitz, 1878–1953) famously argued that because of the absence in our time of evident divine providence, the most extreme of those sanctions against heretics are no longer applicable at all.[16]

In contrast, there were more stringent responses to Reform Judaism that incorporated a rhetoric that went beyond the plain meaning of the controlling texts. Thus, rabbis mobilized the most extreme categories of Jewish law in prohibiting the construction of a synagogue without a platform in the center or the recitation of public prayer in a language other than Hebrew. They did so more categorically than precedent could easily justify, and they subjected all innovation to intense suspicion and scrutiny.[17]

---

[14] See his summary paragraph in Jacob Katz, *The 'Shabbes Goy': A Study in Halakhic Flexibility* (Philadelphia: Jewish Publication Society, 1989), 231. Haym Soloveitchik emphasizes Jewish revulsion at drinking gentile wine as a decisive factor in determining actual behavior in medieval Ashkenaz. See Haym Soloveitchik, *Yeinam: Sahar be-Yeinam shel Goyim: 'al Gilgulah shel ha-Halakhah be-'Olam ha-Ma'aseh* (Tel Aviv: Alma, 2003), 104–21.

[15] For a recent discussion, see Adam S. Ferziger, *Exclusion and Hierarchy: Orthodoxy, Nonobservance, and the Emergence of Modern Jewish Identity* (Philadelphia: University of Pennsylvania Press, 2005), 99–105.

[16] R. Avraham Yeshayahu Karelitz, *Hazon Ish, Yoreh De'ah* (Benei Berak: Harav Grainiman, 1961 or 1962), "Hilkhot Shehitah," 2:16.

[17] See, for example, Jacob Katz, *A House Divided: Orthodoxy and Schism in Nineteenth-*

The imperative of retrieving Jews estranged from tradition created halakhic pressures of its own, which could also elicit either lenient or stringent approaches. Thus, Rabbi Moshe Feinstein and Rabbi Shlomo Zalman Auerbach, two of the twentieth-century's most eminent decisors, took very different positions on the question of organizing events on the sabbath intended for non-observant Jews who would surely travel to the event in a manner that violates the Sabbath.[18] In this instance, Rabbi Auerbach's lenient view required the daring affirmation that the objective of enhancing observance in the long run meant that the organizer of the event is not leading people to sin in the technical sense of the prohibition.

Another historical development with profound ideological freight, religious and otherwise, was the Zionist movement and the state that it produced. Here, there can be no question that the decisor's ideological position can affect his ruling. Once we recognize that a competing religious value can legitimately play a role in reaching a decision, much depends on whether or not the rabbi in question recognizes the legitimacy of that competing value. A striking example of this dynamic is Rabbi Abraham Isaac Kook's letter in response to a rabbi who opposed the strategy of effecting a formal sale of the land of Israel to a non-Jew during the sabbatical year, so that Jews would be permitted to work the land:

> I must stand in the breach against those who besmirch people who come to settle the land of Israel and who, in the absence of an alternative, are forced to depend on this permissive ruling, which has already become widespread and has a basis in the positions of the Talmuds and the decisors. Such besmirching damages the *yishuv* both spiritually and materially. Materially, because it is impossible for all to observe the laws of the sabbatical year without annulment, since if they will not export the goods ... the land will literally become desolate, God forbid.... Spiritually, because publicizing the prohibition will close the door to entry into the land of Israel ... to all loyal Jews, so that only those who throw the religion behind their backs will immigrate.[19]

He goes on to posit that even religious Jews currently living in Israel will in large measure feel unable to abide by the prohibition, in which case they will come to see themselves as sinners and will stop observing the Torah in other respects as well. Although it is true, he concedes, that from a

---

Century Central European Jewry, trans. Ziporah Brody (Hanover: Brandeis University Press, 1998), 77ff.

[18] For a brief summary, see R. David Sperling, "Inviting Shabbat Guests Who Will Drive," www.nishmat.net/article.php?id=5&heading=0. Sperling also points to the permissive ruling of R. Moshe Sternbuch. See also the discussion in R. Yehuda Amital, "Rebuking a Fellow Jew: Theory and Practice," in *Jewish Tradition and the Non-Traditional Jew*, ed. Jacob J. Schacter (Northvale, N.J.: Jason Aaronson, 1992), 127–38.

[19] R. Avraham Yitzhak Hakohen Kook, *Iggerot ha-Re'iyah*, vol. 1 (Jerusalem: Mosad Harav Kook, 1985), no. 311, pp. 346–47.

purely spiritual perspective it would be better to maintain a stringent position, this fails to take into account a reality in which clearheaded people will understand the unacceptable consequences of doing so.[20]

While Rabbi Kook insists in this letter that the old *yishuv* and the new one are intertwined, so that the destruction of the latter entailed by a stringent ruling would also destroy the former, in another letter he explicitly connects his permissive position to his conviction that strengthening and increasing the new Jewish settlement in the land of Israel will hasten the redemption.[21] A rabbi who did not support the Zionist enterprise would have been far more likely to affirm the stringent position that Rabbi Kook himself recognizes as preferable in the abstract. Rabbinic stands on other issues of Jewish law also vary to a significant degree depending on the decisor's attitude toward Zionism and the state, though there is certainly no absolute correspondence across the board. Examples include the propriety of exempting yeshiva students from army service, returning land to Arab states or ceding it to Palestinians, and matters that should theoretically have little or nothing to do with Zionism but operate in its penumbra, such as celebrating one day of a festival rather than two when visiting Israel and accepting the rabbinate's ordinary *kashrut* supervision rather than insisting on a more stringent standard.

In addition to these ideological factors, humanitarian values can also stand in tension with the plain meaning of legal texts. Here, too, historical developments create new situations in which such concerns become acute. Since issues of personal status tend to provide the most poignant illustrations, they will be the focus of our discussion.

Several movements and crises have forced Jews to face the question of whether a significant number of individuals who wanted to contract a marriage but whose status rendered such an action problematic should be permitted to do so. In the case of Karaism, whose adherents deny the authority of the Oral Law, the procedure for marriage was essentially the same as that of Rabbanites, but the divorce document did not meet rabbinic requirements. It appeared, then, that Karaite marriages may be valid and their divorces invalid. For those rabbinic authorities who embraced this position, a terrible consequence followed, to wit, that the child of a divorced woman's second marriage would be the product of an adulterous relationship and hence essentially unmarriageable. This conclusion was captured in a morbid play on words based on the law that garments rent in mourning over one's parents may never be repaired. *Ha-kera'im* (with an *ayin*) *einam mit'ahim le-'olam*. By changing the *ayin* to an *alef*, we produce a tragic variant: *Ha-kara'im einam mit'ahim le-'olam*—"The Karaites can never become brothers."[22] The most plausible argument for avoiding this unfor-

---

[20] Ibid.

[21] *Mishpat Kohen* (Jerusalem: Mosad Harav Kook, 1966), no. 63, p. 129.

[22] See R. Ben Zion Hai Uziel, *Sefer Mishpetei 'Uzzi'el: mahadura tinyana*, 1st ed., part 2, vol. 1 (Tel Aviv: Jacob Levitski, 1935), "Yoreh De'ah," no. 63, p. 218.

tunate conclusion is that Karaite marriages do not take effect *ab initio* because the witnesses are invalid,[23] and we shall have occasion to examine this approach as we proceed.

In the aftermath of the mass conversion of Jews in the crucible of late-fourteenth-and fifteenth-century Iberia, the problem of marriageability arose in a different context, generated by the law of levirate marriage. A childless *converso* couple would leave Spain for a location where they could observe Judaism. Upon the death of the husband, the widow would ask if she could remarry without obtaining the release called *halitzah* from her deceased husband's brother, a *converso* residing in Spain or Portugal. Any argument to permit such a marriage depended perforce on the assumption that the *converso* community is to be seen as a community of sinners, even of willing sinners. Thus, the original witnesses would be delegitimated or, in an even more extreme formulation, the levir would not be classified as a real "brother." In the context of the historians' debate over the beliefs and practices of this community, Yosef Hayim Yerushalmi argued, I think correctly, that one reason for questioning the historical validity of rabbinic assertions in this context that the *conversos* were in fact willing Christians is that the decisors were facing a humanitarian imperative to relieve this woman's suffering. Their desire to achieve this result would incline them to accept judgments about *converso* sinfulness that they might otherwise have examined more critically.[24] This does not mean that their assessment was insincere, or even incorrect, only that we must approach it with care.

An extraordinary expression of the passions that swirled around this question and the role of religious and human considerations that impinged upon it appears in a remarkable outburst by Rabbi Moses Kapsali, the leading Turkish rabbi during the period of the expulsion from Spain. He permitted such women to remarry, and those who, ruling stringently, did not permit them to do so were in his view

> agents of idolatry, whose intention [!] is only to prevent these forced converts from worshipping God, may He be blessed. For if these women will believe after hearing such rulings that they will be unable to marry, they will not return to the worship of God ...and will return to their improper path. And those rabbis are close to being instigators [to idolatry], and it is almost the case that they are subject to the death penalty in accordance with the law that applies to a seducer and instigator.[25]

---

[23] See, for example, R. David b. Solomon ibn Abi Zimra, *She'elot u-Teshuvot ha-Radbaz* I (Jerusalem: Yerid ha-Sefarim, 2004), no. 73, p. 52.

[24] Yosef Hayim Yerushalmi, *From Spanish Court to Italian Ghetto: Isaac Cardoso, A Study in Seventeenth-Century Marranism and Jewish Apologetics*, rev. ed. (Seattle: University of Washington Press, 1981), 25–26.

[25] Quoted in R. Benjamin b. Mattityahu, *She'elot u-Teshuvot Binyamin Ze'ev* (Jerusalem: Defus Safra, 1959), no. 75. The author (no. 76) rejects R. Kapsali's position. Cited along with additional sources by Simcha Assaf, *Be-'Oholei Ya'akov* (Jerusalem: Mosad Harav

In contemporary times, the strategy of invalidating a marriage on the grounds that the witnesses were not observant Jews is associated most prominently with Rabbi Moshe Feinstein, who mobilized it to permit Reform Jews to remarry after a civil divorce, to permit Reform divorcees to marry—or at least to remain married to—men of priestly lineage, and to remove the taint of illegitimacy from the children of the second marriage of Reform divorcees.[26] While some prominent authorities disagreed with this position, it has largely won the day as a result of its humanitarian consequences as well as its preservation of marriageability across denominational lines, and, ironically, because the invalidating of Reform witnesses appeals to the anti-Reform ideology of traditionalist Orthodox Jews who might otherwise have resisted such a lenient decision.

Another ruling promoting Jewish unity has also more or less prevailed in a somewhat ironic fashion. Ethiopian Jews have been declared unequivocally Jewish by Rabbi Ovadiah Yosef on the basis of a sixteenth-century responsum affirming their descent from the tribe of Dan.[27] The historical evidence militates strongly against this position, but Modern Orthodox Jews, who sometimes denounce traditionalist authorities for excluding non-traditional evidence from their purview, are happy to endorse this unhistorical conclusion because it serves needs with which they identify.[28]

Finally, the spectrum of positions on proper standards of conversion also reflects concerns about unity and social cohesion. The classic prohibition against conversion in contemplation of marriage has been dismissed by many authorities as inapplicable in an age where civil marriage and even cohabitation are socially acceptable alternatives to religious marriage. But the question of recognition before or after the fact of a convert who did not genuinely accept the obligation to observe the Torah as Orthodoxy understands it remains a matter of deep contention. *De jure*, and to a growing extent *de facto*, the stringent position dominates, but the Jewish social fabric, especially in Israel, is imperiled in different ways by all the positions, and there is no question that decisors have been influenced by their varying perceptions of the imperatives of national/communal unity.

Have rabbinic decisors, then, allowed their rulings to be affected by economic and communal needs, by ideological commitments, and by hu-

---

Kook, 1943), 178–79.

[26] *Iggerot Mosheh*, "Even ha-'Ezer" (New York: Moriah, 1973), sec. 3, no. 23, pp. 445–46.

[27] *Shu"t Yabbia' Omer*, "Even ha-'Ezer," vol. 8 (Jerusalem, 1995), no. 11, pp. 404–09. The responsum also rules leniently with respect to the question of marriageability, and in the course of the discussion surveys opinions on the marriageability of Karaites as well.

[28] I made this point in "Identity, Ideology, and Faith: Some Personal Reflections on the Social, Cultural, and Spiritual Value of the Academic Study of Judaism," in *Study and Knowledge in Jewish Thought*, ed. Howard Kreisel (Beersheva: Ben Gurion University of the Negev Press, 2006), 25–26, repr. in Berger, *Cultures in Collision and Conversation: Essays in the Intellectual History of the Jews* (Boston: Academic Studies Press, 2011), 17. On the historical evidence, see Steven Kaplan, *The Beta Israel (Falasha) in Ethiopia: From Earliest Times to the Twentieth Century* (New York: New York University Press, 1992).

manitarian concerns? Of course they have. Have these influences operated primarily on a subconscious level? I do not think so. Rabbinic authorities generally know what they are doing, and they are well aware of the factors that they weigh in rendering a decision. Jacob Katz noted a striking interpretation by Rabbi Moses Sofer (Hatam Sofer, 1762–1839) of a prayer that entreats God to provide us our livelihood in permissible rather than forbidden ways. This means, said the Hatam Sofer, that we ask not to be put in a position in which we have to permit something that on a straightforward reading would be prohibited.[29] On rare occasions, we can envision pressures so powerful that Herculean efforts would be exercised to bend the texts toward a predetermined conclusion. To take a contemporary example from the realm of technological change, we need only reflect on the challenges of sabbath observance in a world where lights go on and off as you stroll past homes, walk through the corridors of hotels, or enter the rest rooms of hospitals. In a recent article in a Torah journal about this topic, the author noted with complete candor that he was making extreme efforts to reach barely plausible conclusions in cases where avoiding problematic behavior entailed overcoming the most daunting difficulties.[30]

The goal of maintaining fidelity to the law while striving to accommodate humane concerns is given moving expression in a responsum by Rabbi Feinstein that encapsulates the challenges faced by men of learning and integrity bearing a burden that mere observers have no way of understanding in its fullness. Rabbi Feinstein had been asked by a European rabbi about the marriageability of a pious young woman whose lineage was problematic, and he responded with a permissive ruling. But the rabbi who had sent the initial inquiry was plagued by a guilty conscience, wondering if he had formulated his question in a manner likely to skew the ruling in a direction supportive of a woman whom he so badly wanted to help. And so he sent a second letter sharing these doubts. I conclude with Rabbi Feinstein's reply:

> As to [your] concern about your effort to permit this young woman, who is a precious, wholehearted soul—on the contrary, it is appropriate, decent, and desirable in the eyes of God to exercise effort on behalf of modest and precious women, just as we have been commanded to attempt to permit the marriage of *agunot*, provided that this effort is made in accordance with the laws of the Torah in truth.[31]

There are no magic formulas for the balancing of humanitarian and ideological concerns on the one hand and the straightforward meaning of texts on the other. For this task to be accomplished with integrity from the perspective of Orthodox Judaism, the decisor must genuinely believe in the

---

[29] *Shu"t Hatam Sofer*, no. 59, cited in Katz, *The 'Shabbes Goy*,' 190.
[30] R. Ya'akov Shlomo Mozeson, "Be-'Inyan Halikhah beli kavvanah le-yad 'Ayin Elektroni ve-ha-Mista'ef', *Kovetz Beit Aharon ve-Yisra'el* 72 (Av–Elul, 5757 [1997]): 63–68.
[31] *Iggerot Mosheh*, "Even ha-'Ezer," sec. 3, no. 10, p. 432.

authority of the Torah, in its divine origin, and in its eternal validity. In other words, what is nowadays described as "the halakhic process" rests upon a foundation consisting of theology as well as legal analysis. It is not just that one who does not share the theological premises of Orthodox Judaism is excluded in principle as an authority. The legal arguments themselves become suspect because of the concern that they are unrestrained by the discipline of faith, that one pole of the dialectic between authoritative text and personal or communal need is deficient. Both elements of that dialectic have been essential to the dynamic of Jewish law; to undermine either of them is to distort not only halakhah, but the history of halakhah as well.

"The Time Has Not Yet Come to Repair the World in the Kingdom of God": Israeli Lawyers and the Failed Jewish Legal Revolution of 1948

Assaf Likhovski[1]

Introduction

When we analyze the term "Jewish lawyers," one important question to ask is whether there is something unique about Jewish lawyers and in what ways (sociological, economic, ideological) Jewish lawyers are different from lawyers who belong to other ethnic groups. But there is another question that one might ask: what happens when the two parts of the term—"Jewish" and "lawyer"—are in conflict? This is the question I would like to ask in this chapter. I will answer it by looking at Jewish lawyers in Israel. At certain moments in Israel's legal history, Jewish lawyers were forced to choose between their commitment to the professional interests of their guild and their commitment to Jewish culture and Jewish nationalism.[2] This dilemma was especially apparent in the debates surrounding what can be called the "failed Jewish legal revolution" of 1948.

In 1948, Israelis, generally, and Israeli lawyers, in particular, had to decide whether they wanted to maintain the legal status quo by retaining the legal system that Israel inherited from the British rulers of Palestine, or whether this legal system would be replaced by one that was connected in some way to Jewish law (*halakha*). The demand for linking Israeli law with Jewish law was expressed by certain religious politicians and lawyers. But the desire to use the *halakha*, or a modernized version of it, in Israeli law also reflected the aspirations of many secular Zionists. What choice did the

---

[1] Professor of Law, Tel-Aviv University Faculty of Law; Director, David Berg Foundation Institute for Law and History, Tel-Aviv University. Parts of this chapter are based on my article, Assaf Likhovski, "Beyn Shney 'Olamot: Moreshet ha-Mishpat ha-Mandatori bi-Medinat Yisra'el be-Reshita" (Between Two Worlds), in *Yerushalayim bi-Tkufat ha-Mandat*, ed. Yehoshua Ben Arye (Jerusalem: Yad Ben Zvi Press, 2003), 253–86; and my book, *Law and Identity in Mandate Palestine* (Chapel Hill: University of North Carolina Press, 2006), http://uncpress.unc.edu/books/T-5910.html. This chapter was originally prepared for the "Jews and the Legal Profession conference" at Cardozo Law School, October 2006. I would like to thank the Augusto Levi Fund for their financial assistance in preparing this work for publication, Adar Ortal for her research assistance, and Ari Mermelstein for his comments and editorial assistance.

[2] Of course, one could also analyze the conflict between professional interests and Jewish *ethical* values (rather than Jewish culture or Jewish nationalism). This ethical conflict will not be discussed in this chapter.

Jewish lawyers of Palestine make, and how was this choice received by lay Israelis?

This chapter tells the story of the attempts to create a legal system based on Jewish law in Mandatory Palestine and in Israel immediately after its independence in 1948. It analyzes the reasons for the failure of these attempts. First, it identifies some practical factors that inhibited legal change in 1948. It then examines the role of Jewish lawyers in maintaining the legal status quo which was based on English law. The chapter then argues that the preference of Jewish lawyers for English law on its own cannot explain the failure of the Jewish law project. Instead, the chapter claims that professional opposition to Jewish law succeeded only because it resonated with wider cultural perceptions prevalent among lay Israelis in 1948 and afterwards concerning law in general, Jewish law in particular, and their own society. By manipulating these perceptions, lawyers successfully thwarted the linking of Israeli law to Jewish law.

Specifically, this chapter focuses on the perception that many Israelis had that their society was one in a state of transition. Israeli society was perceived as not yet fully formed. In particular, the term "the desert generation," an allusion to the Israelites who fled slavery in Egypt and wandered in the Sinai desert for forty years, was often used in this context. As long as this society was viewed as incomplete, there was no point, so the argument went, in changing its laws. Some lawyers skillfully used this image to justify adherence to the legal system that Israel inherited from the British Mandate. Thus, in the conflict between being Jewish and being a lawyer, the professional part triumphed. Many lawyers in post-independence Israel were indeed committed to their narrow professional interests more than they were to Jewish cultural nationalism and its legal manifestation—the project of Jewish legal revival.

I. The Law of British Palestine and its Legacy

Before the British occupied Palestine at the end of World War I, the legal system of the country was based on Ottoman law. Prior to the nineteenth century, Ottoman law mainly relied on norms taken from the *Shari'a*—Islamic law. During the nineteenth century, Ottoman rulers reformed their legal system by adopting codes taken from Europe, mainly from France.[3] However, in some areas of the law, most notably in private law, the sultans preserved Islamic law. Here too, however, some Western influence was evident. Ottoman scholars codified the private law norms of

---

[3] See, e.g., Moshe Ma'oz, *Ottoman Reform in Syria and Palestine 1840–1861: The Impact of the Tanzimat on Politics and Society* (Oxford: Clarendon Press, 1968); Esin Örücü, "The Impact of European Law in the Ottoman Empire and Turkey," in *European Expansion and Law: The Encounter of European and Indigenous Law in 19th and 20th Century Africa and Asia*, eds. W. J. Mommsen and J. A. de Moor (Oxford: Berg, 1992), 39–58. See also Avi Rubin, *Ottoman Nizamiye Courts: Law and Modernity* (New York: Palgrave Macmillan, 2011).

the *Shari'a* in a Western style code called the *Mejelle* (*Mecelle* in Turkish). The substance of the *Mejelle* was, thus, Islamic, but its structure was inspired by modern European codes. Consequently, the legal system that the British encountered in Palestine was based on a patchwork of French and Islamic norms and procedures.

British colonial legal policy at the end of the nineteenth century and in the early twentieth century sought to preserve the legal status quo in British colonies, especially in those colonies that had a developed local legal system.[4] However, English law did influence many colonial legal systems through a process known as Anglicization, which was sometimes the result of deliberate design and at other times of sheer coincidence. Some local systems proved more resistant to English influences than others. In some colonies, the British set up a single governmental legal system, but in others (especially those in Africa) they created dual legal systems in which there was an institutionalized distinction between a governmental system that implemented English norms, and a native legal system that was based on local customs (or at least on what the British believed to be local customs).[5] All of these factors led to significant differences in the nature of legal systems throughout the British Empire.

Two legal concepts influenced the process of Anglicization. One was the distinction between substance and procedure, and the other was the distinction between the public and private spheres. The British were not eager to replace local substantive law, but were more interested in replacing procedural law. Using British procedural law served a practical need in that British judges were used to the evidentiary and procedural notions of the common law. Westerners also viewed non-Western legal systems as discretionary and corrupt, so replacement of procedural law was seen as a way to prevent corruption.[6] The English contribution to the colonies, the argument went, was to provide the natives with a system of justice that enforced local

---

[4] See, e.g., T. Olawale Elias, *British Colonial Law: A Comparative Study of the Interaction between English and Local Laws in British Dependencies* (London: Stevens, 1962), 80–82; H. F. Morris, "English Law in East Africa: A Hardy Plant in an Alien Soil," in *Indirect Rule and the Search for Justice: Essays in East African Legal History*, eds. H. F. Morris and James S. Read (Oxford: Clarendon Press, 1972), 73; Konrad Zweigert and Hein Kötz, *Introduction to Comparative Law*, vol. I, 2d ed., trans. Tony Weir (Oxford: Oxford University Press, 1987), 233–45; Diane Kirkby and Catherine Coleborne, eds., *Law, History and Colonialism: The Reach of Empire* (Manchester: Manchester University Press, 2001).

[5] Elias, *British Colonial Law*, 80–81; Morris, "English Law," 233–45; Terence Ranger, "The Invention of Tradition in Colonial Africa," in *The Invention of Tradition*, eds. Eric Hobsbawm and Terence Ranger (Cambridge: Cambridge University Press, 1992), 211, 247–62.

[6] Max Weber, *Max Weber on Law in Economy and Society*, ed. Max Rheinstein (Cambridge, MA: Harvard University Press, 1954), 213; V. G. Kiernan, *The Lords of Human Kind: Black Man, Yellow Man and White Man in an Age of Empire* (New York: Columbia University Press, 1986), 131. But see Haim Gerber, *State, Society and Law in Islam: Ottoman Law in Comparative Perspective* (Albany: State University of New York Press, 1994).

norms, but, unlike local legal systems, did so efficiently. Thus, in British texts one often finds the idea that the British "civilized" local legal systems by imposing the notion of the "rule of law" on native judges and officials, or by importing procedural mechanisms such as the principles of "natural justice," which had not been applied before the British conquest.[7]

Changing substantive law was more difficult than replacing native procedure, but here too Anglicization was at work. Those areas of law defined by the British as most "private" (or "religious")—the law of marriage and divorce, laws of inheritance, and, to a lesser extent, the rules governing land tenure—were usually left unchanged. An intermediate area of law, the rules of contracts and torts, was usually replaced by English rules, but the process sometimes took a long time. Finally, the more "public" areas of law—criminal law and commercial law—were almost invariably anglicized.[8]

It is important to bear in mind that the introduction of English law was not always intentional. When new legal questions appeared, English-trained lawyers and judges naturally turned to English law to solve them, and thereby inadvertently imported this law into the legal system of the colonies.[9] Importation was also the result of lack of familiarity with local law. Sir Anton Bertram, who had been Attorney General of the Bahamas, a judge in Cyprus and the Chief Justice of Ceylon, wrote (no doubt from personal experience), "the most extraordinary feature of our judicial system is ... the diversity of the law which our Courts apply. The judges of our various Supreme Courts pass on promotion from one system of law to another and are required immediately on their arrival in a new territory to administer a system of law ... to which they are completely strange."[10]

This lack of familiarity with local law was certainly evident in Palestine. Not only was Palestine merely one station in the long careers of some British officials, but, more significantly, many of the British officials in

---

[7] Zweigert and Kötz, *Introduction to Comparative Law*, 235, 239, 241; Edward W. Said, *Orientalism* (New York: Pantheon Books, 1978), 37; Martin Chanock, *Law, Custom and Social Order: The Colonial Experience in Malawi and Zambia* (Cambridge: Cambridge University Press, 1985), 5; Nasser Hussain, *The Jurisprudence of Emergency: Colonialism and the Rule of Law* (Ann Arbor: University of Michigan Press, 2003), 3–4.

[8] Elias, *British Colonial Law*, 5, 137, 141, 147; Zweigert and Kötz, *Introduction to Comparative Law*, 235, 241–42; Herbert J. Liebesny, *The Law of the Near and Middle East: Readings, Cases and Materials* (Albany: SUNY Press, 1975), 56; Lawrence M. Friedman, "Law and Social Change: Culture, Nationality and Identity," in *Collected Courses of the Academy of European Law*, vol. IV, book 2 (The Hague: M. Nijhoff, 1995), 253–54; John Strawson, "Revisiting Islamic Law: Marginal Notes from Colonial History," *Griffith Law Review* 12 (2003): 362, 369; Duncan Kennedy, "Two Globalizations of Law and Legal Thought: 1850–1968," *Suffolk University Law Review* 36 (2003): 631, 645–46.

[9] Jörg Fisch, "Law as a Means and as an End: Some Remarks on the Function of European and non-European Law in the Process of European Expansion," in *European Expansion and Law: The Encounter of European and Indigenous Law in 19th and 20th Century Africa and Asia*, eds. W. J. Mommsen and J. A. de Moor (Oxford: Berg, 1992), 15–38.

[10] Anton Bertram, *The Colonial Service* (Cambridge: Cambridge University Press, 1930), 152.

Palestine, especially in the first years of British rule, were amateurs. In addition, Ottoman law, as well as the decisions of the Palestine courts, were objectively difficult to ascertain and even obtain. An unofficial French translation of Ottoman legislation had been made in 1905, but there was no authoritative English version. Moreover, even those copies of the French translation were rare and not all British officials had access to them. Official publication of the reports of the courts of Palestine began only in the mid-1930s. Finally, the physical conditions of work in many courts in Palestine were not conducive to conducting extensive legal research. The courts were described by one observer as "stables" and by another as "dirty and unkempt rooms" with broken chairs and benches, with court clerks who were "shabby and down at heel" and records which were kept on "scraps of paper."[11]

The distinctions between process and substance and between the public and the private that the British employed in many of their colonies also emerged in Palestine. During the three decades of British rule in Palestine, British legislation replaced a large number of Ottoman laws with ordinances and regulations based on English or British-colonial codes.[12] The process of replacement took place in a way that reflected the substance/process and public/private dichotomies. The British began with procedural and public law and gradually moved on to more private/substantive areas of the law. In the 1920s, the British replaced Ottoman commercial laws, the Ottoman code of criminal procedure, and some Ottoman rules of evidence. They also reorganized the land registration system, began a cadastral survey of the land, and promulgated town-planning legislation.[13] In the 1930s, the British replaced the French-based Ottoman Penal Code and the code of Civil Procedure with codes based on English law. Finally, in the late 1940s, when

---

[11] Central Zionist Archives (CZA) 215/155, Harry Sacher to Herbert Samuel, December 10, 1925; Martin Bunton, "Inventing the Status-Quo: Ottoman Land-Law during the Palestine Mandate, 1917–1936," *International History Review* 21 (1999): 28; Gabriel Strassman, 'Otey ha-Glimah: Toldot Arikhat ha-Din be-Erets Yisra'el (Wearing the Robes: A History of the Legal Profession Until 1962) (Tel Aviv: The Lawyers' Association, 1984), 68, 94; Norman Bentwich and Helen Bentwich, *Mandate Memories 1918–1948* (London: Hogarth Press, 1965), 203; Naomi Shepherd, *Ploughing Sand: British Rule in Palestine, 1917–1948* (London: John Murray, 1999), 32–33.

[12] Daniel Friedmann, "The Effect of Foreign Law on the Law of Israel: Infusion of the Common Law into the Legal System of Israel," *Israel Law Review* 10 (1975): 324, 327–52.

[13] See generally Kenneth Stein, *The Land Question in Palestine, 1917–1939* (Chapel Hill: University of North Carolina Press, 1984); Scott Atran, "Le Masha'a et la Question Foncière en Palestine, 1858–1948," *Annales. Économies, Sociétés, Civilisations* 42.6 (1987): 1361–89; Eliezer Malchi, *Toldot ha-Mishpat be-Erets Yisra'el: Mavo Histori la-Mishpat bi-Medinat Yisra'el* (The History of the Law of Palestine: An Introduction to the Law of Israel), 2d ed. (Tel Aviv: Dinim, 1953), 101–5; Henry E. Baker, "Legal System," in *The Israel Yearbook: 1967*, ed. L. Berger (Israel: Israel Yearbook Publications Ltd., 1967), 85–86.

British rule in Palestine was nearing its end, they began to anglicize areas such as tort and labor law.[14]

When the British left Palestine in 1948, the process of Anglicization was only partially completed. Consequently, the legal system that was left behind was a hybrid one, based in part on English law and in part on old Ottoman law. Since 1948, Israeli law has gradually shed parts of its Mandatory heritage. Israelis reformed the private law they inherited from the Ottomans and British, ultimately creating continental-like civil codification.[15] Constitutional, administrative, and commercial laws have also been greatly modified.

However, the Mandatory legal heritage is very much alive in the law of twenty-first century Israel and can clearly be seen in the legal system's general characteristics. Israeli law inherited from its Mandatory predecessor the deference to precedents, the notion that judges should play an important and active role in creating legal norms, an adversarial conception of the role of lawyers, a unitary conception of the structure of the court system and many other general structural features.[16] The relationship between Israeli law and Mandatory law also extends to the details of the legal system, as entire areas of Israeli law are still based on Mandatory legislation. For example, Israel's income tax system is still based on a British Income Tax Ordinance enacted in 1941.[17] Its civil and criminal procedure norms, the rules of evidence used by the legal system, and the Israeli penal code originate in Mandatory laws and regulations.

Finally, the very identity of the system is still firmly English (or Anglo-American). Despite two explicit attempts, in 1948 and in 1980, to sever the ties of Israeli law with the common-law world and replace these ties with a link to Jewish law, Israeli legal identity is still tied to English legal culture. Why is this so? Why was there no "legal revolution" that changed the identity of the Israeli legal system following Israel's independence?

The next two parts of the chapter deal with this question. The second part shows that the potential for a "Jewish legal revolution" did indeed exist in 1948. The third part analyzes some of the reasons why, despite the existence of the potential for a change in the identity of the legal system, this change did not ultimately occur.

---

[14] See generally Assaf Likhovski, "Between Mandate and State: Re-thinking the Periodization of Israeli Legal History," *Journal of Israeli History* 19.2 (1998): 5–34.

[15] See for example the symposium issue on the new civil code in *Mishpat ve-'Asakim* 4 (2006).

[16] See Aharon Barak, "Shitat ha-Mishpat be-Yisra'el: Masortah ve-Tarbutah" (The Israeli Legal System: Tradition and Culture), *Ha-Praklit* 40 (1992): 197, 204; Yoram Shachar, "History and Sources of Israeli Law," in *Introduction to the Law of Israel*, eds. Amos Shapira and Keren DeWitt-Arar (The Hague: Kluwer Law International, 1995), 1.

[17] See generally Assaf Likhovski, "Is Tax Law Culturally Specific? Lessons from the History of Income Tax Law in Mandatory Palestine," *Theoretical Inquiries in Law* 11 (2010): 725–63.

II. The Failed Jewish Legal Revolution of 1948

The "first Israelis" who lived through the months before and immediately after Israeli independence in 1948 felt they were living in a revolutionary period.[18] This is also true of the first Israeli lawyers. The pages of the journal of the Jewish Bar Association of Palestine, *ha-Praklit*, contained many articles that discussed the desired character of Israel's legal system and declared that the legal system of the new Israeli state should be entirely different than the system of the British Mandate and linked in some way to Jewish law. This desired linkage was not a utopian dream that briefly appeared in 1948. It had a long history that went back to the early decades of Zionism.

A. The First Phase of the Jewish Legal Revival Movement

Like many nationalist movements, Zionism sought to revive the Jewish cultural past. The best-known aspect of Zionist cultural activity is the revival of the Hebrew language. But linguistic revival was not the only item on the Zionist agenda. Some Zionists also sought to revive what they called *Mishpat 'Ivri* (literally, "Hebrew law") and make it the legal system of the Jewish community in Palestine. The revival of law, like the revival of a large part of Jewish culture by the Zionist movement, was not so much a continuation of the Jewish past as a break with it; not the restoration of an old tradition, but the invention of a new one.[19] Secular Zionists sought to create a new "Hebrew" person who would be the antithesis of the old exilic Jew.[20] Zionists saw the Jews of the Diaspora as passive, weak, and uprooted. These Jews were the "other" of Zionist culture, a negative template of the new, active, masculine Hebrew person that many Zionists sought to be.[21] Similar-

---

[18] See generally Tom Segev, *1949: The First Israelis* (New York: The Free Press, 1986).

[19] See generally Hobsbawm and Ranger, *The Invention of Tradition*; Benedict Anderson, *Imagined Communities: Reflections on the Origin and Spread of Nationalism*, rev. ed. (London: Verso, 1991). On the history of the Jewish legal revival movement, see, e.g,. Likhovski, *Law and Identity*, 127–54; Ronen Shamir, *The Colonies of Law: Colonialism, Zionism and Law in Early Mandate Palestine* (Cambridge: Cambridge University Press, 2000); Amihai Radzyner, "Jewish Law in London: Between Two Societies," *Jewish Law Annual* 18 (2009): 81–135; idem, "Ha-Mishpat ha-'Ivri beyn 'Le'umi' le-'Dati': Ha-Dilemah shel Ha-Tnu'ah ha-Datit-Le'umit" ("Jewish Law" between "National" and "Religious": The Dilemma of the Religious-National Movement), *Mehkarey Mishpat* 26 (2010): 91–178.

[20] See, for example, Itamar Even-Zohar, "Ha-Tsmihah veha-Hitgabshut shel Tarbut 'Ivrit Mekomit ve-Yelidit be-Erets Yisra'el, 1882–1948" (The Emergence and Crystallization of Local and Native Hebrew Culture in Erets Yisra'el, 1882–1948), *Cathedra* 16 (1980): 165, 171–75; Gabriel Piterberg, "Ha-Umah u-Mesaprehah: Historyografyah Le'umit ve-Orientalizm" (The Nation and its Raconteurs: Orientalism and Nationalist History), *Teoryah u-Vikoret* 6 (1995): 81, 95; Yael Zerubavel, *Recovered Roots: Collective Memory and the Making of Israeli National Tradition* (Chicago: University of Chicago Press, 1995), 18–19; Michael Berkowitz, *Zionist Culture and West European Jewry before the First World War* (Chapel Hill: University of North Carolina Press, 1996).

[21] Even-Zohar, "Ha-Tsmihah," 171; Zerubavel, *Recovered Roots*, 26; Oz Almog, *Ha-Tsabar: Dyokan* (The Sabra: A Portrait) (Tel Aviv: 'Am 'Oved, 1997), 30, 127–32.

ly, when the revivers envisioned the creation of a new legal system it was one based on Jewish law but not identical to it. They used the term *Mishpat 'Ivri* in order to distinguish their modernized notion of Jewish law from the traditional law of Jewish communities in the Diaspora—the *halakha*.

The project of legal revival had its roots in early nineteenth century German nationalism. German thinkers claimed that each nation had its own unique "national spirit" (*volksgeist*) and that every aspect of national culture should reflect this spirit. These ideas were translated into the legal realm in the jurisprudential thought of the Historical School, which held that law was not created "from above" by the rational mind of an enlightened ruler. Instead, law (identified with custom) was produced by "the people" in an organic, silent, and unconscious process. Because law was a creation of the people, it could not be universal. Each nation has its own laws, just as each nation has its own language, and both law and language reflect the unique spirit of the nation, its *volksgeist*.[22]

Such ideas influenced legal movements in many countries and Zionist legal thinkers were no exception.[23] These thinkers, who came mainly from Russia, called for the creation of a national Jewish legal system that would be based on Jewish law.[24] In the beginning of the twentieth century, a number of Russian-Jewish students, educated in central European and Russian universities, decided that the time had come to begin the work of legal revival. Two prominent leaders were Paltiel Dikshtein, a Russian Jew who had studied law at the University of Odessa, and Samuel Eisenstadt, a young Swiss-educated Russian scholar. In 1916, Eisenstadt called for the establishment of a "scientific society for the study of Hebrew law." Such an organization, the Hebrew Law Society (*Hevrat ha-Mishpat ha-'Ivri*), was ultimately established in Moscow in the late 1910s, and immediately began publishing a scholarly journal that advocated legal revival.[25] The turmoil of

---

[22] Freidrich Carl von Savigny, *Of the Vocation of Our Age for Legislation and Jurisprudence*, trans. Abraham Hayward (London: Littlewood and Co., 1834), 24–27. See also "Symposium: Savigny in Modern Comparative Perspective," *American Journal of Comparative Law* 37 (1989): 1; James Q. Whitman, *The Legacy of Roman Law in the German Romantic Era: Historical Vision and Legal Change* (Princeton: Princeton University Press, 1990).

[23] See generally Marc Galanter, "The Displacement of Traditional Law in Modern India," *Journal of Social Issues* 24.4 (1968): 65, 85; idem, "The Aborted Restoration of 'Indigenous' Law in India," *Comparative Studies in Society and History* 14 (1972): 53; idem, *Law and Society in Modern India* (Delhi: Oxford University Press, 1989), 37–53.

[24] See generally Walter Laqueur, *A History of Zionism* (New York: Schocken Books, 1989), 113, 162–66; Ehud Luz, *Parallels Meet: Religion and Nationalism in the Early Zionist Movement (1882–1904)*, trans. Lenn J. Schramm (Philadelphia: Jewish Publication Society, 1988), 138–39; Gideon Shimoni, *The Zionist Ideology* (Hanover, N.H.: Brandeis University Press, 1995), 85–87.

[25] Samuel Eisenstadt, "Hevrah Mada'it le-Hakirat ha-Mishpat ha-'Ivri: Mikhtav Galuy" (A Scientific Society for Research of Hebrew Law: An Open Letter), in Samuel Eisenstadt, *Tsiyon be-Mishpat* (Tel Aviv: Ha-Mishpat, 1967), 31, 33; and "Le-Toldot Hevrat 'Ha-Mishpat ha-'Ivri'" (On the History of the Hebrew Law Society), *Ha-Mishpat* 2 (1927): 220.

the Russian Revolution and its aftermath hindered the activities of the society and by the early 1920s, as conditions in the Soviet Union worsened, the society was disbanded and some of its members immigrated to Palestine.²⁶

Meanwhile in Ottoman Palestine, Zionist immigrants created a system of secular courts for the Zionist Jewish community of Palestine. These courts, called the Hebrew Courts of Arbitration (*Mishpat ha-Shalom ha-'Ivri*), were established in 1909. The main reason for their creation was the practical desire of Zionist Jews not to be subjected to the jurisdiction of Ottoman or rabbinical courts. A secondary reason was the lack of jurisdiction of European consular courts in cases in which the litigants were citizens of different European countries. However, the notion of nationalist legal revival, to which even some left-wing socialist Jews were committed at this stage, may also have played a part in their formation.²⁷

After World War I the amount of litigation in the Hebrew Courts of Arbitration increased dramatically.²⁸ It was also at this time that their activity became fused with the activity of the Hebrew Law Society, newly reestablished in Palestine. Prominent Jewish lawyers like Norman Bentwich, the Anglo-Jewish Attorney General of Palestine, Judge Gad Frumkin, and Mordechai Eliash, a leading member of the local bar association, joined the ranks of the Hebrew Law Society.²⁹

During the 1920s and early 1930s, the revivers published two scholarly journals, *Ha-Mishpat* and *Ha-Mishpat ha-'Ivri*, and founded two legal presses. Using them, the revivers began to consolidate their movement and create a unified agenda for it.³⁰ They compiled a massive bibliography of

---

²⁶ Eisenstadt, "Le-Toldot," 220, 221; "Takanot ha-Hevrah 'ha-Mishpat ha-'Ivri' be-Erets Yisra'el" (Regulations of the "Hebrew Law Society" in Palestine), *Ha-Mishpat* 1 (1927): 196; idem, "Ve'idat Hevrat 'ha-Mishpat ha-'Ivri' bi-Yerushalayim, Sukkot Tarpav" (The Hebrew Law Society Conference in Jerusalem, Succoth 1926), *Ha-Mishpat ha-'Ivri* 2 (1926/7): 232; idem, "Ha-Universitah shel Tel Aviv: Beyt ha-Sefer ha-Gavohah le-Mishpat vele-Kalkalah" (Tel Aviv University: The School of Law and Economics), undated manuscript, CZA, A 212/37, 4.

²⁷ Gdalya Yogev and Yehoshua Freundlich, eds., *Ha-Protokolim shel ha-Va'ad Ha-Po'el ha-Tsiyoni 1919–1929* (Minutes of the Zionist General Council 1919–1929) (Tel Aviv: University of Tel Aviv, 1975), 2:60; Paltiel Dikshtein, *Toldot Mishpat ha-Shalom ha-'Ivri: Megamotav, Pe'ulotav ve-Hesegav* (A History of the Hebrew Courts of Arbitration) (Tel Aviv: Yavneh, 1964), 23–25, 68–69; Eisenstadt, "Mishpat ha-Shalom ha-'Ivri be-Erets Yisra'el" (The Hebrew Courts of Arbitration in Palestine), in Samuel Eisenstadt, *Tsiyon be-Mishpat,* 64; Strassman, *'Otey ha-Glimah,* 39–46; Shamir, *The Colonies of Law,* 32.

²⁸ The British enacted an Arbitration Ordinance, which indirectly recognized the courts as arbitration tribunals and, thus, enabled litigants to use the state apparatus to enforce their judgments. For a discussion of British attitudes to the Hebrew Courts, see generally Shamir, *The Colonies of Law,* 61–63. Even some Arabs used these courts. See, for example, Decision P/687/36 *'Arif al-Mutawali, Grocer, Jerusalem v. Solel Boneh Ltd.*, reported in *Ha-Mishpat* 1 (1927): 252–56, 340; and *Ha-Mishpat* 2 (1927): 168. However, the courts, as well as the revival project, more generally, were an internal Jewish affair in which neither the Arabs nor the British intervened in any significant way.

²⁹ See "Takanot ha-Hevrah 'ha-Mishpat ha-'Ivri' be-Erets Yisra'el" (Regulations).

³⁰ As with any intellectual movement, one can find different notions and contradictory

works on Jewish law, which was published in 1931.[31] They created a calendar of historical events connected with Jewish law.[32] They proposed collaborative research plans which would progress in stages to legal revival.[33] They even suggested measures that would broaden their circle of supporters, such as teaching law in Jewish high schools in Palestine, presumably as a preparatory step to creating a cadre of people committed to the idea of legal revival.[34]

All of these projects, therefore, suggest that in the 1920s, the creation of an autonomous nationalist legal system for the Jews of Palestine seemed feasible. By the early 1930s, however, the movement lost much of its momentum.[35] The journals published by the revivers gradually stopped appearing.[36] Even more damaging to the cause of legal revival was the rapid decline in the use of the Hebrew Courts of Arbitration in the late 1920s and early 1930s. Individual litigants and official Jewish bodies, like the Tel Aviv municipality and the Zionist Executive, refused to litigate in the Hebrew Courts or demanded that these courts rule according to Ottoman and English law instead of the fuzzy notion of Hebrew law.[37]

When the old institutions of the revival project (the courts, the journals, and the society) gradually stopped functioning, the focus of revival activity shifted to legal education. In 1934, the revivers established a law school, the

---

attitudes among members of the society based on different beliefs, ideologies and interests. However, because all members of the society expressed some interest in the project of legal revival, their thinking can be analyzed collectively. On conflicts within the society, see generally Radzyner, "Ha-Mishpat ha-'Ivri beyn 'Le'umi' le-'Dati'."

[31] Samuel Eisenstadt, *'Ein Mishpat: Sefer Shimush Bibliyografi le-Sifrut ha-Mishpat ha-'Ivri* (The Fountain of the Law: A Bibliography of Hebrew Law Literature) (Jerusalem: Ha-Mishpat, 1931), xiii.

[32] For example, in 1930 they marked "nineteen hundred years since the Exile of the Great Sanhedrin." Samuel Eisenstadt, "Yovel la-Mishpat ha-'Ivri" (A Hebrew Law Jubilee), *Ha-Mishpat* 4 (1930): 41.

[33] Paltiel Dikshtein, "Sha'arey ha-Mishpat ha-'Ivri" (Gates of Hebrew Law), *Ha-Mishpat ha-'Ivri: Riv'on Mada'i* 1 (1918): 122; Eisenstadt, "Ve'idat Hevrat 'ha-Mishpat ha-'Ivri'," 236; Asher Gulak, "Tokhnit le-'Avodat Hevrat 'ha-Mishpat ha-'Ivri'," (A Plan for the Work of the Hebrew Law Society), *Ha-Mishpat ha-'Ivri* 2 (1926/7): 196; idem, "Le-Sidur Hayenu ha-Mishpatiyim ba-Arets" (Organizing our Legal Life in Palestine), *Ha-Toren* 33–34 (1930/1): 28; A. H. Freimann, "Diney Yisra'el be-Erets Yisra'el" (Jewish Law in Palestine), in *Ha-Mishpat ha-'Ivri u-Medinat Yisra'el: Leket Ma'amarim*, ed. Y. Bazaq (Jerusalem: Mosad ha-Rav Kuk, 1969), 36.

[34] S. Nehorai, "Limud ha-Mishpat be-Vet ha-Sefer ha-Beynoni" (Teaching Law in Secondary School), *Ha-Mishpat* 1 (1927): 167.

[35] Eisenstadt, *'Ein Mishpat*, xxvi.

[36] *Ha-Mishpat* stopped regular publication in 1929, although irregular issues appeared in 1931 and 1934/5. *Ha-Mishpat ha-'Ivri* was published between 1925/6 and 1927/8, in 1932/3, and, for the last time, in 1936/7.

[37] Norman Bentwich, "The Application of Jewish Law in Palestine," *Journal of Comparative Legislation and International Law* 9 (1927): 59, 65–67; Dikshtein, *Toldot Mishpat ha-Shalom*, 62–63; Strassman, *'Otey ha-Glimah*, 44–46; and Shamir, *The Colonies of Law*, 108–25. The courts, however, did not disappear entirely in the 1930s. See, for example, *Ha-Mishpat* 5.2 (1935): 14; *Ha-Mishpat* 5.3 (1935): 14.

Tel Aviv School of Law and Economics. One of the major goals of the School of Law and Economics, declared its founders, was to "to train jurists, lawyers and judges who could fulfill the ideals of the nation in the field of legal revival."[38] During the 1940s, the School slowly expanded, eventually laying the groundwork for the establishment of Tel Aviv University in the 1950s. But in one respect the school was unsuccessful. It did not fulfill its declared goal of serving as "an academic tool for the revival of Hebrew law." In 1937, the School established a committee for the "codification of Hebrew law," but this committee achieved nothing. Some professors at the School attempted to use Jewish legal sources in their courses (in addition to teaching Ottoman and British-colonial law), but the use of such sources was not universal and in any event did not contribute to the project of revival.[39]

B. The Second Phase: Resurrection and Failure in 1948

While the 1930s saw the revival movement gradually losing momentum, this trend was reversed in the years 1945–1948 as prospects of the establishment of an independent Jewish state in Palestine grew. In 1945, Avraham Haim Freimann, one of the leading scholars of Jewish law in Mandatory Palestine argued that Jewish law (after its reform and modernization) should become the law of the future Jewish state.[40] In a 1946 article entitled "Concern for Tomorrow," Haim Cohn, a leading Jewish lawyer who later became an Israeli Supreme Court justice, also said that preparations should be made for the establishment of a Jewish state, and that Jewish law should be revived by composing "a proposal that demonstrates that it is possible to construct a uniform civil law that would continue our ancient traditions, and which will be unique to the Jewish people, reflecting its character and destiny, and yet will match the advancements and developments of all enlightened nations."[41]

Interest in Jewish law increased as the British hold on Palestine weakened. At the beginning of 1947, the autonomous Jewish court system reappeared in Tel Aviv. Naturally, there was a debate about the law that such

---

[38] Eisenstadt, "Ha-Universitah," 11, 16; CZA, A 212/2 (Tel Aviv University: School of Law and Economics, July 1936); CZA, A212/2, B. Ziv, "Ma Anu Rotsim" (What do We Want?), in *Beyt ha-Sefer ha-Gavohah le-Mishpat ve-Kalkalah* (The School of Law and Economics) (1935).

[39] CZA, A212/2, *Beyt ha-Sefer ha-Gavohah le-Mishpat ve-Kalkalah: Sidrey Limudim, 1944* (School of Law and Economics: Catalogue 1944), 3; Eisenstadt, "Ha-Universitah," 86; CZA, A212/2, *Prospekt li-Shnat ha-Limudim Tartsah* (Catalogue 1937/8), 5–6, 8, 11, 12; CZA, A212/2, *Sefer ha-Shanah*, 1948 (1948 Yearbook), 21; Menachem Elon, interview by author, New York City, New York, November 1995.

[40] See A. H. Freimann, "Diney Yisra'el," 36.

[41] H. H. Cohn, "De'agah le-Yom ha-Mahar," *Ha-Praklit* 3 (1946): 38, 46. On Cohn's changing attitude to Jewish law see also Amihai Radzyner and Shuki Friedman, "Ha-Mehokek ha-Yisre'eli veha-Mishpat ha-'Ivri: Haim Cohn beyn Mahar le-Etmol" (The Israeli Legislator and Hebrew Law: Haim Cohn between Tomorrow and Yesterday) *'Iyune Mishpat* 29 (2005): 167–244.

courts should apply. Some said that these courts should apply Jewish law, in order to "return Jewish law to the path of the natural life of the people and the State."⁴² Moshe Silberg, another future justice of the Israeli Supreme Court, had already called for the codification of Jewish law in the 1930s. In September 1947 he reiterated this call, writing that the Jewish state would have to adopt Jewish law, after its appropriate codification, as its national law.⁴³ Another advocate of Jewish legal revival, Paltiel Dikshtein, also demanded that English law be replaced by Jewish law, as the former was not suited to local conditions because "not everything that cold minds on the banks of the Thames envisioned can be utilized on the banks of the Jordan and Yarkon Rivers, under the blazing subtropical sun."⁴⁴

It is important to note that the advocates of the Jewish legal revolution realized it could not take place overnight. They did not demand replacing Mandatory law with Jewish law in one fell swoop. More modest (and realistic) proposals were suggested. One such proposal recommended integrating norms taken from Jewish law into new Israeli legislation, declaring that there was a link between Israeli law and Jewish law in the constitution of the new state, or enacting a law that would require Israeli judges to turn to Jewish law in cases of lacunas or conflicts in existing laws.⁴⁵

In the first months of 1948, immediately before Israeli independence, calls by both secular and religious Israelis to use Jewish law as the law of the new State intensified.⁴⁶ The demand for the use of Jewish law also had

---

42 E. L. Globus, "'Al Beyt Din 'Ivri," *Ha-Praklit* 4 (1947): 111, 114.

43 M. Silberg, "Ha-Mishpat ba-Medinah ha-'Ivrit" (Law in the Jewish State), *Haaretz* (February 17, 1938–March 14, 1938), reprinted in Z. Terlo and M. Hovav, eds., *Ba'in ke-Ehad: Asufat Dvarim shebe-Hagut uva-Halakha* (Jerusalem: Magnes Press, 1982), 180, 199–200; M. Silberg, "Hidusho shel ha-Mishpat ha-'Ivri" (Renewing Jewish Law), *Ha-Boker* (September 14, 1947), reprinted in Terlo and Hovav, *Ba'in ke-Ehad*, 202, 204.

44 P. Dikshtein, "Hakhrazah 'al ha-Mishpat ha-'Ivri" (Declaration on Jewish Law), *Ha-Praklit* 5 (1948): 3–4.

45 Ron Harris, "Hizdamnuyot Historiyot ve-Hahmatsot shebe-Hesah ha-Da'at: 'Al Shiluvo shel ha-Mishpat ha-'Ivri be-'Et Hakamat ha-Medinah" (Absent Minded Misses and Historical Opportunities: Jewish Law, Israeli Law and the Establishment of the State of Israel) in *Shney 'Evrey ha-Gesher: Dat u-Medinah be-Reshit Darkah shel Yisra'el*, eds. Mordechai Bar-On and Tsvi Tsameret (Jerusalem: Yad Izhak Ben-Zvi Press, 2002), 35. See also P. Dikshtein, "Lo Titakhen Medina 'Ivrit Lelo Mishpat 'Ivri" (A Jewish State is not Possible without Jewish Law), *Ha-Praklit* 4 (1947): 328, 329–30; Dikshtein, "Hakhrazah 'al ha-Mishpat ha-'Ivri" (in which Dikshtein suggested enacting the following provision: "wherever existing legislation does not address a given issue at all, or wherever there are two possible interpretations or where two laws conflict, the courts and other official bodies must use the norms of Jewish law, adjusted to modern times"). For other expressions of the same idea, see Y. Karp, "Ha-Mo'atsah ha-Mishpatit: Reshit 'Alilot Hakikah" (The Legal Council), in *Sefer Uri Yadin: Ma'amarim le-Zikhro shel Uri Yadin*, vol. 2, eds. Aharon Barak and Tana Shpanitz (Tel Aviv: Bursi, 1990), 238, which mentions a proposal by politician Zerah Warhaftig according to which "the decisions of the civil courts would be governed by the laws that were in force on the last day before the end of the British Mandate and in accordance with the principles of the law of the Torah and the rules of justice and equity."

46 A. Karlin, "Le-Heker ha-Mishpat ha-'Ivri" (On the Study of Jewish Law), *Ha-Praklit* 5 (1948): 80; S. M., "Mishpat ha-Shalom ha-'Ivri: Ma Yihyu Tafkidav ba-Medinah ha-

practical consequences. In December 1947 a Legal Council, whose task was to prepare the legal transition from British to Jewish rule, was established. A subcommittee of this Council was created to study the possible uses of Jewish law in the law of the future state.

However, the subcommittee on Jewish law was unable to suggest ways of incorporating Jewish law into Israeli law, partly because its chairman, Avraham Haim Freimann, was killed on his way to the campus of the Hebrew University of Jerusalem.[47] It soon became clear that there would be no "national revolution" in the field of the law, not even the simple declaration that Jewish law should be used to fill in lacunas in existing Mandatory legislation.[48] The first act of legislation after the establishment of the state, the Law and Administration Ordinance of 1948, refrained from explicitly linking the new Israeli legal system with Jewish law. The fading enthusiasm for the use of Jewish law was also reflected in the decisions of the Jewish Bar Association conference in the summer of 1949, which called for "the creation of an advanced legal system" and for "laws ... that would be consistent with the spirit of the revolution that brought about the establishment of the state." Jewish law was not mentioned at all.[49] In September 1949, Paltiel Dikshtein complained about a general trend in the new Israeli legislation to ignore Jewish law.[50] As time passed, interest in legal revolution waned and was only interrupted now and then with vague promises to make use of Jewish law.[51] Thus, within approximately a decade after independence it became clear that Israel's legal system would not be based on Jewish law. In an article written in the late 1950s, Haim Cohn, who in prestate years had been one of the main proponents of the revival of Jewish

---

'Ivrit?" (What Will Be the Role of Jewish Law in the Jewish State?), *Ha-Praklit* 5 (1948): 92; M. Silberg, "Ha-Mishpat ba-Medinah ha-'Ivrit" (Law in the Jewish State), *Ha-Praklit* 5 (1948): 102; P. Dikshtein, "'Atsma'ut Medinit ve-'Atsma'ut Mishpatit" (National and Legal Independence), *Ha-Praklit* 5 (1948): 107; S. Eisenstadt, "Medinah u-Mishpat" (State and Law), *Ha-Praklit* 5 (1948): 113; M. Bar Ilan, "Hok u-Mishpat bi-Medinatenu" (Legislation and Law in our State), *Yavneh* 3 (1949), reprinted in Y. Bazaq, ed., *Ha-Mishpat ha-'Ivri u-Medinat Yisra'el: Leket Ma'amarim* (Jerusalem: Mosad ha-Rav Kuk, 1969), 20.

[47] P. Dikshtein, "Le-Zekher Dr. Avraham Haim Freimann" (In Memoriam: Dr. Avraham Haim Freimann), *Ha-Praklit* 5 (1948): 67; Harris, "Hizdamnuyot"; Karp, "Ha-Mo'atsah," 238.

[48] M. Silberg, "Ha-Mishpat Ba-Medinah ha-'Ivrit," *Ha-Praklit* 5 (1948): 102, 103 (codification of Jewish law would require "half a generation and perhaps even an entire generation").

[49] "Hahlatot ha-Ve'idah ha-13 shel Histadrut 'Orhey ha-Din be-Yisra'el" (Decisions of the Thirteenth Convention of the Bar Association in Israel), *Ha-Praklit* 6 (1949): 125; [Speech of S. Assaf], ibid., 247, 249 ("There are no revolutions in the world of the law," and the process of reviving Jewish law would take "a generation or even generations").

[50] P. D., "Le-Darkhey ha-Hakikah bi-Medinatenu" (On Legislation in our State), *Ha-Praklit* 6 (1949): 144.

[51] For example, Uri Yadin, "Ha-Tikhnun ha-Mishpati be-Sha'ah Zo" (Legal Planning Now), *Ha-Praklit* 7 (1950): 283 (promising that the Justice Ministry plans to draw on foreign and Jewish sources alike in the process of legislation).

law, said that the conservatism of the rabbinical establishment was to be blamed for the fact that "the revival of Jewish law as the law of the state of Israel is no longer on the agenda: This was yesterday's concern."[52] Similarly, an article by Eliezer Malchi, an Israeli lawyer and later judge, written in the early 1960s, reflected the new approach of many Israeli lawyers. Malchi said that "in the previous [i.e., nineteenth] century, there was a tendency to link nationalism and law. Each nation had to have its own legal system. Each legal system tried to differentiate itself as much as possible, so that it would reflect the spirit of the nation. This approach is outdated and is now perceived as artificial. Nowadays, the tendency is to learn from the law of other states."[53]

A final, and much later, attempt to associate Jewish law with Israel's legal system was made in the early 1980s, when the Foundation of Law Act was passed. This act officially severed the connection between Israeli and English law, and instructed judges that in cases in which no answer could be found in Israeli legislation or case law, they should decide the case in accordance with the "principles of freedom, justice, equity, and peace of Israel's Heritage."[54] While some observers had high expectations for the impact of this act, a number of Supreme Court decisions from the 1980s and 1990s made certain that it would have no real influence on the shape of Israeli law.[55]

III. The Reasons for the Failure

A. Practical Explanations

One set of explanations for the failure of the "Jewish legal revolution" in 1948 is practical in nature.[56] First, it is obvious that legal reform was simply not a major issue on the agenda of the first Israelis given the importance of security and economic concerns. With the threats facing Israel in its first years, even those lawyers and statesmen who supported legal reform were

---

[52] H. Cohn, "De'agah shel Yom Etmol" (A Concern of Yesterday), in *Haim Cohn: Mivhar Ktavim*, eds. A. Barak and R. Gavison (Tel Aviv: Bursi, 1992), 25, 31–32, 40; A. Radzyner and S. Friedman, "Ha-Mehokek." From time to time, isolated calls for the revival of Jewish law were reiterated. See S. Eisenstadt, "Kodifikatsyah Hadashah shel Mishpatenu ha-Le'umi" (A New Codification of our National Law), *Mishpat ve-Kalkalah* 5 (1958/9): 162.

[53] A. Malchi, "Ha-Mishpat le-'Atid Lavo" (The Law of the Future), *Ha-Praklit* 20 (1963/4): 410.

[54] 34 *Law of the State of Israel* 181 (1980).

[55] See, e.g., H.C. 1635/90, Jerzewsky v. Rosh ha-Memshalah, PD 45(1), 749. See also Menachem Mautner, *Law and the Culture of Israel* (Oxford: Oxford University Press, 2011), 41–44.

[56] For a list of reasons why "the first Israelis" were uninterested in the law in general and in replacing the Mandatory legal heritage in particular, see, for example, Alfred Witkon, "Ha-Mishpat be-Erets Mitpatahat" (Law in a Developing Country), in *Mishpat ve-Shiput: Kovets Ma'amarim ve-Reshimot*, eds. Aharon Barak et al. (Jerusalem: Schocken, 1988), 39, 43–48.

hard pressed to dedicate much attention to it. Second, Jewish law itself is problematic. It is an ancient and religious legal system whose norms are not easily amenable to incorporation in the law of a modern state. Its use in post-1948 Israel would have required the investment of substantial time and effort.

Third, there were institutional barriers to legal reform. In a study of the legal transition from the Mandatory era to Israeli independence, historian Ron Harris has argued that the fact that Jewish law was not incorporated into the legal system of Israel after its establishment was not the result of any ideological resistance to Jewish law but mainly the result of chance and poor institutional design; namely, the Legal Council charged with preparing the legal system of the state-in-the-making and (among other things) deciding the role of Jewish law in the future Jewish state included too many members and had too many subcommittees. Some of the subcommittees could not convene because of the Arab blockade of Jewish Jerusalem in the early months of the 1948 war. In addition, legal reform was given low priority by major politicians such as David Ben Gurion. These factors, rather than any ideological conflicts between secular and religious Jews, led to the preservation of Mandatory law and prevented any linkage between Jewish law, or a modernized version of it, and the Israeli legal system that came into being in May 1948.[57]

Finally, the absence of a Jewish legal revolution in Israel in 1948 was not necessarily only the result of Israel's specific conditions. It may also have been due to the very nature of law. Even if the practical considerations listed above had not been factors, it would not be realistic to expect Israel to transform its legal system overnight. Legal revolutions are not common and many new countries, even those born of war with foreign occupiers, tend to preserve the occupier's legal system after gaining independence. Law is inherently conservative. Changes made too rapidly undermine the political and economic certainty that the legal system seeks to guarantee. The conservatism of law is especially evident in the common-law world, where law, by definition, is based on reverence for precedents. America is a case in point. For many years after gaining independence, the United States maintained close links to English law. Another common-law legal system, whose history is even closer in some senses to that of Israel, is India.[58] After Indian independence in 1947, there were nationalist calls for abolishing the legal system of British India and replacing it with a uniquely "Indian" legal system. But in India, too, nationalist legal aspirations were not fulfilled.[59]

While one cannot ignore these explanations, it would be inaccurate to say that legal revolutions never occur. There are examples of such revolutions. One such example is late nineteenth century Japan.[60] A legal revolu-

---

[57] Harris, "Hizdamnuyot."
[58] Likhovski, "Between Mandate and State," 68.
[59] Galanter, *Law and Society in Modern India*, 37–53.
[60] Kenzo Takayanagi, "A Century of Innovation: The Development of Japanese Law,

tion also took place in Turkey in the early 1920s, after the collapse of the Ottoman Empire, and in Egypt in the early twentieth century.[61] In addition, one must note that while it would have been unrealistic to expect Israel to change its legal system overnight, it would have been quite easy and costless to enact a less revolutionary provision requiring judges to use Jewish law in cases of lacunas or conflicts in existing Mandatory legislation. However, even this did not occur. Practical concerns, thus, provide only partial explanations for the failure of Israel in 1948 to link its new legal system to Jewish law.

B. Jewish Law as a Threat to the Professional Monopoly of Lawyers

In a book on the autonomous Jewish court system of Mandatory Palestine, sociologist Ronen Shamir argues that one reason for the failure of these courts in the early 1930s was the opposition of the Jewish legal profession. Jewish lawyers in Palestine made their living by mediating between Jewish litigants and the Mandatory legal system. Their monopoly as mediators was based on their knowledge of the English language and their familiarity with English law. These lawyers, therefore, had an interest in preserving the Mandatory legal system and not the autonomous Jewish system that flourished in the 1920s. The autonomous system had used the Hebrew language and was both less formal and less professional than the Mandatory system. For this reason, it threatened the livelihood of Jewish lawyers, and these lawyers did their best to weaken the Jewish courts and to channel their clients toward the Mandatory system.[62] Shamir does not discuss the debates about Jewish law in the 1940s and 1950s, but an analogous argument can be made in discussing the preservation of the Mandatory system in the years following the establishment of Israel. Many Israeli lawyers in the 1940s and 1950s had an interest in preserving the Mandatory system because they were intimately familiar with it and because it was inherently less accessible to laymen than a system in which Jewish law had a major role.

The legal literature published during the first years after statehood contains very few statements in defense of the legal status quo and of English law, perhaps because memories of the bitter conflict between the Jews and the British in late 1940s Palestine were still very much alive, and few lawyers dared to identify themselves with the law of "perfidious Albion." However, we do find a few explicit statements in which lawyers openly support

---

1868–1961," in *Law in Japan: The Legal Order of a Changing Society*, ed. Arthur Taylor von Mehren (Cambridge, MA: Harvard University Press, 1963), 5–40; Hiroshi Oda, *Japanese Law*, 2d ed. (Oxford: Oxford University Press, 1999), 21–29.

[61] Esin Örücü, "Turkey: Change under Pressure," in *Studies in Legal Systems: Mixed and Mixing*, eds. Esin Örücü et al. (The Hague: Kluwer Law International, 1996), 89; Guy Bechor, "To Hold the Hand of the Weak: The Emergence of Contractual Justice in the Egyptian Civil Law," *Islamic Law and Society* 8 (2001): 179.

[62] Shamir, *The Colonies of Law*, 108ff.

the retention of Mandatory law and reject the use of Jewish law in the legal system of Israel.⁶³ One such example is in a 1950 article by Eliezer Malchi in which he described the demands for the replacement of the Mandatory penal code with a code based on Jewish law as "a most dangerous thing, [which] must be left to later generations."⁶⁴ Another lawyer, Aharon Ben Shemesh, wrote an article in which he advocated the preservation of Ottoman land law, which Israelis inherited from the Mandatory era. Ben Shemesh argued that the basic principles of this law were close to those of Jewish law, and this made the need for the use of Jewish law redundant.⁶⁵

One can also find some observers who expressly linked the preservation of the legal status quo to the interests of the professional guild. Gad Tedeschi, a law professor who taught at the Hebrew University, explained that abandoning Mandatory law would not inconvenience the general population, which in any case was not well versed in that law. It would only hurt the lawyers' guild.⁶⁶ In this respect, Israel's legal history is not unique. When India gained its independence, the vested interest of local lawyers in preserving the existing, anglicized, legal system was also one of the main reasons for maintaining the system.⁶⁷

While the interests of lawyers were certainly an important factor in preventing a "Jewish legal revolution" in 1948, this alone cannot explain the preservation of the legal status quo. First, the legal profession during the Mandate and in the first decade of statehood was hardly monolithic. Not all

---

⁶³ See Binyamin Cohen, "Be-Shevah ha-Formalizm" (In Praise of Formalism), *Ha-Praklit* 7 (1950): 324, in which Cohen criticizes the anti-formalistic legal approach, which is the result of "the waves of the national revolution that gave birth to the State of Israel." And compare: K. Vardi, "Ruhot Hadashot be-Veyt ha-Mishpat" (A New Approach in the Courts), *Ha-Praklit* 7 (1950): 324. See also Yehuda Frankel, "Al Mishpat ve-Sidrey Mishpat ba-Medinah" (On Law and Procedure in the State), *Ha-Praklit* 8 (1951/52): 212, in which he decries "the artificial imposition of this or that [foreign] legal system" on Mandatory law, and the "reversion to ancient Jewish law, only out of the desire to create an independent national law."

⁶⁴ E. Malchi, "Al Kodeks Plili Hadash (Li-Ve'ayat Tikun ha-Mishpat ha-Plili ba-Arets)" (On a New Criminal Code), *Ha-Praklit* 7 (1950): 352, 354.

⁶⁵ A. Ben-Shemesh, "Ekronot Mishpatiyim Domim ba-Mishpat ha-'Ivri u-Vehok ha-Karka'ot ha-Otomani, 1858" (Similar Legal Principles in Jewish Law and in the Ottoman Land Law), *Ha-Praklit* 6 (1950): 141, 144.

⁶⁶ Gad Tedeschi, "Al Be'ayot Klitah ve-'Al Mediniyutenu ha-Mishpatit" (On Problems of Reception and on our Legal Policy), *Ha-Praklit* 16 (1960): 348, 379. Some observers also argued that the desire of the legal profession to preserve the status quo matched that of the new Israeli administration. "Our government," said one observer in 1949, "feels much more comfortable with the existing colonial system of laws [which has no constitution and] hardly any provisions that define basic human and civil rights," because this way, "the authorities know that they are powerful and they use this power to advance their goals." Shimon Gratsh, "Be'ayot Konstitutsyoniyot" (Constitutional Problems), *Ha-Praklit* 6 (1949): 130, 140. See also Frankel, "Al Mishpat ve-Sidrey," 216, in which he argues that the Ministry of Justice should focus on passing administrative legislation that would enable increased regulation of the "young administration" of the state, instead of busying itself with the drafting of new civil laws that would replace the existing ones but which are not urgently needed at this time.

⁶⁷ Galanter, *Law and Society in Modern India*, 46.

lawyers were well versed in English law. Many Israeli lawyers were immigrants from Central and Eastern Europe with little knowledge of the English language or of English law. Indeed, most of the key players in Israel's legal system were of German descent, and many of these key players had better knowledge of German than of English law.[68] In addition, many of the leaders of the Jewish bar were deeply committed to the Jewish legal revival project. In particular, Paltiel Dikshtein, editor of the journal of the Jewish Bar Association, was one of the major advocates of the Jewish legal revival project since its inception.

Furthermore, the lawyers were not alone in deciding the outcome of legal reform. In this respect, a comparison between post-independence Israel and India is illuminating. One reason for the failure to revive Hindu law in post-1947 India was that the strong guild of Indian lawyers, whose interest was to preserve Anglo-Indian law, did not face any serious opposition. There was no organized group that stood to gain from the revival of Hindu law nor was there any educational institution that could have produced lawyers with an interest in such a revival.[69] The situation in Israel was different. Both the Hebrew University of Jerusalem and the Tel Aviv School of Law and Economics, the two Jewish higher-education institutes in Palestine where law was taught, were rhetorically (and to some extent practically) committed to the revival of Jewish law.[70] There were also political parties that expressed an interest in such a revival. This is reflected, for example, in the comments made by David Zvi Pinkas, a National-Religious Party member of Israel's parliament (*Knesset*), during the drafting sessions of the abortive Israeli constitution in 1950, who declared:

> We miss Jewish law. We are living—substantially and procedurally—according to a collection of laws that have one thing in common: they are not Jewish, they did not emanate from the soul of this people....We, with our ancient heritage of the loftiest concepts of law and justice, must not drink from foreign streams, from poorly dug wells ... and it is inconceivable that we, in our own state, should imitate other nations and their laws.[71]

---

[68] For a similar (albeit not identical) argument, see P. Dikshtein, "Atsma'ut Mishpatit" (Legal Independence), *Ha-Praklit* 5 (1948): 107. He depicts English law as "lovingly" embraced by only "a thin layer of the population ... almost all of the Diaspora Jews now in Palestine were raised in other legal systems ... Jews from Eastern and Central Europe and from Asia alike, all feel that the English law contains peculiar and unusual attributes with which they cannot agree." On the influence of German-Jewish lawyers, see Fania Oz-Salzberger and Eli Salzberger, "The Secret German Sources of the Israeli Supreme Court," *Israel Studies* 3 (1998): 159–92.

[69] Galanter, *Law and Society in Modern India*, 46.

[70] Likhovski, *Law and Identity*, 106–26.

[71] *Divrey Ha-Knesset* 5 (May 2, 1950): 1262. On the ambivalent attitude of observant Jews to the idea of legal revival, see also Radzyner, "Ha-Mishpat ha-'Ivri beyn 'Le'umi' le-'Dati'."

In conclusion, the fact that many lawyers opposed linking Israeli law to Jewish law was an important factor in preventing such a linkage. However, in order to understand why these lawyers *succeeded*, an additional, cultural set of explanations must be added. The next section shows that this success was partly due to the fact that the lawyers' arguments against legal change resonated with wider cultural perceptions of law and society prevalent among lay Israelis at the time.

C. Why Did the Professional Opposition Succeed? The Role of Culture

Cultural images of Jewish law, of law generally and, most importantly, of Israeli society, were major factors that inhibited the linkage between Jewish and Israeli law. Unlike the Hebrew language, which could easily be separated from religion and, thus, could be adopted willingly by secular Zionists, Jewish law was too strongly tied to religion, and was, therefore, perceived by Zionists as antithetical to their ideology. Despite attempts to secularize Jewish law in the early twentieth century, most Israelis identified (and still identify) Jewish law with religion and with Jewish life in the Diaspora. Zionism was, in essence, a secular movement that attempted to extricate the Jews from the ghetto of religion. Lawyers opposed to the revival of Jewish law manipulated this relationship between Jewish law and the Jewish Diaspora when they described Jewish law as an outdated, petrified religious system, ill suited to life in a modern sovereign secular state.[72]

Another cultural image that may have played a role in the reluctance to effect any transformation of the Mandatory legal system was an image of the nature of law. Israeli culture at the time was dominated by the socialist ideology of the ruling MAPAI party, and this ideology was mainly concerned with traditional Zionist goals such as creating Jewish settlements on Israel's frontiers. Law was considered by many Israelis as a bourgeois pursuit that suited Diaspora Jews. As one contemporary observer put it, law was a matter that simply could not "engender enthusiasm in the hearts of idealists."[73] Therefore, the Mandatory heritage was maintained, in part, because the idea of devoting energy to legal matters simply did not appeal to the first generation of Israelis.

In addition to their perception of law, another important factor inhibiting legal change was the cultural image that Israelis had of their own society. In the 1950s, massive immigration from Europe and the Middle East dramatically changed the demographics of Israel. Many observers described the new immigrants as a "desert generation" and believed that a new Israeli culture and identity would crystallize only once this generation was absorbed by Israeli society.[74] The notion of a "desert generation" carried

---

[72] See, e.g., Malchi, "Al Kodeks," 354; Frankel, "Al Mishpat ve-Sidrey," 212, 216. On the role of such images in the Mandatory era, see Likhovski, *Law and Identity*, 151–53.

[73] Witkon, "Ha-Mishpat be-Erets Mitpatahat," 42–45.

[74] For a general discussion, see, for example, Segev, *1949: The First Israelis*.

both positive and negative connotations. Sometimes it simply meant that no long-term legal change could take place until all the members of the new Israeli society had arrived in Israel. Sometimes the image was more negative—no long-term legal change could take place because the first generation of Israelis was not fit to be governed by new laws.

One well-known use of the "desert generation" argument appeared in the 1948–1950 debate regarding the adoption of an Israeli constitution. The Israeli Declaration of Independence contemplated the election of a constitutive assembly, which would adopt a constitution, but once this assembly—the first Knesset—was elected, it took the position that "the time [for adopting a constitution] has not yet arrived, because we are still busy laying down the material and human foundations of the state."[75] Thus, for example, Knesset Member David Bar-Rav-Hai of the ruling MAPAI party, argued:

> A constitution is created ... not at the beginning of a revolution, but at its end ... whereas we ... are not at the end of our revolution, but at its beginning, because our revolution is not the establishment of the state ... [but] the gathering of the exiles. We are talking about this generation, the generation sitting with us here and in the transit camps of immigrants who have not yet put down roots in this country ... [and] about those who will be coming here in the very near future.[76]

Since not all the immigrants had arrived, there would be no point in enacting a constitution that did not take into account their views. This position eventually led to the famous "Harari Resolution" of June 1950, according to which Israel was to adopt its constitution one chapter at a time; each chapter would constitute a "basic law," and at the end of the process, all these basic laws would be consolidated into a single constitution (which even today, more than sixty years later, has failed to materialize).[77]

The "desert generation" argument was not used only in constitutional debates. It also appeared in general discussions about the retention of Mandatory legal system. Here the argument was used by both opponents and proponents of the legal status-quo. Opponents of Mandatory law argued that its replacement would facilitate the creation of a new Israeli society and a new Israeli identity. Proponents of Mandatory law, on the other hand, explained that while a new Israeli identity was not fully formed,

---

[75] *Divrey Ha-Knesset* 3 (November 21, 1949): 128 (David Ben Gurion).

[76] *Divrey Ha-Knesset* 4 (February 7, 1950): 726–27.

[77] *Divrey Ha-Knesset* 5 (May 2, 1950): 1711–22, 1743. On the constitutional history of Israel, see generally Amnon Rubinstein and Barak Medina, *Ha-Mishpat ha-Konstitutsyoni shel Medinat Yisra'el* (Israeli Constitutional Law), 5th ed. (Jerusalem: Schocken, 1996), 50–53, 367–69, 910. See also Philippa Strum, "The Road Not Taken: Constitutional Non-Decision Making in 1948–1950 and Its Impact on Civil Liberties in the Israeli Political Culture," in *Israel: The First Decade of Independence*, eds. S. Ilan Troen and Noah Lucas (Albany: State University of New York Press, 1995), 83–104.

there was no point in replacing the Ottoman-English legal heritage of the Mandate with a new legal system linked in some way to Jewish law.

The "Desert Generation" Argument as a Reason for Replacing the Mandatory Legal Heritage

Some observers, most notably Israeli Supreme Court Justice Alfred Witkon, called for replacing Mandatory norms, especially those that originated in Ottoman law, with new Israeli norms that would facilitate the absorption of immigrants and speed up the creation of a homogeneous Israeli culture and society. Witkon thus viewed the law as an important tool in achieving a "melting pot" Israeli society. In 1962, he wrote an article in which he said that in a society that was "not homogeneous in terms of its cultural level" the law should serve as "an active educational tool" used to "modernize" the population.[78] Witkon conceded that the values of those groups that opposed "modern" law in Israel (he was apparently referring to Orthodox Jews and to Middle Eastern immigrants) were "not all negative," and, furthermore, were deeply rooted in their "customs, traditions and ways of life." However, he continued:

> We aim for progress. We have seen firsthand, throughout the years of the Mandate, an administration that failed to rejuvenate the face of society and its legal system. It preserved the image of a backward society, the barrenness of the land and the ignorance of the people, the rule of tribal culture and the corruption of the clergy, as though these were sacred values that must not be touched. Must we follow in these footsteps?

Witkon answered this rhetorical question by saying that it was obvious that "law should be on the side of progress." Witkon later expressed his chagrin at the fact that "fourteen years have passed since statehood, and we have not yet had a fundamental reform of the laws of inheritance and personal status; Ottoman laws such as the *Mejelle* and the land law still prevail, imposing difficulties on the daily lives of Israel's citizens."[79] The political discourse and case law of the late 1950s contained additional statements expressing the same desire to use law as a tool for the homogenization of Israeli society.[80]

---

[78] Witkon, "Ha-Mishpat be-Erets Mitpatahat," 49, 51–54.

[79] Ibid., 51–54. See also D. Ben Gurion, "Dvarim ba-Ve'idah ha-13 shel Histadrut 'Orkhey ha-Din be-Yisra'el, Tel Aviv June 5–6 1949," *Ha-Praklit* 9 (1949): 96–97. For a critique similar to Witkon's regarding the legal conservatism of the Mandatory government, see M. Silberg, "Ha-Mishpat ba-Medinah ha-'Ivrit" (Law in the Jewish State) *Ha-Praklit* 5 (1948): 102, 103, in which Silberg criticized the "constant fear of the [Mandatory] legislator that he would trespass the traditional boundaries of the sacred desert."

[80] See, for example, *Divrey ha-Knesset* 4 (February 7, 1950): 734, in which Yisra'el Bar Yehuda states: "We are living in a country of unique circumstances, of a gathering of the exiles, of people from many ethnic origins from all parts of the world, with different

The "Desert Generation" Argument as a Reason for Preserving the Mandatory Legal Heritage

The opposing school of thought, which supported preservation of the Mandatory legal heritage, also made use of the "desert generation" argument. As long as Israeli society was heterogeneous, declared lawyers who opposed legal change, the Ottoman-English law that Israel had inherited from the British must not be replaced.[81]

A 1950 article by Eliezer Malchi serves as a good example of the use of the argument in this way.[82] Malchi rejected demands for the replacement of

---

traditions and ... with various unwritten constitutions ... and we want to create a single nation from this admixture. To do this, we must take all possible actions ... to live together ... and this tendency must also be reflected in the law—by education through a single legal system for everyone." It is important to note that, perhaps contrary to popular belief, the case law of the 1950s does not include many statements reflecting the "melting pot" ideology. For a rare (and now famous) example of the melting pot ideology in the case law of the 1960s, see Criminal Appeal 172/62 *Garame v. Attorney General*, PD 17, 925 and the discussion of this case in Yoram Shachar, "Ha-Adam ha-Savir ba-Mishpat ha-Plili" (The Reasonable Person in Criminal Law), *Ha-Praklit* 39 (1989): 78–107; Menachem Mautner, "Sekhel Yashar, Legitimatsyah, Kfiyah: 'Al Shoftim ke-Mesaprey Sipurim" (Common Sense, Legitimacy and Coercion: On Judges as Story Tellers), *Plilim* 7 (1997): 61.

Another use of the "desert generation" argument in demands for legal change was the call to revise Mandatory law so it would better fit the heterogeneity of Israeli society in this "desert generation" phase of its existence. The argument was that Mandatory law (or rather, the English part of it) was designed for a much more homogeneous society than Israel in the 1950s. For example, in a 1954 court decision, Justice Silberg called upon the Court not to embrace the standard interpretation of the concept of public mischief in English law because "we are living in an era of a gathering of the exiles.... One day, the exiles will become one, and in the melting pot of the state, there shall arise a single nation with a single national culture that will contain a comprehensive set of moral and cultural values shared as much as possible by all the individuals comprising this nation." However, Silberg added, at present, "we have ... a situation in which there is no uniformity among the various ethnic layers of the population, which differ from one another in their opinions, traditions, lifestyles, world views and moral and cultural values." Therefore, Silberg believed the section dealing with "public harm" in the criminal code should be abolished or at least given a narrow interpretation, because as long as the culture was not homogeneous, there would be no uniform agreement as to what constitutes such harm. See Criminal Appeal 53/54, *Eshed v. Attorney General*, PD 8, pp. 785, 820–21. Interestingly, the first Chief Justice of the Supreme Court, Moshe Smoira, also supported the notion of a heterogeneous body of Israeli law (although not as a temporary measure). In the summer of 1949 he spoke of a juridical "gathering of the exiles" in which "we will draw, as much as possible, on our sources," but also make use of "a collection of the excellent systems we have found in exile," in order to create a mixed system comprised of the best of all these systems. See Moshe Smoira, "Dvarim ba-Ve'ida ha-13 shel Histadrut 'Orkhey ha-Din be-Yisra'el," *Ha-Praklit* 6 (1949): 102, 103.

[81] Ironically, this argument echoed similar rhetoric used by some of the British judges toward the end of the Mandate to explain why English norms should not be imported into Palestine. These judges held that "an undeveloped land needs an undeveloped law." See Witkon, "Ha-Mishpat be-Erets Mitpatahat," 40. See also Likhovski, *Law and Identity*, 65.

[82] It was during this time that the Knesset was contemplating the adoption of a constitution and decided that "the time was not ripe" for a comprehensive constitution. It is therefore possible that Malchi's arguments were inspired by the Knesset debates.

the Mandatory penal code (which was based on English law) with an "original" penal code that would draw on the principles of Jewish law to the greatest extent possible. Malchi argued that the Mandatory penal code should be preserved, explaining that, "the character of Israeli society has still not crystallized, and it is undergoing a process that could take an entire generation, until a new generation will replace the hybrid desert generation."[83] Instead of a legal revolution, Malchi proposed a "conservative" approach of preserving the status quo, because "the time has not yet come 'to repair the world in the kingdom of God.'"[84]

The conservative "desert generation" argument, supporting the legal status quo, was used with respect to the Ottoman (as well as the English) part of Mandatory law. For example, in a lecture at the annual conference of the Israeli Bar Association in 1954, one of the speakers, using somewhat bizarre imagery, said that the civil (Ottoman) law that Israel had inherited from the Mandatory era—the *Mejelle*—was not "an attractive bride that we will want to embrace in the long run," but "we cannot, of course, push her over the cliff all at once, as if she were a scapegoat." Instead, he said, we can only "dismember her one piece at a time … the time has not yet come to create the perfect civil code for Israel, since as a nation we are a gathering of exiles … the moral structure of this people and the face of its culture are still being molded … the common national identity that can serve as substantive background for a comprehensive code has not yet been forged."[85]

Echoes of the "desert generation" rationale also appeared in the 1950s debate about abolishing the Ottoman rules that allowed the imprisonment of debtors for civil debt. As historian Ron Harris has noted, one major argument heard during the Knesset debate concerning these rules was that Ottoman norms that allowed the imprisonment of debtors could not be repealed because Israeli society was not yet sufficiently law-abiding. For example, in a Knesset session in 1958, MK Yochanan Bader said that "even now many Israelis still follow oriental traditions, and many of their assets are gold or other objects that can be hidden in their socks." He warned that "Incarceration of debtors must therefore not be abolished, because given the nature of Israel and its inhabitants, other means of collecting civil debt

---

[83] Malchi, "Al Kodeks," 354.

[84] Malchi, "Al Kodeks," 358. Malchi, ibid., 354, 358, further argued that Jewish [penal] law had been "frozen for two thousand years," and that the problems of modernizing Jewish law "were too weighty for our young and inexperienced shoulders." It is, of course, possible that the real reason for his opposition to any legal change was that he was an English-educated lawyer. See also E. Malchi, "Atid ha-Mishpat he-Angli bi-Medinat Yisra'el" (The Future of English Law in the State of Israel), *Mishpat ve-Kalkalah* 5 (1958/59): 47, 49, where Malchi speaks about the State of Israel as being "in an age of transition."

[85] Assaf Goldberg, "Mishpat, 'Am ve-Lashon" (Law, Nation, and Language), *Ha-Praklit* 10 (1953/54): 139, 146–47. See also Tamar Hoffman, "'Tsinor Yevu ha-Din he-Angli la-Arets—Siman 46 li-Dvar ha-Melekh" (A Conduit for Importing English Law to Israel—Article 46 of the King's Order in Council), *Ha-Praklit* 12 (1955/56): 50.

are impracticable."[86] Bader's words implied that Mandatory law (specifically the Ottoman norms that dealt with debt) should not be replaced, not only because the homogeneous Israeli culture that would justify legal change had not yet formed, but also because the Ottoman heritage was more suited to the current circumstances of Israeli society, many members of which had not yet been fully westernized.

Another variant of the conservative approach, which favored the preservation of the legal status quo in this transitory, "desert generation," era, was the argument that the primary requirement of the legal system during this time of the "ingathering of exiles" was to educate the immigrants to uphold the law. By inference, replacing the legal system was not a top priority. For example, in a 1951 speech, Justice Minister Dov Yosef stated:

> [W]e are truly a gathering of the exiles. Hundreds of thousands of Jews have come here from countries in which the law was not rooted deeply enough. In Israel, we want the same attitude toward law and order as seen in developed, enlightened countries. We have the difficult role of absorbing the immigrants spiritually and assimilating them into our midst, so the entire people will reach our level rather than the level of Yemen, Iraq, or North Africa.[87]

His emphasis on the need to teach the new immigrants to comply with the law had the effect of weakening the motivation to work toward comprehensive legal reform, since such reform would have increased legal uncertainty and, thus, indirectly would have led to increased non-compliance with the law.[88] As we saw, the argument could cut both ways, as an argument for legal change as well as an argument for maintaining the status quo. However, more people used it to justify legal conservatism, perhaps because the

---

[86] *Divrey ha-Knesset* 23 (1958): 96, cited by Ron Harris, "Nefilato va-'Aliyato shel Ma'asar ha-Hayavim" (The Fall and Rise of Imprisonment for Debt), *'Iyune Mishpat* 20 (1997): 439, 480.

[87] "Min ha-Na'aseh be-Histadrut 'Orkhey ha-Din: ha-Ve'ida ha-Artsit ha-14" (Events of the Bar Association: The Fourteenth National Convention), *Ha-Praklit* 8.3 (1951/52): 5–8.

[88] This was especially evident in discussions of tax compliance. Officials often explained that tax evasion was prevalent in Israel because of the heterogeneity of the population. See Assaf Likhovski, "Training in Citizenship: Tax Compliance and Modernity," *Law and Social Inquiry* 32 (2007): 686. There are many other examples of the great interest expressed in the concept of the rule of law in the legal and political discourse of the time. See, for example, *Divrey ha-Knesset* 4 (February 7, 1950): 734, in which Yisra'el Bar Yehuda says: "The Jewish people in the Diaspora, because it was persecuted and had no rights, has acquired a characteristic that must be uprooted immediately—the ability to 'handle' the law.... [W]e must educate the people and the authorities to [comply] with our law." See also Criminal Appeal 226/54 *Alufi v. Attorney General*, PD 9 1345 (a case of an official who took bribes, in which it was noted that "with dismay, we see the devastating influence of those with whom [the official] cooperated.... [T]hese were new immigrants who in their countries of origin were not accustomed to civil rights and duties. And this was the civic education philosophy that the appellants and others of their kind were to impart: defraud, cheat, lie, bribe, and use any unlawful means you can to evade your duties as an individual toward the state.").

idea of using law as an educational tool and a tool for social change was definitely a minority position in Israel of the 1950s where formalism and judicial passivity were the dominant legal ideology.[89]

Conclusion

When Israel was established in 1948, many observers expected that the country would replace the Mandatory legal heritage with a new legal system linked in some way to Jewish law. This expected change did not occur. Practical reasons were certainly a factor in the retention of the Mandatory legal heritage. However, another important factor was the opposition of many Jewish lawyers to Jewish law. The professional opponents of Jewish law saw it as a threat to their monopoly on access to the legal system. In their battle to preserve the Mandatory legal heritage, these lawyers made successful use of cultural images prevalent in Israeli society at the time in order to prevent legal change.

In particular, they made use of several prominent cultural images. First, the image of Jewish law as a religious system unfit for a secular Zionist society. Second, an image of law generally as a bourgeois pursuit unfit for the pioneering, idealistic, socialist society that Israel imagined itself to be in the 1950s. Finally, an image of Israeli society generally and the new immigrants that arrived after 1948 in particular, as a "desert generation"—an ingathering of exiles with no common homogeneous basis which would enable the creation of a new legal system based on Jewish law. As long as the process of the formation of a new Israeli society was incomplete, some lawyers such as Eliezer Malchi could argue that "the time has not yet come to repair the world in the kingdom of God," and to link Israeli and Jewish law.

The story told here may contain a general lesson. Lawyers are not totally free to determine the identity of the legal system. While their professional interests play an important role in shaping the law, lay actors such as politicians, intellectuals, and even ordinary citizens also influence the shape of the legal system. In order to achieve their desired goals, lawyers must justify their position in ways that resonate with wider cultural perceptions about law and society. Israeli lawyers in the 1950s succeeded in preventing a "Jewish legal revolution" because they made use of widely held cultural images that supported the retention of the legal status quo. Once the constitutional moment of 1948 was gone and the legal revolution thwarted, inertia guaranteed that Jewish law would have only marginal influence on Israeli law.

---

[89] See generally Mautner, *Law and the Culture of Israel*, 75–90.

ABOUT THE EDITORS

Ari Mermelstein is Assistant Professor of Bible at Yeshiva University. He holds a PhD from NYU's Department of Hebrew & Judaic Studies, a JD from NYU Law School, and a BA from Yeshiva College. Dr. Mermelstein is also the assistant director of the Yeshiva University Center for Jewish Law and Contemporary Civilization at Cardozo Law School and the Israeli Supreme Court Project at Cardozo Law School. He is the author of *The Genesis of Beginnings: Creation, Covenant, and Conceptions of Historical Time in Second Temple Judaism*.

Victoria Saker Woeste is a Research Professor at the American Bar Foundation. She was educated at the University of Virginia (BA) and the University of California-Berkeley, in the interdisciplinary Jurisprudence & Social Policy program (MA, PhD). Her first book, *The Farmer's Benevolent Trust*, won the Law & Society Association's J. Willard Hurst Prize; she is also the author of the acclaimed book *Henry Ford's War on Jews and the Legal Battle Against Hate Speech*.

Ethan Zadoff is a PhD Candidate in the Department of History of CUNY's Graduate Center. He teaches classes in the Hebrew and Hebraic Studies Division of the Department of Classical and Oriental Studies, in CUNY's Hunter College. He holds an MA from the Bernard Revel Graduate School for Jewish Studies, as well as a BA from Yeshiva University.

Marc Galanter is the John and Rylla Bosshard Professor Emeritus of Law and South Asian Studies at the University of Wisconsin-Madison and formerly LSE Centennial Professor at the London School of Economics. He studies litigation, lawyers, and legal culture. He has written extensively on these topics, including *Tournament of Lawyers: The Transformation of the Big Law Firm* and *Lowering the Bar: Lawyer Jokes and Legal Culture*, as well as acclaimed books on the legal system of India.

Visit us at *www.quidprobooks.com.*